THE ESSENTIAL GUIDE TO
WILDERNESS CAMPING
AND BACKPACKING IN
THE UNITED STATES

i

THE ESSENTIAL GUIDE TO
WILDERNESS CAMPING AND BACKPACKING IN THE UNITED STATES

CHARLES COOK

MICHAEL KESEND PUBLISHING, LTD.
NEW YORK

This book is dedicated to each and every person who is taking responsibility, in whatever way, to help protect the natural environment and save our remaining wilderness areas.

The Essential Guide to Wilderness
Camping and Backpacking in the United States
© 1994 by Charles Cook

Library of Congress Cataloging-in-Publication Data:

Cook, Charles, 1945–
The essential guide to wilderness camping and backpacking in the United States/Charles Cook. p. cm. Includes index. ISBN 0-935576-46-0
1. Hiking—United States—Guidebooks.
2. Backpacking—United States—Guidebooks. 3. Wilderness areas—United States—Guidebooks. 4. United States—Guidebooks. I. Title. II. Title: Wilderness camping and backpacking in the United States.
GV199.4.C67 1944   796.5′1′0973—dc20
94-1725 CIP

Cover Design: Kirschner Caroff Design Inc.
Book Design: Jackie Schuman
Map Preparation: Jackie Schuman & Charles Cook

CONTENTS

WHERE TO GO: A COMPLETE GUIDE TO U.S. PARKS AND OTHER NATURAL AREAS OPEN TO WILDERNESS CAMPING, ALONG WITH THE BEST TRAILS FOR BACKPACKING

PREFACE

There are many ways to enjoy the natural world, whether you enter for a few hours, a day, a week, or longer. Even a short visit can be quite refreshing. Without a doubt, however, the richest, most exciting, most memorable experiences await those who choose to remain in the wilderness overnight.

An estimated 13 million Americans went backpacking in 1992, and a much larger number engaged in other forms of primitive or wilderness camping. Up until the early 1970s only a small minority of hardy souls participated in these pursuits. In recent years improved equipment and a widespread interest in nature and healthy activities have led record numbers to join in.

If you're someone who is attracted to nature, feels ready for a dose of real adventure, is reasonably self-sufficient or willing to learn how to be so, and perhaps has an itch to explore some of the most gorgeous, spectacular places to be found on the planet...then I urge you to give these activities a try.

If you're a beginner, this book will get you started and on your way. There's a little homework to be done, but it will pay off a thousandfold in pleasures to come. If you're someone who has wilderness experience, Part II of the book will help you discover many new places to visit throughout the country.

My own initiation into wilderness-oriented activities began back in 1971, when I was first introduced to hiking and backpacking. I was hooked almost instantly, and can say with gratitude that my life hasn't been the same since.

In 1973 I spent five months backpacking the 2,100-mile Appalachian Trail from Georgia to Maine, and over the years have taken other long trips as well. Since 1980 I've led more than 700 hikes and backpacking trips as a licensed guide, in addition to leading canoe, bike, and rafting trips.

Ever since I first became involved in these activities, obtaining camping regulations and other information about parks and wilderness areas has often been a time-consuming process, and sometimes a frustrating one. Many guidebooks omit camping rules and other information needed by backpackers and wilderness campers. Park and forest brochures are frequently inadequate.

This book is the first comprehensive countrywide resource guide for wilderness campers and backpackers. Included is a *complete* listing of locations throughout the United States where wilderness camping and backpacking are allowed, with camping regulations specified for each area. You'll also find a thorough introduction to these activities, along with relevant resources.

The book is a companion to my first book, *The Essential Guide to Hiking in the United States* (Michael Kesend Publishing Ltd., 1992), which presented an overview of hiking areas and trails in all 50 states. While some of the information in the former book will be useful to backpackers, the focus therein was solely on hiking. Camping and backpacking were not addressed.

The present book, in contrast, is entirely about camping—specifically camping in the wilderness, of which backpacking is one popular variant. Everything important about primitive camping as well as where to camp throughout the country will be found here, along with information about the wide range of wilderness-related activities available in addition to hiking.

While this book was in large measure a labor of love, it also proved to be much more of a challenge than I'd imagined. In spite of my ample files and the extensive materials obtained for the earlier book, an enormous amount of additional research was necessary. Adequate information was difficult to come by for some states and regions. A huge amount of correspondence and other efforts were required to successfully accomplish the task.

Every attempt has been made to make the book as complete and accurate as possible. Some parks and agencies did not respond to repeated inquiries, however. While all the important camping areas will be found here, along with hundreds of lesser-known places, at least a handful of smaller areas were omitted because of lack of information. A few listings are unusually brief because the information available was very sparse.

Those who have read *The Essential Guide to Hiking in the United States* may note a small amount of overlap between the two books, but this volume is different in many ways. No material has been reprinted from the first. Some parks and wilderness areas have listings in both books, but the descriptions here were written anew and offer somewhat different information, such as camping regulations and wilderness-related activities available.

Many listings will be found here which do not appear in the first book. These are parks, preserves, and wilderness areas which may offer few or no hiking trails, but have other activities available, and are locations where primitive camping is permitted. At the same time, a number of areas listed in the hiking book are absent because they're off-limits to camping.

As was true with the first book, it has not been possible to personally visit and explore all the areas and trails listed. Such a task would undoubtedly take a great many years, perhaps a lifetime, to accomplish. However, I have in fact visited a substantial number of the locations discussed here, including most National Parks and hundreds of smaller parks and forests.

The overview of wilderness camping and backpacking in Part I was written from my personal experience and what I've learned from others. I avoided consulting other sources while preparing this section (checking afterward, however, to see if there were any irreconcilable differences between my methods and the those of others. I found none of importance).

While my reading on the subject of backpacking and camping has been limited over the years, back in 1971 I was strongly influenced by Colin Fletcher's book *The Complete Walker*. I also read John Hart's *Walking Softly in the Wilderness* in the late 1970s, and have been an occasional reader of *Backpacker Magazine*.

The main portion of the book, Part II, could not possibly have been written without the generous assistance of a great many other people, namely, the numerous park and agency employees throughout the country who sent materials and information. I'm greatly indebted to everyone who helped in this and other ways.

I hope the book will serve you as a useful companion, whether you're about to try wilderness camping for the first time, have some experience and knowledge but wish to learn more, are interested in exploring a wider range of activities, and/or want to expand your repertory of places to go.

It's sometimes easy to forget what a large country this is, and difficult to appreciate how much wild, beautiful, and often spectacular scenery still exists. While camping isn't allowed everywhere, to be sure, the options remain many and varied. Start planning now for the time you have available, then go! I wish you the most fulfilling wilderness adventures possible.

Wilderness camping and backpacking involve venturing out into the wilder places and remaining for a night or an extended stay. It's necessary to be self-sufficient while you're there. A tent usually provides your only shelter. Life becomes simplified. You eat, sleep, and spend days and nights in the fresh air, close to the earth, immersed in the natural world.

Many people are attracted to wilderness camping—sometimes called primitive camping or back-country camping—because it provides such a refreshing escape from our man-made, clock-and-routine-run civilization. Assuming you go about it in the right way, wilderness camping can offer an experience as exciting, memorable, and deeply nourishing as any in life.

Camping has long been popular in this country, but the majority of those who go camping stay at campgrounds ("car camping"), where you can drive right up to your campsite. While it amounts to an enjoyable vacation for many people, and certainly an inexpensive one, this kind of camping doesn't really satisfy when you've tasted the pleasures of sleeping in the wild.

Campgrounds do offer conveniences, and in some areas they provide the only places where you can legally camp. There are drawbacks, probably the greatest of which is the number of people generally present. In addition, the natural landscape has been seriously altered in most campgrounds. Nature usually comes third after people and facilities. Solitude tends to be scarce. You're rarely far from the sounds of others socializing, along with the (hopefully muted) background noise of radios and even TVs.

Some of the campgrounds in National Parks, National Forests, and on other public lands are less developed and more remote. Sites may be situated a good distance apart, providing a sense of privacy, and surroundings are likely to be wilder. Such campgrounds are likely to offer a more congenial experience, especially for people in search of quiet and contact with nature.

To some of us, though, no campground can compare with camping out in the heart of the wilderness. Granted it isn't always easy. To reap the greatest rewards it's helpful to have an adventure-some spirit, a willingness to encounter the unexpected and, most important, the necessary knowledge and ability. You need to have route-finding skills, to bring the appropriate equipment and clothing, and before trying it on your own to have experience in going with others. A few risks are involved. Help may not be readily at hand if something goes wrong.

Primitive or wilderness camping is permitted in a number of parks and forests throughout the United States, especially the larger ones, but in other areas it's not. Regulations vary greatly from place to place. A permit may or may not be required. Sometimes specific backcountry sites must be used. In other cases you can camp freely wherever you wish, usually with a few restrictions—requiring, for example, that your tent be set up no closer than a specified distance from trails and water sources.

Wilderness camping is commonly combined with activities such as hiking, canoeing, kayaking, rafting, mountain biking, cross-country skiing, snowshoeing, horseback riding, rock climbing, mountaineering, and other forms of outdoor recreation. Those who fish and hunt will often camp out as well. Some people go into the wilderness overnight simply to "be there," to commune with nature, without planning any formal activity.

If you enter the wilderness on foot with a full-size backpack, carrying everything you need for an overnight stay or longer, the activity is usually called backpacking. There's an art to successful backpacking, the most important principle being to minimize the weight and bulk of what's brought. Going light usually means maximum freedom and enjoyment.

Most backpackers follow hiking and backpacking trails. A smaller number engage in bush-whacking (off-trail travel). Some backpackers hike long-distance trails, camping in a different site each night along the way, perhaps occasionally staying put for a time after reaching a lovely spot. Others set up a "base camp" and take day hikes from there.

What is it about the wilderness that attracts so

many of us? For one thing, there's the feeling of adventure involved in entering and exploring "nature in the raw." It's a fascinating and endlessly varied environment, with rules (mostly unwritten) unlike those we normally live under. This is a world which isn't human-dominated or controlled. Here people are only visitors, and greatly outnumbered by other species.

Aside from a thin-walled tent at night, there's little to separate you from nature. Some campers find this a little scary at first—to be out in the wilds with so few "crutches" and conveniences—even though there's really little to be seriously concerned about. It can feel liberating to be temporarily free of the routines of civilization, and to do without the countless encumbrances we surround ourselves with in daily life.

It's relaxing and healthful to leave the world of "clock time"—to let your body unwind from accumulated tension, to find your own natural rhythms and get in sync with the rhythms and cycles of life around you. Some people experience the most restful sleep they've ever known (not always at the beginning, since it can take time to be comfortable in a new environment).

Then there's the phenomenal physical beauty of much of the wilderness . . . which may include dramatic high mountain scenery, deep layered canyons on an awesome scale, clear-water lakes and ponds and rivers and streams along with waterfalls, the lushest and richest vegetation imaginable, and beautifully austere desert landscapes. Given the damage already done to much of our environment, it's amazing and gratifying to discover places which remain enormously attractive and still relatively untouched.

Wildlife is of special interest to many people.

While wild animals aren't always as visible and available as some would prefer, sightings and encounters can occur at any time, and there's not much danger as long as you know how to behave in their company. The unexpected viewing of large mammals and other wildlife can be one of the highlights of a trip.

There are also pleasures and challenges provided by whatever activities you might pursue during your stay. Backpackers explore winding trails, wandering through all conceivable kinds of wild terrain. Canoeists and kayakers and rafters negotiate wilderness waterways, floating across placid waters or racing through roaring whitewater. Mountain bikers and (in winter) cross-country skiers view the wilds from still other perspectives. Healthy exercise is among the many benefits of these activities.

Some of the most memorable moments of a wilderness camping trip tend to come in the evening . . . watching the sun set over a wild mountain lake, listening to choruses of crickets and frogs, as waves lap along the shoreline . . . or at night, under a starry moonlit sky, soothed to sleep by the wind blowing softly through pines, with the sounds of a murmuring stream nearby . . . or early morning, awakening to singing birds as the sun slowly rises over a foggy pond, with bright colors of fall foliage materializing in the mist . . .

Heading home after such a trip isn't always easy. Yet it's common to feel infinitely better than when you arrived—often stronger, more relaxed, more centered, and much more attuned to nature and the earth. Any difficulties back at work or home may be easier to deal with now. And however long it will be until you return, it's almost certain that the meaning of those days and nights in the wilderness won't soon be forgotten . . .

HOW TO USE THIS BOOK

In Part I you'll find a discussion of all the important elements of wilderness camping and backpacking, including what to bring on a trip and how to take care of yourself in the wilderness. Read and study this part of the book thoroughly if you're a beginner or have relatively little experience.

Part II lists all the possible places throughout the United States where you can backpack or camp outside of campgrounds. Turn to this section when you're ready to plan a trip or consider where to go. An experienced wilderness camper may want to start with this part of the book. Those who haven't camped in a while may also want to read Part I as a review.

Decide which states and regions are of interest to you, and choose some specific locations or trails which sound interesting. Next, contact each park, forest, or trail association directly for more information. Request up-to-date camping information, since regulations and permit policies are subject to change at any time.

You'll also need to obtain a good map for each area, and if possible a guidebook. For these items check with your nearest outdoor supply store. Guidebooks and maps are also available from some park information centers or gift shops, local bookstores in the vicinity of larger parks and forests, or by mail order.

At the end of each state's chapter in Part II is a "Camping Resources" section. Here you'll find information which may come in handy, including a listing of "Organizations Which Offer Wilderness Camping Trips," in case you want to go with a group, and also "Useful Guidebooks" which are currently available.

Under the heading of "Information About State Park Campgrounds" is an agency to contact for information should you want to stay at a campground in a state park. If you'd like to obtain a complete listing of campgrounds in all 50 states, check your bookstore or camping store for one of the large national campground directories.

If you'll be traveling any distance to reach a particular park or wilderness area, and could use a highway map and/or other travel information, these may be requested from a state's office of travel or tourism. You'll find the address and phone number listed under "State Highway Map and Travel Information."

When you've decided on a destination and taken steps to obtain more information, return to Part I for assistance in preparing and packing for your trip. Consult the checklist provided to make sure you're bringing everything necessary to make your trip as safe and comfortable as possible.

READER RESPONSE

Are you aware of a park, forest, wilderness area, trail, outdoor club, or other resource which belongs in this book? Is there an entry which you believe should be removed? Or have you spotted an error? Please send feedback, corrections, and updates to the address below. Your help in making the next edition of this book complete and accurate will be gratefully appreciated.

Charles Cook
% Michael Kesend Publishing, Ltd.
1025 Fifth Avenue
New York, NY 10028

WILDERNESS TRIPS

From March through November each year Charles Cook leads overnight trips to wilderness areas in New York, Vermont, New Hampshire, Maine, and Virginia—as well as day trips to natural areas in downstate New York, northern New Jersey, and western Connecticut. For literature, including a trip schedule, write to the following address:

Wilderness Trips with Charles Cook
P.O. Box 655
Pomona, NY 10970

PART I

ESSENTIALS OF WILDERNESS CAMPING AND BACKPACKING

ONE

Wilderness
Camping Fundamentals

The wilderness is obviously quite a different world from the one most of us have been brought up in. Assuming you're someone who's new to this realm or relatively inexperienced, there are obviously things to be learned before embarking on an overnight trip. The better informed and prepared you are beforehand, the more likely your trip will be a success. The chapters which follow discuss in detail what's required. This chapter offers an introductory overview, a look at some fundamental concepts and considerations involved in wilderness camping and backpacking.

Wilderness

Few places on the planet are more beautiful, more exciting to visit, more awe-inspiring than wilderness areas. Here nature runs wild and free, undeveloped and relatively untouched by humanity. Spending an extended time in this environment can provide a rich experience for anyone.

Most areas of wilderness are largely or entirely without roads, phones, buildings, bathrooms, and other facilities or conveniences. Some of us consider this to be a major part of the attraction. Among the many positive rewards of wilderness travel is that it's gratifying to be able to get away from *everything* (even some of the things we love or truly enjoy) for a time.

You're obviously more or less on your own when in the wilderness (less so, of course, if you're with an organized group or experienced friends). There may be marked trails or an occasional sign to direct you, but this won't always be the case. Finding the way and staying out of trouble is totally up to you. You might not cross paths with someone else who could assist if you should get lost or otherwise run into difficulty.

Not all wilderness areas are remote. Some relatively wild parks or forests do have networks of roads, meaning you may not be far from a possible escape route, should there be a need for one. In popular areas the trails are so well traveled that help might be quickly available in the event of a mishap. Still, it's wise to be prepared for anything and proceed with caution. Among other skills, it's necessary to know how to use a map and compass, and essential to have those items along or to be with others who do.

Some people enjoy taking on challenges or setting ambitious goals, seeking for instance to hike or paddle long distances, or perhaps climb rugged mountains. While it can be worthwhile and gratifying to stretch oneself at times in the wilderness, it's also important to avoid losing sight of our limitations as human beings. We are indeed mortal, after all. Excessive confidence, ambition, and/or carelessness can lead any person into trouble—in circumstances which could include exhaustion, an accident, or getting lost. Since your life could be at stake, surely it makes sense to take the best possible care of yourself out there.

Equipment

A substantial amount of equipment is normally required for an overnight wilderness trip, much more of course than is needed on a day trip. Major items generally include a backpack (or other type of pack or bag for carrying gear), sleeping bag, and tent. Other appropriate items include a pad or mat to sleep on, a small stove, cookware, and a flashlight.

Each piece of equipment fulfills a particular function or purpose. If you'll be doing much walking or hiking, a backpack is by far the most efficient and comfortable way to carry everything. Other types of packs and bags are designed for activities like canoeing/kayaking, rafting, and cycling. At night a sleeping bag furnishes insulation for warmth while you're sleeping, and a tent provides protection from the elements and from insects.

In earlier times people camped out with much less, and some so-called primitive peoples have long been able to make do with relatively little. You could do so, too, if you really wanted to. One way to learn how would be to train at a school which teaches wilderness survival skills.

Most of us, however, are somewhat soft from the ways of civilization. Camping equipment makes outdoor living easier, safer, more comfortable. It eases the transition for us.

At the same time, there's also a risk of going overboard with equipment. Unnecessary gear can get in the way. There are hundreds of useful and/or gimmicky items available on the market which are supposed to make camping easier or better. Without restraint you could end up knee-deep in gear, creating numerous distractions and barriers between you and nature.

A good practice is to bring only those things which are indispensable to your safety, well-being, and comfort in the wilderness. Leave at home less important items that you won't use very often. A discussion of recommended gear and clothing follows at some length in Chapters 2 through 6.

Beginners often find the subject of equipment to be a little intimidating, and for some it borders on being overwhelming. If that's the case for you, consider going first on a trip with an outfitter, guide, club, or other organization which will furnish most or all of the gear. This will save you the trouble of having to deal with it on your own at the start. Later, after a trip or two, you can decide whether or not you want your own equipment.

Shopping for wilderness-oriented gear isn't the simplest task these days, given the many available brands and designs and models, which change from year to year. If you find the process at all frustrating or difficult, keep in mind that *equipment is a means to an end*. With experience the use of gear becomes easy and automatic. It won't remain the focus of your experience, or require much attention and expenditure of energy on your part, and you'll be free to enjoy yourself in the wilderness each day as you wish.

If you're not sure you're ready to buy, or uncertain of your commitment to wilderness camping, *renting* equipment is another good option. A number of outdoor specialty stores rent gear at reasonable prices. Inquire at your local store, if there's one nearby. In renting you'll get a better feel for what's involved, and afterward will probably be clearer about what you want to buy, should you decide to get your own equipment.

A final option is to *borrow* gear from a friend or acquaintance. Even if you don't happen to know any backpackers or campers, it never hurts to ask around. Millions of people have camping equipment in their closets. While there's no certainty that someone else's gear will be appropriate for your particular needs (the pack might be much too large or the tent too heavy), then again it might be just right for you.

Common Concerns and Fears Among Beginners

In spite of the many attractions of nature and wilderness, the idea of sleeping outside brings up concerns and fears for many people. A significant number of those who love outdoor activities *never* camp out, and for some it's in part because of fears. These include the fear of being seriously uncomfortable, of wild animals (especially bears and snakes), of the unknown.

It's normal to feel anxious or experience fear when we're trying something new, or venturing into an environment which is strange to us. It also seems to be the case that inexperienced people often project all kinds of fears onto the wilderness.

It's easy enough to imagine threats to our safety and well-being out there. The truth is, assuming we know how to take care of ourselves, the wilderness is safer and healthier in most ways than the polluted and sometimes violence-prone world we live in back at home.

Anxieties about the wilderness are undoubtedly intensified by the books and movies and stories we've been exposed to. These often portray nature in a distorted way: as a place of constant adversity, of dangerous animals, of an unceasing array of hazards.

Many wilderness-related fears have a very minimal basis in reality. This is not to deny that there can be real dangers, but these will rarely be encountered. Most wild animals, for instance, have no desire for contact or conflict with human beings. As long as you respect their space they'll generally give you a wide berth. Much of the time you won't even be aware they're around. Unprovoked attacks are rare in the extreme. Millions of Americans camp out safely each year without a problem from animals or other presumed dangers.

Then there's the matter of comfort. We live in a society where many seem to be obsessed with comfort, and advertising encourages this. Some non-outdoorspeople imagine that camping involves considerable discomfort, and to go camping means deliberately courting hardship and turning your back on the benefits of civilization. With such beliefs it's no surprise that many avoid giving wilderness camping a try.

It's unquestionably true that some people have had bad experiences while camping out, but this is usually the result of inadequate equipment and clothing, and/or a lack of appropriate skills. In fact, there's no reason to be seriously uncomfortable in the wilderness these days. There are thick foam pads or mattresses to sleep on, and other items of equipment available today are designed for maximum comfort and ease of use.

Of course, a good many everyday conveniences aren't available in the wilderness. The level of comfort won't necessarily be equivalent to that at home, and you're potentially much more exposed to the elements. At the same time, it's possible to find perfectly adequate protection and warmth during the day using raingear and proper clothing, and at night you can sleep cozily and comfortably inside your tent and sleeping bag.

Other sources of concern involve the possibility of getting lost (totally avoidable if you're careful and know how to use map and compass), having to go to the bathroom without facilities (not difficult to learn), and trying to keep clean without taking a shower (you can always wash up by hand, take a dip in a lake or stream, or use a "solar shower"). Outdoor living does require a change in some habits, including learning a few simpler methods which don't depend on conveniences like plumbing or heating.

Pleasures

The ways of camping are easy enough to learn and surprisingly gratifying. It's satisfying to be self-reliant. Among other things, if you've camped in the wilderness you're likely to be able to weather such back-at-home events as power failures, blackouts, and plumbing problems much better than those who are completely addicted to modern conveniences.

The simplifying which takes place on a wilderness trip ends up being one of the most refreshing elements of the experience. Nothing is complicated. Rarely do you have to do more than one thing at a time. Not only is that appealing and relaxing, but you also return with a sharper perspective—including on what we've gained as well as given up by living in our culture with its endless array of conveniences and complexities.

You may start to appreciate some things more through their absence. At the same time, quite a few of us also come to realize that our lives are overly cluttered—that we might be content with fewer of the things we normally consider important, or tend to surround ourselves with.

One of the delights of a camping trip is that at the end of the day you don't have to return to your vehicle or the highway. There's nowhere to go but to your tent, which more often than not is pitched amid beautiful surroundings. A real feeling of vacation begins here. On a longer trip you may even forget what day of the week it is. The world of civilization feels remote. There are no telephones, newspapers, or TVs, no world news, and none of the other usual sources of stress.

It takes time to unwind, which rarely if ever happens in a day. After several days or more, some people find themselves experiencing a deep and profound feeling of peaceful relaxation, more complete than one might have imagined possible. And as long as you remain, you'll be immersed in one of the most healing environments imaginable.

Backpacking

A backpacking trip is basically an extended hiking trip which involves camping in the wilderness. Everything needed for the duration of the trip is carried in a full-size backpack.

The words "backpacking" and "hiking" have been used loosely over the years and are sometimes confused. Some people use them interchangeably, but they're not quite the same thing. Hiking doesn't necessarily include camping. Millions of Americans hike for a day at a time without camping out. As most of us use it, the word backpacking *always* implies camping.

Non-backpackers often assume that a full-size pack must be heavy and uncomfortable to carry. This isn't usually true, as long as you have a modern pack that fits properly, and you're willing to limit your supplies to the necessary minimum. Most of the top-quality packs available in recent years are designed to be carried with a surprising degree of comfort. The experience of walking with a backpack can even be pleasurable after you've had time to adjust to it.

With a modern backpack most of the weight actually rides on your hips, rather than on the more vulnerable back and shoulders. This is possible because of a hipbelt system which is rigged up to the pack frame. The weight of a properly fitted pack will be felt primarily in the thighs and legs, just as if you'd gained some body weight.

This is not to say that carrying a full-size pack is necessarily easy. Backpacking does put some added demands on the body, and it'll provide a challenging workout when you're hiking steeply uphill or downhill. It's not recommended for those who are seriously out of shape. Hikers and other active people in reasonably good condition should have little difficulty in adjusting to backpacking. As with other activities, it's best to ease into it gently. Start with a short, unambitious trip, and avoid tackling major changes of elevation at first. You can find plenty of challenges later on if you so desire.

The most important principle for successful backpacking is to keep the *weight* and *bulk* of everything to an absolute minimum. On first glance this should seem pretty obvious, but it's far too often ignored, especially by beginners but also by quite a few seasoned backpackers. Weight is the most critical factor by far. Attempting to carry an overly heavy pack is to risk spoiling a trip, or at least turning it into an arduous experience of physical endurance.

The weight of the pack will matter less, of course, if you're only going to walk a short distance with it. When you'll be hiking a few miles or more it's vital to keep that weight down. This is perhaps your most important task in preparing for a trip. What is a reasonable maximum will vary from one person to another. Backpackers who are in top shape will obviously be able to carry more than those who haven't been exercising on a regular basis.

An old rule of thumb suggests that if you're a so-called average person in good condition, carrying a pack which weighs between one-fourth and one-fifth of your body weight should be no problem at all. It's possible to work up to heavier loads, but trying to carry much more than that at first may be asking for trouble. Keeping it within this range will be a special challenge on a longer backpacking trip, but with effort it can be done.

As with any kind of travel, going light with a backpack increases your feeling of freedom. For some people it takes real self-discipline to leave behind all but the bare essentials, which is what's often required to keep the pack light enough. Such "luxury" items as a camera, binoculars, or comfortable camp shoes may seem important enough

to bring, but without considerable restraint the load can easily get out of hand.

What's the special appeal of backpacking? For some of us it's being able to carry everything we need and roam freely along wilderness trails for days at a time—communing with nature and camping where we wish (in those wilderness areas where unrestricted camping is permitted). Backpacking offers a freedom on foot which is unheard of elsewhere in today's world.

There's a real thrill involved in backpacking deeply into a remote and unspoiled wilderness area, which might be days from the nearest highway—the kind of splendid place which relatively few people are likely to ever set eyes on. It's also a delight to view new scenery each day and camp at a different site each night (although you can also set up a base camp, and take day hikes from there if you like). To backpack through a mountain range brings those mountains remarkably to life. Our knowledge of an environment becomes deeply ingrained in a way that's unlikely to leave us.

Many people who lead busy lives tend to limit their excursions to weekends, perhaps taking a longer trip every now and then. A weekend of backpacking or other wilderness activity is certainly sufficient for a person to experience a feeling of refreshment and renewal. Spending a week or more in the wilderness can provide a more profound impact.

It's also possible, if you have the time and inclination, to go out for weeks or even months on end. The relatively small number of backpackers who do so, including those who hike the entire 2,100-mile Appalachian Trail or other major National Scenic Trails each year, often find such a backpacking trip to be a truly life-changing event.

TWO

Major Items of Equipment: Backpack, Sleeping Bag, Tent

BACKPACK

If you're entering the wilderness on foot, the easiest and most sensible way to carry everything is in a backpack. You could probably manage with other kinds of carry-bags if you're not walking very far, but the alternatives are certain to be more cumbersome. When longer distances are involved, a backpack becomes a critically important item of equipment.

Backpacks come in many shapes and sizes and designs. A large "full-size" pack is what's appropriate for most overnight trips. There are also medium-size "weekender" packs available which have enough space for a short overnight trip.

A full-size pack has room for clothing, food, cooking gear, a mini-stove, and everything else you need in order to live in the wilderness for as much as several days or more—including a tent and sleeping bag, which may fit inside or be attached outside.

Getting a Good Fit

It's important that a backpack be *fitted to your body*. Fit and comfort are vital if you'll be carrying the pack for more than a short distance. Not all packs will fit you. Wearing a poorly-fitting or uncomfortable pack is likely to take the joy out of a trip as effectively as the wrong size boots or shoes.

Beware of inexpensive "one-size-fits-all" backpacks. Low-priced packs ($50-$75 or less) are often poorly designed by today's standards, undependable, and sometimes quite uncomfortable. If finances are limited and you're tempted to cut corners, make a compromise with the tent rather than the pack.

Most top-quality packs come in different sizes (although there are a few exceptions, as some modern packs are super-adjustable), to fit people of different body lengths and shapes. With a choice of pack sizes it's easier to find the right fit.

Those who backpacked many years ago—or who have not-so-fond memories of carrying heavy packs in the military—might be amazed at the comfort of a modern pack. It's a far cry from earlier designs, and usually has heavy foam padding in all the right places. Also, just about anything that you'll put inside the pack may now be obtained in lighter-than-ever versions.

People who have never backpacked often assume that wearing a pack must put a considerable strain on the back and shoulders. With the right pack this isn't the case, since much of the weight of a modern backpack actually goes on the pelvis—supported by a padded hipbelt (attached to the pack frame), which is tightened around the hips. The shoulder straps will hold the pack snugly to your back, but they shouldn't carry most of the weight.

You should be able to stand erect and walk in a relatively normal way when carrying a backpack. You'll feel the weight especially in your legs and thighs, and this will be most noticeable when walking steeply uphill or downhill. Carrying the pack shouldn't be a struggle. If it is, you're carrying too much weight, or the pack needs adjusting, or you have the wrong pack

External Frame versus Internal Frame Packs

The most important choice you'll have to make when buying a backpack is between an external frame and internal frame pack. There's been an ongoing debate for many years about which is best, and differences of opinion on the subject still abound.

External frame packs have been around a lot longer than internal frame packs. The former can be easily identified by the external and visible tubular frame which usually extends below and sometimes above the packbag.

Advantages of the external frame pack include: It's easy to fasten items such as sleeping bag and tent to the frame, there's an air space between the pack and your back which makes it comfortable to wear in warm weather, the pack holds its shape when only partially full, and it can be set down in mud without dirtying the packbag. Over the years there's been some consensus that external frame packs balance heavy loads especially well, and are probably the best choice for longer backpacking trips.

An internal frame pack has the frame hidden inside the packbag. The pack is generally not as wide and usually doesn't extend as high as the typical external frame pack. This design was developed to serve a number of different purposes. Unlike external frame packs, internal frame packs collapse well and can often be carried onto airplanes. They're especially suitable for activities where an external frame may get in the way, such as cross-country skiing, mountaineering, or bushwhacking.

Many backpackers still swear by external frame packs, and these packs remain especially suitable for travel on trails. They're also less expensive than most internal frame packs. The advantages of the externals are sometimes unfairly overlooked amid the current popularity of the internals. Many stores now feature a much larger selection of the latter, and a few have even stopped carrying external frame packs.

At the same time, it's true that the most recent generation of internal frame packs have been receiving extremely positive reports from some backpackers and others. Women in particular often get a better fit with an internal frame pack, and quite a few men as well as women testify that the newest models are very comfortable even with heavier loads.

When you're shopping for a pack, try on as many different models of both external and internal frame packs as you can. Remember that comfort and fit are more important than anything else. See what feels best. It'll be necessary to have some weight inside the pack to know how it really feels (some stores have weights available for this purpose). Walk around for a while with the pack on.

Get some assistance from a salesperson, who should be able to help you locate the right size and make adjustments.

If you find more than one that fits you well, and you're having trouble making a decision, choose the pack with the most pockets and compartments. While it's useful to have a good-size main compartment for larger items, in general the more dividers and pockets the better. This makes it much easier to separate and organize your gear, and you'll then be able to locate items quickly when you need to.

Prices for a top-quality backpack currently run from about $80 to $250 and higher. You might find one on sale for somewhat less. A full-size pack which sells for under $50 is almost certainly not of adequate quality. Keep in mind that you could be in a tough spot if the pack should fall apart on your trip, especially if you're far from a highway. Don't take a chance with this important item.

Other Kinds of Outdoor Luggage

There are other kinds of packs and carry-bags available which are appropriate for activities where little or no walking is involved, such as cycling, canoeing, or rafting. These items can be used instead of or in addition to a backpack.

For water-based activities like canoeing, kayaking, or rafting you can bring a traditional duffel bag or other kinds of carry-bags. The fabric should be heavy-duty nylon, if possible, and coated for waterproofness. Add your own external or internal plastic (or nylon) bag as a barrier to insure that no water gets in. On an overnight cycling trip items are typically carried inside "panniers" (bike-bags).

Shoulder bags are popular among some people for short trips on foot. For longer distances, carrying a backpack is much less tiring and makes a lot more sense. This way the load is balanced and you'll have the free use of both arms and hands.

SLEEPING BAG

Few things are more satisfying than a good night's sleep after an active day in the wilderness. A sleeping bag provides protection and insulation from cooler nighttime temperatures, helping to ensure that you will indeed sleep well and comfortably. The importance of this item cannot be overstated.

It's essential to have a sleeping bag which is warm enough for the coldest conceivable temperatures that you might confront on a trip. In some mountain areas it can drop below freezing even in the summer. Not many things will take the fun out of a trip more thoroughly than having to spend a night or two shivering away inside an inadequate sleeping bag. Don't risk spoiling your trip by bringing a bag which may not be up to the task.

An inadequate bag could, however, be improved by wearing extra clothing inside it. If you have any doubts about the warmth of a sleeping bag you already own or have borrowed, and there isn't time to get another bag, bring *plenty* of extra clothing along as insurance.

Temperature Ratings

A good sleeping bag will come with a *temperature rating*, which is an estimate by the manufacturer that the bag should keep a normal person warm when the air temperature is no lower than a stated number of degrees. Shop only at stores which display sleeping bags with the temperature ratings clearly identified. Get a bag with a rating which is lower than any temperature that you could possibly encounter on a trip, and warmer than you think you'll need, especially if you're someone who gets cold easily. The stated ratings are typically for a so-called average person, and should not be trusted completely.

The most versatile sleeping bag for camping in much of the country (in other than areas with a hot climate) will be a so-called "3-season bag," which should normally cover your needs during spring, summer, and fall. A 3-season bag usually has a temperature rating in the range of 15° to 25° F.

There may be times in the summer when it's too warm to get completely into a 3-season bag, but you can unzip it and pull the bag over you like a quilt as needed. Nights in the mountains are sometimes surprisingly cool or even cold, however, so the extra insulation may come in handy more often than you might expect.

Down versus Synthetics

An important factor that has to be considered when selecting a sleeping bag is the *fill*, the insulating material used. Your major choice is between down and synthetics. Each has advantages and disadvantages. Goose or duck down is still the lightest of all possible fills, the least bulky, and also the most compressible. Weight-wise, down is ideal for a long trip. It's also more expensive than the synthetics, although prices have dropped considerably in recent years. Quality varies.

The greatest disadvantage of down is that when wet it's utterly useless for insulation. A down bag

must be kept dry at all costs, or your trip may be finished (and your life may be endangered if the weather's cold and you're far from a road). In addition, down takes a long time to dry out.

Synthetics such as Polarguard weigh more than down, and they don't compress as easily into a stuff sack. Some of the newer synthetics including Hollofil and Quallofil, however, are a bit lighter and more compressible. Aside from price, the greatest advantage of a synthetic sleeping bag is that it can be wrung out when wet and will still provide warmth. It's also easier to wash, quicker to dry, and is less fragile than a down bag.

If you're going on a long trip where a pound or two will make a big difference, you may want to seriously consider a down bag. If you'll be taking mostly shorter trips, however, and/or visiting areas of the country where precipitation is common, your best choice is probably a synthetic bag.

Mummy versus Rectangular Shape

Another decision you'll have to make is regarding the shape of the bag. Best by far for backpacking is a "mummy bag," which is severely tapered and has a hood with a drawstring at the top. Since it closely fits the contours of your body, a mummy bag will keep you warm with the least amount of material and fill, meaning less weight and bulk to carry.

Some people are initially troubled by the idea of a mummy bag, fearing they'll feel too confined. In fact you can move your body any way you want in a mummy bag, although it's true that the bag has to be unzipped if you want to stretch out arms or legs in different directions. While it may not be for everyone, lots of people find contentment in a mummy once they've tried one.

Roomier "modified mummys" are also available, as are tapered bags, which have a shape in between that of a mummy and a rectangular bag. Traditional rectangular sleeping bags are still on the market, and such a bag might pass, especially if you're not concerned about the additional weight and bulk. Because of the shape and the fact it's completely open at the top, however, it isn't likely to be as comfortable in cold weather.

A final consideration is the length or size of the bag. Most sleeping bags come in two or three different lengths. It's sensible to get a bag which is closest in size to your actual height, so that you won't need to carry more weight and bulk than necessary. Most stores will let you get inside a bag to see how it fits and feels, so don't hesitate to do that if you want to.

Top-quality 3-season sleeping bags generally run from under $100 to well over $200. Some cold-weather or winter bags cost much more. A modern sleeping bag has a thin nylon outer shell, and it can be stuffed into a stuff sack, which normally comes with the bag. Stay away from old-fashioned cloth-lined sleeping bags which roll up. While still available at some sporting goods and army-navy stores, many of these bags aren't warm enough for 3-season use, and most aren't durably made.

Storing a Sleeping Bag

Once you own one, never leave a sleeping bag in its stuff sack for any length of time, because this will shorten the life span of the bag. Open it up and store the sleeping bag loosely. Unpack it immediately after each trip so any moisture will evaporate quickly. If you forget, the bag might easily contract a serious case of mold or mildew.

Should you happen to borrow a sleeping bag or have an old one sitting in the closet, shake it vigorously and stretch the bag out on the floor. If it has a reasonably low temperature rating and isn't worn out, the bag should loft up at least several inches from the floor. If it lies there relatively flat, two or three inches above the floor, you can conclude that it's not going to do the job in cold weather.

Sleeping bags do wear out, and a bag that once provided good insulation will eventually lose that ability, particularly if it's left in a stuff sack for long periods. When borrowing a bag, don't place complete trust in someone's claim that it's warm, especially if the bag is old or shows signs of heavy use.

TENT

A tent obviously offers protection from the elements and also from insects. If you're camping during a season or in an area where there's no chance of rain or other precipitation, and there are no bugs, a tent isn't really necessary. You could sleep out in the open air under the stars, as some people prefer to do.

In most regions of the country, however, precipitation is always a possibility, and forecasts can't be trusted very much. Storms and rain can come suddenly at any time, especially in mountain areas. In such locations it's unwise and risky to be without a tent or other shelter at night. If there's a remote chance of precipitation, set up the tent even if you plan to sleep outside (imagine the scenario of being caught by a storm in the dead of night, as you fumble with a flashlight in a state of semisleep and attempt to erect your tent in the pouring rain).

Some people compromise by camping out under a tarp, which is usually a sheet of nylon or plastic. This is typically stretched across a line which is tied between two trees. The tarp will make for an extra light and open shelter, fine as long as insects aren't a problem. Of course, in a heavy, windy rainstorm the tarp isn't going to keep all of the rain out, and you're likely to get wet on such occasions.

There are many kinds of tents on the market these days, ranging from tiny, superlight models to huge, family-size tents you can stand up in. Those that are heavy or bulky can instantly be ruled out for backpacking, cycling, and any other activity where weight and bulk must be minimized. Backpackers will usually want to focus on those tents which lie at the lightest end of the spectrum, preferably in the range of three to six pounds or less.

Most tents are made to hold at least two people, although any tent can be used by a single person. Some tents also come in larger sizes suitable for three, four, or more people. When two people are sharing a tent they can split up the weight, with one person carrying the body of the tent, and the other carrying the fly, poles, and stakes. This makes it feasible for two or more campers to manage with a heavier tent, if necessary.

Tents Suitable for Wilderness Camping

The largest, highest, and roomiest tents are not appropriate for most wilderness camping trips. Such tents are usually much too heavy and bulky to be carried any distance, and require a lot of space for setting up. They're most suitable for car-camping.

For many years the most popular kind of tent for camping in the wilderness was the traditional rectangular "A-frame" tent (so-called because the tent has an "A" shape when viewed from the front or back). These tents are still widely used, but much less so now than in the past. They remain reasonably dependable but require many stakes and tie-lines, take longer to put up than many of the newer tents, and won't withstand high winds as well.

If you already own an A-frame tent, or can borrow one, or buy one at a bargain price, it should fit the bill. Avoid camping in open areas where you might be exposed to high winds, which happens to be a good idea regardless of the tent you have.

Much more popular these days are "dome tents," which are multisided and dome-shaped.

While most of them aren't high enough for a person of average height to stand up in, dome tents still feel very spacious inside. They're also fairly easy to set up, and withstand storms quite well. Most are self-supporting, meaning they don't require stakes, which can be an advantage when camping on sand, snow, or bedrock (a few A-frame tents are also self-supporting). A disadvantage is that many are a little heavy for backpacking, typically weighing from six to 10 pounds or more, and usually require a good-size plot of ground for setting up.

Especially suitable for backpacking are the light-weight "hoop tents" which are somewhat bug-shaped or frog-shaped, often tapering down sharply from front to rear. Headroom in these tents is quite limited and usually found only at the front, and there's not much space for gear when two people are inside (backpacks can be left outside overnight). However, these tents can be erected quickly, and, best of all, they often weigh as little as three to four pounds.

One-person "bivouac tents" are also on the market. These are the lightest of all, but not very popular with most campers because they're so small. There's not enough room for a person to sit up inside, so you wouldn't want to have to spend an extended time in one, which is always a possibility if you encounter severe weather. The tents weigh in at as little as two pounds or less, though, which certainly can't be beat.

There are still other kinds of tents, including some with innovative designs and interesting features which have appeared in recent years. Also, extra sturdy and durable "4-season" tents are available for winter or expedition use. The cost of a regular good-quality two-person tent is usually between $150 and $300, with some of the larger tents and special designs costing much more.

The Rain Fly

Most tents come with a rain fly, a separate tarp which goes over the main body of the tent and is suspended a few inches from the tent walls. The fly is normally made of waterproof nylon, whereas the inner walls consist of breathable nylon.

A substantial amount of water is lost from the human body through exhalation and perspiration during the night. In a tent with a fly, this moisture should pass through the breathable inner wall of the tent, and then may condense on the inside surface of the fly, from there to run off onto the earth.

Budget tents usually have a single wall without a fly, and these tents are famous for condensation problems. When a single-walled tent is zipped up, moisture is likely to condense inside, and then drip and/or form a small pool of water on the tent floor. People in single-wall tents sometimes have the impression that their tent is leaking when it's raining outside, whereas raindrops may actually be dislodging drops of condensation inside. Unless you want to make do with a cheaper tent to save money, you're much better off in getting a tent with a fly.

Setting Up the Tent

After purchasing or borrowing a tent and before departing on a trip, always open it and try to put up the tent in your yard or living room. It's important to make sure all the parts are there, and a good idea to practice setting it up when you have some spare time. Printed directions aren't always easy to understand, and it may take a while to figure things out.

If parts are missing and you don't find out until you're in the wilderness, your trip could be off to a bad start or in real trouble. Also, trying to put up a new tent for the first time on the trip itself can be frustrating, especially if you're tired from a day of travel and manage to arrive at your campsite with as little as a few minutes of daylight remaining.

Most tents aren't difficult to set up. After doing it once or twice you'll probably find it comes more or less automatically. If you run into trouble the first time, and you're still at home, call the store where you bought the tent for some advice over the phone (or go back in person if necessary). Should you be going on a trip with an organized group, others who are experienced will undoubtedly be able to help you set it up. Just be sure all the proper parts are included before leaving.

Tent Care

A tent needs proper care to ensure it has a long life and remains waterproof. "Seam-sealer" should be periodically applied to the seams of most tents to keep them waterproof. The seams are where leaks are likely to develop, since that's where stitching went through the nylon.

Some tent manufacturers recommend applying seam-sealer before you use the tent the first time, and then at least once a year, or more frequently if the tent receives heavy use. If you fail to do this right away, you aren't likely to get badly soaked inside the tent when it rains, but it's possible that some water may work its way through the seams.

In order to protect the floor of your tent from wear and tear (and thus avoid leaks), take your boots off before entering. This also makes it easier to keep things clean. Be extremely careful if you bring your pack inside, or any gear which has hooks, rings, or other parts which might snag on the tent floor.

Keep sharp objects and especially fire away from the tent at all times. Most tents are treated with fire retardant, but will still melt in an open flame, or if sparks from a nearby fire land on it. The same of course holds true for your nylon-shelled sleeping bag, as well as your pack, raingear, clothing, and other equipment. Never build a campfire close to the tent. If it's within fifty feet or so, make sure the fire stays small and is closely tended at all times.

Don't use matches or a candle inside the tent, especially a small one. In a large tent do so with the greatest caution. If any flame should make contact with the vulnerable nylon walls of a tent, the consequences are potentially disastrous—you could sustain serious burns if it ignites. It's best to make it a habit to never use these things inside or near a tent. A good flashlight or other battery-operated lamp will do fine for reading or other use. Also, never use a stove inside a tent (stoves can and sometimes do flare up unexpectedly).

When it's had plenty of use, a tent will eventually show signs of wear and tear and develop multiple leaks. That's obviously the time to replace it. You can prolong the life of your tent by not leaving it set up in direct sunlight for extended periods of time (which ages the nylon), and by always drying and airing it out immediately after returning from a trip.

Storing the tent even slightly damp may attract molds, which can cause serious deterioration along with unpleasant odors. If it's dirty or muddy, rinse the tent off outside with a hose, or in your shower or bathtub. A simple sponging will normally be adequate to keep it clean. Soap may be used if necessary.

THREE

Other Important Items

RAINGEAR

It's essential to bring raingear on any wilderness trip, unless you're visiting an area where rain is considered to be virtually impossible. Even then it wouldn't be completely foolish to pack some minimal form of raingear such as a poncho, just in case the unlikely event does happen during your trip. Remember that unusual weather is far from a rarity in most of the world today, and a storm can occur anywhere.

The possibility of getting wet should never be taken lightly, especially if the temperatures might be in the range of cool to cold. Getting thoroughly soaked to the skin in the rain must be avoided at all costs in cold weather. It would be less of a problem, of course, on a warm or hot day.

Aside from the likelihood of discomfort should you get drenched, you may also be risking hypothermia, which can occur in temperatures as high as 50°-60° F (see Chapter 13 for more about hypothermia).

Perhaps you'll want to listen to weather forecasts before departing on your trip, but don't ever make the mistake of leaving raingear at home because "it's not supposed to rain." Inexperienced people have certainly been known to do such a thing, and sometimes suffer serious consequences because of it.

Any seasoned outdoorsperson who has traveled in areas with variable weather knows that the forecasts are wrong as often as they are right—especially for mountain areas, which tend to have their own unique and sometimes quickly changing weather patterns.

To summarize: Unless you've got extremely good grounds for doing otherwise, *always* bring rainwear, no matter how remote the possibility of precipitation may seem to be. If it does indeed rain, your comfort, safety, and on occasion even your survival might depend on the protection of the raingear.

Poncho

The simplest rainwear you could bring would be a nylon poncho, which hangs loosely down to your knees and has a hood. It should be made of the lightest-weight nylon available if you're backpacking or otherwise want to minimize weight.

Advantages of a poncho include the fact that it's not as confining as most other forms of raingear and allows the passage of some air, meaning you're less likely to overheat in warm weather. It will also double as an emergency tarp (some of them come with grommets). On the other hand, a poncho doesn't do so well in windy, exposed areas, as it may catch the wind and snap.

There are vinyl ponchos which cost under $5, but this kind of poncho is easily torn if you happen to snag it on a branch, and it will quickly fail under any kind of stress. Don't bring such an undependable item on an overnight wilderness trip. A good nylon poncho will generally cost between $20 and $40. Like all other forms of raingear, with wear and tear the poncho will eventually start to leak and need to be replaced.

Another option for backpackers is a "backpack poncho" or "packboard poncho." This is extra long in the back and extends to cover a full-size backpack, in addition to the person wearing it.

Rain Chaps

If you use a poncho it's also a good idea to have some protection for your legs, especially in cool or cold weather. Rain chaps provide a convenient solution. These consist of two separate nylon "pant legs" which attach either to your belt or the belt loops on your pants or shorts. Chaps are more air conditioned than rain pants, can be pulled on over most boots, and will take up little space in your pack when not in use.

Rain Jacket or Suit

Other forms of rainwear include rain jackets and rain suits. A jacket doesn't usually reach down much below the waist, and may or may not have a hood (if not, you'll need a separate rain hat). A full rain suit with pants will provide the most complete protection, which is an important consideration when it's cold. In warm weather, however, when involved in exercise you'll overheat more quickly in a rain suit than in a poncho.

Appropriate rain jackets and suits are normally made of nylon. If you're backpacking, make sure it's the lightest weight nylon available. Avoid all vinyl raingear, which can easily tear or otherwise fail, possibly jeopardizing your safety.

Rainwear made of so-called "breatheable but waterproof" fabrics like Goretex has become very popular in recent years. This kind of raingear is much more expensive, but by supposedly eliminating the perspiration problem, it's said to keep you drier and more comfortable in the rain. At the same time, there are many reports that such garments begin to leak after becoming slightly dirty or worn. Opinions on the subject remain divided. Some people fully endorse and swear by these products, while others feel they don't stand up to the glowing claims made about them, and aren't worth the price.

Pack Raincover

It's important to protect your sleeping bag and all essential clothing from the possibility of getting wet while traveling. Most packs are coated for waterproofness, but it's wise never to trust that a pack or other luggage is in fact totally waterproof, regardless of the manufacturer's claims. You might find out otherwise in heavy rain, or if the pack should somehow fall into water. Even if there aren't leaks in the fabric, moisture can get in through a pack's zippers.

A nylon pack raincover is a good investment for any backpacker, although this item is less essential if you're going to be using a backpack poncho (which covers the pack while it's on your back). A raincover provides an extra layer of protection, some additional insurance that your gear will remain dry. The cover can also be put on your pack at night, assuming you'll be leaving it outside the tent.

A cheap, inelegant, but satisfactory short-term alternative to a nylon raincover is a large garbage bag, which can be pulled over the pack or around any other kind of luggage. Bring several if you're going to use them, as a plastic bag won't stay leak-free for long.

Still another method for keeping your gear from getting wet is to place clothing and other essentials in plastic bags *inside* the pack. The stuff sack for your sleeping bag can also be lined with a plastic bag as an extra barrier against water.

WATER CONTAINERS

Water Bottles/Canteens

You'll normally need containers for carrying a minimum of one to two quarts (or liters) of water, and much more if you're camping in the desert or during hot weather. When visiting an area where water is abundant, two one-quart (liter) containers will usually do. When camping in an arid area or away from water, plan on carrying at least a gallon or more of water per day.

Even when visiting a place where there's ample water, always start out with a minimum of a quart or more water from home, and at least double that if high temperatures are likely, as it could take more time than expected to reach a water source.

Outdoor specialty stores sell some sturdy and durable plastic bottles, and these are especially recommended because they'll take lots of abuse and last for many years. Many of the conventional metal or plastic canteens available are unnecessarily heavy for backpacking, although they may be fine for other activities. Just don't bring a cheap, flimsy plastic bottle that might crack or break if you accidentally step on it. Never bring glass, which obviously can shatter if dropped.

Other Water Containers

In addition to water bottles and canteens, larger containers are available for storing and transporting water. Collapsible plastic water carriers are very useful. They're made in sizes usually ranging from 2 1/2 gallons to 5 gallons, weigh little when empty, and cost just a few dollars each. One or two will come in handy on most trips, especially for those times when you can't camp right next to water and have to walk to reach it.

It's possible to fill one carrier with unpurified water from a lake or stream, and keep this for washing and cooking, and fill another carrier with filtered or purified water for drinking and brushing teeth. If you do this, be sure to label the containers clearly so you'll avoid accidentally mixing them up.

WATER FILTER

It's unfortunate that the purity of most water sources in the wilderness can no longer be trusted.

In the past people drank freely from wild lakes, ponds, rivers, and streams, but the risk of contracting a parasite or ingesting harmful bacteria has grown too high. It's now usually necessary to purify water either by boiling, using tablets, or filtering (see Chapter 10 for more about water and purification).

In recent years a number of portable water filters suitable for camping have appeared on the market. Many people now consider a water filter to be an essential item on a wilderness camping trip. Some filters weigh less than a pound. Most of the better ones will filter out parasites, bacteria, and various pollutants.

A majority of these filters are equipped with a hand pump, and water can be purified rather quickly. Some appealing advantages of filtering are that the taste of the water is not affected, it stays cold, and you can drink the water immediately.

Filters do have to be cleaned and replaced periodically. Always choose the best looking water that you can find for purifying. A filter will clog up rather quickly if you use brackish or silt-filled water. Prices for water filters range from under $40 to $200 and higher.

FOAM PAD OR MATTRESS

Most backpackers and others who camp in the wilderness use a foam pad or mattress under their sleeping bag at night. In most circumstances a pad or mattress of some kind should be considered essential, as it will provide not only comfort, but also insulation from the ground in cool or cold weather (a sleeping bag with synthetic fill will also furnish a bit of cushioning, but usually not enough).

There may well be times when you'll be able to camp on sand or soft ground with pine needles, but this can't always be counted on. It's sometimes necessary to make do with a campsite which is a bit uneven and bumpy, and on occasion even one with exposed tree roots or embedded rocks. A pad will help smooth things out and make for much more comfort.

It's true that some people find they can get used to sleeping on hard or irregular ground without a pad. For those of us accustomed to soft beds, however, this would take some time, and it simply isn't necessary. If you value a good night's sleep, do yourself a favor and bring a pad along.

In cold weather, which is always a possibility in many of the mountain areas, a pad is important

as well for the insulation it provides—reducing the loss of heat from sleeping bag to ground. Also, be aware that the temperature ratings given to sleeping bags are normally based on the assumption that a pad will be used. Without one your bag won't be as effective.

An assortment of foam pads and mattresses, including "self-inflating" ones (which require pressure to roll up, and then expand when unrolled) are available. The self-inflating mattresses have become especially popular in recent years. They're fairly compact when rolled up, are waterproof, and cost from about $40 to over $90 (depending on size and thickness).

"Open cell" foam pads, made of the kind of compressible foam used in furniture and other products, are perfectly suitable as well. These pads are somewhat bulkier when rolled up, but are no heavier than the self-inflating pads, generally cost less, and are quite comfortable.

Thinner "closed cell" pads, which compress very little, have similarly been around for many years. These offer excellent insulation but very little in the way of cushioning. Since they aren't as comfortable, you're probably better off with the alternatives. Sometimes open cell and closed cell foam are combined in one pad, and this product certainly fits the bill.

Traditional air mattresses have limitations which make them unsuitable for most wilderness camping trips. The durable ones are generally too heavy for backpacking, although they may be all right for a trip where weight isn't a consideration. And the inexpensive lightweight mattresses available are totally unreliable.

All conventional air mattresses have the drawback that they can leave you flat during the night when a leak develops, and usually one eventually does. There's a particular kind of lightweight mattress on the market which comes with separately inflatable tubes, however. Since it won't let you down completely in the event of a leak, this kind of mattress is more acceptable.

FLASHLIGHT WITH SPARE BATTERIES AND BULB

After dark you'll usually need a dependable flashlight to find your way around (although on a moonlit night you might be able to manage without one). Nighttime needs can include "answering nature's call" as well as reading. A small, sturdy, lightweight flashlight is your best bet when weight and bulk are important considerations.

Always bring a minimum of two or three extra sets of batteries and at least one spare bulb. Batteries and bulbs can go dead at any time, sometimes at the most inconvenient moment. Without extras you'll be suddenly immobilized in the dark. Try changing the batteries and bulb in the dark (or with your eyes closed) at least once prior to your trip, as this is something you may have to do in the wilderness.

Buy *alkaline* batteries, which last longer, and make sure they have an expiration date on the package, so you know they're reasonably fresh. Batteries wear out much faster in cold weather, so bring more if cold temperatures are likely.

Occasionally you may have to do something after dark—such as set up your tent—requiring a source of light as well as the use of both hands. A small rectangular flashlight has the advantage that it can be gripped by the teeth, freeing your hands. Little round flashlights are also available which can be strapped above the ear, and some come with an attachment that can be held by the teeth. Still another option is a headlamp, which is fastened to the forehead with a headband. It's handy for anyone who needs a mobile light for extended use.

INSECT REPELLENT

Insects can be encountered at any time during the warmer seasons or in mild weather. When in doubt, bring along the bug repellent. A small compact container of repellent should be adequate unless you're going on a lengthy trip.

Some areas of the country have more biting insects than others, but it's often difficult to predict accurately the prevalence of bugs at any particular time and place. Local weather and rainfall may have a marked effect on the insect population, which can vary enormously from year to year.

Generally speaking, few if any bugs are likely to be encountered in cool, windy, or rainy weather. This kind of weather is pretty common in many of the higher mountain areas. Warm or hot days that are muggy are likely to be the buggiest.

Whereas in some places biting insects are rarely much of a problem, in other regions repellent and even a headnet are musts at certain times of year. Sometimes your guidebook or a park brochure will alert you to possible bug problems. If it's a concern, you can also call a park information center and ask.

Commercial insect repellents are reasonably if not totally effective in killing or at least deterring most insects. However, in recent years there have been questions about possible risks from the chemicals in these products. Some of the "all natural" repellents sold in health food stores are probably safer to use.

Wait till you verify that there are indeed biting insects around before applying repellent (the vast majority of bugs in the wilderness or elsewhere don't bother human beings). If you're exercising and sweating, it may have to be reapplied frequently.

It goes without saying that most people don't care much for insects. Some use their dislike of bugs as grounds to avoid going camping, or spending much time in the natural world. While there are times and places where insects can be annoying, they seldom present a serious problem in this country. Rarely should the presence of bugs interfere in a major way with your enjoyment of a trip, as long as you have repellent along and use it as needed.

Attitude is important. It will help a lot if you can learn to tolerate and accept (or at least to ignore) the presence of insects and any other elements of nature (or life) that you may not especially care for. Dwelling on insects or other minor problems can inflate them considerably, giving them the power to dominate and seriously detract from your day.

TOOLS FOR FINDING YOUR WAY AROUND

Compass

Having a compass is a must on any wilderness trip. Never assume that you'll always be able to find your way, that you cannot get lost, no matter how experienced you are. Bringing a compass and knowing how to use it will minimize the chance that you'll ever get seriously disoriented or lost, since you'll be able to confirm as often as you need to that you're headed in the right direction. Any compass sold by an outdoor specialty store should suffice.

If you've never used a compass, read a book on the subject or find someone who can teach you. In an organized group it may not be considered necessary for every participant to bring a compass and map, as the leader and others will be carrying these items. Still, it's a good idea to bring them, just in case you should get lost or separated from the group.

Map

Entering the wilderness without a map is foolhardy, unless you really know your way around an area, or you're traveling with others who have maps. You wouldn't try to travel cross-country by car without maps or a road atlas, nor should you think of attempting to find your way around in the wilds without a good map. Some areas do have frequent signs and well-marked trails, but it's still possible to get lost in such a place.

A map will often show trails, roads, rivers, major streams, lakes, mountains, and other information which could prove useful or necessary in helping you find your way, and perhaps to locate campsites. Specialized maps are sometimes produced for various activities such as hiking, cross-country skiing, or river travel.

One well-known series of maps, available for the entire country, are the U.S. Geological Survey topographic maps. These attractive maps show geographical features in detail, including the shapes of mountains, cliffs, and lakes. A drawback is that trails are often indicated incorrectly or omitted.

Maps of parks and wilderness areas may often be obtained from outdoor specialty stores, some sporting goods stores, and also map stores. Maps are often included with outdoor guidebooks, so they don't always have to be purchased separately. U.S. Geological Survey maps are carried by some stores, and may be obtained through the mail by writing to: U.S.G.S., 1200 S. Eads Street, Arlington, VA 22202 (for states east of the Mississippi), or U.S.G.S., Box 25286, Denver, CO 80225 (for states west of the Mississippi).

Free hand-drawn maps can often be obtained directly from parks and forests. While these maps may offer some useful information, and they're important when other kinds of maps are not available, the quality is often poor. You could request such a map either by mail or at a park information center, but first try to obtain a professional-quality map from other sources.

Guidebook

If a guidebook is available for the area you're planning to visit, it's probably a good idea to get a copy. A guidebook can provide useful and sometimes important information about trails, water routes, and/or campsites. There may be advice which could help make your trip more successful.

It should be mentioned that while some guidebooks are outstanding, not every guidebook is well-written or especially useful. On the other hand, you never really know when the information might come in handy or prove invaluable. When in doubt, get the guidebook and bring it along.

Some of us prefer to avoid reading detailed descriptions of areas in advance, however, and use restraint in consulting the guidebooks we carry. It's a pleasure to be able to discover some things freshly on one's own, and to not always know in advance exactly what everything's going to be like.

SAFETY ITEMS

First Aid Kit

If you take good care of yourself, you'll probably need to open the first aid kit on relatively rare occasions. Should you somehow suffer an accident or injury, however—and happen to be hours or even days from medical assistance—the kit could be a lifesaver. *Always* bring one, no matter how seemingly tame the trip. In any group one or more people should have a kit.

You can buy a ready-made first aid kit in a sporting goods store, outdoor specialty store, or pharmacy. You could also put one together on your own and maybe save a few dollars in the process. Included should be such items as Band-Aids, gauze bandages, adhesive tape, antiseptic cream or lotion, and an elastic-type bandage in case of a knee or ankle injury.

If you'll be walking, hiking, or backpacking, also bring "moleskin," which is a feltlike material with adhesive on the back. Useful as well is "molefoam," similar but made with foam and therefore thicker. Potential blisters can almost always be nipped in the bud if you put moleskin or molefoam over any area on your feet where there's rubbing, and do it early enough. You'll need a knife or small scissors to cut it to size.

Matches

Matches (or a lighter) are obviously necessary for starting your stove or a campfire. It's also a good idea to bring matches along whenever you leave camp on a hike or other excursion. In an emergency, you might need to start a fire for warmth, or to signal for help.

Ordinary matches need to be protected from rain and other moisture. Pack them in small, double plastic bags, tightly closed, and keep them there except when being used. If matches are left out and exposed to moisture on a damp day or night, they'll probably be ruined. Running out of matches or having them get wet would present a real problem, so always have a second supply packed away in plastic just in case. In addition, as extra insurance some campers carry a "match safe," a small waterproof container which holds a few wooden matches for emergency use.

There also also "waterproof matches" for sale, wooden matches which will usually light even when wet. Carrying a supply of these is another way to ensure that you'll be able to start your stove or a campfire in rainy weather. An alternative is a lighter. If you bring one, just make sure it isn't your only source of flame, as lighters can break or otherwise fail.

Fire Starter

Getting a campfire going in wet conditions can be extremely difficult, and yet this could be essential in an emergency. Carry some sort of fire starter—which comes in the form of paste, tablets, or sticks—in case you find yourself faced with the need to start a fire under adverse conditions. It's also useful with some stoves which require priming. Keep the fire starter with your matches and bring it along on any day trip.

Whistle

Carry a whistle for emergency use. If you should get lost or separated from friends or a group, blowing on the whistle could help others to find you. A succession of three blasts is generally recognized as a signal of distress, a call for help. Have the whistle with you at all times. Use only when necessary.

Emergency Thermal Blanket

A small compact "emergency blanket" should be brought and kept with first aid items. When it's wrapped around a person's body, the aluminized blanket reflects most body heat back. This item could save someone's life in a cold weather emergency, such as falling into icy water, or it can provide some added warmth if your clothing or sleeping bag should prove inadequate.

PROTECTION FROM THE SUN

Sunscreen or Lotion

If there's any possibility that you'll be spending more than short intervals in direct sunlight, bring sunscreen or lotion and apply to exposed skin when you're out in the open. Camping in forested areas usually means that you'll be in the shade most of the time. However, this won't be the case if you're in a deciduous forest in late fall or early spring, when the leaves are down.

Be especially careful to avoid overexposure to the sun's rays when traveling extensively in open areas. At higher elevations you can get burned especially quickly. When in areas which are mainly forested, exercise care if you'll be spending time at lakes, large rivers, open meadows, or on mountaintops.

Sun Hat

Bring a hat with a reasonably wide brim when visiting the desert or any other sunny, open area where little shade may be available. Such a hat will help you keep cooler, and protect your face and head from possible sunburn or overexposure.

Sunglasses

Sunglasses are generally recommended for use in sunny areas. However, there's some disagreement about whether they're really necessary and healthy to wear under ordinary conditions (as the eyes do normally have the capacity to adjust naturally to bright sunlight). It's clear, though, that sunglasses or goggles are truly essential when there's snow on the ground and at the same time bright sunshine, especially at higher elevations.

FOUR

Food and Cooking Gear

FOOD

Most wilderness campers bring along complete provisions for the duration of their trip. Quite a few also supplement their diet by fishing or collecting wild edibles. Gathering all your food in the wilderness would require great skill. It's an ability that our ancestors had, but that unfortunately most of us know little of. These days one is also limited by fishing and hunting regulations and restrictions.

If you're in the right place for it, during the appropriate season it's easy to pick berries or do a little fishing. If fishing interests you, check with a local sporting goods store about obtaining the necessary license. Collapsible fishing rods are available which can be carried in a backpack. Learning about edible plants will also expand your mealtime possibilities.

On a car-camping trip there are few limitations regarding what kind of foods you can bring, and how much. Perishable foods can be kept on ice in a cooler. On most kinds of wilderness camping trips, however, a cooler is much too cumbersome to carry. A possible exception is if you're traveling in a good-size boat or canoe, or camping a relatively short distance from your car.

Assuming a cooler is out of the question, it's basically necessary to forgo foods which are quickly perishable, although they can be brought for use the first day. Fresh meat, chicken, or fish, for example, will deteriorate in as little as a few hours when air temperatures are warm or hot. The same is true for some fruits and vegetables, including bananas and tomatoes. Others such as apples, oranges, and carrots will keep for many days. Perishability is, of course, much less of a problem in winter and cold weather.

Dehydrated Foods

Especially suitable for wilderness camping trips are dehydrated (dried) foods. These are essentially non-perishable, don't have a lot of bulk, and weigh relatively little since the water has been removed (water furnishes most of the weight). They might not necessarily win popularity contests, but in truth you can eat quite well with dehydrated foods.

Some common dried foods are available in your supermarket, such as rice, beans, pasta, dried soups, instant potatoes, powdered milk, and dried fruit. A much broader and more interesting selection will be found at most health food stores.

Various prepackaged dehydrated meals are available. Many campers prefer these because the ingredients have already been assembled, and often little in the way of preparation is required. Cooking times vary considerably, so check instructions on packages before buying.

It's a good idea to bring at least some foods which require minimal cooking—in case of possible inclement weather, or if you find that you don't feel much like cooking after a long day. If you'll be involved in activity during the day or otherwise away from camp, bring lunch foods which don't need to be cooked.

Freeze-Dried Foods

The lightest, most compact, and quickest of all foods to prepare are freeze-dried foods. All you have to do is add boiling water, stir, and wait a few minutes before eating. Opinions on freeze-dried foods vary widely. They're more expensive than regular dehydrated foods, and not all are especially tasty, but many campers seem to be satisfied with them. It partly depends on how hungry you are (it's long been said that everything tastes better outdoors, especially after a day of physical activity).

You may want to try freeze-dried foods sometime to decide for yourself. They're available primarily from outdoor specialty stores and larger sporting goods stores. A few freeze-dried items can now also be found in supermarkets and other food stores.

There's no denying that by bringing freeze-dried foods you'll save on weight. This can make a real difference on an extended trip, when food for a week or more may have to be carried. On shorter trips, where an extra couple of pounds would be less of a problem, other dried foods should do as well.

Menu Possibilities

There are lots of possible menus you could follow using dried foods. A few suggestions follow.

Breakfast: granola or oatmeal, with powdered milk, plus dried fruit, crackers (or bread), and a hot drink such as tea, coffee, or hot chocolate.

Lunch: cheese and crackers, small can of tuna or sardines, dried fruit. Snack food for any time of day: "trail mix" or "gorp," a varied mix of nuts, raisins, and/or other dried fruit.

Dinner: dried soup, a prepackaged dehydrated dinner, or a one-pot stew using various dried vegetables, rice, plus dried (or a small can of) fish or meat if desired. Numerous hot and cold drinks may be obtained in powdered form and can be included.

You could also bring some fresh foods, including vegetables—preferably the less-perishable varieties—although these will weigh a great deal more than dried foods. A few slices of fresh vegetable can help bring a stew or other dish to life, so some of us bring small portions of these foods even on longer trips.

Most canned foods should be considered out of the question for backpacking and any other kind of trip where weight must be minimized, since cans are so heavy (due in part to their high water content). The one exception some of us make is in bringing *small-size* cans of tuna, salmon, sardines, or chicken. This is especially worth considering if your other foods may fall short in meeting protein needs—which can occasionally be a problem for campers involved in lots of strenuous exercise. Remember, though, that the weight adds up very quickly even with small cans.

Try to measure out or estimate the portions of food needed for each day's meals, so you'll avoid bringing too much or too little. You may want to have a little extra along in case your appetite increases, particularly if you'll be engaged in challenging physical activity, or in the event that a delay forces you to remain in the wilderness longer than planned. Many campers bring *far* too much food, however, apparently from the fear of

not having enough and running out. When preparing for a backpacking trip it's necessary to use some real restraint here.

Some people package each meal or item in a separate plastic bag, which can minimize the amount of preparation and sorting to be done on the trip itself. The only drawback is the number of plastic bags required and the trash generated. Plastic bags may be washed and re-used, however.

FOOD STORAGE AND PROTECTION

Nylon Food Bag

It's a good idea to keep all food in one place so it doesn't get mixed up with your other gear. A sturdy nylon stuff sack, the kind used for sleeping bags, is perfect for this purpose. In a pinch any strong plastic bag (preferably doubled up) will do.

The food bag can be easily removed from your pack and hung from a tree branch or between two trees, either at night or whenever you're not using it, to keep it out of reach of animals. See Chapter 9 for more about hanging food.

50 Feet of Nylon Cord

A 50-foot length of nylon cord will come in handy for hanging your food as well as other purposes, such as for a clothesline, or to help erect an "emergency shelter" with a poncho or tarp during a storm. You'll probably need to cut the cord into two or more pieces.

Nylon cord of medium thickness is best (heavy rope or thin cord is harder to work with). This kind of cord is incredibly strong, and will easily last a lifetime if you don't lose it. Whenever you cut the cord, light a match to melt the tips, which will keep any strands from unraveling.

Plastic Bags and Food Containers

Plastic bags are useful for protecting food. Use sturdy self-sealing bags, or double the bags up. Do this especially for powdered foods or anything which would be messy if a bag should split open. If they're not self-sealing, close them with a rubber band or tie. Transfer any food which came in cardboard packaging to plastic before your trip. Cardboard boxes are bulky, rarely full when purchased, and will tend to disintegrate when wet.

The price of plastic bags has been steadily rising, and landfills in this country are also filling up with plastic, so consider reusing such bags whenever you can. Always carry plastic out of the wilderness and dispose of it properly. Never throw it

FOOD AND COOKING GEAR

20

into a campfire, as toxic fumes will be released and you'll leave a residue of plastic on the earth.

Another way to carry food is in semirigid plastic containers. These will take up a bit more space and won't pack as easily as plastic bags, but they're useful for storing certain kinds of foods, including meal leftovers. Make sure that the containers are strong, and not likely to break open or leak.

Plastic squeeze tubes are also available, and these are designed to carry potentially messy foods such as peanut butter or honey. To be on the safe side, always keep such tubes and other containers inside a sealed plastic bag in case of leakage.

Never bring food which is still in a glass container, even when you can afford the considerable extra weight involved. If the glass breaks you've got a real mess on your hands, and it can't be left in the wilderness (you'll have to carry it out with your other trash). Transfer anything that comes in glass to plastic before the trip.

Plastic Litter Bag

Bring at least a couple of plastic bags for litter and garbage. Double them up to avoid any possible leakage. If you're backpacking you won't need a full-size garbage bag, since your litter should be relatively compact. A small to medium-size bag will normally do.

The litter-and-garbage bag can be placed inside or next to your food bag when it's hung. Never leave a garbage bag on the ground at night or when you leave the campsite. Animals are almost certain to find it, and may create a real mess with it.

All litter should be carried out with you—except for plain paper, which can be burned. In some parks and regions it's also considered acceptable to toss food scraps or leftovers in the woods. If you do so, make sure they're discarded well away from your campsite and off the beaten path, so no one will step in it.

Leaving leftover food can sometimes have a significant and negative environmental impact, however. In fragile or heavily-used areas all garbage should be carried out. Check regulations and local recommendations for the park or area you're visiting.

COOKING GEAR

Stove

Small portable one-burner stoves have been used by backpackers and other wilderness campers for many years. They're now considered just about mandatory for cooking, since campfires are restricted or prohibited in a growing number of areas. The stoves have a lot to recommend them, and have some advantages over campfires for cooking. They're easier to start and maintain than fires, especially in wet weather, and very efficient to use.

A small number of backpackers and other travelers do without a stove in order to save weight. This means having cold meals, or relying on a campfire when one is permitted and feasible. Since most people value hot meals, stoves are generally carried.

You'll have a number of possible choices when shopping for a stove. Weight and bulk are of course vital considerations for backpackers, but most one-burner stoves tend to be reasonably light and compact. Those that are currently available weigh in between about 8 and 22 ounces (without fuel).

White Gas Stoves versus Cartridge Stoves

The primary decision you'll need to make in buying a stove is between one that uses liquid gas and one that takes fuel cartridges. "White gas" (unleaded, filtered gas, popularly sold as Coleman Fuel) is the most commonly used liquid fuel in this country. Some stoves run on kerosene or alcohol.

Fuel cartridges usually contain either butane or propane gas under pressure. Propane cartridges are relatively heavy and bulky, whereas butane cartridges are much lighter and more compact. Thus, only the latter are appropriate for backpacking.

Stoves which utilize cartridges are especially easy to use. Unlike most white gas stoves, they don't require "priming" at the start (which involves creating pressure to draw up the fuel, accomplished either by using a pump, or lighting some fuel or fire starter on top of the stove). If you want a stove that's especially simple to operate, get one that takes cartridges.

While extremely convenient, these stoves do have a few disadvantages. Cartridges take up considerable space (an important consideration on an extended trip), and the stoves don't function well in below-freezing temperatures. Also, not all kinds of cartridges are widely available, so you might have difficulty resupplying during an extended trip. For most trips during the warmer seasons, however, a cartridge stove should be fine.

White gas stoves are potentially a little messier, as some of them require pouring fuel, and they're slightly more complicated to start because of the necessary priming. Fuel costs are lower, however. Many of these stoves put out a stronger flame, and unlike cartridge stoves they're effective in extreme cold. If you'll be going on a cold-weather trip where very low temperatures are likely, this is the kind of stove to have.

Starting Up the Stove

After purchasing your stove, read the directions carefully before lighting it. Try the stove for the first time at home, not in the wilderness, to make sure it works. Always be attentive when turning the stove on and lighting it. Although stoves are safe when used correctly, proceeding carelessly could lead to a serious injury (just as it could with a kitchen gas range).

Never lean over a stove when lighting it. Some stoves have a tendency to flare up at the start, so keep your face well away, make sure no one else is sitting next to the stove, and that nothing flammable is nearby (such as an open fuel container). If you've spilled any fuel, move the stove elsewhere or light it with extra caution. When starting a cartridge stove, first light your match and hold it in place before opening the fuel valve.

Never use a stove inside a regular-size nylon tent, and only with the greatest care inside a large, family-size tent. It's always best to cook outside and well away from any tent, partly because of the potential for disaster if the stove should flare up, but also since cooking odors and spilled food are likely to attract animals. If you're convinced you must use a stove inside a large tent, keep it well away from the walls, make sure there's plenty of ventilation, and monitor the stove continuously.

Cooksets and Other Cooking Gear

Camping cooksets currently on the market range from very simple to extremely elaborate. If you're backpacking or otherwise need to minimize weight, bring the least amount of cookware that you can get away with. A single small lightweight cooking pot with a cover may be sufficient for one or two people, assuming you're willing to limit entrees to "one-pot meals."

A metal "Sierra Cup" (drinking cup) is a useful item, in part because it will double as a minipot for cooking a side dish, heating soup, or boiling water for a hot drink. While it's possible to bring sets of eating utensils and dishes, weight could also be saved by bringing just a spoon (supplemented, when necessary, by your pocket knife), and either eating right out of the pot or using your cup as a dish.

Some campers like to cook rather fancy meals. Everyone to their own preference, of course, but this will mean more pots and pans, more weight and bulk to carry, and more cleaning to do after meals. If weight is not a problem and you don't mind the cleaning, by all means bring whatever you like.

One useful little item is a "pot gripper," which can be used instead of a handle to grip the rim of a pot. With a pot gripper you'll avoid accidentally burning your hand on a hot handle, and it makes for an especially safe and stable way to carry any pot.

As to the matter of cleaning pots or dishes, you could bring a small sponge, steel wool, and/or a cleaning rag. Yet those who are intent on keeping everything simple and light sometimes omit such items. Leaves as well as fingers will serve as surprisingly effective cleaning aids, believe it or not, and using some warm-to-hot water you can often even manage quite well without soap.

FIVE

Additional Accessories

SMALL PACKS

Day Pack

If you plan to do some day hiking on your trip, or think you might want to venture away from your campsite for any period of time, bring along a day pack or some other kind of carry-bag. A day pack has enough room for lunch or a snack, water, raingear, extra clothing, and emergency items. These should usually be carried if you'll be going more than a short distance from camp.

Beginners are often unaware of how risky it can be to leave a campsite for any length of time without bringing such items as rainwear and extra clothing (where appropriate). In many mountain areas the weather can change quickly, and being caught without protection could put you in a serious spot. In the desert you'd probably want to bring extra water instead of raingear.

When going very far, always include such items as a first aid kit and your flashlight, just in case of a possible injury or some other delay in returning. Temperatures can plunge at night no matter where you are. If for some reason you aren't able to make it back to the campsite, the extra clothing and other gear in your day pack could even help save your life.

Fanny Pack or Belt Pouch

A fanny pack has enough room inside for a few small items. It's worn in back of the waist and secured by a belt. While you won't be able to fit much clothing or a large water bottle in such a pack, it may be adequate if you're not going far or otherwise need to bring relatively little. Fanny packs are popular with cross-country skiers and cyclists as well as hikers.

Little belt pouches are also available. A belt pouch is carried on your belt, or attached to the shoulder strap of a backpack. It can be used to carry such things as a guidebook and/or map, a small camera, binoculars, or other items.

GROUNDSHEET

It's a good idea to use a *groundsheet* under your tent. A groundsheet is a plastic or nylon sheet (tarp), which should be cut to size so it's just a bit smaller than the dimensions of the tent floor. The groundsheet will help protect the bottom of your tent from tiny holes or punctures, which could be caused by sharp twigs, thorns, or spruce needles.

During heavy rain some water is likely to find its way through any holes in the tent floor, so preventing punctures is important. Be careful that the groundsheet doesn't extend visibly beyond the tent wall. If it does, rain may collect in a pool on the sheet underneath your tent and probably find its way inside.

POCKET KNIFE

A pocket knife will come in handy at various times. Any small knife should be adequate. Swiss Army Knives are especially popular, since they include an assortment of useful little tools, including such things as a screwdriver, saw, pliers, can opener, tweezers, and scissors. Carrying a Swiss Army Knife can save you the trouble of bringing some additional items.

KEEPING CLEAN

Toiletries and Personal Items

The choice is yours as to which toiletries and other personal items to bring. Most people will include such items as soap, shampoo, toothbrush, comb or brush, washcloth, and a towel. Some people go overboard in this department and bring too much.

If you're a backpacker or otherwise want to travel light, it's vital to *keep these things to a minimum*. Repackage items like shampoo, using the smallest possible containers. When in doubt, skip the towel and make do with just a washcloth.

Soap

A small container or bar of soap should be sufficient. Remember that even biodegradable soap or shampoo must never be used in water sources. Always wash with water you've transported at least 100 to 150 feet from the source, and rinse soap off onto the earth. If you swim often, or sponge yourself with a washcloth periodically, you may find you don't need to use soap at all.

Plastic Wash Basin

Some campers bring a collapsible plastic wash basin. This simple item weighs very little and makes washing up easier. Water can be heated for the basin if you like.

Solar Shower

Although it's possible to keep reasonably clean in the wilderness, an obstacle to some potential campers in the past has been the inability to take regular showers while camping out. That's no longer the case, as you can now bring along a "solar shower." This is a lightweight and inexpensive item (under $20), consisting of a shower head along with a large vinyl bag which is coated to reflect the sun. You simply fill the bag with water and leave it in the sun for about three hours. Then hang the bag from a tree, and you've got a warm-to-hot shower lasting several minutes or more.

SANITATION

Toilet Paper

Bring an ample amount of toilet paper. While it's always possible that there will be an outhouse or other facility close to where you'll be camping, in many large parks and wilderness areas this is unlikely. Outhouses are most frequently found at established backcountry campsites. Such facilities are otherwise relatively few and far between. If you do happen to camp near one, remember there won't necessarily be toilet paper inside.

Assuming you don't have access to an outhouse, toilet paper is normally buried after use along with your waste (see Chapter 10 for more about sanitation). In a few of the country's most fragile and overused wilderness areas, however, regulations require that toilet paper be carried out (in plastic) along with solid waste.

Small Trowel

A small plastic trowel can be helpful in digging a little hole to bury your waste. This item is carried by camping supply stores. In some areas of the country, however, you'll find that the ground is reasonably soft most of the time. In such areas a sturdy stick may be more than adequate to do the job.

OTHER OPTIONAL ITEMS

Camera/Binoculars

If photography is important to you, and you want a visual record of your trip, you'll obviously want to pack a camera. Lightweight and compact cameras are available which are perfectly suitable for backpacking.

Others who are into bird-watching or wildlife-viewing may consider binoculars to be an essential item. Just as with cameras, there are some light, compact, and high-quality binoculars on the market these days.

Decide how important such items are to you. If something is a high priority for you, and you'd use it on a regular basis, by all means bring it along. If not, skip it.

Reading Material/Notebook

If you want to bring some reading material with you, a single compact paperback book will probably suffice unless you'll be away for a long time. Most people don't do as much reading in the wilderness as they expect to, especially those who are involved in activities. Several books will probably be too many unless you're a voracious reader or on an extended trip.

Some people like to record their experiences in a journal while in the wilderness, and/or do other writing or drawing. A notebook and pens or pencils would come in handy for such purposes. Bring these if you think you'll have use for them.

Watch

It's a good idea to have a watch along, but try consulting it as little as possible on your trip. Getting away from the usual time orientation and rigid schedules that so many of us live and labor under can be a real pleasure, and an eye-opening experience.

If you're taking day trips from your campsite, however, or traveling a considerable distance to another site, it's important to be aware of the general time of day. Don't let yourself get in a situation where the sun is setting and you still have a long way to travel.

When the sun is out it's rather simple to track the day's course, but not so easy on a foggy or overcast day. A watch can help on such occasions. Don't wear it on your arm, though. Keep it in an accessible place like your daypack or pocket, and check the time only when you need to.

Repair Kit

A little repair kit can come in handy if an item of equipment somehow gets damaged or broken, or clothing is ripped. The likelihood of this occurring will be low if you're using top-quality gear and clothing, but accidents do happen, equipment occasionally falls apart, or an important item of clothing gets torn.

Such a kit should be considered mandatory if you're going on an extended trip into a remote area. Include needle and thread, rip-stop tape, extra pins or other parts for your pack and stove, and anything else that could help you to repair broken items and mend clothing.

Folding Scissors

Many camping stores sell small collapsible scissors, and these are easier to use than the tiny ones which come with Swiss Army Knives. Scissors will be useful for such tasks as trimming moleskin or molefoam to size, or cutting tape.

G.I. Can Opener

The so-called G.I. can opener is an inexpensive little item which is no more than two inches long, folds flat, takes up virtually no space, and provides a quick and effective way to open cans. It takes a bit of practice for most people to learn to use this kind of can opener efficiently.

Mirror

While handy for personal use, a small mirror can also be invaluable in an emergency—for signaling (flashing the sun's reflection) to aircraft or others who might be some distance away. Special mirrors designed for signaling are available, but any camping mirror will do. Be sure it's unbreakable.

Hammock

Stretching out in a hammock is a wonderful way to while away some leisure time in the woods.

You can read or nap in it, or even sleep in the hammock at night, although most people prefer to spend the night on solid ground in a tent.

A hammock will provide a simple bed for the night in an emergency (such as not being able to find a campsite, or if an area is flooded). All you need in order to string the hammock are two trees in reasonably close proximity. Suitably lightweight, sturdy, compact, and inexpensive hammocks are available.

Pillow

An inflatable camping pillow can be purchased for nighttime use, or for sitting on hard or wet ground. It's also possible to make a nighttime pillow by putting clothing in a stuff sack—and a foam pad can be used as a cushion to sit on around camp, or a small piece of closed-cell foam may be brought separately for this purpose.

WHAT TO LEAVE AT HOME

Camp Saw, Hatchet, Shovel

Not too long ago these were standard items for many campers, but times have changed. Such tools have legitimate uses, of course, but for the most part they aren't needed and don't belong in the wilderness.

In no park or wilderness area should you ever cut either live or dead standing trees or branches. Cutting (destroying) a living tree is usually against the law in protected areas. Sawing or chopping down a dead tree leaves an unsightly stump, detracting from the wild feel of a place. The same goes for dead branches. Dead trees and branches should be allowed to fall on their own, and only then are appropriate to use for firewood.

Sometimes you'll be able to find enough downed branches for firewood. If not, and wood is truly scarce, you shouldn't build a fire anyway except in an emergency. A hatchet or saw isn't necessary, since fallen branches can be broken by hand or by jumping on them, and large unbroken branches may be fed into the fire a little at a time. A normal-size hatchet or saw will be too heavy to carry on many trips anyway, although lightweight, miniature camp saws are carried by some camping stores.

There's no longer a good reason to bring a shovel into the wilderness. The old practice of digging a trench around the tent is outdated and harmful, as it will damage vegetation and the earth, and may lead to considerable erosion. The only thing you should need to dig is a little latrine hole (usually for one-time use). This can be done using either a small plastic trowel or a sturdy stick. In some areas of the western U.S. authorities recommend digging a pit for a fire, to be filled in afterward.

Many camp stores still stock hatchets, axes, saws and shovels, and some people are obviously still buying them. For the sake of the environment, however, outdoorspeople today need to give up their attachment to the old aggressive pioneer ethic. We all need to learn to minimize our impact, help protect the earth, and act as respectful *caretakers* of the wilderness.

Radios and Cassette Players

Even if it's not turned up full blast, a radio or cassette player can be incredibly intrusive and obnoxious to those who are in the wilderness seeking peace and quiet or the sounds of nature. Radios and cassette players are now banned (except for use with earphones) in quite a few parks and preserves, but they still remain fully legal to use in most areas.

These days some people are apparently so addicted to radio, TV, music tapes, or simply background noise that they find it difficult or impossible to live without such things for even a short time. Those who bring radios often show little interest in natural sounds, and no tolerance for silence. Also, many campers aren't aware of how far sound and noise can travel in the wilderness, which can be up to several miles.

Don't bring a radio or cassette player, plain and simple, however much you may be tempted to. Without them you'll have a much richer experience of nature, and come back infinitely more relaxed (since those things help keep a person "plugged into" civilization and the everyday world). You can listen to and enjoy radio and music as much as you want when you return home.

If you feel nevertheless that you absolutely must bring one, please use earphones or play it at the very lowest possible volume, so you don't disturb wildlife or other campers. You might not be aware of the presence of others camping nearby, but if you have a radio or cassette player they will be aware of you, and probably not happy about it.

Dogs and Other Pets

It's understandable that some people like to bring their pets along on a camping trip, but pets can get into trouble in the wilderness. Many domestic pets find it difficult to resist chasing after wildlife. Unleashed dogs sometimes get quilled by porcupines, sprayed by skunks, or clawed by bears.

Domestic animals don't really belong in the wilderness, and certainly don't fit in well. Even if they refrain from giving chase, pets often have a disruptive effect on wildlife and the environment as a whole. Some of them also foul water sources.

Barking and aggressive dogs are of course unwelcome, and resented by people who are visiting nature in search of rest. A quiet, well-behaved pet will be less of a problem, but his presence will still have more of an impact in the wilderness than many owners realize or acknowledge.

Dogs and other pets are banned in some parks and wilderness areas, and permitted in others. If it's legal and you choose to bring a pet, take responsibility to see that he doesn't molest or disturb other forms of life. If there's a possibility that your pet won't be able to fully practice "low-impact camping," please leave him at home.

SIX

Clothing and Footwear
For The Wilderness

The important function of clothing is of course to protect and insulate the body from cool or cold temperatures and "the elements." It should be obvious that staying adequately warm is absolutely essential to the enjoyment of any wilderness trip.

With the proper clothing you can keep quite comfortable no matter how cold it may be. If you fail to bring enough clothing you'll not only be risking discomfort, but if conditions are severe you might even be putting your life in jeopardy.

A wide range of temperatures and conditions of weather and climate may be encountered around the United States throughout the year. There's no way to accurately predict well in advance what the weather will be in most regions, although the normal range of possibilities is narrower in some places than others.

Remember also that unusual weather and freak storms can and do happen almost anywhere. Don't take chances by leaving items at home which would be critical to your well-being in the event of cold or severe weather, however unlikely such conditions might be. Always bring more clothing than you think you'll need.

Find out what the coldest possible temperatures usually are in the area you'll be visiting, and pack an extra layer or two in addition to what seems appropriate. Backpackers have a special challenge in preparing for a trip, namely how to bring sufficient clothing and yet keep the total weight down. Cut corners on other things, if necessary, but not on essential clothing.

In the summer it's easy to forget what feeling really cold or seriously chilled is like. There may be a temptation to leave most clothing at home, especially when preparing to depart during a heat wave. Don't give in to any such temptation. Never forget that cold is always a possibility in most mountain areas, regardless of what's going on elsewhere, and that in some regions below-freezing temperatures can be encountered in summertime.

Layering

In cool or cold weather the most sensible way to dress is in layers. Bring a number of thinner, lighter items of clothing rather than one or two heavy garments. A hefty parka may be too warm except for standing around in extreme cold. With layering you can add or remove items as needed to find just the right level of warmth, which will vary throughout the day.

While exercising you'll generate heat and undoubtedly have to take off some layers. If you're involved in strenuous activity, such as backpacking on steep trails, it's possible that you'll find yourself getting down to as little as a T-shirt even in temperatures that are below freezing. As soon as you stop, however, you're certain to need many more layers on.

It's important to develop the habit of adding clothing at the *first sign* of being cold. If you wait till you're chilled it may take a long time to warm up, even if you have a campfire nearby or can climb into your sleeping bag. Respond quickly when you start to feel cold. If you're exercising, put on extra layers immediately upon stopping, rather than waiting till you've totally cooled down.

At the same time, it's important to remove clothing whenever you start to overheat, which is likely to happen during most physical activity. Shed sufficient clothing so that you'll be sweating minimally. If you permit your body and clothing to get soaked in perspiration when it's cold, you'll be more susceptible to chilling when you stop.

Failing to pay attention to your body's need for warmth and allowing yourself to get seriously chilled can put you at risk for hypothermia. See Chapter 13 for more about this cold-weather hazard.

Cotton, Wool, and Synthetics

The attributes of different materials and fabrics vary, and it's important to be aware of this when choosing items of clothing to bring on a wilderness trip. The material you're wearing can occasionally be a matter of critical importance.

Cotton clothing, for example, has long been favored by many people, and for overall comfort some would say it's unsurpassed. Cotton has a serious drawback for use on a wilderness trip, however. When wet it provides no insulation or warmth whatsoever.

While it's certainly acceptable to bring and wear some items of cotton, be sure to have at least one full set of clothing made of either wool or synthetics. It's possible to get chilled in surprisingly mild temperatures, and getting wet in cold weather while wearing cotton clothing is a recipe for real trouble.

Cotton jeans are best avoided altogether, even though they remain popular among some outdoorspeople. Jeans can be miserably uncomfortable and even dangerous when wet on a cold day. Bring them only as a spare pair of pants to be worn in dry weather.

Among natural fabrics, wool is by far the best for outdoor use, as it will give you a substantial amount of warmth even when wet. If cool or cold and wet weather is even remotely possible on your trip, pack some wool clothing if you can.

A number of synthetic fabrics have also become popular for outdoor use, and these share with wool the attribute of offering warmth when wet. Some have an advantage over wool, namely in absorbing extremely little moisture.

Polypropylene is currently among the most favored of the synthetics. Others include nylon and polyester. New fabrics also keep appearing on a fairly regular basis. Most synthetics are not quite as comfortable to the touch as cotton, but in damp weather you're much, much better off with them.

BASIC ITEMS OF CLOTHING

The following items of clothing should be brought on virtually any wilderness trip, regardless of local climate or temperatures. Make substitutions, of course, if you have other items which will do as well. Omit something only if you're absolutely *certain* it will be unnecessary.

Whenever you encounter rain, always be sure to keep at least *one complete set of clothing* dry. Then you'll be able to change into these at the end of the day—for use inside your tent, or around the campsite if the rain has stopped.

If a second day is rainy as well, it remains essential to maintain that set of dry clothing. This may mean you'll have to pack away the dry items and put on the previous day's wet clothing. It's vital to avoid letting everything get soaked, a well-known way to help spoil a trip.

Long Pants

Have at least one pair of long pants along, even if you plan to wear shorts every day. Long pants may come in handy for warmth on chilly nights, or for protection from the sun, or from insects. If you're backpacking you might find yourself on a brushy overgrown trail, where pants will keep your legs from getting scratched. They'll also reduce the chances of direct contact with plants like poison ivy or poison oak.

Bring two pair of pants if you can afford the weight. One pair should be synthetic or wool rather than cotton—and when you're caught in the rain, that's the pair to be wearing or to put on, keeping the other protected and dry.

If you have only one pair with you, *never* wear them in the rain. Put your shorts on instead, so you'll have dry pants to change into at the end of the day. Avoid bringing tight jeans or other snug pants which will restrict your freedom of movement. Loose-fitting pants are the most suitable and comfortable.

Shorts

Many people prefer shorts to long pants in warm or hot weather for obvious reasons, including the fact that they're totally unrestrictive. Bring a pair during the warmer seasons. There are times even in summer, however, when you may want to wear long pants or to change into them (see above).

Long-Sleeved Shirt

Carry at least one long-sleeved shirt. Just as long pants are sometimes necessary, a long-sleeved shirt will often be appropriate and useful in helping protect your arms from cold or wind, from exposure to the sun, or from biting insects. You can roll up the sleeves when appropriate.

T-Shirts/Undershirts

In warm weather the ubiquitous T-shirt is seen almost everywhere in the out-of-doors. Any other kind of light short-sleeved shirt will also do. A T-shirt or lightweight shirt may be sufficient by itself when temperatures are warm enough, or it can be worn under other garments, of course.

If there's any chance of cold, wet weather, have at least one T-shirt or undershirt that's made of a material other than cotton. Even in cold but dry weather you're better off not wearing cotton next to your skin while physically active, as you may get chilled from perspiration. T-shirts and undershirts can be easily washed out as needed, so no matter how long the trip, it's not necessary to bring more than two or three.

Underpants

As with other items, if possible, try to have at least one non-cotton pair of undershorts or pants. Two or three pair are plenty, as you can wash them out on your trip. Bringing many changes of underwear is one of numerous possible ways to help create an unwieldy load for yourself to carry.

Socks

Heavy wool ragg socks have long been popular with hikers, backpackers, and many other outdoorspeople. These socks are warm even when wet, and provide an ample amount of cushioning when you walk. Two or three pair should be enough for any trip, since they can be washed out every night or two.

Synthetic socks (such as polypropylene or acrylic) will also be fine, although these aren't normally as thick or warm as heavy wool socks. Avoid cotton socks except in the very mildest climates and conditions. Your feet will often perspire during ordinary walking or other exercise, meaning damp socks, and with cotton socks in cool weather you'll probably have cold feet.

Liner socks are useful for a bit of additional comfort and warmth, and assuming you're on foot they'll also provide some protection from blisters. These thin socks are worn next to the skin under a heavier pair of socks. They lessen the chance of blisters by reducing the amount of friction against your skin, and also wick moisture away to the outer sock. The best materials for liner socks are polypropylene and other synthetics.

Wool Sweater or Shirt

A wool shirt or sweater will come in handy whenever it cools off, and you'll find very few places in this country where there isn't a possibility or likelihood of cool nighttime temperatures. Bring at least one sweater or warm shirt. Two lighter sweaters will be more versatile than a single heavy one.

In recent years "pile" sweaters and jackets have become popular. These synthetic garments are light, soft, warm, and absorb little water. Thus, for insulation and warmth they provide a good alternative to traditional sweaters and light jackets.

Shell Parka or Windbreaker

A shell parka or windbreaker is a thin outer garment which provides protection from the wind, and offers additional insulation from trapped air. When worn over other clothing this item offers a surprising amount of added warmth for little bulk.

Because it's so versatile, a windbreaker or shell parka can be brought on virtually any trip, whatever the climate or time of year. One especially light and compact version is an anorak, a thin waist-length nylon shell with a hood.

COLD-WEATHER CLOTHING

In some parts of the country "cold-weather clothing" will be appropriate only from very late fall through early spring, if at all. In other areas including the high mountains, however, these items may be needed right in the middle of summer.

Keep in mind that if your body becomes acclimated to summer heat, even a temperature like 50°F may feel quite cold. At such times you may need to wear a substantial amount of clothing to be comfortable, especially while sitting around the campsite.

Thermal Underwear

Thermal underwear is obviously appropriate for a wilderness trip involving cold weather, but it's also useful for any trip where nighttime temperatures may be just on the cool side. On a chilly evening thermals will help you stay comfortable around camp. On a really cold night you may want to wear them inside your sleeping bag.

Wearing thermals during the day is a somewhat different matter. If you'll be exercising, your body will probably start to overheat at some point and clothing will have to be removed, probably including the thermal underwear. The problem with thermals is that almost everything else has to be taken off to get to them. Don't leave the thermals on if you're sweating. They should be kept dry for later use.

Except in extreme cold, it may be better to omit thermal underwear for daytime activities, and instead add or remove outer clothing as needed. If you do wear thermal underwear during an active day, make sure it's polypropylene (or other synthetic) or wool, to avoid getting chilled from any perspiration. Wear cotton thermals only when you're at rest in camp and can keep them dry.

One set of thermal underwear (top and bottom) will do for any ordinary cool-to-warm-weather trip. In subfreezing conditions it's probably advisable to bring at least two sets.

Jacket or Vest

A down or synthetic jacket is appropriate for any trip when cold temperatures are likely. Down garments are well known for offering exceptional warmth with relatively little weight, and they also compress well. Thus, a down jacket is especially suitable for an extended backpacking trip, or any other cold-weather trip where you need to minimize your load.

A light down jacket, sometimes called a down sweater, is probably the most versatile garment for a wide range of conditions. A down vest is another alternative, and this should provide the warmth of a thick sweater. Heavy down jackets are normally too warm to wear while active, except in extreme cold. Down garments which come with a thin nylon shell are best for backpacking, since they can be conveniently put away in a stuff sack when not in use.

Down has one major drawback, namely that it's useless when wet and takes forever to dry out. Thus down garments must be carefully protected from rain and other moisture. If your down jacket gets soaked in cold weather and you don't have plenty of other warm clothing along, this could spell disaster.

Synthetic jackets and vests are safer to use since they will offer insulation and warmth when wet. At the same time, most synthetic garments are somewhat bulkier and heavier, and this can make a significant difference on a backpacking trip.

If it's really cold you could also bring a pair of insulated pants, available in some outdoor specialty and sporting goods stores. It's also possible to increase the warmth of any pants by wearing nylon shell pants (wind pants or rain pants) over them.

Knitted Cap

A traditional knitted wool cap or the equivalent is a cold-weather must. Heat is quickly lost from the head when it's cold, and your whole body may actually feel warmer when you wear a cap. These caps are also available in synthetics including polypropylene. While many other kinds of caps and hats are available, the standard knitted cap is among the warmest.

In subzero cold a face mask may be necessary, especially in windy conditions. Also useful is a balaclava, a knitted item which pulls down over and protects the face, leaving a hole for nose and mouth. It will roll up into a cap for warmer days.

Mitts or Gloves

Many kinds of outdoor mitts and gloves are available. Bring along a minimum of a light pair of gloves or mitts on any trip where cool weather is possible, and a heavier pair when it's likely to be colder. It's not unusual for your hands to get cold while sitting around camp, even in relatively mild temperatures.

Mitts tend to be a little warmer than gloves. Among the options are insulated synthetic mitts and gloves, and also wool mitts which can be worn with an overmitt (a nylon shell, which provides additional insulation and protection from moisture). Avoid ordinary leather gloves, as these don't offer much warmth, and they wet through very easily.

FOOTWEAR

The obvious purpose of footwear is to protect the feet, and in some cases to offer support on rough ground. If your feet were tough enough you could go barefoot in the wilderness, and a few hardy souls do so—but that's unrealistic for most of us, whose feet have spent a lifetime inside shoes. Going barefoot is most feasible, of course, on sand or soft earth.

There's an incredibly wide assortment of boots and shoes to choose from these days. The kind of footwear that's right for you will depend on what activities you'll be involved in, when and where you'll be going, and what the conditions are likely to be.

If you're a hiker or backpacker it's advisable to wear hiking boots, which are designed specifically for trail-walking. Lighter outdoor shoes are available for casual walking. There are also specialized shoes made for cycling, rock climbing, running, and other activities. Canoeists usually wear a pair of sneakers or other light shoes. On many wilderness trips it's also appropriate to bring along some more protective footwear, in case you encounter cold, rain, mud, or snow.

Some boots and shoes are designed for wet conditions and completely waterproof. Others are thickly insulated and designed especially for cold or snow. "Pac boots" or "pac shoes," which are rubberized beneath the ankle, are useful for mud, snow, or other wet conditions, although not so appropriate for long-distance walking. So-called "work boots" tend to be suitable for general outdoor use, as are most of the other boots you'll find in sporting goods and army-navy stores.

Hiking Boots

Most backpackers and hikers wear hiking boots, which protect the feet and ankles as well as provide stability on rough ground. It's especially important to have sturdy footwear while carrying a backpack or other load. If you take a bad step, which is bound to happen occasionally, you can lose your balance almost instantly without good footwear. With a pack on your back it's harder to recover from a bad step, meaning a possible fall or an ankle injury. Good boots will help prevent this.

Boots aren't really necessary if you'll be walking mainly on soft earth or sand. However, a great many wilderness areas in this country include rugged terrain. Other kinds of boots can also be used, but a hiking boot typically has extra padding and protection around the ankles. Shoes by definition don't come up over the ankles, and so are normally inadequate for backpacking.

Hiking boots are typically classified by weight, ranging from lightweight to heavyweight. Light to medium weight boots are most appropriate for backpacking. Stay away from ultralight boots which flex easily at the ankles and don't provide adequate ankle support. At the same time, avoid heavyweight boots which flex minimally if at all, and may take forever to break in.

Getting a good fit is more important than all other factors put together. Any boot should feel comfortable right at the start. Shop at a store with knowledgeable salespeople who can help you with the process. A lengthier discussion of hiking boots is found in *The Essential Guide to Hiking in the United States*.

Light Camp Shoes

If you're wearing hiking boots or other sturdy footwear during the day, it's nice to have some light, comfortable shoes to change into at camp. Possibilities include running shoes, moccasins, sneakers, sandals, or slippers. For backpacking bring the lightest and most compact shoes you can find.

While great to have along, camp shoes should normally be placed in the category of less-than-essential items. Consider omitting them if you're already overloaded, especially if your other footwear is already reasonably light and comfortable.

Insulated Booties

When camping in winter or cold weather, nothing is more of a pleasure to wear around the campsite than synthetic or down-filled booties. These puffy little boots, unsuitable for walking more than short distances, will keep your feet warmer than any other kind of footwear.

SEVEN

Planning and Preparing for A Trip

FIRST STEPS FOR BEGINNERS

If you're new to backpacking or primitive camping, it's best to take your first trip or trips with others who are experienced in wilderness travel. There are some new skills you'll need to acquire, and learning these first-hand from others is the easiest and safest way.

If you don't happen to have friends who can take you out and teach you the essentials, find a club or other organized outdoor group that you can go with at least a couple of times. Some organizations which sponsor wilderness trips are listed in Part II, under the "Camping Resources" sections for many states.

Even with experience some people continue to go with an organized group. Camping with the right group can be fun, and an added advantage is that many of the responsibilities involved are either taken care of by a leader or shared with others.

If you've previously spent little time in the wilderness, start with a few one-day trips before trying your first overnight trip. Make sure you enjoy a particular activity (such as hiking, canoeing, or horseback riding) and are more than minimally proficient in it before committing to an overnight trip, especially an extended one, involving the activity.

Avoid making ambitious plans at the beginning. Remember that a considerable level of fitness may be required if you expect to be physically active for as much as several days in a row. The trip is likely to be more enjoyable and successful if you're in good shape and have a healthy reserve of stamina.

Camping Alone

Authorities have long suggested that the minimum safe size of a group in the wilderness is no less than four—so in case of a serious injury, one person could stay with the person and the other two go for help. There's safety in numbers.

Some of us feel, however, that it's a mistake to rigidly adhere to such advice at all times. Under the right circumstances it can be very beneficial to go out into the wilderness alone. The experience can be a wonderfully rewarding one.

Don't even consider camping by yourself, however, unless or until you're completely proficient in the ways of wilderness living, and know how to take care of yourself in virtually all circumstances and conditions.

The requirement is that you know *exactly* what you're doing, and are certain that you can carry it out successfully without a problem or mishap. The risks can never be completely eliminated, but by exercising caution you can keep them to a minimum.

If you believe you're ready for a solo experience and think you'd enjoy the solitude, give it a try. Be willing to take full responsibility for yourself, however, and stay completely attentive and careful. A serious accident or getting lost while alone could literally mean your life. When in doubt, always go with others.

Obtaining Equipment

You may want to consider borrowing or renting equipment rather than buying it at first, if those are available options for you, especially if you're uncertain of your commitment to wilderness camping. Most people who go camping or backpacking more than once or twice want to have their own equipment, but at the beginning renting or borrowing are worth considering. Outfitters and some organized groups also supply equipment for trips, and this service can be attractive to a beginner.

When you're ready to purchase gear, try to locate a store which specializes in top-quality outdoor equipment, and has knowledgeable salespeople who are also experienced campers. Check the yellow pages under "Camping" or "Backpacking" if you don't already know of local stores. Most of the items you'll need to buy or obtain have been covered in Chapters 2 through 6.

Avoid rushing the process once you're in a store. A substantial amount of time may be required if you're outfitting yourself completely. Ask about their return policy, which will vary considerably from one establishment to another. Try to buy from a store that will accept merchandise back as long as it's in resalable condition (in case you find out at home that something doesn't fit correctly, or is somehow the wrong choice).

If you find you're having difficulty making a decision, or start to feel flustered with the process, leave and come back another day. Don't give up! Avoid spending much time studying technical specifications and minutiae, unless you enjoy that sort of thing. Don't worry too much about brands as long as you're in a store which carries only quality merchandise.

It's possible that several different models or designs of a product may be adequate for your needs. Just make sure the item fits properly, when size is an important factor. A good salesperson should be able to assist you in sorting through alternatives, and may be able to help you arrive at a decision.

Choosing A Destination and Obtaining Information

If you're going with an organized group, presumably the destination has already been chosen by others. When it's up to you to decide where to go, this may take some time, and it occasionally requires a little research. Yet the process of trip-planning can also be rather fun and exciting.

Part II of this book offers a comprehensive listing of areas throughout the country where wilderness camping and backpacking are permitted. Select one or several locations which sound appealing and would be convenient for you to visit.

Your next step is to obtain a map or maps of the area, and also perhaps a guidebook, if available. Guidebooks and maps may be obtained from outdoor specialty stores, some sporting goods stores, bookstores, or by mail order. Current guidebooks for many states are listed in Part II under "Camping Resources."

A good guidebook will provide useful and often valuable information about the area you're interested in, including trail data and camping information. Many guidebooks are oriented toward a particular activity like hiking or canoeing. The focus is also usually on a limited geographical area, often a single park or wilderness area, although there are guidebooks which cover an entire state. A guidebook may or may not come with good maps. When maps aren't included you'll have to obtain them separately.

Before visiting any park or area of interest it's wise to call or write directly to ask for current information, including camping regulations (while these are listed here in Part II, rules are always subject to change). If you haven't been able to get hold of a map from other sources, request one, along with any other printed information that is available.

Permits

Camping permits are required in a growing number of parks, especially those that receive heavy use, as well as some private areas. There are still a large number of places in the country where you can camp without a permit, however. Since permits can be introduced at any time, it's always best to check directly with a park regarding current regulations before paying a visit.

Sometimes a permit may be or must be obtained in advance. This can often be done by mail and occasionally by phone. In other cases a permit has to be applied for in person at the start of your trip, or picked up at that time. If you're visiting a large forest or park this could involve a little inconvenience, as you may have to travel out of your way to reach the necessary facility. In a popular park you might have to wait in line for the permit. Try to get it ahead of time whenever possible.

Sometimes the reason for requiring permits is to limit the number of campers in a wilderness area, or within different regions of a large park. There may be a chance that your permit request could be turned down, which is most likely if you've chosen a popular trail or time period. Apply early if you can.

Permits in some parks require that you specify exactly where you'll camp each night for the duration of your trip. For other permits you need only designate a general area, or you may be entitled to camp just about anywhere within a park's boundaries.

Usually there's no charge for a permit, although on occasion a nominal fee is charged for making an advance reservation. Many state parks and private areas do charge a camping fee, however, and this is sometimes on top of an entrance or admission fee.

OTHER CONSIDERATIONS: WEATHER, CLIMATE, AND SEASON

How you'll prepare for a trip and what's appropriate to bring along will depend in part on the climate of the area you're visiting, the season or time of year, and the range of weather which could be encountered.

Weather and Forecasts

Except for a few regions in the country where conditions are relatively constant, as in the desert, it's impossible to predict the weather with great accuracy. Long-range predictions are of dubious value, and even short-term forecasts are often wrong.

Forecasts are especially likely to be off the mark and unreliable in many of the country's higher mountain regions. Sudden changes in weather and temperature are common in these areas. Storms and precipitation can come at any time.

Most experienced outdoorspeople learn not to base long-term plans on forecasts or place much trust in them, except when weather of unusual severity is predicted. If there's any chance of a tornado, hurricane, floods, gale force winds, or other truly dangerous conditions, you'll naturally want to be on the alert. Be prepared to leave quickly or head for safer ground. Perhaps you'll want to remain at home in the first place. These kinds of conditions are relatively rare in most areas.

Since the predictions are so often wrong, it's surely a waste of time to worry about unfavorable-sounding forecasts, or to be especially concerned about the weather in general. The best thing to do is to prepare in advance for every conceivable kind of weather and the widest possible range of temperatures. Raingear and warm clothing should *always* be brought, period.

Find out the lowest temperatures which would normally be expected in the area you'll be visiting. Bring an appropriate amount of clothing plus some additional layers, just in case you should encounter a record cold wave. Of course the weather could also turn out to be consistently fair

and mild. Sooner or later, however, you'll probably take a trip where you need every bit of clothing you brought, and will feel thankful you have it along.

Rain

Always expect rain and be ready for it, keeping rainwear in a conveniently accessible place. Using raingear is a matter of safety as well as comfort. While staying dry is less critical on a warm day, never forget that getting soaked and seriously chilled in cold weather could endanger your life.

Many beginners fear getting caught in the rain, imagining that wet weather will ruin their trip. If you ask an experienced camper about it, chances are you may be told that rain is really "no big thing." In fact, some people actually come to enjoy being out in the rain, and find it refreshing, especially in warmer weather. Try to stay open-minded on the subject.

Rain is of course an important part of the weather cycle in much of the United States. Rain is life-giving. Most life on the planet would cease without it. Appreciate rain's part in the total scheme of things, and rainy days may begin to seem more attractive and interesting to you. As long as you're prepared, you'll probably start to feel less like a victim of the rain, and might even find yourself enjoying the entire range of weather.

Climate and Season

A wide range of climates is to be found throughout this country, and weather sometimes varies dramatically from one season or time of year to another. You'll want to consider these matters in planning a trip, and deciding where to go and when.

It's obvious that less in the way of protective clothing is needed when camping out in the summer, or whenever it's warm or hot. Always bring some extra layers, though, in case the weather is cooler than expected—especially if you'll be at higher elevations, or in an area where conditions are unpredictable.

When going out in the winter or anytime it's cold, a great deal more clothing must of course be worn to be comfortable. Most but not all campers usually attempt to avoid extremes of both cold and heat, conditions which naturally make special demands.

If you want to avoid seasonal extremes, when camping during the summer it makes sense to head for higher elevations and/or the northern regions of the country, and in the winter to travel to southern areas and/or remain at the lowest elevations.

Winter Camping

If you're visiting an area where winters are relatively warm, camping at this time of year won't be much different from that of other seasons. In large areas of the country, however, winter camping means tenting in the snow and/or cold. In some regions extremely low temperatures are possible.

Don't try snow-camping or spending a night out in the cold until you're a thoroughly experienced camper. You should feel at home in the wilderness, and confident that you can deal with any situation which arises. There's not much of a margin for error in the winter. An emergency like getting lost, injured, or falling into icy water could easily be fatal without immediate help.

It's important to be familiar with layering (see Chapter 6), and know how to regulate your body's temperature. You'll need *plenty* of extra clothing, including insulated boots and probably also an extra-warm (subzero) sleeping bag. Getting chilled is especially dangerous in severe cold. Don't take chances with anything you do. Play it especially safe at this time of year.

If more than a few inches of snow are on the ground, you may need snowshoes in order to get around on foot. Crampons might be necessary if it's icy (these attach to your boots and have spikes for gripping ice). Bring both of the above items when in doubt.

Putting up your tent properly in deep snow requires some special techniques. You'll need a dependable winter stove, since starting a campfire and finding firewood can be quite a difficult challenge when there's plenty of snow and ice on the ground. Water sources might be completely frozen, so obtaining water for drinking and cooking can require the time-consuming process of melting snow in a pot on your stove. Water bottles may have to be taken into your sleeping bag at night to keep them from freezing.

It's easy to get lost in the snow under certain conditions, especially during a blizzard. Some snow-covered trails are very difficult to follow if there aren't frequent markers on trees along the way. Never count on being able to retrace your route back to where you started, as tracks can be completely obliterated at any time by wind or fresh snow.

In spite of the added challenges of a winter trip, quite a few people find this to be their favorite season for camping in the wilderness. It's often a time of extraordinary silence, broken only by the sound of the wind, a creaking tree, and an occasional bird. Winter snow has a beauty of its own, which becomes dazzling in bright sunshine. Since not many people camp out at this time of year, you can find plenty of solitude.

There are several books currently available on the subject of winter camping. Read one or more before planning a winter trip and preparing to go out overnight at this time of year.

PREPARING FOR YOUR TRIP

Getting in Shape

If you'll be engaging in strenuous exercise on your trip, it's obviously sensible to be in shape for it. This is a good idea even if you don't expect to be especially active in the wilderness. Once there, you may find you want to do more than originally intended, or on occasion circumstances might force you to hike, paddle, or otherwise travel much farther than planned.

If you don't already exercise on a regular basis, try to start getting in shape at least several weeks or more prior to your trip. What's appropriate in the way of exercise will depend partly on what you'll be doing in the wilderness. Aerobic activities like brisk walking, running or jogging, and cycling are especially recommended.

If possible, try to get out at least a few times prior to your trip to practice the specific activity or activities you'll be involved in. Your body will then have less adjusting to do on the trip itself. You'll reduce the chances of injuring yourself or overdoing it, and will probably enjoy the activity more.

Other Preparations

Preparing and packing for a wilderness trip takes some time, although an experienced camper can usually get ready on short notice. Start early. Only if you're going with an outfitter or group which supplies gear and food will you have little to do, limited perhaps to packing clothing and personal items.

Assuming you're going on your own or with friends, allow ample time to borrow, rent, or buy equipment. Sometimes repeated visits to stores will be necessary to obtain everything you need. Getting ready is always easier once you have your own gear. Then it means only making an occasional trip to a camping store to replenish items such as fuel cartridges or flashlight batteries.

As much as several hours may be required to shop for food and pack it, especially if you're new to the process of planning a camping menu, selecting suitable foods, and deciding on appropriate portions. It's easiest if you opt for prepackaged dehydrated or freeze-dried dinners, but there are also many other options (see Chapter 4). Allow extra time if you want to concoct some interesting homemade meals while in the wilderness.

Although there may be a store near or occasionally right inside the park you'll be visiting, it's usually best to do *all* shopping while still at home. Some stores won't have the kind of food or fuel cartridges you need, and stores located in or next to major parks often charge high prices for supplies.

Also, if you're like most of us, you'll probably want to begin your adventure and head into the wilderness as soon as you can after arriving. Once you're in the area, having to spend part of a day hunting around for necessary items isn't much fun. Get everything you need before leaving home. If you should discover something missing, you can always look for a store on route.

Packing

Begin the actual packing well ahead of time. If you're a beginner, try to get started at least a week or more before your departure. By not being in a rush you'll be able to experiment with the best ways to arrange your gear, and weed out things if your load is too heavy. If you find you've forgotten anything, there will still be time to run out and purchase it.

Packing is especially challenging for a backpacking trip, as well as any other activity which requires keeping the weight and bulk of what you're bringing to an absolute minimum. It's helpful if you know someone who can assist you with this the first time.

If you're going with an organized group, don't worry about showing up with everything masterfully packed. Do the best you can to assemble and pack necessary items, and you'll be able to get assistance from others later if you need it.

One of the most important principles of packing for a wilderness camping trip is to arrange everything in the most orderly way possible. You shouldn't have to constantly dig for what you need. Place essential items where they'll be easily accessible. If you stuff things randomly into your pack or bag, as some beginners do, you'll surely find it impossible to locate necessary items on short notice—such as rainwear in the event of sudden rain, or your flashlight when it's getting dark. Use a checklist (see end of Part I) to make sure nothing is accidentally omitted.

In packing a duffel or cargo bag you'll have the most leeway in arranging clothing and gear as you

wish. Just be sure you know the location of important items, which should be reachable without having to unpack everything else. If your trip involves water travel, bring the most waterproof carry bags available and also pack the clothing and essential items in plastic.

Packing a Backpack

Assuming you'll be carrying it on your back rather than in a canoe, a backpack should be packed in such a way that the load is well-balanced. It will almost certainly be more awkward to carry if the pack is top-heavy or has most of the weight on one side.

Any heavy items such as a stove or cookwear should be packed inside (relatively high up) as close as possible to where your back or spine will be, and not toward the front of the pack. The closer the center of gravity of the loaded pack is to the center of your back, the more likely it will be well-balanced when worn.

Avoid attaching heavy gear such as a tent to the outside front of the pack, or putting it directly inside the front, which is some distance from your back. This would move the pack's center of gravity outward, and could have a tendency to pull you backward and off-balance when you're carrying it.

If your pack has outside pockets, use these for keeping the important items that you'll want easy access to: raingear, flashlight, bug repellent, first aid kit and emergency items, compass, map, guidebook, and water bottle or canteen. Belt pouches or other little zippered bags may also be used to carry smaller items like your compass, knife, small scissors, spare flashlight batteries and bulb, and matches.

Assuming the pack has at least two good-size compartments, use one for clothing and the second for other important items of gear. If there's a single large compartment, consider putting either clothing or nonclothing items in a stuff sack to keep them separate from everything else.

It's highly recommended that all food be kept in its own bag or stuff sack. This will help you to avoid getting any food mixed up with other gear or into your clothing, and to avert disaster should your honey, peanut butter, or any other messy food somehow manage to leak out of its container.

If the pack has an external frame, your sleeping bag and tent will probably be attached to the frame below as well as above the packbag. With an internal frame pack, one or both of these items are usually carried inside, and some items may be attached to the packbag outside.

With time and a little experimentation you'll develop a system to organize your gear and clothing in a way that works for you—and avoid the potential difficulty and frustration that goes with being unable to locate items when you need them.

Some people find their packs are still too heavy, even after careful planning and packing. Unless the trip is going to be a lengthy expedition, however, with effort you can probably find ways to reduce the weight. Chances are that you still have quite a few nonessentials in the pack which could be weeded out. An experienced friend with an impartial eye could help with this.

Typical "problem areas" where people go overboard include: bringing a large kit of personal toiletries (the items could be repackaged in tiny plastic bottles), an arsenal of reading material (one small paperback is probably sufficient, except on an extended trip), many changes of underwear (two or three are enough, since they can be washed out as needed), and far too much food.

Virtually all camping items like flashlights, cooking pots, and stoves come in miniature, extra-light versions these days. Obtaining these will make it much easier to keep the total weight down. If you're only taking short trips, it's not necessary to run out and replace everything you already own with a super-light-and-compact version. If you become committed to this kind of camping, however, you'll want to keep an eye out for such items and accumulate them over time.

Entering the Wilderness

Arriving

The most common way to reach a park, forest, or wilderness area is, of course, by car. Bus or train service is also available for some of the more popular parks, especially those which are relatively close to cities and other population centers.

An entrance or parking fee is charged at many National Parks, state parks, and other visitor-oriented parks where facilities are provided. At other areas, including most National Forests and state forests, such fees are generally not required.

While entry or parking fees may be nominal, at some locations the amount now runs as high as $10 or more per car. During off-season periods the fee may or may not be charged.

If there's an information or visitor center, you may want to stop in for up-to-the-minute details on trail conditions or other information. Perhaps you'll need to pick up a camping permit, when required. If you haven't already obtained maps and a guidebook, these items are sometimes available for sale.

Not all parks and other areas have a visitor or information center, however, or it may not be open the day or hour you arrive. It's best to get any information you need ahead of time.

Parking

In some parks and forests parking is strictly regulated, and permitted only in lots and designated places. In other areas it's allowed freely along roads and elsewhere. To avoid the possibility of your car being ticketed or towed away, make sure it's legal before parking outside of an approved lot.

Parking areas are often located at trailheads, trail crossings, and points where there's easy access to rivers or lakes. At times it's also necessary to travel some distance from a parking spot to get to a particular trail or water route.

Trailheads may or may not be well-marked. Sometimes there are prominent roadside signs, making them almost impossible to miss. Elsewhere trailheads are indicated only by paint blazes or small signs. Some searching may be required to locate the trail.

A map or guidebook will usually be of help here. You might also be able to get directions from a ranger or other park employee. Since trails are occasionally relocated, be aware that older maps and guidebooks may not show the trails correctly.

In certain areas it's wise to ask a ranger about how safe it is leave your car overnight in a particular location. Break-ins are sometimes known to occur, whether in remote regions or near major highways. Such problems are thankfully rare in some parts of the country, but unfortunately much more common in others.

A parking place next to a ranger station or other facility is usually the most secure place to leave a car. If you're visiting an area where break-ins or vandalism have occurred, it's sometimes suggested that you find a nearby resident or business owner who will keep an eye on your car for a nominal fee.

Registering

Whether or not a permit is needed, regulations sometimes require that you sign in at a ranger station or visitor center and indicate how long you'll be in the wilderness. Leaving this information is a good idea even when it's not mandatory, as someone will then know you're missing if you don't return as scheduled.

At many trailheads or a short distance down trails you'll find a trail register. Always sign in at such registers, since this would help others to trace your route if you somehow failed to return. On occasion it's also suggested that a note be left on your car's dashboard, indicating the planned date of your return.

Finding Your Way in the Wilderness

Whether you're on trails, waterways, or elsewhere, staying oriented in the wilderness isn't always a simple matter. Your ability to find the way should never be taken for granted. Awareness and considerable skill are sometimes required.

Following well-marked trails can be easy, but some trails are poorly-marked or unmarked. The route may be unclear at times. Those who choose to bushwhack off the beaten path face even greater challenges in staying oriented.

However you travel in the wilderness, attentiveness is always in order. Even on the best-marked trails it's wise to periodically check map and compass to verify your location. An assumption that you know where you're headed could be mistaken.

It's impossible to overestimate the value of a map and compass. These items should be with you on any wilderness trip, period. If you don't know how to use them, go with others who do. You won't usually need to consult the compass and map constantly, but it should be done every now and then, to confirm that you're indeed where you think you are, and going in the right direction.

In any park or natural area, whether large or small, there's always a possibility that you could somehow get turned around, disoriented, or lost. This happens on occasion to even the most experienced outdoorspeople. Beware of subscribing to a belief that you're immune to such difficulties. If you're conscientious and stay alert, however, you'll have very little to worry about.

Getting Lost

There's really never a good reason for getting seriously lost. It doesn't ever have to happen to you, and it probably won't, as long as you pay adequate attention and can keep from getting careless about staying oriented in the wilderness.

The key is to *always* stop *at the first sign* that you're off the track, or that something is amiss. Respond immediately to any hunch that things don't look quite right. Check map and compass, and if necessary consult your guidebook. Look around.

Never continue ahead if there's some indication that you may have gone astray, that you aren't where you thought you were, and perhaps could have somehow gotten onto a different trail. Only proceed if you're sure of your orientation.

The safest bet is to go back to the last trail marker you can find, or to any other indication that you were on the correct path or headed in the right direction. If necessary, retrace your route all the way back to where you started.

Continuing on when you're uncertain of your whereabouts is a perfect prescription for getting seriously lost. This could mean big trouble, especially without a map and compass along. In a small park the odds are fairly good that you'll stumble across a road and find your way out, but then again maybe you won't. In a large wilderness area your life may be at risk.

If you were to get lost while carrying or transporting your gear, at least you'd have food and shelter, and would be able to keep yourself well and even comfortable for days if necessary. You could either systematically search for a way out, or wait for others to locate you. If you should happen to be separated from most or all of your gear and extra clothing, however, and the weather is cold and wet, you might not survive for very long.

It isn't necessary to waste energy worrying about these things, but try to keep it all tucked away in the back of your mind whenever you venture away from your campsite. Know that your life might be at stake if you couldn't locate the site again and had to spend a night or more without shelter and extra clothing.

By being careful you'll never have to deal with such an event. Most people who get seriously lost are poorly equipped, often without a map and compass, and usually aren't adequately skilled, or have been inattentive or careless.

Taking a course or reading a book on the subject of wilderness survival also wouldn't hurt, just in case you should ever find yourself in a situation of being lost and separated from your gear. Ways of getting through a night without adequate clothing or gear might include making a huge pile of loose, dry leaves and crawling into it, or doing intermittent calisthenics.

For a moment let's assume that an unlikely, unwanted event has indeed occurred. You've reached a point where you're clearly lost and can't find the way back. First sit down for a rest. Take some deep breaths. Do your best to remain calm. Think through recent events and try to remember how you came to be where you are now. See if you can sense which is the right way back.

If you've been traveling with others but are now separated from them, and you're pretty sure they'll be searching for you, stay put right where you are. Above all, don't rush off aimlessly in any direction. You could be relatively close to the trail, and if you head the wrong way this will make matters worse.

Since other people might be within earshot, use your whistle, blowing a series of three short blasts, which is widely known to be a signal of distress. Try shouting as well. If you get a response, move very slowly and carefully in the direction of the voice, carrying all gear along with you.

If you've been traveling alone or are lost with your companions, and believe you may not be far from the trail or your campsite, begin a slow, careful, systematic search from the point where you are. Stay oriented in relation to this spot by constantly sighting back to it (perhaps using a tree).

If you've registered your estimated return time at a ranger station, or others at home are expecting you back on a certain date, a search party may be sent out when you don't return as scheduled. This might not happen for a number of days, of course, assuming you're not due back yet.

Build a large smoky fire (with great care) if you have reason to believe others may be searching for you. Keep an eye out for low-flying aircraft, which you could attempt to signal to using your mirror.

The risk of getting lost is especially high when bushwhacking (traveling cross-country). Don't bushwhack unless you really know what you're doing, and feel absolutely confident that you can avoid losing your way. When bushwhacking keep that map and compass handy and check them constantly.

Staying Oriented During Specific Activities

What's involved in staying oriented varies somewhat with the particular activity or form of wilderness travel you're involved in. Most hiking and backpacking takes place on marked or unmarked trails, of course. Hiking maps which show the trails clearly are available for many but not all areas. As long as you know how to follow a trail, read a map, and use a compass, it's extremely unlikely that you're going to get lost. For more about hiking trails see *The Essential Guide to Hiking in the United States*.

Canoeists, kayakers, and rafters need maps which show waterways in detail. Following a single river or stream may not be a problem, but some rivers fork or lead into lakes. Bays and islands on larger lakes or along the ocean sometimes have a confusingly similar appearance. The map as well as other sources of information will be important in helping you pinpoint where you are, and also the location of potential campsites.

If you're traveling on horseback or by bike, many of the appropriate trails, paths, or old roads you'll use will probably be without signs or markers, or infrequently marked at best. A detailed map will be essential in helping you keep oriented. Best is a map designed for the particular activity you're involved in.

Cross-country ski trails are sometimes but not always marked. For well-known areas special X-C ski maps are often available. When in doubt about your orientation, you could always return by following your own tracks out, and the same option exists when you're snowshoeing. There's a danger here, however, in that wind or fresh snow can obliterate existing tracks at any time. Since getting lost in the winter could easily be life-threatening, always pay extremely close attention to your route.

NINE

Setting Up Camp

LOCATING A SITE

Designated campsites are available in many but not all parks and wilderness areas. These sites are common in National Parks, state parks, and other heavily-used locations. Sometimes the campsites are available by advance reservation. The use of such sites may be optional, or camping may be restricted to them.

If you're visiting a park or forest with designated or established campsites, finding a place to camp should be simple—that is, assuming the campsites aren't all taken, they're well marked, and you have adequate information for locating them.

An obvious advantage of using an approved campsite is that you're spared the trouble of hunting for a suitable spot each day. A potential disadvantage is that designated campsites are often clustered together, meaning the presence of other campers.

Some forests and parks also allow visitors to camp wherever they wish. Here your tentsite could be any suitable open area where others have obviously camped in the past, or it might be a more pristine place that shows no signs of previous use.

Finding an appropriate campsite on your own can be a simple task or a challenge, depending on the terrain, amount of vegetation, and also availability of water. Potential campsites may be abundant in a relatively flat, unrocky region, whereas good sites will be more scarce in steep, mountainous terrain.

Requirements For a Campsite

The most fundamental requirement for a good campsite is a relatively flat area of ground which is largely free of rocks, bumps, and other obstacles. If necessary it's possible to camp on a slight incline, but the more level the better. You'll sleep best on a reasonably flat surface.

It's also desirable, whenever possible, to be close to a spring, stream, river, pond, or lake in order to meet your needs for water. Most of us, of course, are quite attracted to water in a natural setting. Such places are often especially scenic.

Although camping near water is almost always a priority, regulations now generally prohibit setting up your tent right next to it. Many parks and forests throughout the country either request or require that campsites be no closer than 100-200 feet from lakes, streams, and other water sources.

If the terrain is rough or steep, it's possible that at times you may not be able to find a suitable campsite anywhere near a water source. A wilderness trip can also involve crossing a dry region which has no dependable water sources at all, requiring that you transport water for part or all of the trip.

Guidebooks will sometimes offer advice about recommended places to camp in addition to designated campsites. Information about the availability of water and where to find it is essential. This can also be gleaned from a good map.

Never depart on a wilderness trip without knowing for sure whether water is available, and without confirming that it's indeed legal and otherwise feasible to camp in a particular area. If there's no dependable water you might have to carry it for the entire trip, which might mean a very heavy load. If you're planning to venture into an unusually rugged area, verify ahead of time that there's enough level ground for potential campsites.

Those who are canoeing, kayaking, or rafting obviously won't have a problem finding water, and in most cases will camp near or alongside the river or body of water. Even so, there may be major stretches of river or lakeshore without legal or suitable campsites (some of the land might be private, or the terrain along the shore rough). Study a guidebook or obtain other information in advance to confirm the availability of campsites.

When you're in the process of looking for a site, local camping regulations may limit your choices. How far should your campsite be from the trail or water? Must your tent be out of sight of the trail? The rules may or may not be clearly posted in the area. Ignorance of regulations is an excuse that doesn't necessarily sit well with rangers or enforcement officers.

If you fail to inform yourself of the rules or ignore them, your trip could take a very unpleasant turn along the way should a ranger happen by. Admittedly, enforcement of regulations varies greatly. Some parks, forests, and backcountry areas are largely unpatrolled, and there may be little enforcement.

In other parks and areas, however, you can receive a stiff fine or summons and be evicted from the park on the spot. This is not the way any of us wants to end a trip. It's probably not worth taking a chance. Know the rules and observe them—unless a ranger gives you permission to ignore one or more of them.

Other Considerations in Selecting a Site

Avoid camping in a low spot or at the bottom of a depression, which might fill with water if it rains. Be alert if the soil is thin and there appears to be bedrock underneath, meaning any rain would have nowhere to go and the area could be flooded. Likewise, never set your tent up in a dry stream bed or other channel where water might be funneled if it should rain.

Anytime there's even a remote possibility of heavy showers and ensuing flash floods, camping directly alongside a stream or river is potentially risky. It's safer to be on higher ground, at least several feet or more above the waterline. Also, when camping close to the ocean or a large lake, be careful to keep well beyond the reach of tides and possible storm waves.

When you're preparing to set up camp in a forest, look overhead to make sure a dead tree isn't leaning (or a large dead branch hanging) precariously over your potential site, posing a threat if it should fall. While the likelihood of this occurring might be rather slim, it's well within the realm of possibility during a windy storm. When in doubt, pick another spot.

High mountain meadows and mountaintops are attractive places to visit, but they're undoubtedly dangerous for camping because you're completely exposed to the elements—including any severe storms, high winds, and/or lightning. If a storm does blow up, it'll be too late for you to pack your things and leave. Camping in such areas is often illegal anyway, since vegetation at higher altitudes tends to be fragile and easily damaged.

PUTTING UP THE TENT

Setting up a tent usually takes no more than a few minutes. With practice, some of the newer tents will actually go up in as little as a minute or two. Whatever kind of tent you have, assume it will take longer at the start. By far the best place to put up your tent the first time is at home, in case you run into problems. Bring any written directions along on the trip.

Whether you'll be staying at a designated site or have to make your own campsite, plan to reach the intended area while there's still ample daylight remaining. Setting up in the dark with a flashlight can be a hassle if you aren't very familiar with your tent. Sooner or later, though, in spite of your best efforts you'll probably end up having to make camp after dark. An experienced camper can usually manage this without much trouble.

Having to put up the tent while it's raining is another less-than-ideal situation that you're bound to meet with eventually. If it's still early and you have some time to work with, wait a while to see if the rain lets up. But trust that you'll be able to manage whatever the weather.

On occasion you may find yourself in a rocky area where the soil is thin, and it's difficult to get the tent stakes in more than a couple of inches. Self-supporting tents have a real advantage here. If you don't have such a tent, try to look for another site, or use nearby trees or bushes to help tie out the tent. Don't forget that an area with bedrock underneath and poor drainage could flood with water if it rains.

Avoid setting up in meadows and directly on vegetation when there's a choice. Sometimes you won't be able to camp without flattening some grass or small plants. As long as you're not in a fragile area or at high elevations, and are remaining for only a night or two, the damage is probably acceptable. But be aware that your presence is indeed having an effect. The more ways you can reduce your impact on the natural environment, the better.

If your campsite is on hilly or bumpy ground, stretch out on your groundsheet and move around to find the most comfortable way to orient your body. Then set up the tent and situate the door accordingly. If you can't avoid being on an incline, sleep with your head uphill.

After you've set it up, make sure the body of the tent and the fly are taut. There should be a space of at least two to four inches between the fly and inner tent wall, with the two not touching. If they do, you're likely to get some dripping inside from condensation. Also, stakes tend to shift slightly in the earth with time, so they may need to be readjusted later, especially during and after rain. See Chapter 2 for more about tents.

Tents and Food

Cultivate the habit of never bringing food into your tent for any reason. Almost all foods are capable of attracting wildlife. Most animals have an incredibly acute sense of smell, and they may be drawn to your food no matter how it's packaged.

If you try to eat or snack inside the tent, some crumbs will probably be spilled regardless of how careful you are, and these may end up being mashed into the tent floor. In bear country this means putting yourself at risk. Even if there are no bears around, there's still a chance that some other animal will chew or claw a hole in the side of your tent to get in. This is most likely to occur while you're away, but if an animal is hungry enough it could even happen at night when you're inside.

It's best to refrain from keeping or consuming food anywhere near the tent. Establish a cooking and dining area at least 50 to 100 feet away, whenever possible, and limit all food consumption to that location and beyond.

Hanging Food

Heavy-duty coolers and other containers designed for food storage are capable of protecting food from most animals, but such containers are much too cumbersome to bring on most kinds of wilderness camping trips.

The best thing to do with food when it's not being consumed is to store it in a nylon or plastic bag, and hang it high from the branch of a tree, or between two trees. Keep the food hung not only at night, but also during the day at other than mealtimes. Food left anywhere around the campsite is likely to be quickly targeted by chipmunks, squirrels, or larger animals.

There are several ways to hang a food bag. The simplest is to find a branch which is at least 15 feet off the ground—ideally one that's strong enough to hold your food bag but not much else. Take a 25-to-50-foot length of nylon cord, tie a small rock to one end, and heave it over the branch. The line should hang at least three to four feet out from the tree trunk.

With both ends of the cord in your hand, give a good tug to verify that the branch will indeed hold

the weight of your food without breaking. It should bend, which will keep larger animals from climbing out on it.

Release the rock and tie your food bag to one end of the cord, then pull the other end to hoist the bag up at least 10-12 feet off the ground. Don't bring it up too close to the branch, as squirrels or other small animals will be more likely to jump onto the bag or run down the line.

Tie the other end to a different tree, if possible. When you need your food, simply untie the cord and lower the bag, but leave the line where it is so you'll be able to pull the food bag up again. Once the line is in place, re-hanging the food each time is very simple.

Another method is to tie a high horizontal line between two trees, and hang your food bag from the center of the line, tying it off as described above. The horizontal line should be 15 feet or more off the ground and reasonably taut. Put it in place by tossing each end (tied to a rock) over a high branch of a different tree. Then tie the ends around the trunks below.

The methods described above are effective in most areas. However, bears and other animals in some of our National Parks and other popular areas are extremely accustomed to human food, and in quite a few locations they've become unusually aggressive and resourceful in obtaining supplies from campers.

An especially foolproof system is known as "counterbalancing" which requires dividing your food between two bags. Use either a suitable branch or a horizontal line as discussed above. Tie your cord to a rock, toss it over the branch or line, and attach it to one bag. Pulling the bag high, tie the cord's other end to the second bag. Then push it up with a long stick so that both bags hang at least 10 feet off the ground. To retrieve your food, use the stick to pull either of the bags down.

After dark it's unquestionably more difficult to locate a suitable branch and hang your food line. Get in the habit of doing it immediately after setting up your tent, so the task doesn't get forgotten until much later.

LEAN-TOS AND SHELTERS

Lean-tos and other simple shelters provide an alternative to tenting out. These structures are located along trails and waterways in many parks and wilderness areas around the country. Almost all are near water sources.

A lean-to is a simple three-sided structure, open in the front, with a slanting roof. A wooden lean-to which holds four to six people is often called an Adirondack shelter. Other open shelters made of wood or stone sometimes sleep as many as 12 to 14 people.

In a typical lean-to or trail shelter, you simply bed down on the wooden or dirt floor, normally with a groundsheet spread out to keep your sleeping bag and pad from getting dirty. In a few areas shelters have wooden or wire bunks built in.

Since a lean-to is completely open in the front, you're not really separated from nature in any significant way. Staying in a lean-to or other open shelter is usually considered to be another form of camping, an alternative to staying in a tent. It's not the same experience as spending the night in a closed cabin, which may have a wood-burning stove and other comforts.

Sleeping in a shelter or lean-to can be fun if you don't mind a little communal living and sharing your space with fellow-travelers. There won't be any real privacy (unless no one else shows up), as you'll be stretching out right next to others.

A lean-to is a great place to spend time on a rainy day, as there's a roof overhead, and you can cook and socialize as you wish. There will usually be a fireplace or fire circle outside in front, and occasionally a fireplace is built right in.

In some parks lean-tos must be reserved in advance, and a fee is often charged. This is common in many smaller state and local parks. Elsewhere a lean-to or shelter is generally free, and available to anyone who comes along.

When using a regular (unreserved) shelter or lean-to, you're expected to make room for everyone who arrives until the structure is filled to capacity. It's considered very poor form to be unwelcoming and discourage others from staying, or to take over such a lean-to for your own exclusive use. This is also usually illegal. And tents should never be set up inside.

Years ago a major advantage of using trail shelters was that this eliminated the need to carry a tent. The recent popularity of camping, however, has meant that you can never be sure that a shelter will have space available. Except when visiting a place where lean-tos may be reserved, carry a tent or tarp in case.

If you're traveling alone or with just a friend or two, staying at lean-tos offers the benefit that you're likely to meet others and share some good company in the wilderness. This can help make a solo trip especially congenial. On a long trip it's also nice to be spared the need to put up your tent every night.

Some of us have warm memories of nights spent in lean-tos, sharing stories and conviviality with newfound friends. However, be aware that near roads or in popular areas there's also the possibility of encountering rowdy groups, or other people who want to party (this is less likely in remote wilderness areas). One safe option is to set up camp a little distance from a lean-to. Then visit the shelter if and when you feel like socializing or sitting by a campfire, or to cook in rainy weather.

Aside from the risk that you'll have to share the space with noisy neighbors, or possibly with someone who snores loudly at night, lean-tos have some other disadvantages. In warm weather you're exposed to insects, and when it's cold and windy the lean-to won't provide the protection and additional warmth of a tent.

Because of the constant cooking that goes on in lean-tos and the inevitable spilled food, these structures are notorious for harboring a community of mice and/or other nocturnal critters, which you'll hear scampering about at night. Older shelters also sometimes leak. Check the roof carefully if rain seems possible.

After putting up the tent (or settling into a lean-to), hanging food, and perhaps purifying some water (see Chapter 10), your time is your own. Assuming it isn't yet suppertime, you could sit and rest, nap a little, go for a walk or a hike, poke around and explore a bit, take a swim, paddle around in your canoe, do some reading, chat with a friend, sit quietly, listen to the sounds of nature . . . or do anything else that appeals.

TEN

Taking Care of Basic Needs

WATER

It's easy to take water for granted when it comes out of a tap. At home there's no effort or planning required in order to satisfy your need for water. In the wilderness, however, it isn't such a simple matter. Those who spend time out in nature often develop a new appreciation for this precious substance, which is vital to all forms of life on this planet.

Some people have never known real thirst. If you enter a dry area and seriously underestimate the amount of water needed, or forget to bring it at all, you'll probably learn a lot more than you wanted to about thirst. It's the kind of mistake few people make twice—assuming they're fortunate enough to survive it the first time. Your body's need for water is utterly critical.

While in some regions of the country water is a scarce commmodity, in other areas it's everywhere. In planning a wilderness trip you need to know about the availability of water in the park or forest you'll be visiting. This information can usually be obtained from a guidebook, a good map, or a park information center.

When you've confirmed the presence of water, remember there's always a slight possibility that a particular spring or stream won't be running, especially during a period of drought or reduced rainfall. Don't put yourself in a position where you would be in dire straits if a water source should be dry.

You won't need to carry a large supply when visiting areas where water is plentiful, but it's wise to always have at least a quart (liter) or two in your pack. In regions where it's known to be scarce, protect yourself by bringing plenty of extra water. Since water is heavy, when traveling in the desert or any dry area you'll probably be carrying substantial additional weight.

You can normally expect to need at least a gallon of water per day, per person, for drinking and cooking, and even more in hot weather and/or when involved in strenuous exercise. A gallon weighs eight pounds, so it's easy to see how quickly the weight adds up if you have to bring enough for more than a day or two.

Camping near water will not only allow you to lighten your load considerably, but you'll also be furnished with an ample supply for washing—and possibly even swimming, assuming the source happens to be a lake, pond, or river.

Purifying Water for Drinking

Few things taste better than cool, fresh mountain spring water. Pure, clean, delicious water is undoubtedly one of the underrated delights of this world. Sadly, drinking directly from most water sources in the wilderness is now too risky.

Many of us do still drink from high mountain springs, when you can get the water as it emerges from the ground. There's little chance that such a source could be contaminated—as long as you're far from roads and development, at a higher elevation than surrounding areas, and sure there's no possibility of stagnant water or pollution feeding into the spring.

Streams, rivers, ponds, and lakes must always be considered suspect, even though some of these waters undoubtedly remain pure. Remarkably clear and clean-looking water can still harbor parasites. These have been spreading in recent years, as has bacterial contamination.

The chances of getting sick from drinking the water are now much higher than just a decade or two ago. While a parasite won't kill you, it can make life slightly miserable for days, weeks, or longer. Unless a ranger, local resident, or other reliable person can vouch for a water's cleanliness and safety, it's best to purify it before drinking.

Boiling water is the oldest, most tried-and-true method of assuring its potability. This is trustworthy as long as there isn't chemical pollution, which shouldn't be a problem in most wilderness areas. Boiling will kill any possible bacteria or parasites and leave the water completely safe to drink. Contrary to earlier beliefs that it should be boiled for at least several minutes, bringing the water to a full boil will be sufficient.

The only real drawback of this method is that it takes time to boil enough for a day's supply, and you have to wait till it cools down before drinking. Boiling also leaves the water with a slightly flat taste. All water used for cooking can conveniently be boiled, of course, in the process of preparing a meal.

Portable and lightweight water filters have come on the market during the past decade, and for many campers a water filter has now become a standard item of equipment. With just a bit of exertion (most of them involve using a hand pump) you can purify enough water to meet daily drinking needs in a few minutes or less. An advantage of using a filter is that you can drink the water immediately after purifying, it stays cold, and the taste isn't affected. See Chapter 3 for more about water filters.

One other common method of purifying water exists: adding iodine or other chemical tablets to the water. This is the least desirable choice. With tablets you have to wait a while before drinking, they leave an unpleasant taste, may be unhealthy to ingest, and, most important, don't always work adequately (there are cases, one sustained by the author many years ago, where parasites have been contracted even after use of the tablets).

FOOD AND COOKING

Along with water, food is obviously a matter of special importance and necessity. Eating well and satisfying your body's nutritional needs should be placed among your highest priorities.

Food preferences vary enormously, of course, and some people are much more concerned about what they eat than others. It's not uncommon to have emotional issues arise in relation to food prior to and during a wilderness trip. Beginners often worry or fear that they won't bring enough and will end up hungry, or that a diet of mostly dehydrated foods will be unpalatable or boring.

The truth is that anyone can eat extremely well in the wilderness. Depending on the kind of diet you prefer, however, it's probable that you'll have to make some adjustments.

A few campers are determined to bring their favorite foods at any cost. You occasionally run across people in the wilderness cooking giant steaks or preparing elaborate dinners, complete with wine and candles—enjoyable no doubt, but usually at the expense of having to haul some heavy supplies along.

Because of the weight, bulk, and perishability of many common foods, it makes sense to alter your diet a bit to make the overall camping experience easier. However, if you don't have to carry the food and there's room for it, or you simply don't mind the extra weight, there's no reason why you can't bring practically anything you want to.

In Chapter 4 you'll find a more detailed discussion of food and what's most appropriate for a wilderness camping trip. If any of the suggestions sound unappealing to you, try putting together a menu that satisfies your needs better. If your favorite foods are heavy or perishable, however, some adjustment is called for. Once you're in the wilderness you may find that some preferences don't seem as important as you thought.

Fresh foods are especially problematic. Most of these foods are heavy, and spoilage often comes quickly, unless you're out in cold weather. If you love fresh vegetables or fruit, is it worth the weight to carry them along with you? The decision is yours. A compromise is always possible. Perhaps you could bring some but not all of what you'd prefer.

There are people who love to cook and enjoy making rather ambitious meals in the wilderness, not minding the time and effort required. Other campers prefer to do an absolute minimum of cooking. Many bring prepackaged meals which require nothing more than boiling some water, stirring, and waiting five minutes.

How much cooking you'll want to do will almost certainly be affected by how busy and active you are during the day. If your typical day is filled with challenging physical activity, you can expect to be pretty tired by suppertime, and probably much less likely to want to cook than if you've been taking it easy.

In the not-too-distant past virtually all cooking in the wilderness was done over campfires. This has changed, although the practice has by no means died out. Campfires have increasingly been restricted and even banned in a growing number of parks and other areas. Small camping stoves are now standard equipment for cooking (see Chapter 4 for more about stoves).

After a long day's travel, which may include strenuous exercise, it's normal to feel tired and perhaps want to turn in early. Some people jump in the sack right away, skipping supper. Generally speaking, however, it's best to eat something first, to take in some food at the end of (as well as during) a long day. This is especially important in cold weather. The body needs nourishment and refueling when we've been placing demands on it.

ANSWERING NATURE'S CALL

Toilets are pretty scarce in the wilderness, although outhouses are sometimes found at designated campsites, and occasionally other facilities are available in heavily-used areas. More often than not, though, you simply have to "go in the woods," or take care of it somewhere away from your campsite.

Some beginners find this matter a bit intimidating, especially if they've never had the experience of using anything other than a regular toilet. It can serve as another potential obstacle to those who haven't yet tried wilderness camping. In fact, there's actually very little involved in learning to "go to the bathroom" in the wilds (except, perhaps, for the challenges of managing it during a severe storm). With minimal practice it should soon feel like the most natural thing in the world.

Assuming there's nothing available to sit on, the required posture is squatting—as comfortably as possible—in order to take care of business. You could try to find a small log or a large fallen branch to sit on, but squatting is an ancient and perfectly satisfying posture.

For solid waste it's vitally important that you dig a small hole, ideally four to five inches deep, using either a small trowel or a stick. This can be done either before or afterward. Then rake the dirt and some leaves over it, burying your toilet paper as well. There are now some wilderness areas where waste and toilet paper must be carried out in plastic bags, but burying it remains acceptable and the norm in most parks and areas of the country.

Any place you pick should be a good distance from water sources (a minimum of 150 feet), and of course well away from the campsite and any trails. Urinating should likewise be done away from water, but a hole doesn't have to be dug. In the course of taking care of these needs, make sure you don't get lost.

KEEPING CLEAN

We live in a culture where many people are extremely concerned about cleanliness. While for some it's not a matter of extraordinary interest, for others it's virtually an obsession. Undoubtedly the absence of showers and bathtubs deters more than a few from trying wilderness camping. Yet there's no reason you can't keep reasonably clean while in the natural world.

One relatively new option which makes it a little easier is to bring a "solar shower" (see Chapter 5). This item will give you a close approximation to a real shower, with a light spray of warm-to-hot water for up to several minutes.

Otherwise, it's always possible to take a thorough sponge bath, and to wash as often as you wish on a trip. If soap is being used, don't rinse anywhere near a water source. You can either use cold water or heat some on your stove.

If you're camped near a lake, pond, or good-size stream in warm weather, swimming may be an option, or you could at least get into the water every now and then. Taking a dip is not only refreshing, but it will help you stay clean. Just remember that soap or shampoo must never be used directly in a stream or lake.

STAYING WARM AND DRY

Keeping adequately warm and dry should stand near the top of any list of important requirements for wilderness living. Whether you're in transit or at your campsite, it's vital to protect yourself from getting seriously wet from rain, and to be adequately insulated from cool or cold temperatures. This is not just a matter of comfort. At times your life may depend on it (see Chapter 13 for a discussion of hypothermia).

At the very least, the enjoyment of a wilderness experience is likely to be thoroughly dampened if you get soaked to the skin and seriously chilled. Even if you build a fire and have brought a good sleeping bag, it can be difficult to warm up once you're badly chilled. Know about and practice layering in cold weather to minimize the possibility of this happening (see Chapter 6).

Protecting Yourself with Raingear

Even if there's just a 1 percent chance of rain in the area you'll be visiting, bring a waterproof poncho, rain suit, or other rainwear (a detailed discussion of raingear is found in Chapter 3).

Never get in a position where you and your raingear are separated by any significant distance. Storms can sometimes arrive with sudden fury, and rain can be ice cold. If you walk or travel more than a few minutes from your campsite, bring a day pack with raingear, along with some extra clothing, map and compass, and emergency items including a first aid kit.

Whenever you're out in heavy rain, or precipitation continues for a long time, you're bound to get at least a little wet even while wearing raingear. This is especially probable if you're exercising heavily and sweating. The raingear will still provide some warmth, however, and wearing it is always preferable to having cold rain soak your body.

Wet Weather Considerations

Should you happen to be in your tent when it starts pouring or a storm breaks, you could choose to stay put and try to wait it out, assuming you don't have a schedule to adhere to. In time the storm will subside. Cooking or pursuing any activity is naturally a little more difficult during a downpour, although it certainly can be done if necessary, and occasionally must be.

More often than not, inclement weather only amounts to some light rain or drizzle, perhaps with an occasional shower. There's no reason to let this interfere with daytime activities, which can still be comfortably enjoyed as long as you're properly dressed. It's your decision whether to shorten or postpone activities in wet weather. There's surely no harm in taking a rest day and remaining in the tent if you want to.

On the other hand, if you're involved in long-distance travel you may have a schedule to follow, and perhaps will have to proceed whatever the weather. Or you may want to go anyway. Unless rain or other weather creates a truly hazardous condition, however, it shouldn't present a real problem or spoil your trip.

Protecting Your Gear

It's extremely important that essential clothing and gear, including your sleeping bag, be protected from getting wet. This is another truly critical area. It could mean the end of your trip if everything gets soaked. If you're far from civilization, you could be in a difficult and dangerous situation.

Backpackers should either bring a raincover for the pack, or put important items in securely tied plastic bags inside. Use a plastic bag inside your sleeping bag stuff sack as well for extra protection. Another option for protecting your backpack is to wear a "backpack poncho" or "packframe poncho," which covers the pack while you're walking. If you're canoeing or rafting, make sure all luggage is well-protected in case you should capsize.

Whenever you're away from the campsite, whether for a few minutes or many hours, close everything up in case of possible rain. Remember that even the brightest morning can be followed by heavy afternoon showers, and storms come with very little warning in some mountain areas. Inexperienced campers sometimes leave their campsite for many hours with tents half open, clothing hanging on a line, and even a sleeping bag airing out. Never leave things outside that you wouldn't want to get wet.

CAMPFIRES

Building a campfire is among the most ancient of practices, and sitting by one still has almost universal appeal. There's great congeniality in sharing a campfire with others. The setting is especially conducive to sharing stories and/or songs, and discussing the day's activities or what's to follow tomorrow.

A campfire can be a source of special comfort in cold weather, and a fire is usually helpful in keeping insects at bay when it's buggy. You can build a campfire at any time of day, but evening is the most popular and convenient time to have one.

In the past it was almost unthinkable not to have a fire when camping out, but with increased environmental awareness this has been changing. Campfires have a real and visible impact on the wilderness. Many forest fires have begun with a poorly tended campfire, and building new fire circles leaves scars on the earth. Campfires are now restricted or prohibited in a growing number of parks and wilderness areas.

While some people feel cheated if they can't have a campfire, there are some advantages in doing without one. For one thing, you'll discover the night sky much more completely, especially if you're camping out in the open. Sitting or lying stretched out for a spell of star-gazing with friends can be as relaxing and fulfilling as time spent in front of a campfire.

A crackling fire will also tend to obliterate the subtle sounds and sights of the evening and nighttime. Without a fire you may find it easier to feel connected to the natural world at night. Allow your eyes to grow accustomed to the dark. You may find that fear of the night, which is common, will subside at least partially. Even when campfires are permitted, it's nice to occasionally do without one.

Where campfires are legal it's important to be conscientious about building, tending, and putting them out. Try to do this in a way that will have the least impact on the environment. Use a preexisting fire circle, if available, rather than making a new one. Try not to destroy any plant life, and avoid starting the fire directly on organic soil (soft earth). In some regions of the country digging a pit for the fire is recommended.

Gather only dead wood and branches you find on the ground for firewood. Cutting dead trees which are standing or breaking off branches leaves an area looking less wild and attractive. If you've never built a campfire before, have someone teach you, or consult a book on outdoor skills. Keep in mind that some older books will recommend camping methods that are no longer acceptable in the wilderness (including such practices as cutting live branches or digging trenches).

It should be obvious that a fire must never be left untended, yet it still happens all too often. A gust of wind can easily blow ashes around and ignite a spreading ground fire in a matter of moments, especially in dry conditions. That's precisely how many forest fires begin, and the result is much destruction. Take seriously your responsibility to make sure that none of your actions, including fire-building, has any harmful consequences.

If firewood isn't plentiful, keep the fire small. Skip it altogether if there isn't much fuel available in the area. Dead branches and trees normally rot and contribute to the richness of the soil, and to the wilderness environment as a whole.

When you're ready to go to sleep or leave the campsite for any reason, use ample amounts of water to put the fire out completely. Dirt or sand can be used in an area where water is scarce, as long as this doesn't involve damaging or altering the local environment. Don't leave a single spark or a hint of smoke.

All too often a fire which was believed to be out has flared up later and caused destruction, usually aided by the wind. Get in the habit of putting it completely out no matter where you are or what the conditions. Just because everything's calm at bedtime doesn't mean that a stiff wind couldn't blow up during the night, possibly showering the area and your tent with sparks.

Wilderness areas have been undergoing deterioration on many fronts in recent years. Too many signs of past human presence can subtly diminish the wilderness experience for others. Part of practicing "low-impact camping" means taking a fire circle apart and scattering the rocks when you're ready to break camp, or filling in a fire pit, and otherwise obscuring any signs that you were there. Rake some leaves or loose dirt over the area. A lengthier discussion of low-impact camping follows in Chapter 14.

ELEVEN

Wilderness Activities

For most people an overnight wilderness trip involves much more than just camping out. While it can mean a welcome opportunity for some relaxation, catching up on sleep, and slow-paced living, there are also many ways to actively enjoy the wilderness while you're there.

An activity like hiking, canoeing, rafting, or cycling will often serve as the central focus of a trip, or it can be a sideline. This chapter offers a look at some of the numerous possibilities. How much time and energy you spend in such pursuits is totally up to you.

Be sure to get some instruction in advance, when appropriate, for any activity you're unfamiliar with. Try it for the first time in a place close to civilization, and preferably on a one-day trip, just in case everything doesn't go right or you discover it's not for you. Be sure you really enjoy the activity before committing to an extended trip.

If possible, go with an experienced friend or an organized group at first. Keep in mind that skills take time to develop, and avoid challenges which might exceed your level of ability or endurance.

FOOT TRAVEL

Walking

Walking is the oldest and simplest way of getting around in the wilderness, and it's also one of the most satisfying. Walking can be done almost anywhere in the natural world, except, of course, where the land is too wet or under water, or the terrain excessively rugged. It's helpful to have a path, trail, or road to follow, especially when the vegetation is dense or there are other obstacles, but this isn't essential.

You can walk whenever you like and for as long as you like. Walks can range from a short, leisurely stroll in the area around your campsite to a major

dawn-to-dusk trek. Little planning is required, although if you're venturing far from camp it's important to bring extra clothing, water, food, and emergency items. The main risk is the possibility of getting lost, so close attention must be paid to the route you're following. Always bring map and compass, and know how to use them.

Hiking

When a wilderness walk involves a distance of at least a few miles, and is carried out in a reasonably purposeful way, it's usually called a hike. Most but not all hiking is done on hiking trails, which are often marked and sometimes easy to follow. A hike can range from an untaxing afternoon stroll along a gently winding trail to a steep and strenuous trail-climb in mountainous terrain.

Avid hikers will often camp in an area where there are lots of trails, meaning many possible choices for day hikes. Off-trail hiking, or bushwhacking, is another possibility. This is easy to do in open areas, but quite difficult in rugged terrain or dense vegetation. It's also riskier, since there's a greater chance of getting lost, but more solitude is available. See *The Essential Guide to Hiking in the United States* for much more about hiking.

Backpacking

Backpacking refers to walking or hiking into the wilderness with a full-size backpack, carrying everything that's needed for an overnight stay. A backpacking trip can involve hiking a long-distance trail (or series of trails) and setting up camp in a different site each night. Or it can mean staying at a single campsite for the duration of the trip, which could be for one night or many.

Since all clothing, equipment, and food for the trip must be carried on your back, there's a strong incentive to minimize your load. This means bringing the lightest and most compact food and gear available, limiting yourself to what's truly necessary. Backpacking is also discussed in Chapter 1.

WATER-BASED ACTIVITIES

Canoeing

Most people are attracted to water in a natural setting. Among the most ancient means of water travel is canoeing, and it remains a popular and pleasurable way to get around on wilderness waterways. Wherever there are accessible lakes and rivers you're likely to find canoeists. Rentals are often available nearby.

Canoeing can be done in a very leisurely way, which could mean paddling lazily around a beautiful lake or down a slow-moving river, maybe with a little fishing along the way. For those so inclined, canoeing can also involve the excitement of a challenging whitewater run on a fast-moving river, or the physical demands and adventure of long-distance wilderness travel.

Unless your canoeing is confined to a single small lake or river, it's essential to have a map, guidebook, and/or other information. You'll want to know about the difficulty of each waterway, including any possible obstacles, so you don't end up on a river or trip which exceeds your level of skill or ambition. Information about potential campsites will also be useful.

Most people canoe in pairs, although from one to four can occupy a normal-size canoe. There should be at least one experienced person in each canoe, and for reasons of safety as well as enjoyment, everyone should get some formal instruction before attempting a river which includes whitewater.

Make sure that equipment and clothing are well-protected in waterproof luggage, which should be tied to the canoe, in case it capsizes or you take in water. Life vests or jackets should always be brought and worn. For obvious reasons, anyone participating in water-based activities in the wilderness should know how to swim.

Kayaking

A kayak has the appearance of a small and very streamlined canoe. It will go any place a canoe will go, and will often do so faster and more easily. Most kayaks are built to carry a single person. The kayak is propelled and steered using a paddle with a blade at both ends.

A kayak is usually covered on top except for an opening for the occupant. Thus, you're much more protected and less likely to get swamped than in a canoe. Kayaks do turn over easily, however. It's important to get some good instruction before trying kayaking in the wilderness.

Rafting

Rafting is an especially popular activity on many of the country's wild rivers. It's most fun and exciting when whitewater is involved. The best time to go rafting is usually springtime, or at any other time when water levels are reasonably high. On smaller rivers it's often impossible during low-water conditions.

Rafting offers more of a group experience than canoeing or kayaking. Larger rafts hold six to eight or more passengers. Most people who go rafting do so with organized groups, which normally provide guides and instruction on the trip. Paddling and steering involve a cooperative effort on the part of participants.

There are also small rubber rafts which hold two to four people, and some people go out on their own in such rafts. Don't do this without previous rafting experience. You'll also need detailed river maps and probably campsite information. Riding safely and successfully through whitewater requires real skill and plenty of stamina as well. Wear life jackets or vests at all times.

TWO-WHEELED TRAVEL

Bicycling

Tens of millions of Americans have bicycles. People cycle for the exercise and because it's an enjoyable way to get around. Although much riding is done close to home, adventuresome cyclists often head for parks and wild areas and camp out.

Conventional bikes require pavement or a dirt road or path which is in tolerably good shape. Some parks have special bike paths, and many have suitable paved or unpaved roads.

Those who take long-distance bike treks, which may be mainly outside of park boundaries, can still choose to head for a park or forest to camp at night. This could be either at a campground or alongside the road or trail, where permitted. Some knowledge of bike repair is highly recommended before you undertake such a trip, since you'll be far from a bike shop most of the time. Be sure to bring and wear a helmet.

Mountain Biking

During just the past few years the development and success of the mountain bike has created a new kind of biking, one which has experienced an explosion of popularity. A mountain bike is capable of negotiating much rougher trails than a conventional bicycle. Not all mountain bikes are used in wild places, but considerable numbers of people are now heading for parks and wilderness areas with mountain bikes to experience the rewards and challenges of riding on wild terrain.

There are still very few trails designed and marked specifically for mountain biking, but because of demand this is likely to change very rapidly. Currently mountain bikes are allowed on hiking trails in some areas, but many parks now forbid this practice, permitting bikes, however, on other paths and old roads. Most National Parks restrict bike use to regular roads.

Mountain bikes do have a considerable impact on the trail environment, especially when it's muddy or where there's easily-erodable soil, or in areas of fragile vegetation. Bikers should be fully aware of that fact. Refrain from riding on inappropriate trails or in vulnerable areas. It's also essential to ride at safe speeds, especially on multi-use trails, to avoid the possibility of colliding with hikers, horseback riders, or other mountain bikers.

HORSEBACK RIDING

Horseback riding is another activity which is enjoyed in many parts of the country, and is especially popular in western regions of the United States. Riding is not permitted in all parks and wilderness areas, however. Check with a park's information center or headquarters regarding regulations and the availability of suitable trails.

In many parks and forests you'll find bridle paths or equestrian trails for horseback riding. Other paths or old roads may usually be used as well. In addition, many hiking trails in the western United States are open to horses, which is much less frequently permitted in the eastern states.

Sometimes corrals or hitching posts will be situated next to good potential campsites, shelters, or other accommodations. Horse rentals are often available near or adjacent to a park, and occasionally you'll find them right within park boundaries.

Horses can have a major impact on the wilderness environment. Care must be taken to assure that your horse doesn't damage trees (which can happen when horses are tied to them), graze freely on wild plants, tear up the earth, or foul water sources.

WINTER IN THE WILDERNESS

Snowshoeing

Snowshoeing is a form of winter hiking, an ancient way to get around on foot in deep snow, and still one of the best. Often said to look like oversized tennis rackets, snowshoes have sufficient breadth to distribute your weight over a large area and keep you on the surface of the snow. There are bindings attached which allow you to strap the snowshoes onto your boots or other footwear.

No real instruction is necessary. It takes only a few minutes to get used to snowshoes, requiring just a minor change in habits to walk properly. On snowshoes you can follow snowcovered hiking trails, other paths, or old roads. It's also possible to traverse any terrain which isn't overly steep and rugged, as long as there's enough open space (free of brush or other dense vegetation) to walk in. You need at least a few inches and preferably a foot or more of snow.

Snowshoes can and should be brought on any overnight trip where you might encounter deep snow. They're available for rental or purchase at outdoor equipment stores, and also at many cross-country ski centers.

Take special care on any winter or cold-weather trip, as getting lost or sustaining an injury at such times would have especially serious consequences. Use restraint in setting goals, as it takes longer and requires more exertion to walk a distance in snowshoes. On an overnight trip snowshoeing will be strenuous even when you're on level ground, since your pack will be weighed down with warm clothing and winter gear.

Cross-Country Skiing

Like snowshoeing, cross-country skiing (abbreviated X-C), also known as ski touring, goes back a very long time. During the past decade or so it's experienced a rebirth of popularity. X-C skiing remains one of the most enjoyable ways to explore the wilderness in winter. It provides a phenomenally good workout when practiced aerobically, although it can be done in a more leisurely, less strenuous way as well.

For X-C skiing you need a reasonably broad path or trail, preferably one which is free of sharp turns or unusually steep pitches. In snow country you'll find some trails designated and marked for X-C skiing. Easy hiking trails are also very suitable, as are bridle paths, bike paths, and unplowed roads. A few inches of snow will be adequate on a trail which isn't too bumpy, whereas rocky trails require a lot of snow to be skiable.

While downhill skiing receives much more publicity and attention than X-C skiing, undoubtedly because the former is a high-profit industry, X-C skiing has many advantages. It usually costs nothing when practiced on public lands, it's safer, you don't have to stand in lift lines, much more solitude is available, and it furnishes a real wilderness experience.

Cross-country ski centers have sprung up in recent years, and these are good places to learn the sport (you'll pay a moderate entry or trail fee). Adventuresome skiers soon head for the wilderness, however, where relatively few people are to be found in winter. You can enjoy the silence and ski with a backdrop of spectacular scenery.

Combining X-C skiing with camping means an opportunity for a winter adventure of the first order. You'll need to wear a full-size internal frame pack while skiing in to your campsite, undoubtedly weighed down with winter gear and clothing. This kind of trip should only be attempted by someone who is both a skilled skier and an experienced camper.

MOUNTAIN CHALLENGES

Rock Climbing

Whereas hiking sometimes involves ascending steep mountains, by definition a hiking trail usually has adequate footing, and most of the time you can walk in a reasonably normal way. Rock climbing involves a much greater degree of difficulty and challenge. Footing is often minimal or practically nonexistent.

Climbers find routes up vertical cliffs and rock faces which to the untrained eye would seem impossible to scale. Hands, arms, and the upper body play a vital role. Considerable strength and stamina are obviously required. Safe climbing usually involves the use of ropes and other equipment.

This is an especially challenging activity, and for many participants it means dealing with substantial amounts of fear. When practiced properly and responsibly, rock climbing is reasonably safe. As with other outdoor activities, there are occasional accidents. A climbing accident, however, can more easily have serious or fatal consequences.

Always climb with others. Doing it alone is extremely risky and almost certainly foolish. Learn climbing from a reputable school, program, or expert instructor. You'll find such instruction available in many of the country's mountain regions.

Mountaineering

Mountaineering usually refers to ascending a major trail-less mountain or peak. This can take up to several days for a high or difficult mountain, especially if adverse conditions are encountered. Rock climbing skills are required, and camping gear may have to be carried to a relatively high elevation. On occasion it's necessary to bivouac (spend a night) in a precarious place, such as suspended from the side of a cliff. Ice and deep snow are commonly encountered at higher elevations.

Mountaineering is among the most difficult and dangerous of all activities you could pursue in the wilderness, and also probably one of the most thrilling. It's for the select few who are extremely fit, highly skilled (well-trained by a climbing school), who possess unusual quantities of stamina and courage—and who are willing at times to risk their lives in pursuit of an extraordinarily difficult goal.

FISHING AND HUNTING

Fishing and hunting have long provided reasons for many men (and an increasing number of women) to head for wilderness areas. Fishing can be an extremely relaxing way to spend the day. It often means spending quiet hours in a canoe, or sitting alongside (or standing in) a rushing stream. Some people who fish are quite serious and intent on catching something, while for others the end result is less important than simply being out there.

Fresh fish will also make a tasty addition to one's diet in the wilderness. Remember that a fishing license usually must be obtained in advance, and there are regulations regarding the number, kind, and size of fish which can be caught and when. Licenses are available from many sporting goods stores.

Hunting likewise requires obtaining a license and is permitted only during limited seasons, which differ from state to state, and vary depending on the type of animal or bird hunted. Most but not all hunting seasons are in the fall.

In recent decades hunting has increasingly become a focus of controversy and strong feelings. Hunting laws have come under attack in some areas. This is not the place for a discussion of the pros and cons of hunting, as good cases can be made by advocates on both sides of the issue.

While it's common and appropriate to criticize those who practice the sport in a dangerous or inhumane way, most hunters do in fact act responsibly, and many make good use of the meat to supplement their diet. Of course hunting is an age-old activity and tradition, and it's been part of the lives of millions of people in this country until recently. It remains legal in the majority of the country's parks and wilderness areas. An exception is most National Parks, where it's prohibited.

Just as with fishing, not all hunters are concerned with results. Quite a few refrain from shooting or killing, and simply enjoy the process of tracking an animal. For some people hunting season provides an opportunity to head for the wilderness and camp out, to get away from routine and enjoy some outdoor adventure and relaxation.

When entering an area where hunting is going on, for reasons of safety be sure to wear bright colors, preferably Day-Glo orange. If you're a non-hunter, during the designated season you might want instead to visit a park where hunting isn't permitted.

WILDERNESS SURVIVAL

Most of us are very dependent on the equipment and food we bring on a wilderness camping trip. If you should somehow become separated from your gear for a period of a day or more, this would probably mean an emergency situation, especially if it happens during cold or inclement weather.

While such problems should be avoidable, on occasion people do get lost or injured while away from their campsite, or caught in a flood, or manage to lose a canoe or other watercraft with all their equipment in it. If this should happen to you, and you're far from highways and possible assistance, your survival would probably be in question.

There are a number of schools and programs available around the country which teach skills for surviving in the wilderness without gear. Learning these skills has practical value in case you ever find yourself in such a situation, and some of the knowledge may be applicable to other realms of life. For many people the challenges of a survival course also have value in building confidence and fostering personal growth.

Survival schools typically teach such things as how to start a fire without matches, construct an emergency shelter, learn to identify wild edibles, and track animals (if necessary catching them for food), all with few or no tools except perhaps a knife. Often there's a "solo": up to several days spent alone, where you have the opportunity to practice what you've learned.

The best-known organization in this country that teaches wilderness survival is Outward Bound, based in Connecticut and with schools in several locations around the United States. For information contact Outward Bound, 384 Field Point Road, Greenwich, CT 06830; (203)661-0797. Another highly-rated program is offered by the National Outdoor Leadership School, P.O. Box AA, Lander, WY 82520; (307)332-6973.

INNER EXPLORATIONS

Some schools, holistic learning centers, and independent teachers offer trips, courses, and workshops in the wilderness which have a focus on personal and emotional growth, group experience, or spiritual and other "inner explorations."

Included is the so-called "vision quest," a wilderness rite of passage based on Native American ways. This kind of experience can offer an opportunity for dealing with major life transitions, and finding new meaning and purpose. For some participants the effects are profound. Wilderness experiences and courses such as these are often listed in holistic learning center catalogs.

OTHER ACTIVITIES

Swimming is naturally popular during summer, or whenever water and air temperatures are warm enough. A swim can provide a refreshing break in the midst of virtually any activity, assuming you have a suitable ocean, lake, pond, river, or stream at hand. In most wilderness areas you can swim wherever and whenever you want. In smaller and heavily-used parks, however, swimming is sometimes forbidden or restricted to public beaches with lifeguards.

An activity which isn't normally associated with the wilderness but can often be practiced there is jogging or running. If you're a serious runner or simply enjoy jogging, and the activities discussed in this chapter aren't enough for you, you can run on any trail or path or road in passable condition.

There remain still other ways to spend time in the wilderness when you're not involved in active recreation, or anytime you prefer something less physically demanding. The many possibilities include:

- bird watching
- photography

- nature study
- identification of trees, plants, flowers, wildlife, animal tracks and droppings, bugs, etc.
- listening to sounds
- meditating
- thinking and problem solving
- reading
- journal writing

- sketching or painting
- star-gazing
- card and board games
- campfire building
- storytelling or singing
- resting
- lovemaking
- sleeping

TWELVE

Morning, Afternoon, Evening, Night

The structure of each day you spend in the wilderness is to a large extent up to you. How each day unfolds will of course be affected by whether or not you're involved in any particular activities. While constraints may sometimes be provided by weather and other external circumstances, for the most part you can design or plan your day (or *not* plan it) as you wish.

Morning

Some people like to get up at the crack of dawn, have a quick breakfast, and be on their way before other campers have even stirred. This isn't unreasonable if the day will be one of intense activity or long-distance travel. Others prefer to sleep in, start slowly, and enjoy a much more leisurely day, whether or not they'll be participating in an activity.

You can start your day whenever and however you want. Many people do tend to get in the habit of turning in on the early side, and rising relatively early in the morning, especially on an extended trip. When you're living out-of-doors the body tends to adjust easily to the natural cycles of light and dark, and it becomes hard to imagine doing it any other way.

There are only so many hours of daylight, of course, so if you have a full day of activity or travel planned, it makes sense to try to get a relatively early start. In warm or hot weather another advantage in starting early is that you can travel or exercise during the cooler morning hours.

While some people like to have a quick breakfast and be on their way, there's also something to be said for relaxing at breakfasttime and enjoying the beauty of early morning. It's a pleasure to refrain from rushing around the way that too many

of us do in everyday life. Try to avoid overscheduling the day, or letting a wilderness trip turn into a variant on the rat race.

It's possible to remain at a campsite or base camp for up to several nights or more, and taking day trips from there. A day trip can be anything you want it to be, whether a relatively short excursion from camp or an all day, dawn-to-dusk trek.

You could also pack up in the morning and travel to another campsite before day is done. This is what happens most days when you're backpacking along a lengthy trail, canoeing or rafting down a major river, or crossing a stretch of wilderness by some other means. How far you travel each day is completely up to you.

It's always possible to take rest days as well. You can hang around camp and take it easy, perhaps napping, reading, swimming, doing a little exploring nearby, or anything else you'd like to do. Whether you'll want or need rest days will depend in part on how difficult a particular activity is, how far you're traveling, and what kind of shape you're in. If strenuous activity is involved, it's wise to schedule periodic rest days to avoid the risk of burnout or exhaustion.

Sometimes a rainy day will be the best time to take a break from activity. Yet a sunny day can also be appealing for lazing around. For some people, *every* day in the wilderness is basically a rest day, or at least a low-key-kind-of-day. If relaxation is a prime objective, there's no reason it can't be this way for you.

It's great to be able to decide each day what to do and how long you're going to do it, to move on when you feel like it or stay put when that appeals. This is possible as long as you're visiting a park or wilderness area which doesn't require you to specify in advance exactly where you'll be camping each night.

In those places where permits and campsite reservations are necessary, you'll have to decide beforehand how far to travel each day and whether or not to schedule any rest days. This system is definitely not ideal, as weather, a minor injury, or other conditions can make it hard to keep to a schedule.

It's also impossible to know in advance just how energetic or tired you're going to feel, and when you're going to want a rest. However, such requirements simply have to be lived with in order to visit many National Parks and other popular parks and wilderness areas.

If you're taking a trip from the campsite and won't be back by lunchtime, you'll probably want to pack a lunch. The easiest time to do this is at breakfast, while the food is out. Most people on the move eat a cold lunch. If you're remaining at camp, lunch can also be cooked if you want. A stove could be brought along on a day trip, but many of us don't bother because of the extra weight, bulk, and unnecessary trouble involved.

When you leave camp for the day or even a much shorter time, remember to make sure your food is hung or otherwise properly secured, the tent is closed up, and nothing of importance is left outside in case it rains. Always pack raingear, extra clothing, food, ample water, a flashlight, and emergency items to bring along on any day trip. If there's a campfire, make sure it's completely out before you leave.

Afternoon and Early Evening

If you're spending the day away from camp, plan to arrive back at the site by late afternoon if possible, or at least with an hour or two of daylight remaining, so you'll have time for dinner before it gets dark. It's good to leave some extra time in your schedule in case something unforeseen arises, or it simply takes a lot longer than expected to return.

Bring a flashlight with spare batteries and bulb just in case. Without it you could be stranded in the event of a serious delay. This might mean that you'd have to spend a night away from camp, presumably minus your sleeping bag and tent, and with only the clothing and gear you've brought for the day.

Even with a flashlight, progress is usually slower after dark. This isn't an ideal way to travel, since trails are often harder to follow and it's easier to get lost. Returning to camp and having supper while there's still daylight is certainly preferable. If you're someone who's inclined to make ambitious daytime plans, however, there may well

be times when you'll be eating by the light of your flashlight, lantern, or campfire.

When moving on to a new area, leave ample time in the afternoon to look for a campsite and set up your tent. Finding a good site can take time, especially if you're in a hilly or rough area, or one with dense vegetation. It's never much fun if you have to hurry because of dwindling daylight.

Whenever possible, it's always a pleasure to allow for a bit of leisure time before dinner. If you're on an extended trip, once in a while you may want to stop by midday and take the afternoon off. This will give you some extra time for rest, and perhaps for cleaning up, washing some clothes, and/or swimming.

Evening

People who have never camped in the wilderness often ask: "What do you do in the evening?" Most of the popular forms of entertainment such as TV, radio, movies, and recorded music obviously aren't available in this environment (you could bring a radio or tapes, but you're much better off leaving those things at home. See Chapter 5 regarding radios and cassette players).

Those who can't imagine living for a few days without constant entertainment are almost certainly not the best possible candidates for wilderness camping. Nature offers a quieter world, and one where most entertainment has to be self-created.

Some people worry about being bored. The question is, are you likely to find mountains, canyons, rivers, lakes, meadows, plants, flowers, trees, birds, animals, or life in general boring? Those of us who love wilderness camping and backpacking are almost certain to answer with a resounding "No!"

Evening can be a time for thoughtful or spirited conversation, reading, sitting quietly by a campfire, alongside a stream, river, or lake, or stretched out in an open meadow under the stars. You'll probably discover that your experience of time tends to change when you're immersed in nature. Once you're off the treadmill, so to speak, there's no urgency about measuring and filling free time the way people often do back at home.

It's possible to bring conventional diversions like cards or board games, and these are sometimes good for rainy days, but it's also nice to do without such easy distractions. Many of us become satisfied with less "busyness." Just watching the ripples or waves in a lake or a bubbling stream—or listening to natural sounds—can be remarkably relaxing and surprisingly satisfying.

It's great to sit and do absolutely nothing once in a while, or even more often. This may be virtually incomprehensible and unthinkable to a hyperactive person, or even an average American, but it's also one of the healthiest things you could do.

Taking a little walk after supper is often pleasurable. A "night walk" after dark can be an adventure, especially when it's done without a flashlight. Let your eyes adjust to the dark. Even without the moon or stars you can often make out the faint shapes of trees and objects. Proceed very slowly and cautiously to avoid stumbling (place each foot down carefully, shifting your weight only when you feel solid ground underneath).

It's best to have some company when taking a night walk, and preferable that at least one person remain back at the campsite. Then you can call out if you get disoriented, and follow the direction of the response. But don't go far, or try a night walk at all, unless you're very familiar and comfortable with finding your way around in the wilderness.

During the evening some people like to get into intense discussions about the state of the world or the meaning of life, or to share personal stories. Such conversations sometimes have a way of continuing on well into the night.

A little solitude can also be gratifying, even if you're enjoying the experience of camping with others. Some people retire to their tents early—to read, write in a journal, meditate, or simply mull things over. The answers to questions, solutions to problems, or new and needed perspectives sometimes come more easily while in the wilderness.

After Dark

The usual tool for getting around after dark is, of course, a flashlight. On a moonlit night you may not even need one. If you're just sitting around it may be preferable to leave the light off, except when there's something specific you need to focus on. Your eyes will then adjust more completely to the dark.

Candlelight is very pleasant and provides a softer, less intrusive light than a flashlight or other artificial source. As long as the evening isn't breezy or windy, lighting a candle or two will create a very appealing effect, and even provide enough light for certain tasks.

A *candle lantern* is another option favored by some campers, and this item provides a solution to the potential wind problem. It's essentially a windproof little container with glass windows that holds a candle inside. A candle lantern can be used in lieu of a flashlight or headlamp for reading, and hung from a branch or elsewhere. For reasons of safety avoid lighting and using it inside a tent except with the greatest caution.

An assortment of gas-burning and battery-operated lanterns of various sizes are widely available. These lanterns have long been used by car-campers, are often very bright, and surely aren't necessary on a wilderness camping trip. Do you really need a powerful light in the evening? Most people don't. Such lanterns are probably popular for the same reasons as campfires: they provide a sense of security. A superbright light will dominate a large area, and has a considerable impact on the environment at night. Anyone else camping nearby may well find it obnoxious.

There are also some relatively small, compact, less intrusive lanterns being sold. Unless you have a clear need for one, though, avoid bringing a lantern, or at least keep it turned down to a dim setting. If you want to take a lantern into your tent, for safety reasons it should be a battery-operated one.

Except when you want to read, or have a specific task to carry out, try letting a little more of the night into your campsite, rather than trying to shut it out with a bright light. Once you come to feel comfortable in nature at night you may find you prefer to have a minimum of artificial lighting around camp.

Turning in for the Night

If you have a campfire, make sure it's dead out before you get into your tent (campfires are discussed in Chapters 10 and 14). Leaving a campfire burning or smoldering is risking disaster if it should turn windy during the night, which could scatter live ashes in the direction of your tent and elsewhere.

Also be certain that food and cooking gear have been properly hung or otherwise protected before you turn in (see Chapter 9). If necessary, check to make sure no food has been accidentally left in your tent or pack.

Cooking gear should be secured along with the food, since after cleaning there are still likely to be faint odors which could attract wildlife. Also, some animals such as porcupines will often chew on anything made of metal, and occasionally even plastic. If you leave your cooking gear out, don't be surprised if you're awakened in the night to the sound of it being knocked around. And in the morning it may be missing, or full of holes and unusable.

Bring boots and other footwear inside the tent at night. Some animals are known to gnaw on boots for the salt which is deposited from your sweat, and footwear can be damaged. Don't leave other items lying around on the ground at night either.

Your pack can remain outside the tent if you like, which may be essential if your tent is small. Lean the pack up against a nearby tree and pull a rain cover or plastic bag over it. Make sure nothing scented is left inside, including soap, toothpaste, and other toiletries, which should all be hung with your food.

Some people routinely hang clothing out to dry on a clothesline overnight. What isn't dry at sundown, however, is unlikely to be dry in the morning. In fact it may get much wetter from dew (condensation) or a shower during the night. Unless the clothing is already soaked and it doesn't matter, bring the items into your tent or put them in the backpack for the night.

If some clothing is being left outside in the pack, just make sure you've brought enough into the tent to cover your needs should the night turn out to be cold. Also, have raingear handy in case it's raining in the morning, or if you have to answer nature's call during a nighttime shower. Sleep with the flashlight by your side or within easy reach, keeping spare batteries and bulb where you can find them in the dark.

If you do have to get up during the night, be especially careful to avoid getting lost or turned around in the dark. Keep shining your flashlight back toward your tent to orient yourself as you walk away from it. If you're camped near a trail, follow it a short distance away from camp, turn and walk in a direction perpendicular to the trail for a bit, and then stop to take care of your needs. Retrace your steps back to the tent.

Whenever you're outside at night and away from a trail or waterway, always shine your light around and carefully observe the shapes of trees, rocks, or other elements of the landscape. You won't get disoriented if you pay close attention to the surroundings. Should you be camping with others and somehow manage to get lost or turned around nearby, call out for help if necessary. As long as you're not out of earshot, you'll be able to follow the direction of your companions' voices.

Sleep

Not everyone sleeps soundly in the wilderness at first. If you've spent time in nature and/or camping out previously, it probably won't require too much of an adjustment. For a beginner, though, there are lots of unfamiliar sounds, and one's imagination and fears can sometimes run wild. It can also be extremely quiet at times, and for some urban dwellers used to noisy surroundings the silence can initially be unsettling.

Don't assume that you'll have trouble sleeping, but if you do, rest assured that it will most likely be a short-lived problem. There's a good deal about the natural world that's beautiful, relaxing, soothing, and conducive to sleep. Some wilderness campers even discover the deepest, most restful, most satisfying sleep of their lives.

If you're getting lots of exercise during the day and tiring your body out, the probability that you'll sleep soundly at night is even higher. The only possible exception would be if you overdo it to such an extreme that your body is "overtired," sometimes creating the opposite effect.

If you haven't been involved in much physical activity on the trip and sleep isn't coming easily, use this as a cue to schedule more active exercise. Take a long walk or find some other kind of physical pursuit to engage in for at least part of the day.

THIRTEEN

Safety in
the Wilderness

Most people who visit parks and wilderness areas each year do so without getting sick, sustaining injuries, or suffering any other harm. It's not necessary to be excessively concerned about hazards. At the same time, it's important to know how to take care of yourself out there, and to be able to recognize potential problems before they have a chance to develop.

There's no question that spending time in the wilderness does mean taking on some risks. These can be kept to an minimum by attentive and responsible behavior. As in other realms of life, however, the risks can never be completely eliminated.

If you're many miles from a highway, getting seriously hurt or sick would amount to a real crisis, one which must be avoided by every means possible. Medical attention would be hours away at the very least, and in a remote area it might take days to get to a doctor or hospital. Your life could be on the line.

It's essential that you assume full responsibility for yourself and your actions, and completely up to you to keep from getting hurt. Under ordinary circumstances it's unreasonable to blame the park or anyone else if you should have an accident.

In the unlikely event of an injury, your survival may depend on getting out on your own. A rescue or other aid can never be counted on. A considerable amount of time may be required to get the word out that help is needed, and rescues are often expensive. You can be *charged* for the cost of a rescue if a mishap is the result of your own carelessness or unpreparedness.

Every person who embarks on a wilderness trip should be fully aware of the risks, especially when preparing to venture out alone. Unless you're thoroughly skilled in wilderness ways, and feel absolutely certain that you can deal with any situation which arises, it's best to go with knowledgeable friends or a reputable group.

Accidents

Some of us believe that accidents are about 99.9 percent avoidable (the remaining .001 percent being so-called "acts of god" and other circumstances beyond our control). Most accidents happen to people who simply aren't paying attention, don't know what they're doing, and/or have blundered into a dangerous situation and haven't recognized it.

If you're someone who tends to be accident-prone, or you have a feeling that something unfortunate may happen to you in the wilderness, don't go—at least for now. There's always the risk that you might help create a self-fulfilling prophecy.

Should you really want to venture into the wilderness, however, don't let any fears dissuade you. Just learn what to be careful about, and be as prepared as you can. Then try to relax about the whole business, and focus on ways to enjoy yourself.

If you're going on an extended trip into a remote area, it's a good idea to study a book on outdoor first aid before your trip. You may also want to read more about some of the potential problems discussed in this chapter. If you've never had first aid or CPR training, consider taking a course.

Hazards Associated with Specific Activities

Some hazards are associated with particular activities. A twisted ankle, for example, is the most common injury among hikers and backpackers. Care must be taken on rough trails to avoid turning an ankle, or stumbling and falling. Blisters are another problem to watch out for. While they're in no way dangerous, blisters can certainly undermine a good time. If serious enough they can bring your trip to a grinding halt.

Mountain bikers and cyclists need to maintain safe speeds, and exercise special caution during downhill runs to avoid losing control, especially on rough or winding trails. The results of a high-speed accident can obviously be disastrous. Always wear a helmet, and avoid rugged trails if you're not a skilled cyclist.

In white-water canoeing, kayaking, or rafting there's a risk of running into a rock and being tossed into the water (or against the rock), which occasionally leads to an injury or drowning. Don't attempt white-water activities without some first-rate instruction. Know how to swim before getting involved in any water-based sport. It also wouldn't hurt to take a course in water safety. Wear a life jacket at all times when on the water.

Anyone engaged in activities like cross-country skiing, snowshoeing, or winter hiking should know that winter can be merciless to the careless or unprepared person. Getting hurt in a remote area at this time of year would undoubtedly be life-threatening. Watch out for icy trails, and ski at a slow enough speed to be able to stop on short notice.

COLD-WEATHER PROBLEMS

Hypothermia

Commonly referred to as "exposure," hypothermia is a potentially dangerous condition which involves getting severely chilled. It's most likely to occur when you're simultaneously cold and wet. In such circumstances the body has trouble maintaining the necessary core temperature, which begins to drop.

In advanced stages of hypothermia, shivering becomes violent, thinking is muddled, and a person generally loses his or her instinct for self-preservation. Without assistance and external heat, death is likely to be the outcome.

Extremely cold weather is not a requirement for hypothermia. Some cases occur in temperatures as warm as 50°-60° F. It's possible to experience this problem on a cool and wet summer day, weather which is common in higher mountain areas.

Hypothermia can be easily avoided. There's no reason it ever has to happen to you. The key is to never allow yourself to get seriously chilled or cold, especially if you're already wet. Shivering is an important early sign. *Always* respond to shivering by putting on more clothing, finding shelter, or seeking help.

Make every effort to keep from getting soaked to the skin in the rain, or drenched from sweat, especially in cold weather. Wear as little cotton as possible, especially next to your skin, on any cold and wet day. Be sure to have plenty of extra clothing along on a trip, and change into dry clothing when necessary.

Food will help your body to maintain an adequate temperature. Eat regular meals and keep a snack handy. An overtired body is also more susceptible to hypothermia. Get enough sleep each night and avoid exercising to the point of exhaustion.

Frostbite

Generally speaking, frostbite is a winter problem. However, below-freezing temperatures can be encountered at any time of year in some of the higher mountain regions. Flesh will freeze if it's cold enough, and that's what frostbite is all about.

It's important to keep your extremities—hands and fingers, feet, ears, nose—from getting seriously cold or numb. Tissue can be permanently damaged when frostbitten, so it's obviously important to prevent this condition.

Take immediate action if any part of you starts to feel numb or uncomfortably cold. Exercising vigorously will help. Swing arms to warm up hands, or place them under clothing next to your skin. Touch a cold nose or ears with a bare (warm) hand.

Always put on gloves or mitts and extra clothing at the *first sign* of coldness. Cold extremities are sometimes an indication that your entire body could use more clothing. If the temperature is low enough you also may need insulated boots.

Should you sustain a case of frostbite, thawing out must be done very slowly and carefully to minimize tissue damage. Read up on the subject if you'll be involved in winter camping, or visiting an area where extreme cold is a possibility.

HOT-WEATHER HAZARDS

Most people are aware that exercising strenuously in extreme heat can be risky or dangerous. If you're visiting the desert, or any other location where it's very hot during the day, try to limit most physical activity to early mornings and evenings.

Use restraint and change your original plans, if necessary, to avoid overdoing it in the heat. The body ordinarily requires large quantities of water in warm or hot weather, so drink as much as you possibly can, especially when exerting yourself.

If you're careless about water intake, or otherwise let yourself overheat in hot weather, you could be risking a case of heat exhaustion or heat stroke. Pay close attention to any physical symptoms, and respond quickly to signs of overheating.

Heat Exhaustion

This is a condition which can result from inadequate intake of water while exercising in the heat. Symptoms include heavy sweating, dizziness, fatigue, headache, and nausea. A person's skin usually remains cool and pale. Heat exhaustion can be avoided by drinking constantly during any hot-weather activity. Stop immediately if you experience any of the above symptoms. Try to find some shade, drink water, and rest.

Heat Stroke

Heat stroke is a serious business, and in some cases can be fatal. In this condition your temperature has risen so high that the body's thermostat, so to speak, no longer functions properly. The skin is typically very hot and flushed. It's essential that anyone with heat stroke be taken out of the sun and cooled off as quickly as possible, but water shouldn't be given to drink. Prompt medical assistance is normally called for.

ALTITUDE SICKNESS

As you probably know, it takes time to acclimate or adjust to higher altitudes. If you'll be exercising and camping high in the mountains, especially over 9-10,000 feet, start out very slowly. Avoid ambitious plans or intense exercise, giving your body some time to accommodate to the altitude. You'll probably feel short-winded at first, even if you're in great shape.

After a few days at high elevations, you should find your body adjusting. If you go too fast at first, however, you'll be risking a case of altitude sickness. Symptoms of this problem include dizziness, headache, nausea, and extreme fatigue. *Stop* at the first sign of discomfort, and rest for a long time before continuing. If possible, postpone any further activity till another day. Return to a lower elevation, if necessary.

NATURAL HAZARDS

Lightning

There's little to fear from lightning any time you're in a reasonably uniform forest at a low elevation. It's the high, open, and exposed areas you need to be concerned about. Mountaintops are especially likely targets for lightning strikes.

If you're on top of a mountain and can see (or hear) an electrical storm coming, move quickly to a lower elevation, and if possible below treeline. Avoid shallow caves, as lightning can travel inside if it strikes nearby. Never seek shelter under a lone tree or cluster of trees in an open area, or let yourself be the highest object in any exposed place.

A storm can blow up quickly, but you'll usually have at least a few minutes' warning. If you're caught out in the open and there's no time to retreat, kneel down, bend forward and rest your upper body on your thighs and knees. This position is considered safest in the event of a lightning strike, as it minimizes your contact with the ground (lying down is said to be more dangerous, as lightning sometimes travels in a sheet along the ground after striking, and could pass through your body).

Camping in high and open areas is always risky because of the chance of an electrical or other storm, which is possible at any time of day or night. Whenever feasible, it's best to camp at a lower elevation, preferably in a forested area.

Rockslides and Avalanches

Avalanches are mainly a winter or snow-season hazard, and are confined largely to the higher mountain ranges where great masses of snow accumulate. Rockslides or mudslides can occur at any time of year, especially during and after heavy rains.

Use extreme caution about entering an area where avalanches have been known to occur. Heed any warnings of avalanche danger which have been issued or posted. When in doubt, turn around and go elsewhere. Needless to say, avalanches can be fatal.

Rockslides, earthslides, or mudslides are rather rare in much of this country, but common in a few hilly or mountainous areas. Stay especially alert during heavy rain or flooding. If a steep trail or route seems unsafe or unstable in any way, turn back and change your itinerary.

Flood Conditions

Beware of camping close to a river or stream in wet weather, or if there's any likelihood of heavy rains, in case of flooding. Rising waters could overtake your campsite. It's best to seek higher ground, and camp well above the waterway.

Canoeing and rafting are especially hazardous when the water is high and fast, and may be overflowing the river's banks. Know when to stay put and wait it out. You could be risking your life to proceed during high-water conditions.

River Crossings

For foot-travelers, crossing a river can present some danger even at times of normal water levels. While in some wilderness areas it's common to find bridges across the larger streams and rivers, in others this isn't the case. Or you might discover that a particular bridge has been washed away or otherwise destroyed. To continue on your way may require fording the river.

If you prefer not to cross a river, you can always turn back or head in a different direction. The water level is certain to make a difference. Wading may be easy if it's low, or there may be exposed rocks or a large fallen tree to walk across on. But if the river is a raging torrent from heavy rains, or from melting snow in springtime, forget about crossing. Go somewhere else.

Remember that if you ford a river under conditions of low water, heavy rains on subsequent days might make it impossible for you to return the same way. If there's no alternative you could be stranded for as much as several days.

Even slow-moving water should be crossed with care. If it's more than waist-deep you'll have to float your pack across. Don't forget that if your pack should be swept away and all gear is lost, your life could be in danger, especially in cold weather.

There's also the risk that you could be carried away by the current and either injured or drowned. If you'll be visiting a park or region where river crossings are to be expected, consult a good wilderness survival book for detailed instructions on how to ford a river in the safest possible way.

BEASTS AND BUGS

Wildlife

Even though a number of people have fears regarding animals such as bears or snakes, few campers actually encounter any serious problems with wildlife. Attacks on human beings are rare in the extreme (although it's very easy to get a different impression from the media, as reports on the occasional injury or fatality are often overblown and sensationalized). Attacks which do occur are usually provoked in some way by those involved.

There's always a slight chance of meeting almost any kind of animal at close range, and it's important to know how to behave in such an event. If you come face to face with wildlife, keep quiet and back off slowly and gently. Don't shout or do anything which might frighten the animal. In most cases he'll go on his way peacefully.

Never approach a wild animal for any reason, as your action may be interpreted as a threat. Don't attempt to feed wildlife, or to photograph at a close distance. Are you willing to risk your life for a close-up photo? If you respect a wild creature's space, however, you'll have little to worry about.

See *The Essential Guide to Hiking in the United States* for more on the subject of bears, snakes, and other wildlife.

Insects

Insects are relatively harmless to most of us, except of course for those people who experience allergic reactions to bug bites or bee stings. If you're someone who has such a sensitivity or suspect you do, special precautions are in order. Consult your doctor for advice.

Insects can indeed be pesky at times, but they're rarely a real hazard in this country. Bug repellent should be brought on any warm-weather trip, since there's always a possibility of encountering insects when temperatures are mild.

Some regions of the United States are known to have special bug problems at certain times of year, as for example the early-summer blackfly season of the northeastern states. Wearing a headnet or taking other precautions may be advisable if you're going to venture out at such times. Or you could choose to visit a different area during these seasons. See Chapter 3 for more about insects as well as bug repellents.

Ticks

Ticks have an unsavory reputation, and deservedly so, since some of them carry disease. They have an unpleasant way of getting under the skin and resisting being removed.

During the past few years we've heard plenty about Lyme Disease, which is the most-recently-discovered disease carried by ticks. There's fear and even some panic abroad about Lyme Disease.

While it's not to be taken lightly, this is not a fatal disease. Most people who come down with it and receive prompt treatment don't develop complications (but a minority do, as with any illness). And tens of millions of Americans go camping year after year without contracting Lyme Disease.

Check your body periodically if you're camping in an area that's known to harbor ticks. If you do find one on your body, remove the tick right away. It takes at least 48 hours for Lyme Disease to be passed on to you. Not all ticks carry the disease.

A Lyme tick (deer tick) is so small that many people are unaware that they've been bitten. If you come down with flu-like symptoms within a couple weeks of camping out, see your doctor to get tested for Lyme Disease. A round red rash is often found around the area of the bite. If the disease remains untreated, arthritic symptoms sometimes appear weeks or months later.

Ticks are not found in all regions of the United States, and the incidence of Lyme Disease varies greatly from one area to another. Ticks are most likely to be encountered in open, grassy, or bushy places at low elevations. Their season is usually the warmer months between May and October.

The general advice is to wear long, light-colored pants tucked into your socks (as you're most likely to pick up a tick on your lower legs), and to spray your pants and boots with bug repellent. While this will provide the best protection, many outdoorspeople clearly ignore this advice at the present time. Such precautions are probably unnecessary in most parks and wilderness areas, but worth considering in areas known to have a high incidence of Lyme Disease. Some locations where Lyme ticks are present will have warning notices posted.

Poisonous Plants

It's no secret that poison ivy, poison oak, and poison sumac can make life uncomfortable for anyone unfortunate enough to come in contact with them. These plants produce an extremely itchy skin rash which can last up to several weeks. Not everyone is susceptible, however, and the plants are not found in all parts of the country.

Learn to identify each plant from an identification book, or by having someone point it out to you. Be in the habit of paying attention to what vegetation you touch, and watching where you sit. Other plants such as nettles will also produce a short-lived itch, but this amounts to a very minor discomfort.

Safety Regarding Other Human Beings

Given the crime and violence which are reported daily in our media, beginners are often concerned about possible risks from other human beings while camping out. Fortunately, violent crime is extremely rare (although not unheard of) in the wilderness.

Theft and other crime is most common at National Parks and other popular areas. Be especially alert when near highways, and never leave valuables in your car or tent. Packs and other gear are occasionally stolen when left unattended next to roads. Theft of gear from a backcountry campsite remains pretty rare, but when leaving camp on a day trip it makes sense to "close up your campsite," packing away any items which could tempt a passerby.

Hunting Season Safety

Be aware of the dates of hunting seasons, which vary from one part of the country to another. The rifle season for deer and other big game is most often in late fall, and this is the one to pay closest attention to. The dangers may not be as great as many imagine, but given the large number of hunters (including quite a few who are inexperienced and/or careless), accidents do occur.

In some large and remote wilderness areas you may encounter very few hunters during the designated season, whereas in other locations you'll see lots of them. Assuming you're not a hunter but want to camp out during the season, when the option is available you'll most likely be happier and safer visiting a park or other area where hunting isn't allowed.

Hunting is prohibited in almost all National Parks, and in a certain number of state and local parks. It's generally permitted in National and state forests, many larger state parks, and on other public lands. If you choose to visit an area where hunting is taking place, be sure to wear bright clothing, preferably including a Day-Glo orange vest. It's probably safest to stick to well-traveled trails and forgo bushwhacking during hunting season.

FOURTEEN

Practicing Low-Impact Camping

Camping practices have changed greatly over the years, in part because of the impact human beings have had on the environment. We've become aware of the need to tread as lightly as possible on the earth. This is critically important if we're going to keep the environment from being further degraded.

Earlier camping practices like cutting branches, chopping down trees, or digging trenches around a tent are no longer acceptable. Many wilderness areas have been damaged. Much time is required for some of the wounds to heal. For example, it's said that thousands of years will be necessary for high-mountain soil, eroded from recent human impact, to fully regenerate.

It's important that we all become conscious of the effects of our actions on the earth, whether we're in the wilderness or at home. Many Americans behave as if they still aren't fully aware of the harm that's being done to the environment and to all forms of life, ourselves included.

The long-term survival of this planet will probably depend on whether we can learn to change some deep-seated habits—especially in countries like the United States, where waste, littering, and polluting still continue on a massive scale. What's required is that our lives become less self-centered in some ways, that we all take responsibility for the earth and future generations. Change is necessary right now.

What we do while camping out can make a difference. With a little effort we can help reverse the deterioration which has occurred in some wilderness areas during the recent past.

Trash, broken glass, and other eyesores are obviously deplorable, and must be eliminated and prevented to the best extent possible. There are also other problems and subtler signs of damage which aren't always immediately evident to the newcomer, such as badly eroded meadows and mountaintops. When the effects of abuse and misuse are encountered in what was once a pristine environment, the experience is diminished for everyone.

If any additional incentive should be needed to encourage campers to follow responsible practices, damaging the wilderness environment in any way also happens to be illegal in most places. You could be subject to a stiff fine and ejected from a park if you're caught. In some locations punishments are quite severe. However, many people unfortunately still get away with vandalism and other violations. Given current tight budgets and inadequate numbers of rangers, enforcement tends to be spotty.

Low-Impact Camping

Whatever the regulations or accepted practices in any area you might be visiting, it's vital to learn "low-impact camping" (sometimes called "minimal-impact camping" or "no-impact camping"), and to make this your way of being in the wilderness. No matter how careful you are, your presence is going to have at least a small impact on the environment when you camp out. The aim should be to keep that effect close to negligible.

Whenever possible, choose a spot for a campsite where you and your tent will have the least impact. Use a pre-existing site when available. In some parks and forests you'll hear contrary advice, suggesting that you find a new campsite and allow previously-used sites to regenerate as completely as possible.

Avoid camping in meadows or on other vegetation whenever you can. In some low-elevation areas with abundant and fast-growing vegetation this isn't so critical. At higher elevations and in other fragile environments you can cause considerable and long-lasting damage. Also, don't camp right on a riverbank, lakeshore, or in any other location subject to possible erosion.

Be careful where you sit or walk when in a fragile area, treading as lightly as you can. If each step mashes vegetation or leaves a footprint, try to stay on rocks, especially when wearing hiking boots or other rugged footwear. Or change into light shoes to avoid tearing things up.

In the process of breaking camp, do your best to cover all signs that you've been there. Look around for bits of paper or plastic that you (or anyone else) might have inadvertently left, and make sure you're taking everything you arrived with. Unless it's a formal, designated campsite, scatter some leaves over the area where your tent stood. Conceal any evidence of your stay.

Water

Treat all water that you find in the natural world as if it was the most precious of resources, which in fact it is. Make sure you introduce nothing whatsoever into the water supply which doesn't belong there, including soap or food scraps.

All washing of dishes and your body should be done a good distance from water sources. It's fine to swim or splash around in any suitable lake, pond, or stream, just as long as you leave nothing other than body sweat and dirt in the water.

Be especially aware of where you are when "answering nature's call." Always take care of these needs at least 150 feet from water sources. Bury solid waste properly, as discussed in Chapter 10. If you fail to do this, a heavy shower could wash it into the nearest stream or other water supply. It's critical for every camper to take this responsibility in order to keep our water sources from being polluted any further.

Litter and Garbage

Your litter and garbage should be kept in a plastic litter bag. This is normally hung from a tree branch at night along with the food, and carried out at the end of your trip. In some parks it's considered acceptable to toss leftover food in the woods, especially at lower elevations and in regions where organic matter will break down quickly. This is forbidden in other areas, and garbage must be carried out. When in doubt, check with park authorities for local regulations as well as recommendations.

If you do leave food scraps, make sure they don't end up on a potential tentsite, in a place where someone may walk, or in any spot where they would create an eyesore for passersby. Never leave leftovers near water, as the scraps could wash down into it in the event of rain. Food which ends up in water will rot and increase bacterial count, helping to pollute the supply. Pots or dishes which have been used for food should never be rinsed in the water supply, no matter how large the lake or stream.

Use great care to avoid leaving litter anywhere. If you're a smoker, butts should not be buried or left behind. Sadly, it's still not unusual to see smokers tossing cigarette butts, sometimes still lit, as if it was the most natural thing in the world. This is especially irresponsible in the wilderness. Always extinguish butts completely and carry them out like other litter. Picking up refuse left by previous campers is also extremely helpful. Those who haven't much conscience about littering are less likely to toss their trash if an area is completely clean.

Some people believe it's acceptable to burn litter in a campfire. *Only paper*, however, should go into a fire. All other materials must be carried out, as they won't burn completely, may create toxic fumes, and will leave a residue or substance that doesn't belong in the wilderness. Examples are all forms of plastic, foil-lined and plastic-coated paper, and foil packages.

Your trash weighs infinitely less than the original load of food, so there's absolutely no reasonable excuse for being unwilling to carry it out. Granted that organic garbage may start to smell after a few days, but if you have it properly packed and tightly sealed in double plastic bags, this won't be a problem.

Not infrequently one discovers a large bag full of garbage at a lean-to or campsite, as if it was left for a trash pick-up. Surely just about everyone knows that there are no such pick-ups in the wilderness. This kind of inconsiderate behavior means that someone else is stuck with carrying it out.

Before that can happen, however, animals are likely to tear a garbage bag apart in search of food, often scattering the trash around and making a real mess. There's only one place where you should ever desposit litter and garbage on a trip: in a garbage can or receptacle, which is most likely to be found in a parking area or along a highway. If you don't come across a place to deposit your trash on the way out, dispose of it at home.

Campfires

Campfires have ceased to be a necessity for the most part, since lightweight stoves are widely available for cooking. Fires are in fact prohibited in an increasing number of wilderness areas. Having a campfire can no longer be taken for granted.

Campfires can have a considerable impact on the environment, leaving scars on the earth, and through carelessness occasionally sparking a forest fire. Also, fueling a campfire requires lots of dead wood which would otherwise be available to enrich the soil.

In practicing low-impact camping, try to refrain from having a fire except when you've got a good reason for one. Appropriate conditions include uncomfortably cold weather and also serious bug problems. Start and tend a fire with the greatest caution. If having a campfire means seriously disturbing vegetation and leaving a lasting scar, don't build one except in an emergency.

In the coming years campfires are likely to be banned in an increasing number of places, due to their impact and the damage which continues to occur. See Chapter 10 for more about fires.

Noise Pollution

Sound can travel a considerable distance in the wilderness, occasionally up to several miles, and all visitors should be aware of this fact. Many people go into the wilderness in part to "get away from it all," and value highly the peaceful quiet of the natural world. Talking loudly, yelling, or screaming can be very disruptive to others who may be camping nearby. It's certain to disturb animals as well, greatly reducing the likelihood that you'll see any wildlife or much in the way of birdlife.

Groups of kids or adults almost inevitably make some noise while together in the wilderness, especially when enjoying themselves. It's important that group leaders realize how other people may be affected. Making lots of noise when others are camped nearby is inconsiderate at the very least, especially at night. Setting off firecrackers is inexcusable. Groups that want to party, or who find it difficult to keep reasonably quiet, should at the very least try to get off the beaten path and tent in a secluded spot, as far as possible from other campers.

Visual Pollution

Some superbright outdoor clothing has come into fashion in recent years. While it's easier to spot your companions at a distance in such clothing, and it unquestionably makes for safer travel during hunting season, Day-Glo-like colors distract the eye and provide a form of visual pollution in the wilderness.

This is a place where human beings are guests, not permanent residents. How we dress and act have effects on wildlife as well as on fellow-travelers. We have an obligation to minimize the impact of our presence in the wilderness in every way possible.

To reduce your visual impact, bring clothing with muted or less vivid colors. Likewise, select a tent and pack which have natural colors and will blend in with the scenery, so you won't be seen from a long distance by other travelers or wildlife.

The one time this advice should not be followed is, of course, during hunting season. If you're going to be out during that season in areas where hunting is permitted, for safety reasons it's obviously best to wear the brightest clothing you can find.

Alternatives:
Campgrounds and Lodging

While some of us feel that wilderness camping is an unrivaled way to spend time overnight in the natural world, this kind of camping isn't permitted in a significant number of parks and wilderness areas throughout the country. Unless you live nearby, to visit these locations for more than a day means either staying at a campground or finding local lodging.

Where wilderness camping *is* allowed, those who are inexperienced may still find it helpful to spend a night or two at a campground, to become familiar with equipment and "get the bugs out" before venturing into the wilderness overnight.

It's also true that not everyone wants to sleep in the wilderness, or feels ready to, regardless of regulations. Some people simply prefer to limit their camping to campgrounds, or to seek conventional accommodations near a park.

Camping in Campgrounds

There are currently many more car-campers than wilderness campers in the United States. Some people are simply unaware of the options, and know little or nothing about camping in the wilds. Car-camping at campgrounds has received much publicity over the years, and it's what most people think of as "camping."

Many people who use campgrounds are not especially interested in wilderness-related activities. Campgrounds are frequented by travelers, vacationers, and others in search of relaxation. These places are popular in part because they're convenient to use, inexpensive, and offer a taste of outdoor living. For some people that's enough.

Others have a strong interest in the natural world, and the best campgrounds for these people are usually the more remote ones found in a number of public parks and forests. This kind of campground sometimes offers a bit of the flavor of

camping in the backcountry, especially when the sites are spaced well apart.

Facilities in such campgrounds tend to be limited, which makes them less attractive to owners of large recreational vehicles, with some locations inaccessible to these vehicles. A higher percentage of the campers staying there are likely to be involved in wilderness-oriented activities, especially if the park is one which doesn't allow other primitive camping.

Camping at campgrounds has some disadvantages, of course. Most problematic to some of us is the relative lack of privacy and quiet, which is commonly if not universally the case. At the same time, many people do appreciate the sense of security of a campground, along with the availability of conveniences, and also the fact that one's car is nearby if needed.

At all except the most primitive campgrounds you'll have access to bathrooms and showers, public phones, and sometimes a store. Assistance will be available in the event of a problem or emergency. There's certainly no reason why you can't use a campground as a "base camp" for day trips into the wilderness if you want to do things that way.

There are times when it makes good sense to spend a night at a campground at the beginning of a wilderness trip, especially if you've spent the day driving or traveling, and arrive at the park at sundown or after dark. When this happens it's usually much more convenient to sleep at the campground, assuming space is available, and to begin your wilderness adventure the next day.

Upon entering any campground you're normally assigned a site and can set up your tent right away, which shouldn't pose a problem even after dark (car lights can be used, if necessary). In contrast, entering the wilderness at night and trying to find a suitable campsite in the dark can be a rather difficult and time-consuming process. It's not much fun if you're already tired from travel, and definitely not recommended for beginners.

For the most complete listing of public and private campgrounds throughout the country, consult one of the comprehensive campground guides, which are available at most large bookstores and outdoor supply stores. For more information about campgrounds in state parks, look in Part II of this book under "Information About State Park Campgrounds," in the "Camping Resources" section for each state.

Public versus Private Campgrounds

Campgrounds are found in all fifty states. Those on public lands—which include National Parks, National Forests, state parks, and state forests—are generally the most desirable, as the locations tend to be especially beautiful. They also provide the easiest access to wilderness areas.

The campgrounds in National Parks and popular state parks are often in great demand, with advance reservations typically required. Some campgrounds are completely booked weeks or even months ahead of time. Not all campgrounds accept reservations, however, and those in lesser-known areas may rarely be full.

Even campgrounds that take advance reservations sometimes make a number of sites available on a first-come, first-served basis. Always call a campground ahead of time, if possible, to check on space, especially if you're heading for an out-of-the-way place (some don't have a phone, in which case you'll have to take your chances). Without reservations you're more likely to get a space if you arrive by late morning or early afternoon.

Quite a few public campgrounds are free, and some of the others charge a very low fee. These tend to be found in the most remote locations, sometimes accessible only by rough roads, and facilities are usually extremely limited and primitive. Make this kind of campground your first choice if you want to avoid crowds.

Most public campgrounds do charge a fee, and for the majority of locations it currently ranges between about $8 and $15 per night for a site. A typical campsite is large enough for one or two tents and up to several people. The fee will occasionally be as low as $3 to $5 (or free) in places that are well off the beaten path, but it can also be as high as $30 or more per night in popular regions like southern Florida. State residents generally pay less than nonresidents.

Private or commercial campgrounds may be found almost anywhere. Some are next to parks, and pick up the spillover when public campgrounds are full. Others are found far from any sizable natural area. If you're traveling a long distance, a commercial campground may offer a convenient and relatively inexpensive place to bed down en route to your destination.

Some private campgrounds are situated in beautiful places, with as much in the way of natural surroundings as a public campground, but quite a few are found in noisy or less-than-attractive areas, such as next to major highways or commercial districts. Fees are usually higher than at public campgrounds, typically ranging from $15 to $30 per site and sometimes more.

Tent-Camping and Recreational Vehicles

Millions of Americans own recreational vehicles (RVs), large live-in vehicles which serve as mobile homes for travelers. They're abundant in the majority of campgrounds. Undoubtedly many people would testify to the joys of living and "camping out" in them. However, most of us who are tent-campers are happiest when we're able to avoid bedding down near RVs.

While the owners of RVs are often good people who don't mean to be inconsiderate to their neighbors, the particular problem is that these vehicles are the source of an assortment of unnatural sounds: air-conditioning, generators, and usually also TVs or radios. While the noise levels may not be loud, it's often sufficient to drown out or at least overshadow the sounds of nature if you're tenting right next to one. And it's necessary to point out that owners of the larger RVs are bringing a huge and very energy-wasteful hunk of civilization along with them.

Some primitive campgrounds don't permit RVs or attract very few because there aren't hookups for electricity or water available, a good reason why it's worth heading for this kind of campground. Also, some campgrounds set aside a particular area solely for tent-camping. Inquire as to whether or not such an area is available. Let your preferences be known. Perhaps we can encourage more campgrounds to set aside tent-camping areas.

Other sources of noise in campgrounds include public bathrooms and showers. These facilities are often brightly lit and sometimes have doors that bang. Foot-traffic and conversation are common around them even at night. For undisturbed sleep, try to get a site on the outer fringes of the campground, away from facilities as well as the main road. Make your request when you're being assigned a campsite at the time of arrival.

Lodging

If you want indoor accommodations, local options will vary from few to many depending on where you go. Possibilities near a park could include a bed and breakfast, guest house, lodge, hotel, or motel. Limited lodging is sometimes available inside a park as well.

Some people prefer such accommodations for the first and/or the last night of an extended wilderness trip. On the day of arrival it can make for convenience after a long drive, and at the end of a trip it provides an opportunity to shower and enjoy a sumptuous meal.

There are some who prefer indoor accommodations at all times, of course, and who don't camp out at all. Traveling this way has the advantage that much less has to be packed and brought along on a trip. All that's needed is clothing and perhaps some gear for one-day outings, assuming such trips are of interest, and it's possible to eat in a restaurant or cafeteria at the beginning and end of each day. The attractions are obvious.

It adds up to a much more expensive vacation, however. And in the view of those of us who are confirmed campers, if you do this you'll be missing out on plenty—and spending as little as a few hours each day actually outdoors exploring and enjoying nature. In other words, doing it this way basically means trading what is potentially a round-the-clock adventure in the wilderness for a much tamer experience, and probably a less memorable one.

Cabins

Cabins are available for rental by the day, weekend, or week in a number of parks. Some cabins are available on private lands as well. Those that are located in state and national parks are often in great demand, with reservations required many months in advance. Where demand exceeds supply, lotteries are sometimes used to allocate them.

A cabin provides a place for sleeping indoors and offers privacy, but at the same time it's usually a simple dwelling located in a natural setting. Cooking facilities and a fireplace or stove are commonly included. The cabin may or may not be heated, and furnishings can range from primitive to very comfortable. Most often you can drive right up to it. Some cabins, however, are found in wilderness areas, requiring that you travel on foot or by other means to reach them.

A park information center or headquarters will often have brochures or flyers regarding these and other accommodations in the park, when available. They may also be able to advise you about lodging beyond park boundaries—or you could contact the state office of tourism for more information.

CHECKLIST

Major Items of Equipment (Chapter 2)
_____Backpack (or other outdoor luggage)
_____Sleeping bag
_____Tent

Other Important Items (Chapter 3)
Raingear:
_____Poncho
_____Rain chaps
_____Rain jacket or suit (instead of poncho)

Water Containers:
_____Water bottles/canteens
_____Large collapsible water carriers

_____Water filter
_____Foam pad or mattress
_____Flashlight with spare batteries and bulb
_____Insect Repellent

Tools for Finding Your Way Around:
_____Compass
_____Map
_____Guidebook

Safety Items:
_____First aid kit
_____Matches
_____Fire starter
_____Whistle
_____Emergency thermal blanket

Protection From the Sun:
_____Sunscreen or lotion
_____Sun hat
_____Sunglasses

Food and Cooking Gear (Chapter 4)
_____Food

Food Storage and Protection:
_____Nylon or plastic food bag
_____50 feet of nylon cord
_____Plastic bags and food containers
_____Plastic litter bag

Cooking Gear:
_____Stove
_____Cookset

_____Sierra cup
_____Utensils
_____Pot gripper

Additional Accessories (Chapter 5)
Small packs:
_____Day pack
_____Fanny pack or belt pouch

_____Groundsheet
_____Pocket Knife
_____Toiletries and personal items
_____Soap
_____Plastic wash basin
_____Solar shower

Sanitation:
_____Toilet paper
_____Small trowel

Other optional items:
_____Camera/binoculars
_____Reading material/notebook
_____Watch
_____Repair kit
_____Folding scissors
_____G.I. can opener
_____Mirror
_____Hammock
_____Inflatable pillow

Clothing and Footwear for the
Wilderness (Chapter 6)
Basic items of clothing:
_____Long pants
_____Shorts
_____Long-sleeved shirt
_____T-shirts/undershirts
_____Underpants
_____Socks
_____Wool sweater or shirt
_____Shell parka or windbreaker

Cold-weather clothing:
_____Thermal underwear
_____Insulated jacket or vest
_____Knitted cap
_____Mitts or gloves

Footwear:
_____Hiking boots or other outdoor footwear
_____Light camp shoes
_____Insulated booties

PART II

WHERE TO GO: A COMPLETE GUIDE TO U.S. PARKS AND OTHER NATURAL AREAS OPEN TO WILDERNESS CAMPING, ALONG WITH THE BEST TRAILS FOR BACKPACKING

WILDERNESS CAMPING AREAS
AND BACKPACKING TRAILS

The listings which follow consist of all known locations in the United States where wilderness camping and backpacking are permitted. Included among these areas are most National Parks and National Forests, many state parks, as well as other public and private lands where camping is allowed *outside of campgrounds*.

In the process of researching this book, determining whether a particular area qualified for inclusion was not always an easy task. Little or no printed literature is available for some smaller parks and forests. Also, certain terms such as "camping area," "campground," and "primitive" are sometimes used in different ways, creating a potential for confusion. In the interest of clarity, basic terms and concepts are discussed here.

Campgrounds versus Camping Areas

Campgrounds are of course the best-known areas which are used for camping. Most campgrounds are accessible by vehicle, have a substantial number of formal campsites, and offer some facilities such as bathrooms and often showers. In the vast majority of campgrounds a fee is charged for each night's stay.

Those parks and other areas which limit camping to regular campgrounds have not been included in this book. However, it should be noted that campgrounds do vary enormously. Quite a few have campsites that are spaced well apart, and some include "walk-in sites." On occasion such sites are completely out of sight of the main part of the campground, and may even be out of earshot of it. A campground with this kind of walk-in site can offer at least limited privacy and a taste of wilderness camping.

In contrast to a campground, a so-called camping area is usually a simple and informal space for camping, often located some distance from roads, and usually accessible only by trail or waterway. It may or may not have designated (numbered or otherwise identified) campsites. If it does, the total number of sites in such an area is typically small, sometimes as few as one or two. Facilities, if any, are likely to consist of an outhouse.

Frequently no fee is required to use a camping area. When one is charged, it's usually less than at a campground. In some parks camping is allowed almost anywhere, and the use of established camping areas may be optional. Other parks restrict all primitive camping to designated camping areas. For locations where this is the case, the park or forest has been included in this book only if one or more of the camping areas are at least one-third to one-half mile from any road.

A few parks also have a "backcountry campground." This often is simply a medium to large backcountry camping area. Parks where camping is limited to such areas have been included here as long as campsites are not near roads.

Primitive Campsites versus Primitive Campgrounds

More than a little confusion is provided by different uses of the word "primitive" as in primitive camping, primitive camping areas, primitive campsites, and primitive campgrounds.

It's not unusual to see literature from a park or preserve which informs the reader that "primitive camping is available," with no further explanation. At such locations camping might be restricted either to camping areas or a "primitive campground," or on the other hand it may be allowed freely almost anywhere.

A primitive or undeveloped campground is usually a normal campground, reachable by car, which doesn't have electrical hook-ups or modern facilities. When literature is referring to a campground, a statement that "primitive campsites are available" means that the campground has some less developed sites.

As it's commonly used, "primitive camping" is sometimes meant to be more or less synonymous with "wilderness camping." At other times, however, the former is applied specifically to camping in a not-very-wild-or-pristine area, in contrast to camping in a true wilderness.

Wilderness Camping and Wilderness Areas

The word "wilderness" also has different meanings. By the strictest definition, there's very little real wilderness left in the United States. Over the years most areas have been logged, and/or have been heavily affected by human impact. Large and remote wilderness areas are scarce in most parts of the country.

Some people use the word "wilderness," however, to describe any relatively unspoiled area, one which isn't designed and manicured (as is a typical urban or suburban park), with a minimum of man-made improvements. A reasonably wild area of a few thousand acres or more will still offer an experience of being immersed in nature, and certainly is large enough to get lost in.

While some outdoorspeople refer to any camping in a natural area away from roads and facilities as wilderness camping, others prefer to call most such undesignated camping "primitive camping," and reserve the term "wilderness camping" for trips to the vast, remote wilderness areas of the sort one finds in our larger National Parks, and particularly in Alaska.

Major Backpacking Trails

In the state chapters which follow, a number of long-distance trails are singled out for special mention under the heading "Major Backpacking Trails." These are scenic trails, open to backpacking, which are generally at least 40-50 miles long. Camping may be allowed wherever one chooses along the way, or it may be restricted to designated sites.

The most famous and spectacular of long distance trails in this country are our National Scenic Trails. These include the 2,100-mile Appalachian Trail and the 2,600-mile Pacific Crest Trail, both of which are well-established, plus the 3,000-mile Continental Divide Trail and the 3,200-mile North Country Trail, which are partially open but still under construction.

Other brand new supertrails are currently in the works. Undoubtedly first and foremost among these is the 4,800-mile American Discovery Trail, our first coast-to-coast trail. This and other trails which have yet to be fully established or marked are not listed in this book, but when completed the trails will be included in future editions.

See *The Essential Guide to Hiking in the United States* for a discussion of the different kinds of National Trails, along with the defining characteristics of many categories of land: National Parks, National Monuments, Recreation Areas, Historical Parks, Lakeshores and Seashores, National Forests, National Wildlife Refuges, BLM lands, state parks, state forests, county and local parks, private preserves, sanctuaries, and other private lands.

ALABAMA

BEST AREAS FOR WILDERNESS CAMPING

TALLADEGA NATIONAL FOREST—383,841 acres. By far the largest of Alabama's four National Forests, Talladega National Forest consists of two widely separate tracts of land in the west-central and northeastern parts of the state.

The wild and attractive scenery here includes rocky ridges, cliffs, and 2,407-foot Cheaha Mountain, which is the highest point in the state. There's one designated wilderness area, the 7,490-acre Cheaha Wilderness.

Much of the forest consists of oak and pine, plus dogwood and mountain laurel, with numerous creeks and some small lakes. White-tailed deer, fox, and bobcat are among the wildlife.

Activities: The National Forest currently has 156 miles of trails for hiking and backpacking. Included is the 95-mile Pinhoti Trail (see entry page 79). Some trails are open to horses. Fishing is available, and hunting is permitted in season.

Camping Regulations: Camping and campfires are allowed throughout the National Forest, except where posted otherwise. Visitors are asked to camp well away from trails and streams. A permit is required in order to camp outside of campgrounds during deer hunting (rifle) season.

For Further Information: Talladega National Forest, 1765 Highland Avenue, Montgomery, AL 36107; (205)832-4470.

BANKHEAD NATIONAL FOREST—180,173 acres. This scenic National Forest is situated in northwest Alabama. The area includes rocky bluffs and cliffs, a natural stone bridge, many creeks, some gorges and waterfalls, and the 61-mile Sipsey National Wild and Scenic River.

The largest wilderness area in the state, the 25,986-acre Sipsey Wilderness, is located here. Forests are mostly of hardwoods and pine, with a few old-growth stands. Among the wildlife are deer and wild turkey.

Activities: This National Forest has 68 miles of trails, most of which are suitable for backpacking and hiking. There are about 30 miles of equestrian trails. Fishing is possible, and hunting is permitted in season.

Camping Regulations: Camping is allowed almost anywhere, as are campfires, except near day use areas or where posted otherwise. Low-impact camping methods are encouraged, and sites should be well away from water sources and trails. A permit must be obtained in order to camp outside of campgrounds during deer hunting season.

For Further Information: Bankhead National Forest, P.O. Box 278, Double Springs, AL 35553; (205)489-5111.

CONECUH NATIONAL FOREST—83,037 acres. Located in southern Alabama along the Florida border, Conecuh National Forest encompasses an area of low elevations and gently hilly terrain.

The forests are of longleaf pine and hardwoods, with magnolia and dogwood. Included are a large number of streams and some ponds. Deer and alligator are among the wildlife here.

Activities: The one established hiking and backpacking trail in this National Forest is the easy 20-mile Conecuh Trail, which has two major loops. Fishing and hunting are permitted.

Camping Regulations: Camping and campfires are freely allowed throughout the area, except

where otherwise prohibited. Low-impact practices are encouraged.

During deer hunting (rifle) season a permit is necessary in order to camp outside of campgrounds. Fall through spring are the best times to visit, as summers are hot and humid here.

For Further Information: Conecuh National Forest, Route 5, Box 157, Andalusia, AL 36420; (205)222-2555.

TUSKEGEE NATIONAL FOREST—11,073 acres. Located in east-central Alabama, Tuskegee is the smallest of this state's National Forests. The region is hilly but elevations are low. Local wildlife includes deer and wild turkey.

Activities: There's one hiking and backpacking trail in this National Forest, the 8.4-mile Bartram National Recreation Trail, part of what may someday may be a long trail through Alabama, Georgia, and South Carolina. Two large creeks are suitable for canoeing. Fishing and hunting are permitted in season.

Camping Regulations: Camping is allowed just about anywhere, except near day use areas or where posted otherwise. Campfires are not restricted. A permit is necessary in order to camp outside of campgrounds during deer hunting season.

For Further Information: Tuskegee National Forest, Route 1, Box 457, Tuskegee, AL 36083; (205)727-2652.

PINHOTI TRAIL—95 miles. Traversing much of the eastern block of Talladega National Forest, this fine National Recreation Trail will soon be extended to a length of about 130 miles. Connecting with the main route are a couple of side trails.

The trail traverses small mountains and ridges, leads through pine and hardwood forests, crosses a number of streams, and passes several lakes. It's easy to moderate in difficulty for most of the way, with some rough, rocky stretches.

Camping Regulations: Camping is allowed almost anywhere along the trail, as are campfires, although backpackers should set up well off the trail and away from streams. Three trail shelters are available along the way. National Forest regulations in Alabama require visitors to obtain a camping permit during deer hunting (rifle) season.

For Further Information: National Forests in Alabama, 1765 Highland Avenue, Montgomery, AL 36107; (205)832-4470. A free trail booklet and map are available on request.

ORGANIZATIONS WHICH OFFER WILDERNESS CAMPING TRIPS
Sierra Club, Alabama Chapter, 1330 21st Way South, Suite 100, Birmingham, AL 35205. This chapter of the Sierra Club offers some backpacking as well as canoe-camping trips.

INFORMATION ABOUT CAMPGROUNDS IN STATE PARKS
Division of State Parks, Alabama Department of Conservation and Natural Resources, 64 North Union Street, Mongomery, AL 36130; (205)242-3334.

STATE HIGHWAY MAP AND TRAVEL INFORMATION
Alabama Bureau of Tourism and Travel, 532 South Perry Street, Montgomery, AL 36104; (800)ALABAMA.

A L A S K A

BEST AREAS FOR WILDERNESS CAMPING

WRANGELL–ST. ELIAS NATIONAL PARK AND PRE-SERVE—13,200,000 acres. Located near the Gulf of Alaska in the south-central part of the state, adjacent to Canada's Kluane National Park, this gigantic National Park and Preserve was established in 1980. It's the largest National Park in the United States. Two roads provide entry to portions of the backcountry.

Four major mountain ranges fall within the park, including the Wrangell and St. Elias Mountains. Among the many high peaks is 18,008-foot Mount St. Elias, second highest in the country. There are also vast glaciers and icefields, areas of tundra, spruce forests, and many rivers, streams, and alpine lakes. Wildlife includes brown/grizzly and black bear, caribou, moose, Dall sheep, and mountain goat.

Activities: The park has very few established trails, so most hiking and backpacking must be cross-country. Horses are allowed. Rafting and kayaking are available on the Chitina and Copper Rivers, and sea kayaking is possible along the coast.

Cross-country skiing is another option, with spring the best season for this activity. There are also many opportunities for mountaineering. Fishing is available as well. Hunting is permitted in the preserve areas but prohibited in the park.

Camping Regulations: Camping is allowed just about anywhere in this National Park and Preserve, as are campfires, except where otherwise prohibited. No permits are required.

For Further Information: Wrangell–St. Elias National Park and Preserve, P.O. Box 29, Glennallen, AK 99588; (907)822-5235.

DENALI NATIONAL PARK AND PRESERVE—6,000,000 acres. Huge and wild Denali National Park and Preserve in south-central Alaska is the site of 20,320-foot Mount McKinley, highest mountain in the United States, and known as Denali ("the high one") by native peoples. It rises 18,000 feet from the lowlands.

There are also many other mountains in this subarctic wilderness, with glaciers and permanent snowfields, steep slopes and valleys, alpine tundra, many rivers and creeks, and some stands of spruce, aspen, and birch. Wildlife includes grizzly bear, caribou, moose, Dall sheep, wolf, wolverine, and fox.

Activities: The only trail system consists of short trails near the park headquarters and hotel. Most hiking and backpacking must be along river bars, ridgetops, or cross-country.

Mountaineering is available, and those climbing the two highest mountains must register before setting out (registration is recommended for all mountains).

Bike use is restricted to roadways. Limited fishing is possible. Hunting is prohibited in the park except for local residents with permits, but allowed in the preserve.

Camping Regulations: A free backcountry use permit is required in order to camp here, and the permit must be returned before one leaves the area. Zones have been established, and the numbers of campers allowed in each zone is limited.

Campfires are prohibited in some regions of the park. A stove should be brought. Pets are not permitted. Some areas may be closed due to bear or other wildlife activity. Summers here can be wet and cool, with snow always a possibility.

For Further Information: Denali National Park and Preserve, P.O. Box 9, Denali Park, AK 99755; (907)683-2686.

TONGASS NATIONAL FOREST—16,800,000 acres.

This is the largest National Forest in the United States. It's situated on the southeast panhandle of Alaska, and has three separate headquarters. A wide range of spectacular scenery is found on these lands.

Especially notable are Misty Fiords National Monument and Admiralty Island National Monument, both of which fall within the forest boundaries. Access to portions of the National Forest is difficult, and often limited to charter boat or plane.

Terrain includes snow-capped peaks, high ridges, volcanoes, canyons and gorges, rocky outcroppings, glaciers, icefields and snowfields. There are islands and ocean beaches, alpine lakes, fjords, major rivers, and many streams with waterfalls.

Vegetation ranges from virgin rain forests of Sitka spruce and western hemlock, along with lodgepole pine and cedar, cottonwood and alder, to alpine tundra, which begins at 2,500 to 3,000 foot elevation. There are many boggy areas ("muskegs").

Among the wildlife are grizzly and black bear, moose, deer, mountain goat, wolf, wolverine, lynx, and fox. Marine mammals include whale, porpoise, seal, and sea lion.

Tongass National Forest has 14 designated wilderness areas, which add up to over 5,000,000 acres. Among the largest are the 2,142,243-acre Misty Fiords National Monument Wilderness, the 937,396-acre Admiralty Island National Monument Wilderness, the 653,179-acre Tracy Arm–Fords Terror Wilderness, the 448,841-acre Tebenkof Wilderness, the 448,000-acre Stikine–Leconte Wilderness, the 348,701-acre Russell Fiord Wilderness, the 319,568-acre South Baranof Wilderness, and the 264,747-acre West Chichagof-Yakobi Wilderness.

Activities: Hiking and backpacking are possible on over 400 miles of trails, but many of the trails are short and not interconnected. Difficulty ranges from easy to strenuous. Cross-country travel is often feasible.

Canoeing, kayaking, and rafting are available on the Stikine River and other rivers, streams, and ocean waterways. Cross-country skiing and snowshoeing are options during the snow season.

Mountain biking is allowed outside of designated wilderness areas. One may also fish along countless lakes, streams, and rivers. Hunting is permitted in season.

Camping Regulations: Camping is allowed almost anywhere in the National Forest, except where otherwise prohibited. No permits are necessary. In designated wilderness areas campsites should be away from trails and lakeshores. Campfires are legal, but the use of stoves is encouraged.

For Further Information: Tongass National Forest, Chatham Area, 204 Siginaka Way, Sitka, AK 99835; (907)747-6671/ Tongass National Forest, Ketchikan Area, Federal Building, Ketchican, AK 99901; (907)225-3101/ Tongass National Forest, Stikine Area, 201 12th Street, P.O. Box 309, Petersburg, AK 99833; (907)772-3841.

NOATAK NATIONAL PRESERVE, KOBUK VALLEY NATIONAL PARK, CAPE KRUSENSTERN NATIONAL MONUMENT—6,500,000 acres (Noatak National Preserve)/1,700,000 acres (Kobuk Valley National Park)/659,000 acres (Cape Krusenstern National Monument).

Located in the northwestern part of the state and established in 1980, these three parks are known as the Northwest Alaska Areas. They are administered together, with one visitor center for all three. Access is mainly by air taxi.

Within this enormous region are the Baird and De Long Mountains of the Brooks Range, along with some foothills, areas of arctic tundra, northern conifer forests, sand dunes, coastal plain with lagoons, and beach ridges.

There are many rivers, including several National Wild and Scenic Rivers—most notably the Noatak River and its watershed, along with the Kobuk River.

Among the wildlife here are caribou, which number over 300,000, grizzly and black bear, moose, musk oxen, Dall sheep, wolf, wolverine, and lynx. Marine mammals include whale, polar bear, walrus, and seal.

Activities: Backpacking and hiking in these areas is cross-country, as there are no trails. Canoeing, kayaking, and rafting are available on the Kobuk, Noatak, and other rivers from June through mid-September.

Sea kayaking is also feasible along the coast of Cape Krusenstern. Fishing is possible. Hunting is permitted for local residents but forbidden for visitors except in the Preserve.

Camping Regulations: Camping is allowed throughout the region, except where otherwise prohibited, such as in some archeological areas and where subsistence fishing is going on. No permits are necessary, although it's recommended that anyone intending to camp first stop by at the visitor center or a ranger station for up-to-date information.

Campfires are allowed, but a stove should be brought for cooking. Due to the remoteness of the areas, previous camping and wilderness experience are highly recommended. Summer temperatures range from cool to warm, with the weather unpredictable.

For Further Information: Northwest Alaska Areas, P.O. Box 1029, Kotzebue, AK 99752; (907)442-3760.

GATES OF THE ARCTIC NATIONAL PARK AND PRE-SERVE—8,400,000 acres. Created in 1980 and located in north-central Alaska, in the Brooks Range north of the Arctic Circle, this National Park and Preserve was named for two peaks which stand as a gate to the arctic region.

It's in a remote area, and most of the park may be reached only by air taxi. Summer temperatures here range from cool to warm, but it can drop below freezing at any time.

There are mountains as high as 7,000 feet, foothills, areas of alpine tundra, forests of spruce, aspen, and birch, and six National Wild and Scenic Rivers. Wildlife includes caribou, grizzly and black bear, moose, Dall sheep, wolf, and wolverine.

Activities: There are no trails, so backpackers and hikers must find their own routes. Kayaking and canoeing are possible on some of the rivers, as is fishing, and cross-country skiing and snowshoeing are available during the snow season. Hunting is prohibited in the park but permitted in the preserve.

Camping Regulations: Camping is freely allowed throughout this National Park and Preserve, as are campfires, except where otherwise prohibited. No permits are necessary.

For Further Information: Gates of the Arctic National Park and Preserve, P.O. Box 74680, Fairbanks, AK 99707; (907)456-0281.

CHUGACH NATIONAL FOREST—5,800,000 acres. Situated in the southern part of the state, with most lands lying southeast of Anchorage and near or alongside the Gulf of Alaska, this is the second largest National Forest in the United States.

It includes part of the Kenai Peninsula with the Kenai Mountains, the Copper River Delta, and Prince William Sound—which has 3,500 miles of shoreline, and suffered some damage from the 1989 oil spill.

Within this enormous area are spectacular mountains, gigantic glaciers, high lakes and streams, forests of spruce and hemlock, and areas of open alpine tundra above timberline. Wildlife includes brown/grizzly and black bear, moose, Dall sheep, and mountain goat, plus whale and other marine animals.

Unlike Tongass National Forest, Chugach has no designated wilderness areas at the present time. However, there's one huge Wilderness Study Area which is under consideration for possible wilderness designation: the 2,100,000-acre Nellie Juan–College Fiord Wilderness Study Area.

Activities: Over 200 miles of trails are available for backpacking and hiking, including the 39-mile Resurrection Pass National Recreation Trail. The difficulty of most trails varies from easy to moderate. Cross-country travel is also possible.

Canoeing, kayaking, and rafting are feasible on some rivers and streams, and sea kayaking is possible in Prince William Sound. Horses are allowed on trails except during the period of April through June. Cross-country skiing and snowshoeing are winter options here. Hunting and fishing are permitted in season.

Camping Regulations: Camping and campfires are allowed just about anywhere, except near public use areas or where otherwise prohibited. No permits are required. Campers are asked to choose sites which are well off the trail, and utilize pre-existing fire rings whenever possible. Stoves should be used in alpine areas.

For Further Information: Chugach National Forest, 201 East 9th Avenue, Suite 206, Anchorage, AK 99501; (907)271-2500.

GLACIER BAY NATIONAL PARK AND PRESERVE—3,280,000 acres. Situated west of Juneau in southeast Alaska, adjacent to the Canadian border, Glacier Bay National Park and Preserve protects a bay which was covered by a glacier until just 200 years ago. Terrain here is often rocky and rugged. The park is accessible only by boat or plane, with mid-May through mid-September the normal visitor season. Cool and rainy weather is common in the summer.

Within the park is the snow-covered Fairweather Range, with 15,320-foot Mount Fairweather the highest point. There are also many glaciers and fjords (glacier-carved valleys filled with water), icebergs in the bay, and spruce-hemlock forests. Wildlife includes grizzly and black bear, moose, and wolf. Among marine mammals are several species of whale.

Activities: There are no trails in the backcountry here. Hiking and backpacking are possible along beaches, meadows, and other open areas. Glaciers

should be avoided except by those who are experienced in glacier travel.

Kayaking is an option around Glacier Bay, and kayaks may be rented nearby. Rafting is possible on the Alsek River. Fishing is also available. Hunting is allowed in the preserve, which comprises a small part of the total area, but not in the park.

Camping Regulations: Camping is allowed throughout most of the region. It's suggested but not required that a backcountry use permit be filled out before departing. Campsites should be at least 300 feet from freshwater lakes or streams, and out of sight of other campers.

Campfires are permitted only below the high tide line. Pets are prohibited. Some backcountry areas may be closed to the public at times. Camping orientation sessions are held daily at a lodge in the park.

For Further Information: Glacier Bay National Park and Preserve, Bartlett Cove, Gustavus, AK 99826; (907)697-2230.

LAKE CLARK NATIONAL PARK AND PRESERVE— 4,000,000 acres. Established in 1980, this National Park and Preserve is located in southern Alaska, across from the Kenai Peninsula. There are no highways in the region, so access is mainly by small aircraft and occasionally by boat.

The park portion consists of 2,600,000 acres, and the preserve 1,400,000 acres. About 2,400,000 acres have wilderness designation. Dominating the area are the Aleutian and Alaska Ranges, with the incredibly rugged Chigmit Mountains.

There are also two active volcanoes, a number of glaciers, foothills with arctic tundra, forests of spruce, and many lakes and rivers. Brown and black bear, caribou, moose, Dall sheep, wolf, and lynx are among the wildlife. Marine mammals include whale and seal.

Activities: No trails are found here, but backpacking is possible on the open tundra in the western foothills. Cross-country skiing is also feasible, best in March and early April.

Kayaking or canoeing are available on the Mulchatna and Chilikadrotna Rivers. Climbing and mountaineering are other options here. Fishing is possible as well. Hunting is permitted in the preserve but not in the park.

Camping Regulations: Camping is freely allowed in this National Park and Preserve, as are campfires, except where otherwise prohibited. No permits are required.

For Further Information: Lake Clark National Park and Preserve, 4230 University Drive, Suite 311, Anchorage, AK 99508; (907)271-3751.

KATMAI NATIONAL PARK AND PRESERVE—4,000,000 acres. Katmai National Park and Preserve is located on the Alaska Peninsula, in the southwest part of the state. Access is by commercial float plane from nearby King Salmon during summer, or charter plane at other times of year.

There are coastal mountains over 7,000 feet high, with sheer cliffs and beaches, 15 active volcanoes, glacier-carved valleys, large glaciers, and almost 400 miles of Pacific coastline along the Shelikof Strait.

In the region are some forests of spruce, poplar, and birch, areas of alpine tundra, and a large population of brown bear, along with moose, wolf, fox, and marine mammals such as gray whale, sea lion, and sea otter.

Activities: Hiking and backpacking are feasible here on some backcountry routes and elsewhere, although established trails are few. Cross-country skiing is an option during the snow season.

Canoeing and kayaking are available on the Savonoski Loop, which includes rivers and lakes, and canoes may be rented in the area. Fishing is also possible. Hunting is prohibited in the park but permitted in the preserve.

Camping Regulations: Camping is allowed throughout the National Park and Preserve. A free permit is available and recommended for camping in the backcountry, but not required.

Permits may be obtained from the visitor center or park headquarters. Campfires are allowed but discouraged. A stove is suggested for cooking.

For Further Information: Katmai National Park and Preserve, P.O. Box 7, King Salmon, AK 99613; (907)246-3305.

YUKON–CHARLEY RIVERS NATIONAL PRESERVE—2,500,000 acres. This isolated preserve in east-central Alaska protects the Yukon and Charley Rivers. In the region are small mountains with elevations as high as 6,400 feet, hills and canyons, and some other rivers plus many creeks.

Access is via aircraft or by boat on the Yukon River. The climate here is subarctic, with bitter winters and somewhat warm summers. Timberline is around 3,500 feet.

There are vast forests of conifers and hardwoods, along with some tundra. Wildlife includes grizzly and black bear, moose, Dall sheep, fox, and peregrine falcon.

Activities: Backpacking and hiking are possible, but there are no established trails. Kayaking and rafting are available on the Yukon and Charley Rivers, with canoeing feasible only on the Yukon. Fishing is permitted, as is hunting in season.

Camping Regulations: Camping is allowed practically anywhere in this National Preserve. No permits are necessary. For those floating the rivers, sand or gravel bars alongside the waterways are appropriate for campsites. Campfires are permitted, but a stove is recommended for cooking.

For Further Information: Yukon–Charley Rivers National Preserve, Box 167, Eagle, AK 99738.

OTHER RECOMMENDED LOCATIONS

BLM LANDS IN ALASKA—This state has an incredible 90,000,000 acres of BLM (Bureau of Land Management) or public domain lands, far more than any other state, consisting of many separate tracts. Access is often difficult, frequently requiring charter plane. Aside from a few campgrounds there are virtually no facilities.

On the BLM lands in this state there are high mountains, vast stretches of open tundra, forested areas, and six National Wild and Scenic Rivers. Common wildlife includes caribou, moose, bear, Dall sheep, and wolverine.

Of special interest is the 1,200,000-acre Steese National Conservation Area, and also the 1,000,000-acre White Mountains National Recreation Area, Alaska's only National Recreation Area.

Activities: Hiking and backpacking are possible on virtually all BLM lands in Alaska, although only a handful of established trails exist. Two of the most notable are the 27-mile Pinnell Mountain National Recreation Trail (Steese National Conservation Area), and the 19-mile White Mountains Summit Trail (White Mountains National Recreation Area).

Many of the rivers are suitable for canoeing, kayaking, and rafting. Cross-country skiing and snowshoeing are winter options on these lands. Hunting and fishing are permitted in season.

Camping Regulations: Camping and campfires are generally allowed without restriction, except where posted or otherwise prohibited. No permits are required.

For Further Information: Bureau of Land Management, 222 West 7th Avenue, #13, Anchorage, AK 99513; (907)271-5960.

NATIONAL WILDLIFE REFUGES IN ALASKA—There are 16 National Wildlife Refuges in Alaska, all but two of which are over 1,000,000 acres in size. Most of the refuges are accessible only by charter plane or boat. Some receive extremely few visitors.

The two largest are the gigantic 19,624,458-acre Yukon Delta National Wildlife Refuge and the 19,049,236-acre Arctic National Wildlife Refuge—the latter having an 8,000,000-acre designated wilderness area. Wildlife includes caribou, grizzly and polar bear, musk ox, moose, Dall sheep, wolverine, wolf, and walrus.

The refuges encompass mountains and volcanoes, valleys and lowlands, glaciers and grasslands, forests and tundra, rugged coastline and islands. There are wetlands, tens of thousands of lakes, and a great many rivers.

Activities: Hiking and backpacking are allowed in all the refuges, but there are no trails. Travel on foot must be cross-country. Canoeing, kayaking, and rafting are possible on many of the rivers. Hunting and fishing are permitted in season.

Camping Regulations: Camping and campfires are allowed with few restrictions in all of Alaska's National Wildlife Refuges, except where otherwise prohibited. No permits are necessary. Due to the extreme remoteness of some of the areas, extensive previous wilderness camping experience is recommended.

For Further Information: Regional Office, Fish and Wildlife Service, 1011 East Tudor, Anchorage, AK 99503; (907)786-3487.

STATE PARKS IN ALASKA—Alaska has 116 state parks and recreation areas, mainly located in the southern and south-central parts of the state, adding up to over 3,000,000 acres. Unlike other states in the country, camping is allowed freely throughout most of the parks.

A few of the state parks are quite large: 1,555,200-acre Wood–Tikchik State Park, 495,204-acre Chugach State Park, 368,290-acre Kachemak Bay State Park, 324,240-acre Denali State Park, and 254,080-acre Chena River State Recreation Area.

Scenery includes mountains, glaciers, foothills, some rain forests, and areas of alpine tundra. Among the wildlife are grizzly bear, caribou, moose, Dall sheep, mountain goat, wolf, lynx, and bald eagle, plus marine mammals such as whale, seal, and sea lion.

Activities: There are many options for hiking and backpacking, with a large number of maintained trails—more than on other public lands in Alaska except for the National Forests.

Among those parks with sizable trail systems are Chugach State Park, Denali State Park, Kachemak Bay State Park, and the Chena River State Recreation Area, which includes the 29-mile Chena Dome Trail.

Horseback riding is allowed in some areas. Cross-country skiing and snowshoeing are available in the winter. Kayaking, canoeing, and rafting are possible on many of the rivers.

Rock climbing and mountaineering may also be practiced in some parks. Hunting and fishing are generally permitted in season, with restrictions in certain areas.

Camping Regulations: Primitive camping is allowed in most of the parks. Sites should be away from trails and water sources. No permits are necessary. Campfires are restricted to designated areas in almost all parks. A stove should be brought for cooking.

For Further Information: Alaska Department of Natural Resources, Division of Parks and Outdoor Recreation, 3601 C Street, P.O. Box 107001, Anchorage, AK 99510; (907)762-2617.

KENAI FJORDS NATIONAL PARK—580,000 acres. Established in 1980 and located on the southeast Kenai Peninsula, along the southern coast of Alaska, this ruggedly scenic National Park is noted for its coastal mountain fjords. The park is accessible by highway, train, plane, or ferry. Wet weather is very common here in the summer.

There are small mountains, canyons, and steep glacier-sculpted valleys, with some stands of Sitka spruce and western hemlock, along with glaciers and icefields, including 300-square mile Harding Icefield.

Among the wildlife are brown/grizzly and black bear, moose, mountain, goat, wolverine, and bald eagle. Marine mammals include whale, seal, sea lion, and porpoise.

Activities: The park is suitable for hiking and backpacking, but there are only a few short trails, so foot-travelers must normally make their own route. Sea kayaking is available along the fjords, which can be hazardous in inclement weather.

Snowshoeing and cross-country skiing are possible when there's adequate snow. One can cross-country ski on the icefield in summer, although this should only be attempted by experienced skiers. Fishing is permitted, but hunting is not.

Camping Regulations: Camping is allowed throughout the National Park, as are campfires. No permits are required. Camping in the backcountry is not recommended for beginners.

For Further Information: Kenai Fjords National Park, P.O. Box 1727, 1212 Fourth Avenue, Seward, AK 99664; (907)224-3175.

BERING LAND BRIDGE NATIONAL PRESERVE—
2,590,000 acres. Located just south of the Arctic Circle, on northwest Alaska's Seward Peninsula, this isolated National Preserve protects part of what was once a land bridge connecting North America with Asia. Access is mainly by air taxi.

No facilities are available, so total self-sufficiency is required. Temperatures are above freezing from late spring to mid-fall. The sun is up for about 22 hours of the day in summer.

It's a relatively flat area of tundra with some rimless volcanoes and lava beds, lakes, streams, and hot springs. Wildlife includes grizzly bear, moose, wolf, fox, and marine animals such as whale, walrus, and seal.

Activities: Backpacking and hiking are possible here, but the preserve has no trails. Snowshoeing and cross-country skiing are available when there's adequate snow. Hunting and fishing are permitted.

Camping Regulations: Camping is allowed without restriction throughout the preserve, as are campfires. No permits are necessary.

For Further Information: Bering Land Bridge National Preserve, P.O. Box 220, Nome, AK 99762.

ANIAKCHAK NATIONAL MONUMENT AND PRESERVE—
600,000 acres. This is an extremely remote park, located some distance southwest of Katmai National Park and Preserve on the Alaska Peninsula, in the southwestern part of the state.

It's accessible only by charter boat or plane, and visited by a very small number of people each year. There are no facilities. Weather here is often wet and severe in the summer.

The area has some volcanic mountains, including a 6-mile-wide caldera (collapsed volcano), a couple of lakes, and several rivers. Most notable among them is the Aniakchak River, a National Wild and Scenic River.

Activities: Backpacking and hiking are feasible, but there are no trails. Rafting is possible on the Aniakchak River. Fishing is also available in the park and preserve. Hunting is permitted only in the preserve.

Camping Regulations: Camping is allowed without restriction throughout the region, as are campfires. No permits are required.

For Further Information: Aniakchak National Monument and Preserve, P.O. Box 7, King Salmon, AK 99613.

KLONDIKE GOLD RUSH NATIONAL HISTORICAL PARK—
12,990 acres. This park in southeast Alaska preserves many historic sites of the famous gold rush of 1897 in and around Skagway. The setting is an area of mountains, glaciers, lakes, and rivers, with some coastal rainforest, subalpine vegetation, and wildlife which includes bear and moose.

Activities: Of special interest here is the 33-mile Chilkoot Trail, open only to foot travel, which follows the route of the gold rush "stampeders" up over Chilkoot Pass. Part of the trail is steep and challenging, and north of the pass it's in Canada. The trail may be walked in snowshoes during the snow season.

Camping Regulations: Camping and campfires are generally allowed along sections of the Chilkoot Trail within the United States, except near developed areas or where otherwise prohibited. The Canadian portion of the Chilkoot Trail is in Chilkoot Trail National Historic Park. Here camping is restricted to designated sites, and campfires are forbidden except at a couple of locations.

For Further Information: Klondike Gold Rush National Historical Park, P.O. Box 517, Skagway, AK 99840;

ALASKA CAMPING RESOURCES

USEFUL GUIDEBOOKS

Alaska's Parklands: The Complete Guide—Simmerman, Nancy. Seattle: The Mountaineers Books.

Discover Southeast Alaska with Pack and Paddle—Piggot, Margaret. Seattle: The Mountaineers Books.

55 Ways to the Wilderness in South Central Alaska—Nienhueser, Helen and Simmerman, Nancy. Seattle: The Mountaineers Books, 1985.

Glacier Bay National Park—DuFresne, Jim. Seattle: The Mountaineers Books.

Hiker's Guide to Alaska—Swensen, Evan and Margaret. Helena, MT: Falcon Press.

INFORMATION ABOUT STATE PARK CAMPGROUNDS
Alaska Division of Parks and Outdoor Recreation, P.O. Box 107001, Anchorage, AK 99510.

INFORMATION ABOUT NATIONAL PARKS IN ALASKA
Alaska Regional Office, National Park Service, 2525 Gambell Street, Room 107, Anchorage, AK 99503; (907)271-2643.

INFORMATION ABOUT PUBLIC LANDS IN ALASKA
Alaska Public Lands Information Center, 605 West 4th Avenue, Suite 105, Anchorage, AK 99501; (907)271-2737.

STATE HIGHWAY MAP AND TRAVEL INFORMATION
Alaska Division of Tourism, Box E, Juneau, AK 99811; (907)465- 2010.

A R I Z O N A

BEST AREAS FOR WILDERNESS CAMPING

GRAND CANYON NATIONAL PARK—1,215,735 acres. Located in northern Arizona, this spectacular National Park protects the magnificent mile-deep and 200-mile-long Grand Canyon of the Colorado River. The enormous multicolored desert canyon is probably the most famous natural site in this country. It's a thrillingly beautiful area with unequaled views available from the rims.

Elevations range from about 2,400 feet along the river to 7,000 feet and higher along the South and North Rims. Vegetation varies widely from bottom to top, ranging from desert flora through pinyon and juniper to forests of ponderosa pine, spruce, and fir on the rim. Wildlife includes mule deer, coyote, bobcat, and fox.

Activities: There's a large trail network for hiking and backpacking, with some trails quite steep and challenging. Due to the enormous popularity of the park, a few trails receive very heavy use. Horses are allowed on some trails. Mountain bikes are permitted only on park roads and not in the canyon.

The Colorado River is famous for rafting, and many outfitters offer trips. Since numbers are restricted and demand is extremely high, if you want to raft on your own it's necessary to reserve as much as several years in advance. Fishing is permitted. Hunting is prohibited in the park.

Camping Regulations: A free permit is necessary in order to camp in the backcountry here. Permits may be obtained ahead of time via mail by writing to the Backcountry Reservations Office, P.O. Box 129, Grand Canyon, AZ 86023.

Reservations are normally essential, especially from spring through fall, as the number of requests far exceeds available permits. Dates and daily itinerary must be specified in advance. It's necessary to pick up the permit in person upon arriving.

Camping is restricted to designated sites in some parts of the canyon. In other areas it's possible to choose your own site, which must be at least 100 feet from water sources. Campfires are prohibited, so a stove must be used for cooking. Pets are not allowed.

Those who camp in the canyon should keep in mind that the climb back to the rim is very long and strenuous, with little water or shade along the way. Spring and fall are the best times to visit. Summer is not recommended due to the often intense heat in the canyon.

For Further Information: Grand Canyon National Park, P.O. Box 129, Grand Canyon, AZ 86023; (602)638-7888.

TONTO NATIONAL FOREST—2,874,580 acres. This enormous National Forest in arid central Arizona has diverse and outstanding scenery, including steep rugged peaks, precipitous canyons, buttes and mesas, painted cliffs and bluffs, rocky outcrops and pinnacles.

There are several desert mountain ranges, and an area of Indian cliff dwellings is included. Vegetation ranges from saguaro cactus and manzanita to pinyon-juniper and forests of fir and pine. Deer, bear, and mountain lion are among the wildlife.

Tonto has eight designated wilderness areas: the 252,000-acre Mazatzal Wilderness, the 160,000-acre Superstition Wilderness, the 53,500-acre Four Peaks Wilderness, the 36,780-acre Hellsgate

Wilderness, the 32,800-acre Salt River Canyon Wilderness, the 20,850-acre Sierra Ancha Wilderness, the 18,950-acre Salome Wilderness, and 11,450 acres of the 20,000-acre Pine Mountain Wilderness.

Activities: Backpacking and hiking are possible on over 800 miles of trails, including the 51-mile Highline National Recreation Trail, the 29-mile Mazatzal Divide Trail, and the 28-mile Verde River Trail. Difficulty varies from easy to strenuous.

Horses are allowed on many trails. Cross-country skiing is possible at higher elevations during the snow season. Limited rafting and kayaking are available on the Verde and Salt Rivers. Fishing is another option, and hunting is permitted in season.

Camping Regulations: Camping is allowed throughout the National Forest, except where otherwise prohibited. Campfires may be built, but the use of a stove is recommended for cooking. No permits are necessary except for outfitter-guide services. When in wilderness areas, camp at least 300 feet from water sources and away from trails. Summer heat is sometimes extreme, so spring and fall are the preferred times to camp here.

For Further Information: Tonto National Forest, P.O. Box 5348, 2324 East McDowell Road, Phoenix, AZ 85010; (602)225-2500.

APACHE–SITGREAVES NATIONAL FORESTS— 2,004,819 acres. These two National Forests in east-central Arizona are administered together. Elevations range from 3,500 feet to over 10,000 feet. Among the high and rugged mountains here is 10,912-foot Escudilla Peak, third highest in the state.

There are also canyons, plateaus, a number of lakes and streams, and great expanses of desert. Included are forests of ponderosa pine, mountain meadows, and subalpine flora, along with desert vegetation such as yucca and prickly pear. Among the wildlife are antelope, elk, deer, and mountain lion.

Apache–Sitgreaves has three small designated wilderness areas: the 11,000-acre Bear Wallow Wilderness, the 7,000-acre Mount Baldy Wilderness, and the 5,200-acre Escudilla Wilderness. Also here is the 174,000-acre Blue Range Primitive Area, which is managed like a wilderness area.

Activities: Some 875 miles of trails are available for backpacking and hiking, including the 29-mile Eagle National Recreation Trail. Difficulty varies from easy to strenuous. Horseback riding is permitted on most trails. Mountain biking is possible

outside of wilderness areas. Cross-country skiing is a winter option, as is snowshoeing. Skis may be rented nearby. Fishing is available along many lakes and streams, and hunting is permitted in season.

Camping Regulations: Camping and campfires are allowed freely throughout most of the area, except near public recreation areas or where posted otherwise. No permits are required. Maximum group size for camping in the Mount Baldy Wilderness is six.

For Further Information: Apache–Sitgreaves National Forests, P.O. Box 640, Springerville, AZ 85938; (602)333-4301.

CORONADO NATIONAL FOREST—1,780,196 acres. Consisting of a number of separate tracts in southeast Arizona, this scenic National Forest includes twelve mountain ranges. The highest peak is 10,717-foot Mount Graham, with many other mountains over 9,000 feet.

Terrain here is often rugged, with canyons and cliffs, rocky outcroppings and pinnacles. Coronado also has some lakes, streams, and forests of spruce, pine, and fir. Among the wildlife are deer, pronghorn, black bear, bighorn sheep, mountain lion, and bobcat.

There are eight designated wilderness areas: the 87,700-acre Chiricahua Wilderness, the 76,000-acre Galiuro Wilderness, the 57,000-acre Pusch Ridge Wilderness, the 38,600-acre Rincon Mountain Wilderness, the 26,780-acre Santa Teresa Wilderness, the 25,200-acre Mount Wrightson Wilderness, the 20,000-acre Miller Peak Wilderness, and the 7,400-acre Pajarita Wilderness.

Activities: Backpacking and hiking are available on over 900 miles of trails, including a section of the new Arizona Trail (see entry page 94). Difficulty varies from easy to strenuous.

Horses are allowed on most trails. Technical climbing is possible in the mountains here. Fishing is available along streams and lakes, and hunting is permitted in season.

Camping Regulations: Camping is allowed throughout the National Forest, as are campfires, except near public recreation areas or where otherwise prohibited. No permits are necessary.

For Further Information: Coronado National Forest, 300 West Congress, Tucson, AZ 85701; (602)670-6483.

COCONINO NATIONAL FOREST—1,835,913 acres. Located in north-central Arizona, Coconino National Forest encompasses a huge area of diverse scenery, which includes the sometimes snow-covered San Francisco Peaks and the high desert of the Colorado Plateau.

Arizona's highest mountain, 12,633-foot Humphrey's Peak, is here—along with sandstone buttes, rocky cliffs, and colored canyons. Most notable of the canyons are 21-mile-long Sycamore Canyon, plus 16-mile-long and 2,500-foot-deep Oak Creek Canyon. There are a number of lakes and streams, with some desert grasslands, pinyon-juniper woodlands, and forests of conifers. Wildlife includes elk, mule deer, black bear, mountain lion, and coyote.

This National Forest has nine designated wilderness areas: the 44,000-acre Red Rock–Secret Mountain Wilderness, 23,000 acres of the 56,000-acre Sycamore Canyon Wilderness, the 18,200-acre Kachina Peaks Wilderness, the 18,150-acre Munds Mountain Wilderness, the 13,600-acre West Clear Creek Wilderness, the 11,550-acre Fossil Springs Wilderness, the 10,000-acre Strawberry Crater Wilderness, the 6,700-acre Wet Beaver Creek Wilderness, and part of the 6,510-acre Kendrick Mountain Wilderness.

Activities: Hiking and backpacking are possible on over 300 miles of trails, including a 53-mile segment of the 133-mile General Crook State Historic Trail. Difficulty varies from easy to strenuous.

Horseback riding is available on many trails, as is mountain biking outside of wilderness areas. Cross-country skiing is possible here in the winter. Fishing is feasible along many streams and lakes, and hunting is permitted in season.

Camping Regulations: Camping is allowed throughout the National Forest, except near public use areas or where otherwise prohibited. No permits are necessary. Campfires are generally allowed, but they're sometimes banned when conditions are dry.

Campsites in wilderness areas must be away from trails and meadows, and at least one-quarter mile from lakes and other water sources. Summers can be very hot, so fall and spring are the preferred seasons to camp here.

For Further Information: Coconino National Forest, 2323 East Greenlaw Lane, Flagstaff, AZ 86004; (602)527-7400.

PRESCOTT NATIONAL FOREST—1,250,613 acres. This National Forest is made up of two large tracts in central Arizona. It's a region of rugged mountains, huge mesas, limestone canyons, and granite boulders. Elevations range from 3,000 feet to more than 7,000 feet.

There are pinyon-juniper woodlands, forests of fir and pine, and also desert cactus and mesquite, manzanita and chapparral. Wildlife includes deer, black bear, mountain lion, and coyote.

Prescott has eight designated wilderness areas: 25,870 acres of the 56,000-acre Sycamore Canyon Wilderness, the 25,125-acre Castle Creek Wilderness, the 16,000-acre Cedar Bench Wilderness, the 9,800-acre Granite Mountain Wilderness, 8,760 acres of the 20,000-acre Pine Mountain Wilderness, the 7,550-acre Juniper Mesa Wilderness, the 5,750-acre Woodchute Wilderness, and the 5,500-acre Apache Creek Wilderness.

Activities: There are more than 300 miles of established trails for hiking and backpacking, and most trails are also open to horseback riding. Difficulty ranges from easy to strenuous. Rafting and kayaking are available on the Verde River during springtime. Hunting and fishing are permitted here in season.

Camping Regulations: Camping is allowed throughout most of the National Forest, except where posted otherwise. No permits are necessary. Campfires are legal except during periods of drought. When camping in wilderness areas, sites should be at least one-quarter mile from water sources. Since summers are typically hot here, spring and fall are the best times to visit.

For Further Information: Prescott National Forest, 344 South Cortez Street, Prescott, AZ 86303; (602)445-1762.

KAIBAB NATIONAL FOREST—1,556,465 acres. Kaibab National Forest consists of three sizable units both north and south of Grand Canyon National Park, in northern Arizona. In the region are some high peaks, including 10,418-foot Kendrick Mountain.

There are also plateaus, cliffs and canyons, a small portion of the Grand Canyon's rim, subalpine meadows, conifer forests, and some desert. Among the wildlife are elk and mule deer.

Two relatively small wilderness areas are found in this National Forest: 7,000 acres of the 56,000-acre Sycamore Canyon Wilderness, and part of the 6,510-acre Kendrick Mountain Wilderness, which extends into Coconino National Forest.

Activities: Hiking and backpacking are possible on about 77 miles of trails, including 37 miles of the new Arizona Trail (see entry page 94). Difficulty varies from easy to strenuous.

Horseback riding is allowed on most trails. Mountain biking is possible on trails outside of wilderness areas. Fishing is available, and hunting is permitted in season.

Camping Regulations: Camping and campfires are allowed in most parts of the National Forest, except near developed areas or where otherwise prohibited. No permits are required. Spring and fall are the recommended seasons to camp here. Summers are quite hot, especially in the canyons.

For Further Information: Kaibab National Forest, 800 South 6th Street, Williams, AZ 86046; (602)635-2681.

OTHER RECOMMENDED LOCATIONS

PETRIFIED FOREST NATIONAL PARK—93,500 acres. Located in northeast Arizona, this National Park is famous for its impressive display of petrified wood and other fossils, mostly bright reddish-brown in color. Included is part of the Painted Desert, with colored clay hills and badlands, buttes and mesas. Average elevation is about 5,400 feet.

The park has two designated wilderness areas, the 43,020-acre Painted Desert Wilderness and the 7,240-acre Rainbow Forest Wilderness. Vegetation consists of grasslands and desert flora. Deer, antelope, coyote, and bobcat are among the wildlife.

Activities: Backpacking and hiking are allowed throughout the park. There are hardly any developed trails, however, so most travel must be cross-country. Horses are permitted. Hunting is forbidden.

Camping Regulations: A permit is required in order to camp in the backcountry, and may be

obtained from one of the two visitor centers. Camping is restricted to the two wilderness areas, which comprise much of the park. Pets are prohibited.

Campsites must be at least one-half mile from roads. Campfires are not allowed, so a stove must be brought if one wishes to cook. All water must be carried in, and there's no shade. Spring and fall are the best times to visit and camp here.

For Further Information: Petrified Forest National Park, Petrified Forest National Park, AZ 86028; (602)524-6228.

LAKE MEAD NATIONAL RECREATION AREA—896,000 acres in Arizona (1,480,000 acres total). Located in northwest Arizona just west of Grand Canyon National Park, as well as in the southeast corner of Nevada, this National Recreation Area features 110-mile-long Lake Mead and 67-mile-long Lake Mohave. Both were formed by damming up the Colorado River.

In this desert region are mountains, plateaus, canyons, and sandstone formations. With some sandy beaches along the shore, the lake attract many tourists and there's lots of boating. Vegetation includes joshua tree and cactus, with mule deer, bighorn sheep, mountain lion, and coyote among the wildlife.

Activities: Hiking, backpacking, and horseback riding are possible within the National Recreation Area, but most travel must be cross-country since there are few established trails. Fishing is available at the lakes. Hunting is permitted in portions of the area.

Camping Regulations: A large number of established campsites are available along the lakeshores. Backcountry camping and campfires are allowed here as well as elsewhere, except near developed areas or where otherwise prohibited. No permits are required. Since summers are very hot here, the best time to visit is October through May.

For Further Information: Lake Mead National Recreation Area, 601 Nevada Highway, Boulder City, NV 89005; (702)293-8907.

BLM LANDS IN ARIZONA—There are approximately 14,200,000 acres of BLM (Bureau of Land Management) or public domain lands in Arizona, consisting of a great many separate tracts. In recent years no less than 47 wilderness areas totaling 1,400,000 acres have been designated on these lands.

Several of the wilderness areas are quite large, and most are in the western part of the state.

Places of special interest include 3,500-deep Paria Canyon, in the 110,000-acre Paria Canyon-Vermilion Cliffs Wilderness, which has a 37-mile trail.

Elsewhere are 11-mile long Aravaipa Canyon, and also a stretch of the San Pedro River. While brochures are available for some of the most popular areas, little or no printed information exists for many others.

Activities: Backpacking and hiking are possible throughout these lands, as is horseback riding, but there are relatively few established trails. Cross-country travel is often feasible. Mountain biking is permitted outside of wilderness areas. Hunting and fishing are available in season.

Camping Regulations: Camping is allowed on most BLM lands, except where otherwise prohibited. Campfires are also generally permitted but forbidden in a few locations. Bringing a stove is recommended. Permits or registration are required for some of the wilderness areas, and group size is occasionally limited.

For Further Information: Bureau of Land Management, P.O. Box 16563, 3707 North 7th Street, Phoenix, AZ 85011; (602)640-5501.

THE NAVAJO NATION—The enormous Navajo Nation (the Navajo Indian Reservation) in northeast Arizona comprises almost one-fifth of the state. Included is a portion of the Painted Desert, with mountains, canyons, mesas, and plateaus.

Of special note here are famous Monument Valley, with its huge sandstone formations, along with the Little Colorado River Gorge, Marble Canyon, and the canyons of the San Juan River.

Activities: Hiking and backpacking are available on some unmaintained trails and paths. Visitors are asked to stay on trails and established routes. Fishing and hunting are allowed, but a permit is required for these activities.

Camping Regulations: A backcountry camping and use permit must be obtained in order to camp along the trails here. Permits are available in person or by mail, and a fee is charged for each night's stay.

Some areas such as Navajo Mountain are off-limits to campers. Residential areas should also be avoided. Campfires are prohibited. Since summers are hot and winters cold, spring and fall are the best seasons to visit.

For Further Information: The Navajo Nation, P.O. Box 308, Window Rock, AZ 86515; (602)871-4941.

KOFA NATIONAL WILDLIFE REFUGE—665,460 acres. This large National Wildlife Refuge in the southwestern part of the state encompasses an area of desert with two mountain ranges, the Kofa and Castle Dome Mountains. Some of the terrain here is rugged.

About 516,000 acres of the refuge have wilderness status. Vegetation includes cactus, mesquite, and other desert plants, along with some California palm trees in Palm Canyon. Bighorn sheep, mule deer, coyote, and fox are among the wildlife.

Water is generally scarce, but there are a number of waterholes. Roads in the refuge are rough, so 4-wheel drive vehicles are necessary on some routes. Fall through spring are the recommended times to visit. Summers are quite hot.

Activities: Backpacking and hiking are allowed, but there are no established trails other than a 1-mile path. The refuge is open to horses as well. Limited hunting is permitted in season.

Camping Regulations: Camping is allowed almost anywhere in this National Wildlife Refuge, except within 100 feet of roads or one-quarter mile of water sources. Although campfires are permitted, bringing a stove for cooking is recommended.

For Further Information: Kofa National Wildlife Refuge, 356 West First Street, P.O. Box 6290, Yuma, AZ 85364; (602)783-7861.

ORGAN PIPE CACTUS NATIONAL MONUMENT— 330,000 acres. Located in southwestern Arizona along the Mexican border, this National Monument protects an area of the Sonoran Desert. Included are some low mountains and canyons, with organ pipe cactus, saguaro cactus, cholla, and other desert vegetation. Among the region's wildlife are desert bighorn sheep, deer, and coyote.

Activities: Hiking and backpacking are possible, as is horseback riding, but there are only a few maintained trails. Most travel must be cross-country. Hunting is prohibited.

Camping Regulations: A free permit, available from the visitor center, is required to camp in the backcountry. There's one "backcountry campground," and camping is permitted elsewhere as well. Pets are prohibited.

Campsites must be at least one-half mile from any road, historic site, or water source. The maximum stay at any one site is two nights. Campfires are not allowed, so a stove must be used for cooking. October through May are the best times to camp here.

For Further Information: Organ Pipe Cactus National Monument, Route 1, Box 100, Ajo, AZ 85321; (602)387-6849.

SAGUARO NATIONAL MONUMENT—83,651 acres. This National Monument in southern Arizona is divided into two units, which are on opposite sides of Tucson. The Monument was established to protect the giant saguaro cactus, which stands up to 50 feet tall and may weigh eight tons, as well as other flora and fauna of the Sonoran Desert.

Terrain ranges from foothills to mountains and canyons. Included here is the 59,930-acre Rincon Mountain Wilderness. Vegetation varies from desert grasslands and scrub through pine-oak woodlands, with mixed conifer forests at high elevations. Among the wildlife are javelina, coyote, and fox.

Activities: Hiking and backpacking are allowed on over 75 miles of trails in the Rincon Mountain Unit, including 12 miles of the Arizona Trail (see entry page 94). Hiking is also available on a few trails in the smaller western unit. Most trails are open to horses.

Camping Regulations: Camping is restricted to six designated backcountry camping areas in the Rincon Mountain Unit. A free permit is required, and may be obtained in person from the visitor center or by mail or phone.

Campfires are allowed at five of the camping areas, but a stove is recommended for cooking. The recommended time to visit is from October through April, when temperatures are mildest. Summer heat at lower elevations can be intense.

For Further Information: Saguaro National Monument, 3693 South Old Spanish Trail, Tucson, AZ 85730; (602)296-8576.

NAVAJO NATIONAL MONUMENT—Located on Navajo Nation (Navajo Indian Reservation) lands in northeast Arizona, on a high plateau, this National Monument preserves two large cliff dwellings. One of the ruins is Keet Seel, eight miles from the entrance via a rough trail. The site is open only from Memorial Day weekend through Labor Day each year.

Activities: The trail to Keet Seel is open to hiking, backpacking, and horseback riding.

Camping Regulations: Camping is restricted to one primitive campground near the ruins. A free backcountry permit is required, and permits are issued to only 20 people per day. Reservations may be made up to two months in advance by phone or mail. The permit must be picked up in person early the morning of arrival. Campfires are prohibited. Water must be carried in.

For Further Information: Navajo National Monument, HC 71, Box 3, Tonalea, AZ 86044; (602)672-2366.

FORT HUACHUCA—73,000 acres. This U.S. Army Fort in the southern Arizona desert includes a portion of the Huachuca Mountains and several canyons. Highest point is 8,410-foot Huachuca Peak. Forests are found at higher elevations.

Activities: Hiking and backpacking are allowed on a fair-sized trail network. Trails are open to foot travel only. Some trails may be closed at times because of military exercises.

Camping Regulations: Backpack camping is permitted in most areas, except where otherwise prohibited. Visitors must call (602)533-2714 or 533-2622 in advance to inform the Public Affairs Office of their plans, and to check on possible trail closures.

For Further Information: Fort Huachuca, AZ 85613; (602)533-2922.

MARICOPA COUNTY PARKS—Four sizable county parks surround the city of Phoenix: 26,337-acre White Tank Mountain Regional Park, 21,099-acre McDowell Mountain Regional Park, 19,200-acre Estrella Mountain Regional Park, and 14,382-acre Lake Pleasant Regional Park. The scenery here includes mountains up to 4,000 feet, canyons, desert, and 3,500-acre Lake Pleasant.

Activities: Hiking and backpacking are possible on over 50 miles of trails at McDowell Mountain Park, and more than 33 miles of trails at Estrella Mountain Park. Many trails are open to horseback riding. Hunting and fishing are permitted in season.

Camping Regulations: Camping is allowed in backcountry areas of the four parks. A permit must be obtained. Campfires may only be built at designated sites. Very few people currently camp in the backcountry areas of these parks.

For Further Information: Parks and Recreation Department, 3475 West Durango Street, Phoenix, AZ 85009; (602)506-2930.

CABEZA PRIETA NATIONAL WILDLIFE REFUGE— 860,000 acres. Located in southwest Arizona, this large National Wildlife Refuge is in an arid area of rugged terrain, with many mountains and valleys, lava flows, and sand dunes.

The refuge protects wildlife which includes desert bighorn sheep, pronghorn, mule deer, javelina, mountain lion, and bobcat. Cactus, cholla, and mesquite are among the forms of vegetation.

Most of Cabeza Prieta lies within the Goldwater Air Force Range. Low-flying aircraft are possible at any time, and there's a slight risk of encountering unexploded bombs on the ground.

A Refuge Entry Permit is required from the refuge office, and visitors must sign a Military Hold Harmless Agreement. Much of the area is closed to the public during periodic air training exercises.

Activities: Hiking and backpacking are possible throughout the refuge, but there are no maintained trails. Limited hunting is permitted in season.

Camping Regulations: Camping is allowed except where otherwise prohibited. Wood campfires are forbidden. Water must be carried in. A 4-wheel-drive vehicle is necessary to use most refuge roads. Summers are extremely hot here, so fall through spring is the recommended time to visit.

For Further Information: Cabeza Prieta National Wildlife Refuge, 1611 North Second Avenue, Ajo, AZ 85321; (602)387-6483.

MAJOR BACKPACKING TRAILS

ARIZONA TRAIL—This scenic new trail, presently under construction, will be some 700 miles long when completed, and will run the entire length of the state. Portions are currently open for use.

About three-quarters of the Arizona Trail is on National Forest lands. It also passes through Grand Canyon National Park, Saguaro National Monument, and some BLM lands.

The trail is open to hikers, backpackers, and horseback riders. Mountain bikes are allowed on sections outside of wilderness areas. Parts of the trail are also suitable for cross-country skiing in winter.

Camping Regulations: On National Forest lands and BLM lands one may camp almost anywhere, and campfires are generally allowed, except where otherwise prohibited. Campsites should be well off the trail and away from water sources, especially in wilderness areas.

Permits are required to camp in Grand Canyon National Park and Saguaro National Monument. The permits should be obtained in advance, particularly for the Grand Canyon. Designated sites must be used in both of these parks. See the appropriate entries above for complete regulations regarding the two areas.

For Further Information: Arizona Trail Coordinator, Kaibab National Forest, 800 South 6th Street, Williams, AZ 86046.

ARIZONA CAMPING RESOURCES

ORGANIZATIONS WHICH OFFER WILDERNESS CAMPING TRIPS
American Youth Hostels, Arizona–Southern Nevada Council, 1046 East Lemon Street, Tempe,

AZ 85281; (602)894-5128. This AYH council schedules occasional backpacking trips.

Sierra Club, Grand Canyon Chapter, 516 East Portland Street, Phoenix, AZ 85004; (602)254-9330. This Sierra Club chapter sponsors many backpacking trips each year.

USEFUL GUIDEBOOKS

Arizona Trails—Mazel, David. Berkeley, CA: Wilderness Press, 1989.

Grand Canyon Treks—Volumes I, II, & III—Butchart, J. Harvey. Glendale, CA: La Siesta Press, 1983.

The Hiker's Guide to Arizona—Aitchison, Stewart and Grubbs, Bruce. Helena, MT: Falcon Press.

Hiking the Grand Canyon—Annerino, John. San Francisco: Sierra Club Books, 1986.

Hiking Guide to the Santa Rita Mountains of Arizona—Martin, Bob and Dotty. Boulder, CO: Pruett Publishing Co.

Hiking the Southwest—Ganci, Dave. San Francisco: Sierra Club Books, 1983.

Hiking the Southwest's Canyon Country—Hinchman, Sandra. Seattle, WA: The Mountaineers Books.

On Foot in the Grand Canyon—Spangler, Sharon. Boulder, CO: Pruett Publishing Co.

The Sierra Club Guide to the Natural Areas of New Mexico, Arizona, and Nevada—Perry, John and Jane. San Francisco: Sierra Club Books, 1985.

INFORMATION ABOUT STATE PARK CAMPGROUNDS

Arizona State Parks, 800 West Washington, Phoenix, AZ 85007; (602)255-4174.

STATE HIGHWAY MAP AND TRAVEL INFORMATION

Arizona Office of Tourism, 1100 West Washington, Phoenix, AZ 85007; (602)542-TOUR.

ARKANSAS

BEST AREAS FOR WILDERNESS CAMPING

OUACHITA NATIONAL FOREST—1,600,000 acres. This enormous National forest is located in west-central Arkansas and extends into Oklahoma. Some of the terrain here is mountainous, with fine views available from rocky bluffs. Highest point is 2,681-foot Rich Mountain.

There are some beautiful lakes, including gigantic Lake Ouachita, plus many streams and waterfalls. The area is hardwood-forested with stands of old-growth pine.

The Arkansas portion of the National Forest has five designated wilderness areas: the 7,570-acre Black Fork Mountain Wilderness, the 14,430-acre Caney Creek Wilderness, the 6,310-acre Dry Creek Wilderness, the 10,105-acre Flatside Wilderness, and the 10,880-acre Poteau Mountain Wilderness.

Activities: Backpacking and hiking are possible on a number of trails, including 170 miles of the 225-mile Ouachita Trail (see entry page 98) and the 30-mile Womble Trail. There are also many equestrian trails, some of which are open to mountain bikes. Canoeing is available along 45 miles of the Ouachita River. Fishing is also possible, and hunting is permitted in season.

Camping Regulations: Camping is allowed just about anywhere, as are campfires, except near public use areas or where posted otherwise. No permits are necessary. Campsites should be at least 100 feet from trails and streams.

For Further Information: Ouachita National Forest, P.O. Box 1270, Hot Springs, AR 71902; (501)321-5202.

OZARK NATIONAL FOREST—1,300,000 acres. Located in the Ozarks of northwest Arkansas, this National Forest consists of a huge tract which is surrounded by five smaller areas. Some of the terrain is rugged. Included are high rocky bluffs with scenic vistas, caves and caverns, lakes and streams with waterfalls. The highest elevation in the state, 2,823-foot Mount Magazine, is located here. Among the wildlife are black bear and deer.

There are five designated wilderness areas: the 11,094-acre Upper Buffalo Wilderness, with the headwaters of the Buffalo National River, the 10,700-acre East Fork Wilderness, the 15,100-acre Hurricane Creek Wilderness, the 16,900-acre Leatherwood Wilderness, and the 11,800-acre Richland Creek Wilderness.

Activities: Hiking and backpacking are available on over 220 miles of trails, including a 160-mile section of the Ozark Highlands Trail (see entry page 98), the 22-mile Mount Magazine Trail, and the 15-mile North Sylamore Creek Trail.

There are also some horse trails. Canoeing is possible on five rivers in the National Forest, with canoe rentals available nearby, and some rivers are suitable for rafting. Hunting is permitted in season. Fishing is another option.

Camping Regulations: Camping and campfires are allowed almost anywhere, except near public recreation areas or where posted otherwise. No permits are needed.

For Further Information: Ozark National Forest, P.O. Box 1008, 605 West Main, Russellville, AR 72801; (501)968-2354.

BUFFALO NATIONAL RIVER—Flowing through the Ozarks of northwest Arkansas, with lands of Ozark National Forest at either end, the 148-mile Buffalo was designated America's first National

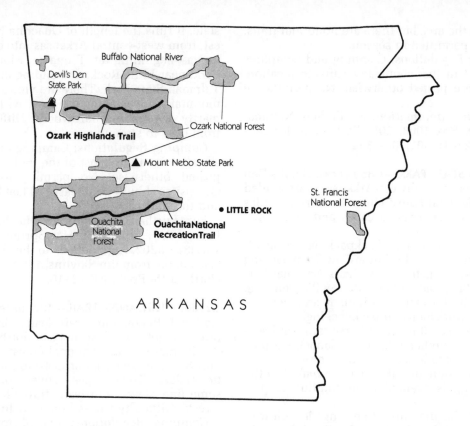

Buffalo National River

Devil's Den State Park

Ozark Highlands Trail

Ozark National Forest

▲ Mount Nebo State Park

St. Francis National Forest

● LITTLE ROCK

Ouachita National Forest

Ouachita National Recreation Trail

A R K A N S A S

River in 1972. Substantial lands are protected in addition to the river itself.

There are sandstone and limestone bluffs up to 500 feet high along the river, other rock formations and caves, many creeks and waterfalls, and oak-hickory forests with willow and cottonwood. Bear, deer, mountain lion, and armadillo are among the wildlife.

Along the National River are three designated wilderness areas: the 22,500-acre Lower Buffalo Wilderness, the 11,300-acre Ponca Wilderness, and the 2,200-acre Upper Buffalo Wilderness.

Activities: Canoeing is very popular on 120 miles of the river, and rafting is also available. Upper sections include whitewater, while lower stretches of the river are mostly calm. Canoes may be rented nearby.

A system of trails for hiking and backpacking is in the process of being developed. Most notable of the trails is the partially completed Buffalo River Hiking Trail, which will eventually extend the length of the river.

There are also some horse trails. Other possible activities include caving and climbing, although the latter is hazardous here on bluffs along the river because of unstable rock. Fishing is also available, and hunting is permitted in season.

Camping Regulations: Camping is allowed almost anywhere along the river, except near developed areas or where otherwise prohibited. No permits are necessary. Those camping by the river are advised to be well above the waterline in case the river rises. No bottles, jars or other glass containers are not allowed. Campfires are permitted, but stoves are recommended for cooking. Pets are prohibited.

For Further Information: Buffalo National River, P.O. Box 1173, Harrison, AR 72602; (501)741-5443.

OTHER RECOMMENDED LOCATIONS

ST. FRANCIS NATIONAL FOREST—20,946 acres. This small National Forest is situated along the Mississippi and St. Francis Rivers on the eastern Arkansas border. It's administered by Ozark National Forest in northwest Arkansas. Much of the region is hilly and hardwood-forested, with two sizable lakes and many creeks, and there are also some riverside flatlands. Wildlife includes deer and turkey.

Activities: Canoeing is available on the rivers here, as is fishing. Hiking and backpacking are possible in the area but there are no formal trails. Hunting is permitted in season.

Camping Regulations: Camping and campfires are allowed in just about any suitable location, except where posted otherwise. No permits are necessary.

For Further Information: St. Francis National Forest, P.O. Box 1008, 605 West Main, Russellville, AR 72801; (501)968-2354.

DEVIL'S DEN STATE PARK—1,850 acres. Devil's Den State Park is in northwest Arkansas, surrounded by Ozark National Forest lands. Scenery includes steep bluffs with overlooks, caves, and rock formations.

Activities: Hiking and backpacking are available on the 14.6-mile Butterfield Backpacking Trail. Much of this trail is in Ozark National Forest, but it starts and ends inside Devil's Den. The park rents backpacking equipment and periodically offers workshops on backpacking.

There are also 20 miles of horse trails and several miles of mountain bike trails. Canoeing is possible on an 8-acre lake and at times on Lee Creek. Canoes and mountain bikes may be rented in the park. Fishing is available, but hunting is prohibited.

Camping Regulations: Camping is allowed along the Butterfield Backpacking Trail, but only outside of the park's boundaries. There are three designated campsites. A free permit must be obtained from the park office. There's also a walk-in camping area within the park, and a fee is charged to camp there.

For Further Information: Devil's Den State Park, 11333 West Arkansas Highway 74, West Fork, AR 72774; (501)761-3325.

MOUNT NEBO STATE PARK—Located in the Ozarks of west-central Arkansas, this state park is situated on top of 1,800-foot Mount Nebo, which offers fine mountain scenery and great views.

Activities: There are 14 miles of trails in the park for hiking and backpacking.

Camping Regulations: Thirteen designated hike-in campsites are located along the 4-mile Bench Trail, which circles the mountain. Camping is restricted to these sites. A fee is charged.

For Further Information: Mount Nebo State Park, Route 3, Box 374, Dardanelle, AR 72834; (501)229-3655.

MAJOR BACKPACKING TRAILS

OUACHITA TRAIL—225 miles. This beautiful National Recreation Trail is the longest trail in the state. It runs the length of Ouachita National Forest, from west-central Arkansas into eastern Oklahoma—beginning at Pinnacle Mountain State Park, near Little Rock, and ending in Oklahoma's Talmena State Park. There are views from rugged mountain ridges along the way, with forests primarily of pine and hardwoods. Difficulty ranges from easy to strenuous.

Camping Regulations: Camping and campfires are allowed along most of the trail, except where posted otherwise. No permits are necessary. Campsites should be at least 100 feet from streams and the trail.

For Further Information: Ouachita National Forest, P.O. Box 1270, Hot Springs, AR 71902; (501)321-5202. A guidebook to the Ouachita Trail is available from Jim Rawlins, 157 Sheridan Road, North Little Rock, AR 72116.

OZARK HIGHLANDS TRAIL—187 miles. This fine National Recreation Trail leads through some rather remote Ozark scenery in northwest Arkansas. It crosses Ozark National Forest, leading from Fort Smith State Park northeast to the Buffalo National River. The trail passes over mountains, with some fine views, and leads through oak-hickory forests. Difficulty varies from easy to strenuous.

Camping Regulations: Except for the westernmost six miles of the trail, camping is allowed along the way, as are campfires. No permits are required. Campsites should be at least 200 feet from water sources and the trail.

For Further Information: Ozark Highlands Trail Association, P.O. Box 1074, Fayetteville, AR 72702; or Ozark National Forest, P.O. Box 1008, 605 West Main, Russellville, AR 72801; (501)968-2354. An *Ozark Highlands Trail Guide* is available from Tim Ernst, 411 Patricia, Fayetteville, AR 72703.

ARKANSAS CAMPING RESOURCES

ORGANIZATIONS WHICH OFFER WILDERNESS CAMPING TRIPS
Ozark Highlands Trail Association, P.O. Box 1074, Fayetteville, AR 72702. This trail association sponsors some backpacking trips each year.

INFORMATION ABOUT TRAILS FOR BACKPACKING
Arkansas Trails Council, One Capitol Mall, Little Rock, AR 72201; (501)682-1301.

STATE HIGHWAY MAP AND TRAVEL INFORMATION
Arkansas Department of Parks and Tourism, One Capitol Mall, Little Rock, AR 72201; (501)682-1301.

CALIFORNIA

BEST AREAS FOR WILDERNESS CAMPING

YOSEMITE NATIONAL PARK—748,542 acres. Located in the mountains of east-central California's Sierra Nevada, Yosemite is one of our most famous and spectacular National Parks. Scenery here includes high rugged peaks and massive granite domes, rock formations and vertical walls, deep canyons and valleys.

Especially renowned is magnificent and awe-inspiring Yosemite Valley. This area has regretfully been overdeveloped and is overused, but the park also has vast areas of wilderness which are much less visited. Top elevation is 13,114-foot Mount Lyell.

Among the high waterfalls is 1,430-foot Upper Yosemite Falls. There are also many lakes and streams, along with forests of fir and pine, giant sequoias, open meadows, and alpine vegetation. Wildlife includes mule deer, black bear, bighorn sheep, mountain lion, and coyote.

Activities: Yosemite has some 800 miles of trails for backpacking and hiking, including sections of the 210-mile John Muir and Pacific Crest Trails (see entries page 113), which coincide in the park.

Difficulty varies from easy to quite strenuous. High trails are often under snow until July. Trails around Yosemite Valley tend to be very crowded during the hiking season.

Many trails are open to horses, which may be rented in Yosemite Valley. Cross-country skiing is possible on a number of trails during the winter. Mountain bike use is restricted to roads and bike paths.

Rock climbing and mountaineering may be practiced on the rock faces and mountains here. Climbing and backpacking instruction are offered in the park. Fishing is available alongside streams and lakes. Hunting is prohibited.

Camping Regulations: A wilderness permit is required in order to camp in the backcountry. Permits may be obtained at the visitor center and several other locations in the park.

Quotas are set for each trailhead. Advance reservations are available and recommended, especially for popular trails and weekends. Reservations may be made by mail only from February 1-May 31, for the period of May 15 through September 15.

An itinerary should be included. Half of the available permits are issued in person on a first-come, first-served basis, and may be picked up 24 hours or less before starting out.

Camping is allowed in most but not all regions of the park. It's not permitted within four miles of either Yosemite Valley or Tuolumne Meadows. Sites chosen should be at least 100 feet from trails and water sources, and one mile from park roads.

Campfires are allowed below 9,000 feet elevation, but are restricted to existing fire rings. A stove is recommended. Groups traveling more than one-quarter mile off the trail are limited to a maximum of eight. Pets are prohibited in the backcountry.

For Further Information: Yosemite National Park, P.O. Box 577, Yosemite National Park, CA 95389; (209)372-0264.

SEQUOIA AND KINGS CANYON NATIONAL PARKS—864,118 acres. Surrounded by National Forest lands in east-central California, and southeast of Yosemite, these two jointly-administered National Parks enclose some of the most magnificent scenery of the High Sierra. Included is 14,495-foot Mount Whitney, highest mountain in the lower 48 states.

Most of the region consists of wilderness, with lofty snow-capped peaks and steep-walled canyons, rivers and lakes, and streams with waterfalls. Among the canyons is 8,000-foot-deep Kings Canyon, said to be the deepest in the United States, with the South Fork Kings River flowing through.

There are many stands of giant sequoia, including the 2,500-year-old General Sherman Tree, believed to be the largest tree on earth, along with virgin forests of mixed conifers, oak woodlands, mountain meadows, and areas of chaparral. Among the wildlife are mule deer, black bear, bighorn sheep, mountain lion, coyote, and bobcat.

Activities: These two National Parks have over 800 miles of trails for hiking and backpacking, including sections of the Pacific Crest Trail and the John Muir Trail (see entries page 113), which coincide. Difficulty ranges from easy to strenuous. High trails may only be snow-free from July to October.

Many trails are suitable for horseback riding, and cross-country skiing is available on some trails in the winter. Bikes are not permitted in the backcountry. Fishing is possible at lakes and streams. Hunting is prohibited.

Camping Regulations: Backcountry camping is allowed in most regions. A wilderness permit is required, and available at ranger stations. A fire permit is necessary as well in order to have a campfire. In some areas camping and campfires are prohibited or restricted to designated sites, especially near lakes.

Quotas are in effect for the number of backpackers allowed to enter daily at each trailhead. Advance reservations may be made by mail. Reservations are taken as of March 1 each year for all dates through the summer.

Whenever possible, campsites should be located at least 100 feet from water sources, and out of sight of trails and other campers. Avoid camping in meadows or on other vegetation.

For Further Information: Sequoia and Kings Canyon National Parks, Three Rivers, CA 93271; (209)565-3307.

SHASTA–TRINITY NATIONAL FOREST—2,159,000 acres. Located in northern California, this enormous National Forest encompasses outstanding high-mountain scenery, with lofty snow-covered peaks, rock pinnacles, lava flows, glaciers, and deep canyons. Highest point is 14,162-foot Mount Shasta, second highest volcano in the Cascades.

There are also beautiful lakes and rivers, streams with waterfalls, mountain meadows, areas of chaparral, and mixed forests of fir, pine, and cedar, including old-growth stands. Among the wildlife are mule deer, black bear, mountain lion, coyote, bobcat, and fox.

The National Forest has five designated wilderness areas: a portion of the 500,000-acre Trinity Alps Wilderness, the 38,200-acre Mount Shasta Wilderness, 37,094 acres of the 109,000-acre Yolla Bolly–Middle Eel Wilderness, the 8,200-acre Chanchelulla Wilderness, and the 7,300-acre Castle Crags Wilderness.

Activities: Some 1,400 miles of trails are available for backpacking and hiking, including a 154-mile section of the Pacific Crest Trail (see entry page 113). Difficulty varies from easy to very strenuous. High trails may be under snow until July.

Horseback riding is allowed on most trails, and cross-country skiing is possible in some areas during the winter. White-water canoeing and kayaking are available on the Trinity River. Mount Shasta and other mountains attract technical climbers. Fishing is another option, and hunting is permitted in season.

Camping Regulations: Camping is allowed throughout most of the National Forest, except near public use areas or where otherwise prohibited. Wilderness permits are required only for camping in the Yolla Bolly–Middle Eel Wilderness.

Campfires are allowed but discouraged, and should be kept small. A stove is recommended for cooking. It's necessary to obtain a fire permit in order to build a campfire or use a stove. Campsites in wilderness areas should be away from meadows and at least 100 feet from water sources.

For Further Information: Shasta–Trinity National Forest, 2400 Washington Avenue, Redding, CA 96001; (916)246-5443.

LOS PADRES NATIONAL FOREST—1,724,000 acres. This huge National Forest consists of two tracts along the coast of south-central California, with lands northwest of Los Angeles as well as in the Big Sur area to the north. There are several mountain ranges here, with 8,831-foot Mount Pinos the highest point.

The rugged scenery in Los Padres includes steep peaks, sculpted rock formations, canyons, and cliffs. A portion of the famous Big Sur coastline falls within the forest boundaries, along with some areas of desert.

In the region are some notable rivers, streams with waterfalls, and hot springs—plus oak woodlands, forests of pine, cedar, and fir, including stands of redwoods, and extensive chaparral. Wildlife includes deer, bear, mountain lion, coyote, bobcat, and fox.

There are five designated wilderness areas: the 164,503-acre Ventana Wilderness, the 149,170-acre San Rafael Wilderness, the 64,700-acre Dick Smith Wilderness, the 21,678-acre Santa Lucia Wilderness, and the 20,000-acre Machesna Mountain Wilderness.

Activities: Backpacking and hiking are possible on about 1,200 miles of trails. Difficulty ranges from easy to strenuous. Some trails receive heavy use.

Horseback riding is allowed on all trails, although a few routes are not advisable for horses. Mountain bikes may be ridden on some trails outside of wilderness areas.

Limited cross-country skiing is available during winter in the Mount Pinos area. Fishing is possible in some streams and rivers, especially in the spring. Hunting is permitted in season.

Camping Regulations: Camping is allowed throughout much of the National Forest, except where otherwise prohibited. Each year about 415,000 acres of the forest are closed to entry, normally from early July through November, due to the fire hazard.

Permits are necessary to enter the wilderness areas at any time of year. Camping in wilderness areas is restricted to designated sites, and campfires are prohibited.

Elsewhere in the forest a fire permit is required to build a campfire or use a stove during the annual period of fire danger. At times campfires are banned or limited to designated sites. Summers are hot and dry in many regions of the forest, so fall through spring are generally the best times to visit.

For Further Information: Los Padres National Forest, 6144 Calle Real, Goleta, CA 93117; (805)683-6711.

SEQUOIA NATIONAL FOREST—1,115,375 acres. This National Forest consists of several tracts near and adjacent to Sequoia National Park, in south-central California. It includes high mountains of the Sierra Nevada, with 12,432-foot Mount Florence the top elevation.

There are rugged peaks, granite domes, rock formations, deep canyons, foothills, and areas of desert here, along with some lakes, rivers, and creeks with waterfalls.

Of special interest are the many giant sequoias, which stand as high as 270 feet, with diameters which occasionally exceed 30 feet. There are also forests of mixed conifers, oak woodlands, and grasslands. Wildlife includes mule deer, black bear, mountain lion, coyote, bobcat, and fox.

Sequoia National Forest has five designated wilderness areas: 142,855 acres of the 305,484-acre Golden Trout Wilderness, the 94,695-acre Dome Land Wilderness, 24,650 acres of the 63,000-acre South Sierra Wilderness, 23,800 acres of the 45,000-acre Monarch Wilderness, and the 10,500-acre Jennie Lakes Wilderness.

Activities: Hiking and backpacking are available on over 900 miles of trails, including a section of the Pacific Crest Trail (see entry page 113), as well as the 40-mile Silver Knapsack Trail. Difficulty ranges from easy to strenuous.

Horseback riding is allowed on most trails. Cross-country skiing is possible on some of the trails during winter. The Kings River is suitable for rafting and kayaking, and fishing is available. Hunting is permitted in season.

Camping Regulations: Camping is allowed throughout most of the National Forest, except where posted otherwise. A wilderness permit, available in person or by mail, is required to camp in the Golden Trout Wilderness or along the Pacific Crest Trail.

Campsites should be at least 100 feet from trails and water sources. A fire permit must be obtained from a forest office in order to use a stove or build a campfire from May 15-October 31.

For Further Information: Sequoia National Forest, 900 West Grand Avenue, Porterville, CA 93257; (209)784-1500.

INYO NATIONAL FOREST—1,798,638 acres in California. Inyo National Forest consists of long and narrow tracts in the Sierras east of Yosemite, Sequoia, and Kings Canyon National Parks. Mountains here include 14,495-foot Mount Whitney, highest point in the lower 48 states.

Terrain consists of steep jagged peaks, deep canyons and cliffs, boulders and rock domes, glaciers, rolling hills, and some desert. There are also meadows with wildflowers, hundreds of lakes, and streams with waterfalls.

In the area is an ancient forest of bristlecone pine, said to be the oldest living things on the earth, along with stands of pine and fir, hemlock and aspen. Wildlife includes deer, black bear, bighorn sheep, coyote, bobcat, and fox.

This National Forest has five designated wilderness areas, consisting of part of the 584,000-acre John Muir Wilderness, 163,145 acres of the 305,484-acre Golden Trout Wilderness, a portion

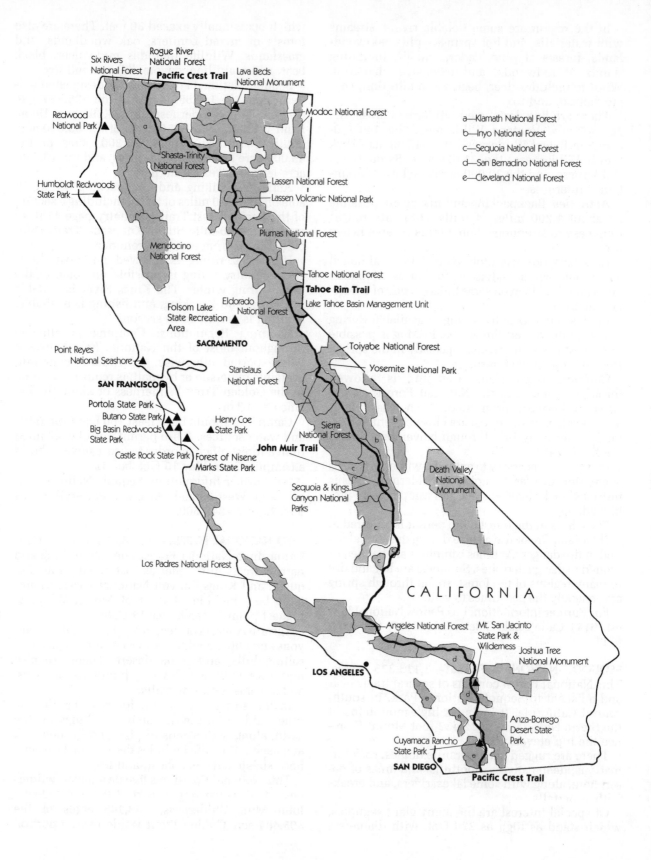

Six Rivers
National Forest

Rogue River
National Forest

Pacific Crest Trail

Lava Beds
National Monument

Redwood
National Park

Modoc National Forest

Shasta-Trinity
National Forest

Humboldt Redwoods
State Park

Lassen National Forest

Lassen Volcanic National Park

Plumas National Forest

Mendocino
National Forest

Tahoe National Forest

Tahoe Rim Trail

Lake Tahoe Basin Management Unit

Folsom Lake
State Recreation
Area

Eldorado
National Forest

Point Reyes
National Seashore

Toiyabe National Forest

SACRAMENTO

Yosemite National Park

Stanislaus
National Forest

SAN FRANCISCO

Portola State Park

Butano State Park

Henry Coe
State Park

Big Basin Redwoods
State Park

Sierra
National Forest

John Muir Trail

Castle Rock State Park

Forest of Nisene
Marks State Park

Sequoia & Kings
Canyon National
Parks

Death Valley
National
Monument

Los Padres National Forest

C A L I F O R N I A

Angeles National Forest

Mt. San Jacinto
State Park &
Wilderness

Joshua Tree
National Monument

LOS ANGELES

Anza-Borrego
Desert State
Park

Cuyamaca Rancho
State Park

SAN DIEGO

Pacific Crest Trail

a—Klamath National Forest
b—Inyo National Forest
c—Sequoia National Forest
d—San Bernadino National Forest
e—Cleveland National Forest

of the 228,500-acre Ansel Adams Wilderness, 38,350 acres of the 63,000-acre South Sierra Wilderness, and 9,507 acres of the 42,800-acre Hoover Wilderness.

Activities: There are more than 1,100 miles of trails for hiking and backpacking, including sections of the John Muir Trail and the Pacific Crest Trail (see entries page 113).

Difficulty ranges from easy to extremely strenuous. Some trails receive heavy use. Trails at high elevations are likely to be free of snow from July to October.

Horses are allowed on most trails. Mountain biking is permitted on many trails outside of wilderness areas. Cross-country skiing is possible in some areas during the winter.

Mountaineering is available in the Minarets Range and elsewhere in the region. Fishing is an option alongside lakes and streams. Hunting is permitted in season.

Camping Regulations: Camping is allowed in most parts of the National Forest, except near public use areas or where otherwise prohibited. Campsites should be at least 100 feet from streams, lakes, meadows, and trails.

A free wilderness permit, which is available from forest offices, is required in order to camp in all wilderness areas except for the South Sierra Wilderness. A quota system is in effect for some areas from late June through mid-September.

Half of the permits may be obtained by advance reservation from March 1-May 31. A small fee is charged for this service. Permits must be picked up in person at the time of entry.

A fire permit is necessary in order to build a campfire or use a stove. Campfires are prohibited in certain areas, and some parts of the forest are closed to camping.

For Further Information: Inyo National Forest, 873 North Main Street, Bishop, CA 93514; (619)873-5841.

SIERRA NATIONAL FOREST—1,303,120 acres. This National Forest stands between Kings Canyon and Yosemite National Parks, in the western Sierras of central California. It's an area of lofty snow-covered peaks, highest of which is 13,986-foot Mount Humphreys, plus small glaciers, rock outcrops, and deep canyons.

There are also many lakes, streams, and rivers—among them the Merced and Kings National Wild and Scenic Rivers—plus hot springs, high meadows and foothills, giant sequoias, and forests of fir, pine, and cedar, including old-growth stands. Among the wildlife are mule deer, black bear, coyote, bobcat, and fox.

The forest has five designated wilderness areas, consisting of about half of the 584,000-acre John Muir Wilderness, 138,660 acres of the 228,500-acre Ansel Adams Wilderness, the 30,000-acre Dinkey Lakes Wilderness, the 22,700-acre Kaiser Wilderness, and 21,200 acres of the 45,000-acre Monarch Wilderness.

Activities: Backpacking and hiking are possible on 1,100 miles of trails, including sections of the John Muir and Pacific Crest Trails (see entries page 113), which coincide here. Difficulty varies from easy to strenuous. High elevations may be under snow until July.

Most trails are open to horses. Some trails are marked for cross-country skiing, and snowshoeing is another winter option. Whitewater rafting and kayaking are available in spring and early summer on the Upper Kings and Merced Rivers. Hunting is permitted in season, and fishing is also possible.

Camping Regulations: Camping is allowed in most of the region, except where posted otherwise. A fire permit is necessary in order to use a stove or build a campfire anywhere in the forest. Campfires may be banned in times of fire danger.

A free wilderness permit is required to camp in all wilderness areas, with a quota system in effect from late June through mid-September for some areas. Campsites should be at least 100 feet from meadows and water sources.

Permits may be obtained from forest offices, and advance reservations are available by mail for a small charge. The permit must be picked up in person at the start of one's trip.

For Further Information: Sierra National Forest, 1600 Tollhouse Road, Clovis, CA 93612; (209)487-5155.

KLAMATH NATIONAL FOREST—1,671,053 acres. Klamath National Forest is made up of two large units in northern California, near or alongside the Oregon border. On these lands are portions of several mountain ranges, with elevations from under 1,000 feet to over 8,500 feet.

There are precipitous peaks, glacier-carved bowls, and rocky canyons here, along with several rivers, and many lakes and streams. Forests are of mixed conifers, with ponderosa pine and old-growth fir, plus some hardwoods.

Also included are large areas of grasslands, and some mountain meadows. Elk, antelope, wild horse, black bear, mule and black-tailed deer, wolverine, and fox are among the wildlife.

The forest has three designated wilderness areas: the 242,000-acre Marble Mountain Wilderness, 15,000 acres of the 500,000-acre Trinity Alps

Wilderness, and the 12,000-acre Russian Wilderness.

Activities: More than 1,100 miles of trails are available for backpacking and hiking, including a section of the Pacific Crest Trail (see entry page 113). Difficulty ranges from easy to strenuous. High-elevation trails may be under snow until July.

Horseback riding is allowed on most trails, and mountain biking is possible on many trails outside of wilderness areas. Some routes are designated for cross-country skiing in winter.

White-water rafting, canoeing, and kayaking are available on the Salmon, Scott, and Klamath Rivers. Canoes, kayaks, and rafts may be rented nearby. It's also possible to fish along the many creeks and lakes, and hunting is permitted in season.

Camping Regulations: Except where posted otherwise, camping is allowed throughout the National Forest. A fire permit is necessary if one wishes to make a campfire or use a stove during the fire season.

A wilderness permit is required for the Trinity Alps Wilderness but not the Marble Mountain or Russian Wilderness areas. Campsites should be at least 100 feet from water sources and away from trails.

For Further Information: Klamath National Forest, 1312 Fairlane Road, Yreka, CA 96097; (916)842-6131.

STANISLAUS NATIONAL FOREST—899,894 acres. This National Forest in central California is situated north and west of Yosemite National Park, in the western Sierras. It's an area of volcanic mountains, rocky ridges, and deep gorges. Highest elevation is 11,520-foot Leavitt Peak.

Stanislaus has several major rivers, many streams, glacial lakes, mountain meadows, alpine vegetation, and forests of fir, cedar, and pine, including some old-growth stands. Among the wildlife are mule deer, black bear, coyote, bobcat, and fox.

There are three designated wilderness areas: the 113,000-acre Emigrant Wilderness, 78,000 acres of the 160,000-acre Carson-Iceberg Wilderness, and 22,000 acres of the 105,165-acre Mokelumne Wilderness.

Activities: Hiking and backpacking are possible on about 700 miles of trails, including a section of the Pacific Crest Trail (see entry page 113). Difficulty varies from easy to strenuous. Some high trails are likely to be snow-free only from July through September.

Horses are permitted on most trails. Some trails are suitable for cross-country skiing and snowshoeing during winter. Whitewater kayaking and canoeing are available on the Tuolumne and Stanislaus Rivers. Hunting and fishing are allowed in season.

Camping Regulations: Camping is permitted in most parts of the National Forest, except where posted otherwise. Campsites should be at least 100 feet from streams and lakeshores. Stoves are recommended for cooking. A fire permit must be obtained in order to use a stove or have a campfire.

A free wilderness permit is required for camping in designated wilderness areas between May 25 and September 30. The permit may be obtained by mail or in person. No quotas are in effect at the current time.

For Further Information: Stanislaus National Forest, 19777 Greenley Road, Sonora, CA 95370; (209)532-3671.

SAN BERNARDINO NATIONAL FOREST—658,664 acres. San Bernardino National Forest consists of two tracts in southern California. Terrain here includes high peaks and ridges, rock gorges and canyons, hilly lowlands, and desert. Highest point is 11,502-foot San Gorgonio Mountain.

There are rivers and creeks, mountain meadows, areas of chaparral, and forests of ponderosa and lodgepole pine, white and Douglas fir, along with juniper and pinyon. Mule deer, black bear, bighorn sheep, mountain lion, coyote, and bobcat are among the wildlife.

This National Forest has five designated wilderness areas: the 54,162-acre San Gorgonio Wilderness, the 31,680-acre San Jacinto Wilderness, 14,200 acres of the 20,000-acre Santa Rosa Wilderness, the 8,581-acre Cucamonga Wilderness, and 2,560 acres of the Sheep Mountain Wilderness.

Activities: Backpacking and hiking are available on 526 miles of trails, including a section of the Pacific Crest Trail (see entry page 000). Difficulty varies from easy to strenuous.

Cross-country skiing and snowshoeing are possible on some trails in winter. Horseback riding is allowed on most trails. Fishing is also available. Hunting is permitted during the appropriate season.

Camping Regulations: Camping is allowed throughout the National Forest, except near public use areas or where otherwise prohibited. A fire permit is necessary in order to have a campfire or use a stove from May 15 until approximately December 15. Some regions may be closed to entry during this period.

A free wilderness permit is required to camp in designated wilderness areas. Daily quotas are in effect. Permits are available in person or by mail up to three months in advance.

For Further Information: San Bernardino National Forest, 1824 South Commercenter Circle, San Bernardino, CA 92408; (714)383-5588.

ANGELES NATIONAL FOREST—652,704 acres. Consisting of tracts north and east of Los Angeles, this National Forest includes rugged peaks of the San Gabriel Mountains, with rock formations and outcrops, cliffs and canyons. Highest point in the forest is 10,064-foot Mount Baldy.

In the region are many streams with waterfalls and several rivers, along with forests of pine, fir, and cedar, some 2,000-year-old Limber pines, plus chaparral and manzanita. Among the wildlife are mule deer, black bear, bighorn sheep, and coyote.

There are three designated wilderness areas: the 44,000-acre Sheep Mountain Wilderness, the 36,000-acre San Gabriel Wilderness, and 8,500 acres of the Cucamonga Wilderness.

Activities: This National Forest has about 525 miles of trails for hiking and backpacking, including 131 miles of the Pacific Crest Trail (see entry page 113) and the 53-mile Silver Moccasin Trail. Difficulty ranges from easy to strenuous. Some routes receive heavy use.

Horseback riding is possible on most trails. Cross-country skiing is available on some trails and roads during winter. Hunting and fishing are permitted in season.

Camping Regulations: Camping is allowed throughout most of Angeles National Forest, except where posted otherwise. Sites should be at least 100 feet from trails and water sources, and 200 feet from other campsites.

A free fire permit is required for the use of stoves and campfires from May 15 until the winter rain season. A wilderness permit is necessary in order to enter and camp in the Sheep Mountain and Cucamonga Wilderness areas, but not in the San Gabriel Wilderness. Permits are available in person or by mail.

For Further Information: Angeles National Forest, 701 North Santa Anita Avenue, Arcadia, CA 91006; (818)574-5200.

TAHOE NATIONAL FOREST—811,740 acres. Situated in the Sierras of north-central California, northwest of Lake Tahoe, this National Forest has high peaks, rocky knobs and outcrops, and deep river canyons with sheer cliffs. Elevations range from 1,500 feet to 9,400 feet.

The North Fork American River, a National Wild and Scenic River, is one of several major waterways here. There are also many streams and small alpine lakes, plus fir, pine, and hemlock forests, including some old-growth stands, along with hardwoods.

Mule deer, black bear, mountain lion, coyote, and bobcat are among the wildlife. The National Forest has one designated wilderness area, the 25,000-acre Granite Chief Wilderness.

Activities: Backpacking and hiking are possible on about 500 miles of trails, including a section of the Pacific Crest Trail (see entry page 113). Difficulty varies from easy to strenuous. Some trails at high elevations are under snow until July each year.

Rafting, kayaking, and canoeing are available on several rivers. Horseback riding is allowed on most trails, as is mountain biking except in wilderness areas. Some trails are designated for Nordic skiing. Fishing is feasible alongside rivers, streams, and lakes. Hunting is permitted in season.

Camping Regulations: Camping is allowed in most areas of the National Forest, except where posted otherwise. Campsites should be well away from water sources and trails.

A fire permit is necessary if one wishes to have a campfire or use a stove from May through the fire season, which usually ends in November. Wilderness permits are not required.

For Further Information: Tahoe National Forest, Highway 49 & Coyote Street, Nevada City, CA 95959; (916)265-4531.

ELDORADO NATIONAL FOREST—668,947 acres. This attractive National Forest is situated in the High Sierra directly west and south of Lake Tahoe, in the north-central part of the state. Among the high mountains here is 9,983-foot Pyramid Peak. There are also canyons and a number of lakes and creeks.

Vegetation includes high meadows with wildflowers and forests of lodgepole pine, whitebark fir, and hemlock, with some old-growth stands. Among the wildlife are mule deer, black bear, mountain lion, coyote, bobcat, and fox.

Eldorado has two designated wilderness areas, consisting of the 63,470-acre Desolation Wilderness and a portion of the 105,165-acre Mokelumne Wilderness.

Activities: About 350 miles of trails are available for backpacking and hiking, including sections of the Pacific Crest Trail and the new Tahoe Rim Trail (see entries page 113). Difficulty varies from easy to strenuous. Some trails receive heavy use.

Most trails are open to horseback riding, and to mountain biking outside of wilderness areas. Cross-country skiing is possible on some trails during the winter. Fishing is available, as is hunting during the appropriate season.

Camping Regulations: Camping is allowed throughout most of the region, except where posted otherwise. A fire permit must be obtained in order to use a stove or build a campfire.

A wilderness permit is also required in order to camp in wilderness areas from May through September. Quotas are in effect. Advance reservations may be made for permits.

For Further Information: Eldorado National Forest, 3070 Camino Heights Drive, Camino, CA 95709; (916)644-6048.

LASSEN VOLCANIC NATIONAL PARK—106,372 acres. Located in the Cascades of northern California and surrounded by lands of Lassen National Forest, this National Park features a number of volcanic mountains, including 10,457-foot Lassen Peak.

The park has craters, cinder cones, lava flows, and deep canyons, with hot springs and other thermal areas, streams, and some lakes. There are also meadows and forests of fir and pine. Deer, bear, mountain lion, and coyote are among the wildlife.

Activities: Backpacking and hiking are available on 150 miles of trails, including a 17-mile section of the Pacific Crest Trail (see entry page 113). Difficulty varies from easy to strenuous. Higher elevations are likely to be free of snow only from July through September.

Some trails are open to horseback riding. Cross-country skiing and snowshoeing are possible on trails in the winter. Fishing is available along the streams and lakes. Bikes are not allowed on trails, and hunting is prohibited.

Camping Regulations: A free wilderness permit is required in order to camp in the backcountry here. Permits may be obtained in person, or requested by mail or phone two weeks in advance. Some areas in the park are closed to camping.

Campsites should be at least 100 feet from water sources and trails, away from meadows and other vegetation, and one mile from roads and developed areas. Campfires are prohibited, so a stove is necessary if one wishes to cook. Maximum group size allowed is 10. Pets are not permitted in the backcountry.

For Further Information: Lassen Volcanic National Park, P.O. Box 100, Mineral, CA 96063; (916)595-4444.

PLUMAS NATIONAL FOREST—1,409,986 acres. Located in the Sierras of northeast California, Plumas National Forest has elevations from 1,000 to 8,000 feet, with rocky mountains and ridges, canyons and cliffs.

There are also lakes, rivers, and creeks with waterfalls—highest of which is 640-foot Feather Falls—along with mountain meadows, conifer forests, and areas of sagebrush and manzanita.

This National Forest has a single designated wilderness area, the 21,000-acre Bucks Lake Wilderness. Wildlife includes mule deer, mountain lion, black bear, coyote, and bobcat.

Activities: There are over 300 miles of trails for hiking and backpacking, including 75 miles of the Pacific Crest Trail (see entry page 113). Difficulty ranges from easy to strenuous.

Horseback riding is possible on most trails. Mountain biking is allowed as well, but not in the wilderness area or on the Pacific Crest Trail. Hunting and fishing are permitted in season.

Camping Regulations: Camping is allowed throughout most of the National Forest, except near public recreation areas or where otherwise prohibited. Wilderness permits are not required.

A fire permit is necessary, however, in order to build a campfire or use a stove. Campsites should be away from meadows and trails, and at least 100 feet from water sources.

For Further Information: Plumas National Forest, 159 Lawrence Street, Quincy, CA 95971; (916)283-2050.

MENDOCINO NATIONAL FOREST—876,236 acres. Located in northwest California, Mendocino National Forest encompasses mountains with elevations as high as 8,000 feet, deep canyons, and lowlands with numerous streams.

There are also meadows, grasslands and brushlands, and forests of fir and pine, hemlock and juniper, including some old-growth trees. Black-tailed deer, black bear, mountain lion, coyote, and bobcat are among the wildlife.

This National Forest has two designated wilderness areas: 73,997 acres of the 109,000-acre Yolla Bolly-Middle Eel Wilderness, which continues on into Shasta–Trinity National Forest, and also the 37,000-acre Snow Mountain Wilderness.

Activities: Backpacking and hiking are possible on about 600 miles of trails. Difficulty ranges from easy to strenuous. Most trails are open to horses, and some of the routes are suitable for cross-country during winter.

Limited canoeing and kayaking are available on a couple of creeks, and fishing is also possible along streams and lakes. Hunting is permitted in season.

Camping Regulations: Camping is allowed throughout most of the National Forest, except where posted otherwise. A fire permit must be obtained to use a stove or build a campfire. A free wilderness permit, which doubles as a fire permit, must be obtained to camp in the Yolla Bolly–Middle Eel Wilderness.

For Further Information: Mendocino National Forest, 420 East Laurel Street, Willows, CA 95988; (916)934-3316.

CLEVELAND NATIONAL FOREST—419,841 acres.

Consisting of tracts in southern California, including one near the Mexican border, Cleveland National Forest is in an arid region of low mountain ranges and deep canyons with seasonal streams. Elevations run as high as 6,000 feet.

There are areas of chaparral, pine-oak woodlands, and forests of conifers at higher elevations. Wildlife includes mule deer, mountain lion, coyote, and bobcat.

Four wilderness areas are found here: the 39,540-acre San Mateo Canyon Wilderness, the 15,900-acre Agua Tibia Wilderness, the 13,000-acre Pine Creek Wilderness, and the 8,000-acre Hauser Wilderness.

Activities: Hiking and backpacking are available on about 200 miles of trails, including a section of the Pacific Crest Trail (see entry page 113). Difficulty varies from easy to strenuous.

Horseback riding is allowed on most trails. Cross-country skiing is possible on some of the higher trails during winter. Fishing is another option, and hunting is permitted in season.

Camping Regulations: Camping is allowed in major portions of the National Forest, but is restricted or prohibited in some areas. Campsites should be at least 100 feet from water sources and meadows. A fire permit is necessary in order to have a campfire or use a stove.

A free wilderness permit, which may be obtained from ranger stations or by mail or phone, is required for camping in all designated wilderness areas. Campfires are prohibited in the wilderness areas, but a stove may be used.

For Further Information: Cleveland National Forest, 880 Front Street, San Diego, CA 92188; (619)557-5050.

SIX RIVERS NATIONAL FOREST—980,285 acres. This

National Forest in northwest California has mountainous terrain and several rivers. Included are portions of the 500,000-acre Trinity Alps Wilderness, the 153,000-acre Siskiyou Wilderness, and the 8,100-acre North Fork Wilderness. Some 200 miles of trails are available, and camping is allowed. Six Rivers did not respond to several requests for information.

For Further Information: Six Rivers National Forest, 507 F Street, Eureka, CA 95501; (707)442-1721.

DEATH VALLEY NATIONAL MONUMENT—2,048,851

acres. Located in south-central California, next to the Nevada border, this enormous National Monument includes famous Death Valley, which has the lowest elevation in the United States: −282 feet at Badwater Basin.

Death Valley is known for extreme temperatures in the summer. In addition to the desert valley, however, there are lofty rugged peaks here—highest of which is 11,049-foot Telescope Peak—along with deep canyons, craters, and sand dunes.

Stands of pine and juniper are found at higher elevations, plus some bristlecone pine. Mule deer, bighorn sheep, mountain lion, and coyote are among the Monument's wildlife.

Activities: There are about 50 miles of trails for backpacking and hiking. Difficulty varies from easy to strenuous. Most trails are primitive and unmaintained. Cross-country travel is feasible throughout much of the Monument.

Climbing and mountaineering are also possible. Climbers should check in at a ranger station before and after the activity. Horseback riding is not recommended here, and hunting is forbidden.

Camping Regulations: Camping is allowed in most areas of the National Monument, except where otherwise prohibited. Camping is not permitted within one-quarter mile of any water source, one mile of a road, or within five miles of a campground.

A permit is not required, but it's suggested that campers fill out a Backcountry Registration Form at a ranger station or visitor center. Pets are not allowed in the backcountry.

Campfires are also prohibited. A stove must be brought if one wishes to cook. Water in the region is very scarce, and it must generally be carried in. Because of the extreme heat, visits between May and October are not recommended.

For Further Information: Death Valley National Monument, Death Valley, CA 92328; (619)786-2331.

LASSEN NATIONAL FOREST—1,060,588 acres. This large National Forest surrounds Lassen National Park in northern California, encompassing mountains of both the northern Sierras and the southern Cascades, with some volcanic peaks and lava formations. Highest point is 8,677-foot Crater Peak.

There are also rugged canyons, caves, plateaus, foothills, meadows, lakes, and ponds, with forests of ponderosa and lodgepole pine, Douglas and red fir. Wildlife includes mule and black-tailed deer, antelope, black bear, mountain lion, and coyote.

Lassen National Forest has three designated wilderness areas: the 41,000-acre Ishi Wilderness, the 20,625-acre Caribou Wilderness, and the 16,335-acre Thousand Lakes Wilderness.

Activities: Backpacking and hiking are available on about 135 miles of trails, including a section of the Pacific Crest Trail (see entry page 113), and also the 30-mile Bizz Johnson Trail.

Difficulty ranges from easy to strenuous. Horseback riding is allowed on most trails. Fishing is possible alongside the lakes and streams. Hunting is permitted in season.

Camping Regulations: Camping is allowed throughout the National Forest, except where posted otherwise. Campsites should be away from meadows and at least 100 feet from trails and water sources.

A fire permit, available from ranger stations, is necessary in order to use a stove or make a campfire. Permits are not currently required for the wilderness areas.

For Further Information: Lassen National Forest, 55 South Sacramento Street, Susanville, CA 96130; (916)257-2151.

TOIYABE NATIONAL FOREST—At 3,856,000 acres, Toiyabe National Forest is the largest National Forest in the United States outside of Alaska. While most of the lands are in Nevada, over 630,000 acres are located in the Sierras of east-central California.

Terrain is mountainous, with elevations as high as 10,000 feet. Parts of the Carson–Iceberg Wilderness, the Mokelumne Wilderness, and the Hoover Wilderness are found here.

Camping is allowed freely in the region, except where posted otherwise. A fire permit is required to use a stove or build a campfire. Wilderness permits must be obtained to camp in designated wilderness areas. See the Toiyabe National Forest listing in the Nevada chapter for more information.

JOSHUA TREE NATIONAL MONUMENT—558,000 acres. Located east of San Bernardino National Forest in southern California's Mojave and Colorado deserts, this large National Monument includes rugged mountains almost 6,000 feet high, canyons, rock formations, and massive boulders.

Some 467,000 acres consist of designated wilderness. There are many stands of Joshua trees in the Monument, along with cactus and other desert vegetation, plus palms at several oases. Bighorn sheep, coyote, and bobcat are among the wildlife.

Activities: Over 50 miles of trails are available for hiking, backpacking, and horseback riding, including 35 miles of the California Riding and Hiking Trail.

Cross-country travel is also possible, although horses must stay on trails or in washes. Rock climbing is a popular activity here. Mountain bike use is limited to roads. Hunting is prohibited.

Camping Regulations: Camping is allowed throughout a large portion of the National Monument, but it's not permitted in several sizable day use areas. Before entering it's necessary to register at one of 12 "backcountry boards" at entry points.

Campsites must be at least 500 feet from trails, one-quarter mile from water sources, and one mile from roads. Washes (dry streams or river beds) should be avoided for camping. Fires are prohibited, so a stove should be brought if one wishes to cook.

Water must be carried in. Since summer heat can be intense, fall through spring are the best times to visit this National Monument. Pets are not permitted in the backcountry.

For Further Information: Joshua Tree National Monument, 74485 National Monument Drive, Twentynine Palms, CA 92277; (619)367-7511.

MODOC NATIONAL FOREST—1,651,232 acres. This extremely large National Forest is made up of tracts in the northeast corner of California. Terrain here is mountainous, with some lofty peaks and volcanoes, cliffs and canyons. Highest point is 9,892-foot Eagle Peak, which is located in the National Forest's one designated wilderness area, the 70,385-acre South Warner Wilderness.

There are glacial lakes and streams, forests of pine and fir, with juniper and sagebrush, plus meadows, grasslands, and alpine vegetation. Wildlife includes mule deer, pronghorn antelope, wild horse, black bear, coyote, and cougar.

Activities: Hiking and backpacking are possible on over 100 miles of trails. Difficulty ranges from easy to strenuous. Horseback riding is allowed on most trails.

Some Nordic skiing and snowshoeing are possible here in the winter. Fishing along the many lakes and streams is another option. Hunting is permitted in season.

Camping Regulations: Camping is allowed in most parts of the National Forest, except near public use areas or where otherwise prohibited. Campsites should be at least 100 feet from water sources and trails. A fire permit must be obtained in order to make a campfire or use a stove.

For Further Information: Modoc National Forest, 441 North Main Street, Alturas, CA 96101; (916)233-5811.

OTHER RECOMMENDED LOCATIONS

BLM LANDS IN CALIFORNIA—California has some 17,200,000 acres of lands in the public domain, administered by the BLM (Bureau of Land Management), and consisting of a great number of tracts scattered around the state. Many of the largest areas are in southeastern California.

On these lands are many major rivers, rugged mountains, deep canyons, badlands with rock formations, and other California Desert scenery. One area of special interest is the 60,000-acre King Range National Conservation Area along the northern coast.

Access to some of the BLM areas is difficult, roads are often not in good condition, and facilities are few. Detailed printed information is not available for many of the locations.

Activities: Most of these lands are open to hiking and backpacking. There aren't many established trails, and those that exist are often short, but the number of trails in California is nevertheless greater than on BLM lands in other states.

Most notable are sections of the Pacific Crest Trail (see entry page 113) and the 35-mile Lost Coast Trail, located in the King Range National Conservation Area. Cross-country travel is feasible in some regions.

Horseback riding is generally allowed, as is mountain biking. Cross-country skiing is an option in areas where there's adequate snow. Rafting, kayaking, and canoeing are available on some of the rivers. Hunting and fishing are permitted in season.

Camping Regulations: Camping is allowed freely on most BLM lands, except near developed areas or where otherwise prohibited. Campsites should be away from trails and water sources. A fire permit is required in order to build a campfire or use a stove. Camping and fires may be restricted or forbidden in some areas.

For Further Information: Bureau of Land Management, 2800 Cottage Way, Sacramento, CA 95825; (916)978-4754.

ANZA–BORREGO DESERT STATE PARK—600,000 acres. Located in the desert region east of Cleveland National Forest, in the southern part of the state, Anza–Borrego is California's largest state park.

There are mountains over 5,000 feet, canyons, badlands, and sandstone formations—with palm oases, some streams, and wildlife which includes bighorn sheep, mule deer, and mountain lion.

Activities: Hiking and backpacking are possible on about 20 miles of short trails, along with segments of the Pacific Crest Trail (see entry page 113) and the California Riding and Hiking Trail. Off-trail travel is also feasible. Horseback riding is freely allowed, whereas bike use is restricted to park roads.

Camping Regulations: This is one of the few state parks in California with minimal restrictions on camping. Some established campsites are available, but with the exception of a handful of locations, one may camp almost anywhere in the park.

Campsites should be well away from water holes and developed areas. Voluntary registration is available at the visitor center, but no permits are necessary. Campfires are prohibited except when built inside metal containers. Water must be carried in.

For Further Information: Anza-Borrego Desert State Park, P.O. Box 299, Borrego Springs, CA 92004; (619)767-5311.

LAVA BEDS NATIONAL MONUMENT—46,239 acres. Lava Beds National Monument is located in northern California, near the Oregon border. It offers a volcanic landscape of lava fields, craters, cinder cones, and nearly 200 lava tubes (caves), with 28,460 acres designated as wilderness.

There are some grasslands and areas of sagebrush, along with stands of ponderosa pine and juniper. Wildlife in the National Monument includes mule deer, mountain lion, and coyote.

Activities: Backpacking and hiking are possible on over 25 miles of trails. Off-trail travel is often difficult. Horses are permitted on three of the trails. Bikes are allowed only on roads.

Caving (spelunking) is available in a large number of underground caves. Registration at the visitor center is recommended before engaging in this activity.

Camping Regulations: Camping is allowed in the backcountry of this National Monument. A free wilderness permit must be obtained from the visitor center.

Campsites must be at least one-quarter mile from trails and roads. Campfires are prohibited, so one should bring a stove in order to cook. Water must be carried in. Pets are not permitted.

For Further Information: Lava Beds National Monument, P.O. Box 867, Tulelake, CA 96134; (916)667-2282.

LAKE TAHOE BASIN MANAGEMENT UNIT—148,000

acres. Located in north-central California, this Forest Service unit was established to protect the lands surrounding famous Lake Tahoe, a 22-mile-long and 6,225-feet-high alpine lake. There's been considerable development nearby.

Elevations in the area are up to 10,000 feet. Included in the unit are small portions of the 63,475-acre Desolation Wilderness, the 105,165-acre Mokelumne Wilderness, and the Granite Chief Wilderness.

Activities: There are over 100 miles of trails for hiking and backpacking, including sections of the new Tahoe Rim Trail (see entry page 113), plus many additional trails in the surrounding National Forests.

Horses are allowed on most trails, as are mountain bikes on trails outside of designated wilderness areas. Cross-country skiing is available in winter. White-water rafting and kayaking are possible on several rivers, as is fishing. Hunting is permitted in season.

Camping Regulations: Camping is allowed in much of the region, except where posted otherwise. A fire permit is required in order to build a campfire or use a stove. Campsites should be at least 100 feet from water sources.

A wilderness permit is necessary in order to enter and camp in the Desolation and Mokelumne Wilderness areas, but not the Granite Chief Wilderness. Permits may be obtained in person or by mail. Quotas are in effect from June 15 through Labor Day. Reservations are available up to 90 days in advance for 50 percent of the permits. Campfires are prohibited in the Desolation Wilderness, but stoves may be used.

For Further Information: Lake Tahoe Basin Management Unit, 870 Emerald Bay Road, Suite 1, South Lake Tahoe, CA 96150; (916)573-2600.

ROGUE RIVER NATIONAL FOREST—While most of

this 638,000-acre National Forest is in Oregon, about 54,000 acres are in the state of California. Terrain here is mountainous, with some elevations over 6,000 feet. Included is a large portion of the 20,234-acre Red Buttes Wilderness.

Camping and campfires are generally allowed throughout the area, except where posted otherwise. A fire permit is necessary in order to have a campfire or use a stove. For more information see the Rogue River National Forest listing in the Oregon chapter.

REDWOOD NATIONAL PARK—106,000 acres. This

long and narrow National Park is located along the coast of northern California. It protects spectacular old-growth stands of redwoods, the tallest trees in the world, reaching as high as 368 feet and as much as 2,000 years old.

Three state parks with redwoods are adjacent to the National Park. Scenery in the region includes rugged coastline with beaches, conifer forests, rivers and streams, and some prairie. Among the wildlife are black-tailed deer, elk, and mountain lion.

Activities: Here and in the state parks are some 150 miles of hiking trails, easy to strenuous in difficulty. Kayaking and canoeing are available on the Smith River. Fishing is possible along some of the rivers and streams. Hunting is prohibited.

Camping Regulations: Backpacking is allowed along just two of the trails. A free backcountry permit is required for the 8.2-mile Redwood Creek Trail, which is fully accessible only from June through September.

Permits are available on a first-come, first-served basis. Camping along the Redwood Creek Trail is limited to gravel bars, as are campfires. Camping is not permitted within one-quarter mile of the Tall Trees Grove.

Camping is also allowed in established sites along the 19.5-mile Coastal Trail. One site only, the Butler Creek Primitive Camp in Prairie Creek Redwoods State Park, requires a permit.

For Further Information: Redwood National Park, 1111 Second Street, Crescent City, CA 95531; (707)464-6101.

POINT REYES NATIONAL SEASHORE—65,303 acres.

Point Reyes National Seashore is on the California coast a short distance north of San Francisco. This area has beautiful beaches, bays, lagoons, and high cliffs, and includes 1,407-foot Mount Wittenberg on the Inverness Ridge.

A sizable portion consist of wilderness. There are forests of fir and pine, plus some grasslands. Among the wildlife are deer, mountain lion, and bobcat, with marine life off the coast.

Activities: The National Seashore has more than 75 miles of trails for hiking and backpacking. Difficulty varies from easy to strenuous. Many trails are open to horses. Mountain bikes are allowed on a few trails outside of the wilderness areas.

Camping Regulations: Camping is restricted to four backcountry camps. A free permit is required, and may be obtained from the visitor center. Maximum stay allowed is four nights. Wood fires are prohibited except on beaches. Pets are not allowed.

For Further Information: Point Reyes National Seashore, Point Reyes, CA 94956; (415)663-1092.

HENRY COE STATE PARK—67,000 acres. Located southeast of San Jose in the west-central part of the state, this is California's second largest state park. It has some steep ridges and canyons, streams, oak woodlands, pine forest, grasslands, and includes a 22,000-acre wilderness area.

Activities: There are 45 miles of trails for hiking and backpacking. Horses are permitted on some but not all trails. Bikes are not allowed on trails.

Camping Regulations: A permit must be obtained from the park museum before camping in the backcountry. It's necessary to use either designated camping areas or camping zones. Horseback riders are required to stay in established horse camps.

A small fee is charged for camping each night. Campfires are prohibited in the backcountry. A stove is necessary for cooking. Pets are not permitted.

For Further Information: Henry Coe State Park, P.O. Box 846, Morgan Hill, CA 95038; (408)779-2728.

HUMBOLDT REDWOODS STATE PARK—51,000 acres. Located close to the coast of northern California, this sizable state park has low ridges, prairies, a stretch of the Eel River, and the largest stands of old-growth redwoods to be found anywhere. Some of the trees are over 300 feet high. There are also forests of Douglas fir and oak, and mule deer are among the wildlife.

Activities: More than 100 miles of trails are available for hiking and backpacking. Horseback riding is possible on a number of old roads. Fishing is feasible along the river.

Camping Regulations: There are five trail camps for backpackers. Camping is restricted to these areas. Advance registration is required, and a small fee is charged for camping each night.

For Further Information: Humboldt Redwoods State Park, P.O. Box 100, Weott, CA 95571; (707)946-2311.

BIG BASIN REDWOODS STATE PARK—16,000 acres. Situated in the Santa Cruz Mountains, south of San Francisco, this state park is noted for 1,500-year-old virgin redwoods, some of which stand over 300 feet tall. There are also streams, mixed conifers, and areas of chaparral and manzanita. Wildlife includes black-tailed deer, mountain lion, and coyote.

Activities: Hiking and backpacking are possible on about 100 miles of trails, including a section of the Skyline to the Sea Trail.

Camping Regulations: There are six trail camps for backpackers, and camping is limited to these designated sites. Reservations must be made at park headquarters.

For Further Information: Big Basin Redwoods State Park, 21600 Big Basin Way, Boulder Creek, CA 95006; (408)338-6132.

CUYAMACA RANCHO STATE PARK—30,000 acres. Located east of San Diego in southern California, this state park includes mountains and mesas, meadows and grasslands, with stands of pine and fir, cedar and oak, and some desert. Highest point is 6,512-foot Cuyamaca Peak. Mule deer, mountain lion, bobcat, and fox are among the wildlife.

Activities: Backpacking and hiking are available on 110 miles of trails, including a section of the California Riding and Hiking Trail. Horses are allowed on most trails.

Cross-country skiing is also possible here when there's adequate snow, and mountain biking is permitted on some trails and old roads. Hunting is prohibited.

Camping Regulations: There are two primitive camps for backpackers, and also one horse campground. Camping is restricted to these areas. A fee is charged for each night. Reservations are recommended and available up to eight weeks in advance.

For Further Information: Cuyamaca Rancho State Park, 12551 Highway 79, Descanso, CA 92016; (619)765-0755.

MOUNT SAN JACINTO STATE PARK AND WILDERNESS—13,000 acres. Located in southern California's San Jacinto Mountains and surrounded by San Bernardino National Forest, this state park includes 10,804-foot San Jacinto Peak and some other high mountains. Over 10,000 acres consist of designated wilderness, and there are forests of fir, pine, and oak.

Activities: Backpacking and hiking are possible on 35 miles of trails, including a section of the Pacific Crest Trail (see entry page 113). Horses are allowed on some trails, and cross-country skiing is available in the winter. Hunting is forbidden.

Camping Regulations: A free permit is required to camp in the Mount San Jacinto State Wilderness. The permit may be obtained in person or by mail up to eight weeks in advance. Quotas are in effect. Advance reservations are advisable in the summer.

Camping is restricted to four designated camping areas, one of which is a larger "wilderness campground." Campfires are not allowed. A stove may be brought for cooking. Pets are prohibited.

For Further Information: Mount San Jacinto State Park & Wilderness, P.O. Box 308, Idyllwild, CA 92349; (714)659-2607.

FOLSOM LAKE STATE RECREATION AREA—18,000 acres. Situated in the Sierra foothills east of Sacramento, this State Recreation Area surrounds a 15-mile-long artificial lake. Included here are some canyons, oak woodlands, and areas of chaparral. Among the wildlife are black-tailed deer, coyote, bobcat, and fox.

Activities: There are about 80 miles of trails for hiking, backpacking, and horseback riding, including the 32-mile Southside Trail. Fishing is available alongside the lake.

Camping Regulations: Twelve "environmental camps," accessible by trail, are located around the lake. Camping is restricted to these sites. Reservations may be made through park headquarters.

For Further Information: Folsom Lake State Recreation Area, 7806 Folsom-Auburn Road, Folsom, CA 95630; (916)988-0205.

PORTOLA STATE PARK—2,600 acres. Portola State Park is located in a canyon in north-central California. The area is forested with mixed conifers, including redwoods. Among the park's wildlife are mule deer, coyote, and bobcat.

Activities: Hiking and backpacking are possible on several trails. Bike use is limited to roads. Horses are not permitted.

Camping Regulations: Primitive camping is restricted to one established trail camp, which is three miles from park headquarters. A fee is charged for camping here each night. Campfires are prohibited. A stove may be used for cooking.

For Further Information: Portola State Park, Box F, Route 2, La Honda, CA 94020; (415)948-9098.

CASTLE ROCK STATE PARK—3,600 acres. Located in the western edge of the Santa Cruz Mountains, in west-central California, this wild state park has elevations from under 1,000 feet to over 3,000 feet. There are steep ridges with rock outcrops and vistas, sandstone caves, meadows, waterfalls, and forests of fir and redwood, oak and pine. Wildlife includes mule deer, coyote, and fox.

Activities: The park has 32 miles of trails for hiking, backpacking, and horseback riding. Included is a section of the Skyline to the Sea Trail. Rock climbing is available on Castle Rock. Hunting is prohibited.

Camping Regulations: Camping is limited to one trail camp, which is located alongside some trails in the center of the park. Campfires are restricted to fire rings provided at the designated sites. Dogs are not allowed, and smoking is forbidden.

For Further Information: Castle Rock State Park, 15000 Skyline Boulevard, Los Gatos, CA 95030; (408)867-2952.

FOREST OF NISENE MARKS STATE PARK—This state park in the Santa Cruz Mountains of west-central California has ridges and canyons, mixed forests, and several creeks. Wildlife here includes black-tailed deer, mountain lion, coyote, and fox.

Activities: There are over 30 miles of trails and fire roads for hiking or backpacking. Horses are allowed in only a small portion of the park. Mountain bikes are restricted to fire roads. Fishing is available along the streams.

Camping Regulations: Camping is limited to one trail camp. Advance reservations must be made for campsites. Campfires are prohibited, but stoves may be used.

For Further Information: Forest of Nisene Marks State Park, 101 North Big Trees Park Road, Felton, CA 95018; (408)335-4598.

BUTANO STATE PARK—2,200 acres. Located in the Santa Cruz Mountains of west-central California, Butano State Park has 400 acres of virgin forest and many redwoods. Mule deer, coyote, and fox are among the wildlife.

Activities: Twenty miles of trails are available for hiking and backpacking.

Camping Regulations: Camping is limited to a single small trail camp, which is located along one of the fire roads some distance from the entrance. Advance reservations are necessary. Campfires are not allowed. A stove must be brought for cooking.

For Further Information: Butano State Park, P.O. Box 9, Pescadero, CA 94060; (415)879-0173.

ENVIRONMENTAL CAMPSITES—Some of California's other state parks now have so-called "environmental campsites," which offer a primitive camping experience. While they are often only a short distance from roads, and some limited facilities may be provided, the sites are normally out of sight of other campsites. For more information contact the California Department of Parks and Recreation, P.O. Box 942896, Sacramento, CA 94296; (916)322-7000.

MAJOR BACKPACKING TRAILS

PACIFIC CREST TRAIL—1,630 miles in California (2,638 total). Extending all the way from Canada to Mexico, the Pacific Crest Trail is one of this country's greatest long-distance wilderness trails. The largest portion is in California, where it runs the length of the Sierras as well as through the southern Cascades.

Scenery along the way couldn't be more magnificent, with high rugged peaks, spectacular vistas, and an endless succession of alpine lakes. Elevations range from 500 feet to 13,200 feet near Mount Whitney. The trail also crosses some desert in southern California.

For most of its length the Pacific Crest Trail is on National Forest, National Park, and BLM lands, along with some state parks and private lands. Difficulty ranges from easy to extremely strenuous. Horses are allowed. Higher elevations are likely to be snow-free only from July through September.

Camping Regulations: Camping is allowed freely along most of the trail, except where posted otherwise. When the trail is on state park or private lands, however, camping is generally restricted to designated sites.

Campsites in National Forests and National Parks should be at least 100 feet from water sources and the trail. Meadows, soft grassy areas, and other vegetation should be avoided in choosing a campsite.

A permit is required to camp in Yosemite as well as Sequoia and Kings Canyons National Parks, and also in many of the National Forest wilderness areas. A single permit may be obtained from a National Forest or National Park office for a trip of any length on the trail.

A fire permit is also necessary if one wishes to build campfires or to use a stove while camping along the trail in this state. Fires are banned in some areas and/or above certain elevations. It's recommended that a stove be carried for cooking.

For Further Information: Pacific Crest Trail Conference, 365 West 29th Avenue, Eugene, OR 97405.

JOHN MUIR TRAIL—210 miles. Running from Yosemite Valley in Yosemite National Park to 14,495-foot Mount Whitney in Sequoia National Park, the John Muir Trail is undoubtedly one of our most wilderness trails. It's the longest trail in the country which isn't crossed by a single road.

Generally remaining at high elevations, the trail passes splendid peaks and a great many lakes, and offers fantastic views along the way. Much of the route is also utilized by the Pacific Crest Trail. Some segments are extremely strenuous.

Camping Regulations: A wilderness permit must be obtained from one of the National Park offices in order to camp along the trail. Some primitive campsites are available, but camping is allowed elsewhere as well along most of the trail.

Campfires are generally permitted below 9,600 feet elevation in Yosemite National Park, below 10,000 feet in Kings Canyon National Park, and below 11,200 feet in Sequoia National Park. A stove is recommended for cooking.

Campsites should be well off the trail and away from water sources and vegetation. Some areas are closed to camping. See the listings for Yosemite National Park as well as Sequoia and Kings Canyon National Parks for complete camping regulations.

For Further Information: Guide to the John Muir Trail—Winnett, Thomas. Berkeley, CA: Wilderness Press, 1984.

TAHOE RIM TRAIL—Currently under construction, this new trail will be about 150 miles long when finished. It encircles huge and spectacular Lake Tahoe, on the California–Nevada border, staying at elevations from over 6,000 feet to 9,600 feet.

Much of the trail has now been completed. Ninety percent is within three National Forests, and it passes through two designated wilderness areas. Small portions are on state park lands. For about 50 miles it coincides with the Pacific Crest Trail.

Terrain in the region is mountainous and generally forested, and there are fine views from the trail. A few sections are rough and rocky. The trail is open to horseback riding and cross-country skiing as well as backpacking and hiking. It's normally free of snow from May through October.

Camping Regulations: Some primitive campsites are available en route, but on National Forest lands one may generally camp elsewhere as well, except where posted otherwise. Campsites should be well off the trail and away from water sources.

A fire permit is required in California in order to use a stove or build a campfire along the trail. A wilderness permit must also be obtained before entering the Desolation Wilderness.

For Further Information: The Tahoe Rim Trail, P.O. Box 10156, South Lake Tahoe, CA 95731; (916)577-0676.

DESERT TRAIL—The Desert Trail is another new long-distance trail which is in the early stages of being built. Some day it should extend all the way from Mexico to Canada, crossing the High Desert of California, Nevada, Oregon, Idaho, and Montana.

Sections totaling about 250 miles have been finished in Oregon, Nevada, and California. Only a small portion of the California route, in the southernmost region of the state, has been completed so far.

For Further Information: Desert Trail Association, P.O. Box 537, Burns, OR 97720. A trail guide for the California section is available from this organization.

CALIFORNIA CAMPING RESOURCES

ORGANIZATIONS WHICH OFFER WILDERNESS CAMPING TRIPS

The following chapters of the Sierra Club sponsor backpacking trips each year. Many chapters offer other kinds of wilderness camping trips as well, and in some cases teach courses in backpacking or wilderness skills.

Sierra Club, Angeles Chapter, 3550 West Sixth Street, Suite 321, Los Angeles, CA 90020.

Sierra Club, Loma Prieta Chapter, 2448 Watson Court, Palo Alto, CA 94303; (415)494-9901.

Sierra Club, Mother Lode Chapter, P.O. Box 1335, Sacramento, CA 95812; (916)557-9669.

Sierra Club, Redwood Chapter, P.O. Box 466, Santa Rosa, CA 95402; (707)544-7651.

Sierra Club, San Diego Chapter, 3820 Ray Street, San Diego, CA 92104; (619)299-1743.

Sierra Club, San Gorgonio Chapter, 568 North Mountain View Avenue, Suite 130, San Bernadino, CA 92401.

USEFUL GUIDEBOOKS

The Anza–Borrego Desert Region—Lindsay and Lindsay. Berkeley, CA: Wilderness Press, 1991.

California Camping—Stienstra, Tom. Helena, MT: Falcon Press.

Carson–Iceberg Wilderness—Schaffer, Jeffrey P. Berkeley, CA: Wilderness Press, 1992.

A Climber's Guide to the High Sierra—Roper, Steve. San Francisco: Sierra Club Books.

Climber's Guide to Yosemite Valley—Roper, Steve. San Francisco: Sierra Club Books.

Desolation Wilderness—Schaffer, Jeffrey P. Berkeley, CA: Wilderness Press, 1985.

Emigrant Wilderness—Schifrin, Ben. Berkeley, CA: Wilderness Press, 1990.

Exploring the Southern Sierra: East Side—Jenkins, J. C. and Jenkins, Ruby Johnson. Berkeley, CA: Wilderness Press, 1992.

Exploring the Yellowstone Backcountry—Bach, Orville E. San Francisco: Sierra Club Books.

Guide to the John Muir Trail—Winnett, Thomas. Berkeley, CA: Wilderness Press, 1984.

The High Sierra: Peaks, Passes, and Trails—Secor, R. J. Seattle: The Mountaineers Books.

Hiker's Guide to California—Adkinson, Ron. Helena, MT: Falcon Press.

Hiker's Hip Pocket Guide to the Humboldt Coast—Lorentzen, Bob. Berkeley, CA: Wilderness Press, 1988.

Hiker's Hip Pocket Guide to the Mendocino Highlands—Lorentzen, Bob. Berkeley, CA: Wilderness Press, 1992.

Hiking the Big Sur Country—Schaffer, Jeffrey P. Berkeley, CA: Wilderness Press, 1988.

Hiking the Bigfoot Country—Hart, John. San Francisco: Sierra Club Books.

Hiking the Great Basin—Hart, John. San Francisco: Sierra Club Books.

Lassen Volcanic National Park—Schaffer, Jeffrey P. Berkeley, CA: Wilderness Press, 1986.

Marble Mountain Wilderness—Green, David. Berkeley, CA: Wilderness Press, 1980.

The Mount Shasta Book—Selters, Andy and Zanger, Michael. Berkeley, CA: Wilderness Press, 1989.

The Pacific Crest Trail—Volume 1: California—Schaffer, Jeffrey P. Berkeley, CA: Wilderness Press, 1989.

Peninsula Trails—Rusmore, Joan and Spangle, Frances. Berkeley, CA: Wilderness Press, 1989.

Point Reyes—Whitnah, Dorothy. Berkeley, CA: Wilderness Press, 1985.

San Bernardino Mountain Trails—Robinson, John W. Berkeley, CA: Wilderness Press, 1986.

Self-Propelled in the Southern Sierra, Vol 2—Jenkins, J. C. Berkeley, CA: Wilderness Press.

The Sierra Club Guide to the Natural Areas of California—Perry, John and Jane. San Francisco: Sierra Club Books, 1983.

Sierra North—Winnett, Thomas and Winnett, Jason. Berkeley, CA: Wilderness Press, 1991.

Sierra South—Winnett, Thomas and Winnett, Jason. Berkeley, CA: Wilderness Press, 1990.

Ski Tours in Lassen Volcanic National Park—Libkind, Marcus. Berkeley, CA: Wilderness Press, 1989.

Ski Tours in the Sierra Nevada: Vols 1-4—Lib-
    kind, Marcus. Berkeley, CA: Wilderness Press.
Starr's Guide to the John Muir Trail and the High
    Sierra Region— Starr, Walter A. San Francisco:
    Sierra Club Books.
The Tahoe Sierra—Schaffer, Jeffrey P. Berkeley,
    CA: Wilderness Press, 1987.
The Tahoe–Yosemite Trail—Winnett, Thomas.
    Berkeley, CA: Wilderness Press, 1987.
Timberline Country—Roper, Steve. San Fran-
    cisco: Sierra Club Books.
Trails of the Angeles—Robinson, John W. Berke-
    ley, CA: Wilderness Press, 1990.

The Trinity Alps—Linkhart, Luther. Berkeley, CA:
    Wilderness Press, 1986.
Yosemite National Park—Schaffer, Jeffrey P.
    Berkeley, CA: Wilderness Press, 1992.

INFORMATION ABOUT STATE PARK CAMPGROUNDS
California Department of Parks and Recreation,
    P.O. Box 942896, Sacramento, CA 94296;
    (916)322-7000.

STATE HIGHWAY MAP AND TRAVEL INFORMATION
California Office of Tourism, P.O. Box 9278, De-
    partment T-99, Van Nuys, CA 91409; (800)862-
    2543, Ext. 99.

COLORADO

BEST AREAS FOR WILDERNESS CAMPING

ROCKY MOUNTAIN NATIONAL PARK—265,000 acres. Located high in the Rockies of north-central Colorado, this superb National Park has no less than 59 peaks over 12,000 feet, with 14,255-foot Long's Peak the highest. A section of the Continental Divide is included. Substantial areas are above timberline, meaning almost unlimited vistas.

Most of the park is wilderness. There are deep canyons and cliffs, some small glaciers, many lakes, streams, and rivers, and forests of spruce and fir, juniper and ponderosa pine. Wildlife includes elk, moose, black bear, mule deer, bighorn sheep, and mountain lion.

Activities: About 355 miles of trails are available for backpacking and hiking, including a section of the Continental Divide Trail (see entry page 122), as well as a trail to the top of Long's Peak. Difficulty ranges from easy to extremely strenuous.

Some trails receive heavy use. Higher trails may only be snow-free from July through September. Allow extra time to adjust to the very high altitudes. Horseback riding is possible on some trails, as is cross-country skiing during the snow season.

Technical climbing is available, with a bivouac permit required to remain overnight. Fishing is another option along streams and some lakes. Hunting is prohibited in the park.

Camping Regulations: A free permit is required for backcountry camping. Permits are available by mail or in person from visitor centers or ranger stations, and must be picked up in person. Phone reservations are accepted from September-May only.

Between June and September visitors may camp a maximum of seven nights, or three nights at any one site. Campfires are prohibited except at small number of designated sites, so a stove should be brought for cooking. Pets are prohibited.

There are some 198 designated campsites located along many of the trails. Dispersed camping is also permitted in 23 trail-less "cross-country zones" in more remote parts of the park. Here tents must be set up at least 100 feet from water sources, and campers may only stay a single night at each site, with a two-night maximum for each zone. Group size in these zones is limited to seven.

For Further Information: Rocky Mountain National Park, Estes Park, CO 80517; (303)586-2371.

WHITE RIVER NATIONAL FOREST—1,960,760 acres. Comprised of two huge tracts in the Rockies of west-central Colorado, White River National Forest includes some outstanding high mountain wilderness, with lofty peaks and some elevations over 14,000 feet.

There are also deep canyons, a 10,000-foot high plateau, many rock formations, conifer-forested slopes, and hilly grasslands, plus numerous lakes and streams. Elk, black bear, mule deer, mountain lion, and coyote are among the wildlife.

The forest has seven designated wilderness areas: 196,360 acres of the 235,230-acre Flat Tops Wilderness, 159,000 acres of the 174,000-acre Maroon Bells—Snowmass Wilderness, 113,000 acres of the 120,000-acre Holy Cross Wilderness, the 74,250-acre Hunter—Fryingpan Wilderness, 51,000 acres of the 134,000-acre Eagles Nest Wilderness,

35,000 acres of the 159,900-acre Collegiate Peaks Wilderness, and 17,000 acres of the 59,000-acre Raggeds Wilderness.

Activities: Backpacking and hiking are possible on more than 1,400 miles of trails, most of which are open to horseback riding. Difficulty varies from easy to very strenuous. Many trails are snow-free only from July through September, and some receive heavy use.

Mountain biking is allowed on trails outside of wilderness areas. Cross-country skiing is available during winter. Limited white-water rafting and kayaking are possible on some of the rivers which run through the forest. Rock climbing is another option. Hunting and fishing are permitted in season.

Camping Regulations: Camping and campfires are allowed throughout most of the forest, except where otherwise prohibited. No permits are necessary. Campsites should be at least 100 feet from trails and water sources. Fires are restricted in some portions of designated wilderness areas. A stove is recommended. Group size is limited to 10 in the Eagles Nest Wilderness.

For Further Information: White River National Forest, P.O. Box 948, Glenwood Springs, CO 81602; (303)945-2521.

RIO GRANDE NATIONAL FOREST—1,851,792 acres. Rio Grande National Forest stretches through south-central and southwestern Colorado, and includes parts of the San Juan, La Garita, and Sangre de Cristo Mountain Ranges. Included are substantial segments of the Continental Divide.

There are many rugged, rocky peaks, with some elevations over 14,000 feet, rock outcrops and natural arches, steep canyons and volcanic cliffs, along with numerous lakes, streams, and rivers, including the source of the Rio Grande.

The region is forested with spruce and fir, pine and aspen, in addition to meadows and areas of alpine tundra. Black bear, mule deer, elk, mountain lion, and bobcat are among the wildlife.

Three designated wilderness areas are found here: 169,000 acres of the 460,000-acre Weminuche Wilderness, 88,000 acres of the 127,000-acre South San Juan Wilderness, and 24,000 acres of the 108,000-acre La Garita Wilderness.

Activities: Hiking and backpacking are possible on over 1,300 miles of trails, including about 235 miles of the Continental Divide Trail (see entry page 122).

Difficulty ranges from easy to quite strenuous. Trails at high elevations are often under snow except from mid-July through mid-September. Horses are permitted on many trails.

Rafting, kayaking, and canoeing are available on the Rio Grande. Cross-country skiing is possible on some trails during the snow-season. Fishing is also feasible, and hunting is permitted in season.

Camping Regulations: Camping is allowed throughout most of the National Forest, as are campfires, except where posted otherwise. No permits are necessary. Camping is restricted in some parts of wilderness areas. Tents should be set up at least 200 feet from trails and water sources. Stoves are recommended.

For Further Information: Rio Grande National Forest, 1803 West Highway 160, Monte Vista, CO 81144; (303)852-5941.

PIKE AND SAN ISABEL NATIONAL FORESTS—2,217,446 acres. Administered together, these two spectacular National Forests in central and south-central Colorado are home to Colorado's highest peaks, with 22 mountains over 14,000 feet.

Among these mountains are the three highest in the state: 14,433-foot Mount Elbert, 14,421-foot Mount Massive, and 14,420-foot Mount Harvard. Also here is famous 14,110-foot Pike's Peak.

Other scenery includes alpine meadows, high lakes and creeks, rock outcrops and talus slopes, steep canyons, and forests of spruce, pine, and aspen. Antelope, elk, deer, bear, mountain goat, and bighorn sheep are among the wildlife.

There are six designated wilderness areas: the 106,000-acre Lost Creek Wilderness, 82,000 acres of the 159,900-acre Collegiate Peaks Wilderness, 34,000 acres of the 74,000-acre Mount Evans Wilderness, the 28,000-acre Mount Massive Wilderness, part of the 41,000-acre Lizard Head Wilderness, and 9,000 acres of the 116,500-acre Holy Cross Wilderness.

Activities: These National Forests have more than 1,200 miles of trails for hiking and backpacking. Included are about half of the 470-mile Colorado Trail and a section of the Continental Divide Trail (see entries page 122), plus the 100-mile Rainbow Trail. Difficulty varies from easy to extremely strenuous.

Many trails are open to horseback riding. Mountain bikes are allowed outside of wilderness areas. Cross-country skiing is available during the snow season. Rock climbing is popular in Elevenmile Canyon, and mountaineering is possible on numerous peaks here. Hunting and fishing are permitted in season.

Camping Regulations: Camping is allowed throughout most of the region, as are campfires, except near public use areas or where otherwise prohibited. Campsites should be at least 100 feet from trails and water sources. No permits are necessary.

For Further Information: Pike and San Isabel National Forests, 1920 Valley Drive, Pueblo, CO 81008; (719)545-8737.

SAN JUAN NATIONAL FOREST—1,860,931 acres.

San Juan National Forest is in southwest Colorado, west of the Continental Divide. It's another area of splendid high rocky peaks which sometimes exceed 14,000 feet, along with steep canyons, mesas, and interesting rock formations.

In the region are spruce and pine forests, high meadows and lakes, and large rivers and creeks with waterfalls. Wildlife includes elk, mule deer, bear, bighorn sheep, and mountain lion.

This National Forest has three designated wilderness areas: 294,000 acres of the 460,000-acre Weminuche Wilderness, 40,000 acres of the 127,000-acre South San Juan Wilderness, and 21,000 acres of the 41,000-acre Lizard Head Wilderness.

Activities: Backpacking and hiking are possible on over 1,100 miles of trails, including a section of the new Continental Divide Trail (see entry page 122). Difficulty varies from easy to extremely strenuous. Some trails receive heavy use. Higher trails may only be snow-free from mid-July through September.

Horses are permitted on most trails, and cross-country skiing is available in winter. Several rivers are suitable for rafting and canoeing. Mountain climbing is popular in the Needle Mountains. Hunting is permitted in season, and fishing is an option on many lakes and streams.

Camping Regulations: Camping and campfires are generally allowed throughout the forest, but are restricted in a few areas. Stoves are recommended for cooking. No permits are required.

For Further Information: San Juan National Forest, 701 Camino del Rio, Room 301, Durango, CO 81301; (303)247-4874.

GRAND MESA, UNCOMPAHGRE, AND GUNNISON NATIONAL FORESTS—2,953,191 acres.

These three National Forests in west and southwest Colorado are administered together. They cover an enormous area of high rocky peaks, deep canyons, plateaus and mesas.

Included is 10,000-foot-high Grand Mesa, largest in the country, as well as some mountains over 14,000 feet along the Continental Divide. There are hundreds of lakes and countless streams, forests of spruce, grasslands, and diverse wildlife.

Eight designated wilderness areas are found here: the 176,400-acre West Elk Wilderness, the 98,000-acre Big Blue Wilderness, 80,000 acres of the 108,000-acre La Garita Wilderness, 49,000 acres of the 119,900-acre Collegiate Peaks Wilderness, 43,000 acres of the 59,000-acre Raggeds Wilderness, 20,000 acres of the 41,000-acre Lizard Head Wilderness, 20,000 acres of the 174,000-acre Maroon Bells–Snowmass Wilderness, and the 16,200-acre Mount Sneffels Wilderness.

Activities: There are hundreds of miles of trails for hiking and backpacking. Most trails are open to horseback riding. Cross-country skiing is possible here during winter.

Canoeing, rafting, and kayaking are available on segments of several rivers. Rock climbing is another option in these National Forests. Hunting and fishing are permitted in season.

Camping Regulations: Camping and campfires are allowed throughout the region, except near public use areas or where otherwise prohibited. No permits are necessary.

For Further Information: Grand Mesa, Uncompahgre, and Gunnison National Forests, 2250 Highway 50, Delta, CO 81416; (303)874-7691.

ARAPAHO AND ROOSEVELT NATIONAL FORESTS—

1,813,493 acres. Located in north-central and northern Colorado, these two co-administered National Forests surround Rocky Mountain National Park. This is a region of splendid high snow-covered peaks, with some elevations over 14,000 feet.

There are steep ridges and deep canyons, with alpine lakes and glaciers. Forests are of fir, spruce, and lodgepole pine. Wildlife includes elk, deer, bear, bighorn sheep, and coyote.

The National Forests have eight designated wilderness areas: 83,000 acres of the 134,000-acre Eagles Nest Wilderness, the 75,000-acre Indian Peaks Wilderness, the 74,000-acre Rawah Wilderness, the 66,600-acre Comanche Peak Wilderness, 40,000 acres of the 74,000-acre Mount Evans Wilderness, the 9,900-acre Neota Wilderness, the 9,380-acre Cache la Poudre Wilderness, and 7,000 acres of the 14,100-acre Never Summer Wilderness.

Activities: Backpacking and hiking are possible on more than 900 miles of trails, including a section of the new Continental Divide Trail (see entry page 122). Horses are allowed on many of the trails. Difficulty ranges from easy to strenuous.

Rafting is available on the Poudre River. Mountain bikes are permitted on trails except in wilderness areas. Cross-country skiing is a winter option.

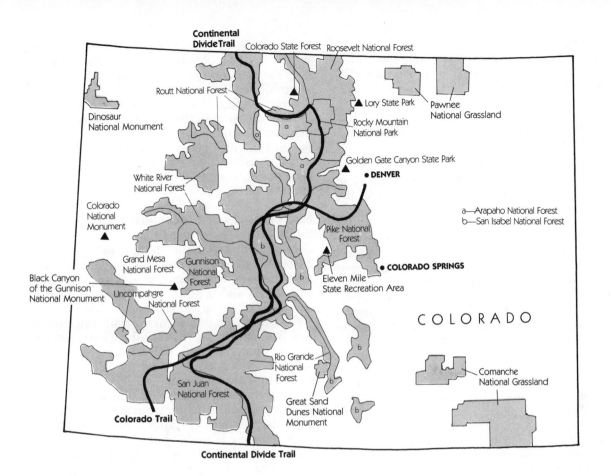

Continental Divide Trail
Colorado State Forest Roosevelt National Forest
Routt National Forest
Dinosaur National Monument
Lory State Park
Pawnee National Grassland
Rocky Mountain National Park
Golden Gate Canyon State Park
● DENVER
White River National Forest
Colorado National Monument
a—Arapaho National Forest
b—San Isabel National Forest
Pike National Forest
Grand Mesa National Forest
Gunnison National Forest
● COLORADO SPRINGS
Black Canyon of the Gunnison National Monument
Uncompahgre National Forest
Eleven Mile State Recreation Area
COLORADO
Rio Grande National Forest
Comanche National Grassland
San Juan National Forest
Colorado Trail
Great Sand Dunes National Monument
Continental Divide Trail

Rock climbing and mountaineering are other possibilities. Hunting and fishing are allowed in season.

Camping Regulations: Camping is generally allowed, except near public use areas or where otherwise prohibited. Campfires are legal but discouraged. A stove is recommended for cooking.

A permit is required to camp in the Indian Peaks Wilderness from June 1-September 30. Quotas are in effect. Permits may be obtained in advance. Camping and fires are restricted or prohibited in some parts of wilderness areas. Permits are also necessary for groups of 10 or more.

For Further Information: Arapaho and Roosevelt National Forests, 240 West Prospect Road, Fort Collins, CO 80526; (303)498-1100.

ROUTT NATIONAL FOREST—1,127,164 acres. Made up of three separate tracts in the Rockies of northwest Colorado, Routt National Forest has rugged scenery including precipitous peaks and deep canyons. Highest elevation here is 12,180-foot Mount Zirkel.

There are many lakes and streams, waterfalls, alpine meadows, and sagebrush hills, plus forests of spruce and fir, pine and aspen. Wildlife includes elk, mule deer, black bear, bobcat, and fox.

Routt has three designated wilderness areas: the 141,000-acre Mount Zirkel Wilderness, 38,870 acres of the 235,230-acre Flat Tops Wilderness, plus 6,700 acres of the 14,100-acre Never Summer Wilderness.

Activities: Over 600 miles of trails are available for backpacking and hiking, including a section of the Continental Divide Trail (see entry page 122). Difficulty varies from easy to strenuous.

Horseback riding is allowed on most trails, as is mountain biking except in wilderness areas. Cross-country skiing is possible here in winter. Rafting is available on the North Platte River. Fishing is another option, as is hunting in season.

Camping Regulations: Camping and campfires are allowed throughout this National Forest, except where posted otherwise. Campsites should be at least 100 feet from trails, lakes, and streams. Stoves are recommended for cooking.

A permit, which may be obtained at the trailheads, is required for camping in the Flat Tops Wilderness. Permits are also necessary for groups of 10 or more. Camping is restricted in some portions of the wilderness areas.

For Further Information: Routt National Forest, 29587 West U.S. 40, Steamboat Springs, CO 80487; (303)879-1722.

OTHER RECOMMENDED LOCATIONS

BLM LANDS IN COLORADO—Colorado has over eight million acres of BLM (Bureau of Land Management) or public domain lands, mainly in the western and west-central part of the state. Included are numerous canyons, 80 miles of the Arkansas River, and 50 miles of the Colorado River. There are a number of "Wilderness Study Areas" on these lands, areas which have been recommended for wilderness designation.

Brochures or other printed literature are available by request for only a few of the many tracts. Public facilities are generally minimal or non-existent, and access to some of the areas is difficult.

Activities: There are very few established trails on BLM lands. Hiking, backpacking, and horseback riding are allowed, but most travel must be cross-country. Nordic skiing is often possible during winter.

Whitewater rafting, kayaking, and some canoeing are available on several rivers, including the Arkansas and Colorado Rivers. Fishing is possible, with hunting permitted in season.

Camping Regulations: Camping is generally allowed on BLM lands, except where posted otherwise. Campsites should be at least 100 feet from streams and lakes. Campfires are allowed, but stoves are recommended. Permits are not required for most areas.

For Further Information: Bureau of Land Management, 2850 Youngfield Street, Lakewood, CO 80215; (303)236-2100.

DINOSAUR NATIONAL MONUMENT—203,815 acres. Located in the northwest corner of Colorado and extending into Utah, this National Monument is named for the fossils of dinosaur bones found here. It's set amid arid desert plateaus, mountains, and canyons.

The monument has two major rivers, the Green and Tampa Rivers. Vegetation includes stands of pinyon pine and juniper, sagebrush, with box elder and cottonwood along the rivers. Bighorn sheep, mule deer, and coyote are among the wildlife.

Activities: Only a few relatively short trails are found here. Cross-country hiking and backpacking are allowed, but foot-travel is difficult due to the rugged terrain.

Rafting is available on the rivers by permit, which must be obtained well in advance due to high demand. Limited fishing is possible. Hunting is prohibited.

Camping Regulations: A free permit is required in order to camp in the backcountry here. Permits may be obtained from headquarters and some ranger stations. Pets are prohibited.

For Further Information: Dinosaur National Monument, Dinosaur, CO 81610; (303)374-2216. 203,815 acres.

BLACK CANYON OF THE GUNNISON NATIONAL MONUMENT—13,672 acres. Situated in west-central Colorado, this National Monument protects 12 miles of the steep and dramatic canyon of the Gunnison River. The area includes pinyon-juniper woodlands and brushlands, with mule deer, elk, and bighorn sheep among the wildlife.

Activities: A few easy hiking trails run along the rim. Backpacking as well as hiking are possible on several unmarked and difficult routes which lead down into the canyon. Horseback riding is limited to one trail along the rim.

Some challenging rock climbing is available on the canyon walls. Climbers must register before and after climbing. Fishing is allowed along the river. Hunting is prohibited.

Camping Regulations: Camping is allowed in the canyon. A free permit must be obtained. Only a limited number of sites are available alongside the river, and quotas are observed. Campfires are prohibited here, as are pets.

For Further Information: Black Canyon of the Gunnison National Monument, 2233 East Main Street, Montrose, CO 81401; (303)249-7036.

GREAT SAND DUNES NATIONAL MONUMENT—38,659 acres. Located at the foot of the Sangre de Cristo Mountains and next to Rio Grande National Forest, in south-central Colorado, this is a huge area of sand dunes. Among them are the highest dunes in the country, nearly 700 feet tall.

Activities: There are a few trails for hiking and backpacking outside of the dune area. Most of the Monument is trail-less, however, requiring cross-country travel. Horseback riding is permitted.

Camping Regulations: Backcountry camping is allowed at two designated sites, and also throughout the western part of the Monument, beyond the main dunes. A free permit must be obtained from the visitor center. Campfires are prohibited.

For Further Information: Great Sand Dunes National Monument, 11500 Highway 150, Mosca, CO 81146; (719)378-2312.

COLORADO NATIONAL MONUMENT—19,919 acres. Colorado National Monument is in western Colorado, not far from the Utah border. It preserves a region of deep, multicolored canyons, along with high rock formations, domes, and arches. There's semidesert vegetation here, with wildlife which includes mule deer, bighorn sheep, and coyote.

Activities: Backpacking and hiking are available on about 45 miles of trails. Horseback riding is permitted on most trails. Cross-country skiing is often possible here during winter. Rock climbing is another option in the Monument.

Camping Regulations: Backcountry camping is allowed almost anywhere, but sites must be at least 100 yards from trails and one-quarter mile from roads. No permits are necessary. Campfires are not allowed, so a stove must be used for cooking. Pets are prohibited.

For Further Information: Colorado National Monument, Fruita, CO 81521; (303)858-3617.

COMANCHE NATIONAL GRASSLANDS—419,000 acres. Administered by Pike and San Isabel National Forests, and consisting of two large tracts in southeastern Colorado, this is a relatively flat area of prairie grasslands, with some rivers and canyons. Wildlife includes white-tailed and mule deer, pronghorn, black bear, mountain lion, and fox.

Activities: Hiking, backpacking, and horseback riding are allowed, but there are few established trails aside from a section of the Sante Fe National Historic Trail. Most travel must be cross-country. Hunting and fishing are permitted in season.

Camping Regulations: Camping and campfires are allowed throughout the National Grasslands, except where posted otherwise. No permits are required.

For Further Information: Comanche National Grasslands, 27162 Highway 287, P.O. Box 127, Springfield, CO 81073; (719)523-6591.

PAWNEE NATIONAL GRASSLANDS—193,000 acres. Administered by Arapaho and Roosevelt National Forests, Pawnee National Grasslands is made up of two units in northeast Colorado. It's an area of shortgrass prairie, with low sandstone buttes amid the flat plains. Wildlife includes deer, antelope, coyote, and fox.

Activities: Backpacking, hiking, and horseback riding are possible throughout the region. Due to the scarcity of trails, most travel is cross-country. Fishing is available, and hunting is permitted in season.

Camping Regulations: Camping is allowed throughout the National Grasslands, as are campfires, except where otherwise prohibited. Permits are not required.

For Further Information: Pawnee National Grasslands, 240 West Prospect Road, Fort Collins, CO 80526; (303)498-1100.

GOLDEN GATE CANYON STATE PARK—10,200 acres. This mountainous and popular state park near Denver has some elevations over 10,000 feet, and includes mountain meadows, pine forests, and outstanding views.

Activities: There are about 60 miles of trails for hiking and backpacking. Difficulty varies from easy to strenuous. Horseback riding and mountain biking are allowed on some trails.

Cross-country skiing and snowshoeing are winter options here. Fishing is available along the streams and at most ponds. Hunting is permitted in season.

Camping Regulations: Camping is restricted to 23 backcountry sites. A permit is required, and must be obtained from the visitor center. A fee is charged to camp here each night. Campfires are not allowed.

For Further Information: Golden Gate Canyon State Park, Route 6, Box 280, Golden, CO 80403; (303)592-1502.

COLORADO STATE FOREST—Colorado State Forest is actually a state park which lies in the mountains northwest of Rocky Mountain National Park. It offers fine alpine scenery, and includes some lakes and streams.

Activities: Hiking and backpacking are possible on over 20 miles of trails. Horses are allowed on many trails. Cross-country skiing and snowshoeing are available during the snow season. Fishing is permitted along lakes and streams, as is hunting during the appropriate season.

Camping Regulations: Backcountry camping is allowed at designated sites here. A permit is required, and must be obtained from park headquarters. A fee is charged for camping each night.

For Further Information: Colorado State Forest, Star Route, Box 91, Walden, CO 80480; (303)723-8366.

LORY STATE PARK—2,479 acres. Located in the foothills of the Rockies in northern Colorado, Lory State Park includes grasslands and a ponderosa pine forest. Mule deer, black bear, and mountain lion are among the wildlife.

Activities: There are about 30 miles of trails for hiking and backpacking. Difficulty varies from easy to strenuous. Horses are allowed on many trails. Cross-country skiing is available in winter. Hunting is permitted in season.

Camping Regulations: Backcountry camping is limited to several designated sites. A permit is required, and may be obtained from the park entrance station. No campfires are allowed, so a stove is necessary for cooking.

For Further Information: Lory State Park, 708 Lodgepole Drive, Bellevue, CO 80512; (303)493-1623.

ELEVEN MILE STATE RECREATION AREA—7,400 acres. Located in an area of grasslands in central Colorado, next to Pike National Forest, this State Recreation Area centers around a 3,400-acre reservoir which was created by damming up the South Platte River.

Activities: Limited hiking is available here, as is cross-country skiing during winter. Fishing is possible along the reservoir. Hunting is permitted in season. Swimming is not allowed.

Camping Regulations: There are 25 primitive walk-in (or boat-in) campsites along the northeast shore of the reservoir. Backcountry camping is limited to these sites. A permit is required, and a fee charged for each night.

For Further Information: Eleven Mile State Recreation Area, Star Route 2, Box 4229, Lake George, CO 80827; (719)748-3401.

MAJOR BACKPACKING TRAILS

COLORADO TRAIL—469 miles. This extremely scenic new trail was dedicated in 1988. It begins near Denver and runs to Durango, traversing seven National Forests and six designated wilderness areas. Much of the time the trail is at high elevations, offering spectacular views.

Portions of the trail are quite strenuous, with many ups and downs. In addition to backpacking and hiking, most of the route is open to horseback riding, mountain biking, and also cross-country skiing during winter.

Camping Regulations: Since it's largely on National Forest lands, camping is allowed freely along most of the trail, except where posted otherwise. Campfires are allowed. It's suggested that campsites be chosen which are well off the trail and at least 100 feet from water sources.

For Further Information: The Colorado Trail Foundation, 548 Pine Song Trail, Golden, CO 80401. Maps and a guidebook for the trail are available from this organization.

CONTINENTAL DIVIDE TRAIL—This major National Scenic Trail hasn't yet been officially designated in Colorado, but a marked "interim route" exists in three of the state's National Forests. While it occasionally runs right along the crest, the trail generally follows beneath the actual divide.

The route is incredibly scenic and magnificent, with many open vistas. Difficulty varies from easy to very strenuous. At highest elevations the trail is under snow for up to 10 months of the year. Horses are allowed on most sections.

Camping Regulations: The trail is mainly on National Forest lands, and along these sections camping and campfires are freely allowed, except where posted otherwise. Whenever possible, choose sites which are well off the trail and at least 200 feet from water sources. Permits are required for camping in Rocky Mountain National Park and also in the Indian Peaks Wilderness of Arapaho and Roosevelt National Forests.

For Further Information: Continental Divide Trail Society, P.O. Box 30002, Bethesda, MD 20814.

COLORADO CAMPING RESOURCES

ORGANIZATIONS WHICH SPONSOR WILDERNESS CAMPING TRIPS

Colorado Mountain Club, 2530 West Alameda Avenue, Denver, CO 80219; (303)922-3708. This 7,500-member hiking and climbing club has chapters throughout Colorado. Numerous scheduled outings including backpacking, canoe-camping, and other wilderness camping trips. In addition, courses which teach wilderness skills are offered.

Sierra Club, 777 Grant Street, Suite 606, Denver, CO 80203; (303)861-8819. This chapter of the Sierra Club offers some wilderness camping trips.

USEFUL GUIDEBOOKS

Bicycling the Backcountry—Stoehr, William L. Boulder, CO: Pruett Publishing Co.

Colorado's Indian Peaks Wilderness Area—Roach, Gerry. Golden, CO: Fulcrum.

Exploring Colorado's Wild Areas—Warren, Scott. Seattle: The Mountaineers Books.

The Floater's Guide to Colorado—Wheat, Doug. Helena, MT: Falcon Press, 1983.

The Hiker's Guide to Colorado—Boddie, Caryn and Peter. Helena, MT: Falcon Press, 1984.

Hiker's Guide to the Mount Zirkel Wilderness Area—Thompson, Jay and Therese. Boulder, CO: Pruett Publishing Co.

Hiking the Southwest's Canyon Country—Hinchman, Sandra. Seattle: The Mountaineers Books.

Hiking Trails of the Boulder Mountain Parks and Plains—De Haan, Vici. Boulder, CO: Pruett Publishing Co., 1979.

Hiking Trails of Central Colorado—Hagen, Mary. Boulder, CO: Pruett Publishing Co.

Hiking Trails of Northern Colorado—Hagen, Mary. Boulder, CO: Pruett Publishing Co.

Hiking Trails of Southwestern Colorado—Pixler, Paul. Boulder, CO: Pruett Publishing Co., 1981.

Mountain Bike Rides in the Colorado Front Range—Stoehr, William L. Boulder, CO: Pruett Publishing Co.

Rocky Mountain National Park Hiking Trails—Dannen, Kent & Donna. Old Saybrook, CT: The Globe Pequot Press.

The Sierra Club Guide to the Natural Areas of Colorado and Utah— Perry, John and Jane. San Francisco: Sierra Club Books, 1985.

The South San Juan Wilderness Area—Murray, John. Boulder, CO: Pruett Publishing Co.

Trails of the Front Range—Kenofer, Louis. Boulder, CO: Pruett, 1980.

INFORMATION ABOUT CAMPGROUNDS IN STATE PARKS

Colorado Division of Parks and Recreation, 1313 Sherman Street, Room 618, Denver, CO 80203; (303)866-3437.

STATE HIGHWAY MAP AND TRAVEL INFORMATION

Colorado Tourism Board, 1625 Broadway, Suite 1700, Denver, CO 80202; (303)592-5410.

CONNECTICUT

BEST AREAS FOR WILDERNESS CAMPING

PACHAUG STATE FOREST—22,937 acres. Located in the eastern part of the state, near the Rhode Island border, Pauchaug is Connecticut's largest state forest. Terrain here is hilly but not steep, with the highest elevations under 500 feet. There are several lakes, many streams, and some swamps and marshes. Wildlife includes deer and fox.

Activities: Three backpacking trails are found in this state forest: the Pauchaug, Nehantic, and Narragansett Trails, which intersect and form a large loop. Horseback riding is also available on some trails and roads in the forest. Fishing is possible, and hunting is allowed in season.

Camping Regulations: Camping is restricted to four separate backpack campsites or camping zones which are located along the trails. Two of the areas have shelters. There's also a special horse camp. Pets are not allowed at campsites.

A camping permit is required, and must be requested at least two weeks in advance by writing to: D.E.P. Eastern District Office, 209 Hebron Road, Marlborough, CT 06447. It's necessary to specify where you wish to camp each night.

For Further Information: Pachaug State Forest, c/o Connecticut Office of State Parks and Recreation, 165 Capitol Avenue, Hartford, CT 06106; (203)566-2304.

MAJOR BACKPACKING TRAILS

APPALACHIAN TRAIL—61 miles in Connecticut (2,100 total). This famous National Scenic Trail enters western Connecticut near the Housatonic River, then parallels and follows alongside the river for a stretch. Terrain through much of the state is hilly, with fine views from some small mountains.

Just before reaching Massachusetts the trail enters one of the wildest and most rugged regions in Connecticut, the southern Taconic Mountains. Here it ascends 2,316-foot Bear Mountain, highest mountain in the state.

Camping Regulations: Several lean-tos and other designated camping areas are located at regular intervals along the trail. Camping and campfires are limited to these approved sites. No permits are necessary.

For Further Information: Appalachian Trail Conference, P.O. Box 807, Harpers Ferry, WV 25425. This organization publishes a *Guide to the Appalachian Trail in Massachusetts—Connecticut.*

TUNXIS TRAIL—Backpacking is permitted on the northern 31-mile portion of the 60-mile Tunxis Trail in north-central Connecticut, leading from near Burlington to the Massachusetts border. It's hilly, scenic, and often wild along the way.

The trail passes through 1,200-acre Nepaug State Forest and 8,600-acre Tunxis State Forest, with hardwood trees as well as some conifers, and offers nice views from open ledges at elevations as high as 1,000 feet.

Camping Regulations: Three backpack camping areas or camping zones are located by the trail, and camping is limited to these areas. A permit must be obtained in advance by mail, and the request should be sent at least two weeks in advance

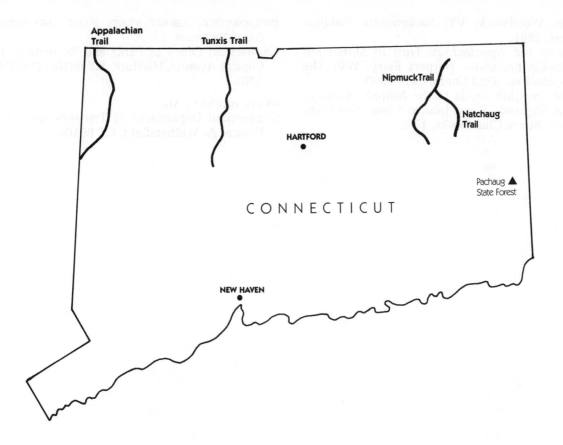

Appalachian
Trail

Tunxis Trail

NipmuckTrail

Natchaug
Trail

HARTFORD
●

Pachaug ▲
State Forest

C O N N E C T I C U T

NEW HAVEN
●

to: D.E.P., Western District Office, Plymouth Road, RFD #4, Harwinton, CT 06791. It's necessary to specify dates and where you want to camp each night. Pets are not allowed in camping areas.

For Further Information: Connecticut Forest and Park Association, 16 Meriden Road, Middletown, CT 06457.

NIPMUCK AND NATCHAUG TRAILS—Backpacking is allowed on these two interconnected hiking trails in northeast Connecticut. The Nipmuck Trail is 26 miles long, extending from Mansfield Hollow State Park to the Massachusetts border, and passing through 8,000-acre Nipmuck State Forest.

The Natchaug Trail is 18 miles long. It runs from J. L. Goodwin State Forest through 13,000-acre Natchaug State Forest, and then intersects with the Nipmuck Trail.

This is hilly, hardwood-forested terrain, with some areas of conifers. The trails utilize old woods roads much of the time, occasionally crossing and following alongside streams.

Camping Regulations: There are three backpack campsites or camping zones along the Nipmuck Trail, and one campsite on the Natchaug Trail.

No pets are allowed. A camping permit must be obtained in advance, and should be requested by mail at least two weeks before a trip. Write to: D.E.P., Eastern District Office, 209 Hebron Road, Marlborough, CT 06447. It's necessary to specify campsites and dates.

For Further Information: Connecticut Office of State Parks and Recreation, 165 Capitol Avenue, Hartford, CT 06106.

CONNECTICUT CAMPING RESOURCES

ORGANIZATIONS WHICH OFFER WILDERNESS
CAMPING TRIPS

Sierra Club, Connecticut Chapter, 118 Oak Street, Hartford, CT 06106; (203)527-9788. This Sierra Club chapter schedules backpacking trips each year.

USEFUL GUIDEBOOKS

Connecticut Walk Book—Middletown, CT: Connecticut Forest and Park Association, 1984.
Fifty Hikes in Connecticut—Hardy, Gerry and

Sue. Woodstock, VT: Backcountry Publications, 1984.

Guide to the Appalachian Trail in Massachusetts–Connecticut— Harpers Ferry, WV: The Appalachian Trail Conference, 1990.

The Sierra Club Guide to the Natural Areas of New England—Perry, John and Jane. San Francisco: Sierra Club Books, 1990.

INFORMATION ABOUT STATE PARK AND FOREST CAMPGROUNDS

Connecticut Office of Parks and Recreation, 165 Capitol Avenue, Hartford, CT 06106; (203)566-2304.

STATE HIGHWAY MAP

Connecticut Department of Transportation, P.O. Drawer A, Wethersfield, CT 06109.

F L O R I D A

BEST AREAS FOR WILDERNESS CAMPING

EVERGLADES NATIONAL PARK—1,400,800 acres. This enormous park at the southern tip of Florida protects an outstanding subtropical wilderness. Due to the effects of development in southern Florida, it's one of our most endangered National Parks. In addition, much of it was severely damaged in 1992 by Hurricane Andrew.

Large areas of the park are wet or under water, and it includes countless keys (small islands) offshore. There are pinelands, cypress and mangrove forests, hardwood hammocks (groves of trees), along with coastal and fresh water prairie.

Among the wildlife are alligator, crocodile, and the Florida panther, plus the manatee. The park is also famous for its exotic birdlife. Winter is the best time to visit, with summer inadvisable due to insects and the heat.

Activities: This National Park is especially suitable for canoeing, and includes some fine marked canoe routes. Most notable is the 99-mile Wilderness Waterway, which extends through much of the Everglades. Canoes may be rented in the park.

There are also many miles of hiking trails, which generally follow old roads, and provide easy walking over nearly level terrain. Trails are often wet during summer and fall.

Biking is possible on some of the trails and roads, as is horseback riding. Freshwater and saltwater fishing are permitted. Hunting is prohibited.

Camping Regulations: A backcountry camping permit is required, and may be obtained from a ranger station. Numerous established campsites are located throughout the park.

Many of the designated campsites consist of "chickees," or raised wooden platforms which may only be reached by canoe or boat. Advance reservations are not available, and numbers of campers are restricted. Campfires and pets are prohibited.

Just a few sites are accessible by hikers, backpackers, or bikers. While camping is allowed at other than authorized sites, possibilities are very limited due to the extensive wet areas. Since hurricane damage in 1992 was extreme in some parts of the park, request up-to-date information before visiting.

For Further Information: Everglades National Park, P.O. Box 279, Homestead, FL 33030; (305)247-6211.

APALACHICOLA NATIONAL FOREST—557,000 acres. Located in the northwestern part of the state, Apalachicola is the largest of Florida's three National Forests. It includes some beautiful pine forests and swamps, grassy savannahs, many creeks, a few small lakes, and several fine rivers.

White-tailed deer, black bear, and alligator are among the wildlife here. There are two designated wilderness areas: the 24,600-acre Bradwell Bay Wilderness and the 8,000-acre Mud Swamp/New River Wilderness.

Activities: The major trail here for hiking and backpacking is the 60-mile Apalachicola Trail, which is part of the Florida Trail (see entry page 132). Difficulty is easy to moderate. Some sections of the trail, especially in the Bradwell Bay Wilderness, are wet for much of the year.

Flatwater canoeing is possible on several rivers, with spring the best time for this activity. Horseback riding is available on the Vinzant Riding

Trail, along with other trails and roads. Fishing is another option. Hunting is permitted in season.

Camping Regulations: Camping and campfires are allowed almost anywhere in the National Forest, except near day use areas or where posted otherwise. Permits are not required. "No-trace camping" is encouraged. During deer hunting season campers must use designated sites.

For Further Information: Apalachicola National Forest, 227 North Bronough Street, Suite 4061, Tallahassee, FL 32301; (904)681-7265.

OCALA NATIONAL FOREST—367,000 acres. Situated in north-central Florida, this National Forest includes hardwood swamps and hammocks, pine forests and prairies, sandy ridges and grassy wetlands.

There are a few rivers and creeks, and a large number of small lakes. White-tailed deer, bear, bobcat, Florida panther, and alligator are among the wildlife here.

Ocala has four designated wilderness areas: the 13,260-acre Juniper Prairie Wilderness, the 7,700-acre Alexander Springs Creek Wilderness, the 3,120-acre Billies Bay Wilderness, and the 2,500-acre Little Lake George Wilderness.

Activities: There's one marked trail for backpacking and hiking, the 66-mile Ocala Trail, which is now also part of the Florida Trail (see entry page 132).

Horseback riding is available on old roads and paths in the forest. Canoeing is feasible on some of the rivers and creeks, as is fishing. Hunting is permitted in season.

Camping Regulations: Camping and campfires are allowed throughout the National Forest, except near public use areas or where otherwise prohibited.

No permits are required. Whenever possible, campsites should be at least 100 feet from trails. During deer hunting season all camping is restricted to designated areas.

For Further Information: Ocala National Forest, 227 North Bronough Street, Suite 4061, Tallahassee, FL 32301; (904)681-7265.

BIG CYPRESS NATIONAL PRESERVE—570,000 acres. Situated northwest of Everglades National Park in southern Florida, huge and wild Big Cypress National Preserve was established in part to help protect the Everglades.

This is an area of marshes and swamplands, pine islands, hardwood hammocks, and prairies. There's a rich birdlife, along with wildlife which includes black bear, deer, Florida panther, and alligator.

Activities: Hiking and backpacking are possible on one marked trail, the Florida Trail (see entry page 132), which forms two loops and stretches over 40 miles. Some sections of the trail pass through private land.

Unlike the nearby Everglades, there are no open waterways here for canoeing, and the area is mainly accessible on foot. Fishing is also available. Hunting is permitted in season.

Camping Regulations: Camping is allowed in the preserve, as are campfires. There are several designated camping areas, two of which are along the Florida Trail. No permits are required, but campers should check in with a ranger before starting out. Winter is the best time to backpack here. Summer is not recommended due to the heat and insects.

For Further Information: Big Cypress National Preserve, Star Route, Box 110, Ochopee, FL 33943; (813)695-2000.

OSCEOLA NATIONAL FOREST—157,000 acres. Located in northeast Florida, Osceola National Forest has cypress and gum swamps, stands of pine, small ponds, and a large lake. There's one designated wilderness area, the 13,600-acre Big Gum Swamp Wilderness. Wildlife includes white-tailed deer, black bear, wild turkey, and alligator.

Activities: The single marked trail here for backpacking and hiking is the 39-mile Osceola Trail, which is now part of the Florida Trail (see entry page 132). Canoeing is available on one river. Fishing is possible, and hunting is permitted in season.

Camping Regulations: Camping and campfires are allowed throughout the region, except near day use areas or where posted otherwise. No permits are necessary. All camping during deer hunting season must be at designated sites.

For Further Information: Osceola National Forest, U.S. Highway 90, P.O. Box 70, Olustee, FL 32072; (904)752-2577.

WITHLACOOCHEE STATE FOREST—123,240 acres. This state forest includes four large tracts of land in west-central Florida. In the area are cypress swamps and sand hills, slash and longleaf pine forests, with magnolia and oak, and also a stretch of the Withlacoochee River. Wildlife includes white-tailed deer, black bear, alligator, and armadillo.

Activities: This is an especially suitable place for hiking and backpacking, with over 100 miles of foot trails. There are three major trails: the 46-mile Citrus Trail, which forms several loops, the

31-mile Richloam Trail, and the 31-mile Croom Trail.

Hiking trails are open to foot travel only, and the trails are closed during part of the hunting season. Canoeing is available on the Withlacoochee River, and horseback riding is possible on several horse trails. Fishing is allowed, as is hunting during the appropriate season.

Camping Regulations: Primitive camping is restricted to designated areas along the trails. There are three established areas along the Citrus Trail, three on the Richloam, and two along the Croom Trail. Campfires are allowed at the sites, but fires should be built for cooking only.

For Further Information: Withlacoochee State Forest, 15019 Broad Street, Brooksville, FL 34601; (904)796-5650.

OTHER RECOMMENDED LOCATIONS

BLACKWATER RIVER STATE FOREST—183,185 acres. Located in Florida's western panhandle, this state forest features a 31-mile stretch of the beautiful Blackwater River, along with three large creeks, four lakes, and some swamps. There are forests of longleaf and slash pine, with cedar and maple. Wildlife includes deer, fox, and wild turkey.

Activities: The main trail here suitable for hiking and backpacking is the 21-mile Jackson Red Ground National Recreation Trail, which is part of the Florida Trail. There's also a 4.5-mile side trail.

Canoeing is available on the Blackwater River as well as on some creeks, and the forest has a number of horse trails. Fishing is another option. Hunting is permitted in season.

Camping Regulations: Camping has been allowed throughout the forest and alongside the Jackson Trail (including at two shelters) up to now, but new rules including permit requirements may be introduced shortly. Contact the forest headquarters regarding regulations. Campfires are limited to designated sites.

For Further Information: Blackwater River State Forest, Route 1, Box 77, Milton, FL 32570; (904)957-4201.

TOSOHATCHEE STATE RESERVE—28,000 acres. Located alongside the St. Johns River in east-central Florida, Tosohatchee State Reserve encompasses an area of pine forests and hammocks, including some virgin pine and cypress. There are also swamps and marshes, and Tosohatchee Creek

flows through part of the reserve. Among the wildlife are white-tailed deer, black bear, bobcat, and fox.

Activities: There's a single trail here for backpacking and hiking, the 27-mile Tosohatchee Trail, which forms several loops. Canoeing is available on the creeks. Horseback riding is possible on appropriate trails. Fishing and limited hunting are permitted in season.

Camping Regulations: Primitive camping is restricted to two backpack camping areas, and there's also a horseback camping area. Campfires are permitted at designated locations. Pets are not allowed in camping areas.

It's necessary to register at reserve headquarters, and a camping fee must be paid for each night. Maximum stay allowed is two nights. Camping is prohibited during hunting season.

For Further Information: Tosohatchee State Reserve, 3365 Taylor Creek Road, Christmas, FL 32709; (407)568-5893.

ST. JOSEPH PENINSULA STATE PARK—2,516 acres. This 10-mile-long and narrow park in Florida's western panhandle is on a peninsula which extends into the Gulf of Mexico. There are lovely wild beaches and dunes here, with salt marshes and pine flatwoods. The outer end of the peninsula (1,650 acres) is protected as a wilderness preserve.

Activities: Hiking and backpacking are available along the shoreline as well as on a road.

Camping Regulations: Camping is allowed throughout the preserve, except on dunes. It's necessary to register and pay a small camping fee before entering. Water must be carried in. A maximum of 20 people are allowed in the preserve each day.

For Further Information: St. Joseph Peninsula State Park, Star Route 1, Box 200, Port St. Joe, FL 32456; (904)227-1327.

MYAKKA RIVER STATE PARK—28,875 acres. Located in the southwestern part of the state, Myakka River is Florida's largest state park. It's an area of pine flatwoods and oak hammocks, marshes and prairie. Included are 12 miles of the Myakka River and a large lake. Deer, bobcat, and alligator are among the wildlife.

Activities: There are about 40 miles of trails for backpacking and hiking. Canoeing and fishing are available on the river. The park also has trails for horseback riding.

Camping Regulations: Camping is restricted to four trailside camping areas. A maximum of 12

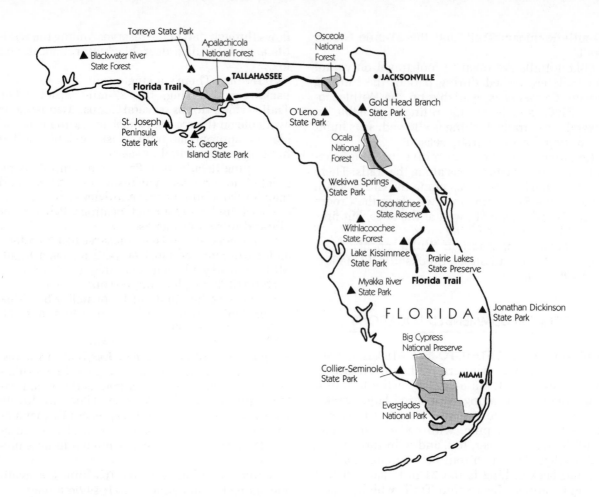

persons are allowed at each area. Campers must first register and pay a small fee.

For Further Information: Myakka River State Park, 13207 SR 72, Sarasota, FL 34241; (813)924-1027.

COLLIER–SEMINOLE STATE PARK—6,423 acres. Collier–Seminole is in southern Florida, northwest of Everglades National Park and west of Big Cypress National Preserve. The Blackwater River flows through the area, along with some other waterways.

Included in the park is a 4,760-acre wilderness preserve, consisting of a mangrove swamp. There are also cypress swamps, marshes, and a tropical hammock. Among the wildlife are black bear, Florida panther, and crocodile.

Activities: Canoeing is available on the Blackwater River and other waterways, and canoes may be rented here. Hiking and backpacking are possible on a 6.5-mile loop trail.

Camping Regulations: One primitive camping area is available for canoeists, and there's another single trailside campsite for backpackers. It's necessary to register before camping, and a small fee is charged. Campfires are allowed at designated sites. Pets are prohibited. Winter is the best time to visit.

For Further Information: Collier–Seminole State Park, Route 4, Box 848, Naples, FL 33961; (813)394-3397.

TORREYA STATE PARK—1,000 acres. This park in northwest Florida has scenery somewhat more typical of states to the north. There are high bluffs and deep ravines, along with swamplands and hardwood hammocks. The Apalachicola River flows through the park. Wildlife includes deer, bobcat, and wild turkey.

Activities: Hiking and backpacking are possible on a 7-mile loop trail, which circles around the park. Fishing is available on the river.

Camping Regulations: Camping is limited to two primitive areas located along the loop trail. One site overlooks the river. A maximum of 12 campers are allowed in each area, and it's necessary to first register and pay a small fee before entering.

For Further Information: Torreya State Park, Route 2, Box 70, Bristol, FL 32321; (904)643-2674.

PRAIRIE LAKES STATE PRESERVE— 8,000 acres. Located in the Kissimmee Valley of east-central Florida, this state preserve includes some small lakes, oak hammocks and marshes, prairies and flatwoods.

Activities: Backpacking and hiking are available on 12 miles of trails, which form two loops.

Camping Regulations: Camping is restricted to two primitive areas, each of which is limited to eight persons. Campfires are allowed in designated spots. Campers must first register and pay a nominal fee.

For Further Information: Prairie Lakes State Preserve, P.O. Box 220, Kenansville, FL 32739; (305)436-1626.

LAKE KISSIMMEE STATE PARK— 5,000 acres. Situated in central Florida, Lake Kissimmee State Park is surrounded by three large lakes. This is an area of marshes, pine flatwoods, and hardwood hammocks, with wildlife which includes deer, bobcat, and alligator.

Activities: Hiking and backpacking are possible on 13 miles of trails, which form two loops.

Camping Regulations: Each trail loop has one authorized primitive camping area, and camping is limited to these two locations. Maximum number of campers allowed at each area is 12. Fires are permitted in the fire circles provided. Registration is required at the park office at the time of entry.

For Further Information: Lake Kissimmee State Park, 14248 Camp Mack Road, Lake Wales, FL 33853; (813)696-1112.

WEKIWA SPRINGS STATE PARK— 6,400 acres. This park in central Florida includes Wekiwa Spring and the Wekiwa River, and there are pine flatwoods and sand hills, swamps and hammocks. Among the area's wildlife are deer, bear, and bobcat.

Activities: The park has 13 miles of trails for hiking and backpacking. Canoeing and fishing are available on the river.

Camping Regulations: Camping is restricted to two designated backpack camping areas along the trails. It's necessary to first register at the park office and pay a nominal fee. A maximum of eight campers are allowed to use each area. Fires are permitted in established fire circles.

For Further Information: Wekiwa Springs State Park, 1800 Wekiwa Circle, Apopka, FL 32712; (407)889-9920.

O'LENO STATE PARK—6,000 acres. O'Leno State Park is in north-central Florida. The area includes sandhills and hardwood hammocks, swamps and flatwoods, and there's a segment of the Sante Fe River, which goes underground for a stretch. Deer, bobcat, and wild turkey are among the wildlife.

Activities: Hiking and backpacking are available on the 12-mile Natural Bridge trail.

Camping Regulations: Camping is limited to one primitive area at Sweet Water Lake. No more than 12 may camp here at one time. It's necessary to first register and pay a small fee. Fires are permitted in a fire circle provided.

For Further Information: O'Leno State Park, Route 2, Box 1010, High Springs, FL 32643; (904)454-1853.

JONATHAN DICKINSON STATE PARK—10,284 acres. Located in southeast Florida, Jonathan Dickinson State Park includes the Loxahatchee River, along with pine flatwoods, dunes, and cypress swamps.

Activities: There's an 8-mile trail for hiking and backpacking. During wet periods the trail may be flooded.

Camping Regulations: Camping is restricted to one authorized camping area along the trail. A maximum of eight persons are allowed to camp here at a time. Campfires are permitted. Campers must first register and and pay a small fee upon entry.

For Further Information: Jonathan Dickinson State Park, 16450 S.E. Federal Highway, Hobe Sound, FL 33455; (305)546-2771.

ST. GEORGE ISLAND STATE PARK—1,883 acres. Accessible by highway, this island park is located in the Gulf of Mexico. It has over nine miles of lovely beaches and dunes, some marshes, and pine and oak forests.

Activities: Hiking and backpacking are possible on a 2.7-mile trail, as well as along the beaches.

Camping Regulations: Primitive camping is limited to one designated area at Gap Point, overlooking a bay, at the end of the 2.7-mile trail. Campfires are allowed. Water must be carried in. Maximum number of campers allowed at one time is 12. Reservations are not available. Campers must register and pay a small fee at the time of entry. Pets are prohibited.

For Further Information: St. George Island State Park, P.O. Box 62, Eastpoint, FL 32328; (904)670-2111.

GOLD HEAD BRANCH STATE PARK—1,480 acres. Located in northeast Florida, Gold Head Branch State Park includes some hardwood and pine forest, a few lakes, and a ravine with a large stream.

Activities: Hiking and backpacking are available on a 3-mile section of the Florida Trail which traverses the park.

Camping Regulations: Along the trail is one designated primitive camping area overlooking Lake Johnson. Camping here is limited to 12 persons. Campfires are allowed. It's necessary to register and pay a small fee for each night.

For Further Information: Gold Head Branch State Park, 6239 SR 21, Keystone Heights, FL 32656; (904)473-4701.

Also, the 4,636-acre Lower Wekiva River State Preserve in central Florida has one canoe-campsite along the Wekiva River. Reservations are required and a small fee is charged. In the near future there will probably also be a primitive campsite for hikers. For more information contact Lower Wekiva River State Preserve, 8300 West Highway 46, Sanford, FL 32771; (407)330-6728.

In addition, Florida has 36 designated canoe trails throughout the state, and camping is allowed along some of the rivers and creeks. For more information, including a listing of canoe clubs and other organizations offering canoe and kayak trips, as well as outfitters and canoe liveries, contact the Florida Department of Natural Resources, 3900 Commonwealth Boulevard, Tallahassee, FL 32399; (904)488-6327.

MAJOR BACKPACKING TRAILS

FLORIDA TRAIL—This ambitious new trail will eventually be 1,300 miles long when completed, running the length of Florida from the western panhandle to Big Cypress National Preserve, just north of the Everglades. Over 700 miles of the trail are currently open. A number of side trails and loops are included.

The Florida Trail passes through some of the state's wildest and most beautiful natural scenery. It's relatively flat and easy. Some sections become quite wet during the rainy season. Winter is the best time to backpack on the trail, with summer not recommended due to insects and the heat.

The trail traverses all three of Florida's National Forests, numerous state parks, and also state forest lands. Other rather lengthy sections are on private land, and these are open only to members of the Florida Trail Association.

Camping Regulations: Within the National Forests camping is allowed almost anywhere, except near public use areas or where posted otherwise. It's suggested that campsites be at least 100 feet from the trail and away from water sources.

Elsewhere along the trail camping is restricted, and campfires are allowed only at authorized sites. On some state lands designated campsites are available, usually requiring registration and the payment of a nominal fee to camp. For other segments of the trail there is currently no legal camping except at nearby campgrounds.

For Further Information: Florida Trail Association, P.O. Box 13708, Gainesville, FL 32604: (904)378-8823/(800)343-1882 (in Florida only).

FLORIDA CAMPING RESOURCES

ORGANIZATIONS WHICH SPONSOR WILDERNESS CAMPING TRIPS

Florida Trail Association, P.O. Box 13708, Gainesville, FL 32604: (904)378-8823/(800)343-1882 (in Florida only). This large association, which has a number of chapters throughout the state, offers a schedule of events including backpacking and canoe-camping trips.

USEFUL GUIDEBOOKS

A Canoeing and Kayaking Guide to the Streams of Florida: Volume I, North Central Peninsula and Panhandle—Carter, Elizabeth F. and Pearce, John L. Birmingham: Menasha Ridge Press, 1985.

A Canoeing and Kayaking Guide to the Streams of Florida: Volume II, Central and Southern Peninsula—Glaros, Lou and Sphar, Doug. Birmingham: Menasha Ridge Press, 1987.

A Hiking Guide to The Trails of Florida—Carter, Elizabeth F. Birmingham: Menasha Ridge Press, 1987.

The Sierra Club Guide to the Natural Areas of Florida—Perry, John and Jane. San Francisco: Sierra Club Books, 1992.

Walking the Florida Trail—Keller, Jim. Gainesville: Florida Trail Association, 1985.

INFORMATION ABOUT STATE PARK CAMPGROUNDS

Florida Department of Natural Resources, Division of Recreation and Parks, 3900 Commonwealth Boulevard, Tallahassee, FL 32399; (904)487-4784.

STATE HIGHWAY MAP AND TRAVEL INFORMATION

Florida Division of Tourism, 107 West Gaines, Suite 543, Tallahassee, FL 32399; (904)488-8230.

GEORGIA

BEST AREAS FOR WILDERNESS CAMPING

CHATTAHOOCHEE NATIONAL FOREST—740,000 acres. Chattahoochee National Forest is located along the northern border of Georgia, in the southernmost reaches of the Appalachian Mountains. It's a wild and beautiful region with terrain which is often quite rugged.

The highest elevation is 4,784-foot Brasstown Bald. There are three designated wilderness areas, consisting of the 37,000-acre Cohutta Wilderness, plus small portions of two other wilderness areas which extend into nearby North Carolina and South Carolina.

Chattahoochee has several major rivers, many creeks and waterfalls, and a few lakes, with mixed forests of pine, hemlock, and hardwoods, as well as rhododendron and mountain laurel. Black bear, deer, wild boar, and fox are among the wildlife.

Activities: Backpacking and hiking are possible on a number of backpacking and hiking trails, including 75 miles of the Appalachian Trail and 50 miles of the Benton MacKaye Trail (see entries page 136), 37 miles of the Bartram National Recreation Trail, and the 31-mile Duncan Ridge National Recreation Trail. Difficulty ranges from easy to strenuous.

There are also trails for horseback riding, and mountain biking is allowed on some trails outside of wilderness areas. Canoeing and rafting are available on the Chattooga National Wild and Scenic River and a few other rivers. Fishing is possible, and hunting is permitted in season.

Camping Regulations: Camping and campfires are allowed throughout the National Forest, except where posted otherwise. No permits are necessary. It's suggested that campers choose sites that are at least 100 feet from streams and trails.

For Further Information: Chattahoochee National Forest, 508 Oak Street N.W., Gainesville, GA 30501; (404)536-0541.

OKEFENOKEE NATIONAL WILDLIFE REFUGE—396,000 acres. This National Wildlife Refuge protects an amazingly vast wilderness swamp in southeast Georgia, near and alongside the Florida border. Most of the refuge (some 354,000 acres) consists of designated wilderness.

Okefenokee has many lakes, marshes, and islands. Much of the area is cypress-forested. There's an abundant bird population, and wildlife includes black bear, deer, and alligator.

Activities: Canoeing is the main activity here, with canoes and camping equipment available for rental nearby. There are also over four miles of hiking trails. Fishing is permitted, but swimming is not.

Camping Regulations: Camping is allowed for canoeists only. A permit is necessary, with a fee charged to camp each night. Maximum stay is five days. Numbers of visitors are strictly limited. Reservations must be made in advance by phone. Camping is restricted to designated sites, which generally include a large wooden platform. Fires are prohibited at some campsites.

For Further Information: Okefenokee National Wildlife Refuge, Route 2, Box 338, Folkston, GA 31537; (912)496-3331.

OCONEE NATIONAL FOREST— 104,000 acres. Consisting of two tracts of wild land southeast of Atlanta, in north-central Georgia, Oconee National Forest is co-administered with Chattahoochee National Forest. It's a relatively flat area (highest point is 654 feet), with a couple of rivers, a number of streams, and an attractive forest of mixed hardwoods and pine, including some old-growth trees. Bear and deer are among the wildlife.

Activities: A few short and easy trails are available for hiking or backpacking. Some trails are open to horseback riding. The Oconee River is suitable for canoeing. Fishing is possible here as well, and hunting is permitted in season.

Camping Regulations: Camping and campfires are allowed almost anywhere, except where posted otherwise. No permits are required. Campers are encouraged to choose sites which are at least 100 feet from trails and water sources.

For Further Information: Oconee National Forest, 508 Oak Street N.W., Gainesville, GA 30501; (404)536-0541.

OTHER RECOMMENDED LOCATIONS

CUMBERLAND ISLAND NATIONAL SEASHORE— 37,000 acres. This 16-mile-long barrier island is located off Georgia's southeast coast. There are many miles of beautiful sandy beach here, along with dunes, saltwater marshes, and some oak and pine forest. Wildlife includes deer and alligator. Ferry service is available from the mainland, and advance reservations are necessary for the ferry.

Activities: Hiking and backpacking are possible on a number of trails, and superb swimming is available. Saltwater fishing is permitted, as is limited deer hunting.

Camping Regulations: The island has four designated backcountry camping areas, with camping restricted to these locations. A backcountry permit is required, and may be obtained from the visitor center. Campfires are prohibited. The island is closed to camping for five short periods between late October and early January to permit deer hunting.

For Further Information: Cumberland Island National Seashore, P.O. Box 806, St. Marys, GA 31558; (912)882-4336.

CLOUDLAND CANYON STATE PARK—2,120 acres. Located on the edge of Lookout Mountain, in the northwest corner of Georgia, Cloudland Canyon State Park has elevations as high as 1,800 feet. Included are ridges and valleys, with a deep canyon gorge, a large creek, and waterfalls. The forest consists of mixed hardwoods and some conifers.

Activities: Hiking and backpacking are available on 11 miles of trails, including a 6-mile Backcountry Trail.

Camping Regulations: Two primitive camping areas are located along the Backcountry Trail. It's

necesssary to register prior to starting and to check out before leaving the park. A small fee is charged for camping each night.

For Further Information: Cloudland Canyon State Park, Route 2, Rising Fawn, GA 30738; (404)657-4050.

FORT MOUNTAIN STATE PARK—1,930 acres. Fort Mountain State Park is located within the Cohutta Mountains of northern Georgia's Chattahoochee National Forest. The park has rugged terrain with some streams, a lake, and a forest mainly of hardwoods, plus dogwood and rhododendron.

Activities: Backpacking and hiking are possible on over 14 miles of trails, including an 8.2-mile Backcountry Trail loop. Fishing is also available.

Camping Regulations: Primitive camping is limited to three separate areas located along the Backcountry Trail, and campfires are allowed at the sites. A small fee is charged for each night.

For Further Information: Fort Mountain State Park, Route 7, Box 7008, Chatsworth, GA 30705; (404)695-2621.

PROVIDENCE CANYON STATE PARK—1,108 acres. Located in western Georgia, Providence Canyon State Park is especially notable for several small and attractive eroded canyons, which are up to 150 feet deep.

Activities: There are 10 miles of hiking trails here, including a 7-mile trail open to backpacking.

Camping Regulations: Primitive camping is limited to five designated areas along the backpacking trail. Campfires are allowed in the fire pits provided.

For Further Information: Providence Canyon State Park, Route 1, Box 158, Lumpkin, GA 31815; (912)838-6202.

VOGEL STATE PARK—280 acres. This little state park is located within Chattahoochee National Forest, in the Blue Ridge Mountains of northern Georgia. It has mixed forests and a 20-acre lake.

Activities: There are 19 miles of trails in the area, with most falling outside of state park boundaries. Included are the strenuous 12.7-mile Coosa Backcountry Trail loop, a section of the Duncan Ridge Trail, and also the Appalachian Trail. Fishing is available, and hunting is allowed in season.

Camping Regulations: Primitive camping is limited to the Coosa Backcountry Trail, along with sections of the Appalachian Trail and Duncan Ridge Trail outside of the park.

A free permit is required to use the Coosa Backcountry Trail, and backpackers should check in upon returning. There are no designated camp-sites, but suitable sites are available along the trail. Campfires are strongly discouraged.

For Further Information: Vogel State Park, Route 1, Box 1230, Blairsville, GA 30512; (404)745-2628.

AMICALOLA FALLS STATE PARK—1,020 acres. Situated next to Chattahoochee National Forest lands, this park centers around 729-foot Amicalola Falls, which is the highest waterfall in Georgia. It also serves as an entry point for those who are back-packing on the Appalachian Trail.

Activities: There are some short hiking trails, and backpacking is available on the 8-mile Approach Trail, which begins in the park and leads to Springer Mountain, southern terminus of the Appalachian Trail. Backpacking equipment rentals are available in the park.

Camping Regulations: A special shelter in the park is for the use of Appalachian Trail hikers. Camping is also available in Chattahoochee National Forest just beyond the park boundary.

For Further Information: Amicalola Falls State Park, Route 1, Dawsonville, GA 30534; (404)265-2885.

In addition, 1,502-acre Black Rock Mountain State Park in northern Georgia has a single campsite (for one party only) along a 7.2-mile Backcountry Trail. Reservations and a permit are necessary. For information contact Black Rock Mountain State Park, P.O. Drawer A, Mountain City, GA 30562; (404)746-2141.

Camping and backpacking are also permitted in some of Georgia's Wildlife Management Areas, used primarily by hunters. For more information contact the Georgia Department of Natural Re-

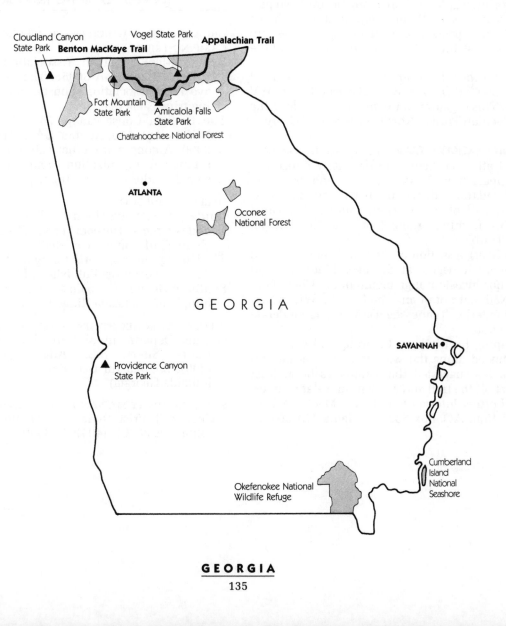

GEORGIA

sources, 205 Butler Street, Suite 1352, Atlanta, GA 30334.

MAJOR BACKPACKING TRAILS

APPALACHIAN TRAIL—76 miles in Georgia (2,100 total). The southern terminus of this important National Scenic Trail is on 3,782-foot Springer Mountain, in northern Georgia's Chattahoochee National Forest. Access is via a trail from Amicalola Falls State Park.

The Appalachian Trail traverses some ruggedly mountainous terrain in this state, with outstanding views from some summits, before crossing into North Carolina. Most of the trail here is moderate to strenuous in difficulty.

Camping Regulations: Shelters are available at regular intervals, and camping as well as campfires are allowed elsewhere along the trail. No permits are necessary. When camping at other than a shelter, backpackers are encouraged to set up camp at least 100 feet from water sources and the trail.

For Further Information: Appalachian Trail Conference, P.O. Box 807, Harpers Ferry, WV 25425. This organization publishes a *Guide to the Appalachian Trail in North Carolina and Georgia.*

BENTON MACKAYE TRAIL—75 miles in Georgia. Named after the man who originally conceived the Appalachian Trail, this new and partially-completed trail will eventually be about 250 miles long. It will offer a western route to the Great Smokies, forming a giant loop with the Appalachian Trail.

The Georgia section of the trail is now finished and open. It begins at Springer Mountain and heads northwest through mountainous Chattahoochee National Forest and the Cohutta Wilderness before entering Tennessee. Difficulty is moderate to strenuous.

Camping Regulations: Camping and campfires are allowed along the way, with no permits required. It's suggested that campsites be at least 100 feet off the trail and away from water sources.

For Further Information: Benton MacKaye Trail Association, P.O. Box 53271, Atlanta, GA 30355.

Also of interest for backpackers is the 37-mile Bartram National Recreation Trail in Chattahoochee National Forest. This trail is part of what may eventually be a long, multi-state trail which traces the route taken by naturalist William Bartram in the 1770s. For information contact the Bartram Trail Conference, 431 E. 63 St., Savannah, GA 31405.

Another trail suitable for backpacking is the 23-mile Pine Mountain Trail, in west-central Georgia, which has nine designated campsites along the way. Much of the trail falls within the boundaries of F.D.R. State Park. For information contact the Pine Mountain Trail Association, c/o Wickham's Outdoor World, Inc., Cross Country Plaza, Columbia, GA 31906.

GEORGIA CAMPING RESOURCES

ORGANIZATIONS WHICH OFFER WILDERNESS CAMPING TRIPS

Benton MacKaye Trail Association, P.O. Box 53271, Atlanta, GA 30355. The Benton MacKaye Trail Association sponsors some backpacking trips each year.

The Georgia Conservancy, 781 Marietta Street NW, Suite B-100, Atlanta, GA 30318; (404)876-2900. Among many other activities, this environmental organization schedules an occasional wilderness camping trip.

USEFUL GUIDEBOOKS

Guide to the Appalachian Trail in North Carolina and Georgia— Harpers Ferry, WV: The Appalachian Trail Conference, 1989.

The Hiking Trails of North Georgia—Homan, Tim. Atlanta: Peachtree Publishers, Ltd., 1987.

Southern Georgia Canoeing—Schlinger, Bob. Birmingham: Menasha Ridge Press, 1989.

INFORMATION ABOUT STATE PARK CAMPGROUNDS

Georgia Department of Natural Resources, 205 Butler Street, S.E., Atlanta, GA 30334; (800)342-7275 (in Georgia) or (800)542- 7275 (outside Georgia).

STATE HIGHWAY MAP AND TRAVEL INFORMATION

Georgia Tourist Division, P.O. Box 1776, Atlanta, GA 30301; (404)656-3590.

HAWAII

BEST AREAS FOR WILDERNESS CAMPING

HAWAII VOLCANOES NATIONAL PARK—229,117 acres. Located on the island of Hawaii, this notable National Park is the home of two volcanic mountains, 13,667-foot Mauna Loa and 4,077-foot Kilauea, which have periodic mild eruptions and active lava flows. The base of the island lies no less than 18,000 feet below the ocean's surface.

Scenery here includes craters, lava shields, steam vents, cinder cones, tubes (tunnels or caves), and some desert, along with rain forest as well as grassy areas. Flora and fauna here are diverse, and there's an especially varied birdlife.

Activities: Hiking and backpacking are available on many miles of trails, including the rugged 18-mile Mauna Loa Trail, which climbs 6,600 feet to the summit of Mauna Loa.

Difficulty ranges from easy to very strenuous. Some trails are open to horseback riding. Visitors are asked to stay on trails. Hunting is prohibited in the park.

Camping Regulations: Shelters, tent sites, and cabins are found at several locations along the trails. Backcountry campers must pre-register at the visitor center and obtain permits, which are available on a first-come, first-served basis.

Maximum stay is seven days, and group size is limited to 12. Campfires are restricted to designated sites. Dogs are not allowed. Campers must check out in person or by phone before leaving the park. Cold weather is possible at any time of year.

For Further Information: Hawaii Volcanoes National Park, P.O. Box 52, Hawaii, HI 96718; (808)967-7311.

HALEAKALA NATIONAL PARK—28,665 acres. This National Park on the island of Maui protects 10,023-foot Mount Haleakala, an inactive volcano which has a crater with a seven mile diameter. The park's landscape includes high cinder cones, lava ash, and other volcanic scenery.

Also in the park is the lush Kipahula Valley, with rainforest, grasslands, and coastal cliffs. There are several streams with waterfalls and pools, and an exotic birdlife, plantlife, and wildlife, including native and non-native species.

Activities: Thirty-six miles of trails are open to backpacking and hiking. Difficulty varies from easy to strenuous. Some trails may be used by horseback riders. Visitors are asked to remain on trails. Hunting is not allowed.

Camping Regulations: Camping in the crater area requires a permit, available from park headquarters on a first-come, first-served basis. Tenting is restricted to two "backcountry campgrounds" or primitive camping areas.

Camping here is limited to two nights in one location, and a maximum of three nights total. Campfires are prohibited, so a stove is necessary if one wishes to cook. Pets are not permitted.

There are also three cabins which are available for a fee. Cabins must be reserved at least 90 days in advance. Since demand is high, a lottery system is used to allocate the cabins.

Camping in the Kipahula Area is limited to a campground which is accessible by car. The Upper Kipahula Valley is completely closed to the public. Weather in the park is often unpredictable, varying from hot to cold at any time of year.

For Further Information: Haleakala National Park, P.O. Box 369, Makawao, Maui, HI 96768; (808)572-9306.

PUU KA PELE FOREST RESERVE—Located in the northwestern part of the island of Kauai, Puu Ka Pele Forest Reserve features 2,000-foot-deep canyons, scenic valleys with stone ruins, streams, and the Waimea River. There are areas of scrub vegetation as well as dense forests here.

Activities: Hiking and backpacking are available on several trails which lead down through Waimea Canyon, Waialae Canyon, and Koaie Canyon. Difficulty varies from easy to strenuous.

Camping Regulations: There are several designated camping areas in the canyons, and camping is restricted to these sites. A permit must be obtained from the Division of Forestry office. It's also necessary to register at the trailhead upon entering and leaving. Maximum stay allowed is four nights.

For Further Information: Puu Ka Pele Forest Reserve, c/o Hawaii Division of Forestry and Wildlife, 3060 Eiwa Street, Room 306, Lihue, Kauai, HI 96766; (808)245-4433.

KULA AND KAHIKINUI FOREST RESERVES—These two forest reserves stand next to Haleakala National Park on the island of Maui. Terrain here ranges from hilly to mountainous and rugged, with elevations from 6,000 to 7,000 feet.

Included are mixed forests of cedar and pine, redwood and ash, plus groves of fruit trees and some grasslands. Wildlife in the reserves includes wild goat and wild pig.

Activities: Backpacking and hiking are possible on more than 30 miles of trails. Seasonal hunting is allowed in the reserves.

Camping Regulations: Camping is limited to several trail shelters and established camping areas. A permit must first be obtained from the Division of Forestry office in order to camp here. Maximum stay allowed is two nights per site.

For Further Information: Kula and Kahikinui Forest Reserves, c/o Hawaii Division of Forestry and Wildlife, P.O. Box 1015, Wailuku, Maui, HI 96793; (808)244-4352.

OTHER RECOMMENDED LOCATIONS

NA PALI COAST STATE PARK—6,175 acres. Located along the coast of the island of Kauai, scenic Na Pali Coast State Park features high rugged cliffs with outstanding views, narrow valleys, streams with waterfalls and pools, and beautiful sand beaches.

Activities: There's one trail for hiking and backpacking, the 11-mile Kalalau Trail, which follows a hilly and sometimes steep route along the coastline—up over cliffs and down through valleys—and dead-ends at a beach. Shorter side trails lead up three of the valleys. Limited hunting is allowed in the park.

Camping Regulations: Three designated camping areas are found along the Kalalau Trail, and camping is restricted to these sites. Maximum stay is five nights. Two consecutive nights are not allowed at two of the camping areas. Group size is limited to 10.

Before entering, a free permit must be obtained by mail or in person from the state park office (address page 139). Permit applications must be received at least a month in advance from May through September, or seven days in advance at other times.

For Further Information: Na Pali Coast State Park, c/o Division of State Parks, 3060 Eiwa Street, Room 306, Lihue, HI 96766; (808)245-4444.

WAIMANU NATIONAL ESTUARINE RESEARCH RESERVE—3,600 acres. This state reserve is located on the northern coast of the island of Hawaii. It includes the Waimanu and Waipio Valleys, at the base of the Kohala Mountains—with small gullies, wetlands, beaches, several streams, and some waterfalls. Portions of the reserve are forested, and there are groves of fruit trees.

Activities: A single trail is available for hiking or backpacking: the 7-mile Muliwai Trail, which runs between Waipio and Waimanu Valleys. The trail is steep and rocky in places, and isn't well-maintained. Seasonal hunting is permitted in the area.

Camping Regulations: There's one shelter about two-thirds of the distance along the trail, and camping is allowed here as well as at some sites in Waimanu Valley. A permit is required.

For Further Information: Waimanu National Estuarine Research Reserve, c/o Hawaii Division of Forestry and Wildlife, 1643 Kilauea Avenue, Hilo, HI 96720; (808)933-4221.

Camping is also allowed along several trails on the island of Oahu. Included are the 7-mile Waimano Trail, the 6-mile Manana Trail, and three shorter trails near Hauula. Scenery includes ridges with beautiful views, valleys, streams, and waterfalls. A camping permit is required. For more information contact the Division of Forestry and Wildlife, 1151 Punchbowl Street, Honolulu, HI 96813; (808)548-8850.

In addition, primitive camping is permitted in one area along the 5.5-mile King's Highway

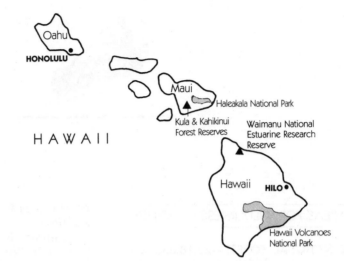

HAWAII

Coastal Trail, on the southern coast of the island of Maui. For more information contact the Division of Forestry and Wildlife, P.O. Box 1015, Wailuku, HI 96793; (808)244-4352.

Finally, camping is allowed in remote Wailau Valley on the north coast of the island of Molokai. Access is possible by boat when waters are calm, or via an unmaintained trail which crosses private land and requires special permission to use. For more information contact the Division of Forestry and Wildlife, P.O. Box 1015, Wailuku, HI 96793; (808)244-4352.

HAWAII CAMPING RESOURCES

ORGANIZATIONS WHICH OFFER WILDERNESS CAMPING TRIPS
Sierra Club, Hawaii Chapter, P.O. Box 2577, Honolulu, HI 96803; (808)538-6616. This chapter of the Sierra Club offers occasional backpacking and other primitive camping trips.

USEFUL GUIDEBOOKS
Hawaii Trails—Morey, Kathy. Berkeley, CA: Wilderness Press, 1992.
Hawaiian Hiking Trails—Chisholm, Craig. Lake Oswego, OR: The Fernglen Press, 1989.
Kauai Trails—Morey, Kathy. Berkeley, CA: Wilderness Press, 1991.
Paddling Hawaii—Sutherland, Audrey. Seattle: The Mountaineers Books.

INFORMATION ABOUT STATE PARK CAMPGROUNDS
Hawaii Division of State Parks, P.O. Box 621, Honolulu, HI 96809; (808)548-7455.

IDAHO

BEST AREAS FOR WILDERNESS CAMPING

NEZ PERCE NATIONAL FOREST—2,218,333 acres. Located in north-central Idaho, this huge National Forest encloses an area of high, rugged mountains and deep canyons. Included is 6,600-foot-deep Hells Canyon on the Snake River, said to be the deepest gorge in the country. Also here are the Selway and Salmon National Wild and Scenic Rivers.

There are many mountain lakes and scores of streams, areas of subalpine vegetation at higher elevations, and forests of ponderosa pine and Douglas fir. Wildlife includes elk, moose, white-tailed and mule deer, black bear, bighorn sheep, and mountain lion.

Nez Perce has four designated wilderness areas: 560,000 acres of the 1,340,000-acre Selway–Bitterroot Wilderness, 105,000 acres of the 2,360,000-acre Frank Church–River of No Return Wilderness, the 206,000-acre Gospel Hump Wilderness, and 34,000 acres of the Hells Canyon Wilderness.

Activities: Backpacking and hiking are available on about 2,600 miles of trails. Difficulty ranges from easy to very strenuous. Trails at high elevations are usually snow-free only from mid-July through September.

Horseback riding is allowed on many trails, as is mountain biking on most trails outside of wilderness areas. Cross-country skiing is possible here during the snow season.

Rafting, canoeing, and kayaking are available on the Selway, Salmon, Snake, and other major rivers in the region. A permit is required to run the Snake River in Hell's Canyon. There are also many possibilities for fishing. Hunting is permitted in season.

Camping Regulations: Camping is allowed throughout the National Forest, as are campfires, except near public recreation areas or where otherwise prohibited. No permits are necessary.

For Further Information: Nez Perce National Forest, Route 2, Box 475, Grangeville, ID 83530; (208)983-1950.

IDAHO PANHANDLE NATIONAL FORESTS—2,479,245 acres. Three of northern Idaho's National Forests (Kaniksu, Coeur d'Alene, and St. Joe) are administered together as the Idaho Panhandle National Forests. There are several rugged mountain ranges in the region, including the Bitterroot Mountains, with elevations over 7,000 feet.

Forests are of pine and fir, spruce and larch, plus old-growth hemlock and cedar. Also here are many lakes, ponds, streams, and rivers, including the St. Joe National Wild and Scenic River. Among the wildlife are grizzly and black bear, moose, caribou, elk, white-tailed and mule deer, mountain goat, and lynx.

Activities: Hiking and backpacking are possible on over 2,000 miles of trails, including a section of the new Idaho Centennial Trail (see entry page 000) and the 41-mile Big Creek Trail. Difficulty ranges from easy to strenuous.

Horses are allowed on most trails, and cross-country skiing is a winter option. Canoeing, kayaking, and rafting are available on the Priest, Coeur d'Alene, and several other rivers. Climbing and spelunking (caving) are other possibilities. Fishing is permitted, as is hunting in season.

Camping Regulations: Camping is allowed throughout the Idaho Panhandle National Forests, except where otherwise prohibited. Campsites should be at least 100 feet from lakeshores and away from trails. Campfires are allowed but discouraged. A stove is suggested for cooking. No permits are necessary.

For Further Information: Idaho Panhandle National Forests, 1201 Ironwood Drive, Coeur d'Alene, ID 83814; (208)667-2561.

SAWTOOTH NATIONAL FOREST—1,347,422 acres.

This National Forest consists of several units in the south-central part of the state. Located here are some of Idaho's most notable mountain ranges, including the Sawtooth, White Cloud, and Boulder Mountains. There are 40 peaks over 10,000 feet, with 12,009-foot Hyndman Peak the highest.

More than half of the National Forest (754,000 acres) has been designated the Sawtooth National Recreation Area, which preserves some of the finest scenery. It's also the location of a major wilderness area: the 217,088-acre Sawtooth Wilderness.

Scenery includes high granite peaks, limestone cliffs, deep canyons, and striking rock formations. There are scores of streams and rivers, over 1,000 lakes, conifer forests, and mountain meadows. Among the wildlife are elk, deer, antelope, black bear, bighorn sheep, and mountain goat.

Activities: Backpacking and hiking are possible on about 1,600 miles of trails, many of which are in the Sawtooth National Recreation Area. Difficulty varies from easy to strenuous. Snow often remains on trails at high elevations until mid-July, and typically returns by late September.

Horseback riding is allowed on most trails. Some trails are designated for cross-country skiing in winter. Mountain biking is permitted on trails outside of the Sawtooth Wilderness.

Rafting, kayaking, and canoeing are available on the Salmon River. Climbing and mountaineering are other options in the mountains here. Fishing is also possible, with hunting permitted in season.

Camping Regulations: Camping is allowed throughout most of the National Forest, except near public recreation areas or where otherwise prohibited. Permits are required for horseback riders and for groups of 10 or more in the Sawtooth Wilderness.

In the wilderness area campsites must be at least 100 feet from trails and water sources. Campfires are generally allowed but discouraged. Fires are not permitted within 200 yards of some lakes, and are prohibited in a few other locations.

For Further Information: Sawtooth National Forest, 2647 Kimberly Road East, Twin Falls, ID 83301; (208)737-3200.

CHALLIS NATIONAL FOREST— 2,516,191 acres.

Enormous Challis National Forest in south-central Idaho encompasses several high mountain ranges, with precipitous peaks, cirque basins, and canyons. Idaho's highest elevation, 12,655-foot Borah Peak, is located here.

There are areas of alpine tundra, meadows, forests of conifers, and grasslands, with many lakes and streams. Wildlife includes elk, deer, moose, black bear, antelope, bighorn sheep, and mountain goat.

Challis has one designated wilderness area, consisting of about 780,000 acres of the 2,361,767-acre Frank Church–River of No Return Wilderness, which extends into five other National Forests, and is the largest wilderness area in the country outside of Alaska.

Activities: Hiking and backpacking are available on over 1,600 miles of trails, including the 59-mile Highline Trail. Many trails are open to horses. Difficulty varies from easy to strenuous. High trails may only be snow-free from July-September.

There's rafting on the Salmon River, a National Wild and Scenic River. Cross-country skiing is available on many trails in winter. Hunting and fishing are permitted in season.

Camping Regulations: Camping is allowed throughout the National Forest, as are campfires, except near public use areas or where posted otherwise. No permits are necessary.

For Further Information: Challis National Forest, HC 63, Box 1671, Challis, ID 83226; (208)879-2285.

PAYETTE NATIONAL FOREST—2,314,436 acres. Located in west-central Idaho and consisting of two huge tracts of land, Payette National Forest covers a wild area of steep and rugged mountains with elevations over 9,000 feet.

There are cirques and horns, rock domes and outcrops, granite walls, and deep canyon gorges, along with countless streams, lakes, and some major rivers, including the Salmon and several other National Wild and Scenic Rivers.

Throughout the region are pine and spruce forests, with fir and aspen, plus meadows and grasslands. Among the wildlife are elk, deer, moose, black bear, bighorn sheep, and mountain goat.

Payette also has 782,000 acres of the largest designated wilderness area outside of Alaska: the 2,361,767-acre Frank Church–River of No Return Wilderness, which continues on into five nearby National Forests.

Activities: There are over 1,400 miles of trails for hiking and backpacking. Difficulty ranges from easy to strenuous. Many trails are open to horseback riding.

Cross-country skiing and ski mountaineering are possible here in the winter. Rafting is available on a section of the Salmon River. Fishing is permitted, as is hunting in season.

Camping Regulations: Camping and campfires are allowed throughout the National Forest, except near public recreation areas or where otherwise prohibited. No permits are necessary.

For Further Information: Payette National Forest, P.O. Box 1026, McCall, ID 83638; (208)634-8151.

TARGHEE NATIONAL FOREST—1,557,792 acres in Idaho (296,448 in Wyoming). Made up of units in southwest Idaho and also Wyoming, this National Forest borders on Wyoming's Yellowstone National Park and Grand Teton National Park, and includes a segment of the Continental Divide.

There are high and rugged mountain ranges here with elevations over 10,000 feet, glacial cirques, steep cliffs and canyons, lakes and ponds, rivers, and streams with waterfalls. Two designated wilderness areas are in the Wyoming portion.

Included as well are areas of alpine tundra and grassy meadows, lodgepole pine and Douglas fir forests, plus sagebrush and semidesert vegetation. Wildlife includes elk, moose, grizzly and black bear, deer, bighorn sheep, and mountain lion.

Activities: Backpacking and hiking are possible on more than 1,200 miles of trails, including a section of the Continental Divide Trail (see entry page 145). Difficulty varies from easy to strenuous. High elevations are normally snow-free only during summer months.

Horseback riding is allowed on many trails, as is mountain biking outside of wilderness areas. Rafting, kayaking, and canoeing are available on the Big Springs National Recreation Water Trail and several rivers.

Cross-country skiing is possible on some trails during the snow season. Rock climbing is also available. Ample fishing is found along streams and lakes, and hunting is allowed in season.

Camping Regulations: Camping is permitted in most of the forest, except where otherwise prohibited. In wilderness areas campsites should be a minimum of 50 feet from streams and 200 feet from lakes.

Campfires are generally allowed, but they're prohibited in some parts of wilderness areas. Permits are necessary only for commercial and organizational groups.

For Further Information: Targhee National Forest, P.O. Box 208, St. Anthony, ID 83445; (208)624-3151.

SALMON NATIONAL FOREST—1,776,994 acres. This National Forest in east-central Idaho encompasses several mountain ranges, including the Salmon River Mountains and Bitterroot Mountains, with jagged peaks as high as 11,000 feet and outstanding views.

A section of the Salmon National Wild and Scenic River flows through the region. There are also many lakes and streams, sagebrush scrublands, meadows, and forests of Douglas fir, spruce, lodgepole and ponderosa pine. Wildlife includes elk, deer, bear, moose, bighorn sheep, and bobcat.

The National Forest has one designated wilderness area, consisting of 427,000 acres of the 2,361,767-acre Frank Church–River of No Return Wilderness—largest such wilderness in the lower 48 states, and shared by five other National Forests.

Activities: There are over 1,200 miles of trails for hiking and backpacking, including a section of the Continental Divide Trail (see entry page 122). Difficulty varies from easy to strenuous. High trails are likely to be snow-free only from July through mid-September.

Most trails are open to horseback riding, and mountain biking is allowed on trails outside of the wilderness area. Cross-country skiing is possible during the winter. Climbing is another option in the mountains here.

White-water rafting, kayaking, and canoeing are available on the Salmon River. A permit is required in advance to float a 79-mile stretch of this river during summer. There's also ample fishing. Hunting is allowed in season.

Camping Regulations: One may camp in most parts of Salmon National Forest, except near public recreation areas or where posted otherwise. No permits are required. Campfires are discouraged but allowed. A stove is recommended for cooking.

For Further Information: Salmon National Forest, P.O. Box 729, Salmon, ID 83467; (208)756-2215.

CLEARWATER NATIONAL FOREST—1,831,374 acres. Situated in Idaho's northern panhandle, Clearwater National Forest includes a portion of the ruggedly beautiful Bitterroot Range. In addition to rocky mountains there are deep canyons, buttes, and grassy prairies, along with the Lochsa and Clearwater National Wild and Scenic Rivers.

Throughout the region are forests of Douglas fir, ponderosa pine, larch, and virgin cedar, plus hundreds of lakes and countless creeks with waterfalls. Wildlife includes elk, moose, deer, black bear, mountain goat, and mountain lion.

There's a single designated wilderness area, consisting of 259,000 acres of the 1,337,900-acre Selway–Bitterroot Wilderness, which is shared by some nearby National Forests.

Activities: Clearwater has about 1,100 miles of trails for backpacking and hiking, including the 35-mile Eagle Mountain Trail. Trails at high elevations are likely to be free of snow only from July through September.

Horses are allowed on many trails, as are mountain bikes except in the wilderness area. Cross-country skiing is available in the winter.

White-water rafting, kayaking, and canoeing are possible on the North and Middle Forks of the Clearwater River, and also the Lochsa River. Fishing is available, as is hunting in season.

Camping Regulations: Camping is allowed freely here, as are campfires, except near public recreation areas or where otherwise prohibited. No permits are necessary. Campsites should be at least 200 feet from lakes.

For Further Information: Clearwater National Forest, 12730 Highway 12, Orofino, ID 83544; (208)476-4541.

BOISE NATIONAL FOREST—2,612,000 acres. This massive National Forest is in west-central Idaho, near Boise. In the region are parts of several mountain ranges, with rocky peaks over 9,000 feet high, plus deep canyons and valleys, and a number of lakes, rivers, and streams.

There are meadows, grasslands, and forests of pine and fir, with aspen. Included are over a half-million acres of old-growth trees. Elk, mule deer, black bear, bighorn sheep, mountain goat, and lynx are among the wildlife.

This National Forest has one designated wilderness area, which consists of 331,600 acres of the 2,361,767-acre Frank Church–River of No Return Wilderness, the country's largest such area outside of Alaska.

Activities: Backpacking and hiking are possible on about 1,000 miles of trails. Difficulty ranges from easy to strenuous. Many trails are suitable for horseback riding, and mountain bikes are allowed on trails outside of the designated wilderness area.

Limited rafting, canoeing, and kayaking are available on several of the rivers here. Cross-country skiing is a winter possibility on some trails.

Fishing is another option, and hunting is permitted in season.

Camping Regulations: Camping is allowed throughout most of Boise National Forest, as are campfires, except near public use areas or where otherwise restricted. No permits are required.

For Further Information: Boise National Forest, 1750 Front Street, Boise, ID 83702; (208)364-4100.

CARIBOU NATIONAL FOREST—1,087,916 acres. Caribou National Forest is comprised of a number of separate tracts in the southeast corner of Idaho, with small sections in Utah and Wyoming. Much of the terrain here is mountainous, with elevations ranging from 5,000 feet to over 9,000 feet. Highest point is 9,953-foot Meade Peak.

There are sagebrush slopes, canyons and ice caves, meadows, forests of Douglas fir and lodgepole pine, rivers and streams. Elk, moose, and deer are among the wildlife. Curlew National Grassland, consisting of 47,658 acres, is also part of this National Forest.

Activities: Hiking and backpacking are available on about 1,200 miles of trails, including the 55-mile High Line National Recreation Trail and the 35-mile Boundary Trail loop. Difficulty varies from easy to strenuous.

Horseback riding is allowed on many trails. Cross-country skiing is possible during the snow season. Fishing is available along the streams and lakes, and hunting is permitted in season.

Camping Regulations: Camping is allowed through the region, except near public recreation areas or where posted otherwise. No permits are necessary. Campfires may be built, but a stove is recommended for cooking.

For Further Information: Caribou National Forest, Suite 282, Federal Building, 250 South 4th Avenue, Pocatello, ID 83201; (208)236-6700.

OTHER RECOMMENDED LOCATIONS

BLM LANDS IN IDAHO—Idaho has 12,000,000 acres of BLM (Bureau of Land Management) or public domain lands, consisting of many separate units. Most are in the south-central and southwestern parts of the state. Included are a number of Wilderness Study Areas, tracts which are under consideration for wilderness status.

BLM lands in Idaho encompass mountains, canyons such as Bruneau River Canyon, caves, and large areas of desert. There are lakes and several whitewater rivers, including stretches of the Payette, Lower Salmon, and Bruneau Rivers.

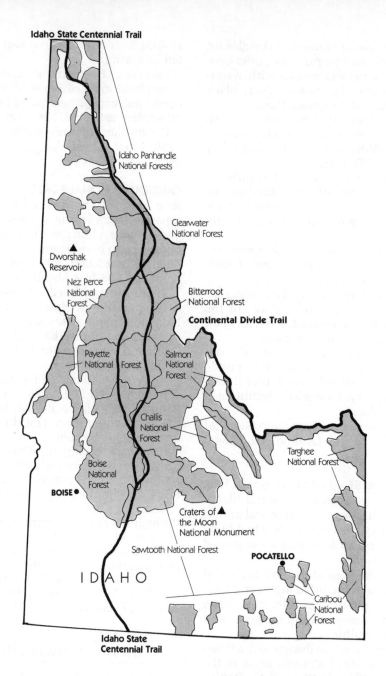

Idaho State Centennial Trail

Idaho Panhandle
National Forests

Clearwater
National Forest

Dworshak
Reservoir

Nez Perce
National
Forest

Bitterroot
National Forest

Continental Divide Trail

Payette
National Forest

Salmon
National
Forest

Challis
National
Forest

Boise
National
Forest

Targhee
National Forest

BOISE

Craters of
the Moon
National Monument

Sawtooth National Forest

POCATELLO

I D A H O

Caribou
National
Forest

Idaho State
Centennial Trail

Access to some of the tracts is difficult, and roads are not always in good condition. Brochures or other printed information are available for very few of the areas.

Activities: Hiking and backpacking are possible on most BLM lands, but there are very few established trails. Cross-country travel is normally required. Horses are allowed, as are mountain bikes in most areas.

Rock climbing and spelunking (caving) are options on some of the lands, with cross-country skiing available during the snow season. Fishing is

possible, and hunting is permitted in season.

Camping Regulations: Camping is allowed freely throughout BLM lands, as are campfires, except where otherwise prohibited. Permits are not generally required.

For Further Information: Bureau of Land Management, 3380 Americana Terrace, Boise, ID 83706; (208)384-3000.

CRATERS OF THE MOON NATIONAL MONUMENT— 53,120 acres. Located in south-central Idaho, this National Monument preserves a somewhat desolate, "moonlike" volcanic landscape, with lava flows, craters, cinder cones, and tubes (caves). The 43,243-acre Craters of the Moon Wilderness comprises the southern part of the park. Wildlife includes mule deer, bobcat, and fox.

Activities: There are about 15 miles of trails for hiking and backpacking. Most trails are short. One may walk elsewhere, but cross-country travel is very difficult on some kinds of lava. A park road which forms a loop is used for cross-country skiing in winter. Hunting is prohibited.

Camping Regulations: A free permit, available from the visitor center, is required in order to camp in the backcountry here. Campfires are not allowed. All water must be carried in. Maximum group size is 12. Pets are prohibited.

For Further Information: Craters of the Moon National Monument, P.O. Box 29, Arco, ID 83213; (208)527-3257.

DWORSHAK RESERVOIR—47,000 acres. Located in the Bitterroot Mountains of northern Idaho and administered by the Army Corps of Engineers, Dworshak is a 19,000-acre reservoir which was created by damming up the North Fork Clearwater River.

Terrain in the region is rugged and often steep, with forests of ponderosa pine, hemlock, and western red cedar. Wildlife includes bear, bobcat, and coyote.

Activities: There are several trails on reservoir lands which may be used for hiking or backpacking. Boating is available on the reservoir, as is fishing. Hunting is permitted in season.

Camping Regulations: A large number of designated campsites are located along the shore, some of them in the numerous inlets. Camping is restricted to these sites. Many of the campsites are accessible only by boat.

For Further Information: Dworshak Project Office, U.S. Army Corps of Engineers, P.O. Box 48, Ahsahka, ID 83520; (208)476-1261.

BITTERROOT NATIONAL FOREST—Most of this 1,113,838-acre National Forest is located in Montana, but some 460,000 acres are in Idaho, along the state's northeast border. Primitive camping and campfires are allowed on these lands, except where otherwise prohibited. See the listing for Bitterroot National Forest in the Montana chapter for more information.

Idaho also has over 250 Wildlife Management Areas and Fishing Access Sites scattered around the state. These lands are used by the public mainly for hunting and fishing. Primitive camping and campfires are allowed in the areas except where posted otherwise. For more information contact the Idaho Department of Fish and Game, 600 South Walnut, P.O. Box 25, Boise, ID 83707; (208)334-3700.

MAJOR BACKPACKING TRAILS

CONTINENTAL DIVIDE TRAIL—325 miles in Idaho (3,100 total). The Idaho portion of this spectacular National Scenic Trail has scenery which includes lofty rugged peaks, with elevations as high as 10,000 feet, and also hilly forests and grasslands. The trail straddles Idaho's border with Montana, and some sections are in that state.

For stretches the trail runs along the actual crest of the Divide, and at other times it follows jeep roads below. Views are often splendid. The route is normally snow-free only from July through September. It's open to horseback riding as well as hiking and backpacking.

Camping Regulations: Since most of the trail in Idaho is on National Forest lands, one may camp freely along the way, except where otherwise prohibited. Campfires are allowed, and no permits are necessary. It's suggested that campsites be well off the trail and away from water sources.

For Further Information: Continental Divide Trail Society, P.O. Box 30002, Bethesda, MD 20814.

IDAHO STATE CENTENNIAL TRAIL—1,200 miles. Officially designated in 1990, the Idaho State Centennial Trail is a new trail which runs the length of Idaho. It utilizes pre-existing trails and some backcountry roads, and is currently in the process of being marked.

The trail passes through some scenic mountainous terrain, running along river canyons and through areas of desert. Most of the route is on National Forest lands, along with some BLM lands in southern Idaho, plus a few areas of private land. Difficulty ranges from easy to very strenuous.

It's multiuse, open not only to backpacking and hiking but also horseback riding, mountain biking, and cross-country skiing. Motorized vehicles are allowed on some sections outside of wilderness areas. Higher elevations are likely to be free of snow only from July through September.

Camping Regulations: Except where otherwise prohibited, trailside camping and campfires are allowed freely where the trail is on National Forest and BLM lands. No permits are required. Camping and fires are generally prohibited on private lands unless one has permission from the landowner.

For Further Information: Idaho Department of Parks and Recreation, Statehouse Mail, Boise, ID 83720: (208)327-7444.

IDAHO CAMPING RESOURCES

USEFUL GUIDEBOOKS

Adventures in Idaho's Sawtooth Country—Stone, Lynne. Seattle: The Mountaineers.

Exploring Idaho's Mountains: A Guide for Climbers, Scramblers, and Hikers—Lopez, Tom. Seattle: The Mountaineers Books.

50 Eastern Idaho Hiking Trails—Mitchell, Ron. Boulder, CO: Pruett, 1979.

Guide to the Continental Divide Trail: Southern Montana and Idaho—Wolf, James R. Bethesda, MD: Continental Divide Trail Society, 1986.

Hiking Trails of the Bitterroot Mountains—Arkava, Morton L. and Leone K. Boulder, CO: Pruett, 1983.

The Hiker's Guide to Idaho—Maugham, Ralph & Jackie. Helena, MT: Falcon Press, 1984.

Hiking Trails of Southern Idaho—Bluestein, S. R. Caldwell, ID: Caxton Printers, 1981.

North Idaho Hiking Trails—Bluestein, S. R. Boise, ID: Challenge Expedition Co., 1982.

Sawtooth National Recreation Area—Linkhart, Luther. Berkeley, CA: Wilderness Press, 1988.

The Sierra Club Guide to the Natural Areas of Idaho, Montana, and Wyoming—Perry, John and Jane. San Francisco: Sierra Club Books, 1988.

Trails of the Sawtooth and White Cloud Mountains—Fuller, Margaret. Edmonds, WA: Signpost Books, 1979.

Trails of Western Idaho—Fuller, Margaret. Edmonds, WA: Signpost Books, 1982.

OUTFITTERS AND GUIDES IN IDAHO

Idaho Outfitters and Guides Association, P.O. Box 95, Boise, ID 83701; (208)342-1919.

INFORMATION ABOUT STATE PARK CAMPGROUNDS

Idaho Department of Parks and Recreation, Statehouse Mail, Boise, ID 83720; (208)334-2154.

STATE HIGHWAY MAP AND TRAVEL INFORMATION

Idaho Travel Council, 700 West State Street, Boise, ID 83720; (800)635-7820.

ILLINOIS

BEST AREAS FOR WILDERNESS CAMPING

SHAWNEE NATIONAL FOREST—300,000 acres. Shawnee National Forest stretches across the southern tip of Illinois between the Mississippi and Ohio Rivers. It's an area of rolling hills with some rugged terrain including steep slopes, cliffs and bluffs, caves, large rock formations and sandstone outcroppings.

There are a number of lakes and streams, with the Big Muddy and Saline Rivers among several larger waterways. Forests are of oak and ash, cedar and pine, along with some dogwood and redbud. Wildlife includes white-tailed deer, fox, and wild turkey.

Seven new wilderness areas were designated in 1990, among them the 5,863-acre Bald Knob Wilderness, the 4,730-acre Clear Springs Wilderness, the 4,466-acre Lusk Creek Wilderness, and the 3,293-acre Garden of the Gods Wilderness.

Activities: The National Forest has over 135 miles of marked trails for hiking and backpacking, along with a larger number of other paths and old roads. Longest is the 47-mile River-to-River Trail. This and some other trails are open to horses.

Canoeing is available on lakes, rivers, and many of the streams. Biking is permitted on some trails outside of wilderness areas. Another option here is spelunking (caving). Fishing is also possible. Hunting is permitted in season.

Camping Regulations: Camping is allowed throughout most of the National Forest, as are campfires, except where posted otherwise. Campers are encouraged to stop by at a forest office before starting out. No permits are necessary.

Within several Special Management Areas one may camp or build campfires only at designated sites. Since extended spells of heat and humidity are common in the summer, spring and fall are the best seasons for camping here.

For Further Information: Shawnee National Forest, 901 S. Commercial Street, Harrisburg, IL 62946; (618)253-7114.

OTHER RECOMMENDED LOCATIONS

SAND RIDGE STATE FOREST—7,500 acres. Situated southwest of Peoria in the central part of the state, Sand Ridge is the largest of four state forests in Illinois. The region is hilly and forested with oak-hickory and pine, and there are also open prairie grasslands. Surprisingly, some desert flora and fauna are found here as well. Deer, coyote, and fox are among the wildlife.

Activities: About 44 miles of hiking, backpacking, and horse trails wind through the forest and form a number of loops. Some trails are used for cross-country skiing in winter. Hunting is permitted in season.

Camping Regulations: Backcountry camping is allowed at 12 separate designated areas along the trails. A permit must first be obtained from forest headquarters. Fires are restricted to established fire pads. Water must be carried in.

For Further Information: Sand Ridge State Forest, P.O. Box 111, Forest City, IL 61532; (309)597-2212.

GIANT CITY STATE PARK—3,694 acres. Located next to Shawnee National Forest lands in southern Illinois, this state park has scenery which includes high sandstone cliffs with rock shelters, oak-hickory forests, some streams and ponds, and a large lake.

Activities: The park has over 20 miles of trails for hiking and backpacking, including the 16-mile Red Cedar Hiking Trail, which circles around the park. Fishing is available in the lake, and hunting is permitted in season.

Camping Regulations: Backpackers may camp along the Red Cedar Hiking Trail. A permit must be obtained from the park office, and a small fee is charged.

For Further Information: Giant City State Park, Box 70, Makanda, IL 62958; (618)457—4836.

PYRAMID STATE PARK—2,527 acres. Located in a hilly region of southern Illinois, Pyramid State Park includes a large number of lakes and ponds. The area is forested with oak and hickory, along with some conifers. Deer are among the park's wildlife.

Activities: There are 17 miles of trails here for hiking and backpacking. Some trails are open to horseback riding, and mountain bikes are also permitted on trails. Canoeing is available on the lakes, and fishing is possible. Hunting is permitted in season.

Camping Regulations: Camping is allowed at a number of designated campsites, located along a couple of the trails. A permit is required, and this must be obtained from the park office. A small fee is charged. Campfires are restricted to established fireplaces.

For Further Information: Pyramid State Park, RR 1, Box 290, Pinckneyville, IL 62274; (618)357-2574.

SILOAM SPRINGS STATE PARK—3,323 acres. Located in west-central Illinois, Siloam Springs State Park has wooded terrain with ridges, valleys, ravines, and a 58-acre artificial lake.

Activities: The park has 12 miles of easy to moderate trails for hiking and backpacking, including the 6-mile Red Oak Backpack Trail. In addition there are 23 miles of equestrian trails, and a 4-mile trail is used for cross-country skiing in winter. Canoeing is available on the lake, and canoes may be rented in the park. Fishing is possible, and hunting is permitted in season.

Camping Regulations: Primitive camping is limited to four designated sites along the Red Oak Backpack Trail. A permit must first be obtained from the park office. Campfires are allowed in established fire rings.

For Further Information: Siloam Springs State Park, RR 1, Box 204, Clayton, IL 62324; (217)894-6205.

MISSISSIPPI PALISADES STATE PARK—2,500 acres. This state park lies alongside the Mississippi River in northwest Illinois. Scenery here includes steep cliffs and rocky bluffs, with caves facing the river. Among the wildlife are white-tailed deer and fox.

Activities: The park has about 15 miles of trails for backpacking and hiking. Trails are closed during the short firearm deer season. Fishing is available along the river.

Camping Regulations: Three backpack camping areas are located along trails in the northern part of the park. Camping is restricted to these sites, which may be used between May 10 and October 31 only. A permit must be obtained from the park office.

For Further Information: Mississippi Palisades State Park, 4577 Route 84 North, Savanna, IL 61074; (815)273-2731.

SAM PARR STATE FISH AND WILDLIFE AREA—1,103 acres. Located in southeastern Illinois, this state fish and wildlife area is dominated by a 183-acre lake. There are hilly forests of oak and hickory, redbud and maple, and deer are among the wildlife.

Activities: In the area are two miles of foot trails and 13 miles of horse trails. Fishing is available, and hunting is permitted here in season.

Camping Regulations: Backpack camping is allowed along one trail in the southeast corner of the park, near the lake, and walk-in campsites are also available west of the lake. A permit must be obtained from the park office.

For Further Information: Sam Parr State Fish and Wildlife Area, RR 5, Box 134, Newton, IL 62448.

MORAINE VIEW STATE RECREATION AREA—1,678 acres. Situated in east-central Illinois, Moraine View State Recreation Area centers around Dawson Lake, a 158-acre artificial lake, and includes a forest of oak and hickory.

Activities: The primary trail here for hiking and backpacking is the 1.5-mile Tall Timber Trail. There are also 10 miles of bridle trails. Fishing is available at the lake, and hunting is permitted in season.

Camping Regulations: Primitive camping is allowed along the Tall Timber Trail. A permit must be obtained from the park office.

For Further Information: Moraine View State Recreation Area, RR 2, Box 110, LeRoy, IL 61752; (309)724-8032.

EAGLE CREEK STATE PARK—2,200 acres. Eagle Creek State Park is located on the west side of Lake Shelbyville, an enormous manmade lake in the woodlands of east-central Illinois.

Activities: There's a 12-mile trail for backpacking and hiking, along with several other trails. Cross-country skiing is possible on some trails in the winter. Fishing is available, and hunting is permitted in season.

Camping Regulations: Camping is allowed at one designated primitive area on the 12-mile backpack trail. It's necessary to register first at the park office before starting out.

For Further Information: Eagle Creek State Park, RR 1, P.O. Box 6, Findlay, IL 62534; (217)756-8260.

SILVER SPRINGS STATE FISH AND WILDLIFE AREA—1,350 acres. Located southwest of Chicago in northern Illinois, Silver Springs State Fish and Wildlife Area includes oak forest and grassy prairie, a stretch of the Fox River, and a few small lakes. Deer and fox are among the wildlife.

Activities: There are several miles of hiking trails and a 7-mile horse trail. Fishing and canoeing are available on the Fox River. Trails are open to cross-country skiing in the winter.

Camping Regulations: Backpack camping is allowed at one designated area overlooking the Fox River, a relatively short distance from a parking area.

For Further Information: Silver Springs State Fish and Wildlife Area, 13608 Fox Road, Yorkville, IL 60560; (708)553-6297.

FERNE CLYFFE STATE PARK—1,100 acres. Surrounded by Shawnee National Forest lands in southern Illinois, this state park is noted for its distinctive rock formations. It also has a large cave, a 100-foot waterfall, and a 16-acre lake. Forests are of hickory, oak, and maple, with redbud and dogwood.

Activities: Hiking and backpacking are possible on 11 miles of trails. There's also an 8-mile horse trail. Hunting and fishing are allowed in season.

Camping Regulations: A single designated backpack camping area is located a half-mile from a parking lot. Primitive camping is restricted to this area.

For Further Information: Ferne Clyffe State Park, P.O. Box 10, Goreville, IL 62939; (618)995-2411.

UPPER MISSISSIPPI RIVER NATIONAL WILDLIFE AND FISH REFUGE—This 200,000-acre National Wildlife and Fish Refuge protects 284 miles of the Mississippi River in four states, with 43,000 acres in Illinois. Offering a corridor of two to five miles wide, the refuge includes wetlands, islands, and river shoreline with some high bluffs and beaches.

The area is not in a wilderness condition, and highways often run close by the river, which has many dams and locks. The refuge nevertheless helps preserve a diverse wildlife, including white-tailed deer, coyote, fox, and bald eagle.

Activities: Canoeing and other boating are possible on the river, as is fishing. Hunting is permitted in season. There are no maintained foot trails.

Camping Regulations: Except where posted otherwise, camping is allowed on the islands and along the shore for up to 14 days. Campfires are permitted.

For Further Information: Upper Mississippi River National Wildlife and Fish Refuge, P.O. Box 415, La Crosse, WI 54601.

In addition, 2,000-acre Castle Rock State Park in northwest Illinois has one designated area along the Rock River for canoe-campers only. For more information contact Castle Rock State Park, 1365 West Castle Road, Oregon, IL 61061; (815)732-7329.

ILLINOIS CAMPING RESOURCES

ORGANIZATIONS WHICH OFFER WILDERNESS CAMPING TRIPS
Sierra Club, Illinois Chapter, 506 South Wabash, #505, Chicago, IL 60605; (312)431-0158. This Sierra Club chapter sponsors a number of backpacking trips, including trips for beginners.

USEFUL GUIDEBOOKS
Illinois Hiking and Backpacking Trails—Zyznieuski, Walter and George. Carbondale, IL: Southern Illinois University Press, 1985.

INFORMATION ABOUT CANOEING AND BICYCLING IN ILLINOIS
Illinois Department of Conservation, Lincoln Tower Plaza, 524 South Second Street, Springfield, IL 62701; (217)782-7617.

INFORMATION ABOUT STATE PARK AND FOREST CAMPGROUNDS
Illinois Department of Conservation, Lincoln Tower Plaza, 524 South Second Street, Springfield, IL 62701; (217)782-7617.

STATE HIGHWAY MAP AND TRAVEL INFORMATION
Illinois Office of Tourism, 310 South Michigan Avenue, Suite 108, Chicago, IL 60604; (312)793-2094/(800)223-0121.

INDIANA

BEST AREAS FOR WILDERNESS CAMPING

HOOSIER NATIONAL FOREST—187,812 acres. Situated in southern Indiana, Hoosier National Forest consists of two very sizable tracts of land, one of which borders on the Ohio River. It's a region of rolling hills and some ridges with nice views.

There are quite a few lakes and many streams. The forests are largely oak-hickory, with pine and cedar, plus redbud and dogwood. Wildlife includes deer and wild turkey.

The National Forest is a patchwork of public and private lands, with no really remote places here, but there's one designated wilderness area: the 12,935-acre Charles C. Deam Wilderness, the largest such area in this part of the country.

Activities: Over 150 miles of trails are available for hiking and backpacking. About half of them are in the designated wilderness area. Difficulty ranges from easy to moderate.

Among the longer trails are the 20-mile Hickory Ridge Trail and the 12-mile Two Lakes Loop, a National Recreation Trail which circles around two large lakes. Many trails are open to horseback riding. Fishing is possible, and hunting is permitted in season.

Camping Regulations: Camping is allowed throughout the National Forest, as are campfires, except near public use areas or where otherwise posted. No permits are necessary.

For Further Information: Hoosier National Forest, 811 Constitution Avenue, Bedford, IN 47421; (812)275-5987.

OTHER RECOMMENDED LOCATIONS

HARRISON–CRAWFORD STATE FOREST—24,000 acres. Located next to the Ohio River in southern Indiana, Harrison–Crawford State Forest has hilly terrain with escarpments overlooking the Ohio and Blue Rivers, plus limestone caves, forests of hardwoods, and wildlife including deer.

Activities: There are 45 miles of trails for hiking and backpacking, including the 25-mile Adventure Hiking Trail. Difficulty is easy to moderate. The forest also has nearly 100 miles of horse trails. Canoeing is possible on the Blue River, and fishing is available as well. Hunting is permitted in season.

Camping Regulations: Camping is restricted to four shelters for backpackers along the Adventure Trail. Visitors should register at the gatehouse or forest office. Campfires are allowed, but a stove is recommended for cooking.

For Further Information: Harrison–Crawford State Forest, 7240 Old Forest Road, S.W., Corydon, IN 47112; (812)738-8232.

JACKSON–WASHINGTON STATE FOREST—This state forest is in southern Indiana, east and south of Hoosier National Forest. It includes a segment of the Knobstone Ridge, which rises over 300 feet above the surrounding forest and offers some nice views. There's a 2,544-acre backcountry area.

Activities: The 58-mile Knobstone Trail (see entry page 153) passes through the forest. There are other trails as well, some of which are open to horseback riding. Horses may not be taken into the backcountry area. Fishing is available, and hunting is allowed in season.

Camping Regulations: Camping and campfires are permitted. Backpackers and others should register at the forest office and specify the area where they will be camping.

For Further Information: Jackson-Washington State Forest, RR 2, Brownstown, IN 47220; (812)358-2160.

SHADES STATE PARK—3,082 acres. Located in west-central Indiana, this largely undeveloped state park has scenery which includes steep sandstone cliffs, ravines, and river-size Sugar Creek. There's a forest of hardwoods plus pine and hemlock, with some virgin stands.

Activities: The park has about 15 miles of easy to moderate trails for hiking and backpacking. Canoeing is available on Sugar Creek, which extends some 90 miles through west-central Indiana. Biking is restricted to regular roads. Fishing is allowed, but hunting is not.

Camping Regulations: Camping is permitted in one backcountry area, a little over two miles from the main parking area via an easy trail. Campers must register at the park office. There's also a canoe-camping area alongside Sugar Creek. Both areas are open to camping from April through October each year. Campfires are allowed in designated spots.

For Further Information: Shades State Park, RR 1, Box 72, Waveland, IN 47989; (317)435-2810.

In addition, there's a backcountry camping area at Pakota Lake, an 8,880-acre reservoir which is

FT. WAYNE

INDIANA

Shades State Park

INDIANAPOL.

Hoosier
National Forest

Jackson-Washington
State Forest

Knobstone
Trail

Harrison-Crawford
State Forest

surrounded by 16,700 acres of state lands near Hoosier National Forest in southern Indiana. Campsites here are out of sight and sound of each other. A fee is charged. The area is managed by the Indiana Department of Natural Resources. For information contact the Pakota Lake Property Office, RR #1, Birdseye, IN 47513; (812)685-2464.

MAJOR BACKPACKING TRAILS

KNOBSTONE TRAIL—58 miles. The Knobstone Trail is the longest hiking and backpacking trail in the state. It winds through southern Indiana's 22,000-acre Clark State Forest, Elk Creek Public Fishing Area, and Jackson–Washington State Forest.

The trail follows the Knobstone Escarpment, a series of somewhat flat-topped ridges over 300 feet high, with some nice views along the way. It also passes several lakes and ponds. Difficulty is easy to moderate, and there are occasional rough stretches. Horses are not permitted on the trail.

Camping Regulations: Camping is allowed on public lands which are traversed by the trail. No permits are required, but backpackers should register at the two state forest offices. Campsites should be out of sight of the trail as well as all lakes, and also must be at least one mile from roads and public use areas. Campfires are discouraged but permitted.

For Further Information: Indiana Division of Outdoor Recreation, 402 W. Washington, Room 271, Indianapolis, IN 46204: (317)232-4070.

INDIANA CAMPING RESOURCES

ORGANIZATIONS WHICH OFFER WILDERNESS CAMPING TRIPS

Central Indiana Wilderness Club, P.O. Box 44351, Indianapolis, IN 46244. This non-profit club sponsors backpacking, canoe-camping, horsepacking, and other wilderness camping trips throughout the year to destinations within Indiana as well as other parts of the country. A backpacking class and beginner's trip is offered each spring.

Indianapolis Hiking Club, c/o Jean C. Ballinger, 7129 Chandler Drive, Indianapolis, IN 46217. This club offers occasional backpacking trips.

INFORMATION ABOUT STATE PARK CAMPGROUNDS

Indiana Division of State Parks, 616 State Office Building, Indianapolis, IN 46204; (317)232-4124.

STATE HIGHWAY MAP AND TRAVEL INFORMATION

Indiana Tourism, One North Capitol, Suite 700, Indianapolis, IN 46204; (800)782-3775; (800)289-6646.

IOWA

BEST AREAS FOR WILDERNESS CAMPING

YELLOW RIVER STATE FOREST—6,550 acres. Yellow River State Forest is located in the northeast corner of Iowa. It's a hilly, mostly-forested area of hardwoods with pine and other conifers, open meadows, and some beautiful creeks. There are also nice views from limestone bluffs. Wildlife includes deer and wild turkey.

Activities: A 20-mile Backpack Trail winds through one unit of the state forest, and there are three shorter hiking trails. Difficulty ranges from easy to moderate, with an occasional steep stretch. Horseback riding is allowed on some trails. Fishing is available as well.

Camping Regulations: Camping and campfires are restricted to nine designated areas along the Backpack Trail, and there are also campsites for horseback riders. Backpackers must sign in at a registration booth before starting out. No fee is required.

For Further Information: Yellow River State Forest, Box 115, McGregor, IA 52157; (319)586-2254.

STEPHENS STATE FOREST— 9,202 acres. This state forest consists of six separate units in south-central Iowa. Included are areas of oak-hickory forest and some prairie, with two ponds and several creeks. White-tailed deer, coyote, and fox are among the wildlife.

Activities: There's a small network of trails in the forest for hiking and backpacking. Cross-country skiing is possible during winter. Fishing is also available. Hunting is permitted in season.

Camping Regulations: Camping is restricted to several designated areas for backpackers along trails in the western part of the 3,256-acre Whitebrest Unit. No fee is necessary.

For Further Information: Stephens State Forest, RR 3, Chariton, IA 50049; (515)774-4559.

UPPER MISSISSIPPI RIVER NATIONAL WILDLIFE AND FISH REFUGE—This 200,000-acre National Wildlife and Fish Refuge protects 284 miles of the Mississippi River in four states. Offering a corridor of two to five miles wide, the refuge includes wetlands, islands, and river shoreline with some high cliffs and beaches.

The area is not in a wilderness condition, and highways often run close by the river, which has many dams and locks. It nevertheless helps preserve a diverse wildlife which includes white-tailed deer, coyote, fox, and bald eagle.

Activities: Canoeing and other boating are possible on the river, as is fishing. Hunting is permitted in season. There are no maintained foot trails.

Camping Regulations: Primitive camping is allowed for up to 14 days on the islands, on sandbars along the shore, and anywhere not posted as closed to camping. Campfires are permitted.

For Further Information: Upper Mississippi River National Wildlife and Fish Refuge, P.O. Box 460, McGregor, IA 52157; (319)873-3423.

Also, a single backpacking campsite is available along one trail in Iowa's 8,772-acre Shimek State Forest, in the southeast corner of the state. Registration is necessary but no fee is charged. For further information contact Shimek State Forest, Route 1, Farmington, IA 52626; (319)878-3811.

IOWA CAMPING RESOURCES

INFORMATION ABOUT CAMPGROUNDS IN STATE
PARKS AND FORESTS
Iowa Department of Natural Resources, Wallace
State Office Building, 900 East Grand Avenue,
Des Moines, IA 50319; (515)281-5145.

STATE HIGHWAY MAP AND TRAVEL INFORMATION
Iowa Division of Tourism, 200 East Grand Avenue, Des Moines, IA 50309; (515)218-3100/
(800)345-IOWA.

KANSAS

BEST AREAS FOR WILDERNESS CAMPING

CIMARRON NATIONAL GRASSLAND—108,175 acres. Located in the southwest corner of Kansas and administered by the National Forest Service, Cimarron National Grassland is the largest area of public land in the state.

It's an area of prairie grasslands, with some major stands of trees, several small ponds, and the Cimarron River—which is dry most of the time except after heavy rainfall.

The National Grassland is open to grazing and has several thousand head of cattle. Some areas are fenced in. Wildlife elsewhere includes white-tailed and mule deer, elk, coyote, prairie dog, pheasant, and wild turkey.

Activities: Several hiking trails run along the Cimarron River, and a 23-mile section of the Sante Fe National Historic Trail traverses part of the Grassland. Hiking and backpacking are also possible on old roads, or one may travel cross-country. Limited fishing is available, and hunting is permitted in season.

Camping Regulations: Camping is allowed throughout the region, except near public use areas or where posted otherwise. No permits are necessary. Campers are encouraged to visit the main office or to phone before starting out. Water is scarce in most parts of the Grassland.

For Further Information: Cimarron National Grassland, P.O. Box J, 242 Highway 56 East, Elkhart, KS 67950; (316)697-4621.

OTHER RECOMMENDED LOCATIONS

FLINT HILLS NATIONAL WILDLIFE REFUGE—18,463 acres. This National Wildlife Refuge lies alongside the John Redmond Reservoir in eastern Kansas. It includes some small lakes and ponds, marshlands, and the Neosho River.

The refuge provides protection for migratory waterfowl and other birdlife such as bald eagle, along with wildlife including white-tailed deer and coyote.

Activities: There are two maintained hiking trails. Fishing is widely available, and hunting is permitted in some parts of the refuge.

Camping Regulations: Primitive and trailside camping is allowed here, as are campfires. Access to some areas is restricted or prohibited at certain times of year.

For Further Information: Flint Hills National Wildlife Refuge, P.O. Box 128, Hartford, KS 66854; (316)392-5553.

CLINTON LAKE— Located west of Kansas City in northeast Kansas, Clinton Lake is a 7,000-acre reservoir which is administered by the Army Corps of Engineers. The area is open to the public for recreational use. Included are oak-hickory forests, with some high bluffs along the shoreline of the reservoir. White-tailed deer, coyote, fox, and beaver are among the wildlife.

Activities: Hiking and backpacking are possible on the 4-mile George Lathan Memorial Trail, which circles around 450-acre Woodridge Park, one of several small Corps of Engineers parks next to the reservoir. Fishing is also available. Hunting is prohibited in Woodridge Park but allowed outside park boundaries.

Camping Regulations: Backpack camping is permitted anywhere in Woodridge Park, and restricted to that park. Campsites should be at least 100 feet from the trail. Elsewhere in the area camping is limited to campgrounds.

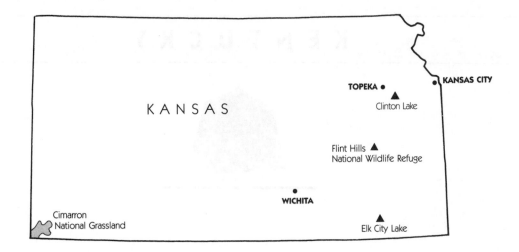

For Further Information: Clinton Lake, c/o U.S. Army Corps of Engineers, Route 1, Box 120G, Lawrence, KS 66044; (913)843-7665.

ELK CITY LAKE—Elk City Lake is another large reservoir administered by the U.S. Army Corps of Engineers. It's located in the southeast corner of Kansas, in an area of rolling hills with hardwood forests and some prairie. There are rock bluffs and outcroppings which offer fine views of the reservoir.

Activities: Backpacking and hiking are available on the 15-mile Elk River Hiking Trail, which runs along the northwest side of the lake and for a stretch up the Elk River.

Camping Regulations: Camping is restricted to three backcountry camping areas along the Elk River Hiking Trail. Campfires are permitted but discouraged. The use of a stove is recommended. Visitors should sign in at trail registers located at trailheads.

For Further Information: Elk City Lake, c/o U.S. Army Corps of Engineers, P.O. Box 567, Independence, KS 67301; (316)331-0315.

Kansas also has a number of "state fishing lakes" of various sizes on public lands throughout the state. These have primitive campgrounds available, but visitors are also allowed to camp away from established sites. For more information contact the Kansas Department of Wildlife and Parks, RR 2, Box 54A, Pratt, KS 67124; (316)672-5911.

KANSAS CAMPING RESOURCES

USEFUL GUIDES
Trails in Kansas—Lefferd, Virginia. Emporia, Kansas: Kansas Trails Council, 1989. This is a booklet which may be obtained from the Kansas Trails Council, 1737 Rural Street, Emporia, KS 66801; (316)342-5508.
Walks and Rambles on the Cimarron National Grassland—Hayward, Stephen and Martha, 1989. This booklet is available from the authors at P.O. Box 963, Elkhart, KS 06950.

INFORMATION ABOUT STATE PARK CAMPGROUNDS
Kansas Department of Wildlife and Parks, RR 2, Box 54A, Pratt, KS 67124; (316)672-5911.

STATE HIGHWAY MAP AND TRAVEL INFORMATION
Kansas Division of Travel and Tourism, 400 West 8th, 5th Floor, Topeka, KS 66603; (913)296-2009.

KENTUCKY

DANIEL BOONE NATIONAL FOREST—664,000 acres. Daniel Boone National Forest consists of two large units of land in eastern Kentucky. The terrain includes some rugged mountains with steep slopes, along with high sandstone cliffs and canyons.

Of special interest is the 25,662-acre Red River Gorge Geological Area, which has over 80 natural arches and bridges, the most of any location east of the Mississippi. Other impressive rocky scenery is found here as well.

The National Forest has six designated state Wild Rivers, many streams with waterfalls, a few large lakes, and forests of hardwoods with pine and hemlock, including some old-growth trees. Among the wildlife are white-tailed deer, fox, and wild turkey.

There are two designated wilderness areas: the 13,300-acre Clifty Wilderness, which is part of the Red River Gorge Geological Area, and also the 4,791-acre Beaver Creek Wilderness.

Activities: Backpacking and hiking are available on over 500 miles of trails. Included is the 257-mile Sheltowee Trace Trail (see entry page 160), a National Recreation Trail which runs the length of the western tract. Others include the rugged 66-mile Redbird Crest Trail, plus the 36-mile Red River Gorge National Recreation Trail, which consists of a series of trail loops.

Horseback riding is allowed on some trails. Cross-country skiing is possible on most trails during the winter. Three of the rivers offer fine white-water canoeing and rafting. Fishing is also available, and hunting is permitted in season.

Camping Regulations: Camping and campfires are allowed throughout the National Forest, except near public recreation areas or where otherwise prohibited. No permits are required. Campsites should be at least 100 feet from trails and water sources, and 300 feet from lakes or roads.

The Red River Gorge Geological Area receives heavy use. Backpackers heading for this area are asked to inform rangers of their plans, and to camp out of sight of trails. In the Geological Area campfires are permitted only at designated sites.

For Further Information: Daniel Boone National Forest, 100 Vaught Road, Winchester, KY 40391; (606)745-3100.

MAMMOTH CAVE NATIONAL PARK— 52,000 acres. This National Park in west-central Kentucky is famous for its spectacular 300-mile-long underground limestone cave system, said to be the largest in the world, and still not fully explored. Aboveground the terrain is hilly, with oak-hickory forests and the Green and Nolin Rivers.

Activities: Hiking and backpacking are possible on 70 miles of hiking trails, 10 miles of which are limited to day-hiking. Horses are allowed on most trails. Canoeing is available on the two rivers. There's also a new 7-mile bike trail. Bikes are not allowed on other trails.

Camping Regulations: In most of the park camping is limited to 12 designated backcountry camping areas, although it's also allowed along river banks and on river islands. Campfires may be built only in preexisting fire rings.

A permit is required to camp in the backcountry, and may be obtained at the park campground entrance. Visitors must sign in at trailhead registers. Access to the backcountry requires taking a ferry across the Green River or driving a long circuitous route.

For Further Information: Mammoth Cave National Park, Mammoth Cave, KY 42259; (502)758-2251.

LAND BETWEEN THE LAKES—170,000 acres. Managed by the Tennessee Valley Authority and surrounded on three sides by two huge lakes (Kentucky Lake and Lake Barkley), this is an enormous, 40-mile-long peninsula which is located both in southwest Kentucky and northwest Tennessee.

Terrain is gently hilly, with elevation differences of no more than 200 feet. There are woodlands, some inland lakes and ponds, and the wildlife includes deer, bison (restricted to a 200-acre range), bobcat, and wild turkey.

Activities: Backpacking and hiking are available on 200 miles of easy to moderate trails. Longest are the 60-mile North-South Trail, which extends the length of the peninsula, and the 26-mile Fort Henry National Recreation Trail, which forms a series of loops. There are also about 30 miles of horse trails. Fishing is possible, and hunting is permitted during the appropriate season.

Camping Regulations: Camping is allowed throughout the peninsula, as are campfires, except where posted otherwise. No fees or permits are required, but backpackers are asked to check in at one of three welcome stations to leave their itinerary. A series of shelters is located along the North-South Trail. When camping elsewhere, sites should be at least 50 feet from trails.

For Further Information: Land Between the Lakes, 100 Van Morgan Drive, Golden Pond, KY 42211; (502)924-5602.

BIG SOUTH FORK NATIONAL RIVER AND RECREATION AREA—120,000 acres. Located in northeast Tennessee and extending into southeast Kentucky, this National River and Recreation Area features the Big South Fork of the Cumberland River, which runs through a rugged cliff-lined gorge, along with several tributaries. Other scenery includes sandstone arches and caves.

Activities: The river is very popular for whitewater canoeing, kayaking, and rafting. Commercial rafting outfits offer trips on the river.

Over 100 miles of trails are available for backpacking and hiking, including a section of the 257-mile Sheltowee Trace Trail (see entry page 160). Difficulty varies from easy to strenuous.

Horseback riding is allowed on trails, and horses may be rented in the park. Fishing is possible along the river and streams, and hunting is permitted in season.

Camping Regulations: Backcountry camping is allowed throughout the area, except where posted otherwise. No permits are required. Campfires may be built, but it's suggested that a stove be used for cooking.

For Further Information: Big South Fork National River and Recreation Area, P.O. Drawer 630, Oneida, TN 37841.

CUMBERLAND GAP NATIONAL HISTORICAL PARK—20,000 acres. This National Historical Park protects the historic gap through the Appalachian

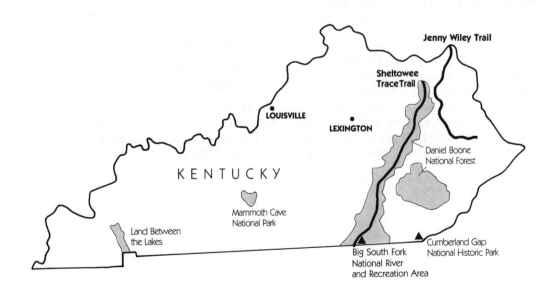

Mountains which was used by early settlers heading westward. While not very large, the park is located in three states: Kentucky, Virginia, and Tennessee. It's dominated by the long ridge of Cumberland Mountain, with elevations over 3,000 feet, and there are several streams.

Activities: The park has more than 50 miles of trails for hiking and backpacking. Among them is the 21-mile Ridge Trail, which extends the length of the park. Horses are permitted on many of the trails, but bikes are not.

Camping Regulations: Backcountry camping is restricted to five authorized areas. A permit is required, and must be obtained from the visitor center. One camping area is designated exclusively for the use of horseback riders (horses are allowed at two other camping areas as well). Campfires are allowed only in established fire rings. Pets are prohibited in the backcountry.

For Further Information: Cumberland Gap National Historical Park, P.O. Box 1848, Middlesboro, KY 40965; (606)248-2817.

Primitive camping is also permitted in some of Kentucky's many Public Wildlife Areas, which are used primarily for hunting and fishing. For information contact the Kentucky Department of Fish and Wildlife Resources, #1 Game Farm Road, Frankfort, KY 40601; (502)564-4336.

MAJOR BACKPACKING TRAILS

SHELTOWEE TRACE TRAIL—257 miles. This National Recreation Trail is Kentucky's longest trail. It stretches the length of Daniel Boone National Forest, in the eastern part of the state, and extends a short distance into Tennessee.

The trail takes in much of the National Forest's finest scenery, including Red River Gorge. Terrain is mountainous and sometimes rugged. Difficulty varies from easy to strenuous. Horses and ORVs (off road vehicles) are allowed on some sections.

Camping Regulations: Camping and campfires are generally allowed along the trail, except where posted otherwise. No permits are necessary.

Campsites should be away from roads, at least 100 feet from the trail, and out of sight of the trail in the Red River Gorge Geological Area.

For Further Information: Daniel Boone National Forest, 100 Vaught Road, Winchester, KY 40391; (606)745-3100.

JENNY WILEY TRAIL—180 miles. Second longest trail in the state, this National Recreation Trail runs from Jenny Wiley State Park, in the eastern part of the state, to South Portsmouth, on the Ohio River at the northeast border of Kentucky.

Most of the time the Jenny Wiley follows a mountain ridge, and almost all of the trail is on private lands. Difficulty ranges from easy to strenuous. It briefly passes within two miles of the Sheltowee Trace Trail, and a short trail connects the two.

Camping Regulations: Trail shelters are located every 10 miles or so along the trail. Camping and campfires are allowed at these shelters, and no permits are required. On private lands camping is restricted to designated sites, except with the landowner's permission.

For Further Information: Kentucky Department of Parks, 12th Floor, Capital Plaza Tower, Frankfort, KY 40601; (502)564-5410.

KENTUCKY CAMPING RESOURCES

USEFUL GUIDEBOOKS
Hiking the Big South Fork—Coleman, Brenda D. and Smith, Jo Anna. University of Tennessee Press.

INFORMATION ABOUT CAMPGROUNDS IN STATE PARKS AND FORESTS
Kentucky Department of Parks, 12th Floor, Capital Plaza Tower, Frankfort, KY 40601; (502)564-5410. A useful "Kentucky Trails Guide" is available from this address.

STATE HIGHWAY MAP AND TRAVEL INFORMATION
Kentucky Department of Travel Development, P.O. Box 2011, Frankfort, KY 40602; (502)564-4930/(800)225-TRIP.

LOUISIANA

BEST AREAS FOR WILDERNESS CAMPING

KISATCHIE NATIONAL FOREST—600,000 acres. Kisatchie National Forest consists of eight separate tracts of land in north-central and northern Louisiana. Scenery here includes some steep 400-foot hills, low mesas, and rocky outcrops with nice views.

There are many lakes and streams, and the 19-mile Saline Bayou National Wild and Scenic River is here as well, along with the Kisatchie Bayou, which has rough rapids and sandy beaches.

Kisatchie has one designated wilderness area, the 8,700-acre Kisatchie Hills Wilderness. Forests throughout the region consist of mixed hardwoods and pine. Among the wildlife are deer and fox.

Activities: There are a number of trails for backpacking and hiking. Included are the 31-mile Wild Azalea Trail (see entry page 182), the 11-mile Whiskey Chitto Trail, the 10-mile Lakeshore Trail, and the 10-mile Big Branch Trail.

Horseback riding is available on the new 12.8-mile Caroline Dormon Hiking and Horse Trail, plus a couple of other trails, as well as on old roads. Biking is another option outside of the designated wilderness area.

Canoeing is possible on numerous lakes, and feasible at times on the Saline Bayou River and the Kisatchie Bayou. Fishing is available, and hunting is permitted in season.

Camping Regulations: Camping and campfires are allowed almost anywhere, except near day use areas or where posted otherwise. No permits are required.

Two Wildlife Management Preserves are located inside the National Forest, and camping within these areas is restricted to designated sites during hunting season (October 1- April 30).

Since summers are usually hot and humid here, and the winters mild, the best period to camp in this National Forest is from fall through spring.

For Further Information: Kisatchie National Forest, P.O. Box 5500, 2500 Shreveport Highway, Pineville, LA 71360; (318) 473-7160.

OTHER RECOMMENDED LOCATIONS

BOGUE CHITTO NATIONAL WILDLIFE REFUGE—26,000 acres. Located north of New Orleans and next to the Louisiana-Mississippi border, this 15-mile-long National Wildlife Refuge is on the floodplain along the Bogue Chitto and West Pearl Rivers. Included here are Bradley Slough and Holmes Bayou.

There are hardwood forests with oak and hickory, elm and sycamore, along with cypress, gum, and ash. White-tailed deer, bobcat, and alligator are among the wildlife.

Activities: Canoeing is available on the refuge's rivers and waterways, as is fishing. Most of the region is accessible only by boat. There are no foot trails. Hunting is permitted in season.

Camping Regulations: Camping is allowed within 100 feet of most of the rivers, and also in some other parts of the National Wildlife Refuge. No permits or fees are required.

For Further Information: Bogue Chitto National Wildlife Refuge, 1010 Gause Boulevard, Building 936, Slidell, LA 70458.

SHREVEPORT

Kisatchie
National Forest

Wild
Azalea
Trail

Chicot State Park

LOUISIANA

BATON ROUGE

Bogue Chitto
National Wildlife Refuge

NEW ORLEANS

CHICOT STATE PARK— 6,000 acres. This attractive park centers around large Lake Chicot in south-central Louisiana, in an area of bottomland hardwoods. It's the only state park in Louisiana where backpacking and wilderness camping are allowed.

Activities: Backpacking and hiking are available on the 10-mile Chicot State Park Trail. Horses and bikes are not permitted in backcountry areas.

Camping Regulations: Camping is limited to five separate designated areas, most of which are located off of blue-blazed spur trails. Campfires are allowed. Pets are prohibited.

A permit is required in order to camp here. Permits are available at the park entrance for a nominal fee. Campers must file a trip plan describing their itinerary, intended campsites, and return time. Daily quotas are observed.

For Further Information: Chicot State Park, Route 3, Box 494, Ville Platte, LA 70586; (318) 363-2503.

Primitive camping is also permitted within several of Louisiana's 38 Wildlife Management Areas, which are scattered around the state and add up to over a million acres of land.

Some of the individual tracts are quite large. Established trails are few. The primary use of these areas is for hunting and fishing, along with nature study and birdwatching.

For more information contact the Louisiana Department of Wildlife and Fisheries, P.O. Box 98000, Baton Rouge, LA 70898; (504) 765-2918.

MAJOR BACKPACKING TRAILS

WILD AZALEA TRAIL—31 Miles. Located in Kisatchie National Forest, southwest of Alexandria, this National Scenic Trail runs from the town of Woodworth to the Valentine Lake Recreation Area, near Gardner.

It's the longest hiking and backpacking trail in Louisiana. Scenic and easy, this trail is famous for the wild azaleas which typically bloom from mid-March to mid-April each year.

Terrain ranges from hilly to flat. Numerous streams are crossed along the way. Of special interest is the Castor Creek Scenic Area, a place of beautiful old hardwood and pine trees.

Camping Regulations: Camping is allowed near the trail with few restrictions. One shelter and an established primitive camping area are located along the way. Campsites elsewhere should be at least 50 feet from the trail.

For Further Information: Kisatchie National Forest, P.O. Box 5500, 2500 Shreveport Highway, Pineville, LA 71360; (318) 473-7160.

LOUISIANA CAMPING RESOURCES

ORGANIZATIONS WHICH OFFER WILDERNESS CAMPING TRIPS

Sierra Club, Delta Chapter, P.O. Box 19469, New Orleans, LA 70179; (504)482-9566. This chapter of the Sierra Club offers some backpacking and canoe-camping trips.

INFORMATION ABOUT STATE PARK CAMPGROUNDS

Louisiana Office of State Parks, P.O. Box 44426, Baton Rouge, LA 70804; (504)342-8111.

STATE HIGHWAY MAP AND TRAVEL INFORMATION

Louisiana Office of Tourism, P.O. Box 94291, Baton Rouge, LA 70804; (504)342-8119 or (800)33-GUMBO (outside Louisiana).

MAINE

BEST AREAS FOR WILDERNESS CAMPING

BAXTER STATE PARK—201,018 acres. Located in north-central Maine, Baxter is one of the finest state parks in the entire country. It's home to massive and spectacular 5,267-foot Mount Katahdin, which is the northern terminus of the Appalachian Trail. Views from above timberline are magnificent.

There's a host of lesser mountains here as well, with steep cirques and valleys, numerous small lakes and ponds, and many streams. The park is maintained in a wilderness condition, minimally developed for tourism. The few roads here are unpaved.

The area includes dense forests of spruce and fir, pine and hemlock, with arctic flora found at higher elevations. Among the wildlife are white-tailed deer, black bear, lynx, and coyote.

Activities: Baxter is primarily a park for backpackers and hikers, with close to 180 miles of trails. Some routes on Mount Katahdin are extremely rugged and steep. Much easier trails can also be found here.

Cross-country skiing and snowshoeing are possible on some trails during the winter. Canoeing is mainly limited to several lakes, with canoes available for rental in the park. Bike use is restricted to roads. Fishing is permitted, but hunting is not.

Camping Regulations: Camping is allowed only at designated campsites and lean-tos, and a fee must be paid for camping each night. Among a number of camping areas are two backcountry campgrounds. Campfires are permitted only at authorized sites.

Advance reservations for campsites may be made by mail, and these are essential for the summer months. Overall demand is very high, and some sites are booked up many months ahead of time. Radios, cassette players, and pets are not allowed in the park.

For Further Information: Baxter State Park, 64 Balsam Drive, Millenocket, ME 04462; (207)723-5140.

ALLAGASH WILDERNESS WATERWAY—Extending 92 miles through the wilds of northern Maine, and surrounded by private North Maine Woods lands, the Allagash is a splendid series of interconnected lakes, rivers and streams. It has National Wild and Scenic River Status.

Given the remoteness of the area, this is not a place for beginners. Access is limited to a few gravel roads or via float plane. The surrounding area is commercial spruce and fir forest, with logging permitted 500 feet or more from the Waterway.

Activities: Canoeing is the most popular activity on the Allagash. There are stretches of whitewater along with flatwater. Trips of from two to ten days are possible. Outfitters, guides, and canoe rentals are available in the region.

Some ice is common through mid-May, so the canoeing season usually begins in late May and runs through October. There are also a few short hiking trails along the Waterway. Fishing is possible here as well, and hunting is permitted in season.

Camping Regulations: Camping is restricted to 75 authorized campsites along the Waterway. A camping fee is charged for each night. Reservations are not available. Fires are allowed only in built fireplaces. Groups are limited to a maximum of 12. Visitors must register at the time of entry, and this may be done at various checkpoints along access roads.

For Further Information: Allagash Wilderness Waterway, Bureau of Parks and Recreation, State House Station 22, Augusta, ME 04333; (207)289-3821.

WHITE MOUNTAIN NATIONAL FOREST—49,000 acres in Maine (798,000 acres in New Hampshire). While most of this National Forest is located in New Hampshire, a sizable tract is in Maine, along the state's western border. The area has a number of rocky peaks and other wild mountain scenery.

Included is 2,906-foot Speckled Mountain, which is in a designated wilderness area: the 12,000-acre Caribou-Speckled Mountain Wilderness. There are hardwood forests with spruce and fir, meadows, streams, waterfalls, and some lakes and ponds.

Activities: This district of the forest has about 160 miles of trails for hiking and backpacking. Cross-country skiing and snowshoeing are available here in the winter. Fishing is also possible. Hunting is permitted in season.

Camping Regulations: Camping is allowed throughout most of the National Forest, except where otherwise prohibited. Campfires are legal but discouraged. Use of a stove is recommended for cooking. No permits are necessary.

Six backcountry shelters are located along several of the trails. When staying at other than established sites, campsites should be at least 200 feet from streams and trails. Group size is limited to a maximum of 10 in the wilderness area.

Camping and fires are restricted in some areas ("Restricted Use Areas"). Camping is not permitted within one-quarter mile of designated camping areas, roads, trailheads, or above treeline (or where trees are under eight feet tall), except on two feet of snow.

For Further Information: White Mountain National Forest, RR 2, Box 2270, Bethel, ME 04217; (207)824-2134.

OTHER RECOMMENDED LOCATIONS

BIGELOW PRESERVE—34,500 acres. Established in 1976, this large state preserve is located next to 20-mile-long Flagstaff Lake in western Maine. It includes Maine's second most impressive mountain, 4,150-foot Mount Bigelow. Terrain here is mountainous and often steep.

Outstanding views are available at higher elevations. The preserve also has some small ponds and streams, and there are mixed forests of spruce, fir, and hardwoods. Wildlife includes black bear, moose, and white-tailed deer.

Activities: This area is mainly suitable for backpacking and hiking. Among several trails here is a section of the Appalachian Trail (see entry page 000), which crosses the mountain. Most trails are moderate to strenuous in difficulty. Fishing is permitted.

Camping Regulations: Camping is allowed throughout the preserve. A fire permit is required in order to have a campfire at other than designated sites. Several lean-tos are available.

For Further Information: Bigelow Preserve, Bureau of State Lands, State House Station 22, Augusta, ME 04333; (207)289-3061.

MAHOOSUC MOUNTAINS MANAGEMENT UNIT—27,250 acres. This State Management Unit is located in western Maine, adjacent to the New Hampshire border and a little north of White Mountain National Forest. It's a ruggedly mountainous area, with Old Speck Mountain (4,180 feet) the highest of several summits. The area has mixed forests of fir and spruce along with hardwoods.

Activities: Hiking and backpacking are the primary activities available on these lands. The Appalachian Trail (see entry page 167) traverses the area, and there are several other trails as well. Much of the hiking here is extremely challenging.

This section of the Appalachian Trail is considered to be one of the most difficult of the entire trail—especially where it descends and passes through Mahoosuc Notch, a deep and rugged gorge. Fishing is possible, and hunting is permitted in season.

Camping Regulations: Camping is allowed in any suitable location. A fire permit is required in order to build a campfire anywhere except at designated sites.

For Further Information: Mahoosuc Mountains Management Unit, Bureau of State Lands, State House Station 22, Augusta, ME 04333; (207)289-3061.

NORTH MAINE WOODS—2,800,000 acres. Occupying a large area in the upper part of the state, the North Maine Woods consists of private lands owned by a number of timber companies and other corporations. The region is open to the public for recreational use.

There are a huge number of attractive lakes, ponds, rivers, and streams. Among the waterways

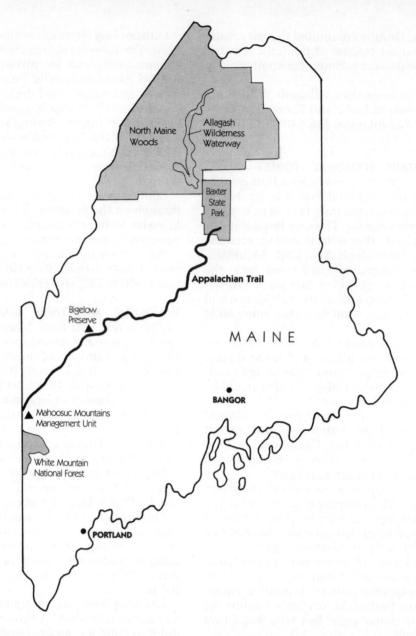

North Maine Woods

Allagash Wilderness Waterway

Baxter State Park

Appalachian Trail

Bigelow Preserve ▲

MAINE

Mahoosuc Mountains Management Unit ▲

White Mountain National Forest

● BANGOR

● PORTLAND

here is the St. John River, which extends over 130 miles through northern Maine.

Extensive logging takes place in the area. Thus it's not a pristine wilderness, but by most other measures it's considered to be rather wild and remote. Access is via unpaved private roads, some of which are in poor condition.

Activities: Canoeing is available on many of the rivers and lakes, as is fishing. There are hardly any developed foot trails, so the options for hiking and backpacking are few. Bikes are prohibited. Hunting is permitted in season.

Camping Regulations: Camping and campfires are allowed at designated sites, which number in the hundreds. A required camping permit is issued at entrance checkpoints. A Maine fire permit is necessary for some but not all sites, and this must be obtained in advance. Fees are charged for camping each night, and there's also an entry fee. Reservations are available and recommended, although these aren't necessary for all campsites.

For Further Information: North Maine Woods, P.O. Box 421, Ashland, ME 04732; (207)435-6213.

GEORGIA–PACIFIC CORPORATION LANDS—450,000 acres. Covering a sizable area in eastern Maine, lands owned by the Georgia–Pacific Corporation are open for public recreation. Active logging takes place on the lands. Included in the region are a number of lakes and rivers.

Activities: Canoeing is available on many of the rivers and lakes, as is fishing. Hunting is permitted in season.

Camping Regulations: Camping is allowed at designated sites, which are located along the St. Croix River and at some of the lakes. A state fire permit is required in order to have a campfire, and this must be obtained in advance.

For Further Information: Georgia-Pacific Corporation Lands, Woodland, ME 04694; (207)427-3311.

OTHER STATE MANAGEMENT UNITS—In addition to the Mahoosuc Mountains Management Unit (see entry page 165), Maine has a number of other so-called Management Units. These undeveloped state-owned lands are found throughout the state, with the majority located in central and northern Maine.

Among the largest are the 25,000-acre Duck Lake Unit, the 22,000-acre Eagle Lake Unit, and the 22,500-acre Richardsontown Unit. Access to many of the units is by old roads, some of which are in barely passable condition.

Activities: Canoeing is feasible on a number of rivers, lakes, and ponds within the areas. Most units have few if any trails for hiking or backpacking. Fishing is often available, and hunting is permitted in season.

Camping Regulations: All units are open to primitive camping. Campfires are allowed only at authorized campsites, and a state fire permit is required for some locations.

For Further Information: Maine Bureau of Public Lands, State House Station 22, Augusta, ME 04333; (207)289-3061.

There are also scores of state-owned islands off the coast of Maine. About 41 of these are currently open for recreational use, and camping is allowed on many of them. A fire permit is necessary in order to have a campfire. Access is by private boat only. For more information contact the Maine Bureau of Public Lands, State House Station 22, Augusta, ME 04333; (207)289-3061.

MAJOR BACKPACKING TRAILS

APPALACHIAN TRAIL—274 miles in Maine (2,100 total). The Maine portion of the famous Appalachian Trail offers some outstanding backpacking.

It enters Maine through the extremely rugged Mahoosuc Range, which provides one of the most difficult sections of the entire trail.

After crossing mountainous western Maine, the trail leads through much easier terrain, passing numerous wild lakes and ponds, and also following some rivers and streams. The trail ends on top of spectacular Mount Katahdin, in Baxter State Park, after a long and steep climb.

Trail difficulty in Maine ranges between easy and extremely strenuous. Backpacking in the western part of the state should only be undertaken by those who are extremely fit and ready for a considerable physical challenge.

Camping Regulations: Camping along the Appalachian Trail in this state is restricted to established campsites and lean-tos, which are spaced every few miles along the trail. No permits are necessary. Campfires are allowed in built fireplaces, which are located at most campsites.

For Further Information: Appalachian Trail Conference, P.O. Box 807, Harpers Ferry, WV 25425.

MAINE CAMPING RESOURCES

USEFUL GUIDEBOOKS

AMC Maine Mountain Guide—Boston: Appalachian Mountain Club, 1988.

AMC River Guide: Maine—Boston: Appalachian Mountain Club, 1986.

Fifty Hikes in Northern Maine—Caputo, Cloe. Woodstock, VT: Backcountry Publications, 1989.

Fifty Hikes in Southern Maine—Gibson, John. Woodstock, VT: Backcountry Publications, 1989.

Guide to the Appalachian Trail in Maine—Harpers Ferry, WV: The Appalachian Trail Conference, 1988.

The Sierra Club Guide to the Natural Areas of New England—Perry, John and Jane. San Francisco: Sierra Club Books, 1990.

INFORMATION ABOUT CAMPGROUNDS ON STATE LANDS

Maine Bureau of Parks and Recreation, State House Station 22, Augusta, ME 04333; (207)289-3821.

STATE HIGHWAY MAP

Maine Department of Transportation, Augusta, ME 04333.

MARYLAND

BEST AREAS FOR WILDERNESS CAMPING

ASSATEAGUE ISLAND NATIONAL SEASHORE—
39,200 acres. This National Seashore is located on a beautiful 37-mile-long barrier island off the coast of southeast Maryland. The southern part of the island is in Virginia and has been designated the Chincoteague National Wildlife Refuge.

Both areas offer wild coastal scenery including sandy beaches and dunes, marshes and forests. White-tailed deer and red fox are among the wildlife, along with two herds of wild ponies, shorebirds, and marine mammals such as dolphin and seal.

Activities: Hiking and backpacking are possible on an unmarked 21-mile Backcountry Trail, which runs along the shoreline of Assateague, along with some shorter trails. The adjacent National Wildlife Refuge has an additional 15 miles of hiking trails.

Canoeing is available around Chincoteague Bay, and canoes may be rented a few miles away. Saltwater fishing is allowed in most areas of the National Seashore, as are clamming and crabbing. Limited hunting is permitted in season.

Camping Regulations: Primitive camping is restricted to seven designated backcountry camping areas in the National Seashore. Four of the areas are located along Chincoteague Bay, making them accessible to canoeists as well as backpackers, and these camping areas may be used from February 1-October 31. The other sites are open throughout the year.

A free permit is required in order to camp here, and a separate overnight parking permit must also be obtained. Reservations are not available. Campfires are limited to fire rings at some campsites. Pets are prohibited in the backcountry. Camping is not allowed in the National Wildlife Refuge across the Virginia line.

For Further Information: Assateague Island National Seashore, Route 611, 7206 National Seashore Lane, Berlin, MD 21811; (301)641-3030.

SAVAGE RIVER STATE FOREST—53,000 acres. Located in the mountainous northwestern part of the state, Savage River is Maryland's largest state forest. Included here is a wildernesslike area, the 3,000-acre Big Savage Mountain Wildland.

There are numerous streams, a couple of rivers, and a 350-acre reservoir. Common trees are oak and hickory, maple and cherry, with some pine and hemlock. Black bear, deer, and bobcat are among the wildlife.

Activities: The forest has about 28 miles of trails for backpacking and hiking, including the 17-mile Big Savage Mountain Trail. Mountain biking is currently allowed on all trails. Cross-country skiing is possible during the winter. The rivers offer good canoeing, and fishing is available. Hunting is permitted in season.

Camping Regulations: There are several designated camping areas. Camping is also allowed along some of the trails, with the requirement that campsites be at least 200 feet from the trail and all water sources. A free camping permit is required, and may be obtained from the forest office.

For Further Information: Savage River State Forest, Route 2, Box A63, Grantsville, MD 21536; (301)895-5759.

GREEN RIDGE STATE FOREST—40,000 acres. This state forest is located near the Potomac River in

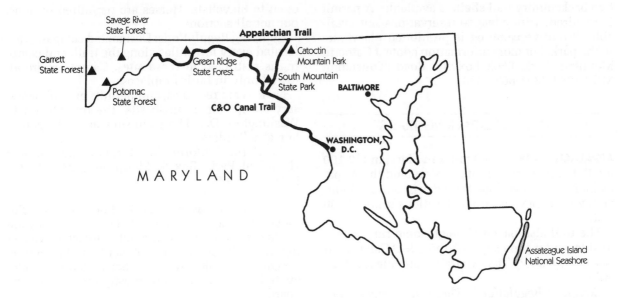

northwestern Maryland. There are fine views from small mountains here, with some elevations over 2,000 feet.

A number of creeks flow through the region, which is forested primarily with oak and hickory, maple and walnut. Wildlife includes white-tailed deer, bear, fox, and wild turkey.

Activities: Hiking and backpacking are possible on several trails, longest of which is the 26-mile Green Ridge Trail. There's also easy access to a section of the nearby C & O Canal Trail (see entry page 170). Fishing is available, and hunting is permitted in season.

Camping Regulations: Camping and campfires are allowed at over 100 designated campsites, which are dispersed along a network of forest roads throughout the area. A camping permit is required, and available from the forest headquarters office. A nominal fee is charged for camping each night.

For Further Information: Green Ridge State Forest, Star Route, Flintstone, MD 21530; (301)777-2345.

POTOMAC AND GARRETT STATE FORESTS—20,000 acres. These two state forests are administered together and consist of multiple tracts in western Maryland. A portion of Potomac State Forest borders on the Potomac River, and this forest includes 3,220-foot Backbone Mountain.

Along with mountains and rock outcroppings there are rolling hills with streams, some ponds and bogs, and forests of oak and hickory, maple

and cherry, with spruce and white pine. Wildlife includes white-tailed deer, black bear, bobcat, and wild turkey.

Activities: The two forests have a number of trails for hiking and backpacking. Some trails are used for cross-country skiing in winter. Fishing is also possible here. Hunting is permitted in season.

Camping Regulations: Trailside camping is allowed for backpackers. A free permit must be obtained from the forest office. Some designated campsites are also available, and a ranger visits these sites and issues the required permit there.

For Further Information: Potomac and Garrett State Forests, Route 3, Box 9305, Oakland, MD 21550; (301)334-2038.

SOUTH MOUNTAIN STATE PARK—10,000 acres. This long and narrow state park is on 40-mile-long South Mountain in west-central Maryland. Elevations are up to 2,000 feet. The park runs the entire length of the mountain in this state. Fine views are available from the ridge.

Activities: Hiking and backpacking are possible on the Appalachian Trail (see entry page 170), which traverses the park.

Camping Regulations: Camping is restricted to shelters along the Appalachian Trail and also a backpackers' camping area. No permits are required.

For Further Information: South Mountain State Park, 21843 National Pike, Boonsboro, MD 21713.

In addition, 5,700-acre Catoctin Mountain Park, administered by the National Park Service, has two backcountry trail shelters available. A permit is required, with advance reservations not available. Primitive camping is prohibited elsewhere in the park. For more information contact Catoctin Mountain Park, 6602 Foxville Road, Thurmont, MD 21788; (301)663-9388.

MAJOR BACKPACKING TRAILS

APPALACHIAN TRAIL—40 miles in Maryland (2,100 total). For most of its route in Maryland the Appalachian Trail runs along the ridge of South Mountain, with nice views from elevations under 2,000 feet.

The trail also passes through some rural countryside, and it connects with the C & O Canal Trail (see entry below). The two trails coincide for three miles.

Camping Regulations: There are several trail shelters and some other designated campsites along this stretch of the trail. Camping and campfires are restricted to these sites. No permits are necessary.

For Further Information: Appalachian Trail Conference, P.O. Box 807, Harpers Ferry, WV 25425. This organization publishes the *Appalachian Trail Guide to Maryland and Northern Virginia*

CHESAPEAKE AND OHIO (C & O) CANAL TRAIL—184 miles. While this is not really a wilderness trail, as it runs near towns and through developed areas, the C & O Canal Trail also traverses some attractive countryside and areas of relatively wild forest.

It's located in the sliver-thin C & O Canal National Historical Park, and follows the old towpath alongside the C & O Canal from Washington, DC to Cumberland, Maryland. The beautiful Potomac River is on one side.

Since the trail is nearly flat, it makes for very easy walking or backpacking. The trail is also open to bicyclists. Horses are permitted on most but not all sections.

Camping Regulations: Designated campsites are located every few miles along the trail, and camping is restricted to these sites. Campfires are allowed only in built fireplaces.

No fees are required, and permits are not necessary except for a single site, the one closest to Washington, DC. The campsites are not open to horseback riders.

For Further Information: C & O Canal National Historical Park, Box 4, Sharpsburg, MD 21782: (301)739-4200.

Maryland also has an important new trail, the Potomac Heritage National Scenic Trail, which could someday become the state's finest backpacking trail. Although it was officially authorized by Congress in 1983, the trail hasn't received adequate funding and is still mostly on the drawing board.

If and when completed, the Potomac Heritage Trail will eventually run 700 miles, utilizing the route of the C & O Canal Trail and continuing on into Pennsylvania. For current information about the trail's status contact the National Park Service, 1100 Ohio Drive, S.W., Washington, DC 20242.

MARYLAND CAMPING RESOURCES

USEFUL GUIDEBOOKS
Appalachian Trail Guide to Maryland and Northern Virginia— Harpers Ferry, WV: The Appalachian Trail Conference, 1989.

INFORMATION ABOUT STATE PARKS AND FOREST CAMPGROUNDS
Maryland Forest, Park, and Wildlife Service, Tawes State Office Building, C-2, Annapolis, MD 21401; (301)374-3771.

STATE HIGHWAY MAP AND TRAVEL INFORMATION
Maryland Office of Tourism Development, 217 East Redwood Street, Baltimore, MD 21202: (800)543-1036.

MASSACHUSETTS

BEST AREAS FOR WILDERNESS CAMPING

MOUNT WASHINGTON STATE FOREST—4,169 acres. Mount Washington State Forest is located in the south Taconic Mountains, in the southwest corner of Massachusetts, adjacent to New York's Taconic State Park. Some of the terrain in this mountainous area is steep and rugged.

Highest point is 2,453-foot Mount Frissell. There are great views available from mountaintops, with high open meadows, rock outcroppings, and streams with waterfalls at lower elevations. Wildlife includes white-tailed deer, black bear, and fox.

Activities: In the forest are about 30 miles of trails for backpacking and hiking, including the scenic 16-mile South Taconic Trail. Limited horseback riding is available, as is cross-country skiing on some trails during winter. Fishing is possible along the streams, and hunting is permitted in season.

Camping Regulations: Backpack camping is allowed at one designated area with a number of campsites, located along a trail in the middle of the forest. A small fee is required for camping each night. There's also a cabin which is open to backpackers.

For Further Information: Mount Washington State Forest, RFD #3, Mount Washington, MA 01258; (413)528-0330.

MONROE STATE FOREST— 4,321 acres. Monroe State Forest is located in a mountainous, hardwood-forested area near the northwest corner of Massachusetts. There are nice views here from ridgetops and rock outcroppings. Highest elevation is 2,730-foot Spruce Mountain.

Activities: Hiking and backpacking are available on 9 miles of trails in the forest. Fishing is also feasible. Hunting is permitted in season.

Camping Regulations: Camping is allowed at three lean-tos and several other designated backpack campsites which are situated along the trails. Campfires may be built at established sites.

For Further Information: Monroe State Forest, c/o Mohawk Trail State Forest, P.O. Box 7, Charlemont, MA 01339; (413)339-6631 (summer); (413)339-5504 (winter).

KENNETH DUBUQUE MEMORIAL STATE FOREST— 7,822 acres. This state forest is situated in the Berkshires of northwest Massachusetts. Some of the terrain in the area is rugged, with elevations up to 1,800 feet. The forest consists mainly of hardwoods and hemlock, with streams and two sizable ponds. Wildlife includes white-tailed deer, black bear, and fox.

Activities: Several hiking and backpacking trails wind through the forest. Some bridle paths are also available. Cross-country skiing is possible here during the winter. Fishing is permitted, as is hunting in season.

Camping Regulations: Primitive camping is restricted to three designated areas which are located along the trails. Shelters are available at these sites. A small fee must be paid for camping each night.

For Further Information: Kenneth Dubuque Memorial State Forest, c/o Mohawk Trail State Forest, P.O. Box 7, Charlemont, MA 01339; (413)339-6631 (summer); (413)339-5504 (winter).

SANDISFIELD STATE FOREST—7,785 acres. Sandisfield State Forest is located in a hilly and forested

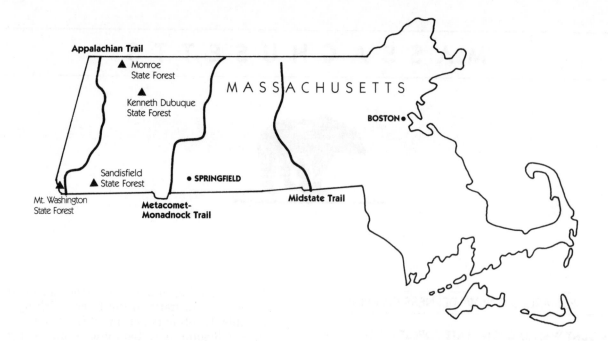

Appalachian Trail

▲ Monroe
State Forest

M A S S A C H U S E T T S

▲ Kenneth Dubuque
State Forest

BOSTON •

Sandisfield
▲ State Forest

• SPRINGFIELD

Mt. Washington
State Forest

Metacomet-
Monadnock Trail

Midstate Trail

area of the Berkshires, in the southwestern part of the state. Included here are streams, swamps, and a 36-acre lake.

Activities: Some trails are available for hiking and backpacking. Horseback riding is allowed on a few trails, as is cross-country skiing in winter. Canoeing and fishing are also possible. Hunting is permitted in season.

Camping Regulations: Primitive camping is restricted to 10 designated backpack campsites which are located 1.5 miles from a parking area. A fee is charged to use these sites.

For Further Information: Sandisfield State Forest, West Street, Sandisfield, MA 01255; (413)528-0904.

There is also a "backpack campground" with over 20 dispersed hike-in campsites at 200-acre Tully Lake, which is in north-central Massachusetts. This area is administered by the Army Corps of Engineers. Hiking trails are available. For more information contact the U.S. Army Corps of Engineers, Tully Lake RR 2, Athol, MA 01331.

MAJOR BACKPACKING TRAILS

APPALACHIAN TRAIL—85 miles in Massachusetts (2,100 total). The Appalachian Trail enters Massachusetts via the south Taconic Mountains, in the southwest corner of the state, where there are some outstanding views from several mountaintops and open ledges.

The trail then heads north through the hilly Berkshires of western Massachusetts. Before reaching the Vermont border, it ascends 3,491-foot Mount Greylock, highest elevation in the state. Difficulty ranges from easy to strenuous.

Camping Regulations: Camping along the Appalachian Trail in Massachusetts is generally restricted to lean-to sites and other designated campsites, located at regular intervals along the way. Campfires are allowed at some but not all campsites. A small fee is charged to camp at a couple of sites. No permits are required.

For Further Information: Appalachian Trail Conference, P.O. Box 807, Harpers Ferry, WV 25425. This organization publishes a *Guide to the Appalachian Trail in Massachusetts-Connecticut.*

METACOMET–MONADNOCK TRAIL—98 miles in Massachusetts (117 miles total). This scenic trail begins in Connecticut, heads north through west-central Massachusetts, and ends on Mount Monadnock in New Hampshire.

At times the trail runs along low ridges and traverses small mountain ranges, with fine views along the way. There are many ups and downs, and the route is sometimes rocky and steep.

Difficulty varies from easy to strenuous. Although it passes through a number of state parks and forests, substantial portions of the trail are on private lands.

Camping Regulations: Camping along the trail is restricted to four shelters and several other established campsites. No permits are necessary.

For Further Information: Trails Program, Department of Environmental Management, 225 Friend Street, Boston, MA 02114; (617)727-3160. A small guide to the trail is published by the Berkshire Chapter of the Appalachian Mountain Club, P.O. Box 369, Amherst, MA 01004.

MIDSTATE TRAIL—89 miles. This trail runs in a north-south direction through the middle of Massachusetts, beginning in Douglas State Forest at the Rhode Island line, and ending at Ashburnham, close to the New Hampshire border. It passes through a hilly, mostly forested region of the state, following old roads much of the time and offering some nice views.

Camping Regulations: Camping is restricted to five designated areas along the trail where there are lean-tos. No permits or fees are required.

For Further Information: Trails Program, Department of Environmental Management, 225 Friend Street, Boston, MA 02114; (617)727-3160.

MASSACHUSETTS CAMPING RESOURCES

ORGANIZATIONS WHICH OFFER WILDERNESS CAMPING TRIPS

Appalachian Mountain Club, 5 Joy Street, Boston, MA 02108; (617)523-0636. This major club has chapters in Massachusetts as well as other northeastern states. Some of the chapters offer backpacking and wilderness camping trips.

USEFUL GUIDEBOOKS

AMC Massachusetts and Rhode Island Trail Guide—Boston: Appalachian Mountain Club, 1989.

Berkshire Trails—Griswold, Whit. East Woods Press, 1983.

Fifty Hikes in Massachusetts—Sadlier, Paul and Ruth. Woodstock, VT: Backcountry Publications, 1983.

Guide to the Appalachian Trail in Massachusetts-Connecticut— Harpers Ferry, WV: The Appalachian Trail Conference, 1990.

The Sierra Club Guide to the Natural Areas of New England—Perry, John and Jane. San Francisco: Sierra Club Books, 1990.

INFORMATION ABOUT STATE PARK AND FOREST CAMPGROUNDS

Massachusetts Division of Forests and Parks, 100 Cambridge Street, Boston, MA 02202; (617)727-3180.

STATE HIGHWAY MAP AND TRAVEl INFORMATION

Massachusetts Office of Travel and Tourism, 100 Cambridge Street, Boston, MA 02202.

MICHIGAN

BEST AREAS FOR WILDERNESS CAMPING

ISLE ROYALE NATIONAL PARK—500,000 acres. This remote National Park is a 45-mile-long island in the northwest corner of Lake Superior, 50 miles from the Michigan shoreline. It's wild, roadless, and accessible by boat or floatplane. The park is open to the public only from mid-May through mid-October each year.

Ninety-nine percent of the park consists of designated wilderness. Terrain is often rocky, with low ridges, and there are several rivers, a number of inland glacial lakes, and some bogs and swamps. The island is forested with hardwoods and conifers. Wildlife includes moose, timber wolf, and fox.

Activities: The main activities available here are hiking and backpacking, with a network of about 170 miles of trails. Included are the 40-mile Greenstone Ridge Trail and the 26-mile Minong Ridge Trail. Difficulty ranges from easy to strenuous.

Off-trail travel is difficult and not recommended. Canoeing is possible on inland lakes, but canoes must be transported to the island. Fishing is another option here. Hunting is prohibited.

Camping Regulations: A free permit, which may be obtained from any ranger station, is required in order to camp in the backcountry. Reservations are not available. A number of designated camping areas are found throughout the park, but it's also possible to camp where one wishes.

Campfires are permitted at some but not all established camping areas, and prohibited elsewhere. A stove should be brought for cooking. Pets are not allowed.

For Further Information: Isle Royale National Park, Houghton, MI 49931; (906)482-0984.

OTTAWA NATIONAL FOREST—Located in a hilly area at the western end of Michigan's Upper Peninsula, Ottawa National Forest has some rugged terrain which includes rocky cliffs and outcroppings. There are forests of pine and hemlock, maple and aspen, with some old-growth trees.

Also here are over 500 lakes, some wetlands, many streams, waterfalls, and a number of rivers—including the Sturgeon National Wild and Scenic River, which has a 300-foot-deep gorge. White-tailed deer, black bear, and fox are among the wildlife.

The National Forest has three designated wilderness areas: the 18,327-acre Sylvania Wilderness, the 16,850-acre McCormick Wilderness, and the 14,139-acre Sturgeon River Gorge Wilderness.

Activities: Hiking and backpacking are possible on 196 miles of trails, including 118 miles of the North Country Trail (see entry page 177). Difficulty varies from easy to moderate.

White-water and flat-water canoeing and kayaking are available on the Sturgeon and other rivers. Canoe outfitters and rentals are located nearby. Cross-country skiing and snowshoeing are possible during winter. Fishing is widely available, and hunting is permitted in season.

Camping Regulations: Camping is freely allowed throughout most of this National Forest, except near public recreation areas or where otherwise prohibited. Campfires may be built, but the use of a stove is recommended.

A permit is required for camping in the Sylvania Wilderness from May 15-September 30, and camping there is restricted to designated sites. Advance reservations may be made for the sites.

For Further Information: Ottawa National Forest, 2100 East Cloverland Drive, Ironwood, MI 49938; (906)932-1330.

HIAWATHA NATIONAL FOREST—879,600 acres. Hiawatha National Forest consists of two large tracts in the central and eastern portions of Michigan's Upper Peninsula, facing three of the Great Lakes.

Terrain includes hills, low ridges, some shallow canyons with rock outcrops and caves, plus swamps, sand dunes, and Lake Michigan beach. There are several rivers, a large number of lakes and streams, and six relatively small designated wilderness areas.

The region is forested with hardwoods, along with pine and hemlock, including some old-growth trees. Among the wildlife are black bear, white-tailed deer, bobcat, fox, and bald eagle.

Activities: Backpacking and hiking are available on over 150 miles of trails, including the 40-mile Bay De Noc–Grand Island Trail, and sections of the North Country Trail (see entry page 177). Difficulty ranges from easy to moderate.

Horseback riding is allowed on some trails, and about 70 miles of trails are designated for cross-country skiing in winter. Canoeing is available on 41 miles of the Sturgeon River, along with several other rivers and on inland lakes. Fishing is also possible. Hunting is permitted in season.

Camping Regulations: There are some established campsites with fire rings. Camping and campfires are allowed elsewhere as well, except near public recreation areas or where otherwise prohibited. A permit is required for campsites at some lakes.

For Further Information: Hiawatha National Forest, 2727 North Lincoln Road, Escanaba, MI 49829; (906)786-4062.

HURON–MANISTEE NATIONAL FORESTS—912,000 acres. These two National Forests in Michigan's Lower Peninsula are administered together. Huron is in the northeast and Manistee in the west-central part of the Peninsula.

Terrain is generally hilly and there are several major rivers, including the 100-mile Pere Marquette National Scenic River and the Au Sable National Scenic River. There are also a great many lakes, streams, and some swamps.

Forests are of northern hardwoods, with hemlock and larch. White-tailed deer, coyote, and fox are among the wildlife. There's one designated wilderness area, the 3,450-acre Nordhouse Dunes Wilderness, which includes a stretch of Lake Michigan shoreline with 140-foot-high sand dunes.

Activities: Over 260 miles of trails are available for backpacking and hiking, including 85 miles of the Shore to Shore Riding–Hiking Trail in Huron National Forest, and more than 60 miles of the North Country Trail in Manistee National Forest (see entries pages 177, 178). Difficulty ranges from easy to moderate.

Canoeing is possible on 66 miles of the Pere Marquette and some other rivers. Canoes may be rented nearby. A free permit is required for canoeing and other boating on the Pere Marquette from May 15-September 10.

Horseback riding is available on some trails, most notably the Riding–Hiking Trail. Cross-country skiing is a winter option on many of the trails. Ample fishing is possible. Hunting is permitted in season.

Camping Regulations: Camping is allowed throughout the two National Forests, as are campfires, except near public use areas or where otherwise prohibited. Some designated campsites may also be used. No permits are necessary.

For Further Information: Huron and Manistee National Forests, 421 South Mitchell Street, Cadillac, MI 49601; (616)775-2421.

OTHER RECOMMENDED LOCATIONS

PORCUPINE MOUNTAINS WILDERNESS STATE PARK—63,000 acres. Located near the northwest corner of Michigan's Upper Peninsula, alongside Lake Superior, this park has been given national wilderness designation. It comprises one of the largest wilderness areas in the Midwest.

The park is in the Porcupine Mountains, a rugged area with some sheer cliffs, bluffs, and fine views. Highest point is 1,958-foot Summit Peak. Included are many creeks and several rivers, waterfalls, wetlands, a few lakes, and some virgin forest of pine and hemlocks. Wildlife includes black bear.

Activities: There are over 90 miles of trails for backpacking and hiking. Difficulty varies from easy to strenuous. About 25 miles of other trails are groomed for cross-country skiing in winter. Hunting and fishing are permitted in season.

Camping Regulations: Backpackers must register and obtain a permit before starting out. A fee is charged for camping here each night. There are some established campsites and three trail shelters (lean-tos) available.

Camping is also allowed elsewhere along the trails, but not within one-quarter mile of any road, shelter, cabin, or scenic area. Campfires are restricted to designated sites. A stove should be brought for cooking.

For Further Information: Porcupine Mountains Wilderness State Park, 599 M-107, Ontonagon, MI 49953; (906)855-5275.

SLEEPING BEAR DUNES NATIONAL LAKESHORE— 71,000 acres. This National Lakeshore is located on the northwest shore of the Lower Peninsula, facing Lake Michigan. It includes 5,260-acre South Manitou Island and 15,000-acre North Manitou Island, which are several miles offshore and may be reached by ferry from May through mid-November.

There are huge sand dunes, along with bluffs over 400 feet high, some inland lakes and streams, and forests of beech and maple. North Manitou Island consists almost entirely of wilderness. White-tailed deer are among the area's wildlife.

Activities: Hiking and backpacking are possible on more than 50 miles of trails in the main part of the Lakeshore, with additional trails found on the islands. Many trails are used for cross-country skiing in the winter.

Canoeing is available on the Platte and Crystal Rivers, and canoes may be rented nearby. Fishing is another option here. Hunting is permitted in season.

Camping Regulations: A free permit is required in order to camp in the backcountry. There are several designated backcountry camping areas within the National Lakeshore.

On North Manitou Island camping is allowed elsewhere as well. It's necessary to be out of sight or sound of trails, inland lakes, and buildings, and at least 300 feet from Lake Michigan. Campfires are generally restricted to designated sites, but also allowed on some beaches. Pets are generally prohibited.

For Further Information: Sleeping Bear Dunes National Lakeshore, P.O. Box 277, Empire, MI 49630; (616)326-5134.

PICTURED ROCKS NATIONAL LAKESHORE—67,000 acres. This long and narrow park, which is next to Hiawatha National Forest in Michigan's Upper Peninsula, protects 40 miles of Lake Superior shoreline. There are sand beaches and dunes here, along with cliffs and caves, arches and other rock formations.

The National Lakeshore encloses a number of small inland lakes, ponds, and streams with waterfalls. Much of the area is forested with northern hardwoods and conifers, including pine and spruce, hemlock and fir.

Activities: Hiking and backpacking are available on almost 100 miles of trails, easy to moderate in difficulty. Among them is the 43-mile Lakeshore Trail, which extends the length of the park and is now part of the North Country Trail (see entry page 177).

Snowfall is abundant here in winter, and 17 miles of trails are groomed for cross-country skiing. Snowshoeing is another option. Canoeing is possible on two inland lakes, with advanced-level canoeing or kayaking also feasible along Lake Superior.

Camping Regulations: A permit is required to camp in the backcountry here. A limited number of permits may be obtained by advance reservation (recommended for July and August).

There are 13 designated camping areas, and these are located at regular intervals along the Lakeshore Trail. Camping is restricted to these sites. Campfires are allowed in fire rings, which are provided at all but two locations. Stoves are recommmended. Pets are prohibited in the backcountry.

For Further Information: Pictured Rocks National Lakeshore, P.O. Box 40, Munising, MI 49862; (906)387-2607.

STATE FORESTS IN MICHIGAN—Michigan has six large state forests: Lake Superior State Forest (1,026,058 acres), Au Sable State Forest (748,458 acres), Mackinaw State Forest (663,843 acres), Pere Marquette State Forest (621,052 acres), Copper Country State Forest (430,291 acres), and Escanaba River State Forest (402,696 acres).

Consisting of northern hardwoods with some conifers, the forests are located in Michigan's Upper Peninsula as well as the northern part of the Lower Peninsula. Terrain ranges from rolling hills to small rugged mountains, and there are a huge number of lakes, streams, and rivers. Included are some lands alongside the Great Lakes.

Activities: The state forests have a total of 64 so-called "Pathways," which are trails for hiking and/or cross-country skiing. Some are suitable for backpacking. Most Pathways form one and sometimes as many as several loops.

Major trails in the state forests include sections of the North Country Trail (see entry page 177), the 70-mile High Country Pathway in Mackinaw State Forest, and the 27-mile Fox River Pathway in Lake Superior State Forest.

Horseback riding is allowed on some designated trails. Canoeing is possible on many of the rivers. Fishing is widely available, and hunting is permitted in season.

MICHIGAN

176

Camping Regulations: Camping is allowed almost anywhere within the state forests, except where posted otherwise. A Camp Registration Card must first be obtained from a Department of Natural Resources office and filled out. Camping is permitted for up to 15 days in a single location.

For Further Information: Michigan Department of Natural Resources, Box 30028, Lansing, MI 48909; (517)373-1220.

MAJOR BACKPACKING TRAILS

NORTH COUNTRY TRAIL—This major National Scenic Trail, currently under construction, will eventually extend some 3,200 miles from New York to North Dakota. The Michigan section will be about 875 miles long, traversing both the Upper and Lower Peninsulas.

So far about 500 miles of the trail have been completed and are open in this state. Substantial portions are on National Forest lands. The trail also passes through state forests, state parks, and some private lands. Difficulty is easy to moderate.

Camping Regulations: Camping is allowed almost anywhere along the trail when it's on National Forest lands. Backpackers are asked to set up camp at least 200 feet off the trail. Camping in state parks and elsewhere is limited to designated camping areas and campgrounds. A permit is re-

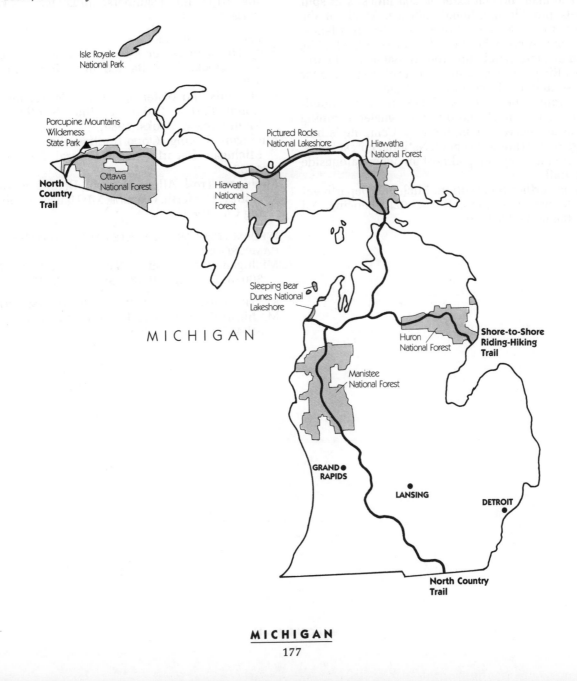

quired to camp in Pictured Rocks National Lakeshore. Campfires are allowed at most established sites.

For Further Information: North Country Trail Association, P.O. Box 311, White Cloud, MI 49349.

SHORE TO SHORE RIDING–HIKING TRAIL—308 miles. Designed for horseback riding as well as hiking and backpacking, this long trail crosses the northern portion of Michigan's Lower Peninsula from Lake Michigan to Lake Huron. One section is utilized by the new North Country Trail (see previous entry). The trail makes for mostly easy backpacking.

The main branch extends 203 miles, and spur trails provide additional mileage. Much of the time it is on National Forest or state forest lands, passing through hardwoods and stands of pine, and at times paralleling the Au Sable and Boardman Rivers. During winter the trail is suitable for cross-country skiing and snowshoeing.

Camping Regulations: There are campground-like "trail camps" and other designated camping areas at intervals along the way. Camping is limited to these areas except on National Forest lands, where one may camp almost anywhere alongside the trail.

For Further Information: Michigan Department of Natural Resources, Box 30028, Lansing, MI 48909; (517)373-1220.

MICHIGAN CAMPING RESOURCES

ORGANIZATIONS WHICH OFFER WILDERNESS CAMPING TRIPS

American Youth Hostels, Michigan Council, 3024 Coolidge, Berkley, MI 48072; (313)545-0511. This AYH chapter sponsors backpacking, canoe-camping, and other wilderness camping trips, and also offers an Introduction to Backpacking class.

Sierra Club, Mackinac Chapter, 115 West Allegan, Suite 10-B, Lansing, MI 48933; (517)484-2372. The Mackinac Chapter of the Sierra Club offers canoe-camping and backpacking trips, including trips for beginners, plus backpacking classes.

USEFUL GUIDEBOOKS

Fifty Hikes in Lower Michigan—DuFresne, Jim. Woodstock, VT: Backcountry Publications, 1991.

Foot Trails and Water Routes of Isle Royale National Park— DuFresne, Jim. Seattle: The Mountaineers Books, 1984.

Michigan Hiking Opportunities—Lansing, MI: Michigan Department of Natural Resources, 1983.

Michigan Trail Atlas—Hansen, Dennis R., and Holley, Danforth. Okemos, MI: Hansen Publishing Co., 1988.

INFORMATION ABOUT STATE PARK AND FOREST CAMPGROUNDS

Michigan Department of Natural Resources, Box 30028, Lansing, MI 48909; (517)373-1220.

STATE HIGHWAY MAP AND TRAVEL INFORMATION

Michigan Travel Bureau, P.O. Box 30226, Lansing, MI 48909; (800)5432-YES.

M I N N E S O T A

BEST AREAS FOR WILDERNESS CAMPING

SUPERIOR NATIONAL FOREST—Stretching for 150 miles along the U.S.–Canadian border, in northeastern Minnesota, Superior National Forest is considered to offer some of the finest canoeing territory in this country—with over 2,000 lakes, countless rivers and streams, and wetlands.

There are also bluffs, ledges, rocky ridges, and small mountains, including 2,301-foot Eagle Mountain, highest point in Minnesota. Forests are of pine, spruce, and fir. Moose, bear, white-tailed deer, timber wolf, and fox are among the wildlife.

This National Forest has an enormous designated wilderness area: the 1,000,000-acre Boundary Waters Canoe Area Wilderness, one of the most visited wilderness areas in the United States.

Activities: Canoeing is the premier activity here, with an almost endless variety of options on the huge number of lakes, rivers and streams. Canoes may be rented nearby, and many outfitters in the area offer organized trips.

Backpacking and hiking are also possible on over 300 miles of trails. Included are the 40-mile Kekekabic Trail, the 38-mile Border Route Trail, and the 55-mile Powwow Trail, which forms a series of loops through part of the Canoe Area Wilderness. Some trails are used for cross-country skiing in winter. Fishing is available, and hunting is permitted in season.

Camping Regulations: Camping is allowed throughout most of the National Forest, as are campfires, except where otherwise prohibited. There are many established sites and lean-tos, but outside of the wilderness area camping is permitted elsewhere as well. Sites should be at least 100 feet from trails and lakes.

A permit is required for camping in the Boundary Waters Canoe Area Wilderness from May 1 through September 30 each year. Reservations for permits are available and advisable, and may be made by mail or phone (218-720-5440). Quotas are in effect, and demand is high. A small reservation fee is charged. The permit must be picked up in person at a forest service office.

There are almost 2,200 designated sites in the wilderness area. Except for some of the more remote portions, camping in this part of the National Forest is generally restricted to established sites. Suggested group size is six, and the limit is 10. Cans and bottles are not allowed in the wilderness area.

For Further Information: Superior National Forest, 515 West 1st Street, P.O. Box 338, Duluth, MN 55801; (218)720-5324.

CHIPPEWA NATIONAL FOREST—600,000 acres. This National Forest in north-central Minnesota has a number of rivers, large areas of wetlands, and over 700 lakes, some with sandy beaches.

There are rolling hills with forests of pine, including several virgin stands, along with cedar, spruce, and aspen. White-tailed deer, black bear, timber wolf, coyote, and bald eagle are among the wildlife.

Activities: Chippewa has more than 200 miles of trails for hiking and backpacking, including 68 miles of the North Country Trail (see entry page 184). Difficulty ranges from easy to moderate. Some trails are suitable for cross-country skiing in winter.

Canoeing is possible on a number of rivers and lakes, including 165 miles of the Big Fork River, and a 120-mile loop which involves some large lakes and rivers. Fishing is also widely available. Hunting is permitted in season.

Camping Regulations: There are numerous established primitive campsites in the forest. Camping and campfires are also allowed almost anywhere else, except near public recreation areas or where otherwise prohibited. No permits are required.

For Further Information: Chippewa National Forest, Route 3, Box 244, Cass Lake, MN 56633; (218)335-2226.

VOYAGEURS NATIONAL PARK—217,000 acres.
Named after the early French-Canadian fur traders who canoed this area, Voyageurs National Park is located in northern Minnesota along the Canadian border, just west of Superior National Forest's Boundary Waters Canoe Area Wilderness.

One-third of the park is covered by water, with over 30 glacial lakes, some of them enormous—plus ponds, streams, marshes, and bogs. The land is forested and sometimes rugged, with low ridges, knobs, and rock formations. Wildlife includes white-tailed deer, black bear, moose, coyote, and timber wolf.

Activities: Canoeing and other boating on the numerous lakes and waterways are the primary activities here. Canoe rentals and outfitters are available near the park.

There are also 18 miles of trails for backpacking and hiking, including the 15-mile Cruiser Lake Trail, which crosses the huge Kabetogama Peninsula. Trailheads are only accessible by boat.

A few other trails here are designated for cross-country skiing in winter, and snowshoeing is also possible. Winter equipment may be rented nearby. Fishing is available extensively throughout the park. Hunting is forbidden.

Camping Regulations: Some 120 designated boat-in campsites are located on the islands and lakeshores, and there are also several established inland sites along the Cruiser Lake Trail.

Campers are asked to use the designated sites, which are available on a first-come, first-served basis. No permits or fees are necessary. Campfires are allowed at many but not all sites. Pets are prohibited.

For Further Information: Voyageurs National Park, P.O. Box 50, International Falls, MN 56649; (218)283-9821.

OTHER RECOMMENDED LOCATIONS

ST. CROIX STATE PARK—33,000 acres. Located in the east-central part of the state, alongside the St. Croix National Wild and Scenic River, this is Minnesota's largest state park.

The area is hilly and includes a mixed forest, with aspen, birch, and pine. The park also includes meadows, marshes, a number of creeks, and the Kettle River. Among the wildlife are white-tailed deer, black bear, coyote, and fox.

Activities: There are 127 miles of trails here for hiking and backpacking, with 75 miles of trails open to horseback riding, and about 21 miles used for cross-country skiing in winter. Included is a section of the multiuse Willard Munger State Trail. Canoeing is available on the St. Croix River, and canoes may be rented. Fishing is allowed, but hunting prohibited.

Camping Regulations: Primitive camping is limited to two backpack camping areas and several canoe-camping areas. Campers must register at the park office.

For Further Information: St. Croix State Park, Route 3, Box 450, Hinckley, MN 55037; (612)384-6591.

ITASCA STATE PARK—32,000 acres. This hilly state park in northwest Minnesota protects the headwaters of the Mississippi River. There are a number of small lakes, ponds, and creeks, plus large Lake Itasca.

The park includes a 2,000-acre wilderness area, with virgin forest of white and red pine, and also meadows and bogs. Deer, bear, coyote, and bald eagle are among the wildlife.

Activities: Hiking and backpacking are possible on about 33 miles of trails. There's also a long bike trail. Canoeing is available on Lake Itasca. Canoes and bikes may be rented.

Camping Regulations: A permit is required for backpack camping, and may be obtained from park headquarters. Camping is limited to several designated sites, where campfires are allowed.

For Further Information: Itasca State Park, Lake Itasca, MN 56460; (218)266-3654.

ST. CROIX STATE FOREST—27,105 acres. Situated in east-central Minnesota and adjacent to the St. Croix River, this state forest includes rolling hills, some small lakes and streams, and the Lower Tamerack River. The region is forested with northern hardwoods, along with some conifers, and there are open grassy areas.

Activities: The forest has many miles of trails for hiking, backpacking, and horseback riding, including a sizable section of the multiuse Willard Munger State Trail. Canoeing is available on the rivers. Hunting and fishing are permitted.

Camping Regulations: There are eight primitive camping areas for backpackers or canoe-campers. Camping is allowed elsewhere in the forest as well, and campfires are permitted.

For Further Information: St. Croix State Forest, Route 2, 701 South Kenwood, Moose Lake, MN 55767; (218)485-4474.

ST. CROIX NATIONAL SCENIC RIVERWAY—This National Scenic Riverway consists of 252 miles of the St. Croix and Namekagon Rivers, including a section of the former which serves as the Minnesota–Wisconsin border.

Primitive camping is allowed at numerous locations along the rivers. For more information see the St. Croix National Scenic Riverway listing in the Wisconsin chapter.

GEORGE H. CROSBY MANITOU STATE PARK—3,400 acres. George H. Crosby Manitou State Park is located in northeastern Minnesota. Notable here is the scenic Manitou River, which crosses the park through a rugged river gorge.

There are rock outcrops, old lava flows, waterfalls, and a glacial lake. Among the park's wildlife are black bear, moose, white-tailed deer, and timber wolf.

Activities: This is a place for backpackers and hikers, with 23 miles of trails. Eleven miles of trails are suitable for cross-country skiing in the winter. Snowshoeing is also possible.

Camping Regulations: Twenty-one backpack campsites are scattered alongside the Manitou River and around Bensen Lake. Camping is restricted to these sites. Visitors must register at the park office. Campfires are allowed in established fire rings.

For Further Information: George H. Crosby Manitou State Park, Box 482, Finland, MN 55603; (218)226-3539.

GRAND PORTAGE NATIONAL MONUMENT—This National Monument in the northeast corner of Minnesota protects a historic 8.5-mile portage route from Lake Superior to the Pigeon River on the Canadian border. A portion of the path passes through an Indian Reservation.

Activities: The 8.5-mile trail is open to backpacking, hiking, and cross-country skiing. Bikes are not allowed.

Camping Regulations: Camping is restricted to one primitive area at the far end of the trail, near the Pigeon River. Campfires are allowed. A free backcountry camping permit must be obtained before starting out.

For Further Information: Grand Portage National Monument, P.O. Box 666, Grand Marais, MN 55604.

SAVANNAH PORTAGE STATE PARK—15,818 acres. This state park in east-central Minnesota preserves a historic 6-mile portage route between the West and East Savannah Rivers, connecting two important watersheds. It's an area of hills, some large bogs, and a number of lakes, with wildlife which includes deer, bear, moose, coyote, and wolf.

Activities: There are 22 miles of easy to moderate trails for hiking and backpacking. Sixteen miles of trails are used for cross-country skiing in winter, and 10 miles are open to mountain biking. Canoeing is possible on the rivers and lakes, and canoes may be rented. Fishing is available along two of the lakes.

Camping Regulations: The park has six backpack camping areas. Primitive camping is restricted to these designated sites.

For Further Information: Savannah Portage State Park, HCR 3, Box 591, McGregor, MN 55760; (218)426-3271.

JAY COOKE STATE PARK—8,813 acres. Located in east-central Minnesota, Jay Cooke State Park encompasses a somewhat rugged area with rock formations, hardwood forests, and the St. Louis River, which flows through a deep gorge. Among the wildlife here are white-tailed deer, black bear, coyote, and timber wolf.

Activities: There are 50 miles of trails for backpacking and hiking. Some trails are open to horseback riding and mountain biking, with about 32 miles used for cross-country skiing in winter. Fishing is also available. Hunting is prohibited.

Camping Regulations: Camping is limited to several backpack campsites along the trails. Campfires may be built in established fire rings.

For Further Information: Jay Cooke State Park, 500 East Highway 200, Carlton, MN 55718; (218)384-4610.

WILD RIVER STATE PARK—7,000 acres. Situated in east-central Minnesota, this long and narrow park extends 18 miles along the western banks of the St. Croix River, the National Wild and Scenic River which forms the Minnesota-Wisconsin border.

In the park are mixed forests of oak and maple, pine and aspen, along with meadows, marshes, and some ponds. White-tailed deer and bald eagle are among the wildlife.

Voyageurs
National Park

Grand Portage
National Monument

Scenic State Park ▲

Superior
National Forest

Chippewa
National Forest

Cascade River
State Park ▲

George Cosby
Manitou State Park

Bear Head
Lake State Park ▲

Split Rock
Lighthouse State Park

Itasca
State Park ▲

DULUTH ●

**Superior
Hiking Trail**

Maplewood
State Park ▲

Savanna Portage
State Park

Jay Cooke State Park

M I N N E S O T A

**North Country
Trail**

St. Croix State Forest

St. Croix
State Park ▲

St. Croix
National Scenic River

Wild River State Park ▲

Lake Maria State Park ▲

MINNEAPOLIS ● ●
ST. PAUL ●

Afton State Park ▲

Minnesota Valley
State Park ▲

Upper Mississippi
River National Wildlife
and Fish Refuge

Myre Big Island
State Park ▲

Activities: Hiking and backpacking are possible on 35 miles of mostly easy trails, which are also groomed for cross-country skiing in the winter. Snowshoeing is another option.

About 20 miles of trails are open to horseback riding. Canoeing and fishing are available on the river, and canoes may be rented in the park. Hunting is prohibited.

Camping Regulations: There are five backpack camping areas and 12 canoe campsites. Primitive camping is restricted to these sites. Visitors must register at the park office.

For Further Information: Wild River State Park, 39755 Park Trail, Center City, MN 55012; (612)583-2125.

MINNESOTA VALLEY STATE PARK—8,000 acres. This state park consists of several tracts alongside the Minnesota River in the southern part of the state. Other lands along the river in this region are part of the Minnesota Valley National Wildlife Refuge.

The river valley includes hills and bluffs, oak forest and prairie, marshes and meadows, and some lakes. White-tailed deer and fox are among the wildlife.

Activities: The 25-mile Minnesota Valley State Trail runs along the river from Belle Plaine to Shakopee, and it will soon be extended. There are also 11 miles of other trails and loops.

Hiking and backpacking are possible on these trails, and some of the trails are also open to horseback riding and mountain biking. Canoeing is available on the river, as is fishing. Limited hunting is permitted in season.

Camping Regulations: A number of canoe campsites are located along the river, and these sites may be used by backpackers as well as canoeists. Camping is restricted to these sites. No fees are charged. Fires are allowed in designated areas.

For Further Information: Minnesota Valley State Park, 19825 Park Boulevard, Jordan, MN 55352; (612)492-6400.

MAPLEWOOD STATE PARK—9,250 acres. Located in west-central Minnesota, Maplewood State Park has hilly terrain with some prairie, forests of hardwoods, plus cedar and tamarack, and many lakes and ponds. Wildlife includes white-tailed deer.

Activities: There are 25 miles of trails for hiking and backpacking. About 15 miles are open to horseback riding, and 17 miles of trails are groomed for cross-country skiing. Canoeing is possible on some of the lakes.

Camping Regulations: Camping and campfires are restricted to three designated backpack camping areas. Two of these areas are next to lakes and useable by canoe-campers as well.

For Further Information: Maplewood State Park, Route 3, Box 422, Pelican Rapids, MN 56572; (218)863-8383.

SCENIC STATE PARK—2,922 acres. A relatively small and hilly park in north-central Minnesota, Scenic State Park has several sizeable glacial lakes. There are also stands of virgin white and red pine.

Activities: In the park are 10 miles of trails for hiking, backpacking, and cross-country skiing. Five miles of trails are open to mountain bikes. Canoeing is available on the lakes, and canoes may be rented here. Fishing is allowed.

Camping Regulations: The park has seven backpack and canoe-camping sites, which are located around the lakes. Camping is restricted to these sites.

For Further Information: Scenic State Park, Bigfork, MN 56628; (218)743-3362.

BEAR HEAD LAKE STATE PARK—4,000 acres. This state park in northeastern Minnesota has rolling hills and some rocky terrain. It's dominated by scenic 674-acre Bear Head Lake and several other lakes. The park's wildlife includes white-tailed deer, moose, and black bear.

Activities: There are several miles of trails for hiking and backpacking, and also the Taconite State Trail, which is open to horseback riding as well. Canoeing and fishing are possible on the lakes, with canoes available for rental. Hunting is prohibited.

Camping Regulations: Camping is limited to five backpack campsites, which are located along the trails next to three of the lakes.

For Further Information: Bear Head Lake State Park, Star Route 2, Box 5700, Ely, MN 55731; (218)365-7229.

CASCADE RIVER STATE PARK—2,813 acres. Cascade River State Park is located in the northeast corner of Minnesota, alongside Lake Superior and adjacent to Superior National Forest lands.

The park includes the Cascade River, several creeks, and the little Sawtooth Mountains, with nice views from 500 feet above Lake Superior. Deer, moose, and wolf are among the wildlife.

Activities: Hiking and backpacking are available on 18 miles of trails, including a section of the Superior Hiking Trail (see entry page 184). Cross-country skiing is possible on 17 miles of trails. Fishing is also available.

Camping Regulations: There are five backpack camping areas in the park. Camping and campfires are restricted to these designated areas.

For Further Information: Cascade River State Park, HCR 3, Box 450, Lutsen, MN 55612; (218)387-1543.

SPLIT ROCK LIGHTHOUSE STATE PARK—1,872 acres. Split Rock Lighthouse State Park includes some rugged terrain alongside Lake Superior in northeastern Minnesota. There are forests of birch and ash, spruce and fir, along with marshlands. Among the wildlife here are white-tailed deer, black bear, and moose.

Activities: The park has over 12 miles of trails for hiking and backpacking, including a section of the Superior Hiking Trail (see entry page 184). Some trails are used for cross-country skiing in winter. Fishing is available in some streams and alongside Lake Superior. Hunting is not allowed.

Camping Regulations: Camping is restricted to several designated camping areas near the Lake Superior shoreline. Campfires are permitted at established sites.

For Further Information: Split Rock Lighthouse State Park, 2010A Highway 16 East, Two Harbors, MN 55616; (218)226-3065.

AFTON STATE PARK—1,699 acres. Afton is a small state park which is located next to the St. Croix River in southeast Minnesota. Some of the terrain here is rugged, with bluffs, rock outcrops, and ravines along the river. There are forests of oak, birch, and aspen, and a few grassy areas. Deer and fox are among the wildlife.

Activities: The park has 18 miles of hiking trails, and these are suitable for cross-country skiing in the winter. Five miles of trails are open to horses, and four miles to bikes. Canoeing is available on the river. Hunting is prohibited.

Camping Regulations: Camping is limited to a large backpack camping area, three-quarters of a mile from a parking lot, with 24 widely dispersed sites. There's also a canoe campsite along the river. Campers must register at the park office.

For Further Information: Afton State Park, 6959 Peller Avenue South, Hastings, MN 55033; (612)436-5391.

LAKE MARIA STATE PARK—1,418 acres. This hilly and forested park in south-central Minnesota has some marshes, ponds, and several lakes, the largest of which is Lake Maria. Terrain is often rough, and consists of terminal moraines (glacial debris including boulders). Among the wildlife here are white-tailed deer and red fox.

Activities: There are 14 miles of trails for hiking and backpacking. The trails are used for cross-country skiing during winter. Seven miles are open to horseback riding. Fishing is available at the lakes. Hunting is not allowed.

Camping Regulations: Eleven designated backpack campsites are located along some of the trails in the southern section of the park. Campers must register at the park office.

For Further Information: Lake Maria State Park, Route 1, Box 128, Monticello, MN 55362; (612)878-2325.

MYRE BIG ISLAND STATE PARK—1,596 acres. Located alongside 2,600-acre Albert Lea Lake, near the southern border of Minnesota, Myre Big Island State Park includes a 116-acre island, rolling hills, wetlands, some prairie, and a hardwood forest on the island. White-tailed deer, fox, and bald eagle are among the wildlife.

Activities: Hiking and backpacking are available on 16 miles of trails. Eight miles of trails are suitable for cross-country skiing during the winter.

Camping Regulations: Four backpack camping areas are located along one trail near the lake. Camping and campfires are restricted to these designated sites.

For Further Information: Myre Big Island State Park, Route 3, Box 33, Albert Lea, MN 56007; (507)373-4492.

In addition, 1,880-acre Glacial Lakes State Park in west-central Minnesota has one primitive camping area which is accessible by a trail. For information contact Glacial Lakes State Park, Route 2, Box 126, Starbuck, MN 56381; (612)239-2860.

STATE FORESTS IN MINNESOTA—Minnesota has 56 state forests, which add up to 3,200,000 acres of land. These are "multiple-use" areas which are open to logging, but they are also available for recreational use.

The activities possible on these lands include hiking, backpacking, canoeing, horseback riding, cross-country skiing, biking, fishing, and hunting. Some of the forests have trail systems, and many of the trails are multiuse.

While state forest literature does not mention or promote camping at other than campgrounds, backpack and primitive camping as well as campfires are generally allowed in the forests, except where posted otherwise.

For Further Information: Minnesota Department of Natural Resources, Division of Forestry, Box 44, 500 Lafayette Road, St. Paul, MN 55155; (612)296-4491.

MAJOR BACKPACKING TRAILS

NORTH COUNTRY TRAIL—Currently under construction, this major new National Scenic Trail will eventually extend some 3,200 miles from New York to North Dakota. The Minnesota section will be about 375 miles long.

The trail here is mostly easy. It runs for 68 miles through Chippewa National Forest, and also several of Minnesota's state parks and forests, plus the Tamarac National Wildlife Refuge. En route it passes a number of beautiful lakes and crosses some rivers. The Chippewa National Forest segment and a few other portions have been completed and are open for backpacking.

Camping Regulations: Where the trail is on National Forest or state forest lands, camping and campfires are allowed almost anywhere, except where posted otherwise. No permits are necessary.

It's suggested that campsites be chosen which are well off the trail and away from water sources. On state park and other lands, camping is restricted to designated sites.

For Further Information: North Country Trail Association, P.O. Box 311, White Cloud, MI 49349. A new guidebook to certified sections of the trail is available from this organization.

SUPERIOR HIKING TRAIL—The Superior Hiking Trail is another scenic new trail in Minnesota. When completed it will be over 250 miles long. The trail follows along the North Shore of Lake Superior from Duluth to the Canadian border, traversing lands of Superior National Forest as well as state parks, state forests, and private lands.

There's some rugged terrain here, with rocky ridges, knolls, bluffs, gorges, and waterfalls, and many panoramic views of Lake Superior. The trail is designed for foot travel. During winter it's suitable for snowshoeing but not cross-country skiing.

Camping Regulations: Campsites have been established every few miles along the trail, and these are available on a first-come, first-served basis.

When the trail is on National Forest or state forest lands, camping is also allowed elsewhere, although campsites should be well off the trail and away from water sources. On state park and private lands, camping is restricted to designated sites.

For Further Information: Superior Hiking Trail Association, P.O. Box 4, Two Harbors, MN 55616; (218)834-4436.

MINNESOTA CAMPING RESOURCES

ORGANIZATIONS WHICH OFFER WILDERNESS
CAMPING TRIPS
Sierra Club, North Star Chapter, 1313 Fifth Street SE, Suite 323, Minneapolis, MN 55414; (612)379-3853. The North Star Chapter of the Sierra Club offers some backpacking, canoe-camping, and other wilderness camping trips each year.
Superior Hiking Trail Association, P.O. Box 4, Two Harbors, MN 55616; (218)834-4436. This organization sponsors an occasional backpacking trip on the Superior Hiking Trail.

USEFUL GUIDEBOOKS
Boundary Waters Canoe Area-Vol. 1—Beymer, Robert. Berkeley, CA: Wilderness Press, 1988.
Boundary Waters Canoe Area-Vol. 2—Beymer, Robert. Berkeley, CA: Wilderness Press, 1991.
Superior National Forest—Beymer, Robert. Seattle: The Mountaineers Books.
Voyageurs National Park: Water Routes, Foot Paths, and Ski Trails—DuFresne, Jim. Seattle: The Mountaineers Books.

INFORMATION ABOUT STATE PARK AND FOREST
CAMPGROUNDS
Minnesota Department of Natural Resources, 500 Lafayette Road, Box 40, St. Paul, MN 55155; (612)296-6157/ (800)766-6000 (in Minnesota only).

STATE HIGHWAY MAP AND TRAVEL INFORMATION
Minnesota Office of Tourism, 375 Jackson Street, 250 Skyway Level, St. Paul, MN 55101; (800)657-3700/ (612)296-5029.

MISSISSIPPI

BEST AREAS FOR WILDERNESS CAMPING

NATIONAL FORESTS IN MISSISSIPPI—Mississippi has six National Forests which are dispersed around the state. Relatively little printed material about these areas is currently available. A new Recreation Guide for the National Forests is expected to be issued in the near future, and this should offer more complete information.

The six Forests are: Bienville National Forest (178,000 acres), De Soto National Forest (501,000 acres), Delta National Forest (60,000 acres), Holly Springs National Forest (147,000 acres), Homochitto National Forest (180,000 acres), and Tombigbee National Forest (66,000 acres).

A considerable range of scenery is found in these forests, with terrain which includes steep slopes as well as flatlands. There are cypress swamps and savannas, bottomland hardwoods and pines, including a 180-acre virgin stand, along with azalea and mountain laurel.

Of particular interest are the 5,000-acre Black Creek Wilderness and the 940-acre Leaf Wilderness, both of which are in De Soto National Forest. A portion of Black Creek, one of several rivers, has National Wild and Scenic River status. There are also some lakes and many streams. Wildlife includes deer, coyote, armadillo, and turkey.

Activities: Of the six National Forests, De Soto has the most hiking and backpacking trails. Especially notable are the 41-mile Black Creek Trail (see entry page 187) and the 22-mile Tuxachanie Trail. Difficulty ranges from easy to moderate.

There are several horse trails, including both the 25-mile Longleaf Trail and the 12-mile Big Foot National Recreation Horse Trail in De Soto, the 23-mile Shockalow Horse Trail in Bienville, and the 18-mile Witch Dance Trail in Tombigbee National Forest.

Canoeing is popular on a 40-mile stretch of Black Creek, along with some other rivers and streams. Kayaking is also possible. Canoe rentals are available nearby. Fishing is another option. Hunting is permitted in season.

Camping Regulations: Camping is allowed almost anywhere in the six National Forests, except near public recreation areas or where posted otherwise. Choose campsites which are at least 100 feet from trails and streams. No permits are necessary.

Campfires are allowed except during periods of forest fire risk. Winters here are relatively warm and summers hot and buggy, so fall through spring are the best seasons to visit.

For Further Information: National Forests in Mississippi, 100 W. Capitol St., Suite 1141, Jackson, MS 39269; (601)965-4391.

OTHER RECOMMENDED LOCATIONS

GULF ISLANDS NATIONAL SEASHORE—137,598 acres. Located both in Mississippi and Florida, this National Seashore consists of several beautiful barrier islands about 10 miles offshore in the Gulf of Mexico, plus areas on the mainland. The islands are accessible only by charter boat.

There are lovely sandy beaches here, along with marshes and pine forests. Horn and Petit Bois Islands are designated wilderness areas. Alligators are among the wildlife, and there are many nesting birds including the Great Blue Heron.

Activities: Beach hiking is an option on 14-mile Horn Island and the other islands. Fishing is permitted, but hunting is not.

Camping Regulations: Camping is allowed on Horn and Petit Bois Islands, as well as on East Ship Island. No permits are necessary. Dune areas are off limits to camping. Water must be carried in. Campfires may be built on beach areas only.

For Further Information: Gulf Islands National Seashore, 3500 Park Road, Ocean Springs, MS 39564.

Primitive camping is also allowed in some of Mississippi's 31 Wildlife Management Areas, which are located throughout the state. These areas are used primarily for hunting. For more information contact the Mississippi Department of Wildlife, Fisheries, and Parks, P.O. Box 451, Jackson, MS 39205.

MAJOR BACKPACKING TRAILS

BLACK CREEK NATIONAL RECREATION TRAIL—41 miles. Located in De Soto National Forest, this easy and scenic trail follows tea-colored Black Creek. It passes through gently hilly terrain, with low ridges, pine and hardwood forests, and some flat floodplain.

At times the trail leads alongside the creek, and for other stretches it runs some distance from the water. About ten miles of the route are within the Black Creek Wilderness Area. Horses and bicycles are not permitted on the trail.

Camping Regulations: Camping is allowed almost anywhere along the trail, except where posted otherwise. No permits are required, and campfires may be built. It's suggested that campsites be at least 100 feet from the trail.

For Further Information: National Forests in Mississippi, 100 W. Capitol St., Suite 1141, Jackson, MS 39269; (601)965-4391.

MISSISSIPPI CAMPING RESOURCES

INFORMATION ABOUT STATE PARK CAMPGROUNDS
Mississippi Department of Wildlife, Fisheries, and Parks, P.O. Box 451, Jackson, MS 39205; (601)364-2120.

STATE HIGHWAY MAP AND TRAVEL INFORMATION
Mississippi Division of Tourism Development, P.O. Box 22825, Jackson, MS 39205; (601)359-3297/(800)647-2290.

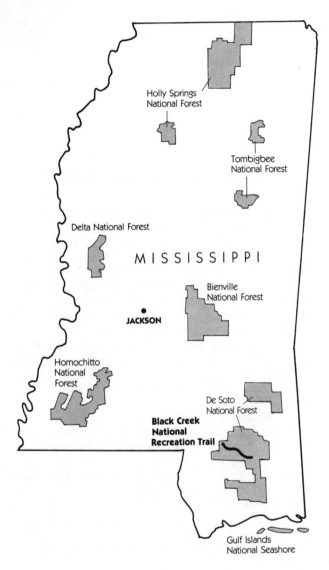

Holly Springs National Forest

Tombigbee National Forest

Delta National Forest

MISSISSIPPI

Bienville National Forest

JACKSON

Homochitto National Forest

De Soto National Forest

Black Creek National Recreation Trail

Gulf Islands National Seashore

MISSOURI

BEST AREAS FOR WILDERNESS CAMPING

MARK TWAIN NATIONAL FOREST—1,500,000 acres. Consisting of nine separate units in the southern part of the state, this enormous National Forest encompasses the Ozarks, the St. Francis Mountains, and the mountains of southwest Missouri.

Terrain ranges from foothills to steep and rugged ridges, with limestone bluffs, rock formations, and caves. Also here are oak-hickory forests with pine and red cedar, and open meadows.

There are some lakes and ponds, plus a number of streams and rivers, including the Eleven Point National Wild and Scenic River. White-tailed deer, bobcat, coyote, and wild turkey are among the wildlife

The National Forest has seven designated wilderness areas adding up to over 63,000 acres, including the 16,300-acre Irish Wilderness, the 12,300-acre Hercules Glades Wilderness, the 9,020-acre Bell Mountain Wilderness, and the 8,120-acre Piney Creek Wilderness.

Activities: Backpacking and hiking are available on hundreds of miles of trails. Included are 200 miles of the Ozark Trail (see entry page 191), the 38-mile Ridge Runner Trail, and the 21-mile circular Cedar Creek Trail.

Other trails have been designated for horseback riding, including the 25-mile Blue Ridge Horse Trail and the 22-mile Victory Horse Trail. Some trails are open to mountain biking, but bikes aren't allowed in wilderness areas.

Canoeing, kayaking, and rafting are possible on some of the rivers and streams. Canoes may be rented nearby. Fishing is also available, and hunting is permitted in season.

Camping Regulations: Camping and campfires are allowed throughout the National Forest, except near public use areas or where otherwise prohibited. No permits are necessary.

For Further Information: Mark Twain National Forest, 401 Fairgrounds Road, Rolla, MO 65401; (314)364-4621.

OZARK NATIONAL SCENIC RIVERWAYS—Administered by the National Park Service and located in southern Arkansas, the Ozark National Scenic Riverways consist of 134 miles of the Current and Jacks Forks Rivers, plus substantial adjacent lands. These wild and beautiful rivers flow between two tracts of Mark Twain National Forest, and the waterways intersect. Riverside scenery includes high limestone bluffs.

Activities: The rivers are popular for canoeing, kayaking, and rafting, with stretches of white-water included. Canoe rentals and shuttle services are available throughout the area. Some portions of the rivers receive heavy use, especially on summer weekends. During dry spells not all sections are canoeable. Conditions after heavy rains can be dangerous.

Backpacking and hiking are possible mainly on the Ozark Trail, which crosses and parallels the Current River for a few miles. Fishing is also available along the rivers.

Camping Regulations: Camping and campfires are allowed near or alongside the rivers. No permits are required. It's possible to camp on gravelbars directly by the river, but one should be on the lookout for rising waters, especially in the event of rain. Campsites should be chosen which offer escape routes on foot.

For Further Information: Ozark National Scenic Riverways, P.O. Box 490, Van Buren, MO 63965; (314)323-4236.

OTHER RECOMMENDED LOCATIONS

CUIVRE RIVER STATE PARK—6,250 acres. Located in the rugged Lincoln Hills of northeast Missouri, this rustic park has two wilderness areas: the 1,675-acre Big Sugar Creek Wild Area and the 1,082-acre Northwoods Wild Area.

Big Sugar Creek runs the length of the park. There are some steep hills and bluffs offering nice views, prairie grasslands, oak-hickory forests with dogwood, and an 88-acre lake. Wildlife includes white-tailed deer and wild turkey.

Activities: Hiking and backpacking are possible on 30 miles of trails. Difficulty ranges from easy to moderate. Horseback riding is permitted on some of the trails.

Camping Regulations: Camping is allowed for backpackers only along the trails. It's necessary to register at the trailhead or park office before starting. Campfires are prohibited.

Campsites must be at least 100 feet from trails, 200 feet from public use areas, and one-quarter mile from entry points. Groups of seven or more must use designated camping areas.

For Further Information: Cuivre River State Park, Route 1, Box 25, Troy, MO 63379; (314)528-7247.

LAKE WAPPAPELLO STATE PARK—1,854 acres. This state park is located alongside Lake Wappapello, an 8,600-acre reservoir in the Ozarks of southeastern Missouri. It's a hilly and somewhat rugged area with nice views, an oak-hickory forest, and wildlife which includes white-tailed deer.

Activities: There are 21 miles of trails, longest of which is the circular 15-mile Lake Wappapello Trail. This trail is for hiking and backpacking, and a section is open to mountain biking. Fishing is available at the lake.

Camping Regulations: Camping is permitted for backpackers only, and it's limited to portions of the Lake Wappapello Trail. Sites must be at least 100 feet from the trail, 200 feet from public use areas, and one-quarter mile from entry points.

Backpackers must register at the park office or trailhead before starting out. Campfires are prohibited. Groups of seven or more must use a designated backpack camping area.

For Further Information: Lake Wappapello State Park, Route 2, Box 102, Williamsville, MO 63967; (314)297-3232.

JOHNSON'S SHUT-INS STATE PARK—2,490 acres. Johnson's Shut-ins State Park is situated in the St. Francois Mountains of southeast Missouri. Shut-ins are steep, canyon-like gorges, which are found here along the Black River.

There is a designated wilderness area in the park, the 1,110-acre East Fork Wild Area. Also included are oak-hickory forests with pine, some talus slopes, and a few rocky, barren, desert-like areas.

Activities: Hiking and backpacking are available on the Ozark Trail (see entry page 191), which has a trailhead in the park.

Camping Regulations: Camping is allowed along some but not all sections of the Ozark Trail. Backpackers are asked to register at the trailhead. Campsites should be at least 100 feet from the trail, 200 feet from public use areas, and one-quarter mile from entry points.

For Further Information: Johnson's Shut-Ins State Park, HC Route 1, Box 126, Middlebrook, MO 63656; (314)546-2450.

SAM A. BAKER STATE PARK—5,168 acres. Located in southeast Missouri's St. Francois Mountains, this state park surrounds 1,300-foot Mudlick Mountain, and includes the 4,180-acre Mudlick Mountain Wild Area. Both the St. Francois River and bluff-lined Big Creek border the park.

Activities: The main trail here is the 12-mile Mudlick Trail, a moderately-strenuous National Recreation Trail which forms a loop around the Wild Area. It's open to hikers, backpackers, and horseback riders. Fishing is possible alongside the creek and river.

Camping Regulations: Camping is allowed only for backpackers, who must register at the trailhead or park office. Campsites must be at least 100 feet from the trail, 200 feet from public use areas, and one-quarter mile from entry points.

Campfires are not permitted. Groups of seven or more are required to camp at designated areas. There are also three shelters which are available for use from October 1 to May 15 each year.

For Further Information: Sam A. Baker State Park, Patterson, MO 63956; (314)856-4411.

ST. FRANCOIS STATE PARK—2,735 acres. St. Francois State Park is in a hilly region of east-central Missouri. It lies next to Big River and includes Coonville Creek. There's a designated wilderness area here, the 1,700-acre Coonville Creek Wild Area.

Activities: Hiking, backpacking, and horseback riding are available on 17 miles of trails. Longest

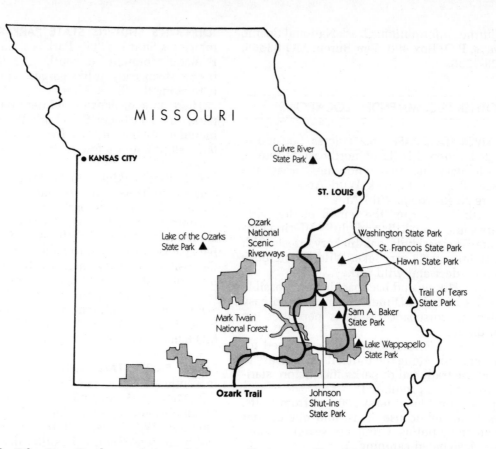

MISSOURI

Kansas City

Cuivre River
State Park ▲

St. Louis

Lake of the Ozarks
State Park ▲

Ozark
National
Scenic
Riverways

Washington State Park
St. Francois State Park
Hawn State Park

Trail of Tears
State Park

Mark Twain
National Forest

Sam A. Baker
State Park

Lake Wappapello
State Park

Ozark Trail

Johnson
Shut-ins
State Park

is the 11-mile Pike Run Trail, consisting of two loops in the Coonville Creek Wild Area.

Camping Regulations: Camping is allowed for backpackers only along the Pike Run Trail. Registration is required at the trailhead or park office. Campsites must be at least 100 feet from the trail, 200 feet from public use areas, and one-quarter mile from entry points. Campfires are prohibited. Groups of seven or more must use designated camping areas.

For Further Information: St. Francois State Park, Bonne Terre, MO 63628; (314)358-2173.

TRAIL OF TEARS STATE PARK—3,415 acres. Located directly alongside the Mississippi River, in southeast Missouri, this hardwood-forested park takes its name from the historic forced Cherokee march which led through these lands. Terrain is hilly with some steep ridges, and 600-foot limestone bluffs line the river.

Activities: The park has 12 miles of trails for backpacking, hiking, and horseback riding. Included is the moderately difficult 10-mile Peewah Trail, which forms several loops.

Camping Regulations: Camping is allowed for backpackers only, who must register at the park office or trailhead before beginning. There's one designated camping area, and camping is also permitted along the trail as long as sites are at least one-quarter mile from entry points, 200 feet from public use areas, and 100 feet from the trail itself. Campfires are prohibited. Groups of seven or more must use the designated camping area.

For Further Information: Trail of Tears State Park, Jackson, MO 63755; (314)334-1711.

WASHINGTON STATE PARK—1,415 acres. Washington State Park is located in the Ozarks of east-central Missouri, alongside Big River. This is an area of oak-hickory forest, with rough terrain including rocky outcrops.

Activities: Hiking and backpacking are possible on 14 miles of trails. Longest is the circular 10-mile Rockywood Trail.

Camping Regulations: Camping is allowed on the western part of the Rockywood Trail loop. There's one designated camping area, and use of this area is required for groups of seven or more. Campsites elsewhere along the Rockywood Trail must be at least 100 feet from the trail, 200 feet from public use areas, and one-quarter mile from entry points. Campfires are not permitted.

For Further Information: Washington State Park, De Soto, MO 63020; (314)586-2995.

HAWN STATE PARK—3,271 acres. Hawn State Park is in a hilly area of the Ozarks of east-central Missouri. Pickle Creek as well as the River aux Vases flow through the park, and there are pine and hardwood forests, with dogwood and wild azalea.

Activities: Hiking and backpacking are available on the 10-mile Whispering Pine Trail, which consists of two loops.

Camping Regulations: Backpackers are allowed to camp along the Whispering Pine Trail. It's necessary to register at the trailhead, and sites must be at least 100 feet from the trail, 200 feet from any public use area, and at least one-quarter mile from entry points. Campfires are prohibited. Groups of seven or more must use designated camping areas.

For Further Information: Hawn State Park, Ste. Genevieve, MO 63670; (314)883-3603.

LAKE OF THE OZARKS STATE PARK—17,152 acres. Situated next to a huge artificial lake in south-central Missouri, this is Missouri's largest state park. It includes rocky hilltops, sheer bluffs, and a number of caves, with oak-hickory forest. Deer are among the wildlife. An arm of Lake of the Ozarks extends through the park. There's also a small wilderness area, the 1,275-acre Patterson Hollow Wild Area.

Activities: The park has 23 miles of trails for hiking, horseback riding, and mountain biking. Backpacking is allowed on one trail only, the 6-mile Woodland Trail, which loops through the Patterson Hollow Wild Area.

Camping Regulations: Camping is allowed for backpackers only along the Woodland Trail. Registration is required at the park office or trailhead. There's a single designated camping area which may be used. Other campsites along the trail must be at least 100 feet from the trail, 200 feet from public use areas, and one-quarter mile from entry points. Campfires are prohibited.

For Further Information: Lake of the Ozarks State Park, P.O. Box C, Kaiser, MO 65047; (314)348-2694.

Missouri also has a number of state forests and wildlife areas of various sizes. These are generally used for hunting, fishing, and other recreational activities. Primitive camping is allowed in some of the larger areas. For more information contact the Missouri Department of Conservation, P.O. Box 180, Jefferson City, MO 65102; (314)751-4115.

MAJOR BACKPACKING TRAILS

OZARK TRAIL—This partially completed trail will eventually extend 500 miles through Missouri's Ozarks, starting near St. Louis and leading southwest to the Arkansas border. There's also an eastern loop through the St. Francois Mountains. It will eventually be connected to the Ozark Highlands Trail of Arkansas.

About 200 miles are in Mark Twain National Forest, and some other sections are on private lands. Scenery along the way is often quite beautiful and wild. There are gratifying views from mountain ridges, and the trail crosses countless streams and follows several rivers. Difficulty ranges from easy to moderately strenuous. Portions of the trail are open to horses.

Camping Regulations: Camping is freely allowed along the trail on National Forest lands, except where posted otherwise. Campsites should be away from scenic spots and at least 100 feet from water sources and the trail. Campfires are legal but discouraged. Elsewhere along the trail camping and campfires are limited to designated sites. No permits are necessary.

For Further Information: Missouri Department of Natural Resources, Ozark Trail Coordinator, P.O. Box 176, Jefferson City, MO 65102; (314)751-2479.

MISSOURI CAMPING RESOURCES

ORGANIZATIONS WHICH OFFER WILDERNESS CAMPING TRIPS

American Youth Hostels, Ozark Area Council, 7187 Manchester Road, St. Louis, MO 63143; (314)644-4660. This AYH council sponsors some backpacking and canoe-camping trips, and offers an introductory course in hiking and backpacking.

USEFUL GUIDEBOOKS

Floater's Guide to Missouri—Cline, Andy. Helena, MT: Falcon Press.

INFORMATION ABOUT CAMPGROUNDS IN STATE PARKS

Missouri Department of Natural Resources, P.O. Box 176, Jefferson City, MO 65102; (314)751-2479/(800)334-6946.

STATE HIGHWAY MAP AND TRAVEL INFORMATION

Missouri Division of Tourism, P.O. Box 1056, Jefferson City, MO 65102; (314)751-4133.

MONTANA

BEST AREAS FOR WILDERNESS CAMPING

GLACIER NATIONAL PARK—1,013,598 acres. Located near and alongside the Canadian border, in northwest Montana, Glacier is one of our most spectacular National Parks. Along with Canada's Waterton National Park it forms the Waterton/Glacier International Peace Park.

This is a region of truly splendid Rocky Mountain scenery, with extremely rugged and steep glacier-carved mountains, cirque basins and valleys, and over 50 glaciers. The Continental Divide extends the length of the park, with elevations over 10,000 feet. Virtually the entire area is wilderness.

There are over 200 lakes, countless streams with waterfalls, alpine meadows, and prairie grasslands. Forests are of spruce and fir, pine and larch. Among the wildlife are elk, deer, grizzly and black bear, moose, bighorn sheep, mountain goat, and mountain lion.

Activities: Backpacking and hiking are possible on over 730 miles of trails. Difficulty ranges from easy to very strenuous. Horses are allowed on some trails. Bikes may only be ridden on established roads, although they are permitted on three trails in neighboring Waterton Park.

Canoeing, kayaking, and rafting are available on the Flathead River. Cross-country skiing is possible throughout the park in winter, as is snowshoeing. Fishing is permitted along streams, rivers, and lakes. Hunting is prohibited.

Camping Regulations: Camping is allowed in the backcountry with a free permit, which is available no more than 24 hours in advance from the park's visitor centers and ranger stations.

There are 63 established backcountry camping areas, and camping is restricted to the designated sites in most parts of the park. Numbers of campers are limited at each site. Campfires are permitted at some but not all locations. Pets are prohibited.

One section of the park includes a wilderness camping zone, and here camping is allowed almost anywhere. In this area campfires are prohibited, and campsites should be away from meadows, at least 100 feet from water sources, and out of sight of trails and other campers. Maximum group size is 12.

For Further Information: Glacier National Park, West Glacier, MT 59936; (406)888-5441.

FLATHEAD NATIONAL FOREST—2,350,508 acres. This enormous National Forest stretches south and west of Glacier National Park, in northwest Montana. It's a magnificent area of high snowy peaks and ridges, deep canyon gorges, and small glaciers. Elevations range from 4,000 feet to 9,820-foot McDonald Peak.

The three-forked Flathead National Wild and Scenic River is here. There are also many lakes, streams with waterfalls, alpine meadows, and forests of fir, spruce, larch, and pine. Wildlife includes grizzly and black bear, elk, deer, mountain goat, and gray wolf.

This National Forest has three designated wilderness areas: the 285,700-acre Great Bear Wilderness, the 73,877-acre Mission Mountain Wilderness, and a large portion of the 1,009,356-acre Bob Marshall Wilderness, Montana's largest, which continues on into Lewis and Clark National Forest.

Activities: Over 2,100 miles of trails are available for backpacking and hiking. Difficulty varies from easy to strenuous. Of special interest is the 15,000-acre Jewel Basin Hiking Area, which is open only to foot travel. Horseback riding is permitted on many other trails.

White-water rafting, canoeing, and kayaking are possible on some of the rivers. Cross-country skiing and snowshoeing are winter options in the region. Mountain biking is allowed outside of designated wilderness areas. Fishing is also available, and hunting is permitted in season.

Camping Regulations: Camping is allowed throughout the National Forest, except near public use areas or where otherwise prohibited. No permits are required. Campfires are normally acceptable, but they're subject to restriction during periods of fire hazard.

For Further Information: Flathead National Forest, 1935 Third Avenue East, Kalispell, MT 59901; (406)755-5401.

GALLATIN NATIONAL FOREST—1,738,138 acres. Located in southwest Montana and bordering on two sides of Wyoming's Yellowstone National Park, this massive National Forest has spectacular Rocky Mountain scenery. There are 25 peaks over 12,000 feet, including 12,799-foot Granite Peak, Montana's highest.

Also here are high plateaus, deep canyons and limestone cliffs, glaciers, alpine meadows, prairie grasslands, and dense forests, along with some major rivers, hundreds of lakes, and a 40-square-mile petrified forest. Among the wildlife are grizzly and black bear, mule deer, moose, and bighorn sheep.

There are two designated wilderness areas, consisting of about 575,000 acres of the 945,000-acre Absaroka–Beartooth Wilderness, and 112,000 acres of the Lee Metcalf Wilderness, both of which extend into other National Forests.

Activities: Backpacking and hiking are available on over 1,800 miles of trails, including the 42-mile Gallatin Divide Trail. Difficulty varies from easy to strenuous. Most trails are open to horses. Mountain bikes are allowed on many trails outside of wilderness areas.

White-water rafting and kayaking are possible on several of the area's rivers. Cross-country skiing is a winter option here, as is snowshoeing. Fishing is also available, and hunting is permitted in season.

Camping Regulations: Camping is allowed throughout the region, except where posted otherwise. No permits are necessary. Campsites should be away from meadows and trails, and at least 200 feet from water sources. Campfires are allowed but discouraged. A stove is recommended for cooking.

For Further Information: Gallatin National Forest, P.O. Box 130, Bozeman, MT 59715; (406)587-6701.

LOLO NATIONAL FOREST—2,091,944 acres. Lolo National Forest consists of several large parcels of land in western Montana, near and alongside the Idaho border. Included is a portion of the Bitterroot Mountains and an area along the Continental Divide, with 10,456-foot Warren Peak the highest point.

There are steep ridges, cirque basins, cliffs and canyons, alpine meadows, high lakes and streams with waterfalls, and forests of fir and pine. Among the wildlife are elk, moose, deer, black and grizzly bear, and mountain goat.

The forest has four designated wilderness areas, consisting of 75,000 acres of the 239,000-acre Scapegoat Wilderness, the 33,000-acre Rattlesnake Wilderness, the 28,000-acre Welcome Creek Wilderness, and a small portion of the 1.3 million-acre Selway–Bitterroot Wilderness.

Activities: Over 1,800 miles of trails are available for backpacking and hiking. Difficulty ranges from easy to strenuous. Horseback riding is allowed on most trails, and many miles of trails are used for cross-country skiing in winter. Fishing is also possible, and hunting is permitted in season.

Camping Regulations: Camping and campfires are allowed throughout the National Forest, except near public use areas or where otherwise prohibited. No permits are required.

For Further Information: Lolo National Forest, Building 24, Fort Missoula, MT 59801; (406)329-3750.

LEWIS AND CLARK NATIONAL FOREST—1,843,397 acres. Lewis and Clark National Forest consists of several tracts in northwest and west-central Montana, with one unit directly east of the Continental Divide. Included are parts of the Front Range, the Little Belt Mountains, and other ranges.

Elevations run from 4,500 feet to over 9,000 feet, with 9,362-foot Rocky Mountain Peak the highest point. Of special interest is the high rock "Chinese Wall," which runs along the Continental Divide.

Along with precipitous peaks, rocky ridges, and steep-walled canyons, there are alpine meadows, grassy prairies, ponderosa pine forests, and numerous lakes, rivers, and streams. Wildlife includes elk, moose, deer, bear, and bighorn sheep.

The National Forest has two designated wilderness areas, consisting of about 300,000 acres of the 1,009,000-acre Bob Marshall Wilderness, Montana's largest, and 84,000 acres of the 239,000-acre Scapegoat Wilderness.

Activities: Hiking and backpacking are possible

on some 1,680 miles of trails, including a section of the Continental Divide Trail (see entry page 197). Difficulty ranges from easy to strenuous. Horseback riding is allowed on most trails.

Cross-country skiing and snowshoeing are winter options on many trails. Rafting, canoeing, and kayaking are available in early summer on the Smith River, which borders a section of the National Forest. Fishing is also possible, and hunting is permitted in season.

Camping Regulations: Camping is allowed almost anywhere in the National Forest, as are campfires, except near developed areas or where posted otherwise. No permits are necessary.

For Further Information: Lewis and Clark National Forest, P.O. Box 869, Great Falls, MT 59403; (406)791-7700.

BEAVERHEAD NATIONAL FOREST—2,148,683 acres. This National Forest consists of several tracts in southwest Montana, northwest of Wyoming's Yellowstone National Park. In the region are a number of spectacular mountain ranges, including lands along the Continental Divide, with some high ridges and craggy peaks over 11,000 feet.

There are also cirque basins and deep canyons, mountain meadows and grasslands, spruce and pine forests, plus many lakes, creeks, and some rivers. Wildlife includes grizzly and black bear, elk, deer, pronghorn, moose, and mountain goat.

Beaverhead has two designated wilderness areas, which extend into nearby National Forests: over 100,000 acres of the 259,000-acre Lee Metcalf Wilderness, and 73,000 acres of the 158,000-acre Anaconda–Pintler Wilderness.

Activities: Backpacking and hiking are available on over 1,600 miles of trails, most of which are open to horseback riding. Mountain biking is allowed on many trails outside of wilderness areas.

Cross-country skiing is possible here in the winter, as is ski mountaineering. Fishing is widely available along many of the streams and lakes. Hunting is permitted in season.

Camping Regulations: Camping is allowed almost anywhere in the National Forest, as are campfires, except where otherwise prohibited. Permits are not required.

For Further Information: Beaverhead National Forest, 610 North Montana, Dillon, MT 59725; (406)683-3900.

BITTERROOT NATIONAL FOREST—1,113,838 acres. Located in the west-central part of the state, with a portion in neighboring Idaho, this National Forest encompasses parts of two major mountain ranges, the Bitterroot and Sapphire Mountains, and includes a section of the Continental Divide.

Highest mountain here is 10,157-foot Trapper Peak. There are also canyons and cliffs, rock outcrops, and boulder fields, and amid the snow-capped mountains are scores of lakes and streams, alpine meadows, and spruce and fir forests. Wildlife includes elk, deer, moose, black bear, bighorn sheep, and mountain lion.

An unusually large portion (almost half) of this National Forest consists of designated wilderness areas:194,000 acres of the 2,364,000-acre Frank Church–River of No Return Wilderness, 41,000 acres of the 158,000-acre Anaconda–Pintler Wilderness, and a portion of the 1,341,000-acre Selway–Bitterroot Wilderness.

Activities: Hiking, backpacking, and horseback riding are possible on over 1,600 miles of trails, including about 50 miles of the Continental Divide Trail (see entry page 197). High trails are often under snow until mid-July.

White-water rafting, kayaking, and canoeing are available on the Selway and Salmon Rivers. Permits and reservations are required in order to float either river from late spring through summer.

Mountain biking is allowed on many trails, but not in wilderness areas. Cross-country skiing and snowshoeing are trail options in winter. Rock climbing and mountaineering opportunities exist here as well. Hunting and fishing are permitted in season.

Camping Regulations: Camping and campfires are allowed throughout the forest with few restrictions, except where otherwise prohibited. No permits are necessary. It's suggested that sites be at least 200 feet from water and away from trails.

For Further Information: Bitterroot National Forest, 316 North Third Street, Hamilton, MT 59840; (406)363-3131.

KOOTENAI NATIONAL FOREST—2,245,000 acres. Kootenai National Forest is located in the northwest corner of Montana, along the state's borders with Idaho and Canada. It covers several mountain ranges, including the Cabinet and Purcell Mountains.

In the region are many rocky ridges, peaks, and canyons. Highest point is 8,738-foot Snowshoe Peak. There are also alpine meadows, grasslands, glacial lakes and streams, and forests of larch and pine.

This National Forest has one designated wilderness area, the 94,272-acre Cabinet Mountains Wilderness. The varied wildlife includes moose, elk, deer, bear, and bighorn sheep.

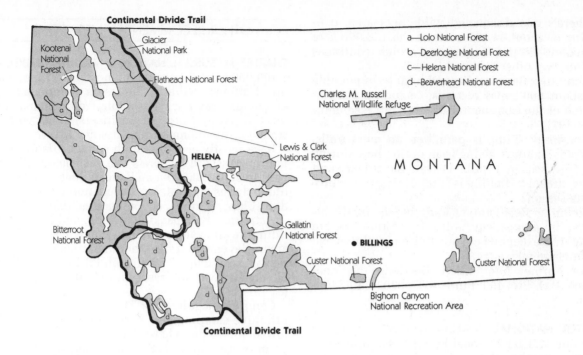

Glacier
National Park

Kootenai
National
Forest

Flathead National Forest

a—Lolo National Forest
b—Deerlodge National Forest
c—Helena National Forest
d—Beaverhead National Forest

Charles M. Russell
National Wildlife Refuge

Lewis & Clark
National Forest

HELENA

MONTANA

Bitterroot
National Forest

Gallatin
National Forest

● BILLINGS

Custer National Forest

Custer National Forest

Bighorn Canyon
National Recreation Area

Continental Divide Trail

Activities: Over 1,300 miles of trails are suitable for backpacking and hiking. Difficulty ranges from easy to strenuous. Most trails are open to horses.

Canoeing, kayaking, and rafting are possible on the Kootenai River. Winter activities include cross-country skiing as well as snowshoeing. Fishing is also available, and hunting is permitted in season.

Camping Regulations: Camping is allowed throughout the forest, as are campfires, except near public recreation areas or where otherwise restricted. No permits are necessary.

For Further Information: Kootenai National Forest, 506 U.S. Highway 2 West, Libby, MT 59923; (406)293-6211.

HELENA NATIONAL FOREST—976,673 acres. Consisting of several units around Helena, Montana, in the west-central part of the state, this National Forest includes a section of the Continental Divide and several mountain ranges. Highest elevation is 9,472-foot Mount Baldy.

There are precipitous peaks, huge cliffs and spires, canyons and rock formations, with open meadows, plus fir and pine forests. Among the wildlife are deer, elk, grizzly and black bear, moose, and antelope.

The National Forest has two designated wilderness areas, consisting of about 83,000 acres of the 239,000-acre Scapegoat Wilderness, which extends into nearby National Forests, and the

28,562-acre Gates of the Mountains Wilderness.

Activities: Hiking and backpacking are available on more than 700 miles of trails, including 120 miles of the Continental Divide Trail (see entry page 197). A section of the Lewis and Clark National Historic Trail is found here as well.

Horses are allowed on most trails. Cross-country skiing is possible in the forest during winter. Hunting is permitted in season, and fishing is also feasible.

Camping Regulations: Camping and campfires are allowed throughout most of this National Forest, except near public use areas or where posted otherwise. No permits are required.

For Further Information: Helena National Forest, 301 South Park, Drawer 10014, Helena, MT 59626; (406)449-5201.

DEERLODGE NATIONAL FOREST—1,195,771 acres. Deerlodge National Forest is made up of several large parcels of land in southwest Montana. Included are a series of mountain ranges and a sizable segment of the Continental Divide. Highest elevation is 10,641-foot Mount Evans.

Along with snow-capped peaks there are massive cirque basins, rock formations, canyons, conifer forests, and numerous glacial lakes and streams. Local mammals include elk, moose, grizzly and black bear, deer, and coyote.

MONTANA

195

There's one designated wilderness area, consisting of about 44,000 acres of the 158,000-acre Anaconda–Pintler Wilderness, which continues on into two other National Forests.

Activities: Backpacking and hiking are possible on about 600 miles of trails, including a major stretch of the Continental Divide Trail (see entry page 197).

Horseback riding is permitted on most trails, and cross-country skiing is an option here during the snow season. Fishing is available at lakes and along streams. Hunting is legal during the appropriate season.

Camping Regulations: Camping is freely allowed in almost any suitable location, as are campfires, except where otherwise prohibited. No permits are necessary.

For Further Information: Deerlodge National Forest, P.O. Box 400, Butte, MT 59703; (406)496-3400.

CUSTER NATIONAL FOREST—1,112,477 acres in Montana. Custer National Forest has a number of tracts in southern Montana, and also administers National Grasslands in North Dakota and South Dakota. Included are the Beartooth Mountains, with 16 peaks over 12,000 feet.

Granite Peak (12,799 feet), Montana's highest mountain, is here. There are also pinnacles, high plateaus, glaciers, and canyons, with alpine tundra, spruce and fir forests, and many lakes and streams. Elk, deer, black bear, moose, bighorn sheep, and mountain lion are among the wildlife.

Within this National Forest is one designated wilderness area, consisting of about 346,000 acres of the 945,000-acre Absaroka–Beartooth Wilderness, the state's second largest. Portions are located in two other National Forests.

Activities: There are about 330 miles of established trails for backpacking and hiking. Difficulty varies from easy to very strenuous. Horses are allowed on most trails. Mountain biking is allowed outside of the designated wilderness area.

White-water kayaking and some canoeing are possible on the Stillwater River. Cross-country skiing is available on trails here in winter. Hunting and fishing are permitted in season.

Camping Regulations: Camping and campfires are allowed throughout most of the forest, except where otherwise prohibited. In some canyons camping is restricted to designated sites. No permits are required.

For Further Information: Custer National Forest, 2602 First Avenue North, P.O. Box 2556, Billings, MT 59103; (406)657-6361.

OTHER RECOMMENDED LOCATIONS

CHARLES M. RUSSELL NATIONAL WILDLIFE REFUGE—1,100,000 acres. Located in northeast Montana, this National Wildlife Refuge is dominated by enormous Fort Peck Reservoir, administered by the U.S. Army Corps of Engineers, along with a stretch of the dammed-up Missouri River.

It's a mostly arid area with some badlands and prairie grasslands. There's one designated wilderness area, the 20,000-acre Bend Wilderness. Wildlife includes elk, antelope, mule and white-tailed deer, bighorn sheep, coyote, and golden eagle.

Activities: Backpacking, hiking, and horseback riding are allowed throughout the refuge, but there are no developed trails other than rough primitive roads for vehicles. Canoeing and fishing are possible on the river and reservoir. Hunting is permitted in season.

Camping Regulations: There's one established primitive camping area here. Camping is also allowed almost anywhere else, as are campfires. No permits are required. Summer visits are not recommended due to the heat.

For Further Information: Charles M. Russell National Wildlife Refuge, P.O. Box 110, Lewistown, MT 59457; (406)538-8707.

BIGHORN CANYON NATIONAL RECREATION AREA—120,000 acres. This National Recreation Area is situated both in southern Montana and northern Wyoming. With steep-walled canyons up to 1000-feet deep, the area includes 71-mile-long Bighorn Lake, which is a dammed-up stretch of the Bighorn River, along with lands on either side. Within the boundaries is a portion of the Prior Mountain Wild Horse Range.

Activities: Hiking and backpacking are possible here, but there are no formal trails. All travel is cross-country. Fishing is available, and hunting is permitted in season.

Camping Regulations: Camping is largely restricted to campgrounds, but backpacking is allowed in the South District of this National Recreation Area. A free permit is required, and may be obtained from visitor centers or ranger stations. Campfires are normally allowed with the appropriate permit.

For Further Information: Bighorn Canyon National Recreation Area, P.O. Box 458, Fort Smith, MT 59035; (406)666-2412.

BLM LANDS IN MONTANA—There are over eight million acres of BLM (Bureau of Land Management) or public domain lands in Montana. Numerous tracts are located throughout the state. Access to the areas is not always easy, roads are sometimes in poor condition, and printed literature is not available for many of the units.

Included on these lands are some major mountains, and 149 miles of the Missouri River, a National Wild and Scenic River which is also a segment of the Lewis and Clark National Historic Trail. There's one designated wilderness area, the 6,000-acre Bear Trap Canyon Wilderness, with a stretch of the Madison River.

Activities: Hiking, backpacking, and horseback riding are possible on BLM lands, but most travel must be cross-country, as there are very few established trails. Canoeing, kayaking, and rafting are available on some of the rivers. Hunting and fishing are permitted in season.

Camping Regulations: Except for a few restricted areas and where posted otherwise, camping and campfires are freely allowed on these lands. Permits are not necessary for most locations.

For Further Information: Bureau of Land Management, 222 North 32nd Street, P.O. Box 36800, Billings, MT 59107; (406)255-2885.

MAJOR BACKPACKING TRAILS

CONTINENTAL DIVIDE TRAIL—961 miles (3,100 total). The Montana section of this important National Scenic Trail offers some magnificent Northern Rockies scenery, with wonderful views from elevations over 10,000 feet. Difficulty varies from easy to strenuous.

The trail traverses Glacier National Park and several National Forests, passing alpine lakes and leading beneath high peaks and cliffs. At times it follows the crest of the Divide and for major stretches runs below, sometimes on jeep roads.

Horses are allowed on the trail, as are mountain bikes and motor vehicles along some sections outside of designated wilderness areas and the National Park. At higher elevations the trail is snow-free only from about mid-July through September.

Camping Regulations: In Glacier National Park a free permit is required, and may be obtained from ranger stations or visitor centers. Camping here is restricted to designated sites. Campfires are allowed only at certain locations.

On National Forest lands camping is allowed almost anywhere along the trail, as are campfires, except where otherwise prohibited. Backpackers are asked to get well off the trail and away from water sources before setting up camp.

For Further Information: Continental Divide Trail Society, P.O. Box 30002, Bethesda, MD 20814.

MONTANA CAMPING RESOURCES

USEFUL GUIDEBOOKS

The Angler's Guide to Montana—Sample, Michael S. Helena, MT: Falcon Press, 1992.

Bitterroot to Beartooth—Rudner, Ruth. San Francisco: Sierra Club Books.

The Floater's Guide to Montana—Fischer, Hank. Helena, MT: Falcon Press, 1986.

Guide to the Continental Divide Trail, Northern Montana—Wolf, James R. Bethesda, MD: Continental Divide Trail Society, 1979.

Guide to the Continental Divide Trail, Southern Montana—Wolf, James. R. Bethesda, MD: Continental Divide Trail Society, 1979.

A Hiker's Guide to Glacier National Park—Nelson, Dick. West Glacier, MT: Glacier National History Association, 1978.

The Hiker's Guide to Montana—Henckel, Mark. Helena, MT: Falcon Press.

The Hiker's Guide to Montana's Continental Divide Trail—Brooks, Tad and Jones, Sherry. Helena, MT: Falcon Press, 1990.

Montana Wilderness—Woodruff, Steve and Schwenneser, Don. Helena, MT: Falcon Press.

The Nordic Skier's Guide to Montana—Sedlack, Elaine. Helena, MT: Falcon Press, 1981.

The Sierra Club Guide to the Natural Areas of Idaho, Montana, and Wyoming—Perry, John and Jane. San Francisco: Sierra Club Books, 1988.

Trail Guide to Glacier National Park—Molvar, Erik. Helena, MT: Falcon Press.

INFORMATION ABOUT OUTFITTERS AND GUIDES

Montana Outfitters and Guides Association, P.O. Box 9070, Helena, MT 59604.

INFORMATION ABOUT CAMPGROUNDS IN STATE PARKS

Montana Department of Fish, Wildlife, and Parks, 1420 East Sixth Avenue, Helena, MT 59620; (406)444-2535.

STATE HIGHWAY MAP AND TRAVEL INFORMATION

Travel Montana, Department of Commerce, 1424 8th Avenue, Helena, MT 59620; (800)541-1447 (out of state)/(406)444-2654 (in state).

NEBRASKA

BEST AREAS FOR WILDERNESS CAMPING

NEBRASKA NATIONAL FOREST /SAMUEL R. McKELVIE NATIONAL FOREST—Nebraska National Forest (140,376 acres) consists of widely separate tracts of land located in central and northwest Nebraska. Samuel R. McKelvie National Forest (115,703 acres) is in the north-central part of the state. These two National Forests are administered together.

The areas include prairie grasslands, rolling sandhills, and scattered stands of hardwoods, with ponderosa pine and cedar. The forests are made up largely of planted trees. Livestock grazing is allowed in both National Forests. White-tailed and mule deer, antelope, coyote, bobcat, and prairie dog are among the wildlife.

Of special scenic interest is the Pine Ridge region in the northwest part of Nebraska National Forest. It's notable for a sandstone escarpment with steep ridges which rise over 1,000 feet above surrounding areas.

There are also rugged buttes, canyons, badlands, some streams, a river, and one designated wilderness area: the 8,100-acre Soldier Creek Wilderness Area. Also in the region is the 6,600-acre Pine Ridge National Recreation Area.

Activities: Hiking and backpacking are possible on about 34 miles of trails in the Pine Ridge region, including the 25-mile Pine Ridge Trail, which has two separate segments.

Aside from a couple of other short trails, most foot-travel must either be on old roads or cross-country, which is very feasible given the relatively open landscape.

Horseback riding is allowed on trails and elsewhere in both National Forests, and some corrals are available. Mountain biking is possible outside of the wilderness area. Canoeing and kayaking are available on the Loup River. Cross-country skiing is a winter option here. Fishing is also feasible, and hunting is permitted in season.

Camping Regulations: Camping is allowed throughout both National Forests, as are campfires, except where posted otherwise. No permits are necessary. Campfires are subject to restriction during dry periods.

For Further Information: Nebraska National Forest and Samuel R. McKelvie National Forest, 270 Pine Street, Chadron, NE 69337; (308)432-3367.

OGLALA NATIONAL GRASSLAND—94,344 acres. This National Grassland is located in the northwest corner of Nebraska, north and west of Nebraska National Forest. It's an area of rolling hills and buttes, and there's badlands scenery which includes sandstone toadstool formations with umbrellalike tops. Livestock grazing is permitted throughout the National Grassland.

Activities: Aside from a one-mile loop trail, there are no designated trails. Cross-country hiking, backpacking, and horseback riding are permitted throughout the area. Fishing is available, and hunting is permitted in season.

Camping Regulations: Camping and campfires are allowed without restriction, except where posted otherwise. Permits are not required.

For Further Information: Oglala National Grassland, HC 75, Box 13A, Chadron, NE 69337.

OTHER RECOMMENDED LOCATIONS

FORT ROBINSON STATE PARK—22,000 acres. Located next to the Soldier Creek Wilderness Area in

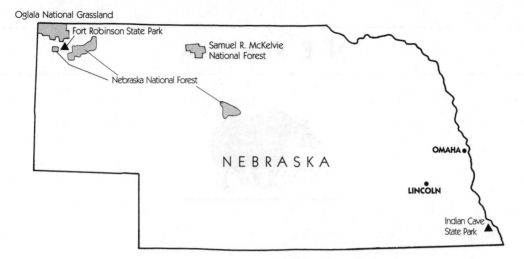

Oglala National Grassland
Fort Robinson State Park
Samuel R. McKelvie National Forest
Nebraska National Forest
NEBRASKA
OMAHA •
LINCOLN •
Indian Cave State Park

Nebraska National Forest, this state park preserves the site of a historic fort. There are open prairie grasslands, rugged piney hills and buttes, some creeks, and a river.

Activities: Hiking and backpacking are available on several trails, and these connect with nearby National Forest trails. Horses are allowed. Cross-country skiing is feasible on some trails during winter. Fishing is possible along waterways.

Camping Regulations: Camping for backpackers is restricted to the northwest part of the park. It's also permitted in the nearby Soldier Creek Wilderness Area and on other National Forest lands. Water must be carried in.

For Further Information: Fort Robinson State Park, P.O. Box 392, Crawford, NE 69339; (308)665-2660.

INDIAN CAVE STATE PARK—3,000 acres. This state park stretches along the Missouri River in southeast Nebraska, in an area with both woodlands and grasslands. The park is noted for a giant sandstone cave which has ancient petroglyphs (Indian picture writings). Deer, coyote, fox, and wild turkey among the wildlife.

Activities: About 20 miles of trails are available for hiking and backpacking. Difficulty ranges from easy to strenuous. Horseback riding is allowed, and some trails are open to cross-country skiing

during winter. Fishing is permitted along the Missouri River.

Camping Regulations: A number of backpacking campsites are located along some of the trails. Several trail shelters may also be used. An entry permit must first be obtained from the park office. Campfires are allowed only in established fire rings.

For Further Information: Indian Cave State Park, c/o Nebraska Game and Parks Commission, P.O. Box 30370, Lincoln, NE 68503.

Primitive camping is also generally permitted in Nebraska's State Wildlife Management Areas, except where posted otherwise. These areas are used primarily for hunting and fishing. For more information contact the Nebraska Game and Parks Commission, P.O. Box 30370, Lincoln, NE 68503.

NEBRASKA CAMPING RESOURCES

INFORMATION ABOUT STATE PARK CAMPGROUNDS
Nebraska Game and Parks Commission, P.O. Box 30370, Lincoln, NE 68503.

STATE HIGHWAY MAP AND TRAVEL INFORMATION
Nebraska Department of Travel and Tourism, P.O. Box 94666, Lincoln, NE 68509; (800)742-7595 (in state)/(800)228-4307 (out of state).

NEVADA

BEST AREAS FOR WILDERNESS CAMPING

TOIYABE NATIONAL FOREST—3,212,545 acres in Nevada (3,855,960 total). This truly enormous National Forest is comprised of several units in central and southern Nevada, along with one tract in California. It's the largest National Forest in the country outside of Alaska.

Scenery includes high and spectacular alpine peaks with elevations over 11,000 feet, mountain meadows, deep rugged canyons and cliffs, desert brushlands with cactus and yucca, plus numerous streams, rivers, and lakes.

There are forests of lodgepole and Jeffrey pine, fir, and aspen. Also here is a large area of bristlecone pine, the earth's most ancient living trees, some of which are thought to be nearly 5,000 years old. Mule deer, wild horse, elk, black bear, bighorn sheep, mountain lion, and bobcat are among the wildlife.

Six designated wilderness areas are found in the Nevada portions of this National Forest: the 115,000-acre Arc Dome Wilderness, the 98,000-acre Table Mountain Wilderness, the 43,000-acre Mount Charleston Wilderness, the 38,000-acre Alta Toquima Wilderness, the 28,000-acre Mount Rose Wilderness, and the 10,000-acre Boundary Peak Wilderness.

Activities: There are approximately 1,165 miles of trails for backpacking and hiking, including the 72-mile Toiyabe Crest National Recreation Trail, and also a section of the new Tahoe Rim Trail. Difficulty varies from easy to strenuous.

Horseback riding is allowed on many trails, and mountain biking is possible outside of designated wilderness areas. Some trails are suitable for cross-country skiing during winter. Climbing and mountaineering are available as well. Fishing is another option, and hunting is permitted in season.

Camping Regulations: Camping is allowed freely throughout most of the National Forest, as are campfires, except near public use areas or where otherwise prohibited. No permits are required.

For Further Information: Toiyabe National Forest, 1200 Franklin Way, Sparks, NV 89431; (702)355-5302.

HUMBOLDT NATIONAL FOREST—2,474,985 acres. Humboldt is a huge National Forest made up of a number of widely scattered tracts in east-central and northern Nevada. On these lands are many scenic mountain ranges, with some elevations over 11,000 feet.

Ruby Dome (11,350 feet) is among the most notable peaks. There are also deep glacial canyons, cliffs, cirque basins, rock formations, rolling hills, plateaus, and arid desert—along with some rivers and streams, and alpine lakes at higher elevations.

The forests are of fir, pine, and aspen, with stands of bristlecone pine. Wildlife includes elk, mule deer, antelope, bighorn sheep, mountain lion, and mountain goat.

The National Forest now has eight designated wilderness areas: the 127,000-acre Jarbidge Wilderness, the 90,000-acre Ruby Mountains Wilderness, the 82,000-acre Mount Moriah Wilderness, the 50,000-acre Grant Mountain Wilderness, the 36,900-acre East Humboldt Wilderness, the 36,000-acre Currant Mountain Wilderness, the 31,000-acre Santa Rosa–Paradise Peak Wilderness, and the 27,000-acre Quinn Canyon Wilderness.

Activities: About 900 miles of trails are available for backpacking and hiking, including the 40-mile Ruby Crest National Recreation Trail. Difficulty ranges from easy to strenuous. Trails at high elevations are likely to be snow-free only from July through mid-September.

Mountain biking is allowed on many trails, but not in wilderness areas. Most trails are open to horseback riding. Cross-country skiing is available during the snow season. Fishing is possible, as is hunting during the appropriate season.

Camping Regulations: Camping is allowed throughout the National Forest, except where otherwise posted. Campfires are permitted, but stoves are suggested for cooking. Campsites in wilderness areas should be at least 200 feet from trails and water sources. No permits are necessary.

For Further Information: Humboldt National Forest, 976 Mountain City Highway, Elko, NV 98901; (702)738-5171.

GREAT BASIN NATIONAL PARK—77,000 acres. Established in 1986 on lands which were previously part of Humboldt National Forest, this new National Park is located in the southern Snake Range, near the eastern border of Nevada. Among a number of high peaks here is 13,063-foot Wheeler Peak.

Scenery also includes limestone canyons and caves, rock outcroppings, and a small glacier. There are Douglas fir forests, along with spruce and aspen, stands of ancient bristlecone pine and limber pine, pinyon-juniper woodlands, and brushlands.

Activities: Backpacking and hiking are available on about 25 miles of established trails. Cross-country travel is possible but difficult in some areas due to vegetation and rugged terrain. Much of the park is only snow-free during the summer months.

Horseback riding is allowed on some trails. Cross-country skiing and snowshoeing are winter options on suitable trails and roads. Mountain bike use is restricted to roads. Fishing is permitted, but hunting is not.

Camping Regulations: Camping is allowed throughout the backcountry here, and no permits are necessary. Registration at the visitor center is recommended but not required.

All campsites should be below timberline, away from bristlecone pine groves, and at least 100 feet from water sources. Campfires are generally permitted but discouraged, and prohibited above 10,000 feet elevation.

For Further Information: Great Basin National Park, Baker, NV 89311; (702)234-7331.

OTHER RECOMMENDED LOCATIONS

LAKE MEAD NATIONAL RECREATION AREA—586,000 acres in Nevada (1,480,000 acres total). Located in the southeast corner of Nevada as well as northwest Arizona, just west of Grand Canyon National Park, this National Recreation Area features 110-mile-long Lake Mead and 67-mile-long Lake Mohave, both formed by damming up the Colorado River.

In this desert region are mountains, plateaus, canyons, and sandstone formations. With some sandy beaches along the shore, the lake attracts many tourists and there's lots of boating. Vegetation includes Joshua tree and cactus, with mule deer, bighorn sheep, mountain lion, and coyote among the wildlife.

Activities: Hiking, backpacking, and horseback riding are possible within the National Recreation Area, but most travel must be cross-country since there are few established trails. Fishing is available at the lakes. Hunting is permitted in portions of the area.

Camping Regulations: A large number of established campsites are available along the lakeshores. Backcountry camping and campfires are allowed here as well as elsewhere, except near developed aras or where otherwise prohibited. No permits are required. Since summers are very hot here, the best season to visit is October through May.

For Further Information: Lake Mead National Recreation Area, 601 Nevada Highway, Boulder City, NV 89005; (702)293-8907.

BLM LANDS IN NEVADA—BLM (Bureau of Land Management) or public domain lands in Nevada are incredibly extensive, adding up to nearly 50,000,000 acres—far more than any other state except Alaska.

There are many separate tracts, and printed literature is available for only a handful. Access is sometimes difficult, and public facilities are rare. Areas of special interest in Nevada include Red Rock Canyon, High Rock Canyon, and the Blue Lakes.

Activities: Backpacking and hiking are possible throughout BLM lands, as is horseback riding, but there are very few established trails. Fishing is also available, and hunting is permitted in season.

Camping Regulations: Camping is allowed in most areas, except where otherwise prohibited. No permits are required. Campsites should be at least 200 feet from water sources and trails. Campfires are allowed, but stoves are recommended.

For Further Information: Bureau of Land Man-

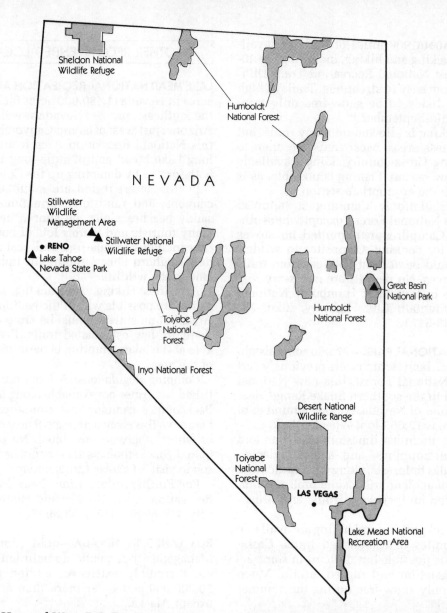

NEVADA

Sheldon National
Wildlife Refuge

Humboldt
National Forest

Stillwater
Wildlife
Management Area

● RENO

▲ Stillwater National
Wildlife Refuge

▲ Lake Tahoe
Nevada State Park

Great Basin
National Park ▲

Humboldt
National Forest

Toiyabe
National
Forest

Inyo National Forest

Desert National
Wildlife Range

Toiyabe
National
Forest

LAS VEGAS
●

Lake Mead National
Recreation Area

agement, 850 Harvard Way, P.O. Box 12000, Reno, NV 89520; (702)328-6300.

DESERT NATIONAL WILDLIFE RANGE—1,588,000 acres. Located in the Mohave Desert of southern Nevada, the primary purpose of this huge National Wildlife Range is to protect desert bighorn sheep. It's the largest wildlife refuge in the country outside of Alaska.

The area encompasses several mountain ranges, with elevations from 2,500 feet to 10,000 feet. The western half of the refuge is an Air Force bombing range, and this portion is closed to the public.

Vegetation includes pine and fir forests at higher elevations, pinyon and juniper woodlands, with Joshua tree as well as yucca and cactus, In

addition to bighorn sheep, there are also mule deer, coyote, mountain lion, bobcat, and fox.

Activities: Backpacking and hiking are possible here, as is horseback riding, although there are few trails. Limited hunting is permitted in season.

Camping Regulations: Established primitive campsites are found in two locations. Camping is allowed elsewhere in most parts of the range, but sites must be at least one-quarter mile from water sources and out of sight of the water. Campers are asked to sign in at the Corn Creek Field Station upon entering and leaving the National Wildlife Range. Campfires are permitted.

For Further Information: Desert National Wildlife Range, 1500 North Decatur Boulevard, Las Vegas, NV 89108; (702)646-3401.

SHELDON NATIONAL WILDLIFE REFUGE—575,000 acres. Located in the northwest corner of Nevada, along the Oregon border, this National Wildlife Refuge is in a semi-desert area, with rolling hills and tablelands intersected by rocky canyons. Elevations range from 4,500 feet to 7,600 feet.

Included here are some lakes, creeks, marshes, grasslands, and brushlands, with stands of aspen and juniper. Among the wildlife are pronghorn antelope, mule deer, mountain lion, bobcat, and coyote.

Activities: The National Wildlife Refuge is open to hiking, backpacking, and horseback riding, but most of the area is trail-less. Travel is generally cross-country. Fishing is restricted to a couple of locations. Limited hunting is permitted.

Camping Regulations: A special use permit is required in order to camp outside of campgrounds. Campfires are allowed, but may be prohibited when the fire hazard is high.

For Further Information: Sheldon National Wildlife Refuge, P.O. Box 111, Lakeview, OR 97630; (503)947-3315.

INYO NATIONAL FOREST—While most of this enormous (1,798,638-acre) National Forest is in California, some 61,000 acres of the forest are located in Nevada. Included here are the White and Excelsior Mountains, with 13,140-foot Boundary Peak the highest point, along with some canyons. Camping is permitted. See the Inyo National Forest listing in the California chapter for more information.

LAKE TAHOE NEVADA STATE PARK—13,000 acres. Located along the northeast shore of large and scenic Lake Tahoe, which is on the California border, this state park has some small mountains, inland lakes, and conifer forests. Wildlife includes mule deer, black bear, and mountain lion.

Activities: Hiking, backpacking, and horseback riding are available on a small trail network, consisting largely of old roads. A section of the new Tahoe Rim Trail also passes through the park. Mountain biking is permitted on some trails. Cross-country skiing is a winter trail option.

Camping Regulations: Camping is restricted to two backcountry camping areas in the park.

Campfires are generally allowed, but are subject to being banned during summer months.

For Further Information: Lake Tahoe Nevada State Park, 2005 Highway 28, P.O. Box 3283, Incline Village, NV 89450; (702)831-0494.

STILLWATER NATIONAL WILDLIFE REFUGE/STILLWATER WILDLIFE MANAGEMENT AREA—This National Wildlife Refuge and adjacent state Wildlife Management Area in west-central Nevada are noted for their abundant and diverse waterfowl. It's a relatively flat region which includes a large number of lakes and reservoirs, along with extensive marshlands and some desert vegetation.

Activities: There are no formal trails, although some foot-travel is possible. Extensive fishing is available. Seasonal hunting is allowed in the Wildlife Management Area but not in the National Wildlife Refuge.

Camping Regulations: Camping is permitted in the state Wildlife Management Area as well as in a portion of the National Wildlife Refuge. No permits are required.

For Further Information: Stillwater National Wildlife Refuge, P.O. Box 1236, Fallon, NV 89406; (702)423-5128.

NEVADA CAMPING RESOURCES

USEFUL GUIDEBOOKS
The Hiker's Guide to Nevada—Grubbs, Bruce. Helena, MT: Falcon Press.
Hiking the Great Basin—Hart, John. San Francisco: Sierra Club Books, 1981.
The Sierra Club Guide to the Natural Areas of New Mexico, Arizona, and Nevada—Perry, John and Jane. San Francisco: Sierra Club Books, 1985.

INFORMATION ABOUT CAMPGROUNDS IN STATE PARKS
Nevada Division of State Parks, Capitol Complex, Carson City, NV 89710; (702)687-4370.

STATE HIGHWAY MAP AND TRAVEL INFORMATION
Nevada Commission on Tourism, Capitol Complex, Carson City, NV 89710; (800)237-0774.

NEW HAMPSHIRE

BEST AREAS FOR WILDERNESS CAMPING

WHITE MOUNTAIN NATIONAL FOREST—798,000 acres. Located in north-central New Hampshire, with an additional tract across the border in southwestern Maine, White Mountain National Forest is one of the finest mountain wilderness areas in the eastern United States.

It's the largest alpine area east of the Mississippi, a ruggedly spectacular region of high, rocky mountains with open summits. Loftiest of the ranges is the Presidential Range, which includes 6,288-foot Mount Washington, highest in the Northeast.

There are 45 lakes and ponds, several rivers, many miles of streams, and numerous waterfalls. Forests are mixed, with spruce, fir, pine, and hardwoods, including some old-growth trees. Moose, deer, black bear, and bobcat are among the wildlife.

The forest has four wilderness areas: the 5,500-acre Great Gulf Wilderness, the 45,000-acre Pemigewasset Wilderness, the 27,380-acre Presidential–Dry River Wilderness, and the 25,000-acre Sandwich Range Wilderness.

The White Mountains are famous for variable and often incredibly severe weather, especially on Mount Washington and other high peaks. Visitors should be prepared for intense storms and cold at any time. The snow season is usually October-May, but summer snowstorms occasionally occur at higher elevations.

Activities: There are over 1,200 miles of trails for hiking and backpacking in this National Forest, including 86 miles of the Appalachian Trail (see entry page 205). Difficulty ranges from easy to extremely strenuous. Many trails are steep and lack switchbacks.

Hundreds of miles of trails are appropriate for cross-country skiing during the winter, and other trails are available for snowshoeing. Some of the rivers are suitable for canoeing, including the Pemigawasett and Saco Rivers. Fishing is possible along rivers, streams, and lakes. Hunting is permitted in season.

Camping Regulations: Camping is allowed throughout most of the National Forest, except near public use areas or where otherwise prohibited. No permits are necessary. Campfires are permitted but discouraged. A stove is recommended for cooking.

There are a number of trail shelters and established camping areas, some of which have wooden tent platforms. Caretakers are present at many of these locations, and a small fee is charged to camp each night at such sites.

Also in the National Forest are nine Appalachian Mountain Club Huts (lodges), which offer overnight accommodations in bunk beds, along with meals. Some are in remote locations. The Huts are popular and advance reservations are essential.

When camping at other than designated areas, sites must be at least one quarter mile from any road, hut, or other facility. Campsites should also be 200 feet from trails and water sources.

Camping is prohibited from May 1-November 1 in a number of "Restricted Use Areas" (RUAs), which are shown on some maps. These are typically fragile areas at high elevations, and included are virtually all locations above timberline.

For Further Information: White Mountain National Forest, Box 638, Laconia, NH 03247; (603)524-6450.

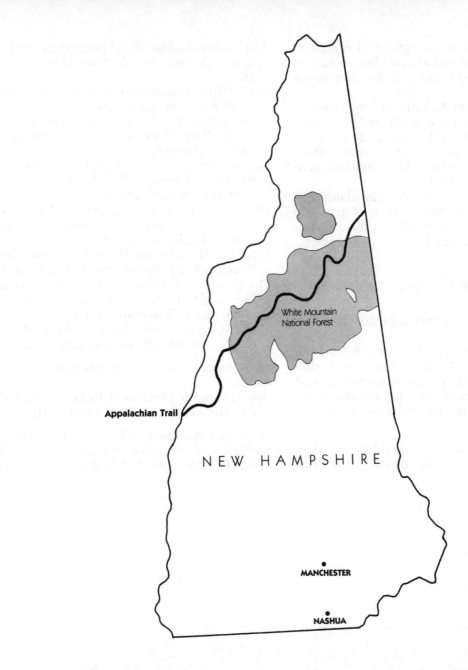

White Mountain
National Forest

Appalachian Trail

NEW HAMPSHIRE

MANCHESTER

NASHUA

Canoe-camping is also available along several rivers in the state, some of which lie outside White Mountain National Forest. For more information contact the New Hampshire Office of Vacation Travel, P.O. Box 856, Concord, NH 03301.

MAJOR BACKPACKING TRAILS

APPALACHIAN TRAIL—157 miles in New Hampshire (2,100 total). This important National Scenic Trail enters New Hampshire from Vermont at Hanover. It winds through White Mountain National Forest, crossing the Presidential and Franconia Ranges, the two highest mountain ranges in the state, and then traverses the less lofty but incredibly rugged Mahoosuc Range at the Maine border.

The scenery throughout this state is magnificent, and the views are some of the finest to be found along the entire Appalachian Trail. The difficulty of the entire New Hampshire portion should not be underestimated, however. Much of the time it's extremely rough and strenuous.

Camping Regulations: Camping and campfires are allowed along the trail at a number of lean-tos and other designated campsites. No permits are necessary.

Within White Mountain National Forest (see entry page 204) camping is also allowed elsewhere along the trail, except in Restricted Use Areas, or within one-quarter mile of roads or facilities. Campsites should also be at least 200 feet from water sources and the trail.

For Further Information: Appalachian Trail Conference, P.O. Box 807, Harpers Ferry, WV 25425. This organization publishes the *Appalachian Trail Guide to New Hampshire–Vermont.*

NEW HAMPSHIRE CAMPING RESOURCES

ORGANIZATIONS WHICH OFFER WILDERNESS CAMPING TRIPS

Appalachian Mountain Club, Box 298, Gorham, NH 03581; (603)466- 2727. This major club sponsors backpacking, canoe-camping, and other wilderness camping trips, and also offers courses and seminars in wilderness skills.

USEFUL GUIDEBOOKS

AMC Guide to Mount Washington and the Presidential Range—Boston: Appalachian Mountain Club.

AMC River Guide: New Hampshire and Vermont—Boston: Appalachian Mountain Club, 1983.

AMC White Mountain Guide—Boston: Appalachian Mountain Club, 1987.

Appalachian Trail Guide to New Hampshire-Vermont—Harpers Ferry, WV: The Appalachian Trail Conference, 1989.

Canoe-Camping Vermont and New Hampshire Rivers—Schweiker, Roioli. Woodstock, VT: Backcountry Publications.

Fifty Hikes in New Hampshire's White Mountains—Doan, Daniel. Woodstock, VT: Backcountry Publications, 1983.

Fifty More Hikes in New Hampshire—Doan, Daniel. Woodstock, VT: Backcountry Publications, 1986.

The Sierra Club Guide to the Natural Areas of New England—Perry, John and Jane. San Francisco: Sierra Club Books, 1990.

25 Ski Tours in New Hampshire—Schweiker, Roioli. Woodstock, VT: Backcountry Publications.

INFORMATION ABOUT CAMPGROUNDS IN STATE PARKS

New Hampshire Division of Parks and Recreation, P.O. Box 856, Concord, NH 03301; (603)271-3254.

STATE HIGHWAY MAP AND TRAVEL INFORMATION

New Hampshire Office of Vacation Travel, P.O. Box 856, Concord, NH 03301; (603)271-2666.

NEW JERSEY

BEST AREAS FOR WILDERNESS CAMPING

WHARTON STATE FOREST—108,000 acres. Wharton State Forest encompasses a considerable portion of New Jersey's Pine Barrens, an enormous wild area in the south-central part of the state. Given New Jersey's relatively small size and high population density, it's rather surprising and gratifying to find such a place here.

This is a region of largely flat terrain with sandy soil, some interesting and diverse vegetation, and a vast forest of pitch pine. There are many lakes and streams, marshes and swamps, and four small rivers. Wildlife includes white-tailed deer and fox.

Activities: Some fine, easy canoeing is available on the Mullica, Batsto, Wading, and Oswego Rivers. Canoe rentals are available nearby. There's one marked trail here for hiking and backpacking, the 51-mile Batona Trail (see entry page 208). Hiking is also possible on old sandy roads, as is horseback riding. Fishing is available, and hunting is permitted in season.

Camping Regulations: Camping and campfires are restricted to nine designated camping areas, some of which are in relatively remote areas. A camping permit is required, and may be obtained at the forest office. Horses are allowed at some camping areas. Pets are prohibited.

For Further Information: Wharton State Forest, RD #9 Batsto, Hammonton, NJ 08037; (609)561-3262.

OTHER RECOMMENDED LOCATIONS

ROUND VALLEY RECREATION AREA—4,003 acres. Located in north-central New Jersey, this state rec-reation area centers around Round Valley Reservoir, which is one mile by three miles in size. Surrounding the reservoir are hilly oak-hickory woodlands. Wildlife includes deer and fox.

Activities: Hiking and backpacking are possible on the 9-mile Cushetunk Trail, which is rough and steep in places. There's also an easy 1-mile trail. Horses and mountain bikes are allowed on the longer trail.

Cross-country skiing is available here in winter when there's adequate snow. Canoeing and other boating are possible on the reservoir, as is fishing. Limited waterfowl hunting is permitted in season.

Camping Regulations: A large number of backpack campsites are located along the Cushetunk Trail. The sites begin about three miles from a parking lot, and continue alongside the trail for a stretch of about three miles. The campsites are also accessible by boat.

Campers must register in person at the park office and obtain a permit. A fee is charged for camping each night. Sites may be reserved in advance by mail or in person. Campfires are allowed in fire rings provided. Pets are prohibited.

For Further Information: Round Valley Recreation Area, Box 45-D, Lebanon-Stanton Road, Lebanon, NJ 08833; (908)236-6355.

In addition, camping for canoeists is allowed at designated sites along 40 miles of the Delaware River, within the Delaware Water Gap National Recreation Area, on New Jersey's northwestern border. No permits or fees are required. For information contact the Delaware Water Gap National Recreation Area, Bushkill, PA 18324; (717)588-2435.

Appalachian
Trail

NEWARK

Round Valley
Recreation Area

N E W

J E R S E Y

TRENTON

Batona Trail

Wharton
State Forest

ATLANTIC CITY

MAJOR BACKPACKING TRAILS

APPALACHIAN TRAIL—72 miles (2,100 total). This famous National Scenic Trail enters New Jersey from Pennsylvania at the Delaware Water Gap. It runs along the northwestern border of the state, following the ridge of the Kittatinny Mountains for about 40 miles. The trail then turns east at High Point State Park, and after some distance crosses into New York.

For much of its length in New Jersey the Appalachian Trail is on state park and state forest lands. Terrain is hilly to mountainous, with some sections quite rocky. Fine views are available from the Kittatinny Mountain ridge. Difficulty varies from easy to moderately strenuous. Horses and bikes are not allowed on the trail.

Camping Regulations: Designated camping ar-

eas and shelters are located at regular intervals along the trail. Camping is generally limited to these sites, and prohibited elsewhere along the trail. Campfires are allowed at established sites. No permits are required.

For Further Information: Appalachian Trail Conference, P.O. Box 807, Harpers Ferry, WV 25425.

BATONA TRAIL—51 miles. This trail traverses a good portion of New Jersey's wild and sandy Pine Barrens, in the south-central part of the state. Much of the trail is within Wharton State Forest, with shorter segments in Lebanon State Forest and Bass River State Forest.

Leading through an endless forest of pine, the Batona Trail parallels the Batsto River for some distance, crosses numerous streams, and passes several ponds. Aside from a few small hills, it's almost flat and thus extremely easy for backpack-

NEW JERSEY

208

ing. Horseback riding and mountain biking are not allowed on the trail.

Camping Regulations: Camping and campfires are restricted to several designated camping areas along the way. A permit must first be obtained from one of the state forest offices.

For Further Information: Wharton State Forest, RD #9 Batsto, Hammonton, NJ 08037; (609)561-3262.

NEW JERSEY CAMPING RESOURCES

ORGANIZATIONS WHICH OFFER WILDERNESS CAMPING TRIPS

University Outing Club, c/o Margaret Smith, 11 Highwood Road, Somerset, NJ 08873. This club schedules occasional backpacking and canoe-camping trips. The club is associated with Rutgers University, but welcomes participants unaffiliated with the university.

USEFUL GUIDEBOOKS

Canoeing the Jersey Pine Barrens—Parnes, Robert. Old Saybrook, CT: The Globe Pequot Press.

Fifty Hikes in New Jersey—Scofield, Bruce; Green, Stella; and Zimmerman, H. Neil. Woodstock, VT: Backcountry Publications, 1988.

Guide to the Appalachian Trail in New York and New Jersey— Harpers Ferry, WV: The Appalachian Trail Conference, 1988.

New York Walk Book—New York–New Jersey Trail Conference. Garden City: Anchor Books, 1984.

INFORMATION ABOUT CAMPGROUNDS ON STATE LANDS

New Jersey Division of Parks and Forestry, CN 404, Trenton, NJ 08625.

STATE HIGHWAY MAP

New Jersey Department of Transportation, 1035 Parkway Avenue, Trenton, NJ 08618.

NEW MEXICO

BEST AREAS FOR WILDERNESS CAMPING

GILA NATIONAL FOREST—3,320,000 acres. This enormous and notable National Forest, one of the country's largest, is located in southwestern New Mexico. The varied terrain here includes rugged high mountains, steep canyons, flat mesas, rock formations, and outcroppings. Elevations range from 4,500 feet to 11,000 feet. About 170 miles of the Continental Divide fall within the forest boundaries.

There are also some major rivers and many mountain streams. Vegetation includes high conifer forests, alpine meadows, grasslands, and desert flora. Among the wildlife are antelope, elk, mule deer, black bear, bighorn sheep, and mountain lion.

This National Forest has three designated wilderness areas: the 558,000-acre Gila Wilderness, the 202,000-acre Aldo Leopold Wilderness, and the 29,300-acre Blue Range Wilderness, which extends into Arizona.

Activities: Backpacking and hiking are available on almost 1,500 miles of trails, including the 33-mile West Fork Trail and the 32-mile Gila River Trail. Difficulty ranges from easy to strenuous. A section of the Continental Divide Trail, still yet to be fully established in New Mexico, will pass through.

Horseback riding is allowed on many of the trails, as is mountain biking. Designated wilderness areas are open to foot travel and horses only. Cross-country skiing and snowshoeing are possible here at higher elevations in the winter.

Canoeing, kayaking, and rafting are available on a couple of rivers, but water levels are usually adequate only in springtime. Fishing is another option. Hunting is permitted in season.

Camping Regulations: Camping is allowed freely throughout most of the National Forest, as are campfires, except near public use areas or where otherwise prohibited. No permits are required. A stove is recommended for cooking.

For Further Information: Gila National Forest, 2610 North Silver Street, Silver City, NM 88061; (505)388-8201.

SANTA FE NATIONAL FOREST—1,567,000 acres. This very large and scenic National Forest consists of tracts both east and west of Santa Fe, in northern New Mexico. Elevations range from 5,300 feet to over 13,000 feet, with several mountain ranges included. Highest point is 13,103-foot Truchas Peak, second highest in the state.

In addition to lofty peaks and ridges, Santa Fe National Forest has deep canyons and mesas, glacial lakes and creeks, and three National Wild and Scenic Rivers. There are forests of ponderosa pine and spruce, fir and aspen, along with grasslands and semidesert vegetation such as cactus. Wildlife includes elk, black bear, mule deer, bighorn sheep, and mountain lion.

In the National Forest are four designated wilderness areas: the 222,000-acre Pecos Wilderness and the 50,000-acre Chama River Canyon Wilderness, small portions of which are also in Carson National Forest, plus the 41,130-acre San Pedro Parks Wilderness, and the 5,200-acre Dome Wilderness.

Activities: Hiking and backpacking are possible on over 1,000 miles of trails, including the 50-mile Skyline Trail. Difficulty varies from easy to strenuous. Some trails at high elevations may only be snow-free from July through September.

Horseback riding is allowed on many of the trails, as is mountain biking outside of designated wilderness areas. The Champa River is suitable for canoeing and rafting. Cross-country skiing and snowshoeing are winter options. Fishing is also available, and hunting is permitted in season.

Camping Regulations: Camping and campfires are allowed throughout most of the National Forest, except near public recreation areas or where posted otherwise. No permits are necessary.

Campsites should be at least 200 feet from trails and water sources. Campfires may be banned when conditions are extremely dry. A few areas such as the lake basins in the Pecos Wilderness are closed to camping and fires.

For Further Information: Santa Fe National Forest, 1220 St. Francis Drive, P.O. Box 1689, Sante Fe, NM 87504; (505)988-6940.

CARSON NATIONAL FOREST—1,500,000 acres. Carson National Forest is comprised of several large tracts in northern New Mexico, including lands along the Colorado border. Parts of the San Juan and Sangre de Cristo ranges are within the forest, and elevations vary from 6,000 feet to over 13,000 feet. Highest point in the state, 13,161-foot Wheeler Peak, is located here.

Terrain includes high rocky peaks and ridges, deep canyons and open mesas, with a number of rivers and lakes, and scores of streams. Vegetation ranges from bristlecone pine and alpine flora at highest elevations, through spruce and fir forests, to sagebrush and pinyon-juniper below. Among the wildlife are elk, black bear, mule deer, bighorn sheep, and mountain lion.

There are five designated wilderness areas: the 20,000-acre Wheeler Peak Wilderness, the 20,000-acre Latir Peak Wilderness, the 18,000-acre Cruces Basin Wilderness, and small portions of the Pecos and Chama River Canyon Wilderness areas, most of which are in Santa Fe National Forest.

Activities: Backpacking and hiking are available on about 330 miles of trails. Difficulty ranges from easy to strenuous. Many trails are open to horseback riding.

Mountain bikes are allowed on most trails except in designated wilderness areas. Cross-country skiing is possible on trails here during the snow season.

Rafting and canoeing are available on a couple of the rivers in springtime. Fishing is also feasible at lakes and alongside rivers and streams. Hunting is permitted in season.

Camping Regulations: Camping is allowed in most parts of the National Forest without restriction, except near public use areas or where otherwise prohibited. No permits are necessary.

Campsites should be away from meadows and at least 300 feet from water sources. Campfires are permitted but discouraged. Bringing a stove is recommended if one wishes to cook.

For Further Information: Carson National Forest, 208 Cruz Alta Road, P.O. Box 558, Taos, NM 87571; (505)758-6200.

CIBOLA NATIONAL FOREST—1,653,000 acres. This National Forest consists of a number of dispersed tracts in central and western New Mexico. Portions of several mountain ranges fall within the forest boundaries. Highest point is 11,301-foot Mount Taylor.

There are also deep canyons with sheer cliffs, rock formations, open mesas, and plains. Vegetation includes forests of mixed conifers and aspen, areas of pinyon-juniper, and open meadows. Elk, black bear, deer, mountain lion, and bobcat are among the wildlife.

Cibola has four designated wilderness areas: the 44,650-acre Apache Kid Wilderness, the 37,232-acre Sandia Mountain Wilderness, the 36,400-acre Manzano Mountain Wilderness, and the 19,000-acre Withington Wilderness.

Activities: About 270 miles of trails are available for backpacking and hiking. Difficulty ranges from easy to strenuous. A section of the as-yet-uncompleted Continental Divide Trail will cross the forest.

Horseback riding is allowed on most trails, as is mountain biking except in wilderness areas. Cross-country skiing is a cold-weather option at higher elevations. Very limited fishing is possible here. Hunting is permitted in season.

Camping Regulations: Camping is allowed with few restrictions throughout the National Forest, except near public use areas or where posted otherwise. No permits are required. Campfires are legal except during periods of high fire danger. Bringing a stove is strongly encouraged.

For Further Information: Cibola National Forest, 2113 Osuna Road NE, Suite A, Albuquerque, NM 87113; (505)761-4650.

LINCOLN NATIONAL FOREST—1,103,000 acres. This National Forest in south-central New Mexico is made up of three large tracts of land, one of which is adjacent to both Carlsbad Caverns National Park as well as Guadalupe Mountains National Park across the Texas border.

There are several mountain ranges in the region, with elevations as high as 11,500 feet. Terrain includes high ridges and deep canyons, rock outcrops, and open plains. Some streams and rivers flow through the forest.

The area also has high meadows and savannahs, stands of pine and madrone, along with pinyon and juniper, plus desert flora. Among the wildlife are elk, mule deer, black bear, mountain lion, and bobcat. There are two designated wilderness areas: the 48,143-acre White Mountain Wilderness, and the 35,800-acre Capitan Mountains Wilderness.

Activities: Hiking and backpacking are possible on over 250 miles of trails. Difficulty varies from easy to strenuous. Horseback riding is allowed on most trails.

Many trails outside of designated wilderness areas are open to mountain bikes. Cross-country skiing and snowshoeing are available at higher elevations during winter.

Spelunking (caving) is popular in an area of caves and caverns. A permit is required for this activity. Fishing is also possible, and hunting is permitted in season.

Camping Regulations: Camping is allowed throughout the National Forest, as are campfires, except near public use areas or where otherwise prohibited. No permits are required.

For Further Information: Lincoln National Forest, Federal Building, 1101 New York Avenue, Alamogordo, NM 88310; (505)437-6030.

KIOWA NATIONAL GRASSLAND—134,000 acres. Administered by Cibola National Forest, this National Grassland consists of two separate units in northeast New Mexico. Elevations are around 5,000 feet. Several thousand head of livestock are allowed to graze here.

Included are rolling prairie grasslands, plus 800-foot deep Canadian River Canyon, along with the Canadian River. Among the area's widlife are antelope, bear, mule deer, coyote, and fox.

Activities: Hiking, backpacking, and horseback riding are permitted throughout the Grassland. The only established trail is a 3-mile section of the Santa Fe National Historic Trail.

Travel on foot or by horse is also possible on old roads, paths, or cross-country. Fishing is available along the Canadian River. Hunting is permitted in season.

Camping Regulations: Camping is allowed without restriction in most parts of the National Grassland, except where posted otherwise. No permits or fees are required.

For Further Information: Kiowa National Grassland, 16 North Second Street, Clayton, NM 88415; (505)374-9652.

OTHER RECOMMENDED LOCATIONS

BANDELIER NATIONAL MONUMENT—32,737 acres. Famous for its cliff ruins of prehistoric Indian shelters, Bandelier National Monument is located in north-central New Mexico, west of Santa Fe. More than 23,000 acres here are designated as wilderness.

Terrain is often rugged, with deep canyons, caves, and mesas. Along with desert vegetation including yucca and cactus there are pinyon-juniper and conifer forests. Elk, mule deer, and coyote are among the wildlife.

Activities: Bandelier has over 70 miles of trails for hiking and backpacking. Horses are allowed on a few trails. Cross-country skiing is sometimes possible here in the winter.

Camping Regulations: Camping is allowed in the backcountry of this National Monument, except where otherwise prohibited. A free permit is required. Some designated sites are available at a base camp, and camping is permitted elsewhere as well.

Campsites must be at least 100 feet from water sources and one-quarter mile from archaeological sites. Campfires are generally allowed but discouraged, and are subject to being banned at times. Bringing a stove is strongly recommended.

Water must be carried in. Group size is limited to 10, and groups must camp at least one-half mile from one another. Pets are prohibited. Spring and fall are the best times to camp here, with summer visits not recommended due to the heat.

For Further Information: Bandelier National Monument, HCR 1, Box 1, Suite 15, Los Alamos, NM 87544; (505)672-3861.

CARLSBAD CAVERNS NATIONAL PARK—46,755 acres. Located next to Lincoln National Forest in southeast New Mexico, this National Park is famous for its enormous underground cave system, one of the largest in the world. Aboveground most of the park consists of wilderness.

Terrain includes rocky ridges and some steep canyons. Vegetation ranges from desert varieties to stands of juniper and pinyon pine. Among the wildlife here are mule deer, mountain lion, and bobcat.

Activities: Hiking and backpacking are available on over 50 miles of trails. Spelunking (caving) is also possible, and requires a permit from the visitor center.

Camping Regulations: Camping is allowed throughout the park's backcountry. A free permit

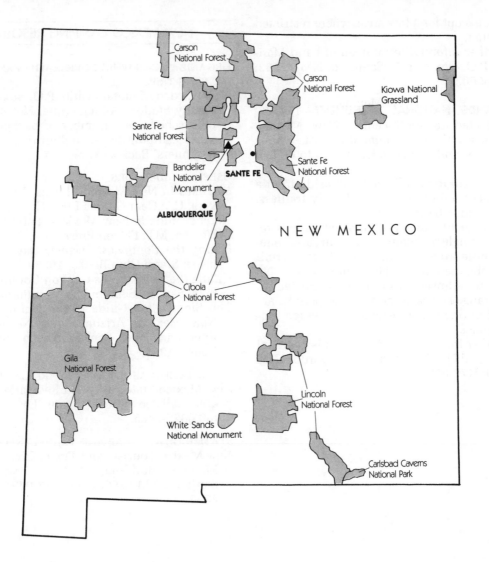

Carson
National Forest

Carson
National Forest

Kiowa National
Grassland

Sante Fe
National Forest

Bandelier
National
Monument

SANTE FE

Sante Fe
National Forest

ALBUQUERQUE

NEW MEXICO

Cibola
National Forest

Gila
National Forest

Lincoln
National Forest

White Sands
National Monument

Carlsbad Caverns
National Park

is necessary, and may be obtained from the visitor center. Water must be carried in. Pets are prohibited. Spring and fall are the best times to camp here.

For Further Information: Carlsbad Caverns National Park, 3225 National Parks Highway, Carlsbad, NM 88220; (505)785-2232.

BLM LANDS IN NEW MEXICO—New Mexico has almost 13,000,000 acres of BLM (Bureau of Land Management) or public domain lands, consisting of a great many parcels of land of all sizes. Included are many mountain ranges, a portion of the Continental Divide, and a section of the Rio Grande, which has National Wild and Scenic River status.

There are two designated Wilderness Areas on BLM lands in northwest New Mexico, and scattered around the state are a number of Wilderness Study Areas, which are currently under consideration for wilderness status.

Access to some of the BLM areas is difficult, roads are not always in good condition, and printed information is available for relatively few of the individual locations.

Activities: Hiking, backpacking, horseback riding, mountain biking, fishing, hunting, and other activities are permitted on most BLM lands. There are few established trails, however, so most travel must be cross-country.

Camping Regulations: Camping is freely allowed on these lands without a permit, as are campfires, except for a few areas where restricted or prohibited.

For Further Information: Bureau of Land Management, P.O. Box 27115, Sante Fe, NM 87502; (505)988-6000.

WHITE SANDS NATIONAL MONUMENT—144,000 acres. Situated in south-central New Mexico, White Sands National Monument protects a huge area of white sand dunes which are up to 60 feet high.

Activities: Hiking is allowed, but aside from a one-mile nature trail, the area is largely trailless. Most travel must be cross-country.

Camping Regulations: Primitive camping is restricted to a single backcountry camping area, one-third of a mile from a parking area. A free permit must be obtained from the visitor center. No campfires are allowed. Water must be carried in. A missile range is located nearby, and permits are not issued during the occasional times when testing takes place.

For Further Information: White Sands National Monument, P.O. Box 458, Alamogordo, NM 88311; (505)479-6124.

NEW MEXICO CAMPING RESOURCES

ORGANIZATIONS WHICH OFFER WILDERNESS CAMPING TRIPS

New Mexico Mountain Club, P.O. Box 4151, University Station, Albuquerque, NM 87196. This club schedules a number of backpacking and other camping trips, including an occasional Beginners' Backpack.

USEFUL GUIDEBOOKS

50 Hikes in New Mexico—Evans, Harry. Pico Rivera, CA: Gem Guides Book Co., 1984.

Hiker's Guide to New Mexico—Parent, Laurence. Helena, MT: Falcon Press.

Hiking the Southwest—Ganci, Dave. San Francisco: Sierra Club Books, 1983.

Hiking the Southwest's Canyon Country—Hinchman, Sandra. Seattle: The Mountaineers Books.

The Sierra Club Guide to the Natural Areas of New Mexico, Arizona, and Nevada—Perry, John and Jane. San Francisco: Sierra Club Books, 1985.

INFORMATION ABOUT STATE PARK CAMPGROUNDS

New Mexico State Parks and Recreation Division, 408 Galisteo Street, Sante Fe, NM 87504; (505)827-7465.

STATE HIGHWAY MAP AND TRAVEL INFORMATION

New Mexico Tourism and Travel Division, Joseph Montoya Building, 1100 St. Francis Drive, Sante Fe, NM 87503; (505)827-0291/ (800)545-2040.

NEW YORK

BEST AREAS FOR WILDERNESS CAMPING

ADIRONDACK PARK—2,400,000 acres of state-owned land (6,000,000 acres including private lands). Dominating the upper part of New York State, this enormous and spectacular state park is the largest park of any kind in the United States outside of Alaska. There's more wilderness here than any location east of the Mississippi.

The publicly-owned portion of the park has been designated the Adirondack Forest Preserve, and these lands are permanently protected and will remain "forever wild." Private landholdings inside the park are subject to possible development, however.

The Preserve has a number of designated wilderness areas where motor vehicles are prohibited. Other regions are classified "wild forest" or "primitive area," and some vehicles as well as a wider range of uses are permitted in these areas.

Predictably, much of the finest scenery is found in the wilderness areas. Most famous and frequently-visited is the rugged High Peaks Wilderness, which is home to the loftiest mountains, including some 46 peaks over 4,000 feet.

Highest is 5,344-foot Mount Marcy. Almost all of the higher mountains offer wonderful open panoramic views above timberline. The other wilderness areas have much smaller mountains and gentler terrain, and these area attract far fewer visitors.

Scattered throughout the park are over 2,700 lakes and ponds, along with a number of rivers and countless streams. There are many swamps and marshes, and forests of conifers and hardwoods. White-tailed deer, black bear, moose, coyote, bobcat, and fox are among the wildlife.

Activities: Backpacking and hiking are available on a vast trail network, offering an incredible number of options. Included is the 132-mile Northville–Placid Trail (see entry page 217). Difficulty ranges from easy to extremely strenuous. Many trails in the High Peaks region are quite steep and challenging, and these trails are also frequently overcrowded.

Outstanding wilderness canoeing and kayaking are to be found on the many rivers and lakes, including the famous chain of lakes and rivers extending over 80 miles from Old Forge to Tupper Lake or Saranac Lake. Canoes may be rented in many locations. Rafting is also possible on some of the rivers.

Cross-country skiing and snowshoeing are widely available in the winter. Some trails are designated for horseback riding, with cycling and mountain biking possible on old roads and some trails. There are also many opportunities for rock climbing. Fishing is another option, and hunting is permitted in season.

Camping Regulations: A large number of lean-tos and other designated campsites are available throughout the park. Camping is also freely permitted elsewhere on Forest Preserve lands within the park, except where posted or otherwise prohibited.

When camping at other than lean-tos or established areas, campsites should be at least 150 feet from trails, water sources, and roads. Good campsites are hardest to find in the High Peaks Wilderness, but there are some sizable designated camping areas. Those in search of solitude are advised to avoid this region.

A permit is required only for groups of 10 or more, or in order to camp for more than three nights at one site. Campfires are allowed, but bringing a stove is highly recommended. Camping is prohibited above 4,000 foot elevation from May 1-December 14.

For Further Information: New York State Department of Environmental Conservation, 50 Wolf Road, Albany, NY 12233; (518)457-2500.

CATSKILL PARK—250,000 acres (700,000 acres including private lands). Second only to the Adirondack Park in size and importance, New York's Catskill Park encompasses a scenic mountain region in the southeastern part of the state.

Public lands within the park comprise the Catskill Forest Preserve. A number of wilderness areas here protect much of the wildest and most beautiful scenery. Motor vehicles are prohibited and other uses restricted within these areas.

Virtually all of the park's terrain is mountainous, with 34 peaks over 3,500 feet elevation. Highest is 4,180-foot Slide Mountain. Superb views are available from mountaintops, open ledges, and clearings. Many valleys consist of private lands.

A large number of streams are found here, and most of the region is hardwood-forested, with spruce and fir at higher elevations. Wildlife includes white-tailed deer, black bear, coyote, bobcat, and fox.

Activities: There are over 200 miles of trails for backpacking and hiking. Difficulty varies from easy to very strenuous, with a majority of trails on the challenging side. A couple of trails are designated for horseback riding.

Cross-country skiing is a winter option on just a handful of the easier trails. Snowshoeing is possible on other trails. Fishing is available along some streams and at the few lakes. Hunting is permitted in season.

Camping Regulations: Camping is allowed on Forest Preserve lands within the park, except where posted otherwise. A number of lean-tos and other designated campsites are available.

When camping at other than a lean-to or established area, campsites must be at least 150 feet water sources, trails, and roads. Campfires are allowed, but bringing a stove is suggested.

No permits are required, except for groups of 10 or more, or to camp for more than three nights at one site. Camping is prohibited above 3,500 foot elevation from March 22-December 20 each year.

For Further Information: New York State Department of Environmental Conservation, 50 Wolf Road, Albany, NY 12233; (518)457-2500.

OTHER RECOMMENDED LOCATIONS

HARRIMAN AND BEAR MOUNTAIN STATE PARKS—54,000 acres. Located in the Ramapo Mountains of southeastern New York, about 40 miles northwest of New York City, these two adjacent state parks are administered together.

Although most elevations here are under 1,300 feet, terrain is quite rocky and rugged. Fine views are available from numerous mountaintops, rocky ledges, and outcroppings.

There are also a number of lakes, ponds, and some large streams. The forest consists mainly of hardwoods, with ample stands of hemlock, plus mountain laurel. White-tailed deer, bear, bobcat, and fox are among the wildlife.

Activities: Hiking and backpacking are possible on 40 different trails totaling over 200 miles. Included is a section of the Appalachian Trail (see entry page 217). Difficulty ranges from easy to strenuous. Some trails receive heavy use.

An additional network of old roads has been designated and marked for cross-country skiing in the winter, although local snowfall is only occasionally adequate for skiing. Fishing is also available. Hunting is prohibited.

Camping Regulations: Open stone shelters are situated along trails at a number of locations in the two parks. Camping is restricted to these shelters and within 100 feet of them. Campfires are allowed in shelter fireplaces. No permits or fees are required.

For Further Information: Harriman and Bear Mountain State Parks, c/o Palisades Interstate Park Commission, Bear Mountain, NY 10911; (914)786-2701.

OTHER STATE LANDS IN NEW YORK—New York also has many state forests, wildlife management areas, and other state-owned lands in addition to state parks. Camping is freely allowed in almost all state forests, as well as on most other lands administered by the New York State Department of Environmental Conservation (DEC).

There are nearly 600,000 acres of state forest lands and over 400,000 acres of other lands. The tracts vary considerably in size. Obtaining information about the individual areas is often difficult, with brochures or other printed literature available for only a few. Hiking guidebooks provide limited information on a handful of units which have hiking trails.

For Further Information: New York State Department of Environmental Conservation, 50 Wolf

Road, Albany, NY 12233; (518)457-2500. The most complete information regarding the lands is available by directly contacting the 16 regional offices of the D.E.C. Addresses and phone numbers of these offices may be obtained from the state headquarters above.

MAJOR BACKPACKING TRAILS

APPALACHIAN TRAIL—94 miles in New York State (2,100 miles total). On its way from New Jersey to Connecticut the Appalachian Trail crosses the southeastern part of New York State, traversing some small but rugged mountains, with attractive scenery and many fine views.

Portions of the trail are in Harriman and Bear Mountain State Parks, including the very first section of the trail which was completed in 1923. It also crosses the Hudson River via the Bear Mountain Bridge, and passes through Hudson Highlands State Park and Fahnestock State Park.

Camping Regulations: Camping along the Appalachian Trail in this state is generally restricted to shelters and other designated campsites, which are spaced at intervals along the trail. Campfires are allowed only in fire rings and built fireplaces at approved campsites. No permits are required.

For Further Information: Appalachian Trail Conference, P.O. Box 807, Harpers Ferry, WV 25425. This organization publishes the *Guide to the Appalachian Trail in New York and New Jersey.*

FINGER LAKES TRAIL—775 miles. The Finger Lakes Trail runs west from the Catskills across the lower part of New York State, passing through the beautiful Finger Lakes region and then down to the Pennsylvania border. Terrain along the way is hilly and occasionally mountainous.

The main stem of the trail is over 500 miles long, with additional mileage provided by seven different branch trails. Almost 400 miles are being utilized as part of the new North Country Trail (see next entry).

The trail is on public as well as private lands. Difficulty ranges from easy to strenuous. In addition to hiking and backpacking, it's suitable for cross-country skiing and snowshoeing in winter. Horses and mountain bikes are prohibited.

Camping Regulations: A number of lean-tos and designated campsites are located along the trail. For some stretches camping is restricted to such sites, and campfires are limited to fire rings provided. A stove is recommended for cooking.

Where the trail is on state forest land, camping and campfires are allowed almost anywhere, but campsites must be at least 150 feet from water sources and the trail. On these lands a permit is required for groups of 10 or more, or to remain at a campsite for more than three days.

For Further Information: Finger Lakes Trail Conference, P.O. Box 18048, Rochester, NY 14618. A series of trail maps and guidebooks are available from this organization.

NORTH COUNTRY TRAIL—This new super-trail, which has National Scenic Trail status, is currently under construction. It will eventually run about 3,200 miles from New York to North Dakota. The New York portion will be about 520 miles long.

The eastern terminus of the trail is at Crown Point on Lake Champlain, in the Adirondacks. From there the trail crosses the Adirondack Park and heads southwest to hook up with the Finger Lakes Trail, which it follows for some 388 miles. The trail then enters Pennsylvania at Allegheny State Park.

Camping Regulations: Camping and campfires are allowed almost anywhere along the trail in the Adirondack Park and in state forests. Campsites should be at least 150 feet from streams, lakes, and the trail. A permit is required only to spend more than three nights at a site, and for groups of 10 or more. In other state parks and on private lands, camping and campfires are restricted to lean-tos and designated campsites.

For Further Information: North Country Trail Association, P.O. Box 311, White Cloud, MI 49349.

NORTHVILLE–PLACID TRAIL—132 miles. This is almost entirely a wilderness trail, and a beautiful one. It runs much of the length of the Adirondack Park, from Northville to Lake Placid, with just a few road crossings—traversing one of the wildest regions in the East.

The trail steers between mountains and is generally quite easy, with just a few sizable hills and occasional rough spots. It passes a large number of lakes and ponds, and follows a couple of rivers for some distance.

Camping Regulations: Lean-tos and designated campsites are located at intervals along the trail. There are few restrictions on other camping, however, except that sites must be at least 150 feet from roads, water sources, and the trail.

Campfires are allowed, but the use of a stove is encouraged. Permits are not required except for groups of 10 or more, or in order to camp over three nights at one location.

For Further Information: New York State Department of Environmental Conservation, 50 Wolf Road, Albany, NY 12233; (518)457-2500.

Another important long-distance trail in New York State is the Long Path, which runs some 225 miles from the George Washington Bridge (New York City) to the northern Catskills, and will eventually be extended to the Adirondacks.

Backpacking is not feasible along major portions of the trail at present. Exceptions are in the Catskill Park, where camping is allowed 150 feet from the trail, and at trail shelters in Harriman and Bear Mountain State Parks.

For more information about the Long Path contact the New York–New Jersey Trail Conference, 232 Madison Avenue, #908, New York, NY 10016. This organization publishes a *Guide to the Long Path.*

NEW YORK CAMPING RESOURCES

ORGANIZATIONS WHICH OFFER WILDERNESS
CAMPING TRIPS
Adirondack Mountain Club, RR #3, Box 3055, Lake George, NY 12845; (518)668-4447. This major club has 27 chapters in New York State. Some of the chapters sponsor backpacking and other wilderness camping trips, including classes and trips for beginners. Trips and courses are also offered through the club's headquarters. For information contact: ADK, Box 867, Lake Placid, NY 12946; (518)523-3441.
Sierra Club, 730 Polk Street, San Francisco, CA 94109; (415)776- 2211. This important national club has a New York chapter as well as a number of local groups. Some groups sponsor backpacking trips, including special trips for beginners. Contact the above address for more information.

INFORMATION ABOUT WILDERNESS GUIDES
New York State Outdoor Guides Association, P.O. Box 916, Saranac Lake, NY 12983.

USEFUL GUIDEBOOKS
Adirondack Cross-Country Skiing—Conroy, Dennis. Woodstock, VT: Backcountry Publications, 1992.
An Adirondack Sampler—Wadsworth, Bruce. Adirondack Mountain Club, 1988.

Canoeing Central New York—Ehling, William. Woodstock, VT: Backcountry Publications.
Discover the Adirondack High Peaks—McMartin, Barbara. Woodstock, VT: Backcountry Publications.
Discover the Central Adirondacks—McMartin, Barbara. Woodstock, VT: Backcountry Publications, 1992.
Discover the Eastern Adirondacks—McMartin, Barbara. Woodstock, VT: Backcountry Publications, 1988.
Discover the Northern Adirondacks—McMartin, Barbara. Woodstock, VT: Backcountry Publications, 1988.
Discover the Northeastern Adirondacks—McMartin, Barbara. Woodstock, VT: Backcountry Publications.
Discover the Northwestern Adirondacks—McMartin, Barbara. Woodstock, VT: Backcountry Publications.
Discover the Southeastern Adirondacks—McMartin, Barbara. Woodstock, VT: Backcountry Publications, 1986.
Discover the South-Central Adirondacks—McMartin, Barbara. Woodstock, VT: Backcountry Publications, 1986.
Discover the Southwestern Adirondacks—McMartin, Barbara. Woodstock, VT: Backcountry Publications, 1987.
Discover the Southern Adirondacks—McMartin, Barbara. Woodstock, VT: Backcountry Publications, 1988.
Discover the West-Central Adirondacks—McMartin, Barbara. Woodstock, VT: Backcountry Publications, 1988.
Fifty Hikes in the Adirondacks—McMartin, Barbara. Woodstock, VT: Backcountry Publications, 1988.
Fifty Hikes in Central New York—Ehling, William P. Woodstock, VT: Backcountry Publications, 1984.
Fifty Hikes in the Hudson River Valley—McMartin, Barbara and Kick, Peter. Woodstock, VT: Backcountry Publications, 1985.
Guide to Adirondack Trails: Central Region—Wadsworth, Bruce. Adirondack Mountain Club, 1986.
Guide to Adirondack Trails: Eastern Region—Tisdale, Betsy. Adirondack Mountain Club.
Guide to Adirondack Trails: High Peaks Region—Goodwin, Tony. Adirondack Mountain Club, 1985.
Guide to Adirondack Trails: Northern Region—O'Shea, Peter. Adirondack Mountain

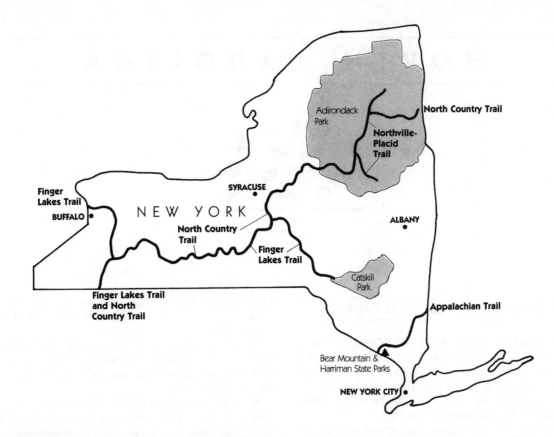

Finger Lakes Trail
BUFFALO

NEW YORK

SYRACUSE

Adirondack Park

North Country Trail

Northville-Placid Trail

ALBANY

North Country Trail

Finger Lakes Trail

Catskill Park

Finger Lakes Trail and North Country Trail

Appalachian Trail

Bear Mountain & Harriman State Parks

NEW YORK CITY

Club, 1986.

Guide to Adirondack Trails: Northville–Placid Trail—Wadsworth, Bruce. Adirondack Mountain Club, 1986.

Guide to Adirondack Trails: Southern Region—Laing, Linda. Adirondack Mountain Club.

Guide to Adirondack Trails: West-Central Region—Haberl, Arthur. Adirondack Mountain Club, 1987.

Guide to the Appalachian Trail in New York and New Jersey— Harpers Ferry, WV: Appalachian Trail Conference, 1988.

Guide to the Long Path—New York–New Jersey Trail Conference, 1987.

Guide to Catskill Trails—Wadsworth, Bruce. Adirondack Mountain Club.

Guide to the Catskills—Adams, Arthur, Coco,

Roger, Greenman, Harriet and Leon. Walking News Inc., 1975.

Hiking the Catskills—McAllister, Lee and Ochman, Myron S. New York-New Jersey Trail Conference, 1989.

New York Walk Book—New York–New Jersey Trail Conference. Garden City: Anchor Books, 1984.

INFORMATION ABOUT STATE PARK CAMPGROUNDS
New York State Office of Parks and Recreation, Empire State Plaza, Albany, NY 12238; (518)474-0456.

STATE HIGHWAY MAP AND TRAVEL INFORMATION
New York State Division of Tourism, One Commerce Plaza, Albany, NY 12245; (518)474-4116/(800)CALL-NYS.

NORTH CAROLINA

BEST AREAS FOR WILDERNESS CAMPING

GREAT SMOKY MOUNTAINS NATIONAL PARK—
275,900 acres in North Carolina (520,000 acres total). This spectacular National Park lies along the western border of North Carolina, and half of the park is in Tennessee. It's the most heavily visited National Park in the entire country.

Consisting of an ancient mountain range, the Great Smokies are among the loftiest and most massive mountains in the East. Top elevation here is 6,643-foot Clingman's Dome, second highest summit east of the Mississippi.

Sixteen other mountains stand over 6,000 feet. Included are some grassy, open "balds." Panoramic views are common. Hundreds of miles of streams flow through the area, with many waterfalls. Most of the park consists of designated wilderness.

Flora and fauna are incredibly varied. There are conifers at higher elevations and deciduous forests below. Included are some old-growth stands. Among the wildlife are black bear, deer, wild boar, bobcat, and fox.

Activities: Backpacking and hiking are available on over 850 miles of trails, including a 69-mile segment of the Appalachian Trail (see entry page 224), which leads along the high ridgetops, and the 43-mile Lakeshore Trail paralleling enormous Fontana Lake.

Some trails are designated for horseback riding. Cross-country skiing is possible on trails here during the winter. Bike use is limited to roads. Fishing is also available. Hunting is prohibited.

Camping Regulations: A free permit is required in order to camp in the backcountry, and may be obtained from any ranger station. It's necessary to specify in advance where one will camp each night. Pets are not allowed.

Scores of designated campsites, including 18 shelters, are scattered throughout the park. All camping and campfires are restricted to these authorized locations.

Reservations are available for some of the shelters and campsites, and may be made by calling (615) 436-1231 up to one month in advance. Reservations are essential for sites which are in heavy demand, including those along the Appalachian Trail.

Permits must be picked up in person. Shelters may be used for one night only, whereas most other campsites are available for up to three nights. Group size is limited to a maximum of eight.

The park's bears are known to be unusually aggressive in trying to obtain food from campers. Extra care should be taken to keep food properly hung and away from tents.

For Further Information: Great Smoky Mountains National Park, Gatlinburg, TN 37738; (615)436-5615.

NANTAHALA NATIONAL FOREST—517,400 acres. Located south of Great Smoky Mountains National Park, in the southwest corner of the state, Nantahala is the largest of North Carolina's four National Forests. It's an area of fine southern Appalachian mountain scenery.

There are some "bald" mountains with grassy meadows and great views. Also in the region are 2,000-foot deep Nantahala Gorge, some large lakes, and several major rivers, including part of the Chattooga National Wild and Scenic River.

Among numerous waterfalls here is 411-foot Whitewater Falls, said to be the highest in the East, along with 250-foot Cullasaja Falls. Of special interest as well is 3,800-acre Joyce Kilmer Memorial Forest, an area of old-growth trees.

Forests are of spruce and fir as well as hardwoods, plus rhododendron, dogwood, and mountain laurel. Wildlife includes black bear, deer, wild boar, and fox.

This National Forest has three designated wilderness areas: the 13,130-acre Joyce Kilmer/Slickrock Wilderness, the 12,080-acre Southern Nantahala Wilderness, and over 3,000 acres of the Ellicott Rock Wilderness, which extends into South Carolina.

Activities: More than 450 miles of trails are available for backpacking and hiking. Included are nearly 90 miles of the Appalachian Trail and 81 miles of the Bartram Trail (see entry page 225), plus the 25-mile Rim Trail. Difficulty varies from easy to very strenuous.

Among trails which are designated for horseback riding is the 17-mile Tsali Horse Trail. Canoeing, kayaking, and rafting are possible on several of Nantahala's rivers. Fishing is also available, and hunting is permitted in season.

Camping Regulations: Camping and campfires are allowed throughout the National Forest, except near public use areas or where otherwise prohibited. No permits are necessary. It's suggested that campsites be located at least 100 feet from trails and water sources.

For Further Information: Nantahala National Forest, 100 Otis Street, P.O. Box 2750, Asheville, NC 28802; (704)257-4200.

PISGAH NATIONAL FOREST—Pisgah National Forest is located on lands near and alongside the Tennessee border, in west-central and northwest North Carolina. It's a scenic region of high rugged mountains and deep canyon gorges, with a number of rivers and many streams with waterfalls.

There are forests of hardwoods as well as spruce, fir, and pine, including some virgin forest—plus dogwood, azalea, and large areas of rhododendron in the Roan Mountain region. Among the wildlife are deer, black bear, bobcat, and fox.

This National Forest has three wilderness areas: the 18,500-acre Shining Rock Wilderness, the 10,970-acre Linville Gorge Wilderness, and the 7,900-acre Middle Prong Wilderness.

Activities: Backpacking and hiking are possible on more than 550 miles of trails, including segments of the Appalachian Trail and the new Mountains-to-Sea Trail (see entry page 225), and

also the 30-mile Art Loeb Trail. Difficulty ranges from easy to quite strenuous.

Many trails are open to horses. Canoeing is available on the French Broad River, and cross-country skiing is possible during the winter. Rock climbing is an option on some of the mountains. There's also ample fishing to be found along streams and rivers. Hunting is permitted in season.

Camping Regulations: Camping and campfires are allowed throughout most of the National Forest, except near developed areas or where otherwise prohibited.

A permit is required for camping in the Linville Gorge Wilderness on weekends and holidays only from May 1-October 31. Permits are free and may be obtained either by mail or in person. Maximum stay in the Gorge is two nights.

For Further Information: Pisgah National Forest, 100 Otis Street, P.O. Box 2750, Asheville, NC 28802; (704)257-4200.

CROATAN NATIONAL FOREST—157,050 acres. Croatan National Forest is located along the coast of North Carolina. This is a relatively flat region with forests of pine and hardwood, as well as cypress. Major areas are boggy and wet. The scenic White Oak River and three other rivers run along the borders of the National Forest, and there are several lakes. Wildlife includes deer, bear, and alligator.

The National Forest has four designated wilderness areas: the 11,000-acre Pocosin Wilderness, the 9,550-acre Sheep Ridge Wilderness, the 7,600-acre Catfish Lake South Wilderness, and the 1,860-acre Pine Wilderness.

Activities: Hiking and backpacking are available on several easy to moderate trails, longest of which is the 22-mile Neusiok Trail. Wet trail conditions are common. Canoeing is possible on some of the rivers here. Saltwater fishing and limited freshwater fishing are other options. Hunting is permitted in season.

Camping Regulations: Camping is allowed almost anywhere, as are campfires, except near public use areas. No permits are necessary. Few suitable campsites will be found in wet areas. Summer camping is not recommended because of heat and insects.

For Further Information: Croatan National Forest, 435 Thurman Road, New Bern, NC 28560; (919)638-5628.

UWHARRIE NATIONAL FOREST—46,880 acres. Situated in central North Carolina, Uwharrie National

Forest is made up of numerous tracts of land in an area of low-lying mountains. There's one designated wilderness area, the 4,790-acre Birkhead Mountain Wilderness.

The region has forests of hardwoods and pine, with dogwood and mountain laurel, and includes many streams and a couple of rivers. Deer and fox are among the wildlife.

Activities: Backpacking and hiking are possible on a few trails here, most of which are easy to moderate in difficulty. Longest is the 20-mile Uwharrie National Recreation Trail. There are also some horse trails. Canoeing is available on the Uwharrie and Little Rivers. Hunting and fishing are permitted in season.

Camping Regulations: Camping and campfires are allowed in most parts of the National Forest, except where otherwise prohibited. No permits are necessary. It's recommended that campsites be at least 100 feet from trails and water sources.

For Further Information: Uwharrie National Forest, Route 3, Box 470, Troy, NC 27371; (919)576-6391.

CAPE LOOKOUT NATIONAL SEASHORE—Cape Lookout National Seashore is comprised of a series of undeveloped barrier islands stretching 55 miles along the coast of North Carolina, just south of Cape Hatteras National Seashore. Access is by ferry or private boat.

Scenery here includes sandy beaches, dunes, areas of salt marsh, grasslands, and maritime forest. The National Seashore has one designated wilderness area, consisting of the island of Shackleford Banks.

Activities: There are no established trails, but one may hike along the island beaches. Canoeing is possible around the islands. Fishing is also available, and hunting is permitted in season.

Camping Regulations: Camping is allowed almost anywhere, except near historic (now-deserted) Portsmouth Village or by a lighthouse. There are no designated sites, and permits are not required. Campfires are allowed only on beaches, below the high tide line. Firewood is very scarce. A stove is recommended.

For Further Information: Cape Lookout National Seashore, 3601 Bridges Street, Suite F, Morehead City, NC 28557; (919)728-2250.

OTHER RECOMMENDED LOCATIONS

MOUNT MITCHELL STATE PARK—1,677 acres. Located within Pisgah National Forest in western North Carolina, this state park surrounds 6,684-foot Mount Mitchell, highest mountain in the eastern United States. There are magnificent views from the top.

The forest includes hardwood trees along with fir and spruce. Some trees have been badly damaged by acid rain. White-tailed deer, black bear, and bobcat are among the wildlife found in the area.

Activities: Hiking and backpacking are available on 18 miles of trails, with many more trails available on National Forest lands around the park.

Camping Regulations: Camping in the park is restricted to one campground, but trail shelters for backpackers are located just outside park boundaries, in Pisgah National Forest.

For Further Information: Mount Mitchell State Park, Route 5, Box 700, Burnsville, NC 28714; (704)675-4611.

STONE MOUNTAIN STATE PARK—11,500 acres. Stone Mountain State Park is in the eastern Blue Ridge Mountains of northwest North Carolina. This is an area of rugged terrain which includes 2,305-foot Stone Mountain, and some rock outcrops.

Also here are the East Prong Roaring River, 200-foot Stone Mountain Falls, and several creeks. The forest consists of mixed hardwoods and hemlock, with rhododendron and mountain laurel. Among the wildlife are white-tailed deer, bear, bobcat, and fox.

Activities: Hiking and backpacking are possible on a number of trails. Rock climbing is allowed on Stone Mountain, but only when conditions are dry. Fishing is permitted in the creeks and river.

Camping Regulations: Camping is restricted to several designated backpack campsites. A permit is required, and must be obtained from the park office. A fee is charged for each night.

For Further Information: Stone Mountain State Park, Star Route 1, Box 15, Roaring Gap, NC 28668; (919)957-8185.

SOUTH MOUNTAINS STATE PARK—7,225 acres. Located in west-central North Carolina, this state park is in an area of steep, rugged mountains. Highest point is 2,894-foot Benn Knob, which offers an outstanding view.

Jacob's Fork River flows through the park, along with a number of streams, and a highlight is 80-foot High Shoals Falls. There's a mixed forest of conifers and hardwoods, with mountain laurel and rhododendron, and deer are among the wildlife.

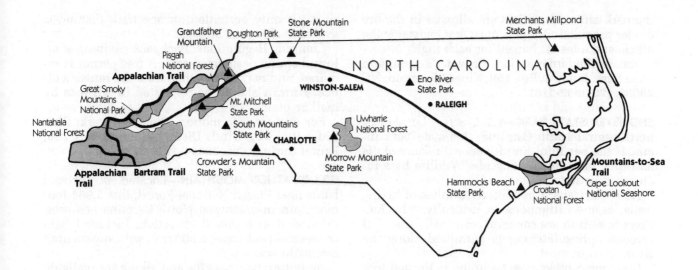

Activities: Many miles of trails are available for backpacking and hiking. Some trails are open to horseback riding. There's also an 18-mile loop for mountain biking. Fishing is possible, but hunting is prohibited in the park.

Camping Regulations: Four camping areas are designated for backpackers, and one for horseback riders. Campfires are allowed at approved sites. A permit must be obtained from the park office, and a fee is charged for camping each night,

For Further Information: South Mountains State Park, Route 1, Box 206, Connelly Springs, NC 28612; (704)433-4772.

HAMMOCKS BEACH STATE PARK—This park consists mainly of 892-acre Bear Island, which lies off the coast of North Carolina. It includes beautiful sandy beaches, dunes, marshes, and a limited amount of forest. There are also shorebirds, with deer and bobcat among the wildlife. Ferry service to the island is available during the summer, whereas access at other times is only by private boat.

Activities: There are no established trails, but hiking is possible along the beach. Fishing is permitted.

Camping Regulations: Camping is allowed at 14 designated sites around the island. Campers must first register and get a permit at the park office, located on the mainland.

A fee is required for camping each night. Campfires are prohibited. The island is closed to camping during full-moon phases in summer, to allow for sea turtle nesting.

For Further Information: Hammocks Beach State Park, 1572 Hammocks Beach Road, Swansboro, NC 28584; (919)326-4881.

MORROW MOUNTAIN STATE PARK—4,600 acres. Morrow Mountain State Park is located in the Uwharrie Mountains of central North Carolina, near Uwharrie National Forest. It includes several small mountains with elevations under 1,000 feet, including Morrow Mountain.

Three rivers flow through the park. The area is largely hardwood-forested with some pine, and also mountain laurel. White-tailed deer, bobcat, and fox are among the wildlife.

Activities: Hiking and backpacking are possible on over 14 miles of trails, and there are also 15 miles of bridle trails. Horses and bikes are not allowed on hiking trails. Fishing is available along the rivers.

Camping Regulations: Primitive camping is limited to four backpack campsites which are located in one area. A fee is charged to camp here each night, and a permit must be obtained from the park office. No campfires are allowed.

For Further Information: Morrow Mountain State Park, Route 5, Box 430, Albemarle, NC 28001; (704)982-4402.

CROWDER'S MOUNTAIN STATE PARK—1,960 acres. Situated amid the King Mountain Range in the southwest corner of the state, this park includes 1,625-foot Crowder's Mountain—with steep cliffs, rock formations, other rugged scenery, and some great views. There's also a 9-acre lake.

Activities: The park has over 10 miles of trails for hiking or backpacking. Difficulty varies from easy to strenuous. Rock climbing is also permitted. Fishing is available at the lake.

Camping Regulations: Primitive camping is restricted to one backpack camping area, a mile from the park office. Campfires are allowed in the fire circles provided. Campers must first register at the office, and a fee is charged for each night.

For Further Information: Crowder's Mountain State Park, Route 1, Box 159, Kings Mountain, NC 28086; (704)867-1181.

ENO RIVER STATE PARK—1,965 acres. Located in north-central North Carolina, this state park includes the beautiful Eno River, with some bluffs and rock formations alongside. Wildlife here includes deer and fox.

Activities: There are almost 20 miles of hiking trails, easy to strenuous in difficulty. The Eno River is suitable for canoeing, especially from fall through spring. Fishing is permitted along the river.

Camping Regulations: Camping is limited to a single designated backpack campsite, which is one mile from the parking lot. A permit must be obtained from the park office, and a fee is charged for each night. Campfires are prohibited.

For Further Information: Eno River State Park, Route 2, Box 436-A, Durham, NC 27705; (919)383-1686.

MERCHANTS MILLPOND STATE PARK—2,700 acres. Merchants Millpond State Park is in northeast North Carolina. Much of the area consists of swamplands, and there's a 760-acre millpond. Trees include cypress and gum, with some stands of hardwoods and pine. Deer are among the wildlife.

Activities: Hiking and backpacking are possible on nine miles of trails. The millpond is open to canoeing, and canoe rentals are available. Fishing is permitted.

Camping Regulations: The park has one backpack camping area, and there's also a canoe-camping area on the millpond. Designated sites must be used. A permit is required from the park office, and a camping fee is charged.

For Further Information: Merchants Millpond State Park, Route 1, Box 141-A, Gatesville, NC 27938; (919)357-1191.

DOUGHTON PARK—6,000 acres. Located on lands along the Blue Ridge Parkway, in the mountains of northwest North Carolina, Doughton Park is administered by the National Park Service. Terrain here is sometimes steep, with nice views from rock outcrops, and there are streams and waterfalls. The area is forested with mixed hardwoods and conifers, and includes rhododendron.

Activities: The park has over 30 miles of hiking trails, easy to strenuous in difficulty. Horseback riding is only permitted on one trail. Fishing is available along the streams.

Camping Regulations: Backpack camping is allowed at one designated area. A free permit is required, and may be obtained from the ranger's office. Permits should be requested in advance by mail or phone.

For Further Information: Doughton Park, Blue Ridge Parkway, Bluffs District, Route 1, Box 263, Laurel Springs, NC 28644; (919)372-8568.

GRANDFATHER MOUNTAIN—Located on private lands near Pisgah National Forest, this 5,964-foot mountain in northwest North Carolina has been developed as a tourist attraction. Included here are several peaks over 5,900 feet, with superb high mountain scenery.

Activities: Backpacking and hiking are available on several trails, some of which are strenuous.

Camping Regulations: Backpack camping is allowed. A permit is required and a fee charged. Designated campsites with fire rings are located along some of the trails. Camping is also permitted elsewhere, but campsites must be out of sight of trails and at least 200 feet from water sources.

For Further Information: Grandfather Mountain, P.O. Box 128, Linville, NC 28646; (704)733-2013 or (704)733-4337.

In addition, Pilot Mountain State Park in northwest North Carolina has two primitive campsites on an island in the Yadkin River, available for canoeists and rafters. For information contact Pilot Mountain State Park, Route 1, Box 21, Pinnacle, NC 27043; (919)325-2355.

MAJOR BACKPACKING TRAILS

APPALACHIAN TRAIL—302 miles in North Carolina (2,100 total). In the course of crossing this state the Appalachian Trail winds through Nantahala National Forest, Great Smoky Mountains National Park, and Pisgah National Forest. For much of the distance it runs along or close to the North Carolina–Tennessee border.

This particular section offers some of the most spectacular backpacking available in the southern Appalachians, including the highest elevations of the entire Appalachian Trail. There are many magnificent views, some of which are from open grassy balds. Difficulty ranges from moderate to very strenuous.

Camping Regulations: Shelters and campsites are located an average of every few miles along the trail. On National Forest lands camping is allowed elsewhere as well, except near public recreation areas or where posted otherwise. When camping at other than designated areas, it's suggested that campsites be at least 100 feet from the trail and away from water sources.

Special rules apply for Great Smoky Mountains National Park. A permit is required, and this should be requested well ahead of time—by calling (615) 436-1231 up to one month in advance. Demand is high, and some permit requests are denied.

Camping along the trail in this National Park is limited to shelters. Tents may be set up outside only when a shelter is full. Maximum stay allowed at shelters is one night.

Only those who are backpacking the Appalachian Trail from well outside the park ("thru hikers") do not need a permit ahead of time. These backpackers may obtain the permit upon entering the park, and do not have to specify shelters in advance.

For Further Information: Appalachian Trail Conference, P.O. Box 807, Harpers Ferry, WV 25425. This organization publishes two guidebooks covering different sections of the Appalachian Trail in North Carolina.

BARTRAM TRAIL—81 miles in North Carolina. This may someday be a long multistate trail, extending about 2,500 miles throughout the southeastern United States. It will follow the approximate route of an expedition taken by 18th century naturalist William Bartam.

Some sections are open in North Carolina, South Carolina, and Georgia. In North Carolina the trail is mostly within Nantahala National Forest, and it connects with the Appalachian Trail. One segment has National Recreation Trail status.

The trail is currently broken in places. Much of the terrain here is mountainous and rugged, and the trail passes through some rather remote areas. Fine views are available along the way. Difficulty varies from easy to strenuous.

Camping Regulations: In Nantahala National Forest camping is allowed in almost any suitable place along the trail, as are campfires. Whenever possible, it's suggested that campsites be at least 100 feet off the trail and away from streams and other water sources. Camping on private lands is prohibited except with permission of the landowner.

For Further Information: North Carolina Bartram Trail Society, Route 3, Box 406, Sylva, NC 28779.

MOUNTAINS-TO-SEA TRAIL—This ambitious new trail will be over 700 miles long when completed, running the length of North Carolina—from Clingman's Dome in Great Smoky Mountains National Park to Cape Hatteras National Seashore on the Atlantic coast.

A 20-mile-wide corridor—within which the trail will run—has been established, and more than a third of the trail is now finished and open. It traverses some rugged mountains, offering outstanding vistas, and also covers much gentler terrain. Difficulty ranges from easy to strenuous.

Camping Regulations: Trailside camping is feasible and legal only along some sections at this time. Where the trail is on National Forest lands one may camp almost anywhere. Campsites should be well off the trail and away from water sources.

A permit is required for camping in Great Smoky Mountains National Park (see the National Park entry page 220 for complete regulations). On private lands camping is prohibited except at approved sites or with the landowner's permission.

For Further Information: North Carolina Division of Parks and Recreation, 512 North Salisbury Street, Raleigh, NC 27611; (919)733-4181.

NORTH CAROLINA CAMPING RESOURCES

USEFUL GUIDEBOOKS

Guide to the Appalachian Trail in North Carolina and Georgia— Harpers Ferry, WV: The Appalachian Trail Conference, 1989.

Guide to the Appalachian Trail in Tennessee and North Carolina— Harpers Ferry, WV: The Appalachian Trail Conference, 1989.

Hiker's Guide to the Smokies—Murlless, Dick, and Stallings, Constance. San Francisco: Sierra Club Books.

Hiking in the Great Smokies—Carson, Brewer. Holston Printing Co.

Hiking Trails of Joyce Kilmer–Slickrock & Citico Creek Wilderness Areas—Homan, Tim. Atlanta: Peachtree Publishers, 1990.

North Carolina Hiking Trails—de Hart, Allen. Boston: Appalachian Mountain Club Books, 1988.

100 Favorite Trails of the Great Smokies and Carolina Blue Ridge—Carolina Mountain Club.

Walks in the Great Smokies—Albright, Rodney and Priscilla. Old Saybrook, CT: The Globe Pequot Press.

North Carolina Division of Parks and Recreation, 512 North Salisbury Street, Raleigh, NC 27611; (919)733-4181.

North Carolina Division of Travel and Tourism, 430 North Salisbury Street, Raleigh, NC 27611; (800)VISIT-NC.

BEST AREAS FOR WILDERNESS CAMPING

THEODORE ROOSEVELT NATIONAL PARK—70,000 acres. Comprised of two widely separate units in west-central North Dakota, Theodore Roosevelt National Park encompasses some rugged and beautiful badlands scenery, with buttes and table-lands, steep slopes and deep canyons.

Included are a petrified forest and a "painted canyon." The Little Missouri River flows through both tracts, along with a number of creeks. Over 28,000 acres have designated wilderness status.

The area includes prairie grasslands and some woodlands, with juniper, yucca, and cactus. Among the wildlife are white-tailed and mule deer, bison, elk, and prairie dog, and there are some wild horses. Extremes of temperature are not unusual in the region, with severe storms some-times occurring.

Activities: There are about 85 miles of trails for backpacking and hiking. Horseback riding is per-mitted on the trails, and horses may be rented in the park during the summer.

Canoeing is available on the Little Missouri River during May and June of each year. Bicycles are allowed on park roads only, not on trails or in the backcountry. Hunting is forbidden.

Camping Regulations: A free permit is required in order to camp in the backcountry. Permits must be obtained in person at the visitor center or ranger station. Campers should also check in at the end of a visit.

There are no designated campsites, and camp-ing is allowed almost anywhere in the park. Sites should be at least 100 feet from water sources.

Fires are not permitted, so cooking must be done on stoves. Maximum group size is 10. Pets are prohibited.

For Further Information: Theodore Roosevelt National Park, P.O. Box 7, Medora, ND 58645; (701)623-4466.

NATIONAL GRASSLANDS IN NORTH DAKOTA— Three separate National Grasslands are located in this state. All are administered by Custer National Forest, which is based in Montana but has a dis-trict office in North Dakota.

Largest is 524,000-acre Little Missouri National Grasslands, which surrounds the two units of The-odore Roosevelt National Park in western and southwest North Dakota.

Included here is some fine badlands scenery, with high buttes, areas of prairie, and trees which include ash and elm, juniper and ponderosa pine. There's also a sizable stretch of the Little Missouri River.

In the southeastern part of the state is 70,180-acre Sheyenne National Grasslands. The Shey-enne River flows through this region, with some elm-basswood forest and other stands of trees amid rolling prairie.

The third area in the state is 6,700-acre Cedar River National Grasslands, which surrounds the Cedar River in southwestern North Dakota, near the South Dakota border.

All of the National Grasslands have major areas of tallgrass prairie, with sandy soil and many wild-flowers. Wildlife includes white-tailed and mule deer, antelope, bighorn sheep, coyote, and prairie dog. Cattle grazing is permitted in some regions.

Activities: The only established trail for hiking and backpacking is a 25-mile section of the new North Country Trail, which passes through Shey-enne National Grasslands.

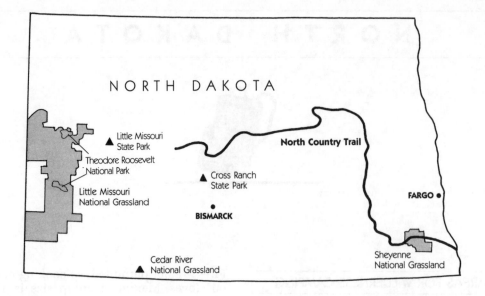

NORTH DAKOTA

Little Missouri
State Park

Theodore Roosevelt
National Park

Little Missouri
National Grassland

Cross Ranch
State Park

North Country Trail

FARGO ●

BISMARCK ●

Cedar River
National Grassland

Sheyenne
National Grassland

Cross-country travel is feasible in most parts of the Grasslands. Horseback riding is allowed. Canoeing and fishing are possible on the rivers. Hunting is permitted in season.

Camping Regulations: Camping and campfires are allowed throughout all the Grasslands, except where posted otherwise. There are no designated campsites. Permits are not required. Campsites should be well away from trails and water sources.

For Further Information: National Grasslands in North Dakota, c/o U.S.D.A.- Forest Service, 1511 E. Interstate Avenue, Bismarck, ND 58501; (701)250-4443.

OTHER RECOMMENDED LOCATIONS

LITTLE MISSOURI STATE PARK—5,748 acres. This state park is located next to Little Missouri Bay, on enormous Lake Sakakawea, in the western part of North Dakota. The park is maintained in a wilderness condition.

Scenery here includes badlands, ridges and buttes, canyons, some intermittent streams, and the Little Missouri River. There are stands of juniper and cedar, with sage and cactus. Among the wildlife are mule deer, coyote, bobcat, and fox.

Activities: Hiking, backpacking, and horseback riding are possible on over 75 miles of trails. Horses may be rented near the park. Fishing is available along the river.

Camping Regulations: Backpack camping is al-

lowed here, as are campfires. Some designated primitive sites are available. A permit is not required.

For Further Information: Little Missouri State Park, c/o Lake Sakakawea State Park, P.O. Box 832, Riverdale, ND 58565; (701)487-3315.

CROSS RANCH STATE PARK—560 acres. Bordering on the Missouri River in central North Dakota, this park features some open mixed-grass prairie, with woodlands which include willow, cottonwood, and burr oak.

Deer, bobcat, and wild turkey are among the park's wildlife. Adjacent is the 6,000-acre Cross Ranch Nature Preserve, owned by the Nature Conservancy, and in this area is a herd of bison.

Activities: There are 15 miles of trails for hiking in the park and nearby preserve. The trails are used for cross-country skiing in winter. Canoeing is available on the Missouri River, which is part of the Lewis and Clark National Historical Trail.

Camping Regulations: A single backcountry camping area is located along the river, over two miles from the visitor center, and camping is limited to that area. Visitors must first check in at the center. Numbers of campers are restricted.

For Further Information: Cross Ranch State Park, Star Route 112A, Hensler, ND 58547; (701)794-3731.

Primitive camping is also allowed, except where posted otherwise, in most of North Dakota's many

Wildlife Management Areas. Located around the state, these areas are used primarily for hunting and fishing, and also offer a limited amount of hiking. For more information contact the North Dakota Game and Fish Department, 100 North Bismarck Expressway, Bismarck, ND 58501; (701)221-6300.

MAJOR BACKPACKING TRAILS

NORTH COUNTRY TRAIL—When completed, this new National Scenic Trail will extend about 3,200 miles from North Dakota to New York. The North Dakota section will run about 435 miles. Portions are now open. Terrain here is sometimes hilly, but the walking is mostly easy.

The trail passes through Sheyenne National Grasslands in southeast North Dakota, follows the Sheyenne River for a long distance into the central part of the state, and terminates at the Missouri River, in Lake Sakakawea State Park.

Camping Regulations: Within Sheyenne National Grasslands there are no designated sites, and one may camp almost anywhere except at trailheads. Tents should be set up well off the trail. Campfires are allowed but discouraged. No permits are required.

Elsewhere the trail passes through state and private lands. Here camping is limited to designated areas. Not much of the trail has yet been completed on these lands, so few established campsites are currently available.

For Further Information: North Country Trail Association, P.O. Box 311, White Cloud, MI 49349.

NORTH DAKOTA CAMPING RESOURCES

INFORMATION ABOUT CAMPGROUNDS IN STATE PARKS AND FORESTS
North Dakota Parks and Recreation Department, 1424 West Century Avenue, Suite 202, Bismarck, ND 58501; (701)224-4887.

STATE HIGHWAY MAP AND TRAVEL INFORMATION
North Dakota Tourism Promotion, Liberty Memorial Building, State Capitol Grounds, Bismarck, ND 58505; (800)437-2077 (out of state)/ (800)472-2100 (in state).

OHIO

BEST AREAS FOR WILDERNESS CAMPING

WAYNE NATIONAL FOREST—178,000 acres. Wayne National Forest is comprised of four separate tracts of land in southern and southeastern Ohio. Two units border on the Ohio River. It's jointly administered with Hoosier National Forest, and forest headquarters are in Indiana.

Large private landholdings exist within the boundaries of this National Forest. There are no designated wilderness areas or really remote places here, but it's nevertheless an area of attractive forest, with hilly countryside and low elevations.

Included are some rugged cliffs, outcrops, and other rocky scenery, along with numerous streams and some rivers and lakes. There are hardwood forests of oak and hickory, cedar and pine, plus dogwood and redbud. Among the wildlife are deer and wild turkey.

Activities: Backpacking and hiking are available on many mile of easy to moderate trails, including over 60 miles of the North Country and Buckeye Trails (see entries page 232), which coincide here through two units of the forest.

Horseback riding is possible on the 18-mile Stone Church Horsetrail and some other trails. Mountain biking is allowed on most trails. Canoeing is available on the Muskingum River and other rivers. Fishing is also possible. Hunting is permitted during the appropriate season.

Camping Regulations: Camping is allowed throughout the National Forest, except near public recreation areas or where otherwise prohibited. Campfires are discouraged but legal. No permits are necessary. Campers are asked to choose sites which are at least 50 feet from any trail.

For Further Information: Wayne National Forest, 3527 10th Street, Bedford, IN 47421; (812)275-5987.

OTHER RECOMMENDED LOCATIONS

SHAWNEE STATE FOREST—60,000 acres. Largest of Ohio's state forests, Shawnee is located west of Wayne National Forest and next to the Ohio River, in the southern part of the state. It's a hilly and somewhat rugged area with many streams and several small lakes.

Almost 8,000 acres are designated as wilderness. There are forests of oak and hickory, maple and poplar, and wildlife includes deer and wild turkey.

Activities: This is one of two state forests in Ohio where backpacking is allowed. The major hiking and backpacking trail here is the moderately-difficult Shawnee Backpack Trail, which forms a 43-mile loop. There are also 15 miles of side trails.

In addition, the forest has over 70 miles of bridle trails. Horses are not permitted on hiking trails. Fishing is possible as well, and hunting is permitted in season.

Camping Regulations: Camping is restricted to designated sites. Eight camping areas are located along the Shawnee Backpack Trail. A free permit is required, and available by self-registration at the parking area. Maximum stay at a campsite is one night. Campfires are allowed at established fire rings. Pets are prohibited.

For Further Information: Shawnee State Forest, Route 5, Box 151C, Portsmouth, OH 45662; (614)858-6685.

BURR OAK STATE PARK—3,265 acres. Situated in southeast Ohio next to Wayne National Forest lands, this state park surrounds Burr Oak Lake, a 640-acre reservoir. Terrain is hilly and there are some caves and rock outcroppings, open meadows, and forests of oak and hickory. White-tailed deer and wild turkey are among the wildlife.

Activities: Hiking is available on several trails here. The longest is open to backpacking: the 29-mile Burr Oak Backpack Trail, which forms a loop around the lake and coincides with the Buckeye Trail (see entry page 232) for a stretch. Difficulty varies from easy to moderate. Cross-country skiing is available on trails during the winter. Fishing is possible alongside the lake, and hunting is permitted in season.

Camping Regulations: Camping is restricted to three designated areas along the Burr Oak Backpack Trail. Backpackers must register before starting, and may stay a maximum of one night at each site. A fee is charged for camping. Campfires are allowed only in fire rings. Pets are prohibited in camping areas. The Burr Oak Backpack Trail is closed during deer hunting season.

For Further Information: Burr Oak State Park, Route 2, Box 286, Glouster, OH 45732; (614)767-3570.

ZALESKI STATE FOREST—26,300 acres. Located near Wayne National Forest in southern Ohio, Zaleski State Forest is in an area of hilly and occasionally steep terrain. Included are many ravines and hollows with streams, a lake, some caves, rock outcrops, and nice views.

Activities: The major trail here for backpacking and hiking is the 23-mile Zaleski Backpack Trail, which loops around the forest. There are also many miles of horse trails. Horses are not permitted on the Backpack Trail. Fishing is available, and hunting is allowed here in season.

Camping Regulations: Camping is restricted to three designated areas along the Zaleski Backpack Trail. A free permit is required, and available by

self-registration at the parking area. A maximum of one night may be spent at each site. Campfires may be built only in the fire rings provided. There's also a special campground for horseback riders.

For Further Information: Zaleski State Forest, Zaleski, OH 45698; (914)596-5781.

EAST FORK STATE PARK—10,580 acres. Dominated by East Fork Lake, a 2,160-acre reservoir created in 1978, this state park is located in the hills of southwestern Ohio. It includes some ravines and streams, remnants of prairie, and hardwood forests of maple and beech.

Activities: Hiking and backpacking are possible on several trails, including a 12-mile Backpack Trail and the 32-mile East Fork Backcountry Trail, which forms a huge loop around the park, and is utilized by the Buckeye Trail for a stretch.

There are also some bridle paths, and the Backcountry Trail is open to horses. Cross-country skiing is a winter option in the park. Fishing is possible, and hunting is permitted in season.

Camping Regulations: Primitive camping is limited to four designated areas along the trails. Each area has tent sites and also two wooden shelters. A permit is required, and it's possible to self-register at the entry point. No fee is charged. Camping is allowed at each site for a maximum of one night. Campfires are restricted to fire rings. Pets are prohibited.

For Further Information: East Fork State Park, P.O. Box 119, Bethel, OH 45106; (513)734-4323.

MAJOR BACKPACKING TRAILS

BUCKEYE TRAIL—1,200 miles. This long trail forms a giant loop around the state of Ohio. It traverses varied terrain, leading through some relatively wild forested areas as well as rural countryside. At times the trail follows old roads and canal towpaths.

It passes through Wayne National Forest and a number of state parks and forests, plus private lands. A major portion is utilized by the new North Country Trail (see next entry). The walking is mostly easy, with hills and a few steep places. Portions of the trail are open to horseback riding, and bikes are permitted when it follows roads. Some segments are suitable for cross-country skiing or snowshoeing in the winter.

Camping Regulations: Camping is generally restricted to designated sites, which are currently available along many but not all sections of the trail. For some stretches one must leave the trail at night. Campfire permits are required in a few locations in order to have a campfire. A stove is recommended.

Within Wayne National Forest camping is allowed anywhere along the trail, except near developed areas or where posted otherwise, and campfires are allowed. Campsites should be at least 50 feet from the trail and away from water sources.

For Further Information: Buckeye Trail Association, Inc., P.O. Box 254, Worthington, OH 43085. A series of trail maps and small guidebooks may be obtained from this organization.

NORTH COUNTRY TRAIL—Currently under construction, this important National Scenic Trail will eventually run about 3,200 miles from New York to North Dakota. When completed the Ohio section will extend some 700 miles, entering Ohio from western Pennsylvania and exiting into southern Michigan.

For much of its route here the North Country Trail follows the Buckeye Trail, circling down through the southern part of the state. It traverses two tracts of Wayne National Forest and a number of state parks, and at times the trail parallels two National Scenic Rivers. Portions are on private lands.

For stretches the trail winds through wild forested areas, with occasional rough spots. It also leads past semideveloped areas, following old roads, railroad beds, and canal towpaths. Difficulty ranges from easy to moderate. Parts of the trail are open to horseback riding and cycling.

Camping Regulations: Camping is generally restricted to designated sites. No permits are necessary. Within Wayne National Forest one may camp almost anywhere except near public use areas, and campfires are permitted although discouraged. Along some sections of the trail legal camping is not currently available.

For Further Information: North Country Trail Association, P.O. Box 311, White Cloud, MI 49349.

OHIO CAMPING RESOURCES

ORGANIZATIONS WHICH OFFER WILDERNESS
CAMPING TRIPS

American Youth Hostels, Columbus Council, P.O. Box 14384, Columbus, OH 43214; (614)447-1006. This AYH council sponsors a number of backpacking trips each year, and also offers a Beginning Backpack Class.

USEFUL GUIDEBOOKS
Backpack Loops and Long Day Trail Hikes in Southern Ohio— Ruchhoft, Robert H. Cincinnati, OH: The Pucelle Press, 1984.
Fifty Hikes in Ohio—Ramey, Ralph. Woodstock, VT: Backcountry Publications, 1990.

INFORMATION ABOUT CAMPGROUNDS IN STATE PARKS AND FORESTS
Ohio Department of Natural Resources, Division of Parks and Recreation, Fountain Square, Building C-1, Columbus, OH 43224; (614)265-7000.

STATE HIGHWAY MAP AND TRAVEL INFORMATION
Ohio Office of Travel and Tourism, 30 East Broad Street, 25th Floor, Columbus, OH 43215; (800)BUCKEYE.

OKLAHOMA

BEST AREAS FOR WILDERNESS CAMPING

OUACHITA NATIONAL FOREST—While most of this large National Forest is located in Arkansas, two sizable units are in southeastern Oklahoma. These tracts include small mountains with scenic views, an area of old beech trees, some pine forest, streams, and 90-acre Cedar Lake.

In this part of the National Forest are two designated wilderness areas: the 9,371-acre Upper Kiamichi River Wilderness, and the 4,583-acre Black Fork Mountain Wilderness, which has an additional 7,568 acres in Arkansas.

There are three other areas of special interest here: the 41,051-acre Indian Nations Wildlife and Scenic Area, the 26,445-acre Winding Stair Mountain National Recreation Area, and the 7,500-acre Beech Creek National Scenic Area and Botanical Area.

Activities: Backpacking and hiking are available on over 40 miles of trails. Included are 31 miles of the 225-mile Ouachita Trail, a National Recreation Trail which runs the length of the National Forest (see the Ouachita Trail entry, Arkansas chapter).

Difficulty ranges from easy to strenuous. There are also some 200 miles of horse trails in the region. Fishing is another possible option. Hunting is permitted in season.

Camping Regulations: Camping and campfires are allowed just about anywhere, except where posted otherwise. No permits are necessary. Campsites should be at least 100 feet from trails and water sources.

For Further Information: Ouachita National Forest, P.O. Box 1270, Hot Springs, AR 71902; (501)321-5202.

NATIONAL GRASSLANDS IN OKLAHOMA—Two National Grasslands are found in western Oklahoma: Black Kettle National Grasslands and a small portion of Rita Blanca National Grasslands, most of which is located in Texas. Both areas are administered by New Mexico's Cibola National Forest.

These tracts consist of mixed grasslands with some rivers and streams. Wildlife includes white-tailed deer, antelope, and wild turkey. Some privately-owned cattle are allowed to graze on the lands. Aside from three small campgrounds, facilities are few.

Activities: Hiking and backpacking are possible, as is horseback riding, but there aren't any established trails. Travel on other than roads must be cross-country. Fishing is available, and hunting is permitted in season.

Camping Regulations: Camping and campfires are allowed throughout the National Grasslands, except where otherwise prohibited. No permits are necessary.

For Further Information: Black Kettle National Grasslands, Route 1, Box 55B, Cheyenne, OK 73628; (405)497-2143. Rita Blanca National Grasslands, P.O. Box 38, Texline, TX 79087; (806)362-4254.

WICHITA MOUNTAINS WILDLIFE REFUGE—This National Wildlife Refuge is located in the Wichita Mountains of southwest Oklahoma, a region of small mountains with elevations over 2,400 feet, rocky outcroppings, canyons, some lakes and streams, oak forests, and areas of mixed grass prairie.

The Wildlife Refuge has two designated wilderness areas: the 5,000-acre Charons Garden Wilderness Area and the 3,500-acre North Mountain Wilderness Area. Wildlife includes elk, bison (buffalo), white-tailed deer, longhorn cattle, and prairie dog.

Activities: Hiking and backpacking are available on 15 miles of trails. Fishing is permitted along the refuge's lakes. Hunting is prohibited.

Camping Regulations: Backcountry camping is allowed by permit only, and is restricted to the Charons Garden Wilderness Area. Sites must be in one of two designated camping zones in the wilderness area. Campfires are forbidden.

Only 10 permits are issued at a time. Visits are limited to a 3-day period, which must commence either on a Friday or Monday. Reservations may be made up to 90 days in advance by mail or phone for a small fee.

For Further Information: Wichita Mountains Wildlife Refuge, RR #1, Box 448, Indiahoma, OK 73552; (405)429-3222.

U.S. ARMY CORPS OF ENGINEERS LANDS—The U.S. Army Corps of Engineers administers many tracts of land in the state of Oklahoma. The areas include a number of large reservoirs and rivers, with grasslands, meadows, and oak-hickory forest. Deer and wild turkey are among the wildlife.

Activities: Several major trails are found on these lands, including a portion of the Jean Pierre Chouteau Trail (see entry page 236), the 24-mile Platter–Lakeside Trail, and the 18-mile Will Rogers Country Centennial Trail.

The trails are open to hiking, and some trails may be used by backpackers as well as horseback riders and mountain bikers. Fishing is generally available. Hunting is permitted in season.

Camping Regulations: Primitive camping and campfires are allowed along some but not all of the trails. Campsites must be at least 100 feet from streams and 300 feet from lakeshores. In many cases camping is restricted to designated sites. A permit is required for a couple of areas.

For Further Information: U.S. Army Corps of Engineers, Tulsa District, P.O. Box 61, Tulsa, OK 74121; (918)581-7349.

OTHER RECOMMENDED LOCATIONS

BEAVERS BEND STATE PARK AND HOCHATOWN STATE PARK—These two state parks stand in close proximity alongside Broken Bow Reservoir, in the southeastern corner of Oklahoma. The area includes small pine-forested mountains along with the Mountain Fork River. White-tailed deer, fox, and wild turkey are among the wildlife here.

Activities: Backpacking and hiking are available on the 24-mile David Boren Trail, which connects the two parks and also crosses Army Corps of Engineers lands.

There are some equestrian trails as well. Canoeing is possible on the river. Canoe and horse rentals are available. Fishing is allowed along the reservoir and river.

Camping Regulations: Camping is restricted to several designated areas near the trail. Two of the sites are primitive, whereas the remainder are developed and accessible by road.

For Further Information: Beavers Bend State Park, P.O. Box 10, Broken Bow, OK 74728; (405)494-6300.

GREENLEAF STATE PARK—Located in eastern Oklahoma, this state park includes part of 930-acre Greenleaf Lake, an artificial lake which was formed by damming up Greenleaf Creek.

Activities: A 20-mile hiking and backpacking trail encircles the lake, passing through the park as well as other public lands. Visitors should stay on the trail. It's closed during deer hunting season and also for occasional military operations. Fishing is permitted alongside the lake.

Camping Regulations: Camping is restricted to lands between the trail and the lakeshore, on the east side of the lake. Sites should be at least 100 feet from the lake and all water sources.

Visitors must sign in at a trail register. Campfires are prohibited, so a stove is necessary if one wishes to cook. It's wise to call in advance to verify that the trail is open.

For Further Information: Greenleaf State Park, Route 1, Box 119, Braggs, OK 74423; (918)487-5196.

ROBBERS CAVE STATE PARK—8,246 acres. Situated in the San Bois Mountains of southeast Oklahoma, and adjacent to the 3,800-acre Robbers Cave Wildlife Management Area, this is Oklahoma's second largest state park. Included are small sandstone mountains up to 1,500 feet, caves, some pine forest, and three lakes. Deer and wild turkey are among the wildlife.

Activities: There are 12 miles of trails for hiking or backpacking, and 25 miles of horse trails. Rock climbing is available. Fishing is possible along the lakes.

Camping Regulations: Primitive camping is restricted to one designated area along a hiking trail. It's necessary to check in at the nature center before starting. Campfires are prohibited.

Rita Blanca
National Grassland

OKLAHOMA

Jean-Pierre
Chouteau Trail

TULSA

OKLAHOMA CITY

Greenleaf
State Park

Black Kettle
National Grassland

Robbers Cave
State Park

Wichita Mountains
Wildlife Refuge

Ouachita
National
Forest

Beavers Bend
State Park

For Further Information: Robbers Cave State Park, P.O. Box 9, Wilburton, OK 74578; (918)465-2565.

Oklahoma also has a number of state Wildlife Management Areas and Public Hunting Areas. Fishing and hunting are the primary use of these areas, but during nonhunting periods other activities like hiking, backpacking, and horseback riding are also permitted.

Unrestricted camping is allowed in some but not all areas. For more information contact the Oklahoma Department of Wildlife Conservation, 1801 North Lincoln, P.O. Box 53465, Oklahoma City, OK 73105.

MAJOR BACKPACKING TRAILS

JEAN PIERRE CHOUTEAU NATIONAL RECREATION TRAIL—While this is not a wilderness trail, primitive camping is allowed along some sections. The Jean Pierre Chouteau Trail is Oklahoma's longest hiking trail, running from Catoosa to Fort Gibson, in northeastern part of the state. It's flat and easy.

The trail follows alongside the McClellan–Kerr Navigation Channel, which consists of canals plus stretches of the Verdigris River. There's some nice scenery along the way, including forested areas and open grasslands. Horses are permitted on some segments of the trail. Fishing is available.

Camping Regulations: Camping is allowed along parts of the trail. A free primitive camping permit is required. Permits may be obtained by mail or in person from the Webbers Falls Project Office, Route 2, Box 21, Gore, OK 74435; (918)489-5541. There are also some park campgrounds near the trail, with a fee charged to camp at these areas from May through September.

For Further Information: Tulsa District, Corps of Engineers, P.O. Box 61, Tulsa, OK 74121.

OKLAHOMA CAMPING RESOURCES

INFORMATION ABOUT STATE PARK CAMPGROUNDS
Oklahoma Division of State Parks: (800)652-6552.

TRAIL INFORMATION, TRAVEL INFORMATION, AND STATE HIGHWAY MAP
Oklahoma Tourism and Recreation Department, 500 Will Rogers Building, Oklahoma City, OK 73105; (405)521-2409 or (800)652-6552.

OREGON

BEST AREAS FOR WILDERNESS CAMPING

WALLOWA–WHITMAN NATIONAL FOREST— 2,383,159 acres. This major National Forest consists of two huge tracts in northeast Oregon, along with some lands in western Idaho. Located here are the Wallowa and Blue Mountains, with snow-capped granite peaks and other rugged terrain. Highest elevation is the Matterhorn, which stands at 9,845 feet.

Part of the 652,488-acre Hells Canyon National Recreation Area lies within the National Forest boundaries. Included are 6,600-foot-deep Hells Canyon, said to be the deepest river canyon in the country, and the Snake National Wild and Scenic River.

Wallowa–Whitman also has other gorges along with steep ridges, rock walls and talus slopes, glaciers, and many lakes and streams. There are ponderosa pine and Douglas fir forests, with spruce and larch. Among the wildlife are elk, mule deer, bighorn sheep, mountain goat, cougar, and coyote.

Four designated wilderness areas are found here: the 358,461-acre Eagle Cap Wilderness, and portions of the 215,000-acre Hells Canyon Wilderness, the 121,800-acre North Fork-John Day Wilderness, and the 19,600-acre Monument Rock Wilderness.

Activities: Backpacking and hiking are available on more than 2,070 miles of trails. Difficulty ranges from easy to strenuous. Trails at high elevations are likely to be snow-free from July through October.

Many trails are open to horseback riding. Mountain bikes are allowed on some trails outside of wilderness areas. Cross-country skiing is possible on trails during the winter.

White-water rafting is available on the Snake River in Hells Canyon. This activity requires a permit from late May through mid-September. Fishing is also possible in the region. Hunting is permitted in season.

Camping Regulations: Camping is allowed throughout the National Forest, as are campfires, except where otherwise prohibited. No permits are necessary.

In wilderness areas campsites should be at least 200 feet from lakes, and campfires are not permitted within one-quarter mile of some lakes. Maximum group size in wilderness areas is 12, but numbers are limited to eight in the Hells Canyon National Recreation Area and six in a portion of the Eagle Cap Wilderness.

For Further Information: Wallowa–Whitman National Forest, P.O. Box 907, Baker, OR 97814; (503)523-6391.

WILLAMETTE NATIONAL FOREST—1,675,407 acres. Located in the western Cascades, in west-central Oregon, Willamette National Forest encloses an area of snow-covered mountains and volcanoes, with 10,495-foot Mount Jefferson the highest point.

There are rock outcroppings and pinnacles, lava fields, craters, cinder cones, and many glaciers—including Collier Glacier, Oregon's largest—along with deep river canyons, hundreds of lakes, a great many streams, and some major rivers.

The area is forested with lodgepole and ponderosa pine, Douglas and silver fir, plus hemlock and cedar, with some old-growth stands. Among the wildlife are Roosevelt elk, black-tailed and mule deer, black bear, cougar, and coyote.

Willamette has eight designated wilderness areas: portions of the 283,402-acre Three Sisters Wilderness, the 111,177-acre Mount Jefferson Wilderness, the 52,516-acre Mount Washington Wilderness and the 52,337-acre Diamond Peak Wilderness, along with the 37,162-acre Waldo Lake Wilderness, 7,500 acres of the 34,900-acre Bull of the Woods Wilderness, the 8,542-acre Mid-Santiam Wilderness, and the 5,033-acre Menagerie Wilderness.

Activities: Hiking and backpacking are possible on over 1,400 miles of trails, including about 100 miles of the Pacific Crest Trail (see entry page 244) and the 27-mile McKenzie River National Recreation Trail. Difficulty varies from easy to strenuous.

Kayaking and canoeing are available on the McKenzie River. Many trails are open to horseback riding, and cross-country skiing is a winter option here. Mountaineering is possible on a number of peaks. There are also many opportunities for fishing along lakes and streams, and hunting is permitted in season.

Camping Regulations: Camping and campfires are allowed freely throughout most of the National Forest, except near public use areas or where otherwise prohibited.

A permit is required to enter and camp in the Three Sisters, Mount Jefferson, and Mount Washington Wilderness areas from Memorial Day Weekend through October 31. Permits are available in person or by mail or phone. Group size is limited to 12 in these areas.

For Further Information: Willamette National Forest, P.O. Box 10607, 211 East 7th Avenue, Eugene, OR 97440; (503)687-6521.

MOUNT HOOD NATIONAL FOREST—1,060,253 acres. Mount Hood National Forest is located in the Cascades of northern Oregon. There are high peaks here, including 11,235-foot Mount Hood, along with steep cliffs and canyons, rock outcrops and pinnacles, cinder cones with lava dikes.

Amid this rugged terrain are some glaciers, many alpine lakes, major rivers, and creeks with waterfalls. Forests are of Douglas fir, with hemlock and some hardwoods, including old-growth stands. Wildlife includes elk, black bear, black-tailed and mule deer, mountain lion, mountain goat, and bobcat.

The National Forest has six designated wilderness areas: the 186,000-acre Mount Hood Wilderness, the 244,000-acre Badger Creek Wilderness, part of the 111,177-acre Mount Jefferson Wilderness, the 44,600-acre Salmon–Huckleberry Wilderness, the 39,000-acre Columbia Wilderness,

and most of the 34,900-acre Bull of the Woods Wilderness.

Activities: Over 1,100 miles of trails are available for backpacking and hiking, including a section of the Pacific Crest Trail (see entry page 000). Difficulty ranges from easy to strenuous. High trails may only be snow-free from mid-July through September.

Horses are allowed on many trails. Mountain bikes may be ridden on some trails outside of designated wilderness areas. Cross-country skiing is possible during the snow season. Mountain climbing is another option here. Fishing is also available, and hunting is permitted in season.

Camping Regulations: Camping is allowed in most areas of the National Forest, except where otherwise prohibited. Campfires are generally permitted but prohibited in parts of some wilderness areas. Campers are encouraged to bring a stove for cooking.

A permit is required for camping in the Mount Jefferson Wilderness. Group size in wilderness areas is limited to 12. Campsites should be away from meadows and at least 100 feet from lakes.

For Further Information: Mount Hood National Forest, 2955 N.W. Division Street, Gresham, OR 97030; (503)666-0771.

UMATILLA NATIONAL FOREST—1,399,342 acres (1,088,197 in Oregon). This National Forest is made up of three large units in the northeastern part of the state, along with some lands in southeast Washington. Dominating the area are the Blue Mountains, with elevations as high as 8,000 feet.

There are also plateaus, high cliffs, rock outcroppings, and deep canyons, with many streams and some major rivers. In the region are forests of Douglas and grand fir, ponderosa and lodgepole pine, and western larch, along with meadows and grasslands. Wildlife includes Rocky Mountain elk, white-tailed and mule deer, bighorn sheep, mountain lion, and coyote.

Umatilla National Forest has three designated wilderness areas: the 177,465-acre Wenaha–Tucannon Wilderness, part of the 121,800-acre North Fork–John Day Wilderness, and the 20,144-acre North Fork Umatilla Wilderness.

Activities: There are about 735 miles of trails for backpacking and hiking. Difficulty ranges from easy to strenuous. Horseback riding is allowed on many trails. Nordic skiing is possible on some trails during winter. Rafting is available on the Grande Ronde River. Streams and rivers are open to fishing, and hunting is permitted in season.

Camping Regulations: Camping is allowed freely throughout the National Forest, as are campfires, except near public recreation areas or where posted otherwise. No permits are required.

For Further Information: Umatilla National Forest, 2517 S.W. Hailey Avenue, Pendleton, OR 97801; (503)276-3811.

UMPQUA NATIONAL FOREST—988,149 acres. This National Forest is in the western Cascades of southwest Oregon, near Crater Lake National Park. Terrain here includes lofty peaks and basins, volcanic rock formations, cliffs and bluffs, and steep canyons. Highest elevation is 9,182-foot Mount Thielson.

In the region are some rivers, small lakes, and many streams with waterfalls. There are stands of old-growth Douglas fir, along with forests of cedar, pine, and hemlock, and open alpine meadows. Wildlife includes black-tailed and mule deer, black bear, Roosevelt elk, mountain lion, bobcat, and fox.

Umpqua National Forest has three designated wilderness areas, consisting of portions of the 55,100-acre Mount Thielsen Wilderness and the 33,200-acre Rogue-Umpqua Divide Wilderness, along with the 19,100-acre Boulder Creek Wilderness.

Activities: Hiking and backpacking are possible on about 600 miles of trails, including most of the 77-mile North Umpqua Trail and 30 miles of the Pacific Crest Trail (see entries page 244). Difficulty varies from easy to strenuous.

Rafting and kayaking are available on some rivers and streams. Horseback riding is allowed on many trails, as is mountain biking except in wilderness areas. Many trails are suitable for cross-country skiing during winter. Fishing is permitted, as is hunting during the appropriate season.

Camping Regulations: Camping and campfires are allowed almost anywhere within forest boundaries, except near public use areas or where otherwise prohibited. No permits are necessary.

For Further Information: Umpqua National Forest, P.O. Box 1008, Roseburg, OR 97470; (503)672-6601.

DESCHUTES NATIONAL FOREST—1,602,809 acres. Deschutes National Forest is located in the eastern Cascades of west-central Oregon. It's an area of high peaks, volcanoes and craters, glaciers, and desert—plus many streams, over 150 lakes, and six National Wild and Scenic Rivers.

There are meadows, forests of ponderosa and lodgepole pine, spruce, and Douglas fir, including old-growth stands. Among the wildlife are elk, mule deer, black bear, and coyote.

This National Forest has five designated wilderness areas, consisting of parts of the 283,402-acre Three Sisters Wilderness, the 111,177-acre Mount Jefferson Wilderness, the 55,100-acre Mount Thielsen Wilderness, the 52,516-acre Mount Washington Wilderness, and the 52,337-acre Diamond Peak Wilderness.

Activities: Hiking and backpacking are available on over 500 miles of trails, including a section of the Pacific Crest Trail (see entry page 244). Difficulty varies from easy to strenuous. Trails at high elevations are likely to be snow-free only from July through September.

Rafting, kayaking, and canoeing are possible on the Deschutes River and several other rivers. Horseback riding is allowed on many trails, and cross-country skiing is available during the snow season. Fishing along the streams, rivers, and lakes is another option. Hunting is permitted in season.

Camping Regulations: Camping and campfires are allowed throughout the National Forest, except where posted otherwise. A free permit is required to camp in the Three Sisters, Mount Jefferson, and Mount Washington Wilderness areas from Memorial Day weekend through October 31.

Maximum group size in wilderness areas is 12. Campsites and campfires should be at least 100 feet from trails and water sources, and one-quarter mile from some designated lakes.

For Further Information: Deschutes National Forest, 1645 Highway 20 East, Bend, OR 97701; (503)388-2715.

ROGUE RIVER NATIONAL FOREST—638,259 acres. This National Forest consists of two tracts in southwest Oregon, one alongside Crater Lake National Park and the other next to the California border, and extending into that state. There are some prominent peaks, with 9,495-foot Mount McLoughlin the highest point, plus cirque basins, deep gorges and steep cliffs, rock formations and massive lava flows.

The beautiful Rogue River is here, along with many lakes, creeks, and waterfalls, including 600-foot Alkali Falls. The area has mixed conifer forests and deciduous trees, with old-growth Douglas fir, pine, and hemlock. Among the wildlife are elk, mule deer, black bear, mountain lion, and bobcat.

There are three designated wilderness areas, consisting of portions of the 116,300-acre Sky Lakes Wilderness, the 33,200-acre Rogue–Umpqua Divide Wilderness, and the 20,234-acre Red Buttes Wilderness.

Activities: Backpacking and hiking are possible on more than 400 miles trails, easy to strenuous

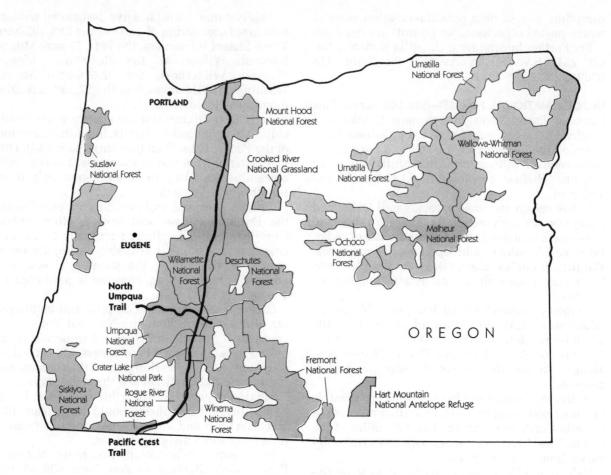

Within the map:
- Umatilla National Forest
- Mount Hood National Forest
- Wallowa-Whitman National Forest
- PORTLAND
- Crooked River National Grassland
- Siuslaw National Forest
- Umatilla National Forest
- EUGENE
- Malheur National Forest
- Willamette National Forest
- Deschutes National Forest
- Ochoco National Forest
- OREGON
- North Umpqua Trail
- Umpqua National Forest
- Crater Lake National Park
- Rogue River National Forest
- Fremont National Forest
- Winema National Forest
- Siskiyou National Forest
- Hart Mountain National Antelope Refuge
- Pacific Crest Trail

in difficulty. Included are a section of the Pacific Crest Trail (see entry page 244) and the 48-mile Upper Rogue River Trail. High trails are likely be snow-free only from mid-July through September.

Horseback riding is allowed on many trails. Cross-country skiing is available when there's snow. Fishing is also possible. Hunting is permitted in season.

Camping Regulations: Camping is allowed throughout the National Forest, as are campfires, except near public use areas or where otherwise prohibited. No permits are necessary.

For Further Information: Rogue River National Forest, P.O. Box 520, Medford, OR 97501; (503)776-3579.

SISKIYOU NATIONAL FOREST—1,093,542 acres. Located in the southwest corner of Oregon, this National Forest includes the Siskiyou Mountains, with rugged canyons and rock outcroppings, mountain meadows, numerous creeks, small lakes, and some rivers—among them the Rogue

and Illinois, both of which are National Wild and Scenic Rivers.

Highest elevation here is 7,055-foot Grayback Mountain. The forests are of mixed conifers and hardwoods, with old-growth Douglas fir and redwood. Wildlife includes elk, mule deer, black bear, mountain lion, coyote, bobcat, and gray fox.

Siskiyou National Forest has four designated wilderness areas: portions of the 179,000-acre Kalmiopsis Wilderness and the 20,234-acre Red Buttes Wilderness, the 36,000-acre Wild Rogue Wilderness, and the 17,200-acre Grassy Knob Wilderness.

Activities: Over 375 miles of trails are available for backpacking and hiking. Included are the 40-mile Rogue River Trail and the 27-mile Illinois River Trail. Difficulty varies from easy to strenuous. Horses are allowed on many trails, as are mountain bikes outside of wilderness areas.

White-water rafting is possible on the Rogue and Illinois Rivers, with permits required to float these two rivers from June 1–September 15. Fishing is also feasible alongside the rivers, streams, and lakes. Hunting is permitted in season.

Camping Regulations: Camping is allowed throughout this National Forest, except near public recreation areas or where otherwise prohibited. No permits are necessary. Campfires may be built but stoves are recommended. Campsites should be well away from meadows and trails.

For Further Information: Siskiyou National Forest, 200 N.E. Greenfield Road, P.O. Box 440, Grants Pass, OR 97526; (503)479-5301.

MALHEUR NATIONAL FOREST—1,458,055 acres. Consisting of extensive lands in east-central Oregon, Malheur National Forest includes high country scenery of the Blue Mountains, with 9,038-foot Strawberry Mountain the highest point.

Common trees include ponderosa pine, lodgepole pine, and fir, with some old-growth stands. There are also meadows and grasslands, alpine lakes, several rivers, and many creeks. Among the wildlife are elk, antelope, mule deer, bighorn sheep, mountain lion, and bobcat.

Two wilderness areas have been designated here: the 68,300-acre Strawberry Mountain Wilderness, along with a portion of the 19,600-acre Monument Rock Wilderness. Also in the National Forest is part of the 29,000-acre Indian Rock–Vinegar Hill Scenic Area, which extends into Umatilla National Forest.

Activities: Hiking and backpacking are possible on over 200 miles of trails. Difficulty ranges from easy to strenuous. Most trails are open to horseback riding, and some are suitable for cross-country skiing in winter. Fishing is available, and hunting is permitted in season.

Camping Regulations: Camping is allowed throughout most of this National Forest, as are campfires, except where otherwise prohibited. Campsites in wilderness areas should be at least 200 feet from lakeshores.

For Further Information: Malheur National Forest, 139 N.E. Dayton Street, John Day, OR 97845; (503)575-1731.

OTHER RECOMMENDED LOCATIONS

CRATER LAKE NATIONAL PARK—183,180 acres. This National Park is located in the Cascades of southwest Oregon. The centerpiece here is Crater Lake, at an elevation of 6,176 feet. It's six miles across and over 1,500 feet deep. The lake lies in the caldera of a collapsed volcano.

Nearby are several mountains, with elevations from under 5,000 feet to over 8,900 feet. Highest point is 8,926-foot Mount Scott. There are old-growth conifer forests of hemlock, fir, and pine. Wildlife includes elk, black bear, coyote, and fox.

Activities: Backpacking and hiking are available on more than 100 miles of trails, including about 25 miles of the Pacific Crest Trail (see entry page 244). Most trails are free of snow from July to October.

Unplowed roads in the park are used for cross-country skiing in winter. Horseback riding is restricted to two trails. Biking is limited to paved roads and one nature trail. Fishing is allowed, but hunting is prohibited.

Camping Regulations: A free permit must be obtained in order to camp in the backcountry here. Permits are available from park headquarters and entrance stations. A self-issuing permit may also be picked up on the Pacific Crest Trail at the place where this trail enters the park. Pets are prohibited.

Campers should use preestablished sites whenever possible, Campsites should be at least one mile from paved roads, away from meadows, and 100 feet or more from trails, water sources, and other campers. Some areas are off limits to camping. Campfires are allowed. Maximum group size is 12.

For Further Information: Crater Lake National Park, P.O. Box 7, Crater Lake, OR 97604; (503)594-2211.

SIUSLAW NATIONAL FOREST—630,584 acres. Situated in western Oregon's Coast Range, Siuslaw National Forest covers an area of small but rugged mountains, with 4,097-foot Marys Peak the highest point. Also included are canyons, lakes, streams, and some Pacific coastline.

Of special interest near the ocean is the 25,658-acre Oregon Dunes National Recreation Area, which has 400-foot dunes and 40 miles of coastline. Elsewhere there are meadows and conifer forests. Wildlife includes elk, deer, bear, and cougar, with whale, seal, and other marine mammals along the coast.

The National Forest has three relatively small wilderness areas: the 9,173-acre Cummins Creek Wilderness, the 7,486-acre Rock Creek Wilderness, and the 5,798-acre Drift Creek Wilderness.

Activities: About 100 miles of trails are available for hiking and backpacking, including a section of the Oregon Coast Trail. Difficulty varies from easy to strenuous. Horses are allowed on some trails. There are many opportunities for fishing alongside lakes, streams, and rivers. Hunting is permitted in season.

Camping Regulations: Camping is allowed throughout the National Forest, as are campfires, except near public use areas or where otherwise prohibited. Some designated sites are also available for use. No permits are necessary.

For Further Information: Siuslaw National Forest, P.O. Box 1148, Corvallis, OR 97339; (503)750-7000.

WINEMA NATIONAL FOREST—1,045,003 acres. Winema National Forest consists of several tracts in the Cascades of southwest Oregon, including lands east of Crater Lake National Park. Highest elevation here is 9,182-foot Mount Thielsen.

Along with volcanic mountains and rock outcrops there are many glacial lakes, rivers, streams, and forests of mixed conifers, plus some meadows. Among the wildlife are elk, mule deer, black bear, mountain lion, and bobcat.

The forest has three designated wilderness areas: the 116,300-acre Sky Lakes Wilderness, part of the 55,100-acre Mount Thielsen Wilderness, and the 23,071-acre Mountain Lakes Wilderness.

Activities: Backpacking and hiking are possible on approximately 100 miles of trails, including a section of the Pacific Crest Trail (see entry page 244). Difficulty varies from easy to strenuous. Most trails are open to horses.

Mountain biking is allowed on some trails outside of wilderness areas. Cross-country skiing is possible here in winter. Canoeing is available on a couple of rivers, and fishing is another option. Hunting is permitted in season.

Camping Regulations: Camping is allowed almost anywhere here, except where otherwise prohibited. No permits are required. Campfires may normally be built, but the use of stoves is encouraged. Campfires may be banned during times of fire hazard.

Group size is limited to 10 in the Mountain Lakes Wilderness, and eight in the Sky Lake Wilderness. Campsites in wilderness areas must be at least 100 feet from water sources.

For Further Information: Winema National Forest, 2819 Dahlia Street, Klamath Falls, OR 97601; (503)883-6714.

OCHOCO NATIONAL FOREST—956,877 acres. This National Forest is comprised of three tracts in central Oregon, with a fourth tract which consists of 111,379-acre Crooked River National Grassland (see entry page 243). It's an area of mountains, steep cliffs, canyons, rolling hills, and high desert.

Top elevation is 7,163-foot Snow Mountain. There are small lakes and streams, meadows and grasslands, areas of sagebrush-juniper, and forests of ponderosa pine and fir, including some old-growth stands. Elk, antelope, mule deer, wild horse, and cougar are among the wildlife.

This National Forest has three designated wilderness areas: the 17,400-acre Mill Creek Wilderness, the 13,400-acre Black Canyon Wilderness, and the 5,400-acre Bridge Creek Wilderness.

Activities: There are currently 86 miles of trails for hiking and backpacking. Difficulty varies from easy to strenuous. Horseback riding is allowed on most trails, as is mountain biking except in wilderness areas. Cross-country skiing is possible here in the winter. Hunting and fishing are permitted in season.

Camping Regulations: Camping and campfires are allowed throughout the National Forest, except near public use areas or where otherwise prohibited. No permits are necessary.

For Further Information: Ochoco National Forest, P.O. Box 490, Prineville, OR 97754; (503)447-6247.

FREMONT NATIONAL FOREST—1,196,000 acres. Located in the eastern Cascades of south-central Oregon, with lands along the California border, Fremont National Forest consists of high desert with mountains and ridges, volcanic domes, rock formations and pinnacles, canyons and steep cliffs.

Elevations range from 4,100 feet to over 8,000 feet. There are meadows, small lakes, streams, a few rivers, and a single designated wilderness area, the 22,823-acre Gearhart Mountain Wilderness. Forests are of ponderosa pine, white fir, and aspen. Wildlife includes elk, antelope, mule deer, and mountain lion.

Activities: About 77 miles of trails are available for backpacking and hiking. Difficulty varies from easy to strenuous. Horseback riding is allowed, as is mountain biking on trails outside of the wilderness area.

Both cross-country skiing and snowshoeing are possible with sufficient snowfall in the winter. Fishing is available along the streams, rivers, and lakes. Hunting is permitted in season.

Camping Regulations: Camping is allowed throughout the National Forest, as are campfires, except near public recreation areas or where otherwise prohibited. No permits are required.

For Further Information: Fremont National Forest, 524 North G Street, Lakeview, OR 97630; (503)947-2151.

HART MOUNTAIN NATIONAL ANTELOPE REFUGE— 275,000 acres. Situated in south-central Oregon, this National Antelope Refuge encompasses an area which includes 8,065-foot Hart Mountain, along with steep rocky cliffs and bluffs, ridges, and deep canyon gorges.

There are also hilly grasslands and brushlands, with a number of creeks and lakes, even though the region is mostly arid. Among the wildlife are pronghorn antelope, mule deer, bighorn sheep, coyote, bobcat, and golden eagle.

Activities: Hiking and backpacking are allowed throughout the refuge. There are no established trails, so travel must be cross-country. Horseback riding is also possible, and Nordic skiing is a winter option. Fishing is limited to two creeks. Hunting is permitted in season.

Camping Regulations: A free permit is required in order to camp in the backcountry. Campfires are generally allowed, but are subject to being banned when fire danger is high. Parts of the refuge may be closed to entry at certain times of year.

For Further Information: Hart Mountain National Antelope Refuge, P.O. Box 111, Lakeview, OR 97630; (503)947-3315.

CROOKED RIVER NATIONAL GRASSLAND— 111,379 acres. Located in the high desert of central Oregon and administered by Ochoco National Forest, Crooked River National Grassland is on a plateau with some steep 600-foot canyons, buttes, and rolling hills.

Included are both the Deschutes and Crooked Rivers, along with some streams and several reservoirs. Vegetation consists of grasslands with sagebrush and juniper. Among the wildlife are antelope and mule deer.

Activities: The National Grassland is open to hiking and backpacking as well as horseback riding, but there are no established trails. Most travel must be cross-country. Hunting and fishing are permitted in season.

Camping Regulations: Camping is allowed throughout the Grassland, as are campfires, except where posted otherwise. No permits are required. Visitors are asked to camp at least 100 feet from water sources.

For Further Information: Crooked River National Grassland, P.O. Box 687, 155 North Court, Prineville, OR 97754; (503)447-9641.

BLM LANDS IN OREGON—There are 15,700,000 acres of BLM (Bureau of Land Management) or public domain lands in the state, consisting of a great many separate tracts—especially in south-central, east, and southeast Oregon. Included are

a large number of Wilderness Study Areas, under consideration for wilderness status.

Locations in the western part of the state are generally forested, with some stands of old-growth trees, and a number of major rivers and streams with waterfalls. Most of the remaining lands are arid areas of high desert, with rugged mountains and steep canyons, buttes, and rock formations.

Access to some BLM areas is difficult, roads may not be in good condition, and facilities are generally few or nonexistent. Brochures and other printed information are available for only a small number of tracts.

Activities: Backpacking, hiking, horseback riding, and mountain biking are allowed on these lands. Among the relatively few established trails are short sections of the Pacific Crest Trail (see entry page 244) and the 40-mile Rogue River Trail. Most travel on BLM lands must be cross-country.

White-water rafting, kayaking, and canoeing are available on several of the rivers. Cross-country skiing is also possible at high elevations. Hunting and fishing are permitted in season.

Camping Regulations: Camping is allowed freely on BLM lands, as are campfires, except where posted otherwise. Limited restrictions apply in a few areas. No permits are required.

For Further Information: Bureau of Land Management, 1300 NE 44th Avenue, P.O. Box 2965, Portland, OR 97208; (503)280-7002.

STATE FORESTS IN OREGON—Oregon has a number of state forests, several of which are sizable. The three largest are 364,000-acre Tillamook State Forest, 92,000-acre Elliott State Forest, and 47,721-acre Santiam State Forest. These lands are used primarily for tree-harvesting. Some of the areas include rugged terrain.

Activities: The state forests are open to recreational use such as hunting and fishing, and also offer some limited opportunities for hiking, backpacking, and horseback riding. Tillamook State Forest has 25 miles of trails, far more than the other forests. Most have few or no established trails.

Camping Regulations: Primitive camping is generally allowed in the state forests, except where posted otherwise. Campfires should only be built at designated campsites.

For Further Information: Oregon Department of Forestry, 2600 State Street, Salem, OR 97310; (503)378-2560.

In addition, Ecola State Park in the northwest corner of Oregon has a single designated primitive camping area along the Oregon Coast Trail, two miles from a parking area. For more information contact Ecola State Park, c/o Fort Stevens State Park, Hammond, OR 97121; (503)861-3170.

Also, Oswald West State Park in northwest Oregon has a walk-in campground which is one-third mile by trail from a parking area. For information contact Oswald West State Park, c/o Nehalem Bay State Park, 8300 R Third Street Necarney, Nehalem, OR 97131.

MAJOR BACKPACKING TRAILS

PACIFIC CREST TRAIL—462 miles in Oregon (2,638 total). This important National Scenic Trail traverses some of the wildest, most spectacular, and most remote mountain scenery of Washington, Oregon, and California, with many magnificent views available along the way.

The trail stays mainly in the Cascades as it crosses Oregon, running from the Washington–Oregon border at the Columbia River to the California line. Most of the time it's on National Forest lands, and it also passes through Crater Lake National Park.

Difficulty ranges from easy to very strenuous. Sections of the trail at high elevations are likely to be snow-free only during August and September. Horses are allowed on the trail.

Camping Regulations: Camping is allowed almost anywhere on National Forest lands along the trail, except where posted otherwise. Campsites should be well off the trail and away from water sources.

A "self-issuing permit" is required for Crater Lake National Park, and this permit may be obtained at the two locations where the trail enters the park. Campfires are allowed along most stretches of the trail in this state, but a stove is recommended.

For Further Information: Pacific Crest Trail Conference, 365 West 29th Avenue, Eugene, OR 97405.

NORTH UMPQUA TRAIL—This new trail, which is currently under construction, follows alongside or near the beautiful North Umpqua River in southwest Oregon. When completed it will be about 77 miles long. Much of the trail is now open.

It stays mainly within Umpqua National Forest, but there's also a section on BLM lands. The trail traverses two designated wilderness areas, the Boulder Creek Wilderness and the Mount Thielsen Wilderness, and intersects with the Pacific Crest Trail.

It's open to horseback riding, and mountain biking is allowed outside of the two wilderness areas. Difficulty is easy to moderate, and there are a couple of steep stretches of trail.

Camping Regulations: Camping is allowed along the trail, as are campfires, except where posted otherwise. Campers should set up well off the trail and away from the river, and avoid meadows.

For Further Information: Umpqua National Forest, P.O. Box 1008, Roseburg, OR 97470; (503)672-6601.

DESERT TRAIL—Someday this new trail should extend all the way from Mexico to Canada, crossing the western High Desert of California, Nevada, Oregon, Idaho, and Montana. So far sections totaling about 250 miles have been completed in Oregon, Nevada, and California.

The Oregon segments include desert areas with mountains and canyons in the eastern and southeastern parts of the state. Much of the trail here is on BLM (Bureau of Land Management) lands, and it also crosses some National Forests.

Camping Regulations: Camping and campfires are freely allowed on BLM and National Forest lands, except where otherwise prohibited. No permits are necessary.

For Further Information: Desert Trail Association, P.O. Box 537, Burns, OR 97720. Guides to several sections of the trail are available from this organization.

Oregon also has a new 360-mile trail, the Oregon Coast Trail, which follows the coastline for the length of the state. Some of the shoreline is wild and very beautiful, but at times the trail also follows roads and passes through developed areas.

Camping along the way is mainly limited to campgrounds, with "hiker-biker camps" at some locations next to the campgrounds. While most of the trail doesn't offer a true wilderness camping experience, it may be of interest to some backpackers.

For more information contact the Trail Coordinator, Oregon State Parks, 525 Trade Street SE, Salem, OR 97310; (503)378-5012.

OREGON CAMPING RESOURCES

ORGANIZATIONS WHICH OFFER WILDERNESS CAMPING TRIPS
Desert Trail Association, P.O. Box 537, Burns, OR 97720. This organization offers backpacking

and other wilderness camping trips each year. Most trips are along the Desert Trail.

Mazamas, 909 Northwest 19th Avenue, Portland, OR 97209; (503)227- 2345. Mazamas is a mountain climber's club, with a schedule which also includes backpacking, whitewater rafting, horsepacking, ski-mountaineering, and other wilderness camping trips.

Obsidians, P.O. Box 322, Eugene, OR 97440. This group sponsors some backpacking and climbing trips.

Trails Club of Oregon, P.O. Box 1243, Portland, OR 97207. The Trails Club of Oregon offers occasional backpacking and other wilderness camping trips.

OUTFITTERS AND GUIDES

Oregon Guides and Packers Association, P.O. Box 3797, Portland, OR 97208; (503)234-3268.

USEFUL GUIDEBOOKS

Crater Lake National Park—Schaffer, Jeffrey P. Berkeley, CA: Wilderness Press, 1983.

Exploring Oregon's Wild Areas—Sullivan, William L. Seattle: The Mountaineers Books.

50 Hikes in Oregon's Coast Range & Siskiyous—Ostertag, Rhonda and George. Seattle: The Mountaineers Books, 1989.

Hiker's Guide to Oregon—Aitkenhead, Donna. Helena, MT: Falcon Press.

Hiking the Bigfoot Country—Hart, John. San Francisco: Sierra Club Books.

Hiking the Great Basin—Hart, John. San Francisco: Sierra Club Books.

100 Hikes in Oregon—Ostertag, Rhonda and George. Seattle: The Mountaineers Books.

Oregon Coast Hikes—Williams, Paul, & Spring, Ira. Seattle: The Mountaineers Books, 1985.

The Pacific Crest Trail—Volume 2: Oregon & Washington—Schaffer, Jeffrey P. and Selters, Andy. Berkeley: Wilderness Press, 1990.

The Sierra Club Guide to the Natural Areas of Oregon and Washington—Perry, John and Jane. San Francisco: Sierra Club Books, 1983.

INFORMATION ABOUT STATE PARK CAMPGROUNDS

Oregon State Parks, 525 Trade Street S.E., Salem, OR 97310; (503)378-5012.

STATE HIGHWAY MAP AND TRAVEL INFORMATION

Oregon Tourism Division, 775 Summer Street N.E., Salem, OR 97310; (800)547-7842 (out of state)/ (800)233-3306 (in state).

PENNSYLVANIA

BEST AREAS FOR WILDERNESS CAMPING

ALLEGHENY NATIONAL FOREST—506,000 acres. Located on the Allegheny Plateau in northwest Pennsylvania, this attractive National Forest includes rolling hills and valleys, with many streams and some ponds, plus the Allegheny River and the Allegheny Reservoir. Some of the terrain is rocky and steep, with rock formations, ledges, and outcrops.

There are forests of oak, black cherry, maple, pine, and hemlock, including some old-growth trees, along with rhododendron, dogwood, and mountain laurel. Among the wildlife are white-tailed deer, black bear, fox, and wild turkey.

Within the National Forest are two designated wilderness areas: the 8,500-acre Hickory Creek Wilderness and the 400-acre Allegheny Islands Wilderness. Also in the region are three National Recreation Areas and two Scenic Areas.

Activities: There are some 170 miles of established trails for backpacking and hiking, including 95 miles of the new North Country Trail (see entry page 251). In addition, cross-country travel is feasible in some parts of the forest.

Canoeing is available on the Allegheny River and Reservoir, the Clarion River, and several streams. Snowshoeing and cross-country skiing are possible in winter when there's adequate snow, generally the case during January and February. Fishing is also available. Hunting is permitted in season.

Camping Regulations: Camping and campfires are allowed throughout the National Forest, except where posted otherwise. Camping is restricted or prohibited in Scenic Areas and a few other locations, and camping is not allowed within 1,500 feet of the Reservoir. No permits are necessary.

For Further Information: Allegheny National Forest, 222 Liberty Street, Box 847, Warren, PA 16365; (814)723-5150.

TIADAGHTON STATE FOREST—204,600 acres. This state forest consists of several tracts of land on both sides of the Susquehanna River, in north-central Pennsylvania. Included here are rock formations and other rough terrain, ridges with vistas, valleys, and areas of plateau.

Tiadaghton is forested with oak, black cherry, beech, and some virgin hemlock. There are also swamps and large creeks. Wildlife includes deer, bear, bobcat, fox, and wild turkey.

In the forest are three designated Wild Areas: the 7,498-acre McIntyre Wild Area, the 6,962-acre Wolf Run Wild Area, and the 3,727-acre Algerine Wild Area.

Activities: Hiking and backpacking are available on some 200 miles of trails. Included are the circular 42-mile Black Forest Trail, the 27-mile Old Loggers Path, and 14 miles of the 59-mile Loyalsock Trail (see entry page 253).

Cross-country skiing is possible on over 40 miles of designated trails. Pine Creek is suitable for white-water canoeing. Fishing is available along the creeks, and hunting is permitted in season.

Camping Regulations: Camping is allowed throughout most of the forest, as are small campfires, except where restricted or posted otherwise. Campsites should be at least 100 feet from trails and 200 feet from roads.

Permits are not required as long as the maximum stay at each campsite is one night. A permit must be obtained if one wishes to remain for two or more nights at a single campsite.

For Further Information: Tiadaghton State Forest, 423 East Central Avenue, South Williamsport, PA 17701; (717)327-3450.

SPROUL STATE FOREST—280,000 acres. Located on the Allegheny Plateau in the north-central part of the state, this is the largest of Pennsylvania's state forests. There are steep and rugged slopes here with elevations up to 2,300 feet, and some areas are remote.

Included are oak forests, many streams, the West Branch of the Susquehanna River, and two designated Wild Areas: the 5,000-acre Fish Dam Wild Area and the 2,200-acre Burns Run Wild Area. Among the wildlife are deer, black bear, fox, and wild turkey.

Activities: Trails for hiking and backpacking in this state forest include the 53-mile Donut Hole Trail (see entry page 253) and the 50-mile Chuck Keiper Trail, which forms two loops. Difficulty varies from easy to strenuous.

Horseback riding is available on a 15-mile loop trail, as well as on old roads. A 14-mile trail is designated for cross-country skiing in winter. Canoeing is possible in springtime on the West Branch of the Susquehanna River. Fishing is another option here. Hunting is permitted in season.

Camping Regulations: Camping is allowed in most parts of the forest, except where posted otherwise. Campsites should be a minimum of 100 feet from trails and 200 feet from roads.

A permit is necessary for camping more than one night at a site, but is otherwise not required. Campfires are legal but discouraged, and sometimes banned during periods of fire hazard.

For Further Information: Sproul State Forest, HCR 62, Box 90, Renovo, PA 17764; (717)923-1450.

SUSQUEHANNOCK STATE FOREST—262,000 acres. Situated in north-central Pennsylvania, Susquehannock State Forest includes rough and steep terrain, with some elevations over 2,500 feet. Of special interest here is the 31,000-acre Hammersley Wild Area.

There are also a number of streams, and the region is forested with oak, birch, cherry, and some old-growth hemlock. White-tailed deer, bear, coyote, and fox are among the wildlife.

Activities: Backpacking and hiking are available on the 85-mile Susquehannock Trail (see entry page 252), which forms a large loop. This trail connects with the Black Forest Trail in Tiadaghton State Forest and the Donut Hole Trail in Sproul State Forest. There are also many unmarked trails.

Cross-country skiing is possible in winter on segments of the Susquehannock Trail and some other trails. Fishing is available along streams. Hunting is permitted in season.

Camping Regulations: Camping is allowed throughout most of the area, as are campfires, except where posted otherwise. Sites should be at least 100 feet from trails and 200 feet from roads. A permit is required to stay more than one night at a campsite.

For Further Information: Susquehannock State Forest, P.O. Box 673, Coudersport, PA 16915; (814)274-8474.

BALD EAGLE STATE FOREST—195,624 acres. This state forest in central Pennsylvania encompasses some 2,300-foot sandstone ridges, with rock outcroppings, talus slopes, and valleys with many streams.

Within Bald Eagle's boundaries is the 3,581-acre White Mountain Wild Area, along with several designated Natural Areas. Forests are of mixed hardwoods, plus some virgin pine and hemlock. Wildlife includes deer, bear, fox, and wild turkey.

Activities: There are a number of trails for hiking and backpacking, including a 60-mile section of the 168-mile Mid State Trail (see entry page 252). Most other trails here are minimally maintained.

Horseback riding is allowed on some trails. Many roads and trails are suitable for cross-country skiing in winter. Canoeing is possible on Penns Creek. Fishing is also available. Hunting is permitted in season.

Camping Regulations: Camping is allowed throughout most of the forest, except in Natural Areas or where posted otherwise. Campsites must be at least 100 feet from designated trails, 200 feet from forest roads, and 500 feet from paved roads.

Small campfires are generally allowed, but they're subject to being banned during periods of high fire danger. A free permit, obtainable in person or by mail, is required if one wishes to stay at any campsite for more than one night.

For Further Information: Bald Eagle State Forest, P.O. Box 147, Laurelton, PA 17835; (717)922-3344.

TUSCARORA STATE FOREST—91,000 acres. This state forest consists of three parcels of land in the Tuscarora Mountain area of south-central Pennsylvania. It's a region of low mountain ridges and valleys with numerous streams.

Included is a designated Wild Area, the 5,382-acre Tuscarora Wild Area. There are forests of oak, virgin hemlock, and pine, along with mountain laurel and azalea. Among the wildlife are white-tailed deer, black bear, fox, and wild turkey.

Activities: Backpacking and hiking are possible on about 200 miles of trails, including 23 miles of the 105-mile Tuscarora Trail (see entry page 252). Cross-country skiing is available during winter on a system of established trails. Fishing is feasible along some of the streams, and hunting is permitted in season.

Camping Regulations: Camping is allowed throughout most of the forest, as are campfires, but these are restricted in a few areas. Some trail shelters are available. Stays of longer than one night at any campsite require a permit, which may be obtained from the forest office.

For Further Information: Tuscarora State Forest, RD 1, Box 42A, Blain, PA 17006; (717)536-3191.

TIOGA STATE FOREST—160,000 acres. Located on the Allegheny Plateau in the north-central part of the state, and with some rugged terrain, Tioga State Forest is noted for 800-foot-deep Pine Creek Gorge, known as Pennsylvania's Grand Canyon. The area is hardwood-forested, with oak, black cherry, birch, and some hemlock. Wildlife includes white-tailed deer, black bear, and fox.

Activities: There's one major marked and maintained trail here for hiking and backpacking: the 30-mile West Rim Trail, which follows the west rim of Pine Creek Gorge and offers fine vistas.

White-water canoeing and kayaking are available on Pine Creek in April and May of each year. Cross-country skiing is possible on a 7-mile trail. Hunting and fishing are permitted in season.

Camping Regulations: Camping is allowed in most regions of the forest, with a few areas restricted. Campsites should be at least 100 feet from trails and 200 feet from roads. A permit is required for stays of more than one night per campsite. Campfires are permitted except during periods of fire hazard.

For Further Information: Tioga State Forest, P.O. Box 94, Route 287 South, Wellsboro, PA 16901; (717)724-2868.

MICHAUX STATE FOREST—85,000 acres. Situated in the south-central part of the state, including lands close to the Maryland border, Michaux State Forest is dominated by South Mountain and other mountain ridges, with some elevations over 2,000 feet.

There are also valleys with many creeks, several reservoirs, and forests of oak, pine, and hemlock, plus rhododendron. Among the wildlife here are deer, bear, and fox.

Activities: Backpacking and hiking are available on a 40-mile section of the Appalachian Trail (see entry page 251), along with other trails. Cross-country skiing is possible on some trails in winter. Hunting and fishing are permitted in season.

Camping Regulations: Camping and campfires are allowed throughout most of the forest, except where restricted or prohibited. Campsites should be at least 100 feet from trails and 200 feet from roads. A permit is required for stays of two nights or more at a single campsite.

For Further Information: Michaux State Forest, 10099 Lincoln Way East, Fayetteville, PA 17222; (717)352-2211.

BUCHANAN STATE FOREST—75,000 acres. This state forest consists of several tracts in south-central Pennsylvania, including lands next to the Maryland border. There are low mountain ridges here, along with hills, valleys, and some streams.

Of special interest is the 11,500-acre Martin Hill Wild Area, which has some rugged terrain. Common trees are oak and hickory, with virgin pine and hemlock. White-tailed deer, black bear, bobcat, and wild turkey are among the wildlife.

Activities: Hiking and backpacking are available on a number of trails, including a section of the Tuscarora Trail (see entry page 252), which follows the ridge of Tuscarora Mountain.

Horseback riding is possible on a few trails and many roads. Some trails are suitable for cross-country skiing during winter. Fishing is another option. Hunting is permitted in season.

Camping Regulations: Camping and campfires are allowed in most parts of the forest, except where posted otherwise. Campsites must be at least 100 feet from trails and 200 feet from roads. A permit must be obtained if one wishes to camp for more than one night at any location.

For Further Information: Buchanan State Forest, RD 2, Box 3, McConnellsburg, PA 17233; (717)485-3148.

ROTHROCK STATE FOREST—94,000 acres. Consisting of a 79,000-acre tract along with other units in central Pennsylvania, this state forest covers a number of mountain ridges—with sandstone formations, other rugged terrain, and views from elevations as high as 2,400 feet.

Included are the 4,800-acre Thickhead Wild Area and five small designated Natural Areas, with streams, swamps, and the Juniata River. There are forests of oak, spruce, and fir, with some virgin hemlock and white pine, plus rhododen-dron and mountain laurel. Among the wildlife are deer, bear, and fox.

Activities: A number of trails are available for hiking and backpacking, including a 40-mile section of the Mid State Trail (see entry page 252). Cross-country skiing is possible on some trails in the winter. Fishing is permitted, as is hunting in season.

Camping Regulations: Camping is allowed on most of these lands, as are campfires, except where restricted or posted otherwise. Campsites must be at least 100 feet from trails and 200 feet from roads. A permit is necessary if one chooses to camp for more than one night at a single location.

For Further Information: Rothrock State Forest, P.O. Box 403, Huntingdon, PA 16652; (814)643-2340.

OTHER RECOMMENDED LOCATIONS

FORBES STATE FOREST—50,000 acres. Forbes State Forest is made up of a number of tracts in the Laurel Ridge area of southwestern Pennsylvania. The highest point in the state, 3,213-foot Mount Davis, is located here as part of the 581-acre Mount Davis Natural Area.

Also of note are the 4,675-acre Quebec Run Wild Area and the 3,593-acre Roaring Run Natural Area. There are rock formations, streams with waterfalls, and mixed oak forest, with maple and tulip trees, plus mountain laurel and rhododendron. Wildlife includes deer, bear, and bobcat.

Activities: Hiking and backpacking are possible on a number of trails, including a section of the Laurel Highlands Trail (see entry page 252), and some trails in the Quebec Run Wild Area. Cross-country skiing is available here in winter. Fishing is another possibility, and hunting is permitted in season.

Camping Regulations: Camping and campfires are allowed in most regions of the forest, except where otherwise prohibited. Campsites should be at least 100 feet from trails and 200 feet from roads. A permit must be obtained from the park office in order to camp for more than a single night at any location.

For Further Information: Forbes State Forest, P.O. Box 519, Laughlintown, PA 15655; (412)238-9533.

DELAWARE STATE FOREST—63,479 acres. Delaware State Forest consists of several tracts in the Poconos of northeast Pennsylvania, near the Delaware River. This is an area of mountain plateau, with some lakes and ponds, swamps and bogs, and streams with waterfalls.

There are five designated Natural Areas here. Most of the land is hardwood-forested, with oak, aspen, birch, and some conifers. Wildlife includes deer, black bear, bobcat, and fox.

Activities: Backpacking and hiking are available on the Thunder Swamp Trail System, which includes the rather easy 28-mile Thunder Swamp Trail and side trails. Horseback riding is allowed on roads and some trails. The Little Bushkill Stream is suitable for canoeing.

Camping Regulations: Camping is allowed throughout most of the forest, as are campfires, except where restricted or posted otherwise. A free permit must be obtained from the forest office in order to camp here. Campsites should be at least 100 yards from trails and roads. A stove is recommended for cooking.

For Further Information: Delaware State Forest, 474 Clearview Lane, Stroudsburg, PA 18360; (717)424-3001.

WYOMING STATE FOREST—40,708 acres. This state forest in north-central Pennsylvania has ridges and plateaus, valleys with streams, a few ponds, and scenic Loyalsock Creek. There are two designated Natural Areas. Forests are of cherry, maple, beech, and other northern hardwoods. Wildlife includes deer, bear, and fox.

Activities: There's one major trail here for backpacking and hiking, a portion of the 59-mile Loyalsock Trail (see entry page 253). Cross-country skiing is possible on some trails in winter. Whitewater canoeing is available on Loyalsock Creek. Hunting and fishing are permitted in season.

Camping Regulations: Camping is allowed in most parts of the forest, as are campfires, except where posted otherwise. Campsites should be at least 100 feet from trails and 200 feet from roads. A permit is required only for campers who choose to spend more than one night at any campsite.

For Further Information: Wyoming State Forest, Old Berwick Road, Bloomsburg, PA 17815.

GALLITZIN STATE FOREST—15,336 acres. Consisting of two tracts of land in southwest Pennsylvania, hilly Gallitzin State Forest has mixed hardwood forests, streams, and wildlife including black bear. There's a designated Wild Area, the Clear Shape Wild Area, and the Charles F. Lewis Natural Area features a gorge with waterfalls.

Activities: Backpacking and hiking are possible on several easy to moderate trails. Cross-country skiing is a winter option here. Fishing is available, and hunting is permitted in season.

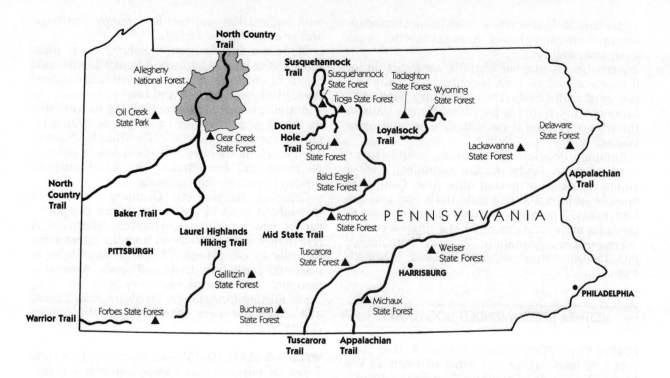

Map of Pennsylvania showing trails and state forests, including North Country Trail, Allegheny National Forest, Oil Creek State Park, Clear Creek State Forest, Susquehannock Trail, Susquehannock State Forest, Tioga State Forest, Tiadaghton State Forest, Wyoming State Forest, Delaware State Forest, Donut Hole Trail, Sproul State Forest, Loyalsock Trail, Lackawanna State Forest, Appalachian Trail, Bald Eagle State Forest, Baker Trail, Laurel Highlands Hiking Trail, Mid State Trail, Rothrock State Forest, PENNSYLVANIA, PITTSBURGH, Tuscarora State Forest, Weiser State Forest, Gallitzin State Forest, HARRISBURG, Michaux State Forest, PHILADELPHIA, Forbes State Forest, Buchanan State Forest, Warrior Trail, Tuscarora Trail, Appalachian Trail.

Camping Regulations: Campers are asked to call or visit the forest office for information and to register plans, indicating where they will be camping and when. Maximum stay allowed is two nights. It's recommended that group size be limited to four.

Most parts of the forest are open to camping, but there are restricted areas. Campsites must be at least 50 yards from trails and 200 yards from roads and water sources. Campfires are generally allowed, but may be prohibited when conditions are dry.

For Further Information: Gallitzin State Forest, 131 Hillcrest Drive, Ebensburg, PA 15931; (814)472-8320.

CLEAR CREEK STATE FOREST—10,000 acres. Clear Creek State Forest is made up of several units in northwest Pennsylvania, including lands adjacent to Allegheny National Forest and along the Allegheny River. In the region are hardwood forests with streams, and among the wildlife are white-tailed deer, black bear, and wild turkey.

Activities: Hiking and backpacking are available on about 47 miles of easy to moderate trails, and there are some 11 miles of trails for cross-country skiing. Horseback riding is also possible, and canoeing on the river is another option. Hunting and fishing are permitted in season.

Camping Regulations: Camping and campfires are generally allowed, except where posted otherwise. Campsites should be at least 100 feet from trails and 200 feet from roads. Camping more than one night at any campsite requires a permit.

For Further Information: Clear Creek State Forest, P.O. Box 705, Clarion, PA 16214; (814)226-1901.

LACKAWANNA STATE FOREST—8,100 acres. This state forest in northeast Pennsylvania includes small forested mountains, with a number of creeks and spruce bogs. Deer, bear, and wild turkey are among the wildlife.

Activities: The main trail here for backpacking and hiking is the 23-mile Pinchot Trail. Limited cross-country skiing is also available. Hunting and fishing are permitted in season.

Camping Regulations: A free camping permit is required, and available from the forest office in person or by mail. Maximum stay is two nights. Camping is allowed in most areas of the forest, except where posted otherwise.

Campsites must be at least 50 yards from trails and 100 yards from roads. Groups should be no larger than four. Campfires are generally permitted, but sometimes are banned during dry periods.

For Further Information: Lackawanna State Forest, State Office Building, Room 401, 100 Lackawanna Avenue, Scranton, PA 18503; (717)963-4561.

OIL CREEK STATE PARK—7,007 acres. Located in northwestern Pennsylvania, this state park has hilly terrain with hardwood and hemlock forests, swamps, and a number of creeks. Included are 12 miles of Oil Creek, a large and scenic stream.

Activities: There's a 36-mile loop trail for hiking and backpacking. The trail runs along both sides of Oil Creek. Some 15 miles of additional trails are available for cross-country skiing in winter. Canoeing is possible on Oil Creek, and fishing is another option. Hunting is permitted in a portion of the park.

Camping Regulations: Camping is restricted to two designated camping areas which are located along the main trail. Each area has several shelters. Reservations must be made through the park office prior to using the sites. Maximum stay allowed at each camping area is one night.

For Further Information: Oil Creek State Park, RD 1, Box 207, Oil City, PA 16301; (814)676-5915.

WEISER STATE FOREST—17,961 acres. This state forest in eastern Pennsylvania consists of eight relatively small tracts of land. The forested terrain includes some rugged mountain ridges and valleys, with several streams.

Activities: Hiking and backpacking are available on a short section of the Appalachian Trail and a few other trails. Fishing is possible, and hunting is permitted in season.

Camping Regulations: Backpack camping is allowed in the forest. A permit is not required, but camping is limited to one night per site. The only designated campsite is a shelter along the Appalachian Trail.

Small campfires are permitted except when forest fire danger is high. Backpackers must be careful not to stray onto adjacent State Game Lands, where camping is strictly prohibited.

For Further Information: Weiser State Forest, P.O. Box 99, Cressona, PA 17929; (717)385-2545.

In addition, camping for canoeists is allowed at designated sites along 40 miles of the Delaware River, within the Delaware Water Gap National Recreation Area, on Pennsylvania's eastern border. No permits or fees are required. For information contact the Delaware Water Gap National Recreation Area, Bushkill, PA 18324; (717)588-2435.

MAJOR BACKPACKING TRAILS

APPALACHIAN TRAIL—230 miles in Pennsylvania (2,100 total). This important National Scenic Trail enters Pennsylvania from Maryland, crosses the southeastern part of the state, and exits into New Jersey. It passes through state forest, state park, and state game lands.

The trail follows low mountain ridges, offering nice views and scenery along the way. Elevations rarely exceed 2,000 feet, and are generally under 1,600 feet. Difficulty is mostly easy to moderate, but the footing is often extremely rocky.

Camping Regulations: A number of shelters and established campsites are located along the trail. Campfires are allowed at these sites but discouraged. A stove is recommended for cooking.

When the trail is on state forest lands, camping is allowed almost anywhere, but campsites should be at least 100 feet from the trail, 200 feet from roads, and well away from water sources. Camping in state parks is limited to designated sites.

On state game lands camping is allowed only within 200 feet of the Appalachian Trail. Campsites must also be at least 500 feet from water sources. Campfires are not allowed on game lands, and the maximum stay per site is one night.

For Further Information: Appalachian Trail Conference, P.O. Box 807, Harpers Ferry, WV 25425.

NORTH COUNTRY TRAIL—Currently under construction, this major National Scenic Trail will some day run 3,200 miles, stretching from New York to North Dakota. The Pennsylvania portion will be about 180 miles long, traversing the northwestern part of the state, an area of rolling hills and valleys.

Difficulty generally ranges from easy to moderate. The major section now completed and open is the 95-mile segment through Allegheny National Forest. The trail also passes through three state parks, and crosses state forest and private lands. It coincides with the Baker Trail (see entry page 252) for a distance.

Camping Regulations: Some established campsites are located along the trail. In Allegheny National Forest camping is allowed elsewhere as well, except where posted otherwise. Campsites should be well off the trail and away from water sources.

Similarly, in state forests it's possible to camp where one wishes. Here campsites should be at least 100 feet from the trail and 200 feet from roads. In state parks and on private lands, however, camping is restricted to designated sites.

For Further Information: North Country Trail Association, P.O. Box 311, White Cloud, MI 49349.

MID STATE TRAIL—168 miles. The Mid State Trail crosses a portion of central Pennsylvania, following rocky and narrow ridges through several state forests, along with some state parks and state game lands. There are many views. Difficulty ranges from easy to strenuous.

Camping Regulations: Much of the trail is on state forest lands. Here camping and campfires are generally allowed, except where posted otherwise. Campsites should be at least 100 feet from the trail and 200 feet from roads. A permit is required only if one wishes to stay for more than one night at any campsite.

Camping is prohibited in some locations, such as the designated state forest Natural Areas which the trail passes through. It's also not allowed on state game lands. Camping is restricted to campgrounds in the state parks.

For Further Information: Mid State Trail Association, P.O. Box 167, Boalsburg, PA 16827. A trail guidebook with maps is available from this organization.

BAKER TRAIL—141 miles. This trail winds through forests, woodlands, and farmlands in western Pennsylvania, following old roads and paths. Much of the trail is on private lands. It connects with the North Country Trail in Allegheny National Forest.

Camping Regulations: There are 10 shelters located on side trails along the way. The shelters are not indicated by signs, so a trail guidebook may be essential in locating them. Other established sites are found along the trail as well.

Where the trail is on private lands, camping is restricted to these designated sites. Camping is prohibited on state game lands. Campfires should be built only in existing fire rings, and a stove is recommended. Groups should be kept to a maximum of 10.

For Further Information: Baker Trail Chairperson, AYH, Pittsburgh Council, 6300 Fifth Avenue, Pittsburgh, PA 15232. A guidebook with maps is available from this organization.

TUSCARORA TRAIL—105 miles. The Tuscarora Trail runs through southern Pennsylvania, connecting with the Appalachian Trail as well as Maryland's Big Blue Trail. Terrain along the way is sometimes rugged, and the underbrush is often thick.

About 40 miles of the trail are on Tuscarora Mountain. It traverses Tuscarora State Forest and Buchanan State Forest, and also passes through two state parks, some state game lands, and private lands. Difficulty ranges from easy to strenuous.

Camping Regulations: There's just one shelter along the trail, but camping and campfires are allowed elsewhere. Camping is limited to designated sites, however, when the trail is in state parks, on state game lands, and on private lands.

In the state forests camping is allowed almost anywhere, except where posted otherwise. Campsites should be at least 100 feet from the trail and 200 feet from roads, and a permit is required in order to stay for more than one night at a campsite.

For Further Information: Keystone Trails Association, Box 251, Cogan Station, PA 17728. A guidebook to the Tuscarora Trail is available from this trail association.

SUSQUEHANNOCK TRAIL—85 miles. This trail forms a huge loop in Susquehannock State Forest, which is located in north-central Pennsylvania. The trail is relatively easy, as it follows fire trails and old logging roads much of the way. It also intersects with the Black Forest and Donut Hole Trails.

Camping Regulations: Camping and campfires are allowed along most sections of the trail, except where posted otherwise. There are no designated campsites or shelters.

Campsites should be at least 100 feet from the trail and 200 feet from roads. A permit is necessary if one chooses to remain for more than one night at a campsite.

For Further Information: Susquehannock Trail Club, P.O. Box 643, Coudersport, PA 16915. A trail guide with maps may be obtained from this club.

LAUREL HIGHLANDS HIKING TRAIL—70 miles. This scenic and popular trail follows 2,700-foot Laurel Ridge in southwest Pennsylvania, running from the Conemaugh River Gorge to the Youghiogheny River Gorge. Included are fine views and some rugged terrain. Difficulty ranges from easy to strenuous.

Substantial portions of the trail fall within 13,625-acre Laurel Ridge State Park, which consists of a number of separate tracts along the ridge. It also crosses state forest and state game lands

About 35 miles of the trail are suitable for cross-country skiing in winter.

Camping Regulations: Eight designated camping areas are located along the trail at regular intervals. Each consists of several shelters as well as tentsites. Camping and campfires are restricted to these areas. Maximum stay allowed in each area is one night.

Those who wish to backpack along the trail must make advance reservations, available by phone or mail up to 30 days ahead of time. It's also necessary to register for specific camping areas, which may be done at the park office upon arrival or by phone.

For Further Information: Laurel Ridge State Park, RD 3, Box 246, Rockwood, PA 15557; (412)455-3744. A guidebook for this trail is available from the Sierra Club, P.O. Box 8241, Pittsburgh, PA 15217.

LOYALSOCK TRAIL—59 miles. The Loyalsock Trail traverses state forests, a state park, and some private lands in north-central Pennsylvania. It follows mountain ridges and alongside streams, and also passes a few lakes and ponds. Some of the route is rugged, with some fine vistas. Difficulty ranges from easy to strenuous.

Camping Regulations: Camping and campfires are allowed freely along the trail when it's on state forest lands, except where posted otherwise. Campsites should be at least 100 feet from the trail and 200 feet from roads.

A permit is required in order to remain more than one night at any campsite in a state forest. In Worlds End State Park camping is restricted to a campground. Camping is prohibited on the private lands which the trail passes through.

For Further Information: Alpine Club of Williamsport, P.O. Box 501, Williamsport, PA 17703.

DONUT HOLE TRAIL—59 miles. This trail arcs around the northern part of Sproul State Forest, in north-central Pennsylvania. Elevations along the trail range from 810 feet to 2,100 feet—with a few steep climbs, wild scenery, and some nice views. One section coincides with the Susquehannock Trail, and it connects with other trails as well.

Camping Regulations: Camping and campfires are allowed almost anywhere along the trail, except where posted otherwise. Campsites should be at least 200 feet from roads and 100 feet from the trail. A permit is required if one wishes to stay for more than a single night at any campsite.

For Further Information: Sproul State Forest,

HCR 62, Box 90, Renovo, PA 17764; (717)923-1450.

WARRIOR TRAIL—67 miles. Running over rolling terrain and along a ridge, this trail follows an ancient route used by Indians. It crosses the southwest corner of Pennsylvania and then enters West Virginia, terminating at the Ohio River. For most of its length the trail is on private property.

Camping Regulations: Four trail shelters are located along the trail, and these are available on a first-come, first-served basis. Camping is restricted to these sites.

For Further Information: Warrior Trail Association, c/o Lucille Phillips, RD 1, Box 35, Spraggs, PA 15362.

PENNSYLVANIA CAMPING RESOURCES

ORGANIZATIONS WHICH OFFER WILDERNESS CAMPING TRIPS

American Youth Hostels, Pittsburgh Council, 6300 Fifth Avenue, Pittsburgh, PA 15232. This AYH council sponsors a number of backpacking, canoe-camping, cross-country skiing, and other trips involving wilderness camping.

Appalachian Mountain Club, Delaware Valley Chapter, c/o Alan Kahn, 1601 School House Road, Gwynedd Valley, PA 19437. Beginners Backpacker Workshops as well as backpacking and other overnight trips are offered by this AMC chapter.

Sierra Club, Allegheny Group, P.O. Box 8241, Pittsburgh, PA 15217. The Allegheny Group of the Sierra Club offers a Basic Backpacking course and some backpacking trips.

USEFUL GUIDEBOOKS

Fifty Hikes in Central Pennsylvania—Thwaites, Tom. Woodstock, VT: Backcountry Publications, 1985.

Fifty Hikes in Eastern Pennsylvania—Hoffman, Carolyn. Woodstock, VT: Backcountry Publications, 1982.

Fifty Hikes in Western Pennsylvania—Thwaites, Tom. Woodstock, VT: Backcountry Publications, 1983.

Guide to the Appalachian Trail in Pennsylvania—Keystone Trails Association, 1989.

Hiking Guide to Western Pennsylvania—Sundquist, Bruce. American Youth Hostels, 1986.

Pennsylvania Hiking Trails—Cogan Station, PA: Keystone Trails Association, 1987.

INFORMATION ABOUT STATE PARK CAMPGROUNDS
Pennsylvania Bureau of State Parks, P.O. Box 8551, Harrisburg, PA 17105; (800)63-PARKS.

STATE HIGHWAY MAP AND TRAVEL INFORMATION
Pennsylvania Department of Commerce, P.O. Box 61, Warrendale, PA 15086; (800) VISIT-PA.

SOUTH CAROLINA

BEST AREAS FOR WILDERNESS CAMPING

SUMTER NATIONAL FOREST—360,000 acres. Sumter National Forest consists of three separate parcels of land in northwest South Carolina. Much of this part of the state is hilly, and near the North Carolina border the terrain is ruggedly mountainous.

There are numerous streams and waterfalls here, along with a major stretch of the Chattooga National Wild and Scenic River, which runs along the Georgia border. Forests include hardwoods and pine, with a few small stands of old-growth trees.

Sumter has one designated wilderness area, the 7,012-acre Ellicott Rock Wilderness, which extends into nearby North Carolina and Georgia. Deer, fox, and wild turkey are among the wildlife found in this National Forest.

Activities: Backpacking and hiking are possible on over 200 miles of trails. Included are a portion of the 75-mile Foothills Trail (see entry page 256), a section of the Bartram Trail, and 16 miles of the 37-mile Chattooga Trail, which follows the Chattooga River. Difficulty ranges from easy to strenuous.

Among other trails in this National Forest are the 26-mile Long Cane Trail loop and the 28-mile Buncombe Trail loop, which are also open to horseback riders and mountain bikers.

The Chattooga River is famous for whitewater rafting, canoeing, and kayaking, and has some challenging stretches. Canoeing is available on some other rivers and streams as well. Fishing is possible, and hunting is permitted in season.

Camping Regulations: Designated campsites are found along many of the trails. Camping is allowed elsewhere, as are campfires, but a free permit is generally required for camping at other than established sites. Low-impact practices are strongly encouraged. Groups should be no larger than 10.

An exception to the permit policy is made for two areas. No permit is required for camping in the Ellicott Rock Wilderness, or in the Chattooga River corridor, which extends one-quarter mile on either side of the river. One may camp almost anywhere in those areas, but sites must be at least 50 feet from streams, trails, and the river, and at least one-quarter mile from roads.

For Further Information: Sumter National Forest, P.O. Box 2227, Columbia, SC 29202; (803)765-5222.

FRANCIS MARION NATIONAL FOREST—250,000 acres. Situated in southeastern South Carolina, near the Atlantic coast, Francis Marion National Forest has elevations just above sea level. There are four small designated wilderness areas here. The region includes many swamps and boggy areas, along with attractive forests of hardwoods and longleaf pine. Deer, bear, and wild turkey are among the wildlife.

Activities: This National Forest has two major trails for hiking and backpacking: the 20-mile Swamp Fox National Recreation Trail and the 20-mile Jericho Trail. The latter is open to horses. These trails tend to stay very wet during rainy seasons.

Canoeing is available on some creeks and rivers in the area, and fishing is also possible. Hunting is permitted in season, but only in some parts of the National Forest at any one time.

Camping Regulations: There are some established campsites, and camping as well as campfires are allowed at these sites without a permit.

Camping is also allowed elsewhere in the forest, but a free permit must first be obtained from a forest office. Low-impact practices are recommended.

For Further Information: Francis Marion National Forest, P.O. Box 2227, Columbia, SC 29202; (803)765-5222.

OTHER RECOMMENDED LOCATIONS

MOUNTAIN BRIDGE WILDERNESS AND RECREATION AREA—11,000 acres. Located in the northwest corner of South Carolina, the Mountain Bridge Wilderness and Recreation Area consists of two state parks—7,476-acre Caesars Head State Park and 3,346-acre Jones Gap State Park—along with three small nature preserves.

Caesars Head State Park includes mountainous terrain with rocky outcroppings, whereas Jones Gap State Park is in a valley. Of particular interest is Raven Cliff Falls, a 420-foot cascade. Much of the area is hardwood-forested, with rhododendron and mountain laurel. Among the wildlife are deer, bear, and fox.

Activities: There are over 25 miles of trails for hiking and backpacking, and the 85-mile Foothills Trail (see entry below) terminates here. Difficulty ranges from easy to strenuous.

Fishing is available along the river, and limited seasonal hunting is permitted in a portion of the area. Mountain biking is restricted to roads.

Camping Regulations: Camping is allowed along just one trail, the 5.3-mile-long and moderately-strenuous Jones Gap Trail, which follows the beautiful Middle Saluda River.

Campers must register at one of the two park offices at either end of the Jones Gap Trail. There are 17 designated campsites along the trail, and these are assigned in advance. A nominal fee is charged. Existing fire rings must be used for campfires. No-trace camping practices are encouraged.

For Further Information: Mountain Bridge Wilderness and Recreation Area, c/o Caesars Head State Park, 8155 Geer Highway, Cleveland, SC 29635; (803)836-6115.

KEOWEE–TOXAWAY STATE PARK—1,000 acres. This small state park is located in the foothills of the Blue Ridge Mountains, in the northwest part of South Carolina. It's on the shore of 18,500-acre Lake Keowee. There are hills and rock outcrops, with oak-hickory forest and some pine, plus many streams. Wildlife includes deer and bobcat.

Activities: Hiking and backpacking are possible on the easy-to-moderate 4-mile Raven Rock Trail, along with two shorter trails. Fishing is available along the lakeshore. Hunting is prohibited.

Camping Regulations: Trailside camping is permitted only at designated sites along the Raven Rock Trail. Campfires are limited to authorized fire circles. It's necessary to register at the park office, and a nominal camping fee is charged.

For Further Information: Keowee–Toxaway State Park, 108 Residence Drive, Sunset, SC 29685; (803)868-2605.

CAPERS ISLAND—2,250 acres. Capers Island is a relatively pristine 3.3-mile-long Barrier Island which is located off the coast of South Carolina, just south of Francis Marion National Forest. Access is only by private boat.

The island has some beautiful sandy beach, dunes, freshwater ponds, marshes, swamps, and forested areas. Wildlife includes white-tailed deer and alligator. The island suffered damage from Hurricane Hugo in 1989.

Activities: Hiking is available along the beach and on old roads. Hunting and inland fishing are not permitted.

Camping Regulations: Camping and campfires are restricted to two designated camping areas. A camping permit is required, and this may be obtained by mail. Pets are prohibited.

For Further Information: Capers Island, c/o South Carolina Wildlife and Marine Resources Department, P.O. Box 12559, Charleston, SC 29422; (803)795-6350.

MAJOR BACKPACKING TRAILS

FOOTHILLS TRAIL—75 miles. This National Recreation Trail is South Carolina's longest trail. It runs from Oconee State Park to Table Rock State Park, crossing the area north of 7,656-acre Lake Jocassee, in the northwest corner of the state. A spur trail connects it to Caesars Head State Park.

A section of the trail is in Sumter National Forest, and it also enters North Carolina's Nantahala National Forest. Fully half of the trail is on Duke Power Company lands. Some of the area's terrain is rugged, and the scenery often outstanding.

The trail crosses a number of rivers and passes near the upper part of 800-foot Whitewater Falls, a series of cascades and falls, said to be the highest in the East. Difficulty ranges from easy to strenuous. Horses and mountain bikes are not allowed on the trail.

Mountain Bridge
Wilderness and
Recreation Area · Foothills Trail

· GREENVILLE

Keeowee-Toxaway
State Park

Sumter
National Forest

SOUTH CAROLINA

· COLUMBIA

Francis Marion
National Forest

Capers Island

Camping Regulations: A number of designated campsites are available along the trail. On some sections camping is allowed elsewhere as well, although sites should be at least 100 feet from the trail and preferably out of sight. In the state parks and Sumter National Forest, camping and campfires are restricted to established sites. No permits are necessary.

For Further Information: Foothills Trail Conference, P.O. Box 3041, Greenville, SC 29602. A trail guidebook with maps is available from this organization.

SOUTH CAROLINA CAMPING RESOURCES

ORGANIZATIONS WHICH OFFER WILDERNESS
CAMPING TRIPS
Sierra Club, South Carolina Chapter, P.O. Box 12112, Columbia, SC 29211; (803)256-8487. This Sierra Club chapter offers backpacking, canoe camping, and other wilderness camping trips. Included are trips for beginners.

USEFUL GUIDEBOOKS
Guide to the Foothills Trail—Greenville, SC: The Foothills Trail Conference, 1988.
South Carolina Hiking Trails—de Hart, Allen. Charlotte, NC: The East Woods Press, 1984.

INFORMATION ABOUT CAMPGROUNDS IN STATE
PARKS
South Carolina Division of State Parks, Edgar Brown Building, 1205 Pendleton Street, Columbia, SC 29201; (803)734-0156.

STATE HIGHWAY MAP AND TRAVEL INFORMATION
South Carolina Division of Tourism, Box 71, Columbia, SC 29202; (803)734-0235.

SOUTH DAKOTA

BEST AREAS FOR WILDERNESS CAMPING

BLACK HILLS NATIONAL FOREST—1,200,000 acres. Located in the Black Hills of west and southwest South Dakota, this National Forest is a scenic area of high mountains, rocky knobs and needles, limestone cliffs and canyons. It's home to 7,242-foot Harney Peak, highest elevation east of the Rockies.

The famous Mount Rushmore National Memorial is located within the National Forest boundaries. Also here is the 27,760-acre Norbeck Wildlife Preserve, which includes a designated wilderness area, the 10,700-acre Black Elk Wilderness.

There are numerous small streams, a few lakes, meadows and grasslands, and forests of ponderosa pine and spruce, oak and aspen. Wildlife includes white-tailed and mule deer, bighorn sheep, elk, and mountain goat.

Activities: Hiking and backpacking are available on over 180 miles of trails, including 63 miles of the 111-mile Centennial Trail (see entry page 260). Difficulty ranges from easy to strenuous.

Many trails are open to horseback riding and mountain biking. Cross-country skiing is possible during winter. Fishing is also available, and hunting is permitted in season.

Camping Regulations: Camping is allowed throughout the forest, except near public recreation areas or where posted otherwise. No permits are necessary. Campfires are prohibited. Campsites should be at least 100 feet from streams, and preferably out of sight of trails.

For Further Information: Black Hills National Forest, RR 2, Box 200, Custer, SD 57730; (605)673-2251.

BADLANDS NATIONAL PARK—244,000 acres. Situated in southwest South Dakota, this National Park includes the largest area of prairie wilderness in the United States. It's surrounded by the lands of Buffalo Gap National Grasslands and the Pine Ridge Indian Reservation.

The unusual landscape here includes barren badlands, with knife-edged ridges, rock forms and spires, steep buttes and deep canyons, with a few creeks. There's one designated wilderness area, the 64,250-acre Sage Creek Wilderness Area.

The park has extensive stretches of mixed-grass prairie, with some juniper and cottonwood trees, plus yucca and cactus. Wildlife includes bison, bighorn sheep, pronghorn antelope, mule deer, and coyote.

Activities: Backpacking and hiking are possible here, but there are only about 10 miles of established trails. Most of the park, including the Sage Creek Wilderness Area, is trailless. Cross-country travel is feasible on the open prairie. Horseback riding is allowed, and cross-country skiing is a winter option when there's enough snow.

Camping Regulations: Camping is allowed almost anywhere in this National Park, except within one-half mile of roads. Permits are not required, but it's recommended that backpackers check in at the visitor center before starting out. Campfires are prohibited. A stove must be brought if one wishes to cook. Drinking water must also be packed in.

For Further Information: Badlands National Park, P.O. Box 6, Interior, SD 57750; (605)433-5361.

WIND CAVE NATIONAL PARK—28,232 acres. Located next to Black Hills National Forest and Custer State Park, this National Park has a large system of underground limestone caves. Aboveground are prairie grasslands, forests of ponderosa pine, and a couple of creeks. Wildlife includes bison, elk, pronghorn, and mule deer.

Activities: About 28 miles of trails are available for backpacking or hiking. Included is a 6-mile segment of the 111-mile Centennial Trail (see entry page 260), which begins in this park. Difficulty varies from easy to strenuous. Horseback riding and mountain biking are not permitted in the backcountry.

Camping Regulations: Camping is allowed in most areas of the park. A backcountry camping permit is required, and may be obtained from the visitor center. Campfires are prohibited, so a stove should be carried for cooking.

For Further Information: Wind Cave National Park, Hot Springs, SD 57747; (605)745-4600.

NATIONAL GRASSLANDS IN SOUTH DAKOTA—South Dakota has three National Grasslands: Buffalo Gap National Grassland (556,997 acres) in southwest South Dakota, Fort Pierre National Grassland (115,998 acres) in the central part of the state, and Grand River National Grassland (162,086 acres) in the northwest.

Grand River National Grassland is administered by Custer National Forest in Montana, and the other two National Grasslands in the state are administered by Nebraska National Forest. All of the tracts are open to livestock grazing.

Within these areas are a few reservoirs, some streams, and several major rivers. The grasslands consist mainly of rolling mixed-grass prairie, with sagebrush, and some trees including cottonwood, elm, and ash along the waterways.

Grand River National Grassland also has ponderosa pine-covered buttes with massive rock formations, ridges and ravines, and badlands. Wildlife in the region includes white-tailed and mule deer, antelope, coyote, fox, prairie dog, and golden eagle.

Activities: Hiking, backpacking, and horseback riding are allowed, but there are no formal trails. Travel on other than old roads and paths must be cross-country. Canoeing is possible on the Grand River and a few other waterways. Fishing is available, and hunting is permitted in season.

Camping Regulations: Camping is generally unrestricted throughout the National Grasslands, except where posted otherwise. Campfires are allowed, but are subject to being banned during the dry season. No permits are necessary.

For Further Information: Buffalo Gap National Grassland and Fort Pierre National Grassland, c/o Nebraska National Forest, 270 Pine Street, Chadron, NE 69337; (308)432-3367. Grand River National Grassland, c/o Custer National Forest, P.O. Box 2556, Billings, MT 59103; (406)657-6361.

OTHER RECOMMENDED LOCATIONS

CUSTER STATE PARK—73,000 acres. Custer State Park is located in southwest South Dakota, adjacent to Black Hills National Forest. Portions of the park are mountainous, and there are also areas of

rolling prairie grasslands. Highest point is 6,023-foot Mount Coolidge.

Some of the more rugged terrain includes steep mountain ridges, rock pinnacles and formations, and deep canyons. An area of special scenic interest in the park is the 2,200-acre French Creek Natural Area.

There are also four lakes, a number of creeks, forests of ponderosa pine, and some hardwoods. Among the wildlife are bison, elk, bighorn sheep, pronghorn antelope, and deer.

Activities: Hiking and backpacking are possible on over 50 miles of trails, including 22 miles of the 111-mile Centennial Trail (see entry to right). Difficulty varies from easy to strenuous. Horseback riding is allowed on many trails. Rock climbing is popular on the granite pinnacles here. Fishing is available, and hunting is permitted in season.

Camping Regulations: Camping is restricted to two designated areas in the French Creek Natural Area. It's necessary to register at the visitor center before starting out. The number of campers allowed to use each area is limited.

A nominal fee is charged for camping each night, and a park entrance license fee must also be paid. Campfires are permitted only in the firegrates provided at the two camping areas.

For Further Information: Custer State Park, HC 83, Box 70, Custer, SD 57730; (605)255-4515.

BLM LANDS IN SOUTH DAKOTA—South Dakota has 280,000 acres of public lands which are administered by the BLM (U.S. Bureau of Land Management). Most of the acreage is in northwest South Dakota, and some of the areas are open to livestock grazing and forestry.

Camping and campfires are freely allowed on these lands, with the exception of a couple of small areas. For further information contact the Bureau of Land Management, 310 Roundup Street, Belle Fourche, SD 57717; (605)892-2526.

In addition, primitive camping is permitted along the shoreline of the Missouri River, which runs down through central South Dakota, and includes several reservoirs. This river is part of the Lewis and Clark National Historic Trail.

For information about canoeing and camping on the Missouri and other rivers in South Dakota, contact the South Dakota Department of Game, Fish, and Parks, 445 E. Capitol Ave., Pierre, SD 57501; (605)773-3391.

MAJOR BACKPACKING TRAILS

CENTENNIAL TRAIL—111 miles. This fine trail was opened in 1989. It runs in a north-south direction through western South Dakota, leading from Bear Butte State Park to Wind Cave National Park. Scenery and vegetation along the way are quite varied.

Over half of the trail is on Black Hills National Forest lands, with other segments in Wind Cave National Park, Custer State Park, Bear Butte State Park, and the Fort Meade Recreation Area, which is administered by the Bureau of Land Management.

Difficulty ranges from easy to moderate. Horseback riding is permitted along the trail outside of Wind Cave National Park. Mountain biking is likewise allowed except in Wind Cave National Park and the Black Elk Wilderness of Black Hills National Forest.

Camping Regulations: Camping is allowed almost anywhere along the trail on National Forest lands, except where posted otherwise. A permit is required for Wind Cave National Park, and in Custer State Park camping is restricted to designated sites.

Trailside camping is not allowed in Bear Butte State Park or the Fort Meade Recreation Area. Campfires are permitted only at designated camping areas or in established campgrounds.

For Further Information: South Dakota Department of Game, Fish, and Parks, HC 83, Box 70, Custer, SD 57730; (605)255-4515.

SOUTH DAKOTA CAMPING RESOURCES

INFORMATION ABOUT STATE PARK CAMPGROUNDS
South Dakota Department of Game, Fish, and Parks, 445 E. Capitol Avenue, Pierre, SD 57501; (605)773-3391.

STATE HIGHWAY MAP AND TRAVEL INFORMATION
South Dakota Division of Tourism, 711 Wells Avenue, Pierre, SD 57501; (800)843-1930 (out of state)/(800)952-2217 (in state).

TENNESSEE

BEST AREAS FOR WILDERNESS CAMPING

GREAT SMOKY MOUNTAINS NATIONAL PARK— 244,100 acres in Tennessee (520,000 acres total). This spectacular National Park lies along the eastern border of Tennessee, and half of the park is in North Carolina. It's the most heavily visited National Park in the entire country.

Consisting of an ancient mountain range, the Great Smokies are among the loftiest and most massive mountains in the East. Top elevation here is 6,643-foot Clingman's Dome, second highest summit east of the Mississippi.

Sixteen other mountains stand over 6,000 feet. Included are some grassy, open "balds." Panoramic views are common. Hundreds of miles of streams flow through the area, with many waterfalls. Most of the park consists of designated wilderness.

Flora and fauna are incredibly varied. There are conifers at higher elevations and deciduous forests below. Included are some old-growth stands. Among the wildlife are black bear, deer, wild boar, bobcat, and fox.

Activities: Backpacking and hiking are available on over 850 miles of trails, including a 69-mile segment of the Appalachian Trail (see entry page 264), which leads along the high ridgetops, and the 43-mile Lakeshore Trail paralleling enormous Fontana Lake.

Some trails are designated for horseback riding. Cross-country skiing is possible on trails here during the winter. Bike use is limited to roads. Fishing is also available. Hunting is prohibited.

Camping Regulations: A free permit is required in order to camp in the backcountry, and may be obtained from any ranger station. It's necessary to specify in advance where one will camp each night. Pets are not allowed.

Scores of designated campsites, including 18 shelters, are scattered throughout the park. All camping and campfires are restricted to these authorized locations.

Reservations are available for some of the shelters and campsites, and may be made by calling (615) 436-1231 up to one month in advance. Reservations are essential for sites which are in heavy demand, including those along the Appalachian Trail.

Permits must be picked up in person. Shelters may be used for one night only, whereas most other campsites are available for up to three nights. Group size is limited to a maximum of eight.

The park's bears are known to be unusually aggressive in trying to obtain food from campers. Extra care should be taken to keep food properly hung and away from tents.

For Further Information: Great Smoky Mountains National Park, Gatlinburg, TN 37738; (615)436-5615.

CHEROKEE NATIONAL FOREST—625,000 acres. Made up of tracts both north and south of Great Smoky Mountains National Park, this National Forest stretches along the Tennessee–North Carolina border from Georgia to Virginia. The mountainous region includes rugged terrain.

There are five major rivers, a number of lakes, and many streams and waterfalls. Forests consist of hardwoods as well as conifers, and there's rhododendron and mountain laurel. Black bear, white-tailed deer, and wild boar are among the wildlife.

Designated wilderness areas here include the 15,000-acre Citico Wilderness, the 5,000-acre Big Frog Wilderness, the 3,900-acre Bald River Gorge Wilderness, plus several smaller wilderness areas.

Activities: Hiking and backpacking are possible on over 640 miles of trails, including more than 130 miles of the Appalachian Trail (see entry page 264), and also the 16-mile John Muir National Recreation Trail. Difficulty ranges from easy to very strenuous.

The five rivers have stretches of white-water, and are suitable for canoeing, kayaking, and rafting. A number of local outfitters offer river trips.

Some trails are open to horseback riding. There are eight miles of designated bike trails, and mountain biking is possible on old roads and some other trails. Fishing is available along rivers, streams, and lakes. Hunting is permitted in season.

Camping Regulations: Camping and campfires are freely allowed throughout this National Forest, except near public use areas or where posted otherwise. No permits are required.

For Further Information: Cherokee National Forest, P.O. Box 2010, 2800 North Ocoee Street, Cleveland, TN 37320; (615)476-9700.

BIG SOUTH FORK NATIONAL RIVER AND RECREATION AREA—120,000 acres. This National River and Recreation Area features the Big South Fork of the Cumberland River and several tributaries. It's located near and alongside the northeast border of Tennessee, and extends into southeast Kentucky.

The river flows through a rugged cliff-lined gorge, and there's a large area of protected land on either side. Included here are sandstone arches, caves, and creeks with waterfalls.

Activities: The Cumberland River is very popular for white-water canoeing, kayaking, and rafting. Commercial rafting outfits run trips on the river.

There are over 100 miles of trails for backpacking and hiking, including a section of the 257-mile Sheltowee Trace Trail (see entry page 160). Difficulty varies from easy to strenuous.

Some trails are open to horseback riding. Horses may be rented in the area, and guided horse trips are available. Fishing is possible along the river and streams. Hunting is permitted in season.

Camping Regulations: Camping is allowed throughout the area, as are campfires, except where otherwise prohibited. No permits are required. A stove is recommended for cooking.

For Further Information: Big South Fork National River and Recreation Area, P.O. Drawer 630, Oneida, TN 37841.

LAND BETWEEN THE LAKES—170,000 acres. Managed by the Tennessee Valley Authority, and surrounded on three sides by two huge lakes (Kentucky Lake and Lake Barkley), this is an enormous, 40-mile-long peninsula. It's located both in southwest Kentucky and northwest Tennessee.

Terrain here is gently hilly, with a maximum elevation change of only 200 feet. There are woodlands, some inland lakes and ponds, and wildlife including deer, bison (which are restricted to a 200-acre range), bobcat, and wild turkey.

Activities: Backpacking and hiking are available on some 200 miles of easy to moderate trails. Included are the 60-mile North–South Trail, which extends the length of the peninsula, and the 26-mile Fort Henry National Recreation Trail, which forms a series of loops. The area has about 30 miles of horse trails. Fishing is available, and hunting is permitted in season.

Camping Regulations: There's a series of trail shelters along the North–South Trail. Camping is allowed elsewhere as well on the peninsula, as are campfires, except where posted otherwise. No permits or fees are required. Campsites should be at least 50 feet from trails. Backpackers are asked to check in at one of three welcome stations and leave their itinerary.

For Further Information: Land Between the Lakes, 100 Van Morgan Drive, Golden Pond, KY 42211; (502)924-5602.

OTHER RECOMMENDED LOCATIONS

SOUTH CUMBERLAND STATE RECREATION AREA— 12,000 acres. Situated at the southern end of the Cumberland Plateau, in south-central Tennessee, this scenic state recreation area consists of seven separate tracts of land. Largest by far is the 11,400-acre Savage Gulf Natural Area.

Savage Gulf includes virgin forest and three deep "gulfs" (gorges) overlooked by sandstone cliffs, with large streams and waterfalls. Throughout the recreation area are oak-hickory forests with pine and hemlock, plus mountain laurel. Deer, bobcat, and fox are among the wildlife.

Activities: Hiking and backpacking are possible on 85 miles of trails in the area. Difficulty ranges from easy to strenuous. Rock climbing is available by permit from the ranger station. Limited hunting is allowed in season with a permit. Some trails are closed during deer hunting season.

Camping Regulations: Camping is restricted to nine backcountry camping areas in the Savage

Gulf Natural Area, and also three primitive camping areas by the 12-mile Fiery Gizzard Trail, which runs alongside the deep gorge of Fiery Gizzard Creek.

A camping permit is required, and may be obtained from a ranger station. A separate fire permit is necessary in order to have a campfire, which may be built only in established fire rings. Campfires are not allowed at some sites, and may be banned altogether in dry weather.

For Further Information: South Cumberland State Recreation Area, Route 1, Box 144-H, Tracy City, TN 37387; (615)924-2980.

FALL CREEK FALLS STATE RESORT PARK—15,800

acres. Fall Creek Falls State Resort Park is on the Cumberland Plateau of eastern Tennessee. The park is noted for some deep gorges with several waterfalls, including 256-foot Fall Creek Falls, and also has a large lake.

Forests are of oak and hickory, hemlock and popular, with mountain laurel and rhododendron. There are some stands of old-growth trees in Cane Creek Gorge. White-tailed deer, bobcat, and fox are among the wildlife.

Activities: The major trail here for backpacking and hiking is the 25-mile Cane Creek Overnight Trail, which forms two large loops, along with several miles of other trails. Horseback riding is possible on some trails, and horses may be rented in the park. Fishing is available, but hunting is not allowed.

Camping Regulations: Backcountry camping is restricted to three designated areas along the Cane Creek Overnight Trail. A permit must be obtained from the park nature center. A separate fire permit is required in order to have a campfire, which is allowed only in established fire rings. Pets are prohibited.

For Further Information: Fall Creek Falls State Resort Park, Route 3, Pikeville, TN 37367; (615)881-3297.

NATHAN BEDFORD FORREST STATE HISTORICAL

AREA—3,000 acres. Located in western Tennessee alongside 200,000-acre Kentucky Lake, which was created by damming up the Tennessee River, this state historical area has rugged ridges, hills, and hollows with creeks. The region is hardwood-forested, with azalea and dogwood. Wildlife includes deer and fox.

Activities: Hiking and backpacking are possible on over 30 miles of trails, including the 20-mile Tennessee Forrest Trail. Fishing is available by the lake. Seasonal hunting is allowed.

Camping Regulations: Camping is limited to several designated sites along the Tennessee Forrest Trail. A permit must be obtained from the park office. A fire permit is also necessary in order to build a fire. Bringing a stove is recommended.

For Further Information: Nathan Bedford Forrest State Historical Area, Eva, TN 38333; (901)584-6356.

BIG HILL POND STATE RUSTIC PARK—4,500 acres.

This state park in southwest Tennessee includes low hills, meadows, swamps, some small lakes and ponds, Cypress Creek, and the Tuscumbia River. It's forested with oak and elm, cypress and gum. Deer and wild turkey are among the wildlife.

Activities: There are 19 miles of trails for hiking and backpacking. Horses and pets are not allowed on trails. Fishing is available by permit. Hunting is possible in a portion of the park during the appropriate season.

Camping Regulations: Four shelters are located along the trails, and camping is restricted to these sites. Campers are asked to check in with a ranger at the time of entry. Campfires are allowed at the shelters, but bringing a stove is recommended.

For Further Information: Big Hill Pond State Rustic Park, Route 1, Pocahontas, TN 38061; (901)645-9275.

MONTGOMERY BELL STATE RESORT PARK—5,000

acres. Montgomery Bell State Resort Park is located west of Nashville, in west-central Tennessee. This is an area of hilly and hardwood-forested terrain, with some streams and several lakes. Deer and fox are among the wildlife.

Activities: There's a new 12-mile backpacking trail, and hiking is also allowed on 7 miles of other trails. Fishing is possible at the lakes. Hunting is prohibited.

Camping Regulations: Camping is limited to three shelters along the backpacking trail. A camping permit must be obtained from the park information office. Advance reservations are available and recommended.

A fire permit is required in order to build a campfire, and a special permit is required for groups of more than six. Stoves are recommended for cooking. Pets are not allowed.

For Further Information: Montgomery Bell State Resort Park, Burns, TN 37029; (615)797-9052.

LONG HUNTER STATE PARK—2,400 acres. Long

Hunter is located along the shore of J. Percy Priest Lake, a large reservoir which is east of Nashville, in central Tennessee. There are bluffs and rock

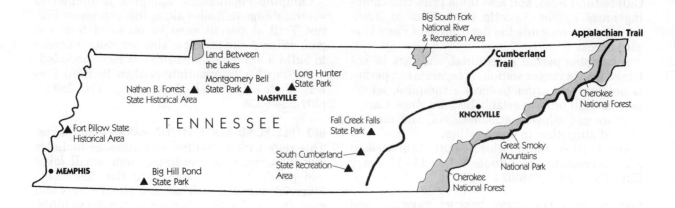

outcrops along the reservoir, and a forest of hardwoods with cedar.

Activities: Hiking and backpacking are possible on about 10 miles of trails. Fishing is available at the reservoir as well as along 100-acre Couchville Lake.

Camping Regulations: Backpack camping is allowed in one area of the park, along the Volunteer Trail in the 1,000-acre Bakers Grove Primitive Use Area. A permit is required, and may be obtained from the visitor center.

For Further Information: Long Hunter State Park, 2910 Hobson Pike, Hermitage, TN 37076; (615)885-2422.

FORT PILLOW STATE HISTORIC AREA—1,650 acres. Located along the Mississippi River in western Tennessee, this park protects an area which was historically important during the Civil War. Terrain is hilly, with hardwood forests and a small lake. Wildlife includes deer and wild turkey.

Activities: The park has 15 miles of trails for hiking or backpacking. Fishing is available by the river.

Camping Regulations: Primitive camping is allowed at a single designated area, one-half mile along the Chickasaw Bluff Trail, and situated on a bluff which overlooks the Mississippi River. A free permit is required from the park office. Campfires may be built in the fire rings provided.

For Further Information: Fort Pillow State Historic Area, Route 2, Box 108B-1, Henning, TN 38041; (901)738-5581.

Camping is also allowed along an 11-mile backpacking trail in 1,720-acre Cumberland Mountain State Park, in east-central Tennessee. For more information contact Cumberland Mountain State

Park, Route 8, Box 322, Crossville, TN 38555; (615)484-6138.

In addition, there's a single backpack camping area along an 8-mile trail loop in 1,067-acre Bob's Creek Pocket Wilderness, which is owned by the Bowater Corporation. For an informational booklet contact the Bowater Corporation, Calhoun, TN 37309.

Lastly, one trail in western Tennessee's Natchez Trace State Resort Park is open to backpacking, with primitive campsites available. For information contact Natchez Trace State Resort Park, Wildersville, TN 38388; (901)968-3742.

MAJOR BACKPACKING TRAILS

APPALACHIAN TRAIL—This important National Scenic Trail runs through northeast Tennessee for about 70 miles, then follows the Tennessee–North Carolina border for more than 200 miles. Included is a 70-mile stretch in Great Smoky Mountains National Park, with the highest elevation of the entire trail at Clingman's Dome (6,643 feet).

The mountainous and often rugged route in this state is among the most scenic sections of the whole trail. A number of open grassy "balds" offer magnificent panoramic views, and the trail traverses some unusually remote wilderness in the Smokies. Portions of the trail are quite steep and strenuous.

Camping Regulations: Shelters and other designated campsites are located every few miles along the trail. Much of the trail in Tennessee is on National Forest lands, and here camping is allowed almost anywhere, as are campfires. When camping at other than shelters or established areas, sites should be at least 100 feet from the trail and away from water sources.

Special rules apply for Great Smoky Mountains National Park. A permit is required, and it should be requested in advance (see the National Park entry page 220). Demand is high, and some permit requests for the Appalachian Trail are denied.

Backpackers must stay at trail shelters in the park, and tents may be set up outside only when a shelter is full. Shelters may be used for one night only. Trailside camping elsewhere along the Appalachian Trail is not permitted in this park.

Those who are backpacking the Appalachian Trail from well outside the park ("thru hikers") do not need to make reservations in advance. A permit may be obtained at the time of entering the park, and shelters do not have to be specified in advance.

For Further Information: Appalachian Trail Conference, P.O. Box 807, Harpers Ferry, WV 25425. *A Guide to the Appalachian Trail in Tennessee and North Carolina* is available from this organization.

CUMBERLAND TRAIL—This new State Scenic Trail, which is currently under construction, will be over 200 miles long when completed. It runs from Cumberland Gap National Historic Park, on the Kentucky and Virginia borders, to Signal Point National Military Park and Prentice Cooper State Forest, which are along the Tennessee River gorge near the Alabama and Georgia borders.

About half of the trail is now open. Difficulty ranges from easy to strenuous. It follows the mountainous eastern escarpment of the Cumberland Plateau, crossing some rugged terrain. Portions of the trail are on state lands, with some stretches along roads.

Camping Regulations: Camping is available at designated sites, which are located at intervals along the trail. Campfires are allowed at authorized campsites only, and may be prohibited during dry weather. A stove is recommended for cooking. Sections of the trail may be closed during deer hunting season.

For Further Information: Cumberland Scenic Trail Manager, Route 2, Box 505, Caryville, TN 37714; (615)566-0901.

TENNESSEE CAMPING RESOURCES

ORGANIZATIONS WHICH OFFER WILDERNESS CAMPING TRIPS

Smoky Mountains Hiking Club, P.O. Box 1454, Knoxville, TN 37901. This hiking club offers a few backpacking trips to the Smokies and other areas each year.

Tennessee Eastman Hiking and Canoeing Club, P.O. Box 511, Kingsport, TN 37662; (615)229-2005. The Tennessee Eastman club offers some backpacking and canoe-camping trips, and has limited camping equipment available. The club was organized for employees of the Tennessee Eastman Company, but others are welcome to join.

Tennessee Trails Association, P.O. Box 41446, Nashville, TN 37204. This trail association sponsors some backpacking trips, including trips for beginners.

USEFUL GUIDEBOOKS

Guide to the Appalachian Trail in Tennessee and North Carolina— Harpers Ferry, WV: The Appalachian Trail Conference, 1989.

Hiker's Guide to the Smokies—Muriless, Dick and Stallings, Constance. San Francisco: Sierra Club Books.

Hiking in the Great Smokies—Brewer, Carson. Great Smoky Mountains Natural History Association.

Tennessee Trails—Means, Evan. Chester, CT: The Globe Pequot Press, 1989.

Walks in the Great Smokies—Albright, Rodney and Priscilla. Old Saybrook, CT: The Globe Pequot Press.

INFORMATION ABOUT STATE PARK CAMPGROUNDS

Tennessee Division of Parks and Recreation, 701 Broadway, Nashville, TN 37243.

STATE HIGHWAY MAP AND TRAVEL INFORMATION

Tennessee Tourist Development, P.O. Box 23170, Nashville, TN 37202; (615)741-2158.

TEXAS

BEST AREAS FOR WILDERNESS CAMPING

BIG BEND NATIONAL PARK—708,200 acres. Bordering on the Rio Grande in southwest Texas, alongside the U.S.–Mexican boundary, Big Bend National Park contains the state's largest area of wilderness. Included here are the Chisos Mountains and other mountain ranges.

Highest point is 7,825-foot Emory Peak. There are also deep canyons with cliffs, rock formations, some badlands, open desert, grasslands, and wooded areas. Among the wildlife are mule deer, mountain lion, and bobcat.

Activities: Over 150 miles of trails are available for backpacking and hiking. Only about 30 miles of the trails are well-marked and easy to follow. Difficulty ranges from easy to strenuous. Hunting is not allowed in the park.

Camping Regulations: A free permit is required for backcountry camping. Permits must be obtained in person. A few parts of the park are closed to camping, and in the popular Chisos Mountain region camping is restricted to designated sites.

In other regions camping is allowed almost anywhere, but campsites must be at least 100 yards from trails and water sources, and one-half mile from roads and developed areas. Campfires are not permitted. A stove must be used if one wishes to cook. Water must normally be carried in. Pets are prohibited.

Weather changes in the park are sometimes dramatic. Since summer heat is often intense, and winter is often cold in the mountain regions, fall and spring are the best times to visit.

For Further Information: Big Bend National Park, TX 79834; (915)477-2251.

GUADALUPE MOUNTAINS NATIONAL PARK—76,920 acres. Situated in the Guadalupe Mountains of west Texas, this beautiful National Park includes steep ridges and peaks, numerous deep canyons, and areas of desert. The highest mountain in Texas, 8,749-foot Guadalupe Peak, is located here.

Vegetation ranges from desert varieties, such as yucca and cactus, to canyon hardwoods including maple and ash, madrone and pine, and highland conifers. Mule deer, black bear, elk, coyote, and mountain lion are among the wildlife.

Activities: There are about 80 miles of trails for backpacking and hiking. Some trails are not well-marked and may be difficult to follow. Horses are allowed on most trails.

Camping Regulations: Backcountry camping is restricted to 10 designated camping areas along trails in various parts of the park. A free permit must be obtained from one of the visitor centers or ranger stations. There are no advance reservations.

Campfires are prohibited, so a stove must be used for cooking. Water is scarce, and must usually be carried in. Pets are not allowed in the backcountry.

For Further Information: Guadalupe Mountains National Park, HC 60, Box 400, Salt Flat, TX 79847; (915)828-3251.

SAM HOUSTON NATIONAL FOREST—158,600 acres. Sam Houston National Forest is located in east Texas, in an area of almost flat terrain, with numerous streams and some lakes. It's forested primarily with pine and hardwoods. Wildlife includes bobcat, fox, and armadillo. There's one designated wilderness area, the Little Lake Creek Wilderness.

Activities: Hiking and backpacking are possible on the 140-mile Lone Star Trail (see entry page 271), which traverses the National Forest and includes a number of loops. There are also some shorter trails. Horses are allowed on trails, and woods roads are open to mountain biking. Fishing is available along streams and lakes. Hunting is permitted in season.

Camping Regulations: Camping and campfires are allowed almost anywhere, except near public recreation areas and where posted otherwise. No permits are necessary. Camping is restricted to designated areas during deer hunting season.

For Further Information: Sam Houston National Forest, Homer Garrison Federal Building, 701 North First Street, Lufkin, TX 75901; (409)639-8501.

BIG BEND RANCH STATE NATURAL AREA—263,905

acres. Located along the Big Bend of the Rio Grande, in southwest Texas, this huge State Natural Area has small mountains and mesas, deep canyons and caves, volcanic rocks, and other rugged Chihuahuan Desert scenery.

Vegetation includes grasslands along with yucca, cactus, and agave, and also some stands of trees. Among the wildlife here are mule deer, mountain lion, javelina, and golden eagle.

Activities: Backpacking and hiking are possible on about 30 miles of trails, including the 19-mile Rancherias Loop Trail. White-water rafting is available by permit on the Rio Grande, and fishing is also allowed along the river.

Camping Regulations: A permit is required in order to camp here, and visitors must specify an itinerary. Some established campsites are located along the trails.

It's also possible to camp elsewhere, except for a few areas which are off-limits to camping. Sites must be at least 300 feet from water sources and historic structures. Avoid drainages.

Campsites along the Rio Grande should be well above the high water mark. Campfires are not permitted, so a stove must be brought if one wishes to cook. Pets are prohibited.

For Further Information: Big Bend Ranch State Natural Area, P.O. Box 1180, Presidio, TX 79845.

DAVY CROCKETT NATIONAL FOREST—161,470

acres. This National Forest in east Texas has forests of hardwoods and pine, boggy areas, many creeks, some lakes, and includes the Neches River. There's one designated wilderness area, the 3,000-acre Big Slough Wilderness.

Activities: The longest trail here for hiking and backpacking is the 20-mile 4-C National Recreation Trail. This trail is closed to horses, but horseback riding is allowed on the Pine Creek Horse Trail, which forms several loops.

Canoeing is possible on some of the lakes, and also along the Big Slough Canoe Trail, which circles around the Big Slough Wilderness and includes a section of the Neches River. Canoes may be rented. Winter and spring are the best times for canoeing here. Fishing is another option. Hunting is permitted in season.

Camping Regulations: Camping and campfires are allowed throughout the National Forest, except near public recreation areas or where posted otherwise. No permits are required. Camping is limited to designated sites during deer hunting season.

For Further Information: Davy Crockett National Forest, Homer Garrison Federal Building, 701 North First Street, Lufkin, TX 75901; (409)639-8501.

BIG THICKET NATIONAL PRESERVE—84,550 acres.

Consisting of a number of separate tracts in east Texas, Big Thicket National Preserve was established to protect an area of diverse flora and fauna.

There are longleaf pine, cypress, and hardwood forests here, with some virgin pine. Also included are meadows, sandhills, swamps, a number of creeks, and a major stretch of the Neches River. Among the wildlife are coyote, bobcat, and armadillo.

Activities: Four of this preserve's units have trails for hiking and backpacking. Horses are allowed on a single trail, the 18-mile Big Sandy Horse Trail. Canoeing is available on the Neches River as well as several creeks. Fishing is also possible. Limited hunting is permitted in season.

Camping Regulations: Backcountry camping requires a permit, which must be obtained before entering. Camping is allowed in designated camping zones, which are found in most of the preserve's units, as well as along much of the Neches River.

Campsites must be at least 200 feet from trails and roads, and 25 feet from water sources, except along the river. Campfires are allowed by the river and forbidden elsewhere.

Maximum stay permitted is five days. Group size is limited to eight. Pets are prohibited. All but a portion of one unit is closed during hunting season, usually from October 1-January 15.

For Further Information: Big Thicket National Preserve, 3785 Milam, Beaumont, TX 77701; (409)839-2689.

PADRE ISLAND NATIONAL SEASHORE—Located on the Gulf Coast of south Texas, 65-mile-long Padre Island National Seashore protects a sizable portion of a long barrier island. It has one of the greatest expanses of wild seashore in the country.

The island has beautiful sandy beaches, dunes, and some grasslands. Deer and coyote are among the wildlife, along with shore birds and marine life which includes dolphin and whale.

Activities: Fifty-five miles of roadless beach are open to backpacking and hiking, and also to 4-wheel drive vehicles. The swimming here is superb. Fishing is allowed, but hunting is not.

Camping Regulations: Camping as well as campfires are allowed along the entire beach except for one 4-mile stretch. No permits or fees are required. Dunes and grasslands are off-limits for camping and fires.

All drinking water must be carried for the duration of one's trip. Summers here are quite hot and winters mildly cool. Fall through spring are the best times to visit.

For Further Information: Padre Island National Seashore, 9405 South Padre Island Drive, Corpus Christi, TX 78418; (512)937-2621.

SABINE NATIONAL FOREST—189,450 acres. Largest of this state's National Forests, Sabine is situated along the eastern border of Texas, next to enormous Toledo Bend Reservoir. There's one designated wilderness area, the 9,946-acre Indian Mounds Wilderness. Throughout the forest are many creeks, with several developed recreation areas located alongside the reservoir.

Activities: Only a few short hiking and nature trails are found here, although backpacking is allowed anywhere in the National Forest. Hunting and fishing are permitted in season.

Camping Regulations: Camping and campfires are allowed throughout the region, except near public use areas or where otherwise prohibited. No permits are required. Camping is limited to designated areas, however, during deer hunting season.

For Further Information: Sabine National Forest, Homer Garrison Federal Building, 701 North First Street, Lufkin, TX 75901; (409)639-8501.

ANGELINA NATIONAL FOREST—156,150 acres. Angelina National Forest is located on both sides of huge Sam Rayburn Reservoir in east Texas, on the Gulf Coastal Plain. Included here are the Neches and Angelina Rivers, along with some creeks.

There are areas of "piney woods" forested with longleaf pine and bald cypress, with magnolia and dogwood, and two designated wilderness areas: the 12,650-acre Upland Island Wilderness, and the 5,286-acre Turkey Hill Wilderness.

Activities: Canoeing is available on the Neches and Angelina Rivers. Horseback riding is allowed. Hiking and backpacking are mainly limited to short trails. Longest is the 5.5-mile Sawmill Hiking Trail, which runs alongside the Neches River. Fishing is also available, and hunting is permitted in season.

Camping Regulations: Primitive camping is allowed throughout the National Forest, as are campfires, except near recreation areas and where otherwise prohibited. No permits are necessary.

Campsites in wilderness areas should be at least 100 feet from trails and water sources. A stove is recommended for cooking. Camping is restricted to designated areas during deer hunting season.

For Further Information: Angelina National Forest, P.O. Box 756, Lufkin, TX 75902; (409)634-7709.

CADDO/LBJ NATIONAL GRASSLANDS—These two National Grasslands in northeast Texas are administered together. Lyndon B. Johnson National Grassland (20,320 acres) consists of a number of tracts in close proximity, and includes two sizable lakes.

Caddo National Grassland (17,796 acres) has a mix of public and private lands, with three lakes and a recreation area. Deer and wild turkey are among the wildlife found here.

Activities: Hiking, backpacking, and horseback riding are allowed, but aside from a couple of established trails, most travel must be on roads, old paths, or cross-country. Limited fishing is available. Hunting is permitted in season.

Camping Regulations: Camping and campfires are allowed throughout the National Grasslands, except near recreation areas or where otherwise prohibited. No permits are necessary.

For Further Information: Caddo/LBJ National Grasslands, P.O. Box 507, Decatur, TX 76234; (817)627-5475.

OTHER RECOMMENDED LOCATIONS

HILL COUNTRY STATE NATURAL AREA—5,400 acres. This State Natural Area is located west of San Antonio in south-central Texas. It's currently open to the public for five days, from Thursday through Monday, each week.

Activities: About 30 miles of trails are available for hiking, backpacking, horseback riding, and

mountain biking. Visitors must stay on trails. Limited fishing is possible.

Camping Regulations: Several camping areas are located along the trails. A small fee is charged to camp here. Campfires are not allowed, so cooking requires a stove.

For Further Information: Hill Country State Natural Area, Route 1, Box 601, Bandera, TX 78003; (512)796-4413.

COLORADO BEND STATE PARK—5,000 acres. This state park in central Texas includes six miles of the Colorado River, with hills and rocky canyons, woodlands and savannas, caves and creeks. Among the wildlife are white-tailed deer, armadillo, and bald eagle. A portion of the park is currently closed to the public.

Activities: Hiking and backpacking are possible on about 12 miles of trails, nine of which are open to mountain biking. Fishing is available along the river, and hunting is permitted in season.

Camping Regulations: Camping is limited to designated areas along one trail next to the Colorado River. Campfires are not allowed, so a stove is necessary in order to cook.

For Further Information: Colorado Bend State Park, Box 118, Bend, TX 76824; (915)628-3240.

BASTROP STATE PARK—3,503 acres. Located in the hills of East Texas, this state park has scenery which includes woodlands of loblolly pine, some small ponds, and a 10-acre lake.

Activities: Backpacking and hiking are available on an 8.5-mile trail, which forms a large loop.

Camping Regulations: Camping is allowed along those sections of the trail which are east of a primitive road. A fee is charged for camping each night. Campsites should be at least 50 feet from the trail and 100 feet from water sources. Campfires are prohibited. A stove should be brought if one wishes to cook.

For Further Information: Bastrop State Park, P.O. Box 518, Bastrop, TX 78602; (512)321-2101.

LOST MAPLES STATE NATURAL AREA—2,208 acres.
Lost Maples State Natural Area is in the hills of East Texas. Scenery here includes forests of bigtooth maple, oak, and juniper, a limestone canyon, grasslands, creeks, and the Sabinal River. Among the area's wildlife are white-tailed deer, mountain lion, bobcat, and armadillo.

Activities: There are 10.5 miles of trails for hiking and backpacking.

Camping Regulations: Eight designated camping areas are located along the trails. A fee is charged for camping each night. Advance reservations are available and recommended, as numbers of campers are restricted. Campfires are prohibited, so a stove is necessary for cooking. Fall and spring are the best times to visit.

For Further Information: Lost Maples State Natural Area, HC01, Box 156, Vanderpool, TX 78885; (512)966-3413.

LAKE SOMERVILLE STATE PARK—Located in east-central Texas, this park is comprised of two units alongside the Somerville Reservoir. Terrain consists of rolling hills, and there are oak-hickory forests. Wildlife includes white-tailed deer, coyote, fox, and armadillo.

Activities: A 21-mile trail system known as the Lake Somerville Trailway extends through the area. The trail is open to hiking, backpacking, horseback riding, and cycling.

Camping Regulations: Six designated primitive camping areas are located along the trail. Camping is restricted to these sites. Campfires are allowed in fire rings.

For Further Information: Lake Somerville State Park, Route 1, Box 499, Somerville, TX 77879; (409)535-7763.

DINOSAUR VALLEY STATE PARK—1,523 acres. Noted for its fossil dinosaur tracks, this state park in north-central Texas includes a stretch of the Paluxy River, with limestone outcrops. There are mixed stands of trees here, as well as prairie grasslands. White-tailed deer, coyote, bobcat, and wild turkey are among the park's wildlife.

Activities: Hiking and backpacking are available on 5 miles of trails. Fishing is also possible along the river.

Camping Regulations: There are seven primitive camping areas for backpackers, and camping is restricted to these sites. Campfires are prohibited. A stove may be used for cooking.

For Further Information: Dinosaur Valley State Park, P.O. Box 396, Glen Rose, TX 76043; (817)897-4588.

ENCHANTED ROCK STATE NATURAL AREA—1,643 acres. Situated in south-central Texas, this State Natural Area is noted for its granite-domed hills, mushroom-shaped rock formations, and a large cave. The region also has oak and hickory woodlands and grasslands. Wildlife includes white-tailed deer, armadillo, and wild turkey.

Activities: There are several miles of trails for hiking and backpacking. Rock climbing is also possible here.

Camping Regulations: Backpack camping is allowed in three designated areas accessible by trail. A fee is charged for each night. Advance reservations are available. Campfires are prohibited, so a stove must be used if one wishes to cook. Water must be carried in. Fall and spring are the best times to visit.

For Further Information: Enchanted Rock State Natural Area, Route 4, Box 170, Fredericksburg, TX 78624; (915)247-3903.

CAPROCK CANYONS STATE PARK—13,906 acres.
This state park in north-central Texas has an escarpment of white caprock, with steep bluffs and exposed red sandstone. There are canyons and badlands, woodlands, a 120-acre lake, some creeks, and two prongs of the Little Red River. Wildlife includes mule deer, wild sheep, coyote, and bobcat.

Activities: Hiking, backpacking, and horseback riding are possible on about 16 miles of trails. Fishing is also available.

Camping Regulations: Camping is restricted to two designated areas along the trails. Each area is about a mile from parking. Campfires are not allowed. A stove is recommended for cooking.

For Further Information: Caprock Canyons State Park, P.O. Box 204, Quitaque, TX 79255; (806)455-1492.

PEDERNALES FALLS STATE PARK—4,800 acres. Pedernales Falls State Park in south-central Texas features a 6-mile stretch of the Pedernales River, which runs through a rugged gorge and has some

waterfalls. There are also canyons with creeks, oak woodlands, and wildlife including deer, bald eagle, and wild turkey.

Activities: The park has about 20 miles of trails for hiking or backpacking. Fishing is available along the river.

Camping Regulations: Camping is limited to one designated area, which is located along the 7.5-mile Wolf Mountain Trail.

For Further Information: Pedernales Falls State Park, Route 1, Box 450, Johnson City, TX 78636; (512)868-7304.

BRAZOS BEND STATE PARK—4,897 acres. Bordering on the Brazos River, in east Texas, this state park has several lakes, a sizable creek, and some hardwood forest along with prairie. Armadillo and alligator are among the wildlife here.

Activities: Hiking and backpacking are possible on over 20 miles of trails. Some trails are open to bikes. Fishing is available at the lakes.

Camping Regulations: A single designated camping area is located along one of the trails. Backpack camping is restricted to this area.

For Further Information: Brazos Bend State Park, 21901 FM 762, Needville, TX 77461; (409)553-3243.

FAIRFIELD LAKE STATE PARK—1,400 acres. Fairfield Lake State Park is located alongside Fairfield Lake, a large reservoir in a hilly forested region of east-central Texas. In the area are woodlands of oak, hickory, and elm, with cedar and pine, plus some grassy prairie. Wildlife includes deer and bald eagle.

Activities: The park has six miles of trails for hiking or backpacking. Fishing is possible along the reservoir.

Camping Regulations: Primitive camping is restricted to one designated area, which is 2.5 miles via trail from a parking area. A fee is charged for each night's stay.

For Further Information: Fairfield Lake State Park, Route 2, Box 912, Fairfield, TX 75840; (903)389-4514.

LAKE MINERAL WELLS STATE PARK—2,800 acres. Located in north-central Texas, this state park surrounds 640-acre Lake Mineral Wells.

Activities: There are 21 miles of trails here for hiking and backpacking, including a 12-mile trail which is also open to horses and mountain bikes. Rock climbing is available, and climbers must check in at park headquarters. Canoes may be rented for use on the lake. Fishing is also possible.

Camping Regulations: Backpacking campsites are located at the end of a 2.5 mile trail, and primitive camping is restricted to this area. Campfires are not allowed, so a stove is necessary for cooking. Water must be carried in.

For Further Information: Lake Mineral Wells State Park, Route 4, Box 39-C, Mineral Wells, TX 76067; (817)328-1171.

INKS LAKE STATE PARK—1,200 acres. Stretching alongside 800-acre Inks Lake, in south-central Texas, this state park has some rock outcroppings, woodlands of oak and cedar, and wildlife which includes deer and armadillo.

Activities: Hiking and backpacking are possible on 7.5 miles of trails. Canoeing and fishing are available on the lake.

Camping Regulations: Campsites are located in a single area along one of the trails, about a mile from park headquarters. Camping is restricted to that area.

For Further Information: Inks Lake State Park, Route 2, Box 31, Burnet, TX 78611; (512)793-2223.

In addition, camping is allowed along the 14-mile Cross Timbers Hiking Trail on the shore of enormous Lake Texoma, which is on the Texas–Oklahoma border north of Dallas. The lands are administered by the U.S. Army Corps of Engineers. Camping and campfires are restricted to three designated primitive sites along the trail. A permit is required, and available in person or by writing to the Resident Engineer, Denison Dam-Lake Texoma, P.O. Box A, Denison, TX 75020. For more information contact the U.S. Army Corps of Engineers, Texoma Project Office, P.O. Box 60, Cartwright, OK 74131; (903)465-4990.

MAJOR BACKPACKING TRAILS

LONE STAR TRAIL—140 miles. The longest trail in the state, the Lone Star Trail runs the length of Sam Houston National Forest in East Texas. It includes a number of loops, and a portion of the trail has National Recreation Trail status.

The trail leads through forests of hardwoods and pine, and crosses a number of creeks, with some deep ravines. Most of the terrain here is nearly flat, so it makes for easy backpacking.

Camping Regulations: Designated campsites are available in some locations along the trail. Camping is allowed elsewhere as well, as are campfires, except where posted otherwise. No permits are required.

Camping is restricted to designated spots during deer hunting season. Since summers are typically hot and humid, fall through spring are the best times for backpacking on this trail.

For Further Information: National Forests in Texas, Homer Garrison Federal Building, 701 North First Street, Lufkin, TX 75901; (409)639-8501.

TEXAS CAMPING RESOURCES

ORGANIZATIONS WHICH OFFER WILDERNESS
CAMPING TRIPS

Sierra Club, Rio Grande Chapter, P.O. Box 9191, El Paso, TX 79983. This chapter of the Sierra Club has several regional groups. Some of the groups sponsor backpacking trips and courses for beginners.

USEFUL GUIDEBOOKS

Camper's Guide to Texas Parks, Lakes, and Forests—Little, Mickey. Houston: Lone Star Books.

Hiker's Guide to Texas—Parent, Laurence. Helena, MT: Falcon Press.

Hiker's Guide to Trails of Big Bend National Park—Big Bend Natural History Association, 1978.

Hiking and Backpacking Trails of Texas—Little, Mickey. Houston: Gulf Publishing Co., 1990.

Hiking the Southwest—Ganci, Dave. San Francisco: Sierra Club Books, 1983.

INFORMATION ABOUT STATE PARK CAMPGROUNDS
Texas Parks and Wildlife Department, 4200 Smith School Road, Austin, TX 78744; (512)389-4800.

STATE HIGHWAY MAP AND TRAVEL INFORMATION
Texas Division of Tourism, P.O. Box 12728, Austin, TX 78711; (512)462-9191/(800)888-8839.

UTAH

BEST AREAS FOR WILDERNESS CAMPING

WASATCH–CACHE NATIONAL FOREST—1,302,523 acres. This National Forest in the northern part of Utah is made up of numerous tracts, including lands near Salt Lake City. In the region are the Wasatch and Uinta Mountains, with many elevations over 10,000 feet. Highest point is 13,442-foot Gilbert Peak.

Scenery includes rugged, snow-capped mountains, rock outcroppings, steep ridges, and deep canyons, with hundreds of lakes and streams. There are forests of spruce, fir, pine, and aspen. Among the wildlife are elk, moose, antelope, mule deer, black bear, bighorn sheep, mountain goat, and bobcat.

Wasatch–Cache has seven designated wilderness areas: a portion of the 460,000-acre High Uintas Wilderness, the 44,350-acre Mount Naomi Wilderess, the 25,500-acre Deseret Peak Wilderness, the 23,850-acre Wellsville Mountain Wilderness, the 16,000-acre Mount Olympus Wilderness, the 13,000-acre Twin Peaks Wilderness, and about 8,900 acres of the 30,000-acre Lone Peak Wilderness.

Activities: Backpacking and hiking are available on about 1,050 miles of trails, including a section of the Great Western Trail (see entry page 278). Some trails receive heavy use. Difficulty ranges from easy to strenuous. Trails at high elevations may only be snow-free from July through September.

Horseback riding is allowed on many trails. Cross-country skiing is possible during winter on a variety of trails. Fishing is also available, and hunting is permitted in season.

Camping Regulations: Camping is allowed throughout the National Forest, as are campfires, except where otherwise prohibited. No permits are necessary.

Special regulations apply for some of the designated wilderness areas and a few other locations. Here campsites must be at least 200 feet from water sources, food scraps must be carried out, swimming is not allowed, and pets are prohibited.

For Further Information: Wasatch–Cache National Forest, 8234 Federal Building, 125 South State Street, Salt Lake City, UT 84138; (801)524-5030.

DIXIE NATIONAL FOREST—1,883,745 acres. Consisting of four units in south-central and southwest Utah, including lands next to Bryce Canyon and Zion National Parks, this is the largest National Forest in the state. Elevations range from under 4,000 feet to over 11,000 feet, with 11,322-foot Bluebell Knoll the highest point.

There are canyons with steep cliffs, colorful rock formations and pinnacles, plateaus and mesas, along with a number of lakes and streams. Forests are of fir and pine, plus pinyon and juniper. Elk, pronghorn antelope, mule deer, black bear, and mountain lion are among the wildlife.

Dixie National Forest has three designated wilderness areas: the 50,000-acre Pine Valley Mountain Wilderness, the 26,000-acre Box-Death Hollow Wilderness, and the 7,000-acre Ashdown Gorge Wilderness.

Activities: Hiking and backpacking are possible on some 640 miles of trails, including a section of the new Great Western Trail (see entry page 278). Difficulty ranges from easy to strenuous.

Horses are allowed on most trails, as are mountain bikes outside of wilderness areas. Cross-country skiing and snowshoeing are available when there's adequate snow. Fishing is possible along lakes and streams, and hunting is permitted in season.

Camping Regulations: Camping is allowed throughout the National Forest, as are campfires, except near public use areas or where otherwise prohibited. No permits are necessary.

For Further Information: Dixie National Forest, 82 North 100 East, P.O. Box 580, Cedar City, UT 84720; (801)586-2421.

ASHLEY NATIONAL FOREST—1,288,422 acres. Ashley National Forest is in northeast Utah, and has a small tract in Wyoming. Especially notable here are the Uinta Mountains, with a number of rugged peaks including 13,528-foot Kings Peak, the highest elevation in Utah.

There are also high alpine basins and glacial canyons, meadows, many lakes, streams, and rivers, with some forests of fir, spruce and pine. Wildlife includes antelope, elk, moose, deer, bear, bighorn sheep, mountain lion, and lynx.

This National Forest has one designated wilderness area, consisting of a large portion of the 460,000-acre High Uintas Wilderness, which continues on into Wasatch–Cache National Forest. It also encloses part of the 200,000-acre Flaming Gorge National Recreation Area, which extends well into Wyoming.

Activities: Hiking and backpacking are available on over 750 miles of trails, including the 53-mile Highline Trail. Difficulty varies from easy to strenuous. High trails may only be free of snow from July through September.

Horseback riding is permitted on most trails, and cross-country skiing is possible on trails during the winter. Rafting is available on a section of the Green River, in the Flaming Gorge National Recreation Area. Fishing is another option, and hunting is permitted in season.

Camping Regulations: Camping is allowed in most of Ashley National Forest, except near public recreation areas or where posted otherwise. Campfires are allowed, but bringing a stove is strongly recommended. No permits are necessary. Some parts of the Flaming Gorge National Recreation Area are closed to camping.

For Further Information: Ashley National Forest, 355 North Vernal Avenue, Vernal, UT 84078; (801)789-1181.

UINTA NATIONAL FOREST—812,787 acres. Consisting of units in north-central Utah, Uinta National Forest includes lofty peaks and high desert, basins with lakes, deep canyons and cliffs, valleys and foothills, streams with waterfalls. Among the notable mountains here are 11,877-foot Mount Nebo and 11,750-foot Mount Timpanogos.

Vegetation ranges from sagebrush to alpine tundra, and there are spruce and fir forests, along with aspen, oak, and maple. Wildlife includes elk, moose, mule deer, black bear, mountain goat, and cougar.

This National Forest has three designated wilderness areas: the 28,000-acre Mount Nebo Wilderness, about 21,000 acres of the 30,000-acre Lone Peak Wilderness, and the 10,750-acre Mount Timpanogos Wilderness,

Activities: More than 500 miles of trails are available for hiking and backpacking, including a 65-mile section of the new Great Western Trail (see entry page 278). Difficulty ranges from easy to strenuous. Some of the trails receive heavy use.

Horseback riding is allowed on most trails. Mountain biking is possible outside of wilderness areas. Some trails are designated for cross-country skiing during winter. Fishing is found along lakes and streams. Hunting is permitted in season.

Camping Regulations: Camping and campfires are freely allowed throughout the National Forest, except near public use areas or where posted otherwise. No permits are required.

For Further Information: Uinta National Forest, P.O. Box 1428, Provo, UT 84603; (801)377-5780.

ZION NATIONAL PARK—147,000 acres. Located near the southwest corner of Utah, this magnificent National Park encompasses an area of high-walled and multicolored canyons up to 3,000 feet deep. Also here are sandstone formations, plateaus, mesas, a petrified forest, and 310-foot Kolob Arch, said to be the world's largest natural arch.

A centerpiece is provided by enormous Zion Canyon, with the lovely Virgin River flowing through (and also a highway). Vegetation includes stands of ponderosa pine and fir, pinyon and juniper, along with cottonwood and willow, plus desert flora. Among the wildlife are mule deer, mountain lion, bobcat, and fox.

Activities: Over 140 miles of trails are available for hiking and backpacking. Difficulty varies from easy to strenuous. Horseback riding is allowed on many trails. Rock climbing is permitted, with climbers encouraged to register at the visitor center. Limited fishing is possible. Hunting is prohibited.

Camping Regulations: A free permit is required to camp in the backcountry here, and may be obtained at the visitor center. Some areas in the park are closed to camping. Campfires are not allowed, so a stove must be carried if one wishes to cook.

Campsites chosen must be a minimum of one mile from roads and trailheads. Whenever possible, sites should also be at least one-quarter mile from springs, 100 feet from other water sources, and out of sight of trails.

Group size is limited to a maximum of 12. Bikes are not permitted in the backcountry, nor are pets. Since summer is often very hot here, spring and fall are the best times to visit.

For Further Information: Zion National Park, Springdale, UT 84767; (801)772-3256.

CANYONLANDS NATIONAL PARK—337,570 acres. This wild and undeveloped National Park is situated on the Colorado Plateau in southeast Utah. Elevations here range from 3,600 feet to almost 7,000 feet. It's an arid land of deep canyons and multicolored rock formations, with needles and spires, arches and balanced rocks.

The Colorado and Green Rivers flow through the park. An area of special interest is the Maze, a complex of canyons. Much of the vegetation consists of desert varieties, with pinyon-juniper. Wildlife includes deer, bighorn sheep, coyote, and fox.

Activities: Hiking and backpacking are possible on over 80 miles of trails, which range from easy to strenuous. Horses are allowed on some trails. Cross-country travel is feasible as well.

Canoeing, kayaking, and rafting are available by permit on the Green and Colorado Rivers. A permit is also required in order to engage in rock climbing, with some areas restricted. Mountain bike use is limited to roads. Hunting is prohibited.

Camping Regulations: A free permit is necessary in order to camp in the backcountry. Permits are available from visitor centers. Campsites should be at least 300 feet from water sources and out of sight of trails.

In some parts of the park camping is restricted and campfires prohibited. A stove should be brought for cooking. Pets are not allowed. Spring and fall are the best times to camp here. Summer heat can be quite intense.

For Further Information: Canyonlands National Park, 125 West 200 South, Moab, UT 84532; (801)259-7164.

CAPITOL REEF NATIONAL PARK—241,865 acres. Situated in south-central Utah, long and narrow Capitol Reef National Park encompasses the Waterpocket Fold, an enormous eroded uplift of land. There are deep desert canyons of multicolored slickrock sandstone here.

The scenic and varied terrain includes mesas and rock pinnacles, arches and bridges, outcroppings and caves. There's desert vegetation, with pinyon-juniper woodlands. Among the wildlife are black bear, mule deer, mountain lion, and coyote.

Activities: Hiking and backpacking are the primary activities available in this National Park, with about 75 miles of trails. Difficulty varies from easy to strenuous. Some trails are minimally marked.

Camping Regulations: Camping is allowed in most parts of the park. A free backcountry permit is required, and may be obtained from a ranger. Campsites should be out of sight and sound of any trail, road, or developed area. Summers are often extremely hot here, so the best seasons for camping are spring and fall.

For Further Information: Capitol Reef National Park, Torrey, UT 84775; (801)425-3791.

FISHLAKE NATIONAL FOREST—1,425,126 acres. Consisting of four separate tracts of land in south-central Utah, Fishlake National Forest includes some high mountain ranges, plateaus, and deep red-rock canyons. Among several mountains over 12,000 feet is 12,173-foot Delano Peak, the highest. There are no designated wilderness areas.

In the region are many streams, lakes, and ponds, along with open meadows, alpine vegetation, and desert flora—plus stands of fir and spruce, pine and aspen, and pinyon-juniper. Wildlife includes elk, antelope, deer, black bear, mountain goat, and mountain lion.

Activities: There are 1,040 miles of trails for backpacking and hiking, including a section of the Great Western Trail (see entry page 278). Difficulty varies from easy to strenuous. High trails may be under snow until July.

Most trails are open to horseback riding, and many may be used for mountain biking. Cross-country skiing is possible during the snow season. Mountaineering is also available. Some streams and lakes are suitable for fishing. Hunting is permitted in season.

Camping Regulations: Camping is allowed throughout most of the National Forest, as are campfires, except near public use areas or where otherwise prohibited. No permits are required.

For Further Information: Fishlake National Forest, 115 East 900 North, Richfield, UT 84701; (801)896-9233.

BRYCE CANYON NATIONAL PARK—37,102 acres. This National Park is on a high eroded plateau in

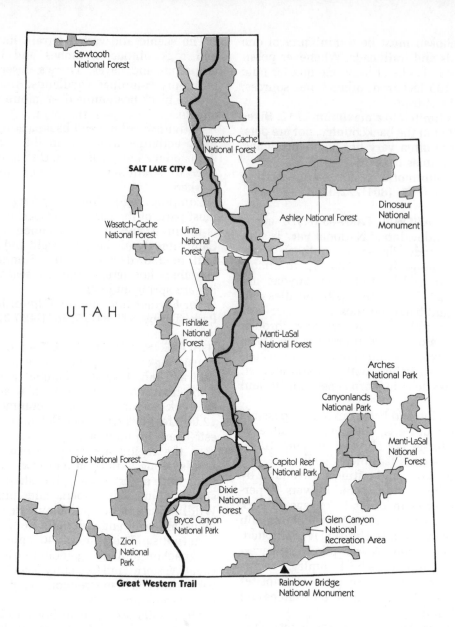

Sawtooth
National Forest

Wasatch-Cache
National Forest

SALT LAKE CITY ●

Wasatch-Cache
National Forest

Uinta
National
Forest

Ashley National Forest

Dinosaur
National
Monument

U T A H

Fishlake
National
Forest

Manti-LaSal
National Forest

Arches
National Park

Canyonlands
National Park

Manti-LaSal
National
Forest

Dixie National Forest

Capitol Reef
National Park

Dixie
National
Forest

Bryce Canyon
National Park

Glen Canyon
National
Recreation Area

Zion
National
Park

Great Western Trail

Rainbow Bridge
National Monument

southwest Utah. Scenery here includes a number of canyons, along with an endless variety of multi-colored rock pinnacles, spires, and other sculpted limestone forms.

Elevations are from under 7,000 feet to over 9,000 feet. Outstanding views are available from many vantage points. There are forests of ponderosa pine and fir, along with aspen, and wildlife includes mule deer, coyote, and prairie dog.

Activities: Bryce Canyon has about 65 miles of trails for backpacking and hiking. Difficulty ranges from easy to strenuous. Visitors are asked to limit backcountry travel to established trails.

Horseback riding is allowed on many trails. Cross-country skiing and snowshoeing are possible here during the winter, and snowshoes are available for loan free of charge from the visitor center. Biking is restricted to roadways.

Camping Regulations: A free permit, which may be obtained from the visitor center, is required in order to camp in the backcountry. The park has a number of established backcountry camping areas, and these designated sites should be used.

Campfires are not allowed, so a stove is necessary for cooking. Pets are prohibited. Summer temperatures are moderate, so the usual camping season here is spring through fall.

For Further Information: Bryce Canyon National Park, Bryce Canyon, UT 84717; (801)834-5322.

ARCHES NATIONAL PARK—73,389 acres. Located in the red rock country of southeast Utah, this National Park protects a great number of natural sandstone arches and bridges, which are up to 290 feet long. The park has over 1000 arches, more than anywhere else in the world.

There are also many spires and pinnacles. This is an area of desert, with some pinyon pine and juniper trees. Wildlife includes mule deer, fox, and golden eagle.

Activities: Just a few short trails are available, totaling about 12 miles, and none reach far into the backcountry. Most hiking and backpacking involves cross-country travel.

Rock climbing is permitted but restricted, and dangerous due to crumbling rock. Mountain bike use is limited to roads. Hunting is forbidden.

Camping Regulations: Camping is allowed in the backcountry with a free permit, issued at the visitor center. There are no established campsites. Campfires are not permitted, so a stove should be brought. Group size is limited to 12. Pets are prohibited. Due to summer heat, fall and spring are the recommended times to camp here.

For Further Information: Arches National Park, P.O. Box 907, Moab, UT 84532; (801)259-8161.

OTHER RECOMMENDED LOCATIONS

MANTI–LASAL NATIONAL FOREST—1,265,423 acres. This National Forest consists of a large unit of land in central Utah, along with two tracts in the southeastern part of the state. On these lands are the Abajo and Lasal Mountains, with peaks over 12,000 feet, and also the high Wasatch Plateau.

There's one designated wilderness area, the 45,000-acre Dark Canyon Wilderness. Scenery throughout the National Forest includes cirque basins, narrow canyons with red rock cliffs, mesas, ridges, hills, and some creeks.

Vegetation ranges from cactus and sagebrush to pinyon-juniper and forests of spruce-fir, ponderosa pine, and aspen. Among the wildlife are elk, moose, mule deer, black bear, mountain lion, and coyote.

Activities: Some 200 miles of trails are available for backpacking and hiking, including an 85-mile section of the new Great Western Trail (see entry page 278). Difficulty ranges from easy to strenuous.

Horses are allowed on most trails. Cross-country skiing is possible here when there's adequate snow. Fishing is another option. Hunting is permitted in season.

Camping Regulations: Camping is allowed throughout most of the National Forest, as are campfires, except near public use areas or where otherwise prohibited. No permits are necessary.

For Further Information: Manti–Lasal National Forest, 599 West Price River Drive, Price, UT 84501; (801)637-2817.

BLM LANDS IN UTAH—Utah has no less than 22,000,000 acres of BLM (Bureau of Land Management) or public domain lands, located throughout most of the state. Access to BLM areas is sometimes difficult, and printed literature exists for very few of the tracts.

On these lands are desert mountains, scores of canyons and gulches, mesas and plateaus, arches and bridges, and an endless variety of colored rock formations.

Included are the Henry Mountains, the Deep Creek Mountains, Paria Canyon, and a stretch of the Colorado River. There's a section of the 19,954-acre Paria Canyon–Vermilion Cliffs Wilderness, along with a number of Wilderness Study Areas—locations which have been recommended for wilderness designation.

Activities: Hiking, backpacking, horseback riding, and mountain biking are allowed on most BLM lands, but there are few established trails. Most travel must be cross-country. Fishing is available, and hunting is permitted in season.

Camping Regulations: Camping and campfires are normally allowed, except near public use areas or where otherwise prohibited. While permits are not necessary for most areas, they are required for a few popular locations. Campsites should be at least 100 feet from springs, in order to allow wildlife access to water. Campers are asked to refrain from building new fire rings.

For Further Information: Bureau of Land Management, 324 South State Street, P.O. Box 45155, Salt Lake City, UT 84145; (801)539-4001.

GLEN CANYON NATIONAL RECREATION AREA—1,158,000 acres. Established in 1972, this National Recreation Area was created by damming up the Colorado River in Glen Canyon to create 186-mile-long Lake Powell. Although the headquarters are located in Arizona, almost all of the area is in southern Utah.

This is arid canyon country, with high buttes and mesas, deep canyons with precipitous cliffs.

Vegetation consists of desert varieties such as cactus and yucca. Wildlife includes deer, coyote, and fox.

Activities: There are many options for hikers and backpackers, but few established trails. Travel must be through canyons or cross-country. Mountain biking is limited to roads.

Canoeing and kayaking are possible on Lake Powell, and fishing is available. River trips through the Grand Canyon also begin here. Demand for these trips is so high that the required permit must be obtained up to several years in advance.

Camping Regulations: Camping is allowed throughout most of this National Recreation Area, except near public use areas. Campers are asked to choose sites which are free of vegetation, out of sight of trails, and at least 100 feet from water sources. A free permit is required to camp in the Escalante River area.

Campfires are generally allowed but strongly discouraged. A stove should be carried. Maximum group size is 12. Since summers tend to be hot, spring and fall are the best times to visit.

For Further Information: Glen Canyon National Recreation Area, P.O. Box 1507, Page, AZ 86040; (602)645-2511.

RAINBOW BRIDGE NATIONAL MONUMENT—160 acres. This small National Monument adjacent to Glen Canyon National Recreation Area is surrounded by lands of the Navajo Nation (Reservation). At the center of the monument is Rainbow Bridge, largest natural bridge in the world, made of sandstone and 275 feet long, 290 feet high, and 42 feet thick.

Activities: The National Monument and bridge are accessible only by two rough trails, or by water from Lake Powell in Glen Canyon National Recreation Area. One of the trails is 13 miles and the other 14 miles long, and they're both on Navajo Nation lands. The trails are open to foot travel and horses only.

Camping Regulations: A permit is required to backpack and camp along the trails, and costs a nominal fee. The permit must be obtained from the Navajo Nation, Recreational Resources Department, Box 308, Window Rock, AZ 86515.

There are several designated camping areas along the trails. Campfires should be built only in preexisting fire sites. Spring and fall are the best times to camp here.

For Further Information: Rainbow Bridge National Monument, c/o Glen Canyon National Recreation Area, P.O. Box 1507, Page, AZ 86040.

SAWTOOTH NATIONAL FOREST—Most of this 1,347,422-acre National Forest is in Idaho, but 71,182 acres are located in the northwest corner of Utah. Included here are the Raft River Mountains, with elevations over 9,000 feet and outstanding views, along with some canyons and streams. Camping and campfires are permitted. See the Sawtooth National Forest entry in the Idaho chapter for more information.

DINOSAUR NATIONAL MONUMENT—Dinosaur National Monument is based in Colorado and most of the lands are there, but about 38,000 acres are in northeast Utah. The region includes Split Mountain Canyon and a stretch of the Green River. Backcountry camping is available by permit. See the Colorado chapter for more about this National Monument.

Utah also has extensive "state trust lands" scattered throughout the state, adding up to some 5,000 separate tracts. These are undeveloped and open to primitive camping and other recreational uses such as hiking. Hunting is allowed as well.

Little in the way of printed literature is available regarding these lands. For more information contact the Utah Division of State Lands and Forestry, 355 West North Temple, 3 Triad Center, Suite 400, Salt Lake City, UT 84180; (801)538-5508.

MAJOR BACKPACKING TRAILS

GREAT WESTERN TRAIL—This new trail may eventually run all the way from Canada to Mexico, extending some 2,400 miles. So far the main portion being constructed is in Utah, with some sections now finished. Along the way is some outstanding mountain and desert scenery.

For most of its length the trail utilizes preexisting trails and roads. The trail is multiuse, with horses, mountain bikes, and motorized vehicles allowed on some segments. There will be parallel routes for different uses part of the way.

Most of the time the trail is on National Forest lands, and it passes through five of Utah's six National Forests. A small portion is on BLM lands. Some of the route is at high elevations. Difficulty ranges from easy to strenuous.

Camping Regulations: On National Forest and BLM lands camping and campfires are allowed practically anywhere, except near recreation areas or where otherwise prohibited. It's suggested that campsites be chosen which are well off the trail and away from water sources. No permits are required.

For Further Information: Great Western Trail Association, P.O. Box 1428, Provo, UT 84602.

UTAH CAMPING RESOURCES

ORGANIZATIONS WHICH OFFER WILDERNESS CAMPING TRIPS

Wasatch Mountain Club, 888 South 200 East, Salt Lake City, UT 84111. This outdoor recreation club schedules some backpacking and other camping trips each year.

OUTFITTERS AND GUIDES

Utah Guides and Outfitters, P.O. Box 111, Jensen, UT 84035; (801)789-4952.

USEFUL GUIDEBOOKS

Cache Trails—Schimpf, Ann and Davis, Mel. Salt Lake City: Wasatch Publishing, 1978.

High Uinta Trails—Davis, Mel. Salt Lake City: Wasatch Publishing, 1974.

The Hiker's Guide to Utah—Hall, Dave. Billings, MT: Falcon Press.

Hiking the Great Basin—Hart, John. San Francisco: Sierra Club Books.

Hiking the Southwest's Canyon Country—Hinchman, Sandra. Seattle, WA: The Mountaineers Books.

Hiking in Zion National Park, The Trails—Lineback, Bob. Zion Natural History Association.

The Sierra Club Guide to the Natural Areas of Colorado and Utah— Perry, John and Jane. San Francisco: Sierra Club Books, 1985.

Utah's National Parks—Adkison, Ron. Berkeley, CA: Wilderness Press, 1991.

Wasatch Trails, Volume I—Bottcher, Betty, and Davis, Mel. Salt Lake City: Wasatch Publishing, 1973.

Wasatch Trails, Volume II—Geery, Daniel. Salt Lake City: Wasatch Publishing, 1976.

Utah Valley Trails—Paxman, Shirley and Monroe; Taylor, Gayle and Weldon. Salt Lake City: Wasatch Publishing, 1978.

INFORMATION ABOUT STATE PARK CAMPGROUNDS

Utah Division of Parks and Recreation, 1636 West North Temple, Suite 116, Salt Lake City, UT 84116; (801)538-7220.

STATE HIGHWAY MAP AND TRAVEL INFORMATION

Utah Travel Council, Council Hall/Capitol Hill, Salt Lake City, UT 84114; (801)538-1030.

VERMONT

BEST AREAS FOR WILDERNESS CAMPING

GREEN MOUNTAIN NATIONAL FOREST—340,000 acres. Consisting of two tracts in the beautiful Green Mountains of central and southern Vermont, this scenic National Forest has a few elevations over 4,000 feet, with steep cliffs, rocky ledges, as well as some gentler terrain. It's by far the largest area of public land in the state.

Included is the 36,400-acre White Rocks National Recreation Area. In the region are lakes and ponds, streams with waterfalls, a section of the White River, and forests of mixed hardwoods, plus hemlock, spruce, and fir. Among the wildlife are white-tailed deer, moose, black bear, coyote, bobcat, and fox.

The forest has six designated wilderness areas: the 21,480-acre Breadloaf Wilderness, the 15,680-acre Lye Brook Wilderness, the 6,920-acre Peru Peak Wilderness, the 6,720-acre Big Branch Wilderness, the 5,060-acre George D. Aiken Wilderness, and the 3,740-acre Bristol Cliffs Wilderness.

Activities: There are over 500 miles of trails for backpacking and hiking. Included are about 125 miles of the 270-mile Long Trail (see entry page 282), which crosses both tracts, along with a section of the Appalachian Trail (see entry page 283) in the southern unit. Difficulty ranges from easy to strenuous.

Cross-country skiing is possible on some designated trails, and snowshoeing is another winter option. Horses are allowed on some trails and old roads. Canoeing and kayaking are available on the White River. Fishing is possible alongside a number of streams and ponds. Hunting is permitted in season.

Camping Regulations: Camping is allowed freely throughout most of the National Forest, except near public use areas or where posted otherwise. No permits are necessary except for organized groups, which must obtain an Outfitter-Guide Special Use Permit. Campfires may be built, but a stove is recommended.

There are designated campsites in some areas. Included are lean-tos, located at regular intervals along the Appalachian and Long Trails. Campsites elsewhere should be at least 200 feet from trails, water sources, and roads.

For Further Information: Green Mountain National Forest, 151 West Street, P.O. Box 519, Rutland, VT 05702; (802)773-0300.

OTHER RECOMMENDED LOCATIONS

MOUNT MANSFIELD STATE FOREST—40,333 acres. Consisting of 11 blocks of land in northern Vermont, this sizable state forest is home to 4,393-foot Mount Mansfield, Vermont's highest and most massive mountain, which takes the shape of a human face in profile.

Terrain near the top is incredibly rocky and rugged, with substantial areas of artic-alpine vegetation. On clear days the views are magnificent. Visitors are many, due mainly to an auto road which ends just short of the summit.

The region is forested with hardwoods as well as conifers, including spruce, fir, and pine. There are also some streams and ponds. Among the wildlife are white-tailed deer, black bear, moose, bobcat, and fox.

Activities: A large network of trails is available on the mountain for hiking or backpacking, including a section of the Long Trail (see entry page 282). Difficulty ranges from easy to very strenuous. Some other trails in the forest are marked for cross-country skiing. Fishing is also possible, and hunting is permitted in season.

Camping Regulations: Several established campsites, including lean-tos and closed cabins, are located along the Long Trail. Camping is allowed elsewhere as well, but only at elevations below 2,500 feet. Campfires are permitted.

Nondesignated campsites must be at least 2,500 feet from roads and shelters, 200 feet from trails or property lines, and 100 feet from water sources. Maximum stay allowed in one location is three nights. Some areas in the forest are off-limits to camping.

For Further Information: Mount Mansfield State Forest, RFD, Stowe, VT 05672; (802)253-4014.

CAMEL'S HUMP FOREST RESERVE—19,500 acres. Situated in north-central Vermont, this state forest reserve is the home of 4,083-foot Camel's Hump—the wildest and least developed mountain in the state, and second highest. Superb views are available from open areas near the top.

Terrain at higher elevations is quite rugged, with rock formations and arctic-alpine tundra near the summit. Below are hardwood forests with old-growth fir and other conifers, plus some streams. Wildlife includes white-tailed deer, black bear, coyote, and fox.

Activities: There are several trails for backpacking and hiking, including a section of the Long Trail (see entry page 282). Difficulty ranges from easy to strenuous. Limited cross-country skiing is available during the winter. Fishing is possible, and hunting is permitted in season.

Camping Regulations: Camping is allowed at established sites, which include two tenting areas with platforms and two closed cabins. One may also camp elsewhere, although only at elevations under 2,500 feet. Campfires are permitted, but the use of a stove is recommended.

Nondesignated sites must be at least 100 feet from water sources, 200 feet from trails, and 2,500 feet from roads, shelters, or developed areas. A few parts of the forest are off-limits to camping. A permit is required for groups of 11 or more.

For Further Information: Camel's Hump Forest Reserve, Department of Forests, Parks, and Recreation, 103 South Main Street, 10 South, Waterbury, VT 05676; (802)828-3375.

GROTON STATE FOREST—25,645 acres. Located in north-central Vermont, Groton State Forest has some rugged terrain, with several medium-size mountains, rock outcrops, and smaller hills. The highest elevation is 3,348-foot Signal Mountain.

Scenery includes some ponds, wetlands, and 414-acre Lake Groton. Forests are of northern hardwoods, with yellow and white birch, plus pine and spruce. Moose, black bear, deer, and fox are among the wildlife.

Activities: Over 40 miles of trails are available for hiking, backpacking, and cross-country skiing. Fishing is another option, and hunting is permitted in season.

Camping Regulations: Camping is allowed at elevations below 2,500 feet. All campsites must also be at least 2,500 feet from roads, 200 feet from trails and property boundaries, and 100 feet from water sources.

Campfires are allowed as well. Maximum stay in one location is three nights. Groups of 11 or more must obtain a permit. Camping is prohibited in a few areas of the forest.

For Further Information: Groton State Forest, Marshfield, VT 05658; (802)584-3820.

CALVIN COOLIDGE STATE FOREST—18,000 acres. Consisting of a number of tracts in south-central Vermont, Calvin Coolidge State Forest has terrain which ranges from hilly to mountainous, with several sizable peaks.

There are hardwood forests along with some conifers, and wildlife includes white-tailed deer, black bear, and wild turkey.

Activities: Hiking and backpacking are possible on several established trails. Some trails and roads are suitable for cross-country skiing during winter. Fishing is available, and hunting is permitted in season.

Camping Regulations: Campsites must be at elevations under 2,500 feet, and also at least 100 feet from water sources, 200 feet from trails and property lines, and 2,500 feet from roads or developed areas. Some areas are off-limits to camping. Groups of 11 or more must obtain a permit. Campfires are allowed.

For Further Information: Calvin Coolidge State Forest, HCR Box 105, Plymouth, VT 05056; (802)672-3612.

OTHER STATE FORESTS IN VERMONT—Primitive camping is allowed in more than half of Vermont's state forests, adding up to 19 different areas. In addition to those discussed above, other state forests include 12,585-acre Putnam State Forest,

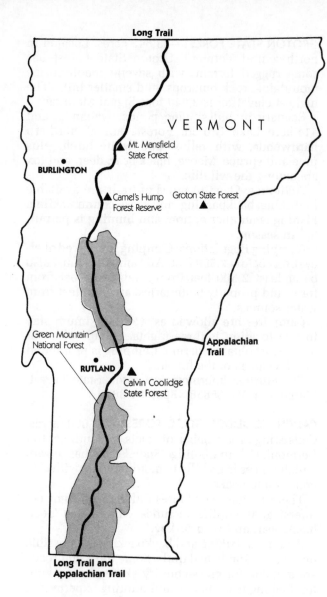

Long Trail

VERMONT

Mt. Mansfield
State Forest

BURLINGTON

Camel's Hump
Forest Reserve

Groton State Forest

Green Mountain
National Forest

Appalachian
Trail

RUTLAND

Calvin Coolidge
State Forest

Long Trail and
Appalachian Trail

7,422-acre Willoughby State Forest, 5,509-acre Roxbury State Forest, and 4,513-acre Okemo State Forest.

Most of the remaining areas are under 1,000 acres, and some are quite small. Visitors should be aware that parts of the forests are open to logging. A true wilderness experience should not be expected, but the scenery is often attractive.

Terrain is typically mountainous or hilly. Access to some of the areas is difficult. Little or no printed literature is currently available for most of the state forests.

Activities: Hunting and fishing are popular in many of the forests. Hiking, backpacking, and cross-country skiing are possible on a limited

number of established trails. Horseback riding is feasible in some areas.

Camping Regulations: Call to check on current regulations, as some changes are anticipated by 1993. It's also advisable to find out whether logging is going on in any particular location.

Primitive camping is presently allowed in major parts of the forests, but it's prohibited in some areas. Campfires are generally permitted. The maximum stay in a location is three nights.

Camping is limited to elevations below 2,500 feet. Sites must also be at least 100 feet from water sources, 200 feet from trails or property lines, and 2,500 feet from roads, shelters, and developed areas. Groups of 11 or more must obtain a permit, which should be requested at least 10 days in advance by mail.

For Further Information: Vermont Department of Forests, Parks, and Recreation, 103 South Main Street, 10 South, Waterbury, VT 05676; (802)828-3375.

MAJOR BACKPACKING TRAILS

THE LONG TRAIL—270 miles. This extremely scenic and well-maintained trail runs the length of Vermont along the spine of the Green Mountains, from Massachusetts to the Canadian border. It's said to be the oldest long-distance hiking trail in the country.

The Long Trail ascends many of Vermont's highest mountains, among them 4,393-foot Mount Mansfield and 4,083-foot Camel's Hump, and it crosses some of the wildest territory in the state.

In the process the trail traverses Green Mountain National Forest, some state lands, and large privately-owned areas. For 98 miles it coincides with the Appalachian Trail.

Difficulty ranges from easy to strenuous. Some sections are quite rugged and strenuous. Group size should be kept to a maximum of 10. The recommended season is June through October.

Camping Regulations: Lean-tos, established tenting areas, and some closed cabins are located at regular intervals along the trail. Camping is limited to these sites where the trail is on private lands, as well as some state lands. At quite a few camping areas a caretaker is on duty, and a small fee is charged.

When the trail is on state forest lands, primitive camping is generally permitted below 2,500 feet elevation. Here sites must also be at least 2,500 feet from roads and shelters, 200 feet from the trail, and 100 feet from water sources.

Within Green Mountain National Forest camping is allowed almost anywhere, with the exception of a few areas where designated sites must be used. Campsites should be at least 100 feet from water sources and 50 feet from the trail.

Campfires are discouraged but allowed at most designated sites, and also elsewhere when on National Forest lands. It's recommended that a stove be brought for cooking.

For Further Information: The Green Mountain Club, P.O. Box 889, Montpelier, VT 05602; (802)223-3463.

APPALACHIAN TRAIL—137 miles in Vermont (2,100 total). This famous trail coincides with the Long Trail (previous entry) for 98 miles, from the Massachusetts border to Sherburne Pass, where the Appalachian Trail turns east and heads toward New Hampshire.

The trail crosses the southern unit of Green Mountain National Forest, as well as state-owned areas and private lands. It traverses a number of mountains over 3,000 feet, some of which offer fine views, and passes several beautiful mountain ponds. Difficulty varies from easy to strenuous.

Camping Regulations: Trail shelters and designated camping areas are found every few miles along the trail. At several locations there's a caretaker on duty and a small camping fee is collected. Where the trail is on private or state lands, camping is restricted to established sites.

On National Forest lands camping is allowed almost anywhere, except in a few areas where authorized sites must be used. When choosing non-designated sites, campsites should normally be at least 100 feet from water sources and 50 feet from the trail.

Campfires are permitted at most established sites, and are allowed in much of the National Forest, but they're prohibited in a few locations. A stove is recommended for cooking.

For Further Information: Appalachian Trail Conference, P.O. Box 807, Harpers Ferry, WV 25425.

VERMONT CAMPING RESOURCES

USEFUL GUIDEBOOKS

AMC River Guide: New Hampshire and Vermont—Boston: Appalachian Mountain Club, 1983.

Appalachian Trail Guide to New Hampshire-Vermont—Harpers Ferry, WV: The Appalachian Trail Conference, 1989.

Canoe-Camping Vermont & New Hampshire Rivers—Schweiker, Roioli. Woodstock, VT: Backcountry Publications.

Fifty Hikes in Vermont—Sadlier, Heather and Hugh. Woodstock, VT: Backcountry Publications, 1985.

Guidebook of the Long Trail—Montpelier, VT: The Green Mountain Club, 1990.

The Sierra Club Guide to the Natural Areas of New England—Perry, John and Jane. San Francisco: Sierra Club Books, 1990.

25 Mountain Bike Tours in Vermont—Busha, William J. Woodstock, VT: Backcountry Publications.

25 Ski Tours in Vermont—Wass, Stan. Woodstock, VT: Backcountry Publications.

Vermont Mountain Biking—Mansfield, Dick. Woodstock, VT: Backcountry Publications.

INFORMATION ABOUT STATE PARK AND FOREST CAMPGROUNDS

Vermont Department of Forests, Parks, and Recreation, 103 South Main Street, Waterbury, VT 05676; (802)828-3375.

STATE HIGHWAY MAP AND TRAVEL INFORMATION

Vermont Travel Division, 134 State Street, Montpelier, VT 05602; (802)828-3236.

VIRGINIA

BEST AREAS FOR WILDERNESS CAMPING

SHENANDOAH NATIONAL PARK—195,363 acres. This scenic National Park stretches 80 miles through the Blue Ridge Mountains of northern Virginia. Included here are many mountains in the 3,000-4,000 foot range, with countless views. Highest point is 4,051-foot Hawksbill Mountain.

There are cliffs, rocky knobs, outcroppings, and some small canyons. The park also has a large number of streams and waterfalls, open meadows, and forests of hardwoods, with some hemlock and fir, plus mountain laurel and pink azalea. Among the wildlife are black bear, white-tailed deer, bobcat, and fox.

Much of Shenandoah is preserved as wilderness. The park is just a few miles wide on the average, however, and the Skyline Drive runs down the middle, providing easy access, but limiting the remoteness of most areas.

Activities: Hiking and backpacking are available on 500 miles of trails, including a 95-mile segment of the Appalachian Trail. Difficulty ranges from easy to strenuous. Most trails here are graded, with switchbacks. Relatively few are truly steep.

About 200 miles of trails are open to horseback riding, and cross-country skiing is possible on many trails during winter. Bike use is restricted to public roads. Fishing is also available. Hunting is prohibited.

Camping Regulations: Camping is allowed in most areas of the park, but campsites must be completely out of sight of trails, shelters, roads, and other campers. It's also necessary to be at least 25 feet from streams, 250 yards from roads, and one-half mile from public use areas.

A backcountry camping permit is required, and may be obtained either by mail or in person from park headquarters, visitors centers, or self-registration centers. Maximum stay allowed at a campsite is two nights. Group size is limited to 10.

While there's a system of trail shelters in the park, these may no longer be used for camping except in severe weather or emergencies. Campfires are allowed only at shelter fireplaces. Glass containers may not be carried into the backcountry.

For Further Information: Shenandoah National Park, Luray, VA 22835; (703)999-2266.

JEFFERSON NATIONAL FOREST—690,000 acres. Consisting of a number of separate tracts, Jefferson National Forest sprawls across a large region of the Blue Ridge Mountains in west-central Virginia. It's an area of many sizable mountains and rocky ridges, with wonderful views.

Of special interest is the 154,000-acre Mount Rogers National Recreation Area, which encloses some of the forest's finest scenery. Highest point in the state, 5,729-foot Mount Rogers, is located here. Other notable mountains include 5,530-foot White Top Mountain and 5,526-foot Pine Mountain.

There are some "balds" (grassy-topped mountains) as well as a profusion of streams and waterfalls—along with mixed forests of hardwoods, with spruce and fir at higher elevations, plus dogwood and rhododendron. Among the wildlife are bear, white-tailed deer, and red fox.

The National Forest has a number of designated wilderness areas: the 8,703-acre James River Face

Wilderness, the 8,253-acre Mountain Lake Wilderness, the 6,375-acre Beartown Wilderness, the 5,730-acre Lewis Fork Wilderness, and several smaller wilderness areas.

Activities: Backpacking and hiking are available on more than 900 miles of trails, including over 300 miles of the Appalachian Trail (see entry page 287). Difficulty ranges from easy to strenuous.

Horseback riding is possible on some trails, including the 68-mile Virginia Highlands Horse Trail, the 40-mile Iron Mountain Trail (a previous route of the Appalachian Trail) and the 34-mile Virginia Creeper National Recreation Trail.

Some trails outside of wilderness areas are open to mountain biking. Cross-country skiing is a winter option at higher elevations. Fishing is also available. Hunting is permitted in season.

Camping Regulations: Camping and campfires are allowed throughout the National Forest, except near public use areas or where otherwise prohibited. No permits are required.

A Virginia law specifies that campfires may be made only from 4 P.M. to midnight each day between March 1 and May 15. Low-impact camping practices are strongly recommended.

For Further Information: Jefferson National Forest, 210 Franklin Road, S.W., Roanoke, VA 24001; (703)982-6270.

GEORGE WASHINGTON NATIONAL FOREST—

1,330,000 acres. This enormous National Forest is the largest in the eastern United States. It's made up of several parcels of land in northern and northwest Virginia, along with two in West Virginia. Terrain is largely mountainous here, with many rock outcrops, ledges, and some deep gorges.

Highest elevation is 4,472-foot Elliott Knob. Outstanding views are numerous. The Shenandoah Valley south of Shenandoah National Park falls within this National Forest. Designated wilderness areas include the 10,090-acre Saint Mary's Wilderness, the 9,300-acre Rough Mountain Wilderness, the 6,725-acre Ramsey's Draft Wilderness, and three smaller areas.

There are countless creeks and waterfalls. Among them is Crabtree Falls, highest in the state, which drops 1,200 feet over multiple cascades. The region is forested with hardwoods, along with pine and hemlock, including some old-growth stands, plus rhododendron and mountain laurel. Wildlife includes white-tailed deer, black bear, bobcat, and wild turkey.

Activities: Hiking and backpacking are possible on over 500 miles of trails, including 70 miles of the Appalachian Trail (see entry page 287). Some trails are open to horseback riding. Canoeing is available on several rivers, and on a few streams in springtime. Fishing is permitted, as is hunting in season.

Camping Regulations: Camping is allowed throughout the National Forest, as are campfires, except near developed areas or where posted otherwise. No permits are required. By Virginia law, campfires are allowed only from 4 P.M. to midnight during the period of March 1 through May 15 each year.

For Further Information: George Washington National Forest, 101 North Main Street, P.O. Box 233, Harrisonburg, VA 22801; (703)433-2491.

OTHER RECOMMENDED LOCATIONS

CUMBERLAND GAP NATIONAL HISTORICAL PARK— 7,526 acres in Virginia (20,270 acres total). This scenic park centers around historic Cumberland Gap, an important early gateway through the Appalachians. While based in Kentucky, it includes lands in the southwest corner of Virginia as well as in Tennessee.

Terrain here is rugged, with fine views from rocky outcrops. There are caves, creeks, and forests of oak-hickory, with some conifers. Deer and fox are among the wildlife.

Activities: About 50 miles of trails are available for hiking and backpacking, including the 21-mile Ridge Trail, which follows along the Kentucky–Virginia border. Difficulty ranges from easy to strenuous. Horses are allowed on many trails.

Camping Regulations: Camping is restricted to five designated backcountry camping areas in this National Historical Park. One area is a horse camp. Two of the camping areas are in the Virginia portion of the park. A backcountry camping permit is required, and must be obtained from the visitor center.

For Further Information: Cumberland Gap National Historical Park, P.O. Box 1848, Middlesboro, KY 40965; (606)248-2817.

PRINCE WILLIAM FOREST PARK—18,571 acres. Located in northern Virginia, southwest of Washington DC, Prince William Forest Park is administered by the National Park Service. This is an area of flat to hilly terrain, with a forest consisting of oak, hickory, beech, and pine. Several creeks run through the park. Among the wildlife are white-tailed deer, fox, and wild turkey.

Activities: Hiking is possible on over 35 miles of trails, easy to moderate in difficulty. Cross-country skiing and snowshoeing are available in winter. Bikes are not allowed on trails. Fishing is permitted, but hunting is not.

Camping Regulations: Primitive camping is allowed only in the Chopawamsic Backcountry Area, which is separate from and a bit south of the main park. Designated campsites must be used.

A permit is required. Permits may be applied for in advance but must be picked up in person. Campfires are prohibited, as are pets. Water must be carried in.

For Further Information: Prince William Forest Park, P.O. Box 209, Triangle, VA 22172; (703)221-7181.

FALSE CAPE STATE PARK—4,321 acres. This remote park is located along Virginia's coast, south of Virginia Beach and just north of the North Carolina border. It may be reached by a 5-mile hike or bike ride through Back Bay National Wildlife Refuge, or by private boat. Overnight parking is not allowed at the National Wildlife Refuge.

The park is on a mile-wide barrier spit along the ocean. Included here are sandy beaches and dunes, with oak and pine forests, marshes and swamps. Water must be carried in.

Activities: There are about nine miles of trails for hiking or backpacking. Some trails are open to bikes. Visitors are asked to stay on trails or walk along the beaches, and to avoid the dunes.

Camping Regulations: Camping is allowed in four designated beach areas. A permit is required, and must be obtained in person from Seashore State Park, 2500 Shore Drive, Virginia Beach, VA 23451; (804)481-2131. Campfires are prohibited. The park is closed to camping for one week in October each year.

For Further Information: False Cape State Park, 4001 Sandpiper Road, Virginia Beach, VA 23456; (804)426-7128.

FAIRY STONE STATE PARK—4,868 acres. Named after the distinctive crystals which are found here, this park is located in the foothills of the Blue Ridge Mountains, in south-central Virginia.

The region is forested with oak, hickory, and some hemlock, along with rhododendron. Included here is a 168-acre lake. White-tailed deer are among the wildlife.

Activities: There are over 25 miles of hiking trails. Difficulty varies from easy to strenuous. Included is a bike trail. Fishing is permitted in the park.

Camping Regulations: Primitive camping is allowed in one designated area, located about 1.5 miles from a parking area via some moderately difficult trails. A permit is necessary in order to camp here, and a fee is charged. Campfires are allowed in fire rings at the sites. Pets are prohibited.

For Further Information: Fairy Stone State Park, Route 2, Box 723, Stuart, VA 24171; (703)930-2424.

SKY MEADOWS STATE PARK—1,618 acres. Situated in northern Virginia, along the eastern edge of the Blue Ridge Mountains, Sky Meadows State Park

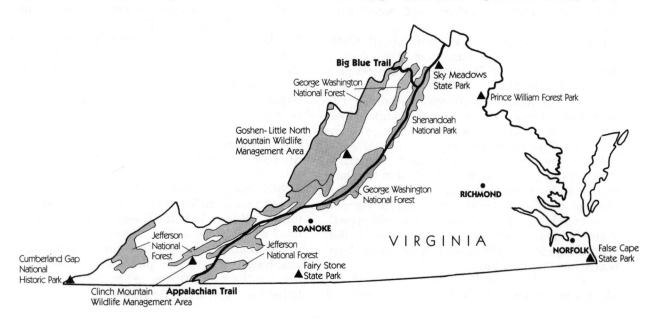

is a hilly area of old pastures and woodlands, with some streams and a couple of ponds.

Activities: Hiking is available on about nine miles of trails, including a 3.6-mile section of the Appalachian Trail (see entry below).

Camping Regulations: There's a small primitive campground with 12 sites and some shelters about a half mile down one trail. Camping is restricted to this area. Campfires are allowed in the fire rings provided.

For Further Information: Sky Meadows State Park, Route 1, Box 540, Delaplane, VA 22025; (703)592-3556.

GOSHEN–LITTLE NORTH MOUNTAIN WILDLIFE MANAGEMENT AREA—33,000 acres. Administered together, these two state Wildlife Management Areas are located in west-central Virginia, adjacent to George Washington National Forest. There are some rugged mountains, numerous streams, and hardwood forests here, with rhododendron. Wildlife includes bear, deer, and wild turkey.

Activities: Hiking and backpacking are possible on several trails, mostly moderate to strenuous in difficulty. Horseback riding is allowed. Hunting and fishing are permitted in season.

Camping Regulations: Primitive camping is allowed for up to seven days anywhere except where posted. No permits are necessary. Campfires are allowed only in designated areas.

For Further Information: Goshen–Little North Mountain Wildlife Management Area, Route 6, Box 484-A, Staunton, VA 24401.

CLINCH MOUNTAIN WILDLIFE MANAGEMENT AREA—25,000 acres. This state Wildlife Management Area is situated next to Jefferson National Forest lands in southwest Virginia. Terrain here is mountainous, with a forest of oak-hickory and other hardwoods, plus rhododendron and mountain laurel. There are several large creeks and a 300-acre lake. Black bear and white-tailed deer are among the wildlife.

Activities: Backpacking and hiking are available on several unmarked trails and also old roads. Difficulty ranges from easy to strenuous. Fishing is permitted, as is hunting in season.

Camping Regulations: Camping is allowed freely thoughout the area from September through mid March only. The remainder of the year camping is restricted to a campground. No permits are necessary. Camping is prohibited within 100 yards of the lake.

For Further Information: Clinch Mountain Wildlife Management Area, Department of Game

and Inland Fisheries, 4010 West Broad Street, Richmond, VA 23230.

Primitive camping is also permitted in most of Virginia's other Wildlife Management Areas, except where posted otherwise. Maximum stay is seven days. Camping is prohibited within 100 yards of state fishing lakes or boat ramps. For more information contact the Virginia Department of Game and Inland Fisheries, 4010 West Broad Street, Richmond, VA 23230; (804)367-1000.

In addition, camping is allowed at one backcountry area in Rock Castle Gorge, along the 10.8-mile Rock Castle Gorge Trail, on Blue Ridge Parkway lands in southern Virginia. A free permit is required. For more information contact the Blue Ridge Parkway, 200 BB & T Building, One Pack Square, Asheville, NC 28801.

MAJOR BACKPACKING TRAILS

APPALACHIAN TRAIL—550 miles in Virginia (2,100 total). After entering the state from Tennessee, this famous National Scenic Trail follows the ridges of the Blue Ridge Mountains in a northeasterly direction across Virginia to the Maryland border.

About one-quarter of the entire Appalachian Trail is located within this state. For most of its route here the trail is on lands of Jefferson National Forest, George Washington National Forest, and Shenandoah National Park.

There's some fine mountain scenery en route, with many superb views available. Difficulty ranges from easy to strenuous. Much of the trail in Virginia is graded, so steep ascents are relatively uncommon.

Camping Regulations: Trail shelters are spaced at regular intervals along the trail. Camping and campfires are limited to these shelters and other authorized campsites when the trail runs outside of National Forest and National Park lands.

Camping and campfires are allowed almost anywhere else, except where posted otherwise, when the trail is on National Forest lands. Campsites should be well off the trail and away from water sources.

Special rules apply for camping in Shenandoah National Park. A permit is required, and may be obtained in advance by mail or in person. Campfires are prohibited. Shelters in the park may no longer be legally used for camping except in emergencies or severe weather. See the Shenandoah National Park entry page 284 for complete regulations.

For Further Information: Appalachian Trail Conference, P.O. Box 807, Harpers Ferry, WV 25425. This organization publishes three separate guidebooks for different sections of the Appalachian Trail in Virginia.

BIG BLUE TRAIL—78 miles in Virginia (144 total). This trail originated as an alternate route to the Appalachian Trail. The Big Blue begins at an intersection with the Appalachian Trail in Shenandoah National Park, and runs north to Hancock, Maryland, where it connects with the C & O Towpath and Tuscarora Trails.

Difficulty ranges from easy to strenuous. Some of the terrain is mountainous and rugged, offering challenging backpacking. At other times the trail follows old country roads. A sizable portion of the Virginia section is in George Washington National Forest, with other parts on private land.

Camping Regulations: Camping and campfires are allowed almost anywhere along the trail when it's on National Forest lands. A permit is required for Shenandoah National Park, where special camping rules apply (see the Shenandoah National Park entry page 284).

When the trail is on private lands, camping is restricted to authorized sites. A couple of trail shelters and some regular campgrounds are also available along the way. Virginia law specifies that between March 1 and May 15 each year, campfires are allowed only between the hours of 4 P.M. and midnight.

For Further Information: Potomac Appalachian Trail Club, 718 N Street, N.W., Washington, DC 20036. *The Big Blue—A Trail Guide* is available from this address.

VIRGINIA CAMPING RESOURCES

ORGANIZATIONS WHICH OFFER WILDERNESS
CAMPING TRIPS
Natural Bridge Appalachian Trail Club, P.O. Box 3012, Lynchburg, VA 24503. This Appalachian Trail club sponsors an occasional backpacking trip.
Old Dominion Appalachian Trail Club, P.O. Box 25283, Richmond, VA 23260. The Old Dominion Appalachian Trail Club offers some backpacking and canoe-camping trips each season.
Tidewater Appalachian Trail Club, P.O. Box 8246, Norfolk, VA 23503. This club schedules a Seminar for Beginner Backpackers two to three times each year.

USEFUL GUIDEBOOKS
Appalachian Trail Guide: Central and Southern Virginia—Harpers Ferry, WV: The Appalachian Trail Conference, 1988.
Appalachian Trail Guide: Shenandoah National Park—Harpers Ferry, WV: The Appalachian Trail Conference, 1986.
Appalachian Trail Guide to Maryland and Northern Virginia— Harpers Ferry, WV: The Appalachian Trail Conference, 1989.
The Big Blue—A Trail Guide—Washington, DC: Potomac Appalachian Trail Club, 1987.
Hiker's Guide to Virginia—Johnson, Randy. Helena, MT: Falcon Press.
Hiking Virginia's National Forests—Wuertz-Schaefer, Karin. Old Saybrook, CT: The Globe Pequot Press.
Hiking the Old Dominion: The Trails of Virginia—de Hart, Allen. San Francisco: Sierra Club Books, 1984.

INFORMATION ABOUT CAMPGROUNDS IN STATE PARKS
Virginia State Parks, 203 Governor Street, Suite 306, Richmond, VA 23219; (804)786-1712.

STATE HIGHWAY MAP AND TRAVEL INFORMATION
Virginia Division of Tourism, 1021 East Cary Street, Richmond, VA 23206: (804)786-4484.

WASHINGTON

BEST AREAS FOR WILDERNESS CAMPING

WENATCHEE NATIONAL FOREST—1,618,287 acres. This huge National Forest in north-central Washington has high peaks and ridges, steep slopes, glaciers and snowfields. There are also mountain meadows with wildflowers, some rivers, many small lakes, plus 50-mile-long Lake Chelan.

Highest point is 10,541-foot Glacier Peak. Included in the region are forests of pine and Douglas fir, with spuce and hemlock. Among the wildlife are elk, deer, moose, black bear, bighorn sheep, mountain goat, mountain lion, coyote, and fox.

Wenatchee has six designated wilderness areas, consisting of about half of the 464,000-acre Glacier Peak Wilderness, 184,000 acres of the 304,000-acre Alpine Lakes Wilderness, and parts of the 146,000-acre Lake Chelan–Sawtooth Wilderness, the 105,600-acre Goat Rocks Wilderness, the 103,000-acre Henry M. Jackson Wilderness, and the 51,000-acre Norse Peak Wilderness.

Activities: Backpacking and hiking are available on more than 2,500 miles of trails, including a section of the Pacific Crest Trail (see entry page 000). Difficulty ranges from easy to strenuous. High trails are usually only snow-free from July through September.

Most trails are open to horses, and mountain bikes are allowed on many trails outside of wilderness areas. Cross-country skiing and snowshoeing are possible during the snow season. Kayaking and canoeing are available on the Wenatchee River. Fishing is another option. Hunting is permitted in season.

Camping Regulations: Camping and campfires are permitted in most but not all areas of the National Forest. Meadows should be avoided. A permit is required for portions of designated wilderness areas from June 15-October 15. Nightly quotas have been established.

A limited number of permits may be reserved in advance by mail. A nominal fee is charged for the permit, which must be picked up in person. Campfires are prohibited within one-quarter mile of lakes over 5,500 foot elevation in the Alpine Lakes Wilderness. Maximum group size in wilderness areas is 12.

For Further Information: Wenatchee National Forest, 301 Yakima Street, P.O. Box 811, Wenatchee, WA 98807; (509)662-4335.

MOUNT BAKER–SNOQUALMIE NATIONAL FOREST— 1,700,000 acres. This scenic National Forest is made up of large tracts in north and south-central Washington, including lands around both Mount Rainier National Park and North Cascades National Park. Highest point is 10,778-foot Mount Baker.

Along with steep volcanic mountains, there are many glaciers and snowfields, alpine meadows, and old-growth forests, with hundreds of lakes and streams, and also the Skagit National Wild and Scenic River. Forests are of spruce and fir, hemlock and cedar. Wildlife includes deer, elk, black bear, mountain goat, mountain lion, coyote, and bobcat.

There are eight designated wilderness areas: about half of the 464,000-acre Glacier Peak Wilderness, 120,000 acres of the 304,000-acre Alpine Lakes Wilderness, the 118,000-acre Mount Baker

Wilderness, parts of the 103,000-acre Henry M. Jackson Wilderness and the 51,000-acre Norse Peak Wilderness, plus the 49,000-acre Boulder River Wilderness, the 14,000-acre Clearwater Wilderness, and the 14,000-acre Noisy–Diobsud Wilderness.

Activities: Hiking and backpacking are possible on over 1,400 miles of trails, including a section of the Pacific Crest Trail (see entry page 294). Difficulty varies from easy to strenuous. High trails may only be snow-free during August and September.

Horseback riding is allowed on most trails, as is mountain biking outside of wilderness areas. Many trails are suitable for cross-country skiing and snowshoeing during winter. Whitewater kayaking and canoeing are available on several rivers. Climbing is another option in the mountains here. Fishing is possible along lakes and streams, with hunting permitted in season.

Camping Regulations: Camping is allowed throughout most of the National Forest, as are campfires, except near public use areas or where otherwise prohibited. No permits are required at this time. Campsites should be at least 100 feet from lakeshores. Group size in wilderness areas is limited to 12.

For Further Information: Mount Baker–Snoqualmie National Forest, 21905 64th Avenue West, Mountlake Terrace, WA 98043; (206)744-3409.

OKANOGAN NATIONAL FOREST—1,706,000 acres.
Okanogan National Forest consists of tracts in north-central and northeast Washington, including lands in the eastern Cascades near North Cascades National Park. Some of the terrain here is rugged, with steep jagged peaks. Highest elevation is 8,974-foot North Gardner Mountain.

There are also deep gorges, creeks with waterfalls, and lakes, along with grasslands and alpine vegetation. Much of the region is forested with Douglas fir and ponderosa pine, including old-growth stands. Among the wildlife are mule deer, black bear, moose, coyote, mountain lion, and bobcat.

This National Forest has two designated wilderness areas: the 530,031-acre Pasayten Wilderness and 95,976 acres of the 146,000-acre Lake Chelan–Sawtooth Wilderness.

Activities: More than 1,550 miles of trails are available for hiking and backpacking, including a 63-mile segment of the Pacific Crest Trail (see entry page 294). Difficulty varies from easy to strenuous. Many of the trails are open to horses.

Mountain biking is allowed on some trails outside of wilderness areas. Cross-country skiing is

possible here during winter. Mountaineering is another option. Fishing is available along lakes and streams, and hunting is permitted in season.

Camping Regulations: Camping is freely allowed throughout most of the National Forest, except near public recreation areas or where otherwise prohibited. No permits are necessary at the present time. Campfires may be built, but a stove is recommended.

Group size in wilderness areas is limited to 12. Campsites should be at least 200 feet from water sources and trails, and 500 feet from other campers. Visitors are asked to use preexisting sites whenever possible, and to camp away from meadows and lakes at higher elevations.

For Further Information: Okanogan National Forest, 1240 South Second, P.O. Box 950, Okanogan, WA 98840; (509)422-2704.

GIFFORD PINCHOT NATIONAL FOREST—1,251,160
acres. Gifford Pinchot National Forest is located in the Cascades of southwest Washington. It's now famous for 8,365-foot Mount Saint Helens, which was previously 9,677 feet high before erupting in 1980. Also here is 12,307-foot Mount Adams, second highest mountain in the state.

Mount Saint Helens is part of the Mount Saint Helens National Volcanic Monument, which protects a sizable area around the crater and dome. There are still major signs of devastation, and access to the area remains restricted.

Elsewhere in the region are other volcanoes and old lava flows, high peaks and ridges, snowfields, lakes, creeks with waterfalls, and forests of conifers including old-growth Douglas fir and hemlock, along with cedar. Among the wildlife are elk, deer, bear, mountain goat, mountain lion, bobcat, and fox.

The National Forest has seven designated wilderness areas: parts of the 168,000-acre William O. Douglas Wilderness and the 105,600-acre Goat Rocks Wilderness, along with the 46,800-acre Mount Adams Wilderness, the 21,000-acre Indian Heaven Wilderness, the 15,800-acre Tatoosh Wilderness, the 6,000-acre Trapper Creek Wilderness, and the 3,000-acre Glacier View Wilderness.

Activities: There are about 1,165 miles of trails for hiking and backpacking, including a section of the Pacific Crest Trail (see entry page 294), and the 32-mile Boundary National Recreation Trail. Difficulty ranges from easy to strenuous. High trails are likely to be snow-free only from late July through mid-September.

Horseback riding is allowed on many trails, and cross-country skiing is possible during the winter.

Mountain biking is permitted on trails outside of wilderness areas. Canoeing and kayaking are available on some of the rivers.

Climbing is another option, with a permit required to climb above 4,800 feet. There are also opportunities for spelunking (caving). Fishing is available, as is hunting in season.

Camping Regulations: Camping and campfires are allowed throughout most of the National Forest, except where otherwise prohibited. Permits are now required to enter and camp in the designated wilderness areas here. Some designated campsites are available. Elsewhere sites must be at least 100 feet from lakes, and 200 feet from the Pacific Crest Trail.

For Further Information: Gifford Pinchot National Forest, 6926 East 4th Plain Boulevard, P.O. Box 8944, Vancouver, WA 98668; (206)696-7500.

OLYMPIC NATIONAL PARK—908,720 acres. This beautiful National Park is located on the Olympic Peninsula in northwest Washington. Included in the region are the rugged Olympic Mountains, with precipitous peaks, rocky ridges, and talus slopes.

Highest point is 7,965-foot Mount Olympus. There are also cliffs and canyons, 60 glaciers, many streams and rivers, high waterfalls, lakes, hot springs, old-growth rain forests, and 57 miles of wilderness beaches.

Among the trees are Douglas fir and Pacific silver fir, Sitka spruce, western hemlock, and cedar. Wildlife includes elk, deer, bear, mountain goat, coyote, and cougar, plus marine mammals such as whale, sea lion, and seal.

Activities: About 600 miles of trails are available for backpacking and hiking. Difficulty ranges from easy to strenuous. Horseback riding is allowed on some trails. Bike use is limited to roads.

Kayaking and canoeing are possible on the Hoh River. Cross-country skiing and snowshoeing are options during the snow season. Fishing is also available. Hunting is prohibited.

Camping Regulations: A free permit is required for backcountry camping. Permits may be obtained from visitor centers, ranger stations, and at trailheads. Pets are prohibited. Camping is allowed in most but not all parts of the park. In some areas camping is restricted to designated sites.

Elsewhere campers are asked to use existing campsites whenever possible, and avoid setting up on vegetation. Sites must be at least 100 feet from water sources and one-half mile from trailheads. Campfires are allowed in some lower-elevation areas, but prohibited elsewhere in the park. Maximum group size is 12.

For Further Information: Olympic National Park, 600 East Park Avenue, Port Angeles, WA 98362; (206)452-4501.

NORTH CASCADES NATIONAL PARK—504,780 acres. North Cascades National Park consists of two tracts in the Cascades of northern Washington, with some lands alongside the Canadian border. It's part of a park complex which includes the 107,000-acre Ross Lake National Recreation Area and the 62,000-acre Lake Chelan National Recreation Area.

Over 90 percent of the park and recreation areas have been designated as the Stephen Mather Wilderness Area. Scenery includes jagged alpine peaks with elevations over 7,000 feet, spires, talus slopes, cirque basins, steep cliffs, and deep mountain passes.

Also in the region are alpine lakes, streams, waterfalls, and no fewer than 318 glaciers. There are old-growth forests of Douglas fir and western red cedar, plus lodgepole pine and hemlock. Among the wildlife are grizzly and black bear, blacktail and mule deer, mountain goat, wolverine, bobcat, fox, and lynx.

Activities: Backpacking and hiking are available on over 360 miles of trails, including about 14 miles of the Pacific Crest Trail (see entry page 294). Difficulty ranges from easy to strenuous. Higher trails may be under snow until July.

Horseback riding is allowed on some trails. Many trails are suitable for cross-country skiing and snowshoeing during winter. Climbing and mountaineering are popular in the park. Climbers must register before starting out.

The upper Skagit River offers good rafting, and canoeing is possible in the Lake Chelan and Ross Lake areas. Fishing is another available option. Hunting is prohibited in the National Park, but permitted in parts of the National Recreation Areas.

Camping Regulations: A free permit must be obtained in order to camp in the backcountry here. There are almost 100 designated camping areas, including 30 for campers with horses.

Reservations are available by mail 30 days or less in advance for up to 50 percent of the designated sites. Permits must be picked up in person at a ranger station or visitor center.

Camping is also allowed elsewhere, but it's necessary to be at least one-half mile from trails and one mile from established sites. Camping is not permitted in high meadows. Campfires are restricted to authorized sites. Group size is limited to 12. Pets are prohibited except on the Pacific Crest Trail.

For Further Information: North Cascades National Park, 2105 Highway 20, Sedro Woolley, WA 98284; (206)856-5700.

MOUNT RAINIER NATIONAL PARK—235,404 acres.

This National Park in west-central Washington is dominated by magnificent 14,410-foot Mount Rainier, a massive volcanic mountain which is the highest peak in the Cascades.

Also in the park are alpine meadows, lakes and hot springs, rivers and streams with waterfalls, ice caves, and 26 glaciers—including Emmons Glacier, largest in the lower 48 states.

Forests are of hemlock and Douglas fir, spruce and western red cedar, with some old-growth stands. Among the wildlife are deer, elk, bear, mountain goat, mountain lion, and cougar.

Activities: Hiking and backpacking are possible on over 300 miles of trails. Included are the 93-mile Wonderland Trail, which circles around Mount Rainier, and a section of the Pacific Crest Trail (see entries page 294).

Difficulty varies from easy to strenuous. About 100 miles of trail are open to horses. Most trails at higher elevations are snow-free from mid-July through mid-October.

Cross-country skiing is available in the winter. Climbing is possible on Mount Rainier, with climbers asked to register before and after trips. Fishing is allowed, but hunting is prohibited.

Camping Regulations: A free backcountry permit is necessary, and may be obtained from visitor centers, hiker's information centers, and ranger stations. There are no advance reservations.

"Trailside camps" (camping areas) are located along some of the trails, including at regular intervals along the Wonderland Trail. It's also possible to camp elsewhere in the backcountry, but sites must be at least 100 feet from water sources and one-quarter mile from trails, roads, and any lake with designated campsites. Subalpine meadow areas are off-limits for camping.

Campfires are not allowed in the backcountry. There are designated horse camps for the use of horseback riders. At other than established group sites, groups are limited to a maximum of five. Pets are prohibited except on the Pacific Crest Trail.

Camping at high elevations is allowed only at designated sites or on permanent ice or snow. During the snow season, campsites are required to be at least 200 feet from roads, 100 feet from trails. Groups may be as large as 12 during winter.

For Further Information: Mount Rainier National Park, Tahoma Woods, Star Route, Ashford, WA 98304; (206)569-2211.

COLVILLE NATIONAL FOREST—1,095,368 acres.

Colville National Forest consists of several units in the northeast corner of the state. Terrain includes some rocky peaks, canyons, and glacier-carved valleys, with a number of lakes and streams. Highest point is 7,309-foot Gypsy Peak.

There's a single designated wilderness area, the 41,350-acre Salmo–Priest Wilderness. Forests are largely of mixed conifers, with Douglas fir, lodgepole pine, and old-growth ponderosa pine, plus hemlock and cedar. Wildlife includes white-tailed and mule deer, moose, black bear, mountain lion, and lynx.

Activities: About 310 miles of trails are available for backpacking and hiking, including the 29-mile Kettle Crest Trail and the 22-mile Shed Roof Divide National Recreation Trail. Difficulty ranges from easy to strenuous.

Horseback riding is allowed on many trails, as is mountain biking except in the wilderness area. Cross-country skiing and snowshoeing are available during winter here. Fishing is also possible. Hunting is permitted in season.

Camping Regulations: Camping is allowed throughout most of the National Forest without restriction, except near public recreation areas or where otherwise prohibited. No permits are required. Campfires are allowed, but the use of stoves is encouraged.

For Further Information: Colville National Forest, 695 South Main, Federal Building, Colville, WA 99114; (509)684-3711.

OLYMPIC NATIONAL FOREST—631,514 acres.

Consisting of several tracts of land surrounding Olympic National Park, on the Olympic Peninsula in northwest Washington, this National Forest has scenery which ranges from lush rain forests to rugged mountains over 7,000 feet.

A number of lakes, rivers, and streams with waterfalls are found here, along with some deep canyons, high meadows, hot springs, and cedar swamps. There are forests of Douglas fir, western red cedar, and hemlock. Wildlife includes elk, deer, bear, mountain goat, cougar, and coyote.

The National Forest has five designated wilderness areas: the 45,600-acre Buckhorn Wilderness, 17,000-acre The Brothers Wilderness, the 15,700-acre Mount Skokomish Wilderness, the 12,000-acre Colonel Bob Wilderness, and the 2,300-acre Wonder Mountain Wilderness.

Activities: Backpacking and hiking are possible on over 200 miles of trails, some of which connect with trails in Olympic National Park. Difficulty ranges from easy to strenuous.

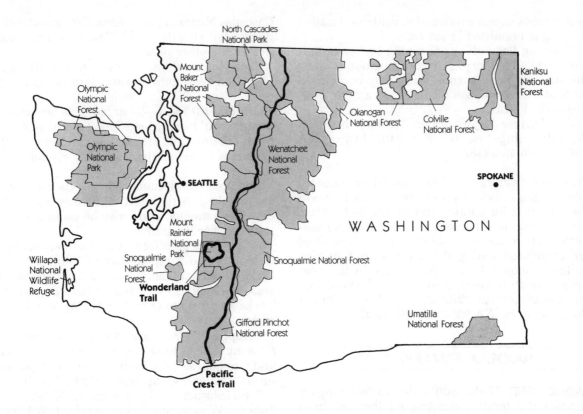

Cross-country skiing is a winter option. Horse-back riding is available, as is mountain biking on some trails outside of wilderness areas. The Humptulips River is suitable for canoeing. Fishing is possible along the numerous lakes, rivers, and streams. Hunting is permitted in season.

Camping Regulations: Camping and campfires are allowed throughout the National Forest, except where otherwise prohibited. No permits are necessary. Visitors are asked to camp at least 100 feet from water sources, and to use existing sites whenever possible.

For Further Information: Olympic National Forest, 801 South Capitol Way, P.O. Box 2288, Olympia, WA 98507; (206)753-9534.

OTHER RECOMMENDED LOCATIONS

UMATILLA NATIONAL FOREST—While 1,399,342-acre Umatilla National Forest is based in Oregon, with the majority of lands in that state, about 311,000 acres of the forest are in the southeast corner of Washington.

This tract is in the Blue Mountains, and includes 6,387-foot Oregon Butte, 6,379-foot Diamond Peak, and over 110,000 acres of the 177,000-acre Wenaha–Tucannon Wilderness.

Camping and campfires are allowed in most areas of the National Forest. See the Umatilla National Forest listing in the Oregon chapter for more information.

IDAHO PANHANDLE NATIONAL FORESTS—About 283,000 acres of Kaniksu National Forest, which is part of the Idaho Panhandle National Forests, are located in the northeast corner of Washington next to Colville National Forest.

Included here are some mountains over 6,000 feet. Camping and campfires are allowed. See the Idaho Panhandle National Forests entry in the Idaho chapter for more information.

WILLAPA NATIONAL WILDLIFE REFUGE—11,000 acres. This National Wildlife Refuge in southwest Washington preserves the land and wildlife around Willapa Bay, and includes 5,000-acre Long Island. Access to the island is by private boat.

There are ocean beaches and sand dunes, grassy areas with shrubs, salt marshes, and some coastal forest with a 274-acre stand of old-growth western red cedar. Among the wildlife here are elk, deer, bear, marine animals, plus a diverse birdlife.

Activities: The refuge is open to foot travel only. There are just a few short trails, along with some gravel roads which are closed to vehicles. Limited hunting is permitted in season.

Camping Regulations: Camping and campfires are restricted to five primitive campgrounds along the shore of Long Island. These may be reached by boat. Campsites are available on a first-come, first-served basis.

For Further Information: Willapa National Wildlife Refuge, HC 01, Box 910, Ilwaco, WA 98624; (206)484-3482.

Primitive camping is also allowed in most of Washington's State Wildlife Areas. Primary use of these areas is for hunting and fishing, but hiking, backpacking, and horseback riding are also permitted. There are no established trails. Campfires are prohibited during the dry season. Camping policy is subject to possible change in the near future. For more information contact the Washington Department of Wildlife, 600 North Capitol Way, Olympia, WA 98501; (206)753-5700.

MAJOR BACKPACKING TRAILS

PACIFIC CREST TRAIL—500 miles in Washington (2,638 miles total). Extending all the way from Canada to Mexico, with National Scenic Trail status, the spectacular Pacific Crest Trail is one of this country's great long-distance wilderness trails.

In Washington the trail crosses the Cascades, passing through North Cascades National Park and Mount Rainier National Park. It also traverses several National Forests with a total of eight designated wilderness areas.

Much of this wild and often remote trail is at high elevations, and the route is likely to be snow-free only during the months of August and September. Difficulty ranges from easy to quite strenuous. Horses are allowed on the trail.

Camping Regulations: Camping is allowed just about anywhere in the National Forests along the way, except where posted otherwise. Permits are not currently required on these lands.

Backpackers are asked to use preexisting campsites whenever possible. Sites should be well off the trail, away from meadows and areas with vegetation, and at least 100 feet from water sources. Campfires are allowed but discouraged. It's recommended that a stove be brought for cooking.

A wilderness permit is required for camping in the two National Parks. Either designated campsites should be used, or sites must be at least one-quarter mile from the trail (Mount Rainier National Park) or one-half mile from the trail (North Cascades National Park). Campfires are allowed at designated sites in North Cascades, and prohibited in the other park.

Trail Information: Pacific Crest Trail Conference, 365 West 29th Avenue, Eugene, OR 97405.

WONDERLAND TRAIL—93 miles. This beautiful and popular trail forms a large loop around 14,410-foot Mount Rainier, in Mount Rainier National Park. There's a wide variety of scenery available along the way.

Included are alpine meadows, glaciers, and areas of old-growth forest. Difficulty varies from easy to strenuous. Food may be cached at ranger stations near the trail.

Camping Regulations: A free wilderness permit is required to camp in Mount Rainier National Park. "Trailside camps" or designated camping areas are spaced every few miles along the trail. These are likely to be full on Friday and Saturday nights.

Camping is also allowed elsewhere, but campsites must be at least 100 feet from water sources and one-quarter mile from the trail. Campfires are prohibited, and group size is limited to five.

Trail Information: Mount Rainier National Park, Tahoma Woods, Star Route, Ashford, WA 98304; (206)569-2211.

WASHINGTON CAMPING RESOURCES

ORGANIZATIONS WHICH OFFER WILDERNESS CAMPING TRIPS

The Mountaineers, 300 Third Avenue West, Seattle, WA 98119. This large and well-known club offers a wide range of activities, including many backpacking trips, and also introductory backpacking classes.

Inter-Mountain Alpine Club, P.O. Box 505, Richland, WA 99352. This hiking and climbing trip sponsors some backpacking trips each year, with equipment available for rental.

INFORMATION ABOUT OUTFITTERS AND GUIDES

Washington Outfitters and Guides Association, 22845 N.E. 8th, Suite 331, Redmond, WA 98053; (206)392-0111.

USEFUL GUIDEBOOKS

Cross-Country Ski Tours, Vol 1 & 2—Kirkendall and Spring. Seattle: The Mountaineers Books.

55 Hikes in Central Washington—Spring, Ira and Manning, Harvey. Seattle: The Mountaineers Books, 1990.

50 Hikes in Mt. Rainier National Park—Spring, Ira and Manning, Harvey. Seattle: The Mountaineers Books, 1988.

The Hiker's Guide to Washington—Adkinson, Ron. Helena, MT: Falcon Press.

Hiking the North Cascades—Darvill, Fred T. San Francisco: Sierra Club Books.

Mount St. Helens National Volcanic Monument—Williams. Seattle: The Mountaineers Books.

Olympic Mountains Trail Guide—Wood, Robert L. Seattle: The Mountaineers Books, 1988.

100 Hikes in the Alpine Lakes—Spring, Vicky and Ira and Manning, Harvey. Seattle: The Mountaineers Books, 1985.

100 Hikes in the Glacier Peak Region—Spring, Ira. Seattle: The Mountaineers Books, 1988.

100 Hikes in the Inland Northwest—Landers, Rich, & Dolphin, Ida Rowe. Seattle: The Mountaineers Books.

100 Hikes in the North Cascades—Spring, Ira and Manning, Harvey. Seattle: The Mountaineers Books, 1988.

100 Hikes in the South Cascades and Olympics—Spring, Ira and Manning, Harvey. Seattle: The Mountaineers Books, 1985.

The Pacific Crest Trail—Volume 2: Oregon & Washington—Schaffer, Jeffrey P. and Selters, Andy. Berkeley: Wilderness Press, 1990.

The Sierra Club Guide to the Natural Areas of Oregon and Washington—Perry, John and Jane. San Francisco: Sierra Club Books, 1983.

Washington Whitewater—North, Douglass A. Seattle: The Mountaineers Books.

INFORMATION ABOUT STATE PARK CAMPGROUNDS
Washington State Parks and Recreation Commission, 7150 Cleanwater Lane, KY-11, Olympia, WA 98504; (206)753-2027.

STATE HIGHWAY MAP AND TRAVEL INFORMATION
Washington Tourism Development Division, 101 General Administration Building, AX-13, Olympia, WA 98504; (800)544- 1800/ (206)586-2102.

WEST VIRGINIA

BEST AREAS FOR WILDERNESS CAMPING

MONONGAHELA NATIONAL FOREST—901,000 acres. Located in the eastern part of West Virginia, Monongahela National Forest encompasses areas of both the Appalachian and Allegheny Mountains. The often wild and rugged scenery includes steep mountain slopes with rocky terrain, some caves, many creeks and waterfalls, and several major rivers.

The state's highest elevation, 4,862-foot Spruce Knob, is here in the 100,000-acre Spruce Knob–Seneca Rocks National Recreation Area. The Seneca Rocks are jagged and sheer-walled rocks which are almost 1,000 feet high.

There are also high plains, with heath barrens and bogs, and hardwood forests of oak and hickory, maple and birch—with some spruce, including old-growth stands, plus dense rhododendron and mountain laurel. Among the wildlife are white-tailed deer, black bear, bobcat, and wild turkey.

This National Forest has five designated wilderness areas: the 35,860-acre Cranberry Wilderness, the 20,000-acre Otter Creek Wilderness, the 12,200-acre Laurel Fork North and South Wilderness areas, and the 10,215-acre Dolly Sods Wilderness.

Activities: Backpacking and hiking are available on more than 850 miles of trails, including about 120 miles of the Allegheny Trail (see entry page 298). Difficulty ranges from easy to strenuous. A few trails receive heavy use.

Horseback riding is allowed on some trails, as is mountain biking outside of wilderness areas.

Cross-country skiing is an option during the winter. Canoeing is possible on several of the rivers. The Seneca Rocks area is popular for rock climbing. Fishing is also available, and hunting is permitted in season.

Camping Regulations: Camping is allowed almost anywhere in the National Forest, except near developed areas or where posted otherwise. Campsites should be at least 100 feet from trails and water sources, and well away from roads. Campfires may be made, but bringing a stove is recommended. No permits are necessary.

For Further Information: Monongahela National Forest, 200 Sycamore Street, Elkins, WV 26241; (304)636-1800. A *Hiking Guide to Monongahela National Forest and Vicinity* may be obtained from the West Virginia Highlands Conservancy, P.O. Box 306, Charleston, WV 25321.

OTHER RECOMMENDED LOCATIONS

GEORGE WASHINGTON NATIONAL FOREST—101,000 acres in West Virginia (1,300,000 total). While most of this huge National Forest is in Virginia, two sizable tracts are located in the northeastern part of West Virginia.

Terrain here is mountainous, and it's an area of hardwood forest with some pine and hemlock. Hiking and backpacking are possible on over 90 miles of trails in the West Virginia units.

Camping and campfires are allowed throughout the region, except near roads or developed areas. No permits are necessary, and no fees required. For more information see the George Washington National Forest entry in the Virginia chapter.

NEW RIVER GORGE NATIONAL RIVER—63,000 acres. Situated in the southern part of the state, this National River consists of 53 miles of the scenic New River, which flows through a deep gorge, and there are also 40 miles of tributaries. Included nearby are the Gauley River National Recreation Area and the Bluestone National Scenic River.

Activities: The river is suitable for canoeing, kayaking, and rafting. Included are varying levels of whitewater as well as flatwater. Outfitters and canoe rentals are available nearby.

Hiking and limited backpacking are possible on over 20 miles of trails on lands of the National River, and several adjacent state parks have many additional trails. Horses and bikes are not allowed on trails. Fishing is permitted.

Camping Regulations: Camping is generally allowed alongside and near the river, but not in all areas. Some riverside lands are privately owned. Campsites chosen along the river should be above the high water line. No permits are required.

For Further Information: New River Gorge National River, P.O. Box 246, 104 Main Street, Glen Jean, WV 25846; (304)465-0508.

JEFFERSON NATIONAL FOREST—18,175 acres in West Virginia (690,000 acres total). Most of Jefferson National Forest's acreage is in Virginia, but there's a small tract in the mountains of southeast West Virginia.

Camping and campfires are allowed freely in the region, except where otherwise prohibited. No permits are necessary. Low-impact practices are encouraged. For more information see the listing for Jefferson National Forest in the Virginia chapter.

WATOGA STATE PARK—10,100 acres. Located alongside the Greenbrier River and next to Monongahela National Forest in the southeastern part of the state, this is West Virginia's largest state park.

Terrain here is mountainous, with mixed hardwood forests including oak and hickory, birch and pine, and some rhododendron. There are several streams and an 11-acre lake. Among the wildlife are white-tailed deer, black bear, and fox.

Activities: The park has over 30 miles of trails for hiking and backpacking, including a 5-mile segment of the Allegheny Trail. Horseback riding is also available, and horses may be rented in the park.

Canoeing is possible on the Greenbrier River. Some trails and roads are designated for cross-country skiing in the winter. Fishing is allowed at the lake or along the river.

Camping Regulations: Camping is permitted at two designated primitive camping areas, and restricted to these locations.

For Further Information: Watoga State Park, Star Route 1, Box 252, Marlinton, WV 24954; (304)799-4087.

HOLLY RIVER STATE PARK—8,292 acres. Holly River is situated in a valley in central West Virginia, with mountains on either side. Near the park boundary is 2,480-foot Potato Knob, which offers great views, and there are dense hardwood forests, two rivers, some streams, and several waterfalls. Wildlife includes deer, bear, and bobcat.

Activities: Hiking and backpacking are possible on 33 miles of trails. Difficulty varies from easy to strenuous. Fishing is available along the rivers and streams.

Camping Regulations: Primitive camping is limited to two designated areas. No fee is required for camping here.

For Further Information: Holly River State Park, P.O. Box 70, Hacker Valley, WV 26222; (304)493-6353.

MAJOR BACKPACKING TRAILS

ALLEGHENY TRAIL—This scenic trail will be about 300 miles long when completed. Most of the trail is now open for use. It stretches from northern West Virginia, near Coopers Rock State Forest, to a point near the Virginia border in the southeastern part of the state.

The trail is mainly on public lands. A major portion is in Monongahela National Forest, and it also crosses West Virginia's two other National Forests, plus several state parks and forests. Difficulty ranges from easy to strenuous.

Camping Regulations: Camping is allowed almost anywhere when the trail is on National Forest lands, except near roads or developed areas,

and campfires are allowed. Campsites should be at least 100 feet from water sources and the trail. On state and private lands camping is restricted to designated sites.

For Further Information: West Virginia Scenic Trails Association, P.O. Box 4042, Charleston, WV 25364. This organization publishes *A Hiking Guide to the Allegheny Trail*, which may be obtained from the following address: Hiking Guide, 633 West Virginia Ave., Morgantown, WV 26505.

BIG BLUE TRAIL—66 miles in West Virginia (144 total). The Big Blue Trail runs from the C & O Canal Trail in Maryland, heading southwest through West Virginia into Virginia, where it turns southeast and terminates in Shenandoah National Park.

This trail connects with the Appalachian Trail twice—in Shenadoah National Park, and again via the Tuscarora Trail in Pennsylvania—thus forming a huge 250-mile loop. Difficulty varies from easy to strenuous.

It traverses some rugged terrain, with wild mountain scenery along the way, and for stretches the trail also follows old country roads. A portion is within George Washington National Forest, while other parts of the trail are on private lands.

Camping Regulations: Camping and campfires are allowed almost anywhere in George Washington National Forest, except where otherwise prohibited. Along other sections of the trail camping is generally restricted to designated sites.

For Further Information: Potomac Appalachian Trail Conference, 1718 N Street, NW, Washington, DC 20036; (202)638-5306. *The Big Blue—A Trail Guide* is available from this organization.

GREENBRIER RIVER TRAIL—80 miles. While this is not really a wilderness trail, it runs alongside the Greenbrier River through some attractive rural and riverside scenery of southeast West Virginia, including some small towns. The trail follows an old railroad bed, and thus makes for easy backpacking. It's also open to bicycling, horseback riding, and in the winter cross-country skiing.

Camping Regulations: A number of primitive camping areas are located along the trail, and camping is limited to these sites. Permits are not required, and except at a regular campground in Watoga State Park, no fees are charged.

For Further Information: Greenbrier River Trail, c/o Watoga State Park, Star Route 1, Box 252, Marlinton, WV 24954; (304)799-4087.

WEST VIRGINIA CAMPING RESOURCES

USEFUL GUIDEBOOKS
Hiking Guide to the Allegheny Trail—West Virginia Scenic Trails Association.
Hiking Guide to Monongahela National Forest and Vicinity—West Virginia Highlands Conservancy.
Hiking the Mountain State—de Hart, Allen. Boston: Appalachian Mountain Club, 1986.

INFORMATION ABOUT STATE PARK AND STATE FOREST CAMPGROUNDS
Travel West Virginia, Department of Commerce, State Capitol, Charleston, WV 25305; (800)CALL-WVA.

STATE HIGHWAY MAP AND TRAVEL INFORMATION
Travel West Virginia, Department of Commerce, State Capitol, Charleston, WV 25305; (800)CALL-WVA.

WISCONSIN

BEST AREAS FOR WILDERNESS CAMPING

CHEQUAMEGON NATIONAL FOREST—850,000 acres. This scenic National Forest is made up of three separate tracts of land in the mostly unspoiled reaches of northern Wisconsin. Terrain here is hilly, with some small mountains, outcroppings, and rock walls. Highest point is 1,600-foot St. Peter's Dome.

There are hundreds of lakes and a number of rivers and streams, plus some swamps and bogs. The region is forested with northern hardwoods, along with pine and hemlock. Wildlife includes white-tailed deer, black bear, coyote, and fox.

Chequamegon has two designated wilderness areas: the 6,600-acre Rainbow Lake Wilderness and the 4,200-acre Porcupine Lake Wilderness—along with 12 "Semi-Primitive Non-Motorized Areas," adding up to 52,000 acres, where motor vehicles are prohibited.

Activities: Backpacking and hiking are available on approximately 200 miles of trails, including 60 miles of the North Country Trail and a 41-mile segment of the Ice Age Trail (see entries pages 304, 305).

Some trails are appropriate for cross-country skiing, and snowshoeing is another winter option. Biking is possible on roads and suitable trails outside of wilderness areas. Excellent canoeing and kayaking are available on many of the rivers and lakes, as is fishing. Hunting is permitted in season.

Camping Regulations: Camping and campfires are allowed throughout the National Forest, except near public recreation areas or where otherwise prohibited. No permits are necessary. Sites should be at least 50 feet from trails, lakes, and streams.

For Further Information: Chequamegon National Forest, 1170 Fourth Avenue South, Park Falls, WI 54552; (715)762-2461.

NICOLET NATIONAL FOREST—661,000 acres. Located in northeastern Wisconsin, this National Forest has hilly and occasionally rugged terrain with some rock formations. Elevations range from 860 feet to 1,880 feet, and fine views are available.

Several major rivers flow through the forest, which also has a large number of streams, over 1,200 lakes, and some swamps and bogs. Trees include hardwoods along with hemlock and pine. Black bear and white-tailed deer are among the region's wildlife.

There are three designated wilderness areas: the 20,000-acre Headwaters Wilderness, the 7,500-acre Whisker Lake Wilderness, and the 5,890-acre Blackjack Springs Wilderness—plus several additional "Non-Motorized Areas" where vehicles are prohibited.

Activities: About 100 miles of hiking and backpacking trails are available in the forest. Many of the trails are used for cross-country skiing in winter, and snowshoeing is also possible.

There are numerous opportunities for canoeing, kayaking, and rafting on the rivers here, as well as on many lakes. Fishing is also available. Hunting is permitted in season.

Camping Regulations: A number of established primitive campsites are located throughout the forest. Camping is allowed elsewhere else as well, except near public use areas or where posted otherwise. No permits are required.

Campfires are legal, but the use of a stove for cooking is recommended. Visitors are encouraged to camp at least 100 feet from lakes and streams, and away from trails.

For Further Information: Nicolet National Forest, Federal Building, 68 South Stevens Street, Rhinelander, WI 54501; (715)362-3415.

APOSTLE ISLANDS NATIONAL LAKESHORE

APOSTLE ISLANDS NATIONAL LAKESHORE—This National Lakeshore consists of 21 of the 22 Apostle Islands in Lake Superior, off the northern shore of Wisconsin, and also 2,500 acres on Bayfield Peninsula. The islands are accessible by excursion boat or water taxi during the summer.

Scenery includes sandstone cliffs and sandy beaches, lagoons and bogs, and forests of northern hardwoods, with oak, maple, and birch, plus some hemlock and pine. Among the National Lakeshore's wildlife are white-tailed deer, black bear, coyote, and fox.

Activities: A number of the islands have trails for hiking, with cross-country skiing and snowshoeing possible in the winter. Fishing is available on Lake Superior. Hunting is prohibited.

Camping Regulations: A permit must be obtained from the visitor center or a ranger station before camping here. Campfires are allowed but restricted to established fire rings or pits. Campers are asked to check in with a ranger at the start and end of a visit. Winter campers must register at park headquarters.

There are designated primitive campsites on most of the islands. In addition, camping is allowed away from established sites on some but not all of the islands.

When camping at other than designated areas, campsites must be at least 100 feet from water sources, out of sight of trails and buildings, and one-quarter mile from established campsites. Groups of seven or more must use authorized group camping areas.

For Further Information: Apostle Islands National Lakeshore, Route 1, Box 4, Bayfield, WI 54814; (715)779-3397.

ST. CROIX NATIONAL SCENIC RIVERWAY

ST. CROIX NATIONAL SCENIC RIVERWAY—This National Scenic Riverway is comprised of 252 miles of the St. Croix and Namekagon Rivers. Both of these rivers have National Wild and Scenic River status, with the St. Croix River forming part of the Wisconsin–Minnesota border.

Along the Riverway are some high cliffs, as well as forests, marshes, swamps, and pools. The rivers are dammed in several places. Among the area's wildlife are bear, coyote, and fox.

Activities: The Riverway is especially suitable for canoeing, with outfitters and canoe rentals available nearby. Limited hiking is possible on some trails, most of which are short. Fishing is allowed, and hunting is permitted in season.

Camping Regulations: There are primitive campsites at many locations along the shore and on islands. Visitors are asked to use these established sites, although camping is also allowed at nondesignated areas along the way. No permits or fees are required. Campfires may be built, but only in established fire rings. It's recommended that a stove be brought for cooking.

For Further Information: St. Croix National Scenic Riverway, P.O. Box 708, St. Croix Falls, WI 54024; (715)483-3284.

NORTHERN HIGHLANDS–AMERICAN LEGION STATE FOREST

NORTHERN HIGHLANDS–AMERICAN LEGION STATE FOREST—220,000 acres. Located in the northern part of the state, Northern Highlands–American Legion is by far the largest of Wisconsin's state forests.

There are over 900 lakes here, some of which are remote, along with several rivers, numerous streams, and some swamps. Wildlife includes deer, black bear, coyote, fox, and bald eagle.

Activities: The forest has more than 18 miles of trails for hiking and backpacking, including the 15-mile Lumberjack Trail, and over 30 miles of trails designated for cross-country skiing during the snow season. Snowshoeing is another winter option.

Canoeing is available on many of the lakes and some streams. Canoes may be rented nearby. Biking is allowed on old roads in the forest but not on hiking trails. Fishing is also possible, and hunting is permitted in season.

Camping Regulations: Backpack camping is allowed along both the Lumberjack Trail and a state snowmobile trail. In addition, there are 118 designated sites for canoe-camping along waterways in the forest. Maximum stay at these campsites is one night. A permit must be obtained for canoe-camping and backpacking.

Thirteen other primitive wilderness campsites are available by reservation, some of them accessible only by canoe or boat. A fee is charged for these campsites, but not for other backpack camping or canoe-camping sites. Campfires are allowed.

For Further Information: Northern Highlands–American Legion State Forest, P.O. Box 440, Woodruff, WI 54568; (715)356-5211.

FLAMBEAU RIVER STATE FOREST

FLAMBEAU RIVER STATE FOREST—88,000 acres. Flambeau River State Forest in northern Wisconsin includes over 60 miles of the North and South

Forks of the Flambeau River. There are also many streams, several lakes, and a number of ponds. Among the wildlife are white-tailed deer, black bear, and bald eagle.

Activities: The most popular recreational activity in this state forest is canoeing on the Flambeau River, along with kayaking and rafting. Some stretches of white water are included.

Cross-country skiing is available on a network of trails. Backpacking and hiking are allowed, but there are no trails designated specifically for these activities.

Some little-used roads, snowmobile trails, and cross-country ski trails provide the best access on foot. Fishing is possible by the rivers and lakes. Hunting is allowed in season.

Camping Regulations: A free permit is required in order to camp in this forest. For those floating the Flambeau, camping is allowed for one night only at designated sites along the river. Fires are restricted to established fire rings.

For Further Information: Flambeau River State Forest, W1613 County W. South, Winter, WI 54896; (715)332-5271.

BLACK RIVER STATE FOREST—65,000 acres. This state forest in west-central Wisconsin includes some sandstone ridges and bluffs, along with a number of lakes, ponds, and streams. There are forests of pine, oak, and aspen, with deer among the wildlife. As in other state forests, logging takes place in some areas.

Activities: Canoeing is available on the Black River during spring and early summer. There are 27 miles of cross-country ski trails which are groomed during the winter, and also about 20 miles of horse trails.

The forest has no designated hiking or backpacking trails. Foot-travelers may use cross-country ski trails and other paths or roads. Fishing is possible, with hunting allowed in season.

Camping Regulations: A permit is required in order to camp in the forest, and may be obtained by mail or in person from the state forest office. Campfires are allowed. Some canoe campsites are available on an island in the Black River. There's also a small horse campground.

For Further Information: Black River State Forest, 910 Highway 54 East, Black River Falls, WI 54615; (715)284-1426.

OTHER RECOMMENDED LOCATIONS

GOVERNOR KNOWLES STATE FOREST—32,000 acres. Fifty-five-mile-long Governor Knowles State Forest, in northwest Wisconsin, protects a narrow band of land on the eastern side of the St. Croix National Scenic Riverway, along the state's border with Minnesota.

Activities: Two 22-mile-long trails parallel the river, and these are suitable for hiking or backpacking. Canoeing is available on the river, with canoe rentals nearby. About ten miles of the area's trails are used for cross-country skiing in winter, and there's a 26-mile trail for horseback riding. Fishing is possible as well.

Camping Regulations: Camping is allowed along portions of the trails, and there are also a few designated canoe-campsites by the river. A free camping permit must be obtained from forest headquarters. Campfires are allowed.

For Further Information: Governor Knowles State Forest, P.O. Box 367, Grantsburg, WI 54840; (715)463-2898.

KETTLE MORAINE STATE FOREST/NORTHERN UNIT—27,300 acres. Located in southeastern Wisconsin, Kettle Moraine State Forest's northern unit has a hilly glacial landscape. The area is forested with oak, maple, and other hardwoods, plus pine and cedar, and there are some lakes and streams. Wildlife includes deer, coyote, and fox.

Activities: The forest has about 70 miles of trails for backpacking and hiking, including the 29-mile Glacial Trail. Cross-country skiing is possible during winter on many of the trails.

There are also designated horse trails, including the 33-mile Kettle Moraine Bridle Trail, and horses may be rented nearby. Canoeing is available on the lakes as well as some streams, as is fishing. Hunting is permitted in season.

Camping Regulations: Primitive camping is limited to six different backpack camping areas, located along two of the trails. Shelters are available at these sites.

Registration is required and a fee is charged for each night. Campers may stay a maximum of one night at each location. Advance reservations for the sites are available and recommended.

For Further Information: Kettle Moraine State Forest/Northern Unit, Box 410, Campbellsport, WI 53010; (414)626-2116.

KETTLE MORAINE STATE FOREST/SOUTHERN UNIT—19,000 acres. The southern unit of Kettle Moraine State Forest, in southeastern Wisconsin, has hilly terrain with many lakes and ponds. There are oak forests, meadows, and wildlife which includes white-tailed deer.

Activities: Hiking and backpacking are possible on about 75 miles of trails, including 36 miles of

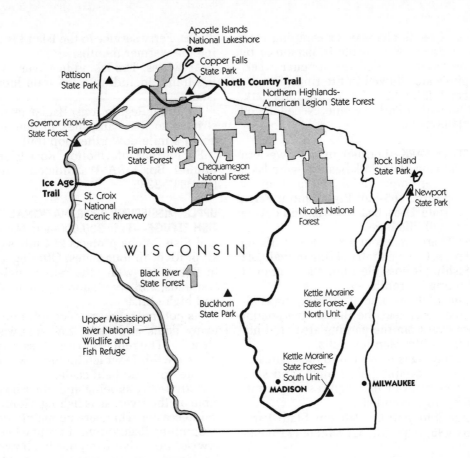

Apostle Islands
National Lakeshore

Copper Falls
State Park

North Country Trail

Pattison
State Park

Northern Highlands-
American Legion State Forest

Governor Knowles
State Forest

Flambeau River
State Forest

Rock Island
State Park

**Ice Age
Trail**

Chequamegon
National Forest

Newport
State Park

St. Croix
National
Scenic Riverway

Nicolet National
Forest

W I S C O N S I N

Black River
State Forest

Buckhorn
State Park

Kettle Moraine
State Forest-
North Unit

Upper Mississippi
River National
Wildlife and
Fish Refuge

Kettle Moraine
State Forest-
South Unit

● MILWAUKEE

● MADISON

the Ice Age Trail (see entry page 304). There are also three loop trails in the forest for horseback riding.

Several trails are designed for cross-country skiing in the winter, and some trails may be used for snowshoeing as well as mountain biking. Fishing is available along the streams and lakes, and hunting is permitted in season.

Camping Regulations: Backpack camping is allowed only along the Ice Age Trail, and restricted to three designated areas with lean-tos. There's also a horse camp.

A permit must be obtained before starting out, and a fee is charged for camping, with a limit of one night per site. Advance reservations are available. Campfires are allowed in fire rings.

For Further Information: Kettle Moraine State Forest/Southern Unit, Highway 59, Eagle, WI 53119; (414)594-2135.

NEWPORT STATE PARK—2,300 acres. Located in northeastern Wisconsin, near the tip of a peninsula extending into Lake Michigan, this wild state park includes 11 miles of Lake Michigan shoreline.

Activities: There are 28 miles of trails for hiking and backpacking. Most trails are used for cross-country skiing in winter. Snowshoeing and winter hiking are allowed on two trails.

Camping Regulations: Along the trails are 16 designated backpack campsites, most of them near the lakeshore. A permit is required to camp here, and may be obtained from the park office. A fee is charged for each night. Campfires are allowed but discouraged. A stove is recommended for cooking.

For Further Information: Newport State Park, 475 South Newport Lane, Ellison Bay, WI 54210; (414)854-2500.

BUCKHORN STATE PARK—3,200 acres. Situated in the south-central part of the state, at the intersection of the Wisconsin and Yellow Rivers, this park includes a number of islands and some sandy beaches.

Activities: Hiking and backpacking are possible on about five miles of trails. Some of the trails are suitable for cross-country skiing in winter. Canoeing is available on the rivers, as is fishing. Hunting is permitted in season.

Camping Regulations: Nine backpack campsites are located along the rivers, and accessible on foot or by canoe. A fee is charged for camping each night. Reservations are available in person or by mail, and are recommended for summer weekends. Campfires are allowed in fire rings.

For Further Information: Buckhorn State Park, West 8450 Buckhorn Park Avenue, Necedah, WI 54646; (608)565-2789.

PATTISON STATE PARK—Located in northwestern Wisconsin, Pattison State Park has a 27-acre lake, a river with a deep gorge, and a couple of lovely waterfalls, including 165-foot Big Manitou Falls, highest in the state. Deer, bear, moose, and coyote are among the wildlife here.

Activities: There are about six miles of hiking trails in the park. Cross-country skiing is available in winter. Fishing is possible along the river or at the lake. Hunting is prohibited.

Camping Regulations: Backpack camping is allowed at three areas near the Black River, about 1.6 miles via trail from the parking area, and not far from 30-foot Little Manitou Falls.

Primitive camping is restricted to these sites. A fee is charged for camping each night, and sites may be reserved in advance. Campfires are permitted in the fire rings provided.

For Further Information: Pattison State Park, Route 2, Box 435, Superior, WI 54880; (715)399-8073.

COPPER FALLS STATE PARK—This state park in northern Wisconsin has two lakes and an 8-mile stretch of the Bad River, with waterfalls and a couple of steep canyons. The forest is of hemlock and cedar, maple and aspen. Deer, bear, and coyote are among the area's wildlife.

Activities: In the park are seven miles of hiking trails, including a section of the North Country Trail (see entry page 305), and also 14 miles of cross-country ski trails. Fishing is available along the river. Pets are not allowed on trails.

Camping Regulations: Backpack camping is restricted to one designated area, located along a trail near the river. Fires are allowed in fire rings. A fee is charged for camping each night. Advance reservations by mail are available and recommended.

For Further Information: Copper Falls State Park, Box 438, Mellen, WI 54546; (715)274-5123.

ROCK ISLAND STATE PARK—900 acres. Rock Island State Park consists of a forested island in Lake Michigan, located off a peninsula in northeastern Wisconsin. Scenery includes limestone cliffs, some rocky shoreline, and a sandy beach with dunes. Ferry service to the island is available during the warmer months.

Activities: The island has over 10 miles of hiking trails, including a 6.5 mile loop around the island.

Camping Regulations: Backpack camping is restricted to five campsites in one area, which is about a mile down the loop trail.

For Further Information: Rock Island State Park, Route 1, Box 118A, Washington Island, WI 54246; (414)847-2235.

UPPER MISSISSIPPI RIVER NATIONAL WILDLIFE AND FISH REFUGE—This 200,000-acre National Wildlife and Fish Refuge protects 284 miles of the Mississippi River in four states. Offering a corridor two to five miles wide, the refuge includes islands, wetlands, and river shoreline with some beaches and high cliffs.

It's not in a wilderness condition. The river has many dams and locks, and highways often run close by. The refuge nevertheless helps preserve a diverse wildlife which includes white-tailed deer, coyote, fox, and bald eagle.

Activities: Canoeing and other boating are possible on the river, as is fishing. Hunting is permitted in season. There are no maintained foot trails.

Camping Regulations: Except where posted otherwise, primitive camping is allowed on the islands and along the shore for up to 14 days. Campfires are permitted.

For Further Information: Upper Mississippi River National Wildlife and Fish Refuge, P.O. Box 415, La Crosse, WI 54601.

MAJOR BACKPACKING TRAILS

ICE AGE TRAIL—Currently in the process of being built, this major new National Scenic Trail will eventually be about 1000 miles long. About a third of the trail is now finished and open.

Difficulty varies from easy to moderate. The trail extends from the shore of Lake Michigan to the St. Croix River at the Minnesota border, winding throughout much of the southern and central regions of Wisconsin.

It follows along glacial moraines (ridges formed by debris deposited during the last ice age). A small portion of the trail is in Chequamegon National Forest, and it also passes through some state parks, state forests, and private lands.

Camping Regulations: Within Chequamegon National Forest camping is allowed almost anywhere along the trail, except where posted otherwise, and campfires are allowed.

Designated campsites must generally be used on state lands, and a camping fee is sometimes charged. Legal campsites are not available at the present time along some stretches of the trail.

For Further Information: Ice Age National Scenic Trail, National Park Service, 1709 Jackson Street, Omaha, NE 68102.

NORTH COUNTRY TRAIL—This important new National Scenic Trail will eventually be 3,200 miles long, stretching from New York to North Dakota. The Wisconsin section, which crosses the northwest corner of the state, will extend about 155 miles.

Some 60 miles of the trail fall within Chequamegon National Forest, and it also traverses state park and forest lands. For about 40 miles it parallels the St. Croix National Scenic Riverway. Difficulty ranges from easy to moderate.

Camping Regulations: On state lands camping is normally restricted to designated sites, and a camping fee is sometimes required. In the National Forest one may camp almost anywhere along the trail, and campfires are allowed, with the exception of posted areas. Legal campsites are not currently available for some segments of the trail, including those on private lands.

For Further Information: North Country Trail Association, P.O. Box 311, White Cloud, MI 49349.

WISCONSIN CAMPING RESOURCES

ORGANIZATIONS WHICH OFFER WILDERNESS CAMPING TRIPS

American Youth Hostels, Wisconsin Council, 2224 West Wisconsin Avenue, Milwaukee, WI 53233; (414)933-1155. This AYH council schedules several canoe-camping trips each year.

INFORMATION ABOUT STATE PARK AND FOREST CAMPGROUNDS

Wisconsin Department of Natural Resources, Bureau of Parks and Recreation, P.O. Box 7921, Madison, WI 53707; (608)266-2181.

STATE HIGHWAY MAP AND TRAVEL INFORMATION

Wisconsin Tourist Information Center, 123 West Washington Avenue, P.O. Box 7606, Madison, WI 53707; (608)266-2161/ (800)432- TRIP (out of state)/ (800)372-2737 (in state).

WYOMING

BEST AREAS FOR WILDERNESS CAMPING

YELLOWSTONE NATIONAL PARK—2,020,625 acres in Wyoming (2,219,736 acres total). Located in the northwest corner of Wyoming, with small portions in Montana and Idaho, Yellowstone is our largest National Park outside of Alaska. The park is slowly recovering from the damage suffered during the major forest fires of 1988.

Most of the area is managed as wilderness. The park is most famous for Old Faithful, Mammoth Hot Springs, and literally thousands of other geysers and hot springs. Also notable are gigantic Yellowstone Lake and the 1,500-foot-deep Grand Canyon of the Yellowstone River, which has a 308-foot waterfall.

Crossing the region is a section of the Continental Divide. Highest elevation is 11,358-foot Eagle Peak. Along with numerous mountain ranges there are high plateaus, open meadows, conifer forests, and some sagebrush desert. Among the wildlife are grizzly and black bear, elk, antelope, mule deer, moose, and bighorn sheep.

Activities: Backpacking and hiking are available on over 1,100 miles of trails. Difficulty varies from easy to strenuous. Bushwhacking or cross-country travel is not recommended due to thermal hazards and also the denseness of the forest.

Horseback riding is allowed on many but not all trails. Use of horses before July 1 must be approved by a ranger. Bikes are permitted on park roads only, and prohibited in the backcountry.

Cross-country skiing is a winter option on trails in the park. Canoeing is possible on Yellowstone Lake. Fishing is available by permit, but hunting is not allowed.

Camping Regulations: A free permit is required in order to camp in the backcountry and to make campfires. A large number of designated campsites are located throughout the park, and camping is restricted to these established sites.

Permits must be obtained in person from a ranger station no more than two days in advance. Numbers of campers are limited for each site, and the maximum stay allowed at campsites ranges from one to three nights. Since there's snow here from fall through spring, summer is the main camping season.

Some regions of the park are restricted or closed to camping for part of the year to minimize the possibility of encounters with bears. Campfires are allowed only in established fire pits, and prohibited at some sites. Pets are not permitted.

For Further Information: Yellowstone National Park, P.O. Box 168, Yellowstone National Park, WY 82190; (307)344-7381.

GRAND TETON NATIONAL PARK—310,520 acres. Surrounded by National Forest lands, spectacular Grand Teton National Park is located directly south of Yellowstone National Park, in northwest Wyoming.

This wilderness park centers around the magnificent Tetons, high and jagged mountains which rise precipitously from the plain of Jackson Hole. Highest is 13,770-foot Grand Teton, and eight other peaks are over 12,000 feet.

There are also steep canyons, high alpine meadows, forests of spruce, pine, and fir, some lovely lakes, plus a stretch of the Snake River. Wildlife includes grizzly and black bear, bighorn sheep, elk, pronghorn antelope, moose, and mule deer.

Activities: Hiking and backpacking are possible on over 200 miles of trails. Difficulty varies from easy to very strenuous. High trails are usually only snow-free from late July through September.

Horseback riding is allowed on most but not all trails. Rafting, kayaking, and canoeing are available by permit on a section of the Snake River. Cross-country skiing and snowshoeing are winter options here. Bikes are not permitted on trails.

Mountaineering is possible in the park by permit. Fishing is available on the lakes and rivers. Contrary to the policy in most National Parks, hunting is allowed here in season.

Camping Regulations: A free permit is necessary in order to camp in the backcountry, and may be obtained from a visitor center or ranger station. A limited number of permits are issued up to several months in advance, and the remainder are available on a first-come, first-served basis.

There are designated sites at some of the lakes, and camping is also allowed within several camping zones. When at other than established sites, it's necessary to camp at least 100 feet from water sources, and out of sight of trails and other campers.

Campfires are not permitted except at some lakeshore campsites. Pets are prohibited. Maximum group size is 12, and groups must use designated group sites.

For Further Information: Grand Teton National Park, Drawer 170, Moose, WY 83012; (307)733-2880.

BRIDGER–TETON NATIONAL FOREST—3,400,309 acres. This truly massive National Forest is the second largest in the United States outside of Alaska. It lies east and south of Grand Teton National Park, in western Wyoming.

Included here are the Wind River Range of the Rockies and the Gros Ventre Mountains. A section of the Continental Divide crosses the National Forest, and a number of mountains are over 11,000 feet. Highest point is 13,804-foot Gannett Peak.

Along with rugged rocky peaks the region has high plateaus, glaciated canyons, legions of lakes and streams, and the Gros Ventre River. There are mountain meadows and forests of spruce, fir, pine, and aspen. Wildlife includes elk, deer, moose, antelope, bighorn sheep, bison, and bear.

This National Forest has three huge designated wilderness areas: the 585,468-acre Teton Wilderness, the 428,169-acre Bridger Wilderness, and the 287,000-acre Gros Ventre Wilderness.

Activities: Backpacking and hiking are available on no fewer than 2,800 miles of trails, including some 200 miles of the Continental Divide Trail (see entry page 310), along with the 70-mile Wyoming Range National Recreation Trail.

Difficulty ranges from easy to strenuous. High trails may only be snow-free from mid-July through September. Horses are permitted on many trails, as are mountain bikes, but the latter are not allowed in wilderness areas.

Canoeing, kayaking, and rafting are possible along a section of the Snake River. Cross-country skiing is available on some established trails in winter. Fishing is another option. Hunting is permitted in season.

Camping Regulations: Camping is allowed throughout the National Forest, except where posted otherwise. Campsites should be away from meadows and alpine tundra. Campfires are generally permitted but discouraged. A stove is recommended for cooking.

In wilderness areas campsites must be at least 200 feet from trails and lakes. Here group size is limited to 10, and permits are required for organized groups. Campfires are banned during summer in some parts of the wilderness areas.

For Further Information: Bridger–Teton National Forest, P.O. Box 1888, Jackson, WY 83001; (307)733-2752.

SHOSHONE NATIONAL FOREST—2,433,029 acres. Enormous Shoshone National Forest is in western and northwest Wyoming, with some lands alongside the eastern border of Yellowstone National Park. Over half of the acreage consists of designated wilderness.

It encompasses parts of several high and spectacular mountain ranges, including a section of the Continental Divide. Wyoming's highest mountain, 13,804-foot Gannett Peak, stands on Shoshone's border with Bridger–Teton National Forest, and there are 20 other mountains over 13,000 feet.

Scenery also includes high plateaus and deep canyons, alpine meadows, sagebrush flats, and conifer forests, with hundreds of lakes and streams, several major rivers, and 156 glaciers—the most of any location in the country outside of Alaska. Among the wildlife are elk, bighorn sheep, moose, deer, black and grizzly bear, and mountain goat.

There are five large wilderness areas: the 704,529-acre Washakie Wilderness, the 350,488-acre North Absaroka Wilderness, the 198,838-acre Fitzpatrick Wilderness, the 101,991-acre Popo Agie Wilderness, and 23,750 acres of the 921,000-acre Absaroka–Beartooth Wilderness.

Activities: Hiking and backpacking are possible on over 1,500 miles of trails. Difficulty ranges from easy to strenuous. Higher trails may only be snow-free from mid-July through September.

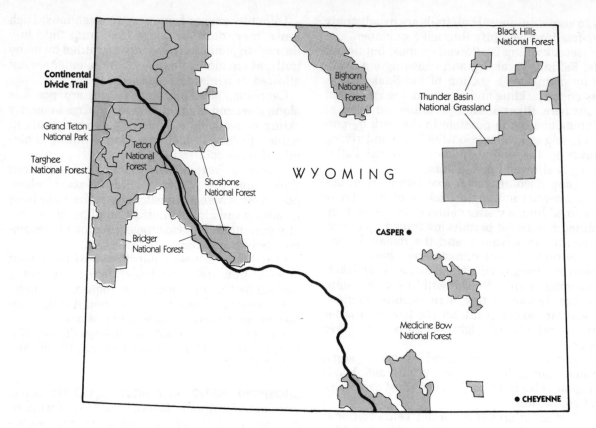

Continental
Divide Trail

Grand Teton
National Park

Targhee
National Forest

Teton
National
Forest

Shoshone
National Forest

Bridger
National Forest

Black Hills
National Forest

Bighorn
National
Forest

Thunder Basin
National Grassland

W Y O M I N G

CASPER ●

Medicine Bow
National Forest

● CHEYENNE

Many trails are open to horseback riding, and cross-country skiing is available in winter. Limited rafting is possible on the Shoshone River. Fishing is permitted, as is hunting in season.

Camping Regulations: Camping is allowed throughout most of the National Forest, except where posted otherwise. Campfires may be made, but a stove is recommended for cooking. Permits are required only for large organized groups.

For Further Information: Shoshone National Forest, 225 West Yellowstone Avenue, P.O. Box 2140, Cody, WY 82414; (307)527-6241.

OTHER RECOMMENDED LOCATIONS

BIGHORN NATIONAL FOREST—1,107,670 acres. This National Forest in north-central Wyoming is located in the Bighorn Mountains, an area of high rocky peaks, steep canyons, and glaciers, along with some major rivers and hundreds of lakes and streams.

There are also alpine meadows and forests of spruce, fir, pine, and aspen. Wildlife includes elk,

moose, deer, black bear, bighorn sheep, and coyote.

Bighorn has one designated wilderness area: the 195,500-acre Cloud Peak Wilderness, which surrounds 13,167-foot Cloud Peak, highest point in the National Forest.

Activities: More than 600 miles of trails are available for hiking and backpacking. Many trails are open to horses. Difficulty ranges from easy to strenuous. High trails are usually under snow from late September through early July.

Mountain biking is allowed on trails outside of the wilderness area. Many trails are suitable for cross-country skiing and snowshoeing during the long snow season. Fishing is another option here, and hunting is permitted in season.

Camping Regulations: Camping and campfires are allowed freely throughout the National Forest, except where posted otherwise. No permits are required, but campers entering the Cloud Peak Wilderness should register at trailheads. Campsites should be at least 100 feet from trails and water sources.

For Further Information: Bighorn National Forest, 1969 South Sheridan Avenue, Sheridan, WY 82801; (307)672-0751.

MEDICINE BOW NATIONAL FOREST—1,090,300
acres. Medicine Bow National Forest is made up of four separate tracts in southeast Wyoming. Included here are several scenic mountain ranges, with 12,013-foot Medicine Bow Peak the highest point.

Along with rocky peaks there are precipitous canyons, rolling high plateaus, meadows, pine forests, many lakes and streams, and some rivers. Wildlife includes elk, pronghorn, deer, black bear, bighorn sheep, and mountain lion.

This National Forest has four relatively small wilderness areas: the 31,300-acre Huston Park Wilderness, the 22,363-acre Platte River Wilderness, the 15,260-acre Savage Run Wilderness, and the 10,400-acre Encampment River Wilderness.

Activities: Hiking, backpacking, and horseback riding are possible on close to 300 miles of trails, most of which are relatively short. Difficulty varies from easy to strenuous. Higher trails may only be snow-free from mid-July through September.

White-water rafting, kayaking, and limited canoeing are available on the North Platte River. During winter there are opportunities for cross-country skiing on some trails. Fishing is possible along lakes, rivers, and streams. Hunting is permitted in season.

Camping Regulations: Camping is allowed throughout the region, as are campfires, except where otherwise prohibited. Visitors are asked to camp at least 100 feet from lakes and trails. A stove is recommended for cooking.

For Further Information: Medicine Bow National Forest, 605 Skyline Drive, Laramie, WY 82070; (307)745-8971.

BLM LANDS IN WYOMING—Wyoming has about
17,800,000 acres of BLM (Bureau of Land Management) or public domain lands. This is about one-fourth of the state's total area, and consists of numerous tracts scattered throughout Wyoming. Many are in the central and western regions.

Included are many mountains, buttes, mesas, scenic canyons such as Sweet Water Canyon, caves, badlands, areas of desert, and grasslands. About 345 miles of the Oregon and Mormon National Historic Trails pass through the lands. Access to some areas is difficult, and detailed brochures or other printed information are not available for most locations.

Activities: Almost all BLM lands are open to hiking and backpacking, as well as horseback riding, but established trails are few. Cross-country travel is often feasible. Mountain biking is generally allowed. Cross-country skiing and snowshoeing are possible in the winter.

White-water canoeing and rafting are available on the North Platte, Green, and other rivers, as is fishing. Rock climbing is an option in mountain areas, and spelunking (caving) is possible in certain locations, this activity sometimes requiring a permit. Hunting is allowed in season.

Camping Regulations: Camping is permitted freely throughout most BLM areas, as are campfires, except where otherwise prohibited. Permits are not necessary for most locations.

For Further Information: Bureau of Land Management, 2515 Warren Avenue, P.O. Box 1828, Cheyenne, WY 82003; (307)775-6256.

THUNDER BASIN NATIONAL GRASSLAND—572,000
acres. Thunder Basin National Grassland is located in northeast Wyoming, in the Powder River Basin between the Black Hills and the Bighorn Mountains. This is an area of open rolling prairie and plateau, with some steep slopes, ridges, and knobs. Most of the lands are open to livestock grazing.

There are several rivers and some intermittent streams. In addition to grasses, vegetation includes sagebrush and some pine and juniper. Among the wildlife are white-tailed and mule deer, antelope, elk, mountain lion, coyote, and fox.

Activities: Hiking, backpacking, and horseback riding are possible throughout the grassland, but there are no established trails. Most travel must be cross-country. Fishing is available along the rivers, with hunting permitted in season.

Camping Regulations: Camping is allowed in most areas, except near water sources, facilities, and where posted otherwise. Campfires are legal but there's little firewood. Bringing a stove is recommended. No permits are necessary.

For Further Information: Thunder Basin National Grassland, 809 South 9th Street, Douglas, WY 82633; (307)358-4690.

TARGHEE NATIONAL FOREST—296,000 acres in
Wyoming (1,557,792 acres total). While most of this National Forest is in Idaho, a sizable unit is located in northwest Wyoming, west of Grand Teton National Park. There are two designated wilderness areas: the 116,535-acre Jedediah Smith Wilderness and the 10,820-acre Winegar Hole Wilderness.

Camping is allowed throughout the National Forest, except where otherwise prohibited. Campfires are not permitted in a few areas. Campsites in wilderness areas should be at least 200 feet from lakeshores and 50 feet from streams. Permits are required for commercial groups and guides. See the Idaho chapter listing for more information about Targhee National Forest.

BLACK HILLS NATIONAL FOREST—175,000 acres in Wyoming. This 1,200,000-acre National Forest is based in South Dakota, with most of the acreage there, but a few tracts are located in the northeast corner of Wyoming. One sizable unit includes 6,650-foot Bear Lodge Mountain.

Camping is allowed throughout the National Forest, except near public use areas or where posted otherwise. See the Black Hills National Forest entry in the South Dakota chapter for more information.

MAJOR BACKPACKING TRAILS

CONTINENTAL DIVIDE TRAIL—When completed, this important National Scenic Trail will extend over 3,000 miles from Canada to Mexico. So far only the Montana and Idaho sections have been officially designated and marked. The route in Wyoming still remains tentative.

For most of its length here the trail is on National Forest lands, and it also passes through Yellowstone National Park. The trail follows near or next to the Continental Divide, and occasionally runs directly along the crest. It generally remains at high elevations, of course, and scenery along the way is often magnificent. Horseback riding is allowed on the trail.

Camping Regulations: Camping is allowed almost anywhere along the trail when it's on National Forest lands, except where otherwise prohibited. Campfires are generally permitted. Sites should be well off the trail and away from water sources.

In Yellowstone National Park special rules apply. A permit is required, and designated camp-sites must be used. See the Yellowstone National Park entry above for complete regulations.

For Further Information: Continental Divide Trail Society, P.O. Box 30002, Bethesda, MD 20814.

WYOMING CAMPING RESOURCES

USEFUL GUIDEBOOKS
Climbing and Hiking in the Wind River Range—Kelsey, Joe. San Francisco: Sierra Club Books.
Guide to the Continental Divide Trail: Wyoming—Wolf, James R. Bethesda, MD: Continental Divide Trail Society, 1986.
Hiker's Guide to Wyoming—Hunger, Bill. Helena, MT: Falcon Press.
Hiking the Teton Backcountry—Lawrence, Paul. San Francisco: Sierra Club Books.
Hiking the Yellowstone Backcountry—Back, Orville E., Jr. San Francisco: Sierra Club Books.
The Lakes of Yellowstone—Pierce, Steve. Seattle: The Mountaineers Books.
Paddle and Portage: The Floater's Guide to Wyoming Rivers—Lewis, Dan. Helena, MT: Falcon Press.
The Sierra Club Guide to the Natural Areas of Idaho, Montana, and Wyoming—Perry, John and Jane. San Francisco: Sierra Club Books, 1988.
Wind River Trails—Mitchell, Finis. Salt Lake City: Wasatch Publishing Co.
Wyoming Hiking Trails—Sudduth, Tom and Sanse. Boulder, CO: Pruett.
Yellowstone Trails, A Hiking Guide—Marschall, Mark. Helena, MT: Falcon Press.

INFORMATION ABOUT STATE PARK CAMPGROUNDS
Wyoming State Parks and Historic Sites, Barrett Building, 3rd Floor, 2301 Central Avenue, Cheyenne, WY 82002; (307)777- 7695.

STATE HIGHWAY MAP AND TRAVEL INFORMATION
Wyoming Travel Commission, I-25 at College Drive, Cheyenne, WY 82002; (307)777-7777.

INDEX